Washington and Lee University, 1930–2000

For Jim, '66, with thanks for the class of
1946 gift in support of this book and for
preservation of W&L's history.
Best Regards, Blaine, '65

Washington and Lee
UNIVERSITY
1930–2000

TRADITION AND TRANSFORMATION

BLAINE A. BROWNELL

LOUISIANA STATE UNIVERSITY PRESS

BATON ROUGE

Published by Louisiana State University Press
Copyright © 2017 by Louisiana State University Press
All rights reserved
Manufactured in the United States of America
FIRST PRINTING

Designer: Barbara Neely Bourgoyne
Typefaces: Requiem, display; Whitman, text
Printer and binder: TK

With gratitude to the Washington and Lee University Class of 1966 whose
financial support through its 50th reunion class gift to collect and preserve the
University's history made possible the publication of this book and the
reprint of Ollinger Crenshaw's *General Lee's College*.

LIBRARY OF CONGRESS CATALOGING-IN-PUBLICATION DATA

Names: Brownell, Blaine A., author.
Title: Washington and Lee University, 1930–2000 : tradition and transformation /
Blaine A. Brownell.
Description: Baton Rouge : Louisiana State University Press, [2017] |
Includes bibliographical references and index.
Identifiers: LCCN 2017008821| ISBN 978-0-8071-6698-7 (cloth : alk. paper) |
ISBN 978-0-8071-6699-4 (pdf) | ISBN 978-0-8071-6700-7 (epub)
Subjects: LCSH: Washington and Lee University—History.
Classification: LCC LD5873 .B76 2017 | DDC 378.755/853—dc23
LC record available at https://lccn.loc.gov/2017008821

FOR

My Grandchildren
Blaine Sorensen, Davis, Eloisa, Mateo, Ana Luz

———

My Mentors
Ollinger Crenshaw, George Brown Tindall,
George E. Mowry, David Herbert Donald

———

My Classmates

But we have been resilient, and part of our genius—the secret of our survival, in fact—is that we have made of adversity the source of growth and development.

⤚

Professor Sydney M. B. Coulling III to President John Wilson,
December 21, 1983

CONTENTS

Photo inserts follow pages 126 and 294

PREFACE

It has always struck me that history is not real life, literature, yes, and nothing else,
But history was real life at the time when it could not yet be called history . . .

—Jose Saramago, *The History of the Siege of Lisbon*

REAL LIFE IS MESSY, complicated, charged with detail, and experienced variously—even uniquely—by each individual. Every person associated with Washington and Lee harbors particular memories and impressions that are personal, real, and important. This book cannot encompass or even validate them all. It is, rather, a framework for such experiences, an institutional history that offers a broader perspective, with a focus on the major issues, challenges, policies, decisions, and personalities that determine the direction of the university.

Washington and Lee (W&L) has special characteristics, but it has always been immersed in the larger society and economy. To a remarkable degree, especially since 1930, its experience has mirrored that of American higher education generally. Beyond that, the challenges of the 1970s, '80s, and '90s are almost alarmingly similar to those still resonant today on the nation's campuses. Of course, institutions did not all respond in the same way or navigate successfully the treacherous shoals of the twentieth century. W&L's longevity and tradition contributed both burdens and impetus to its journey, placing particular importance on the loyalty of its graduates and the quality of its leadership. In this regard, especially, the university was particularly fortunate. Tradition and purpose have not always been secured through transformation.

This book is written from the perspective of the president, who is responsible to the trustees for everything that goes on in the university, as well as for assessing needs, setting priorities, responding to the many constituencies, and planning for the future. From 1930 to 2000, Washington and Lee's presidents were remarkable and unusually capable individuals, each making different but significant and lasting contributions to the institution at critical times. In contrast to some models of organizational leadership foisted inappropriately on higher education, W&L's presidencies were authoritative but also collaborative, with deep respect for the nature of the academic community, its processes, and its diverse members and groups. The institution moved forward with its presidents' guidance and benefited from their search for a shared vision. As every president knows, success depends on the capabilities and support of others—vice presidents, deans, department chairs, faculty members, and student leaders—to literally make things happen. W&L was very fortunate in this regard, as well.

Of course, many stories remain to be told. One frustration of writing any history is the necessary neglect of many interesting side paths and tributaries—personal stories, particular fraternities or athletic teams, secret societies, and even rumors and tall tales. What I have neglected or misjudged will hopefully provide inspiration for others to fully explore more of these stories some day. In particular, the history of the School of Law, in all its richness and detail and with ample resources available in its own archives, deserves to be written.

The university invited me to undertake this work, with the understanding that it would be an accurate account situated in the context of national and regional history and the larger story of American higher education. I was especially honored to work on this project because I was a student of Ollinger Crenshaw, who supervised my honors thesis and guided me toward graduate study in US history. Asked why his account in *General Lee's College* ended around 1930, he reportedly said that he didn't wish to write about people who were still alive. Obviously, I have neglected to follow this advice, though to be objective I have treated historical actors as if they were dead even when, thankfully, many are still very much alive. I also appreciate that, as one approaches events of the present day, "real life" cannot yet be called history.

I am a loyal alumnus with great affection for Washington and Lee University. But I have tried to honor the university's wish and tell this story—the good and the bad—as objectively and honestly as I can. I am happy to conclude that W&L's many achievements are even more clearly defined and appreciated against a background of realities, challenges, setbacks, and missteps. The story is still evolving, of course, but it has thus far led to an institution that is stronger than it has ever been. As the United States endures intense political disagreements about its nature and purpose, Washington and Lee's traditional values of honor, integrity, and civility have never been more important.

Washington and Lee University, 1930–2000

PROLOGUE

THE EDUCATIONAL INSTITUTION that became Washington and Lee University was established in 1749 near Greenville, Virginia, southwest of Staunton. This "peripatetic Latin school" was begun by Robert Alexander, a native of Ulster in Northern Ireland, "largely to start boys toward study for the Presbyterian ministry"; it evolved into an academy and eventually college and university.[1] Alexander's Augusta Academy was a direct outgrowth of the eighteenth-century migration of Ulster Scots, or Scotch-Irish, into Virginia and North Carolina beyond the Blue Ridge Mountains, at that time the western colonial frontier. The institution was not formally affiliated with any religion, denomination, or sect, since it requested and received a charter from the Virginia legislature in 1782, and brief efforts to renew church connections and establish a theological seminary ended by 1796. But it had strong Presbyterian connections from the beginning and identified itself as a "Christian" institution well into the twentieth century.

The early years of this small, rural school are obscured by a lack of formal institutional records and must be deciphered from letters and church documents. Over time, and as settlement in the Shenandoah Valley became more established, the beginnings of the modern institution took shape. In 1776 a more permanent endeavor, Liberty Hall Academy, was established with support from the presbytery, and around 1779 it moved south to a site near Lexington, a newly founded village named in honor of the Massachusetts site of the Minutemen's clash with the British. The academy continued to struggle, financially and otherwise. The first bachelor's degrees were conferred in 1785.

The first defining moment in the institution's history occurred in 1796, when President George Washington donated one hundred shares of stock in the James River Company, valued at $20,000, to the fledgling academy. He received these shares from the legislature in recognition for his earlier support for efforts to extend westward development through river improvements, canals, and commerce. Washington accepted the gift with the condition that he could apply it to a worthy public purpose, and he chose to support an educational endeavor west of the Blue Ridge. This was the largest single gift to an educational institution in North America up to that time, and it immediately raised the stature and prospects of the school, wisely renamed Washington Academy by the trustees. In 1813 it became Washington College.

Despite Washington's generosity, however, the college continued to struggle financially. The trustees even sought in 1817 to be designated the "central university" of the Commonwealth proposed by Thomas Jefferson. While this effort would have garnered significant financial support, it would have ended the institution's independence from public control. In any event, it was unsuccessful; Jefferson was not about to see his grand vision placed so far from Charlottesville, nor, especially, in the hands of Presbyterians.

Through the antebellum era the institution expanded, and by the 1840s the now-famous row of red-brick, white-columned buildings—the Colonnade— had emerged on a hilltop overlooking the town. The curriculum expanded but remained "dominated by the classics and suffused with religion." A president and a few professors provided all instruction, governed by a board of trustees composed mostly of local men connected one way or another with the Presbyterian church. The college thus remained a de facto Presbyterian institution but without formal ecclesiastical control (similar to the College of New Jersey, now Princeton, as it was at the same time).

As a prominent feature in the town, the college was caught up in local politics, church disputes, conflicts with the newly established Virginia Military Institute (founded in 1839), and the issues and controversies leading up to secession and war in 1861. President Henry Ruffner had a rather turbulent twelve-year tenure before resigning in 1848. He was a vocal opponent of slavery and its expansion, but his successor—George Junkin, former president of Lafayette College and of Miami University in Ohio, and of Scotch-Irish stock—defended the peculiar institution and attacked the abolitionists. Junkin was, however, also a staunch pro-Unionist, and when secession came he resigned amid much turmoil and returned to Pennsylvania.[2]

In the 1850s, according to Ollinger Crenshaw, "Washington College . . . was predominantly pro-Whig, moderate in regard to the sectional controversy, mildly pro-slavery, and vigorously pro-Union. In general, however, abolitionists were abhorred and condemned, and members of the faculty, including the president, were slaveholders." But as "emotions rose, divisions that had appeared only as differences of opinion came to be viewed in terms of good and evil." Throughout the South, allegiances were reckoned and lives reshaped by circumstances leading swiftly to war, and so it was in Lexington.

Washington College remained open during the conflict but without a president and with a much-reduced schedule and program. Its enlistees in the Confederate Army constituted the Liberty Hall Volunteers, part of Thomas J. "Stonewall" Jackson's brigade in the Army of Northern Virginia, and fought from First Manassas to Appomattox. A Federal force commanded by Gen. David Hunter attacked Lexington in June 1864, shelling the town and ransacking the college, but threats to burn it to the ground were not implemented. (Two officers in Hunter's force were future US presidents Rutherford B. Hayes and William McKinley.)

The war left the South in a shambles, and Washington College discouraged and dilapidated. But the trustees were determined to forge ahead and only months after the surrender at Appomattox, on August 4, 1865, voted unanimously to offer the presidency of the institution to Gen. Robert Edward Lee. Although Lee had served as superintendent at West Point, he had no other academic leadership experience, and the trustees had not even discussed the job with him. But his reputation for honesty, integrity, and nobility of character, and the deep loyalty and affection he inspired in his troops and the southern populace, far overshadowed ordinary hiring concerns. On August 24, Lee accepted, and on September 18 he rode into town alone on his horse Traveler. He was formally inaugurated on October 2, in ceremonies that he insisted be simple and brief. Thus began the second great defining moment in the university's history.

Lee's presence generated enormous interest in Washington College throughout the South and brought new enrollments and energy to the educational program and financial support from key donors like Cyrus McCormick and George Peabody. He also proved to be a remarkably prescient and effective educator, focusing from the beginning on the crucial importance of education—especially practical and applied subjects—for the postwar rebuilding of the South. In a "Report of the Faculty" submitted to the trustees in April 1867, Lee proposed reorganizing the college into nine departments, awarding undergraduate and advanced degrees, imposing higher standards for graduation, and hiring additional faculty to cover a revised, expanded curriculum. Added to the traditional, classical subjects were new offerings in applied mathematics, physical science, modern languages (including French, German, Spanish, and Italian), English philology, and modern history. In 1868 the faculty proposed "the broadest and most thorough development to the practical and industrial Sciences of the Age," including study in mining, manufacturing, agriculture, and commerce. Some of these initiatives took shape quickly, others only in subsequent decades, and some fitfully or not at all. Lee's hope for a full-fledged school of agriculture was never realized. A program to prepare printers and journalists (with a strong emphasis on typography and production), which would take full shape only in the next century, was the first academic program in journalism at the collegiate level in the United States. The Lexington School of Law, founded by Judge John W. Brockenbrough, was annexed to the college in 1866, and though it remained largely autonomous for some time it would eventually become the institution's major professional school.

Student life in the late 1860s was less dominated by religion and rigid rules (dancing was even permitted) and characterized more by the "gentlemanly" behavior the president expected and modeled. Lee ended compulsory chapel attendance in 1868 (but regularly attended himself), and his emphasis on personal honor and integrity was the core of what became the Honor System, perhaps the most distinctive feature of the institution in later years. The influx of veterans following the war also brought greater maturity and academic commitment to the student population. By all accounts, Lee enjoyed warm relationships with students and was universally recognized as principled and fair.

Lee's major impact on the institution was due less to his curricular innovations, academic vision, or administrative abilities than to his character and personal charisma, which made an enormous and lasting mark on the college and has been invoked by every succeeding president. Lee's personality and reputation, and his five-year tenure as president of Washington College, are arguably his greatest legacies to subsequent generations up to the present day. Within weeks of his death on October 12, 1870, the trustees changed the name of the institution to Washington and Lee University and named his son, George Washington Custis Lee, then a professor at Virginia Military Institute (VMI), as his successor.

A new Lee was at the helm—one with academic experience and knowledge of his father's work—but his presidency was lengthy and troubled. Diffident to the point of shyness, Custis Lee was also given to doubts concerning his own thoughts and abilities. He requested frequent leaves of absence, suffered from various illnesses, and submitted his resignation on numerous occasions. (It was consistently refused by the trustees.) As Crenshaw concluded, "a modern physician would undoubtedly discern the physical effects of mind and emotion in the unhappy experience of this reticent man, overshadowed by his father, the beneficiary of an undesired nepotism." Finally, in 1896, after twenty-six years in office, his resignation was accepted. He retired to "Ravensworth," the Fitzhugh family estate in Fairfax County, and maintained good relations with the university until his death in 1913. His gift of the Charles Wilson Peale portraits of Washington and Lafayette was perhaps his greatest legacy to the university.

While in relatively good financial condition for a southern institution in 1870, due largely to Robert E. Lee's prominence, the university faced problems in enrollment and finances through the rest of the nineteenth century. The situation became so serious that the faculty and the board even discussed the possibility of coeducation in the spring of 1896. The law school also struggled through the 1870s and 1880s, with sometimes fewer than twenty students and only one professor. It began to come into its own with vigorous leadership from John Randolph Tucker, reaching an enrollment of sixty-three in 1892. Two of the university's most distinguished graduates emerged from this period—John W. Davis, the Democratic nominee for president in 1924, and Newton D. Baker, who would become mayor of Cleveland and secretary of war under President Woodrow Wilson. Upon Tucker's death in 1897, his son—Henry St. George Tucker—was appointed to the faculty and would later become dean and acting president. The cornerstone of a new law-school building, Tucker Hall, was laid in 1899.

Religious issues emerged after Lee's death concerning the sectarian affiliation of the institution. Though they were still predominant, Presbyterians lamented the influence of Episcopalians on the faculty and board. In September 1873, the trustees issued a statement that the university was nonsectarian and that no denomination should receive "any preponderance or influence in the University to the exclusion or injury of any other" (including the appointment of faculty). They sought "a University free alike from all complications of church and state, which should represent at once the highest and largest interests of Education, & the noblest remembrances of Christian Heroism and devotion." This statement did not end the matter, given the institution's strong Presbyterian associations, but the Alumni Association endorsed it, and the most heated discussions died down.

Six presidents served after Custis Lee and before 1930, though only two enjoyed tenures of a decade or more: George Hutcheson Denny (1901–11) and Henry Louis Smith (1912–29). William Lyne Wilson, a Confederate veteran and former postmaster general under Grover Cleveland, was inaugurated president in 1897. Though his tenure was brief, his administration brought vigor and modernity to an institution much in need of both. He noted the prevalence of sectarianism at the university and a tendency toward hero worship of General Lee (though he himself venerated Lee and was with him at Appomattox), as well as a need to look toward the future, with special attention to the curriculum, especially the social and natural sciences. He established a chair of economics, whose incumbent was to launch a department and bring new energy and spirit to the faculty, and he was more involved than his predecessors in key faculty appointments generally. He also instituted weekly (and compulsory) assemblies, not for religious instruction but for wide-ranging discussions of national issues and subjects of general interest, and these were continued by his successor. His national contacts and recognition aided his active fund-raising efforts. Early on, he encountered the campus fixation with football and felt compelled to remind students that their principal purpose at the institution was academic study. Of the students he wrote, "I would wish that they would concentrate their energies on baseball and tennis, as football is too dangerous a game, especially for youths so young and light as most of ours are." This matter would trouble his successors to an even greater degree.

Wilson's death in October 1900 was greeted by some as a calamity equal to the passing of General Lee. (Crenshaw later concurred with this judgment and noted the irony that the football field was named after him.) The search for Wilson's successor took nearly a year and was unusually contentious. The divisions on the board were exacerbated by the denominational predominance of Presbyterians in the institution and efforts by the Southern Presbyterian Church to make Presbyterian affiliation a formal condition for all new presidents. But many resisted this idea and were especially opposed to selecting a clergyman as president. Ultimately, George Hutcheson Denny, the thirty-year-old son of a Presbyterian minister, with a PhD In Latin from the University of Virginia, was elected president in 1901. Though his early years in office were marred by the disaffection and resignation of two unsuccessful internal candidates for the job—including the acting president, Henry St. George Tucker—Denny brought energy and aplomb to the position and successfully completed the fund drive named for President Wilson.

Through Denny's "sheer intelligence and unremitting attention to duties," as well as his "personal charm," Crenshaw observed, he quickly won over young and old alike. He impressed the trustees with his energy and commitment to the university's values and the students when he declared "football to be the greatest of college sports." Indeed, he was exceptionally popular with students, whose names he committed to memory. Enrollment expanded to the point that perhaps more students were admitted than should have been; it reached 418 in 1907, the highest in the university's history, and climbed to 570 in 1909. This was a financial boon, but it also drew a reprimand from the Carnegie Foundation for the Advancement of Teaching, which refused to include Washington and Lee on its "accepted" list in 1909. Much of the problem, according to Crenshaw, was the lack of proper academic preparation at the time, especially in the South. Some students were admitted to take courses but not pursue degrees, and a substantial number of students admitted to the College of Engineering and the law school had not graduated from high school. The Carnegie Foundation's executive committee stated flatly that Washington and Lee was a college, not a university, and had no business offering degrees in engineering and law, which were offered at the University of Virginia, "a much stronger school than Washington and Lee can ever hope to be."

Denny defended the admissions and enrollment policies, and could point to the establishment of a chapter of Phi Beta Kappa at the university in 1910 as a testament to academic quality. Also during his tenure, two major features of university life first emerged—the Fancy Dress Ball and the Mock Convention. Denny's financial management achieved a balanced budget and his fund-raising generated some notable gifts—but nothing on the order of what he sought (due partly to the "banker's panic" of 1907). He also presided over the dramatic, and nationally noted, appearance at W&L of Charles Frances Adams Jr. on the centennial celebration of Lee's birth in 1907. In a rousing speech, Adams praised Lee and characterized the gathering as a testament to national reconciliation.

In 1911, Denny resigned his post in Lexington to accept the presidency of the University of Alabama, where Denny Chimes and Denny Stadium (a football arena now also bearing the name of former coach Paul "Bear" Bryant) remain prominent campus features recognizing his successful tenure there. W&L students, faculty, and trustees, local townspeople, and others throughout the Commonwealth prevailed upon Denny to stay, but without success. His popularity remained such that he was enthusiastically welcomed back to campus on visits and even offered the presidency again in the fall of 1928 when his successor's term was ending. While Denny declined to resume his post, he remained connected to Lexington, where he returned to live in retirement.

Denny's decade in office left the university in the strongest position it had enjoyed since General Lee's administration, though the criticism of its lenient admissions policy continued to rankle. The search for a new president turned up a number of candidates, this time without animosity, sectarian or otherwise. In January 1912, the trustees selected Dr. Henry Louis Smith, president of Davidson College and a physicist with a PhD from the University of Virginia. Like his predecessor, Smith was the son of a Presbyterian minister.

Smith's inauguration in May 1913 was a grand affair. The new president's remarks noted the need for "Christian leadership" in the future but introduced an educational program focused primarily on engineering, business, and journalism. In these and later remarks, he lamented the tendency to frivolity in undergraduate life—including the attention to intercollegiate athletics and the "Gentlemen's D"—and called upon faculty to serve as character role models and give primary attention to teaching. Like many other college leaders of his time, Smith commented forcefully on national and world issues. An ardent Wilsonian, he supported the president's war policies, the League of Nations, and national prohibition. He advocated strong bodies as well as minds but had little enthusiasm for organized athletic competition. Though he lacked the warmth and personal charm of Denny, his writing and oratorical gifts garnered widespread respect and promoted the university's name and reputation.

Some notable advances in academic programs and institutional finances marked Smith's tenure. He established new departments in accounting and statistics, education and psychology, and journalism—the latter an effort to recognize and implement Lee's early interest in adding this subject to the curriculum. New buildings were constructed, and a fund-raising campaign added almost a million dollars to the endowment. The new president also moved to curtail enrollment to a point that could be more reasonably sustained by the university's facilities and faculty. The 700 students in 1911-12 were consequently reduced to 478 in 1914-15, and enrollment increased thereafter only in proportion to the size of the faculty. Also, in 1914, several students founded Omicron Delta Kappa, the honorary leadership fraternity that remains highly visible on campus.

Law school enrollment, which reached 207 in 1911, was also pared back, and the faculty took steps to strengthen the curriculum and academic requirements. In 1906, in line with national educational reforms, the trustees mandated two years of study for a degree and changed the designation from BL to LLB; in 1908 they required a minimum number of academic credits for admission. A three-year program was offered as an option and soon made mandatory. After World War I, the faculty numbered five professors, the curriculum was modernized, the "case system" was adopted, and the law school was admitted into the Association of American Law Schools in 1920. Five years later, the American Bar Association gave W&L a "Class A" rating, placing it among only thirty-nine other law schools in the nation so designated.

One less successful—and quite controversial—effort by the national office of the United Daughters of the Confederacy, which Smith supported, was the incorporation of the modest Lee Chapel within the construction of a much larger and grander memorial chapel to General Lee. But vigorous opposition, especially locally, eventually prevailed, and the trustees abandoned the notion in January 1924.

Smith also faced the university's first wartime crisis since the 1860s. Hostilities in Europe led to heated debates in the United States among those advocating pacifism, isolationism, or engagement against the German "menace." Vituperative anti-German feeling and rhetoric appeared in Lexington, and blows to the national economy led to reductions in enrollment. In April 1917, the United States entered the war, and the campus mobilized, with students and faculty members volunteering for service. After unofficial drills under the supervision of VMI officers, W&L got its first regular officers' training unit in February 1918. While the curriculum remained much the same during 1917-1918, the following year's fall term was dominated by the presence of hundreds of Student Army Training Corps trainees and the offering of courses directly supporting this training and the overall war effort. The armistice in November 1918 brought these unusual and confusing conditions to an end.

Over six hundred W&L students and faculty served in the war, and a number did not survive (including a son of President Smith). Perhaps the most notable battlefield contribution from the university was an ambulance unit composed of students, faculty, and townspeople that arrived in France in 1918. The unit as a whole was cited three times by the French government and—along with individual members—was awarded the Croix de Guerre.

Smith served as president for seventeen years, but most of his notable contributions occurred before the summer of 1924, when he was seriously injured in an automobile accident. He had consolidated many of the gains realized by President Denny, increased the size of the faculty and the endowment, and brought the university through the Great War into the heady days of the 1920s and the opportunities and problems of the modern age.

⟨flourish⟩

THE CAMPUS IN 1930 was compact and intimate, facing east toward the small town of Lexington and enjoying an expansive view to the west of House Mountain and the Appalachians. Washington Hall and the buildings on either side formed the core of the Colonnade, the university's iconic center, which sat on the crest of the hill overlooking the town. This ensemble was joined on the south by Newcomb Hall and the President's House, and to the rear by Reid Hall, the Carnegie Library, and the Lees and Graham Dormitories. Doremus Gymnasium was at one end of the concrete Memorial Bridge spanning Woods Creek and a deep railroad cut, and it connected the main campus with Wilson Field and the tennis courts. Many faculty members lived on campus, not quite in the fashion of the pavilions interspersed among student rooms on the Lawn in Thomas Jefferson's "academical village" in Charlottesville, but very much in that spirit. An array of faculty residences, some rather large and others modest, were scattered on either side of the Colonnade and at the bottom of the hill backing up to Lower Main Street; in 1933, they housed the president, treasurer, and eighteen faculty members.

By 1930, Washington and Lee had established what it held to be venerable traditions. The legacy of Lee had been a dominant element in the university's identity since his appointment as president in 1865, and the code of personal conduct he espoused took institutional shape in the Honor System. Other characteristics of the "W&L experience," while not as defining as the Honor System, were nonetheless important. These included the small enrollment, the system of social fraternities (and the camaraderie and formidable socializing they fostered), the role of student governance, the Mock Convention, and the Fancy Dress Ball—all of which were woven into the fabric of the institution.

Even George Washington's gift was overshadowed by the presidency of Robert E. Lee and the institution's subsequent identification with him. Whatever Lee's renowned Virginia lineage and his life and career before the Civil War, he was primarily known as the South's most famous military leader during a failed rebellion against the United States he had previously sworn to serve. His remarkable military exploits in the face of superior forces assumed even greater weight in the hagiography of the "Lost Cause." The moralistic and even religious tone of this southern effort to reclaim regional pride and overturn the political and social consequences of Reconstruction transformed Lee into a legend—a blameless, saintly figure. This cannot be blamed on Lee, who did nothing to glorify himself or continue the sectional struggles beyond Appomattox. On the contrary, he quickly adjusted to postwar life by devoting himself completely to education and sectional reconciliation. But his remarkable self-control, modesty, and rectitude further reinforced the notion in some quarters that he was a sort of artificial totem created to satisfy the needs of others.

The iconic image of Lee may seem inauthentic to modern perception, informed as it is about the revealed flaws of virtually all famous personages, but this idealized image can also obscure his true nature and remarkable character. Indeed, Robert E. Lee was a flesh-and-blood man of his time, with ambitions, challenges, choices, and family problems. Yet he exemplified throughout his life an unwavering commitment to personal honor, duty, honesty, integrity, and fairness, and he deserved his reputation for rectitude, modesty, and professional competence. These elements of character, particularly the concepts of personal honor and integrity, were what the university that now bears his name chose to emphasize in its mission and purpose, and as defining characteristics of the educational experience it offered young men. His successors rarely missed an opportunity to pay tribute to Lee's example.

Many of the principal elements of life and study at Washington and Lee derived from Lee's example, but it is perhaps more accurate to say that they derived from values and behaviors, already considered worthy, that Lee reinforced. The most notable of these elements was a gentleman's code, generally understood in the nineteenth century but with few written rules, that evolved into the W&L Honor System, overseen and enforced completely by students themselves and based resolutely on the principal of the "single sanction"—if you were deemed to be dishonorable, the sole and necessary penalty was immediate expulsion from the university community. Lee did not impose a full-fledged, formal honor code on the campus. He simply voiced the expectation that all students and faculty should think and behave as "gentlemen," which by his definition encompassed the qualities of personal honor, fairness, and civility. A more formal system emerged, and over time its details changed but not its essential character. Certainly, a major part of the university's story in the twentieth century is the persistence of the Honor System, which has had enormous support among alumni and students, even when it was severely challenged by changing attitudes in the 1960s and after. To this day, the overwhelming majority of current and former students will identify the Honor System as the central component of their experience at the university. Among other things, it permitted a remarkable degree of trust and freedom on campus, manifested in unproctored tests, individually scheduled exams, and the security of personal property.

The small size of the university was often determined by circumstances—financial and otherwise—beyond the administration's control. But it was also intentional because the intimacy of the campus permitted richer personal relationships and closer contact between students and faculty. The "speaking tradition" (greeting every person one encountered on campus, by name if possible) prevailed through much of the twentieth century, enabled by a smaller campus population. Some efforts to expand the university's size (the consideration of a second campus in the 1960s and a larger enrollment to accommodate coeducation in the 1980s) either failed or were adjusted to meet the widespread expectation that the university remain an intimate academic community.

Social fraternities have long been a mainstay of life at W&L, with their members accounting for a large majority of the student population, especially during the freshman and sophomore years. Fraternities were so important, in fact, that the university relied on them to provide housing and board for student populations that would otherwise have required residence and dining halls. Fraternities also facilitated strong friendships, group identification, social interactions, and opportunities for leadership. Alumni tend to regard fraternity affiliation and activities as a significant factor in their time at W&L. On the downside, social fraternities also tended to fragment an already small student population, foster exclusion and cliques as much as acceptance, dominate campus politics, and encourage unsanctioned social functions, alcohol abuse, harmful hazing practices, and the often irresponsible behaviors associated with adolescent males, most from privileged families. It also severely reduced the social options available to students who did not join fraternities, voluntarily or otherwise, and was among the main reasons students gave for transferring elsewhere. Later in the century, the fraternity system had deteriorated to the point where the university's leadership contemplated its elimination.

Following upon the emphasis on personal honor and responsibility was student participation in governing aspects of student life, at least those outside the purely academic realm. Students had virtually exclusive dominion over the requirements and functioning of the Honor System, but their role in other university affairs varied over time, gradually growing as the in-loco-parentis responsibilities of colleges and universities faded and social mores became more permissive. In general, students were increasingly permitted to govern and discipline themselves.

Many universities have political straw polls or even nominating-convention exercises that express the students' political preferences. Washington and Lee's Mock Convention—first held in May 1908—was from the beginning intended to predict the outcome of the actual political convention itself rather than the preferences of the student participants. It is as much an educational activity as an occasion for parades, parties, and a welcome break from regular classes. The Mock Convention has been remarkably accurate in predicting the actual nominee of the major party seeking to reclaim the White House; thus far, there have been only six incorrect predictions in twenty-four mock conventions since 1908. This task has become less relevant, however, as the national nominating conventions themselves have been increasingly overshadowed by early caucuses and state primaries. A host of prominent political figures have addressed these campus conventions—including Harry Truman, Richard Nixon, Barry Goldwater, Mario Cuomo, and Bill Clinton.

The Fancy Dress Ball at Washington and Lee had its earliest origins in the 1907 "Bal Masque," the brainchild of Miss Annie R. White, the university librarian, though it did not assume its modern proportions until 1913 and afterwards. Such social occasions can be traced back to the masked balls of the eighteenth century or the Victorian period in England. The essential elements are costumes, music, and a chosen theme that inspires the dress and decorations. Fancy Dress was for many years the highlight of the campus social season, the largest of the annual "dance sets" that delineated the social calendar, and was often reported in regional and national publications. The dances were skipped during the war years and were out of fashion during the turmoil of the late 1960s and early 1970s, but they were resurrected and remain a vivid memory for many who attended, and were at least acknowledged as notable, if anachronistic, by many who did not. Over the years, social life and notions of decorum changed, but even in the days when faculty served as chaperones, the party could get rather boisterous. The chosen theme was often a source of comment, and sometimes controversy, as it might clash with more modern sensibilities. Dress and decorations celebrating the Old South or stereotypical notions of Africa were especially dicey. But Fancy Dress was likely to come up whenever students at other colleges were asked about Washington and Lee.

*   *   *

THE LAST SEVEN DECADES of the twentieth century brought significant changes to almost every aspect of American—and American collegiate—life and were perhaps especially challenging to older, more traditional institutions such as Washington and Lee. Traditions that had sustained the university and shaped its identity had to be rethought, reframed, or adapted to new circumstances and expectations. Washington and Lee's story during these decades—a story of both tradition and transformation—could well rank as the most challenging and important in the university's long history.

CHAPTER ONE

A NEW LEADER IN CHALLENGING TIMES

THE ACADEMIC PROCESSION emerged from the shadows of the Colonnade into a bright, crisp fall day. At the head of the group, Francis Pendleton Gaines started down the sloping walkway, strewn with fallen leaves, from Washington Hall toward Lee Chapel, where he would take the oath of office as the seventeenth president of Washington and Lee University, the ninth since the death in 1870 of the Confederate general whose character and legacy buttressed the institution and whose body reposed beneath the stage where the oath would be administered.

The inaugural ceremonies on October 25, 1930, unfolded with exercises in Doremus Gymnasium, two luncheons, a football game against St. Johns College, and an evening dance. Providing inaugural remarks were John W. Davis, the Democratic Party presidential nominee in 1924 and W&L's most famous living alumnus; William John Cooper, the US commissioner of education; J. H. Kirkland, chancellor of Vanderbilt University; and Frank Porter Graham, president of the University of North Carolina and the best-known higher-education leader in the South. John H. Finley, editor of the *New York Times,* was the luncheon speaker. All in all, it was a splendid tribute to the small liberal arts college and its new president—though W&L lost the football game 7 to 0.

Gaines's remarks exhibited the florid, old-style oratory for which he was already renowned. He lamented changes in college life after a decade of financial and social excess. Where once "a small band of heroic youth . . . annually set forth on the pilgrimage of knowledge, isolating themselves in vales of quietness; now the browning of the leaves see in exodus a nation of youth never quite detached from the larger world." Once rather routine, student life is now "colored and noisy with the frolic pageantry of campus styles." Where once "the objective was the training of the mind; now the objective is to make money." However, he added, "to think of Washington and Lee is to believe in an ideal." The ideal he portrayed doubtless contained familiar aspects of university life, but they were in large measure his own ideals for higher education—including the idea that character and what he later loosely termed "personality" were on a par with academic achievement. The power of the university was "to achieve a distinctive purpose; to reach beyond the monotony of instruction, beyond the formulas of fact, forever widening and forever intensifying, forever important and forever trivial, to reach beyond these and deposit in the life of a boy something a little finer than culture, a little rarer than competence, a little nobler than success; to quicken a dream within the young brain prepared for dreams by the agony of the aeons, to formulate within the tenderness of the heart some coherence for its own compulsions, to furnish a young personality with potency and with poise."[1] One always remembered a Gaines speech, if not for the precise content then certainly for the grand words, unique phrasing, and swelling cadences.

Frank Gaines was born in Due West, South Carolina, on April 21, 1892. Before his first birthday, the family moved to Lebanon, Virginia, and then to Wytheville, where his father—a Baptist minister—took up new appointments. He graduated from Fork Union Military Academy in 1909 and received his AB degree from Richmond College in 1912 and a MA from the University of Chicago two years later. He taught English at Mississippi Agricultural and Mechanical College (now Mississippi State University) between 1914 and 1923, while also pursuing doctoral work at Columbia University in New York. He was awarded the PhD in 1924. While in Starkville he met and married Sadie duVergne Robert, daughter of the dean, in 1917. He was fond of recalling how this contributed to the progress of his career: "If you can't do it any other way, marry the dean's daughter, the boss's daughter, particularly if, as I did, you love her."[2] During his career, he made hundreds of speeches and published scores of articles. *The Southern Plantation* (1924) was his major scholarly contribution, based on his doctoral dissertation. A fulsome admirer of Robert E. Lee, Gaines usually worked the general into his speeches, whatever the topic, as well as in dedicated pieces like *Lee: The Final Achievement* (1933). He saw his own presidency as a continuation of Lee's work and example.

Of medium height and solid build, Frank Gaines possessed an engaging personality, personal warmth, and a flair for the dramatic. He was, as Professor Ollinger Crenshaw put it, "young and debonair," with a penchant for walking canes—he possessed over a hundred—which he waved and even twirled when striding across campus, flicking errant leaves from the sidewalks. A favorite was his "National Cane," made of wood from the cabin in which Lincoln was born, occasionally carried by President Woodrow Wilson and presented to Gaines by his friend, Mrs. Edith Wilson. He remarked, "A little piece of wood from the home where Lincoln was born has come to rest in the home where Lee died."[3] As Virginius Dabney observed, "This stocky, companionable man can be called a virtuoso with the cane, for he swings one as jauntily as a drum major heading a parade."[4] Though Gaines and his wife would suffer from periodic bouts of illness and injury, sometimes requiring recuperative absences from the campus, his personality and authority always conveyed a sense of vigor and purpose.

Gaines came to W&L after three years as president of Wake Forest College, located in Wake County, north of Raleigh, North Carolina. (The college moved to Winston-Salem in 1956.) His tenure there was rather brief, especially given that his predecessor and successor each served in the position for twenty years or more. Gaines sought to further Wake Forest's role as a "cultural college" and a "Christian college," but he also insisted that it be a "small college" with selective admissions. The overall enrollment declined during his administration from 742 to 617. The board of trustees, however, favored enrollment growth and an admissions policy similar to other institutions in the state.[5]

Always drawn to smaller institutions with high academic standards, Gaines turned down the presidency of the University of Minnesota and saw a promising opportunity at W&L, not least because he revered the life and legacy of Lee. He accepted the new challenge before ever visiting Lexington or meeting with the faculty. He was favorably remembered at Wake Forest for his "enthusiastic spirit and helpful disposition" and his oratorical gifts. Professor George Washington Pascal, a friend and university historian at Wake Forest, noted that Gaines was a "ready speaker on many subjects—religion, education, literature, athletics, college affairs, dedications of buildings and stadiums, and was heard gladly whatever his subject, and his services were in constant requisition."[6] These qualities obviously impressed the W&L search committee and the trustees, especially John W. Davis, who played a central role in Gaines's selection. Davis explained that he preferred Gaines because he believed in "the cultural view of education and [was] quite averse to putting Washington and Lee in competition with technical schools."[7]

On February 24, 1930, Robert Henry Tucker, the acting president, wrote to Gaines, congratulating him on his appointment and assuring him that he had "all along been a strong favorite with the members of the faculty." Gaines replied that neither he nor Mrs. Gaines "has ever seen Washington and Lee and we are anxious, of course, to get in our mind the picture of our future home." On matters of academic policy during the transition, "I am perfectly willing to accept the judgment of the faculty."[8] Tucker kept him apprised of policy matters, noting among other things that the limited money available for faculty salaries would "be distributed as widely as possible among the instructors in the lower salary scales." Gaines noted in this correspondence that Mrs. Gaines had become "critically ill," suffering from "extreme nervousness," and had been under the care of a nurse for a month. He had cancelled many engagements to be with her. Her full recovery was expected in another two or three months. He added that she "is much more than a partner to me, perfect as I think she is in that relation; she is an asset to the institution with which I am connected, a much finer asset than I myself am."[9] Mrs. Gaines recovered, and they arrived on campus in time for the beginning of the fall semester.

The longest presidential terms in the university's history up to that time were George Addison Baxter's thirty years in the early nineteenth century, followed by the immediate successor to Robert E. Lee, his son George Washington Custis Lee, who held the post for twenty-six years, from 1871 to 1897. At the age of thirty-eight, Gaines was on his way to becoming the second-longest-serving president of Washington and Lee, and one of the most successful. But his tenure began during a challenging time for the country and the university.

Higher education in the United States in 1930 was stronger and more extensive than it had ever been. It was also, like everything else in the country, on the verge of national economic depression. The number of eighteen-year-olds entering college had grown steadily since the 1870s. Enrollment surged during the prosperous 1920s, fueled by an increasingly widespread notion that college training was essential for entry into the professions and for social mobility generally.[10] In 1929–30, more than 1,400 higher education institutions in the United States enrolled over 1.1 million students, an increase of at least 84 percent since the beginning of the decade; these institutions employed 82,000 faculty and academic staff. Some 19,300 students enrolled in Virginia institutions in 1930, 80 percent more than in 1919–20.[11] Truly extraordinary growth in the size of public colleges and universities would not occur for another thirty years, but the larger institutions—public and private—had already begun to compete for students and also for recognition in finances, in academics, and on the playing field.

The college curriculum—once dominated by philosophy, classics, and languages in preparation for the ministry or teaching—expanded exponentially with the addition of many new specializations attached to other careers. Faculties became more professionalized and organized in disciplinary departments, with greater authority for defining the curriculum, setting academic policy, and selecting their colleagues. A core curriculum based on a notion of unified knowledge was largely abandoned in many universities, replaced with narrow specialties, electives, and loose distribution requirements. By 1920, higher education was increasingly shaped by organizations such as the American Council on Education, regional accrediting bodies, and philanthropic foundations, all of which sought to bring order and consistency to the overall enterprise through common standards for admission, degree requirements, and organization. A functioning system of higher education arose, though at some expense to institutional variety, and without reference to what students were actually learning.

Most private institutions admitted students based on a wide range of criteria and by no means strictly on academic merit. Elite universities were sensitive to the "type" of students they enrolled, effectively resulting in ethnic, religious, or socioeconomic quotas and with preferences for alumni legacies, graduates of prestigious preparatory schools, and children of the well-to-do. Athletic ability already counted heavily in admissions as performance on the playing field continued to grow more and more important in American college life.

Fund-raising campaigns were launched and new programs and facilities added in colleges and universities across the country in the 1920s; most notable was construction of large football stadiums, but there were also additions of auditoriums, laboratories, museums, and classrooms. Complaints familiar to modern ears were voiced in many quarters—that business managers had displaced the faculty as institutional decision makers, that faculty were neglecting students to focus on research, that too many unqualified students were enrolled, that colleges were merely reaffirming social inequities rather than acting to eliminate them, and that curricula were watered down with too many options.[12] As higher education became a goal for more people, it became more diversified but also the subject of greater scrutiny. As the nation entered the throes of economic travail after 1930, the campus construction boom and big fund-raising drives were stopped or greatly reduced, and the institutions that provided pathways to social mobility and stable occupations were themselves struggling to cope.

Washington and Lee offered professional study in law, commerce, and engineering, and added new programs, courses, and facilities during the two decades prior to 1930. The faculty solidified its already considerable influence in academic policies and decisions, but the overall administrative organization remained much the same as it had been. The university's essential character persisted, and its enrollment remained modest, though it did reach record numbers in 1930–31 and 1935–36. The increasing competition for students, funding, and recognition was a palpable concern at W&L, as it was elsewhere in higher education, stimulating the need to cultivate alumni and develop a professional fund-raising operation that would take further shape, sometimes fitfully, in the 1930s and beyond.

The Depression severely challenged all of higher education but perhaps especially the small, struggling colleges with modest endowments and the large, established institutions that had expanded so much in the 1920s. Indeed, the great majority of colleges founded before the Civil War no longer existed by 1930. Washington and Lee responded to these challenges by drawing on its limited endowment, the support of alumni, and student enrollments to maintain its economic viability without sacrificing quality. It relied also on the character, intelligence, and ingenuity of its new president and his administration, a small but committed faculty, and an experienced board of trustees.

Washington and Lee was governed by a self-perpetuating board of trustees, whose members served without term limits and appointed new members when existing ones died or resigned. The board's principal duties were to appoint a president, review and approve other appointments (including faculty members as well as senior administrators), review all university policies, and discharge its fiduciary duty in oversight of institutional finances and commitments. The trustees were definitely involved in all key university decisions and functioned much like other institutional governing bodies in the United States, though self-perpetuating ones were becoming less common.

Most W&L board members were drawn from the local area or from the South, and most were doctors, lawyers, judges, and businessmen. With few exceptions, all were graduates of the university. No religious affiliation was required for appointment, but most were Presbyterian or Episcopalian, and the denomination of all trustees, and even new faculty appointments, was publicly noted well into the twentieth century. The board reflected the institution's deep roots in the Shenandoah Valley and, increasingly, its appeal to students from other regions, especially the Northeast and Midwest. Complaints emerged from time to time, especially from administrators, about the narrow compass and provincialism of some trustees, especially as the university responded to new challenges and attempted new things. President Henry Louis Smith complained of "village views and sects" that undermined the university's development. "A tiny ultra-patriotic group of little-business, home-grown, home-loyal, utterly sectarian villagers," he wrote to John W. Davis, "can neither visualize, long-for, manage, or build up a 20th century inter-state institution. They will instinctively feel hostile toward plans and people that are different from OURS and US."[13] On the other hand, former W&L president George Denny, then serving as president of the University of Alabama, lamented in 1930 that the W&L board and the university, had perhaps drifted too far from their southern and Presbyterian roots. He suggested that no more than a quarter of the student body should come from outside the South and saw no reason to go "to the ends of the earth" to recruit trustees. He noted the number of current trustees from New York, Cleveland, and St. Louis. "They are fine, able men, but I shudder to think what would become of the institution if their views regarding its control were carried into execution." He also noted that the board had just appointed a Baptist as the new president, though he appeared to be an "excellent man."[14]

Despite Denny's objections, W&L definitely benefited from trustees with distinguished national reputations. In 1930 the board's twelve members collectively reflected the university's local and traditional roots, as well as its national aspirations. The rector, or chair, was George Walker St. Clair of Tazewell, Virginia, the ranking member who had served on the board since 1901. Especially notable board members included John W. Davis and Newton D. Baker, as well as William McChesney Martin, president of the Federal Reserve Bank in St. Louis.

Davis, who served as a trustee for twenty-seven years, was arguably the most distinguished and well-connected individual ever to hold this office. He remained a significant presence at the university even beyond his time on the board. With deep connections to W&L, he enjoyed the friendship and respect of innumerable national figures, especially in the law, and from his earliest years was known for fairness, integrity, a noble bearing, and a graceful and modest manner. His father, John J. Davis, had in 1854 attended Judge J. W. Brockenbrough's Lexington law school, opened a practice in Clarksburg, and was an anti-secession delegate to the Virginia General Assembly in 1860–61. His son, John William, entered Washington and Lee as a sophomore in 1889 and then the W&L School of Law in 1894, studying with its two distinguished faculty members, John Randolph Tucker and Charles A. Graves. Tucker was the grandson of the annotator of Blackstone's *Commentaries* and had served in the US Congress for twelve years and as president of the American Bar Association. Deeply influenced by both men, Davis acquired a life-long devotion to Thomas Jefferson and the sanctity of the Constitution. He was appointed assistant professor of law at W&L in 1896. When Dean Tucker became ill, Davis was invited to continue on the faculty, but he longed to practice law and ended his work as an academic after one year.[15]

Davis launched a distinguished legal and political career, eventually serving in the US Congress from West Virginia, as solicitor general of the United States, US ambassador to the Court of St. James, president of the American Bar Association, president of the Council on Foreign Relations, and, as previously noted, Democratic nominee for president in 1924. But his true love was the law, and from his firm in Manhattan, where he moved in 1921, he pursued a career as a superb courtroom orator and effective litigator. He argued over 140 cases before the US Supreme Court (a record for the time) and reportedly turned away several opportunities to join that body in favor of active practice. His conservative inclination grew stronger as his practice became more lucrative and the social and economic reforms of the New Deal seemed, to him, to promote "statism" at the expense of individual rights. A strong defender of religious freedom (and supporter of Al Smith) he also represented the financier J. P. Morgan, was a founding member of the Liberty League, and argued the case against President Harry Truman's seizure of the steel industry in 1952. In his last major case, he represented the state of South Carolina before the US Supreme Court, arguing against Thurgood Marshall and the National Association for the Advancement of Colored People's (NAACP) support for racial desegregation of the schools. The unanimous 1954 decision in *Brown v. Board of Education* left Davis stunned and disappointed, and most definitely on the wrong side of history. But he retained the respect and admiration of all his colleagues, including Marshall.

Davis gave freely of his time to the university and was a major force in selecting Frank Gaines as president and in helping W&L to retain him. Davis was an astute adviser to presidents, deans, and his fellow trustees, and as a graduate of the College and the law school he understood as well as anyone the university's values, aspirations, and shortcomings. In his later years, the challenge of traveling by train to Lexington from New York precluded his regular attendance at board meetings, and he declined the invitation to serve as rector in February 1940.

Newton D. Baker, who was a class ahead of Davis in the law school, also went on to a distinguished national career. He served two terms as "reform" mayor of Cleveland, Ohio, and as secretary of war throughout Woodrow Wilson's administration, he presided over the marshaling of American resources for World War I. A Wilsonian idealist and avid supporter of the League of Nations, he was generally a moderate progressive on local and national issues. He was also a leading lawyer for the utility industry and, like Davis, increasingly put off by the policies of the New Deal. He was a reliable champion of many charitable causes and known for having an open mind and offering wise counsel on the board of trustees.

William McChesney Martin Sr. was also a graduate of Washington and Lee and a contemporary of Davis and Baker. He had been highly involved in student activities and was editor of the *Ring-Tum Phi*. He became a prominent banker in St. Louis and served as president of the Federal Reserve Bank in that city from 1929 to 1941. His close friends included Sen. Carter Glass and Benjamin Strong, president of the New York Federal Reserve. (His son and namesake attended Yale and enjoyed a long tenure as chair of the board of governors of the Federal Reserve System.)

Given its relatively small size and unlimited terms of office, the board was, unsurprisingly, a rather stable group. During the 1930s, it remained much the same except for the passing of Baker in 1937 and George St. Clair in 1939. Herbert Fitzpatrick of Huntington, West Virginia succeeded St. Clair as rector.

The experienced administration that Frank Gaines joined was dominated by Henry Donald Campbell, dean of the university since 1906; Robert Henry Tucker, newly appointed dean of the College and the acting president prior to Gaines's arrival, and three other deans—Glover D. Hancock of the School of Commerce (since 1920), James Lewis Howe of the School of Applied Science (since 1921), and William H. Moreland of the School of Law (since 1923). Paul Penick had been treasurer since 1913, Earl S. Mattingly the registrar since 1920 (appointed when he was an undergraduate student), and Blanche P. McCrum the university librarian since 1922. The School of Engineering, established in 1866, became the School of Applied Science in 1913, but engineering degrees continued to be offered at W&L until 1937. The School of Commerce, also envisioned in Lee's time, was established in 1905 as one of the earliest business schools at an American college or university and also one of the earliest to be professionally accredited. The School of Science and the College were consolidated into the new College of Arts and Sciences in 1939.

The faculty, numbering fifty ranked members (including five in law) and seven instructors, conducted most of the university's work, including academic policy and much of university governance. Eighteen faculty committees, all appointed by the president (who served as an ex officio member), covered virtually every aspect of university life, ranging from admissions to athletics, fraternities, and student social functions. The most important was the executive committee of the faculty, consisting of the president, the deans, and two elected faculty members. The Faculty Discussion Group, an important, but unofficial, regular forum for discussing faculty affairs and academic policies, was also the local chapter of the American Association of University Professors.

The Washington and Lee faculty was unusually stable and relatively small, thus leading to long-term relationships, mostly compatible. The list of faculty in 1930 included some who would figure prominently in years to come. Professor Edgar F. Shannon joined the English department in 1914, and his son would grow up on campus, attend W&L, and become president of the University of Virginia and an influential W&L trustee. Lucius J. Desha (Chemistry) was a major leader in the sciences and later served as dean of the College. Rupert N. Latture joined the faculty in 1920 and, though lacking a PhD, reached the rank of associate professor, was a cofounder of the Omicron Delta Kappa honorary fraternity, and served as an important source of counsel and a continuing, familiar presence on campus. William Gleason Bean (History) and Fitzgerald "Fitz" Flournoy (English), both in the early stages of their appointments, would enjoy long and distinguished teaching careers. Frank J. Gilliam (English), an alumnus and World War I veteran, joined the faculty in 1926 and would make his mark as a significant and much beloved university leader, especially in admissions and student life; students and their parents, as well as presidents and deans, valued his advice. And Ollinger Crenshaw, who graduated from W&L in 1925, joined the history faculty the following year, coached the tennis team from 1934–40, taught generations of students over forty-three years, and wrote the definitive history of the university, *General Lee's College*, published in 1969.

Faculty members were called upon to make sacrifices in their salaries and teaching duties during the 1930s, and they knew from their contacts with students in and outside the classroom of the economic distress and uncertainty that afflicted many families at the time. The teaching load at W&L compared favorably with those of similar institutions, requiring a substantial commitment to classroom instruction with little designated time for or emphasis upon research. The average class size in 1933 was 22.2 students (16.6 in laboratory sections), and faculty members taught an average 12.7 credit hours (roughly four classes of three hours each) and about eighty-five students per semester.[16]

AS FRANK GAINES OBSERVED, the 1930s "saw a world in tumult." The decade "began with a nation-wide fright because of economic upheaval on [an] unprecedented scale, and closed with nation-wide fright, even deeper and not so immediate, because of the peril of a war that menaces all humanity."[17] It was a challenging time to begin a new college presidency.

The stock market crash on October 29, 1929, signaled an end to the giddy prosperity of the 1920s and led eventually—but not immediately—to the Great Depression. Only a few months later, the market seemed to rebound in what many assumed, or at least hoped, was part of a normal business cycle. But by 1932, consumer spending and investment had plummeted and the country was gripped in a deflationary spiral. Unemployment rose to 10 million, interest rates fell, and institutional endowment earnings declined. President Herbert Hoover, who was reluctant to provide relief directly to citizens, nevertheless began to appreciate the extent of the problem and initiated a variety of measures to fund public works and bolster credit in the banking system. The Reconstruction Finance Corporation, for example, extended loans to banks and railroads as a means of economic stimulus, but this and other measures were simply not enough.

The economic crisis was especially grave between late 1932 and early 1933. Industrial production plunged, thousands of banks closed, and virtually all others were under state restrictions. Bank runs and currency hoarding were common. President Franklin D. Roosevelt's inauguration in March 1933 marked a major turning point in the nation's response to the emergency, ushering in a "New Deal" that provided relief and reform in virtually every aspect of the economy—shoring up the banking system, abandoning the gold standard, launching public works, directly (and through outright grants to the states and localities) employing many jobless, providing agricultural subsidies and land banks, and establishing major regional agencies such as the Tennessee Valley Authority. The courts overturned some of these actions, and free-market purists and the economic elites opposed nearly all of them, but their overall impact helped to restore national confidence and lay the foundations for a recovering economy. Roosevelt's efforts to rein in government spending and address the national debt precipitated another economic downturn in 1937—one that would not be completely overcome until the onset of massive public expenditures in World War II. The decade's economic troubles were more serious in the South, which Roosevelt termed "the nation's number one economic problem."

Colleges and universities were, of course, caught up in the economic crisis—buffeted by lower income, declining enrollment and tuition, and shrinking endowments. University leaders were forced to reduce budgets and staffing levels, loosen standards for admission, reallocate funds from operations to scholarships, and find new ways to generate revenue—all while attempting to preserve the values, reputations, and competitive positions of their institutions. At W&L, economic uncertainties precluded any sense of stability as trustees, administration, and faculty struggled to move the university forward. Indeed, positive changes were made in many aspects of university life, and Frank Gaines could always be counted upon to explain, exhort, cajole, and reassure alumni, faculty, and students in sonorous phrases and with an eye on what W&L was all about.

News about the economy cast a darkening shadow over the country, but the full dimensions of the problem were not apparent in 1929–30. W&L's enrollment totaled 912, including 102 law students. The endowment earned an average of 6.12 percent, or $88,621 (over $1.26 million in today's dollars) and contributed almost 25 percent of the university's operating budget. The next year was even better, with a record overall enrollment of 932 and a 6.14 percent return on the endowment.[18] But the onset of sustained deflation by 1931 undermined any hopes of recovery and was accompanied by major declines in virtually all national economic indicators.

As Gaines recalled, "In the early years of the decade, the income declined, slowly at first, then precipitately, until only three dollars were found to do the work for which four dollars had previously been available. A considerable fraction of our investments, formerly deemed secure, ceased to pay income, then reverted, often with accompanying costs which represented further drain upon diminishing revenues." At the same time, he was concerned that the efforts to ameliorate economic crisis might actually harm private colleges and universities. He noted that "some of the processes set in motion to relieve the national distress proved further handicaps to colleges and universities of private control. . . . [Public] Institutions of higher education in Virginia alone were aided by approximately twelve million dollars in these governmental grants. Various forms of new taxation, intended to guarantee security for the nation's toilers, have threatened, and still threaten, to prove dangerous items of cost, without appreciable benefit, to colleges of our type."[19]

Income from student fees, which contributed almost 63 percent of W&L's

operating budget in 1930, dropped significantly beginning in 1931, then gradually recovered after 1934. Rates of return on the endowment reached a low of 3.12 percent, while earnings decreased by 40 forty percent, to a low of $54,031 in 1935. The deflationary spiral exaggerated these losses, but they nevertheless posed a major challenge to sustaining the educational program. As Gaines commented in 1933, the major challenge for the university was "to live within its income and yet to maintain that distinction of service which justifies its existence."[20] In anticipation of just such a challenge, the trustees, at their meeting on January 19, 1932, authorized the executive committee, upon recommendation of the president, to "consolidate the work of the University and to dispense with the services of any employee, to reduce salaries, effect economies, and to do such things as, in their judgment, will promote the economical administration of the affairs of the University."[21]

The losses incurred in the university's real estate holdings (especially mortgages, typically considered a safe and stable investment) were the biggest hits on the endowment. The amount of past-due interest owed to the university reached $12,428 in 1932, and losses in the following year climbed to $176,327, with an additional $135,120 for real estate in foreclosure. In March 1934, the foreclosed loans of endowment funds on real-estate mortgages came to 17.6 percent of all endowment investments. This unanticipated downturn exceeded budget expectations and, as Treasurer Paul Penick reported, "salary cuts were not made early enough to prevent a large deficit" of $12,548 by 1933. A total of $39,000 was transferred from the endowment fund, partly to cover university operations. Though W&L monitored its properties and sought to sell those with some market value, many continued as a drag on the endowment portfolio, both in terms of expense and in decreasing its capacity to generate future income. Endowment-owned foreclosed properties also required additional maintenance and repair, payment of back taxes, and other expenses.

The administration was determined to avoid fiscal deficits and generally succeeded after 1933, largely through cuts and other savings. In fact, a budget surplus of $9,264 was recorded in 1934. Gaines reported that this resulted "by no increase in income but by severe measures of economy in administration. The total loss of income has amounted to about 17 percent. It was no small task to reduce cost of operation proportionately." He provided reassurance that "during the entire course of the depression the excellence of academic work has been sustained and the validity of the Washington and Lee degree has been in no sense impaired."[22] The trustees, of course, welcomed this affirmation.

These "severe measures of economy" included consolidating small class sections, offering advanced courses every other year rather than annually, and reducing the teaching staff. They also included cuts in salaries from the highest levels on down. In 1931–32, Washington and Lee reported a total of fifty-eight faculty members: twenty-one full professors, eleven associate professors, eighteen assistant professors, and eight instructors. These numbers would remain relatively stable over the next few years, but by 1933–34 the total had dropped to fifty-six, with reductions in compensation that included the senior administration.

Noting a budget deficit of "about $25,000" because of reduced student fees and endowment income, the board ordered a 5 percent reduction in salaries for all employees, effective on November 1, 1932. (The executive committee had determined during the summer that President Gaines would be paid $1,000 in addition to his regular salary to mitigate the effect of the reduction for him.) As the decade wore on, the board and administration adjusted and readjusted salaries in light of revenues and anticipated revenues. An additional 2 percent reduction across the board was approved for April 1, 1933, and the cut funds were restored on September 1, 1934. Gaines again received special attention from the trustees; his beginning salary in 1931–32 of $7,500 was increased in June 1935 to $12,000, though it was subject to the general 10 percent reduction for all employees. In November 1935, one half of that general cut, or 5 percent, was restored.[23] Though some reductions were eventually restored, the institution's "educational salaries" during the throes of the Depression were cumulatively reduced by almost 25 percent.[24] The real nature of these reductions, in terms of purchasing power, were mitigated somewhat by deflation, which also reduced prices, interest rates, and earnings. But the clear message was that fiscal prudence was paramount.

The size of the faculty was reduced slightly but not, as Gaines observed, in a manner to harm the traditional educational program: "the preparation and competence of the teaching staff shall not be invaded by a policy of employing instructors simply because they are cheap."[25] And as finances improved toward the end of the decade, adequate faculty compensation was again addressed. The board approved a new salary scale—intended also to address matters of equity—in January 1939.[26]

Overall university enrollment declined steadily from 1930–31 through 1934, reaching 827, an 11.3 percent drop. This situation led to understandable concern because of W&L's heavy reliance on student fees to support operations, even when measured against comparable institutions. "It is enough now to say," Gaines observed in 1932, "that herein is the chief peril of the University and that almost every problem we confront grows out . . . of these unhappy circumstances." At the same time, he reiterated his conviction "that there are some essential principles governing admission which cannot be sacrificed for any financial contingency."[27]

Fortunately, the numbers rebounded, reaching a new record enrollment of 954 in 1935–36 and generally holding steady at around 940 or higher until the onset of World War II. Law school enrollment fluctuated, ranging from a low of 78 in 1934–35 to a high of 112 two years later. At the end of the decade, 68 percent of those who completed undergraduate applications enrolled at W&L.

LIBERAL ARTS COLLEGES and smaller universities, in particular, tended to define themselves through a curriculum that, while less extensive and diverse than those at larger institutions, professed some particular focus. For its size, Washington and Lee maintained an unusual institutional mix of the liberal arts and professional programs, but the liberal arts were always considered the foundation. Soon after his arrival, Gaines sought to avoid spreading the faculty's effort too thinly across too many areas of study. The professional programs introduced in Lee's time to aid a recovering South were particularly difficult to sustain in a time of increased competition and limited funding. The School of Law was retained as a distinctive administrative and academic entity, but the School of Engineering was eliminated, journalism was reduced from a school to a department, and business study was largely confined to the third and fourth years. Despite his reassurances that economic challenges had not diminished W&L's offerings, Gaines believed that an overall tightening of the "scope of work" was needed to give more focus to the curriculum and also to help meet the resource challenges of the Depression decade. In 1939, he took pride in the fact that W&L had managed to increase its endowment and reduce the breadth of its curriculum at the same time.

Developing a liberal arts curriculum involved both the conception of the liberal arts—their composition, value, and purpose—and how they were implemented. Most often, the critical element for implementation resided in the "core" or general degree requirements that all students must meet regardless of major, mostly in the first year or two of study. How Washington and Lee went about structuring, and restructuring, the educational experience of its students in the seven decades after 1930 reveals a good deal about the institution and its academic culture.

The liberal arts were traditionally thought to constitute the foundation for more specialized study and to develop educated individuals with analytical skills and shared knowledge of history, literature, philosophy, and the scientific method. In the nineteenth century, these included a heavy dose of the classics and study of ancient languages like Latin and Greek. Over time, more emphasis was placed on science, politics, psychology, and economics. In any event, study in the liberal arts was presumed to result in "well rounded" persons who could function effectively in many fields and occupations. Beyond that, the details specific to each institution were important, as was the fully articulated outcome. At W&L, the curriculum was important not only for imparting knowledge but for developing character. Frank Gaines was never hesitant to share his views on the matter.

Gaines was a man of his time, and his romantic sense of the region and its history was linked with his vision for the liberal arts college and its curriculum. Reacting against the materialism of the previous decade and the economic travail that occurred at its end, he looked to the liberal arts to reveal the finer points of life and character that he believed were so desperately needed. He looked to the antebellum South as a model. In a speech to the Southern Society of New York City in December 1930, just months after he had assumed the W&L presidency, he expounded on the popular and idealized notion of the Old South—replete with Southern belles, Uncle Remus tales, and paeans to life on the plantation. "But the ideal of the actual Old South was something nobler," he said, based on "a fierce individualism, an affirmation of the everlasting right of the unit of personality. The ideal included vigor of personality, charm of personality, and liberty of personality. The conformities of this leveling machine age were inconceivable." By "personality" Gaines meant what might also be termed "character" or "nature." In his view, this was the truly distinguishing feature of the "mode of life" of the Old South—a "lofty epicureanism . . . the most spacious and most gracious manner of existence yet achieved upon this continent." In this quite anachronistic and mawkish portrayal, southerners doted on leisure, beauty, and the cultivation of character, in contrast to people in the modern age of materialism and striving, "marked by universal Babbittism, by the inanities of conformity and false standards," a time "when we have worshipped the great tribal god, Success, only to find the fruits upon his altar bitter to our taste."[28] (While the realities of Babbittism were evident, Gaines did not acknowledge in his speech many realities of the Old South—especially slavery.)

The liberal arts college, especially in the South, should therefore, according to Gaines, cultivate and expand individual character rather than focus solely on specialized knowledge and occupational preparation. In an address to the Association of Virginia Colleges in 1933, Gaines noted the higher salaries earned by college graduates but lamented that education was too focused on the narrow goal of "economic competence." Lashing out at the "superficial prosperity" of 1929, he referred to the "lack of personal culture, the provincialism, the callousness of social conscience, the selfishness that issued into unparalleled crime" that had revealed economic and educational problems. The liberal arts college could remedy these by preparing students for "citizenship in the larger world, the broadest world of understanding of all common human problems and sympathy for all human aspiration."[29] In a 1940 address to the same organization, he regretted the increasing role of educational accrediting organizations in fostering standardization and professional specialization, and he reiterated his opposition to a curriculum "designed chiefly to prepare government clerks and in extra-curricular endeavor dedicated to the one ultimate accolade, an invitation to send a football team to a bowl." As war raged in Europe and threatened to spread, Gaines claimed that "the significant single development of our day is the inter-weaving of all human destiny into one problem, the new solidarity of the human race," regardless of national boundaries and policies." He urged that students be prepared for leadership in this world with values "that do not rise and fall with the stock market."[30]

The faculty ultimately shaped W&L's curriculum. While faculty members might not have concurred with Gaines's entire philosophical view and historical allusions, they did agree that the liberal arts curriculum should prepare students for life and leadership rather than for "technical tasks" and specific occupations that seemed increasingly paramount in higher education. As Gaines observed, "the aim of mental training is not so much to give a student a definite group of facts as to form in him attitudes and habits of approaching and handling knowledge."[31] Ultimately, professionalization and specialization became centered in postgraduate programs, and liberal arts preparation for these became more important and less an end in itself.

The W&L curriculum never contained a specific course or group of courses that all students were required to take, such as "Contemporary Civilization," introduced at Columbia University (the "core") in 1919 and joined by "Literature Humanities" in 1947. Neither did it mandate the study of designated texts (the "great books") that Robert Hutchins and Mortimer Adler instituted at the University of Chicago.[32] Rather, W&L followed the prevailing practice of requiring study across a range, or distribution, of regular departmental courses to achieve a combination of breadth and depth as a foundation for more intensive study in the major. In 1930, W&L students pursuing the BA degree enrolled in prescribed first-year courses: two in English, one each in foreign language, mathematics, and modern civilization, and two in science, along with a two-semester course in physical education and hygiene. The catalogue stated that this "group system, while preventing the abuses of the elective system, leaves still to the student a wide range of choice in the selection of his studies."[33]

The BA required 126 semester credit hours, distributed in four general disciplinary and subject matter groups (including languages and sciences), with a minimum number in advanced courses. A major in one department was to be selected after the sophomore year. A student could begin work toward a law degree after completing ninety-eight semester hours of credit toward the BA, and undergraduate programs could also be arranged to prepare for postgraduate study in medicine. In 1933, the minimum requirement for work to be taken in the junior and senior years was raised from thirty to forty-two hours, to ensure more emphasis on advanced study. Gaines also mentioned the need for exposure to "the significant arts of our civilization," in order, as he phrased it, to "endow personality with the capacity for adequate and enriching appreciation of the fineness achieved in our upward struggle."[34] The university's effort to do more in the fine arts would increase after World War II and remained a goal through the remainder of the century.

The School of Commerce offered a BS degree, based on a liberal arts curriculum with advanced courses in accounting, statistics, and business administration. A BS degree was also offered with a general engineering concentration, introduced in 1934, but was terminated, along with the engineering department, at the end of the 1936–37 academic year.[35] W&L also awarded a Master of Arts degree, which was phased out in 1948. Gaines presided over significant changes to tighten the "scope of work." As he wrote John W. Davis in August 1936, "We are moving this curriculum to the unified program of the small college of arts and sciences; since I have been here we have reduced 'the School of Journalism' to a department of no more importance than any other department, and we have abandoned 'the School of Engineering' as outside the legitimate field of our endeavor. This leaves us with a fairly coherent program of the arts and sciences and, of course, of the School of Law."[36]

WASHINGTON AND LEE, unlike most small colleges, attracted students from all corners of the United States, including many from the Northeast who were drawn to "General Lee's college." Virginia accounted for the largest number of W&L students from any single state in 1929 (190), but New York registered the second-highest number (68), followed by West Virginia (50) and Florida (48). Roughly 59 percent of W&L students hailed from southern states (including West Virginia and Texas), 20 percent from the Northeast (including Maryland), and 16 percent from the Midwest. The largest declared denominational religious affiliation among students was, not surprisingly, Presbyterian. Sixty percent of undergraduate students were Presbyterian, Methodist, or Episcopalian, with similar distributions in the law school. Only thirty-two students said they were Roman Catholic in 1929, and fifty-four Jewish.[37] Virtually every student declared a religious affiliation.

These numbers did not change dramatically over the course of the decade. In 1940, almost 30 percent hailed from the Northeast, and 53 percent from the South. This decline in regional enrollment, though modest, did cause Dean of Admissions Frank Gilliam to lament in 1939 "the almost alarming shrinkage in freshmen admitted from the south this session." He suggested that competitive full-tuition scholarships be offered, "possibly under some such name as the Robert E. Lee Scholarships, to students living in the eleven states that composed the Southern Confederacy."[38] Gaines reported in 1940 that due to a large overall number of applications, "we have found it necessary to set unofficial geographical quotas for certain sections of the country" and to send "representatives of the Committee on Admissions, usually the Dean of Students, several times a year to the great centers of population."

African Americans were not admitted, and none applied. While it was not an explicit university policy to exclude them, it was a long-standing and deeply embedded practice. But except for the category of race and an occasional "unofficial" geographical preference, there is little evidence that W&L employed or imposed admissions quotas, religious or otherwise. The task of filling each undergraduate class and attracting qualified applicants to the law school was challenge enough. Washington and Lee students were drawn overwhelmingly from middle- and upper-class backgrounds and were graduates of public high schools as well as private preparatory schools. A strong preference was accorded to children of alumni. Most students paid full tuition and aspired to careers in the professions and business (with a smattering of would-be journalists, clergymen, and teachers). Many, of course, were uncertain what career they wished to pursue, and some were steered into college by families hoping they would gain a sense of direction and purpose. In any event, the effects of economic depression were felt even among those students and families who previously had been relatively secure.

Frank Gaines saw the university's role in shaping young men as a noble calling. In his first *Report of the President*, released in May 1931, he noted that while W&L had more applications than it could accept, it should "widen the scope of our appeal to the type of student we earnestly court" and avoid those "who are utterly unresponsive to the enthusiasms, the codes, the standards which are the peculiar heritage of this University." Unlike institutions that "aspire toward pretentiousness and magnitude . . . We shall be content with smallness if thereby we may achieve fineness and genuineness." The successful preparation of such students depended on "the happiness and the loyalty and the harmony of a faculty," which were "not less important than its competence." This faculty, he pointedly noted to the trustees, was roughly half the size, relative to enrollment, of faculty at comparable universities.

As Gaines welcomed new students to the campus in September 1933, he reviewed the hard times the university had survived during its long history and invited them to look on the bright side. If "the world around us is gloomy with sick fancies, then we should cherish all the more the privilege we have, to gather upon this green loveliness, to walk the ancient cloisters where heroic feet have trod before, to delight in good companionships, to live in the reality of great ideas, to shape our own dreams." He lamented the paucity of financial support for students—a "demand for ten dollars for every one"—and promised that not all of the available funds went for athletes. He exhorted students who were better off to understand the plight of their less advantaged fellows, and he warned of the corrosive effects of economic travail on student life. "I wish that in this period of great economic distress we could hold down to reasonable limits the standards of student living," he said, appealing "to the boys of comfortable means to abstain from standards that . . . drive their fellows to bankruptcy or despair. I am saying frankly that we have fifty per cent of our students who [sic] parents are hard put to it to meet the necessary expenses of keeping the boys here." Washington and Lee, he concluded, "is trying above all things to keep this depression from lowering the standard of personality which characterizes our student body—our most precious contemporary opportunity."[39]

Administrators complained continually about the lack of adequate funds for scholarships, a concern that grew steadily through the Depression years and into the 1960s and beyond. Most aid was in the form of loans, with interest. In 1930, over $10,000 was available to lend, but with endowment earnings dropping, the university relied on other limited funds to provide some student financial assistance. In 1935–36, approximately 15 percent of tuition revenue was allocated to help about thirty percent of the student body. This policy, as Gaines put it, "is made necessary if Washington and Lee is not to become a rich man's school," a very real threat in the throes of the times. Later in the 1930s, the university received private donations designated for student financial aid and also relied on "work study" funding from the Federal Emergency Relief Administration and the National Youth Administration. (This source provided about $14,000 to 137 students in 1935–36.)

About half of new students chose to attend Freshman Camp, and all participated in a subsequent week of orientation, wearing the blue beanies familiar to generations of freshmen until the 1960s. Among the innovations driven by Gaines and Gilliam during the 1930s were designated faculty advisors; resident upperclassmen counselors in the dormitories; a program of meetings throughout the year, led by the director of freshman work under the overall leadership of the dean of students; and a continuing emphasis on "the validity of the abiding student traditions," as Gaines put it, "such as the honor system, the emphasis upon courtesy, the inculcation of friendliness, and the broadly democratic recognition of the worth of every individual."[40] Gilliam was especially insistent that an organized program of "guidance" and "freshman adjustment" was essential in preparing students to cope with the demands of college life and personal independence, as well as to inculcate university traditions. (These efforts presaged the organized first-year programs implemented widely throughout the country beginning in the 1970s to get students off on the right foot and help them persist toward earning a degree.) Housing all freshmen in a single facility was integral to such a process, but at the end of the decade only about 70 percent of an entering class could be accommodated in the existing dormitories.

The undergraduate culture at W&L during the 1930s was similar to that of other small, all-male colleges. Students generally fit the mold of the "college man" of the era: "someone with an intense loyalty to his institution; a special mode of dress; the expectation that he drank socially, if not to excess; a devil-may-care attitude regarding young women; and a marginal association with the life of the mind—the latter being exemplified by the 'gentleman's C.'"[41] The academic environment at W&L was not overly rigorous but did demand reasonable attention. Failure to maintain a certain overall academic standard (spelled out in the terms of the "Automatic Rule") could result in probation or expulsion. Social life revolved around fraternities, more or less overseen by the faculty and administration (especially at the major dances and social events like the Fancy Dress Ball) to the degree expected in a time of in loco parentis. Young women visiting on weekends stayed in approved homes or boarding houses in Lexington and were expected to observe a late-night curfew. Nonetheless, W&L men were known for their high spirits (often due to whiskey and beer), and the tales of curfew violations among the young women were legion, if perhaps exaggerated. Most students did not have automobiles on campus, though they could if granted parental permission. Even in the 1930s the tradition of traveling "down the road" to nearby women's colleges was already established.

Fraternities provided much of the student housing and dining services, as well as social activities that often tested the limits of safety, taste, and decorum. The university administration devoted considerable time and attention to these organizations and their behavior. Dean Gilliam reported to Gaines in 1936 that the practice of "Hell Week" in fraternity initiations had been abolished, along with the Vigilance Committee, which Gaines called, much too hopefully, the "last relic of any kind of hazing." These steps coincided with the faculty decision to require that all fraternities have housemothers beginning in 1936–37. For his part, Dean Robert Henry Tucker claimed to detect in student government and other activities, especially fraternity initiation practices, "a perceptible growth in the sense of responsibility on the part of the students." He declared, also too optimistically, that the "idea that the American student is essentially a playboy is rapidly becoming obsolete."[42]

The most elaborate single social event at the university was the Fancy Dress Ball, the largest of the major dances held in the fall, winter, and spring, and among the various dance sets held just after examinations ending the fall semester. In January 1935, the Columbia Broadcasting System transmitted a live broadcast from Doremus Gymnasium to ninety-three radio stations across the country. The decorations and dress became increasingly elaborate (white tie was required for faculty), and national headliners often supplied the music. In January 1938, for example, the theme was the antebellum South, and the gym was decorated like a garden in Charleston, South Carolina, with professionally costumed students posing as characters discussed in a historical note prepared by Professor Ollinger Crenshaw.

The quadrennial Mock Convention was correct again in 1928 with the nomination of Al Smith and in 1932 with Franklin D. Roosevelt. In six tries (no convention was held in 1920) the Mock Convention had predicted the eventual nominee of the party not inhabiting the White House on five occasions. The Republican conventions of 1936 and 1940 broke the record with two incorrect choices—a close selection of Arthur Vandenburg rather than the eventual nominee Alf Landon in 1936 and Charles L. McNary rather than Wendell Willkie in 1940. The tradition would again be interrupted by war and a much depleted student population in 1944.

In 1930 it cost $250 a year (almost $3,600 in 2015 dollars) to attend Washington and Lee, which also covered up to seven days in the local hospital ($2.75 a day after that) and most of the standard fees, including $5 set aside for "wanton or accidental damage" to college property "by students who can not be identified." Two hundred dollars of the fee would be remitted for "the son of any minister of religion who is actually engaged in such" or retired because of physical disability. A special university fund covered fees for "candidates for the Christian ministry," subject to application and endorsement by "competent authority." Fees were also remitted for students from Rockbridge County.

Lodging in the Lees and Graham Dormitories—offering single and double rooms, as well as some suites with common study rooms—ranged from $50 to $100 per student per semester, without board, and the University Dining Hall, accommodating 140 people, charged up to $27.50 per month for a meal plan. Lodging and board in university-approved private homes was also available, sometimes at lower cost.

Students were accustomed to strict attendance policies, which generally prevailed until the changes in student culture of the late 1960s and 1970s. In 1930, freshmen were permitted no absences at all in the first semester (unless excused for illness or other reasons), a prohibition that continued for students on probation or those who earned less than a "C" average in the previous semester. In the sophomore year and beyond, students on the dean's list were generally exempt from limited absences. Professors were required to submit "daily reports of every absence" to the registrar's office, which some faculty considered an onerous burden.

All W&L students knew about the "Automatic Rule" stipulating that a student could not continue in the university if he "fails to pass in nine semester-hours of work or receives grade F in six semester-hours." A student who failed to meet certain benchmarks in the sophomore and junior years would also be expelled. Students could petition the president for readmission on probation, which would be decided by a special committee. New students were warned that the "loss of five or six per cent of the student body in a single year by such elimination is quite common."

Gaines was pleased at the end of the decade by the quality and extent of student extracurricular activity, including religious life. He remarked about the "perfect maze of these student activities on and about the campus," including formal and informal clubs, student publications, literary societies, glee club, college band, dramatic and musical performances, debates and public speaking, and intramural sports. Harry M. Philpott, Director of Religious Activities (who would later leave W&L and become president of Auburn University), led a program that energized the most active student participants (approximately eighty in 1939). Speakers came to campus from near and far, "deputation teams" were dispatched to other colleges and churches to conduct worship services, musical concerts were staged, and parties held with a focus on nonfraternity men.[43]

Many students still failed to attain a degree. A faculty study of the 1935 entering class revealed that only 39 percent had graduated in four years. In offering explanations for this "discouraging figure," Gaines noted that W&L's record in this regard was better than the national average (which included less selective institutions), and that illness, financial exigency, and leaving early for law school were possible reasons for students' failure to graduate. He also observed that the students who dropped out tended to be the least prepared upon entering college. "We should also recall," he wrote the trustees, "that the ultimate contribution of a college is not to be measured exclusively in terms of the men who actually receive a degree; some of our finest alumni left this campus without taking a degree."[44]

Athletics were an important part of student life—indeed, university life. By the beginning of the twentieth century, collegiate sports in the United States were diverging from their European counterparts in terms of defining the student experience and attracting attention from alumni and the general public. While athletic programs were still a far cry from the enormous enterprises they would become in the latter half of the century, they nevertheless exhibited some domineering characteristics early on, including a good deal of hoopla and chicanery.

As they did at most other universities, intramural sports garnered the most student participants at W&L. The role of the classic "student athlete" was evident across campus. E. Parker (Cy) Twombly, Assistant Professor of Physical Education, on the faculty since 1923 and long-time athletic director, reported that 680 students participated in intramural sports in 1937. These activities "sought to instill a better understanding of the physical life and the basic experiences that are conducive to fuller living," and a dedicated field for these sports was desperately needed. But intercollegiate football was clearly the dominant spectator sport.

Spending a fall afternoon watching the Generals play on Wilson Field was a regular weekend social activity, replete with students in raccoon coats and sweaters, carrying blankets and flasks, with their school spirit on full display. Unfortunately, the football team's record was usually mediocre, reaching a low point under Coach James DeHart in 1932, when they won only one game and lost nine. Coach W. E. "Tex" Tilson took over in 1933 and managed a 7–3 record two years later, along with a conference championship. But things declined after that, and Coach Tilson left in 1940, with an overall record in eight seasons of 31–35–6.

W&L was competing at a high level. It was one of fourteen charter members of the Southern Conference, which formed in Atlanta in February 1921 and included most of the members of the future Southeastern and Atlantic Coast Conferences, formed in 1933 and 1953, respectively.[45] Six new members joined the Southern Conference in 1936: the Citadel, Davidson, Furman, George Washington, the University of Richmond, and William and Mary. Clearly, universities were sorting themselves out into public and private, large and small, and perhaps most important, those that could subsidize student athletes and those that could not.

Gaines was ambivalent about intercollegiate sports, as were many university leaders then and now. In 1935, he pointed to the four Southern Conference championships won by W&L teams, touting "this important division of student effort" under "the control of men who are themselves sympathetic with the ideals and purposes of the University," and praising the students involved as "thoroughly representative of the best in our group."[46] He was also increasingly confronted (he might have preferred the term "afflicted") with the dilemmas presented by intercollegiate athletics throughout his long presidential tenure, and especially by football—the high coaches' salaries, financial aid for athletes, the declining academic performance of players, and the persistent call among alumni for better teams and winning records.

Not all alumni were enthusiastic about intercollegiate competition, though—especially when it seemed to undermine academic pursuits—and Gaines was usually caught in the middle. He responded in 1935 to a complaint from trustee Herbert Fitzpatrick about the football coach's salary, concurring that it was "almost ridiculous that a coach should receive more money than one of the most valued professors" but pointing out that the situation was dictated by "supply and demand." Indeed, another Southern Conference member was reportedly paying its coach more than twice as much.[47] Most disagreements centered on the degree of financial subsidy for athletes. Some eager alumni offered to pay the tuition of skilled athletes who had already been admitted to the institution. Clarence Sager, president of the Alumni Association, took great exception to this, noting that he considered "the athletic scholarship idea wholly incompatible with the conception and purpose of the Alumni Fund." He was also concerned that "secret subsidization" would occur outside the bounds of either the Alumni Fund or the university administration. Gaines listened conscientiously to all parties in this dispute and longed for an agreeable compromise: "I am not sure that my own ideas will prevail; but I do believe that some system can be brought about that will be in accord with the heritage transmitted to us, that will offer hope of harmony and not of the bitter divisiveness that seems to follow in the wake of athletic discussion."[48] But he was loathe to permit scholarship funds awarded specifically for athletic ability at a time when the endowment struggled to provide general scholarships for worthy and needy students.

Gaines, along with many of his peers, was continually bedeviled by the fact that faculty, students, and alumni held "varying shades of opinion" on intercollegiate athletics. Largely at his prodding, the board appointed in 1939 a Special Committee on Athletic Policies and Procedures, consisting of three representatives each of trustees, alumni, faculty, and students. In April, the committee issued its report, recommending that athletes not be subsidized but that the university continue its existing policy of granting, on the recommendation of alumni chapters, twenty-five awards of $250 to be applied toward tuition for students who met admission criteria and demonstrated need or were "meritorious in terms of personal character." Recipients must maintain an average grade of "C" in their academic work, and renewal of their award would involve consultation with the alumni chapter. Gaines welcomed this affirmation of academic standards and encouraged the alumni chapters to "be engaged more seriously to discover and encourage boys who would be worthy of aid from the University's normal budget for scholarship purposes." For his part, Gaines always emphasized broad student participation in a variety of sports, as opposed to focusing on high-profile intercollegiate athletics. As he reported in 1940, "with due regard to the hunger of the spectators for gladiatorial combat, our effort has been consistently to promote the interest in those branches of sport that may be called continuation sports, the games a boy may carry on to the later years, swimming, golf, tennis, and the like." But the issue of intercollegiate athletics—especially subsidization—was hardly resolved.[49]

—————

WHEN JOHN W. DAVIS graduated in 1895, the W&L School of Law was one of only eight in the country that allowed its students to complete their studies in one year. He was also one of only two law students to hold a bachelor's degree, and some students were even admitted without high school diplomas. The story of the law school for the next three decades would reflect efforts to raise academic standards, build a faculty large enough to diversify the curriculum, adequately fund the law library, and achieve professional recognition while also sustaining the enrollment that financed the whole enterprise.

The trustees voted in 1906 to require the prior completion of at least two years of college-level study prior to admission and specified a minimum number of academic credits in 1908. These efforts paid off; Washington and Lee was admitted to the Association of American Law Schools (AALS) in 1920. W&L had also elected to comply with the recommendation of the American Bar Association (ABA) in 1921 that law schools require at least three years of work and maintain a law library of at least 7,500 volumes. With understandable pride, the law school achieved these standards and was ranked "Class A" by the ABA in 1923, along with only thirty-eight other schools in the country and four in the South. The challenge, especially in poor economic times, was to maintain that position, especially in meeting AALS standards for at least ten thousand volumes and meeting certain minimum levels of library purchases.

Legal education was evolving but still retained its traditional character, emphasizing apprenticeships supervised by experienced lawyers. In 1930, the small but capable law faculty consisted of four professors and one associate professor. Professor William H. Moreland, a Hampden-Sydney graduate with a 1906 W&L law degree and dean since 1923, was succeeded in 1946 by Clayton E. Williams.

Law school enrollment fluctuated more than that of W&L as a whole, primarily because as a professional school it was more sensitive to economic circumstances and shifting employment opportunities for lawyers. (Even the dean wondered in 1930 whether it was "advisable to turn out a great number of

young lawyers. The country does not seem to be in any urgent need of them.")
Law school enrollment remained around one hundred throughout the 1930s,
except when it decreased to seventy-eight in 1934. Around a third of law students hailed from Virginia and, of the remainder, about three-quarters were
from other southern states. In 1934, 58 percent of the students had done their
collegiate work at W&L, and most law students had not received a baccalaureate degree before beginning their legal studies. After the enrollment drop
in 1934, W&L began offering a $100 reduction in tuition for those admitted
holding the bachelor's degree, both to increase enrollment and to attract better-
prepared students.

Dean Moreland observed that improvements in academic quality had taken
a financial toll on the law school. Faculty struggled with the enrollment of 207
in 1911–12, a number due in part to comparatively lower academic standards
and allowing men to complete their studies in two years. But the subsequent
decrease in admissions was, as Moreland put it, also "a matter of grave concern"
because of its fiscal impact. The law school's place in the overall financial picture of the university was perhaps an especially sensitive matter at a time when
the undergraduate curriculum was becoming more focused and other professional programs, such as engineering and journalism, were being eliminated
or cut back. The law school's academic standards had also not been beyond
question. On the other hand, it had many loyal and some quite distinguished
graduates and a long-standing role at the institution. While these tensions were
kept in-house, they involved matters that the president and the trustees had to
consider.

Moreland's report in 1931 was lengthy and explicit: "The Law Faculty feels . . .
that we should lay before the administration a very frank comment upon the
present condition of the Law School—how it compares with other law schools
as to equipment, teaching force, and quality of work done; whether it is maintaining its position among such law schools; and if it is not, what we must do
in the future to maintain that position."[50] The school had accomplished a great
deal, considering its "meager faculty, equipment and financial support, and
a small student body." Given the choice between high enrollments and high
standards, the law school had "deliberately cast in its lot with the best" and was
challenged to keep up with its peers. Moreland observed that W&L had "not at
any time complied with the rule for expenditures" for law library acquisitions
set by the AALS, which had recently boosted its requirements to holdings of
ten thousand volumes and expenditures of at least $10,000 over five years.

W&L met the first standard but was falling further behind on its expenditure, resulting in an inadequate supply of textbooks and incomplete sets of US State Reports, as well as English, Scots, and Irish Reports.

Moreland also regularly reminded the president and the trustees that W&L had fewer law faculty members than its peer institutions (Virginia had seven faculty, North Carolina eight, and Duke nine) and was thus forced to offer a restricted and rigid curriculum. The addition of only one more faculty member would permit the offering of additional courses, "thereby giving the students an opportunity to specialize somewhat in their second and third years." Improving the curriculum required an increase in faculty, and both were necessary to ensure a favorable comparison with competing law schools. (By 1941, the regular faculty included three additional ranked members, though one professor was already on leave for military service.) Nor did the dean neglect to mention the law school facilities. Tucker Hall "has been in use now for thirty-two years, and it has been, since the day of its completion, an eyesore to the campus." From faculty offices to the lighting system, the building was "ill-adapted to the uses of a law school."[51]

With obvious frustration, Moreland observed that other W&L departments had been expanded, while "the one separate and distinctive school of the University, the only one which awards its own degree, has been left unimproved and undeveloped for at least ten years." In his opinion, the university's reputation "is carried and maintained to a greater degree by its law graduates than by any of its other alumni." In 1935, he reiterated the need for additional faculty, lamenting that "at this time, we have less teaching resources than we had fifteen years ago," since one faculty member was also teaching in the School of Commerce. "In the meantime, each of our competitors has been gradually adding to its teaching force."[52] The frustration was understandable but perhaps not entirely appreciated in other quarters of the university at a time of restricted budgets.

As the economic depression deepened and enrollment declined further, it became difficult for the university to allocate more resources to the law school. One of these enumerated needs had to be addressed, however, when Tucker Hall was destroyed by fire on the morning of December 15, 1934. The pile of gray stone, built in 1900, which broke from the red brick and white columned style of the Colonnade, was engulfed in flame by the time Lexington fire fighters arrived. Fortunately, W&L and VMI students, as well as some townspeople, were on the scene and saved as many books and belongings as they could from the first floor. Nevertheless, all the books and papers of three faculty members, the books and notes of many students, and the entire contents of the law library were lost. Law students were dismissed early for the Christmas holidays.

Steps were taken immediately to find accommodation for the law school, with classes offered in rooms throughout the campus and the law library relocated to a large space in the engineering building. Funds were provided for new library materials, and local law offices opened their libraries to students and faculty members. Remarkably, these emergency measures enabled law school classes to resume on January 3, 1935. Almost as quickly, the administration and trustees determined to construct a new home for the law school in the same location. With the help of alumni gifts, the new Tucker Hall was completed a little more than a year after the fire and was occupied in February 1936. For the many people who thought the old building a large gray monstrosity totally out of keeping with its environs, the new structure was an improvement, as it rather perfectly extended the red-brick facade of the Colonnade. Dean Moreland celebrated both an increase in enrollment in 1936, due in part to the $100 scholarships for college graduates, and a "beautiful new building" that "has proved to be most adequate and comfortable, being a source of great pride to the faculty and students and of admiration to all who have inspected it." While the law library was "not quite the equivalent of the one we lost , . . . it is nearly so."[53]

The law school continued to attract a high proportion (42 percent in 1939) of students whose previous collegiate work had been done at other institutions, and the establishment of the W&L *Law Review* by the trustees in 1938 was a significant addition to the academic program and helped attract favorable outside attention.

THE DROP IN TUITION REVENUE, the declining return on endowment, and the general absence of public financial support for independent institutions like Washington and Lee highlighted the critical importance of private gifts. While notable contributions came from donors not connected to the university, alumni were the most likely and consistent source of support.

The trustees were all W&L graduates, and other alumni regularly weighed in on institutional policies and direction through letters, telegrams, visits, and meetings of alumni groups. The alumni secretary supervised an office, edited the alumni magazine, and generally boosted the university to this constituency. Harry K. ("Cy") Young, '17, arguably the greatest of all W&L athletes, took the office in June 1930 and combined the usual duties with active student recruiting in concert with local alumni groups; he also coached as an assistant in the athletics program. As the decade wore on, the university's reliance on organized former students increased. President Gaines reported in 1933 that an annual appeal to alumni had been launched, with permanent class secretaries appointed for most classes and the expenses covered "by a small group of generous sons of Washington and Lee." By 1934, the alumni office had located more than 90 percent of all living alumni (including many who had attended but not graduated) and boasted thirty active chapters (ten of which Gaines had personally visited during the previous year). The new Tucker Hall was mostly funded from alumni contributions. By 1936 the class secretary and local chapter arrangements were better organized but still a work in progress: 2,000 alumni responded to class letters and 644 sent contributions totaling $3,440 (rising to $5,700 in 1938).[54]

In 1939, the alumni board of trustees asked for an increase in appropriation that, along with funds raised in the annual class-agent campaign, would employ "Cy" Young as a full-time alumni secretary. Gaines supported this idea and referred it for consideration to a special committee of the university trustees— noting that it was important to have a long-range plan for alumni work and to keep the director of such work as "an officer of University administration." He wanted the alumni office to be focused more on overall communication rather than just fund-raising, and he did *not* want alumni affairs to proceed as a separate volunteer or corporate entity outside the university (already an issue at some institutions). Young was appointed to this new full-time university position, which Gaines hoped would promote "the unbroken sustaining of the best relation, reciprocally helpful, between students and their Alma Mater," adding that to "achieve any such purpose, this work needs centralized, consistent, expert, and devoted direction."[55]

THE ALUMNI FUND WAS the most important continuing source of gifts to the university for its operations and endowment, especially during the Depression years. But some of the larger gifts were from those who never attended W&L. These included the Robert P. Doremus bequest, established in 1916 and valued at $141,177 (including $42,500 for the Memorial Gymnasium) and an additional $1,490,766 in 1936 upon Mrs. Doremus's death. The bequest of the entire Doremus estate famously resulted from the kindness of an anonymous (and still unknown) student who offered to guide Mr. and Mrs. Doremus around campus during an unannounced visit. Even though they were not otherwise connected to the university, they expressed appreciation for its beauty and friendliness, and were among its most generous supporters. Another generous non-alumnus was John Barton Payne, who in 1931 made W&L one of three heirs to his estate. Upon his death in 1935, the bequest was valued at $256,116. The family of Cyrus McCormick had long been associated with W&L and added $90,000 in 1925 to the $110,000 they had already donated, and Cyrus Mc-Cormick Jr. gave $102,240 in International Harvester Company securities to the university in 1939. These contributions, coming as they did during tough economic times, seemed even larger. The final Doremus gift in 1936 actually doubled the university's endowment, to almost $3 million.

Trustees and administrators worried constantly about maintaining university buildings and facilities, especially after the Tucker Hall fire. A relatively stable enrollment precluded sudden demands to accommodate more students, but older facilities like laboratories and residence halls became less suitable for academic purposes over time, and normal wear and tear required maintenance and, eventually, renovation. The historic buildings at W&L, particularly the Colonnade, required preservation and posed special maintenance challenges that could not wait for the nation's economic recovery.

By the end of the decade, over a million dollars had been invested in the physical plant, not including more than $150,000 of improvements made to the fraternity houses. Gaines boasted "that not a penny of the money spent has been from any government sources." A number of projects were completed in 1936. The Washington College group, including Washington, Payne, and Robinson Halls, was remodeled and fireproofed (a consultant referred to the conditions of these buildings in 1935 as "deplorable"); the necessary funds for the renovation drew heavily from the Payne bequest (amortized as renovations were completed, with the remainder placed in endowment). Newcomb Hall was also remodeled to better "fit" with the design of the new Tucker Hall. The Carnegie Library was enlarged and the stacks fireproofed, and a new Student Union was constructed at the corner of Washington Street and Lee Avenue (currently the site of Evans Dining Hall). In response to the oft-repeated pleas of Dean Gilliam and President Gaines that the university provide on-campus accommodations for the entire freshman class, the Graham and Lees Dormitories were refurbished, and a new residence hall was in the works in 1940. A new power plant was also completed in time for the beginning of classes in 1938. Some properties adjacent to campus were also acquired—including fifteen acres around the Liberty Hall ruins and 210 acres along the north side of campus.[56]

At the end of the decade, even with projects underway, the list of unfilled needs included an auditorium to accommodate events and convocations, a new classroom building and dining hall, and completion of the chemistry building. In 1938, Gaines wrote to several trustees that the library was a top priority: "As a matter of fact, because of the increasing appreciation of the function of the library in education, Washington and Lee will soon be in the sad position of having the most archaic and most inadequate library of any of the leading colleges in this state."[57] Gaines also informed the trustees a year later that the Faculty Discussion Group had unanimously passed a resolution for more comfortable seats in Lee Chapel. One faculty member "jestingly requested the president and the trustees to sit on those seats during a long session and find out the sensations."[58] Perhaps not so much in jest.

THE ECONOMIC and social challenges of the 1930s led to significant, often controversial political and policy changes. Many conservatives, initially stunned by the extent of the economic collapse, became increasingly appalled by what they considered the economic and political heresy of President Franklin Roosevelt's New Deal. They saw the specter of socialism in measures to achieve price stability, shore up banks, and provide social security. The conservative leanings of Washington and Lee alumni, dominated by businessmen and professionals, became increasingly apparent. Nonetheless, a majority of trustees approved an application to the Public Works Administration (PWA)—created by the National Industrial Recovery Act of 1933 and headed by Harold L. Ickes— for a grant to help rebuild the law school building. Gaines had spoken out against the materialism and freewheeling financial practices that had led to the Depression, and he welcomed actions to shore up the economy, but after it and university finances became more stable in the mid-1930s, he grew increasingly skeptical about the breadth and character of New Deal reforms. He was doubtless influenced by notable board members like John W. Davis, who consistently opposed the acceptance of any federal funding to private institutions, on constitutional and practical grounds, and who rued the appearance of any "New Dealism" on campus. Like other university presidents, Gaines had to cope with disagreements among concerned alumni, faculty members, and students.

James N. Veech of Louisville, Kentucky, a contemporary of Davis and Newton Baker at W&L, was dismayed in 1935 that a "socialist club" was being formed by students at W&L and that Lucy Mason, an associate of Secretary of Labor Frances Perkins and Secretary of Agriculture Henry Wallace, had been invited to speak on the campus. In a letter to Davis, Veech opined, "Ye Gods— in the name of Old Ran, Old Jim, Custis Lee and the conservative University that we know. I protest." Professing his understanding about "tolerance and the right to debate public questions," Veech nonetheless complained, "you as a member of the Board of Trustees are allowing this set of bunk fakers to lead astray with false philosophy the youths sent to the University because you gentlemen are in charge."

Baker forwarded to Gaines a copy of the letter, along with his response to Veech. "I am really not very much disturbed about the radical tendencies at Washington and Lee," Baker wrote. "The fact is that if radical political theo- ries are not discussed openly in our American colleges, the boys and girls will bootleg the discussion and be much worse off. The ideal situation seems to me to have complete freedom of discussion among sincere persons with the cor- rective of a very sane point of view on the part of the president of the univer- sity to whom the boys can turn if they are disturbed by what they hear. This I think we have at Washington and Lee." He concurred that trustees had some responsibility in such matters. Without being specific, he observed that "most of our troubles . . . come from professors who lack manners and intellectual humility rather than from professors who have dangerous notions."[59]

Gaines felt compelled to send a memorandum to the board of trustees on April 2, detailing the efforts of six students ("no one of them being particularly influential") to form a chapter of the Student League of Industrial Democ- racy—doubtless the "socialist club" referred to in Veech's letter. Descended from the Intercollegiate Socialist Society, the League became more prominent in the early days of the Depression and had chapters on 124 college campuses in 1935. Gaines reassured the board that the Faculty Executive Committee had approved the W&L chapter, primarily because failing to do so might lead to unfavorable publicity and generate sympathy among other students. The organizers were also warned, in apparent contradiction to an institutional commitment to free expression, that "we would not tolerate for a minute any student propaganda subversive to our basic forms of government or disloyal to the fundamental ideals upon which this government was founded."[60] This episode reflects the lack of student activism, much less radicalism, at W&L during the decade, and the sensitivity of the president and the board of trustees to any such tendencies.

Faculty members were more likely to harbor sympathies for New Deal reforms, but—despite a "Red scare" in the law school in the 1920s—there is little evidence of faculty activism on campus. In 1943, Gaines notified the board that Rupert Latture and Dean Robert Henry Tucker had requested permission to serve as arbitrators of labor disputes for the US Department of Labor. This reasonable and even innocuous request to work with a federal cabinet department produced a vitriolic howl from some prominent trustees. Homer A. "Rocky" Holt, governor of West Virginia from 1937 to 1941, pointed to the threat of "labor racketeers" and deemed the Department of Labor "so partisan, unreasonable and vindictive of our concept of fair dealing and good procedure as to make it unwise for any of our people to be identified therewith." He believed that W&L "should not in any way, however innocent superficially, become identified with or be used as an instrumentality in furthering the key New Deal labor philosophies." C. R. Avery added that "the government has too many so-called college professors in key positions who are men who have no practical knowledge of business, and who are merely trying to put a lot of theory into effect." On the other hand, Joseph T. Lykes, a business leader in New Orleans, responded that, "as a policy, it seems to me that such outside activity on the part of any of our University officials would enhance rather than endanger the prestige of our institution."[61]

It is not clear whether Latture and Tucker ever received approval to serve as labor arbitrators. However, W&L never experienced any serious outbreak of leftist political action, nor did the university act explicitly or formally to deny the rights of free speech or assembly to anyone in the academic community—in large part because it was unnecessary. As Gaines assured Davis, "in this period of great confusion of public thinking, our institution is conservative without in any sense being reactionary or hide-bound. We seek to permit reasonable academic freedom, but no radical views are championed on this campus, and, so far as I know, there is no danger in the world that this institution will swing from the moorings of its great background."[62] No doubt himself a political conservative, Gaines sought—like most university presidents—to satisfy all constituencies while avoiding controversy.

AFTER A DECADE IN OFFICE, Frank Gaines was a familiar fixture in Lexington and the universally acknowledged public face of Washington and Lee. His widespread national connections in and outside the academy, his dedication to the institution, his talent for public speaking, and his effusive representations on behalf of the university solidified his leadership. Seemingly peripatetic, he accepted only a small percentage of the invitations he received. He knew that his presence on campus was important, and he kept the trustees aware of his activities. In 1939 he reported that during one academic session alone he spoke to eleven alumni groups and three educational associations; gave the honors day address at the University of Pittsburgh and commencement addresses at the University of the South, Florida State College, and North Carolina State College; and served on the executive committee of the Carnegie Endowment for International Peace, as chair of the public relations committee of the Association of American Colleges, and as vice president of the Southern Council on International Relations.[63] During the 1930s, he served at one time or another as chairman of the Federal Emergency Relief Administration of Virginia, member of the Board of Visitors of the US Naval Academy, and president of the Southern University Conference. This schedule took its toll on his health (including bouts with psoriasis), resulting in periodic absences from the office and the cancellation of speeches and appointments.

Gaines's prominence led, not surprisingly, to overtures from other universities in search of an experienced, articulate, energetic leader. In most cases, these were turned away. Over the course of his long tenure at W&L, it became apparent that Gaines was indeed attached to the small liberal arts university in Lexington and was not using it as a stepping-stone to bigger and greater challenges. Occasionally, however, an opportunity would arise that piqued his interest. Such was the case when Tulane University offered him its presidency in 1936. The largest private university in the South, with a $10 million endowment, in a large and culturally rich port city was an obvious temptation.

In a letter to members of the board, major donors, and other interested parties, Gaines confirmed his interest in this offer, which included "a much larger salary than the one I am receiving." His interest, he claimed, was not a matter of money or prestige, however; he looked upon Tulane as a "larger opportunity," while his current position in Lexington offered greater "personal happiness." To leave "Lee's school," although it was smaller and less well endowed, would cause "a curious disturbance of soul." He asked recipients to ponder his dilemma and offer advice if they had any, since he had promised Tulane a decision by April 11. Predictably, and as he doubtless expected, Gaines received many telegrams wishing him well and urging him to remain at Washington and Lee. His friend Nicholas Murray Butler, president of Columbia University, wired on April 9 that he had recommended Gaines to Tulane as the "best possible man for the post." He added, "You must I think decide this matter on personal grounds taking into account historical association climate health and opportunity for public service during the next quarter century." Gaines responded, "I hope you will not think me foolish when I say that I decided to remain here." He noted with obvious pride that the trustees had held a special meeting, with personal entreaties from Baker and Davis (who made a special trip to Lexington for the purpose). The faculty also held a special meeting and passed a unanimous resolution asking that he remain at his post. "Virtually every boy in the student body went off to his room and wrote me a personal letter begging me to stay." Always prone to sentimentality, Gaines exclaimed to Butler, "It is just a little college in these blue-grass hills, but it may legitimately be considered the symbol of Washington's dream and it is the fruit of Lee's last desperate effort to do something in the way of healing and of hope for his people—who happen also to be my people."[64] Thus, Francis Pendleton Gaines, buoyed by the outpouring of affection and support he had himself partly generated, determined to remain at Washington and Lee and lead the university through two more decades that would pose challenges for even this most able leader.

CHAPTER TWO

WAR, RECOVERY, AND EXPANSION

THE UNITED STATES emerged in 1918 after the Great War as the least damaged, in casualties and treasure, of the major combatants. But the conflict, which seemed even more inexplicable after it was over, left enormous carnage in its wake, with lingering national animosities and economic instability that threatened throughout the next twenty years to roil the waters yet again. During the prosperous 1920s and the worldwide economic travail of the 1930s, strong authoritarian and nationalist movements appeared in Germany, Japan, and elsewhere, feeding on national grievances over postwar reparations. The Spanish Civil War further accentuated the deep-seated acrimony between Germany and Russia, Fascism and Communism. This drew considerable interest across the Atlantic, but even as the late 1930s approached and another worldwide conflagration seemed increasingly possible and even probable, American sentiment—if not isolationist—was still largely committed to avoiding foreign entanglements.

World events impinged on America's desire to stay out of harm's way. Japan's invasion of Manchuria in 1937 signaled its determination to exert regional dominance in Asia. Germany's invasion of Poland on September 1, 1939, revealed the full power of the Wehrmacht and dealt a severe blow to hopes that the butchery of World War I had laid the foundations for long-term peace. Within another year and a half, Nazi Germany had swept over most of continental Europe and launched an invasion of Russia in June 1941. Full-scale war in Europe was at hand. Could the United States remain aloof?

American attention to international affairs certainly had increased in academic and policy circles, but the popular feeling generally supported maintaining world peace and stability rather than intervening militarily. Professions of desire for world peace were expressed by new organizations and political leaders, and on campuses across the country, including Washington and Lee. President Gaines led the way as a board member of the Carnegie Commission for World Peace and a frequent speaker on peace and reconciliation on campus and elsewhere. This was a mostly noncontroversial activity, a reflection of American idealism (even for those opposed to Woodrow Wilson's League of Nations), and was frequently aligned in the academic community with growing interest in international affairs. But the hopes for a peaceful world were being rapidly eroded by reality. Gaines was clearly worried, both for the state of the world and for the possible consequences for W&L. These consequences—leading up to, during, and immediately following World War II—would be sudden, extensive, and extremely volatile, testing the university's ingenuity to an extent not felt since the Civil War.

In September 1940, the US Congress passed and President Roosevelt signed into law the first peacetime conscription in the nation's history, requiring all men between the ages of twenty-one and thirty-five to register with local draft boards. In October, Gaines notified the trustees and university community that W&L had been "deeply affected by the disturbance of world conditions with its consequent emphasis upon accelerated national defense." In particular, he was concerned about the effect on future enrollment, since many prospective students were already favoring institutions with options for military training, allowing them to prepare for possible military service while at the same time continuing their education. "We have tried to keep alert to the duty of the University," Gaines wrote, "in an hour of crisis, an hour that has suggestions of hysteria." A faculty committee was contemplating the possibilities and options.[1]

During the following year, the university added special courses with particular relevance for the evolving situation, though none were strictly in military science. The physical education curriculum was altered to emphasize conditioning in line with Selective Service requirements. In May 1941, Gaines recommended that because of "the uncertainty governing the immediate future" no faculty promotions should be made and automatic salary increases should be suspended.[2] Later that year, he noted the "heavy clouds that hang upon our future" and that of "all non-military, liberal arts colleges." While those enrolled in military training might be allowed to continue their studies, others were liable to be called up for service.[3] Dealing with this situation became a continuing preoccupation.

Even with the dire news from abroad, US sentiment remained substantially opposed to direct involvement in the conflict, with strong resistance in some quarters to American assistance to England through the Lend-Lease program and other means. An extension of the requirement for one year of service under the draft was barely approved: it passed in the House of Representatives by one vote. But the national demeanor changed dramatically on December 7, 1941, with the Japanese attack on the US Pacific fleet in Pearl Harbor, Hawaii.

The news came with surreal suddenness, injecting an immediate sense of uncertainty, if not outright crisis, into all dimensions of normal routine. The fall semester was drawing to a close. Tony Parker and his orchestra had played for the opening dance set in October and also for the Sophomore Prom in November. Football coach Riley Smith's contract was renewed for another year, though the team had a mediocre record and ended the season with a 6–0 loss to Maryland. The theme for the Fancy Dress Ball in January was announced—"Night in Monte Carlo"—with Woody Herman and Teddy Powell and their bands scheduled on the first two nights. And the Assimilation Committee decided that all freshmen should continue to wear their caps because of "negligence" in observing the tradition.

On the first weekend in December, W&L students were anticipating the upcoming Christmas holiday and enjoyed or contemplated road trips to surrounding women's colleges. The news of the devastating Japanese attack came in special news bulletins that interrupted regular radio programs. Students and faculty clustered to discuss these events and discern their meaning. Some students immediately sought special passes to witness President Roosevelt's appearance before a joint session of Congress, and classes were ended early so that all students could listen to the proceedings on radio.

With the United States now formally at war with Japan and Germany, students focused on the immediate implications for their education and future plans. They scrambled to contact local Selective Service boards for more information. Congress quickly expanded the draft so that registration was now required of all men between the ages of eighteen and sixty-five, with those between eighteen and forty-five eligible for military service. Washington and Lee thus became instantly vulnerable to drastic declines in student enrollment (which stood at 941 in 1940–41) and reductions in faculty and staff.

President Gaines and Dean Tucker issued statements to the campus community, urging patience and caution in sifting through the abundant rumors and asking everybody to await official word from the government on matters that would affect students and faculty. Above all, they wanted to encourage students to stay in school, focus on their academic work, and not jump to conclusions, abandon their courses, and pack their bags. The administration was well aware that the university itself faced a most uncertain future.

New national imperatives increasingly intruded into the fabric of normal campus life, chipping away at long-time routines and traditions. The W&L variety show, an original musical comedy entitled "Say It Again," opened on December 12 after four weeks of rehearsals. Plans for Fancy Dress continued, but the Dance Board began considering "modifications" to the festivities on January 29–31 so as to avoid "ostentatious display" during "a grave national emergency"—mostly by curtailing expenditures on corsages, flowers, and favors.[4] Fourteen students failed to return for the spring semester because they were called up for military service, and the *Ring-tum Phi* was reduced in size and format in anticipation of a decline in advertising revenue. The faculty immediately began considering an accelerated academic schedule in support of the war effort. Some four hundred students and three hundred of their dates reveled at Fancy Dress, knowing that this would likely be the last such event for years to come. Social activities throughout the campus for the remainder of the semester—including the winter and spring house parties—were canceled or curtailed.

By early February, twenty-five students were enlisted in the Class V-7 program of the Naval Reserve, to finish their studies and be commissioned as ensigns upon graduation. Fourteen faculty members and 244 students between the ages of twenty and forty-five lined up to register with the university Selective Service on February 16. In the space of a few weeks, the campus was already being reshaped by the demands of an enveloping war, marked painfully by the crowds of well-dressed young men gathered downtown to board chartered busses to transport them to military duty.

During this greatest yet of all military conflicts—a world war that was truly global in scope, pitting population against population—W&L men served across the world, in every military branch and in many government posts. They could be found in destroyers, cruisers, submarines, battleships, and fighter planes in the Pacific; at most of the great battles from Leyte Gulf, Saipan, Iwo Jima, and Burma to the Ardennes, Italy, North Africa, and Omaha Beach in Normandy; everywhere from recruiting offices to military intelligence, from the Judge Advocate General (JAG) Corps to the liberation of Paris and dangerous missions behind enemy lines in China; and as prisoners of war. They were stationed in

Pearl Harbor when it was attacked, on the USS Missouri when the Japanese surrendered, and in the V-J Day celebration in Times Square. They held ranks from private first class to senior officers and served with soldiers and civilians from all parts of the country and all walks of life, sharing boredom, bad food, rough seas, thick mud, sleepless nights, horrific combat, injury, and death.[5] Taken together, the economic depression of the 1930s and the war in the 1940s were cauldrons of common experience that fashioned the postwar generations and the American political and economic landscape well into the 1970s. It was the last great "people's war" the United States would wage, with virtually universal participation, bringing together men and women from different economic and geographic backgrounds in a common national enterprise. As students, faculty, and alumni contributed in one way or another to the far-flung war effort, their university in Lexington struggled to support the war and also to keep its doors open.

New special courses were added in 1941–42, including a general survey, "Military Fundamentals," as well as math courses relevant to military engineering. Students could learn about explosives and chemical warfare in chemistry, map reading and topographical features in geology, or military photography and airplane flight in physics. There were also offerings in naval history, the geography of the Pacific area, military preparedness and physical fitness, and citizenship and defense in political science. Some new and existing courses were clustered into a new major in industrial management, relevant to mobilization and national defense. The curriculum was combed for all courses with a potential relevance to wartime demands.[6]

The academic calendar was drastically revised, as it was at other colleges and universities, to enable students to complete their work in the shortest period of time and thus proceed to military service or other wartime duties. The "accelerated" schedule, beginning with the spring term of 1942, eliminated most holidays, compressed examination periods, extended class times by half, and offered the first summer session—divided into two terms—in the university's history. Students could enter in June, September, or February and in many cases complete the work for graduation in three years. Degrees were awarded whenever work for the degree was completed. Two notable characteristics of the first summer session were the faculty's willingness to offer one term of instruction without additional compensation, and the fact that, of the 299 students enrolled, 27 were women, who were admitted only for the summer session and only if they had completed one year of college work. The trustees made clear that this policy was temporary.

The faculty approved provisions that permitted fourth-year students who were called to duty before the end of their final semester to be awarded degrees if they were in good academic standing, and awarded credit to students pulled from school within two or three weeks of the end of a term. (Some of these "special diplomas" were later conferred in a ceremony in Lee Chapel during 1940s class reunions.) Students returning from military service might also be awarded credit for their work and experience, decided on an individual basis. A special faculty Committee on Defense, chaired by Walter A. Flick, professor of education and psychology, advised students and communicated with local draft boards. It evolved into the War Service Committee, which included members from the student body and the community, and oversaw a college and community forum, a library of war information, and a speaker's bureau.

THE UNDERGRADUATE STUDENT BODY declined slightly to 895, or by 5 five percent, as the fall term began in 1942, but withdrawals during the semester were more than twice the usual number, soon bringing enrollment down to 665. The 1942–43 academic year began with 678 enrolled; another 285 had dropped away by session's end. At its lowest point during 1943–44, only fifty-four regular students matriculated at Washington and Lee. The impact on the law school was even more dramatic: from 104 students in 1940–41, only five were enrolled during 1943–44 (and none at all by the end of the term). In 1944–45, only two students (both new) had registered. The School of Commerce was also hit hard.

In April 1943, President John L. Newcomb of the University of Virginia (UVA) rode the bus from Charlottesville to Staunton to meet Gaines for lunch. They discussed Newcomb's proposal that UVA and W&L combine to teach law students until the end of the war. The proposal was based on the apparently successful collaboration between Wake Forest College and Duke University, with students from the former attending classes in Durham. Gaines had explored the details of this arrangement with the Wake Forest president, confiding that it might not work as well because "the distances are greater between UVA and W&L, and a mountain range that can be very slick in winter interposes itself."[7] UVA continued to pursue the possibility, and a year later, in April 1944, Gaines consulted with the trustees, who preferred that W&L maintain its "independent school" if at all possible. William McChesney Martin advised that in light of low enrollments the law school could be "suspended" until the end of the conflict.[8]

W&L's decision not to enter into the arrangement with Virginia also involved considerations of postwar enrollment. As Gaines wrote to Newcomb on May 1, conveying the board's decision to proceed independently, "It was felt that the psychological advantages, particularly with regard to post war prospects, probably outweighed the many desirable arguments for a coalition of our efforts."[9]

Every college and university faced upheavals of various kinds during the war, but the levels of enrollment in larger and coeducational institutions were more easily maintained. Those institutions with military training programs and those designated for educational activities—short term or until graduation—of the Army, Navy, or Marine Corps were cushioned to some degree from enrollment volatility. But the faculty and staff felt the effect everywhere, though in different ways.

Some twenty-two W&L faculty and staff members (sixteen faculty out of about sixty) had departed for war service by October 1942, representing approximately 25 percent of the university's total personnel. A year later about half the faculty were gone, thirty-one to the armed services and nine to auxiliary activity. Of all these, twenty-eight were on leave and a dozen had resigned from the university.[10] The expansion of course offerings with more technical content was especially challenging, since faculty with the technical expertise were most likely to be called into service. Somehow, faculty and course assignments worked out, but not without extra teaching and extra work on the parts of remaining faculty members and a few special hires.

Faculty and staff members with previous military service and special expertise were called up the earliest. Law professor Charles P. Light Jr. held a reserve commission as a lieutenant in the US Army and was called to duty in the JAG Department. Other reserve officers were Dr. Reid White, who left for the Army Medical Corps, and L. C. Pettit, assistant professor of geology. Professor O. W. Riegel in Journalism was called to duty almost immediately to work in the Division of Foreign Propaganda in the Office of Information. Almand R. Coleman (Accounting) left for the Army and Lawrence E. Watkin (English) and W. Magruder Drake (Assistant Registrar) for the U.S. Navy. Law professor Charles R. McDowell had served in World War I and was appointed lieutenant commander in the Navy Air Corps Reserve. Some faculty departed in 1942 or earlier for other tasks. M. H. Stow (Geology) was a technical adviser to the US Bureau of Mines and Herbert Trotter (Physics) conducted special research for the Navy in the Smithsonian Institution.[11] This exodus would continue until the war was over.

In "A Message to Alumni," published in the February 1942 *Bulletin*, Gaines alerted the broader university community to events on campus and the further changes that were to come. W&L's loss of enrollment—with more doubtless ahead—translated directly into loss of university income, which "comes at a time when it hurts most, when the cost of living goes up steadily." He pointed out the special challenges facing "the colleges of men, particularly of those colleges which have neither the authorized military departments nor the strongly specialized scientific divisions." He described how the university was responding to the national emergency—including the accelerated calendar, expanded course offerings, and the summer program—and asked that alumni understand the university's situation, identify and guide suitable students to enroll, and be generous with their financial support.[12] In this climate of uncertainty, every financial gift was welcomed. Gaines hailed a contribution of $25,000 from Joseph T. Lykes in 1942 "as a life-saver thrown out to strugglers in a big ocean."[13] (The metaphor was fitting; the Lykes family owned a major shipping line in New Orleans.)

In a confidential memorandum to the trustees in March 1942, Gaines addressed the problems and discussed some possible responses. Students pursuing certain subjects would be permitted to defer military induction; these included premedical studies and industrial management. Each military service had established programs allowing continued study for those already inducted, promised reserve commissions, or to be inducted after a period of time. Eighteen students were already enrolled at W&L in the Marine Corps Reserve program that had been in place for several years. Other W&L men enlisted in US Navy programs designed to allow students to continue their college work for various periods of time before being called to duty. The Navy's V-12 program, introduced in the summer of 1943, eventually supported some 125,000 sailors at 131 colleges and universities, including the University of Virginia, University of Richmond, Tulane, Vanderbilt, and the University of the South. But W&L's efforts to be designated a Navy V-12 program site were not successful, even though a number of its students participated in the programs at other universities. W&L was thus eager to cooperate in "some comparable plan for the Army," the military service with the largest contingent. As chair of a special committee of the Association of American Colleges, Gaines made every effort to develop a suitable plan for institutions like W&L. "To this effort," he wrote, "I have given more time than to any other one thing in the last ninety days, for it is the most important consideration now before Washington and Lee and similar schools."[14] Fortunately, the efforts with the Army were more successful than those with the Navy.

W&L hosted its first contingent of the US Army Specialized Training Program (ASTP) in August 1943, which at its height enrolled 250 pre-engineering and fifty premedical students, most of them from other universities and with no previous knowledge of W&L and Lexington. These "students" were military personnel assigned for further studies to various colleges and universities. Their tuition was paid by the military (at rates that basically covered university expenses); they wore uniforms, were subject to military regulations and discipline, and were often seen marching in formation to classes. As Gaines put it, these were "soldiers here on campus, not college boys in uniform," but they were housed, fed, and taught by the university, further increasing demands on the faculty and curriculum. Specialized courses and teachers were added—especially in math, physics, and chemistry. Although the students were tested for proficiency, they varied considerably in their backgrounds and abilities. Gaines noted, in his unique way, that some lacked "what might be termed an evenness of receptivity."[15] These students also posed challenges for maintaining all elements of the Honor System and other university traditions and customs. One ASTP student from Marblehead, Massachusetts, who had attended a Midwestern college before enlisting, recalled arriving in Lexington, which seemed like "the end of the earth." But it and W&L turned out to be an "Eden" and "a dream beyond belief for any dogface. We were welcomed into the community in an overwhelming way and W&L could not have been friendlier." He found the faculty "so approachable and the teaching was so superb, unrivaled by any I had had before." When he learned that he could receive his BA with only a year's additional study, he gladly returned to campus in July 1946 to major in political science and history.[16]

One W&L freshman student in 1942–43 recalled this period "as a strange and unsettling time. I watched the student body dwindle almost weekly as, one after the other, my classmates and men in other classes were called up or left Washington and Lee to enlist. Uniforms began to appear on campus, worn, in some cases by W&L men already in service but returning for visits before going overseas, in other cases by the early arrivals of the Special Service troops assigned to W&L. For me and the others who knew we would not be back next year, the spring of '43 was a strained and uneasy interlude. . . . And I remember standing on Letcher Avenue . . . Looking toward the Colonnade, wondering whether I would ever be back, and hoping that I might."[17]

In May, Gaines confided to the trustees, "Every activity and every person on our campus now moves in the shadow of this war." He took solace in historical perspective. "Over and over again, during the nineteen decades of the institution's life, the bugles of a national involvement have sounded, near to us or afar. It is not on record that the school ever failed to prove responsive." He was quick to reassure the trustees of the patriotic fervor of W&L men, though it is unclear why he felt such reassurances were necessary. "It comforts me to recall—and you will allow me to remind you—that in the confused and somewhat aimless years of the last decade, where on many campuses of our country there were the bewildered groups of students organized into little clubs that would now be called 'subversive,' there was not only no such group on this campus, there was not even a student of that disposition, so far as I ever knew."[18]

Gaines and Tucker remarked on the "deepened sense of responsibility developed by the war" that shaped the atmosphere on campus. World crisis and national defense, especially when they had such an intimate connection to the lives and futures of all concerned, certainly helped to focus and intensify academic effort for many students, though class work could also be a victim of uncertainty. The administration chose to emphasize the positive. Students who "had been bred intellectually upon a philosophy that war is futile," Gaines observed, had suffered a great shock. "But the recovery had been a creditable and a heartening thing. These boys on our campus have accepted, somewhat grimly but without flinching, this new duty."[19] A great reduction in extracurricular activity and the normal atmosphere of collegiate life accentuated this sense of purpose.

The University of Virginia continued some sports throughout the conflict, including football. But intercollegiate athletics at Washington and Lee were suspended, though the intramural program continued and physical fitness activity was enhanced. The Troubadour Theater and some other student organizations proceeded, but many—including most publications—were put on hold. The *Ring Tum-Phi* was temporarily replaced by the weekly *Columns*, which included VMI news and was published every Friday from September 24, 1943, to August 23, 1946. The Interfraternity Council authorized the suspension of all fraternity functions throughout the war, and fraternity houses were either assigned for use by the Army School or for freshmen students who were displaced by war-related activities. The student government continued to operate but placed the funds of the Student Body, the Publication Board, and the Dance Board in trust for the duration of the war. Members and leaders of student organizations experienced unprecedented turnover. Formal dances gave way to modest social events, and road trips to women's colleges were significantly curtailed by the shortage of gasoline and tires.

Rupert Latture, then serving as dean of students, reported in October 1943 that at the end of the previous summer session, freshmen lived and took their meals in the Phi Kappa Psi, Sigma Alpha Epsilon, and Lambda Chi Alpha houses, each with a housemother and upperclassman student counselor. "Unavoidably," he wrote, "the students today are missing many enriching and appealing features of college life." Nevertheless, he reported that they were maintaining W&L traditions and customs and supporting the university's contributions to the war effort.[20]

With the dearth of regular students, university revenues were gravely threatened. The university's ability to keep the doors open during the war was due not only to ingenuity and faculty sacrifice but to subsidy by the military services, in particular a substantial contract with the Army School of Special and Morale Services. It was also gratifying that in the midst of war and so soon after the economic doldrums of the 1930s, the financial support from alumni grew even stronger. By June 1943, the annual Alumni Fund campaign had raised $12,266 from 1,337 contributors, the largest amount of money from the greatest number of donors to that point in the history of the fund.

THE US ARMY SCHOOL for Special and Morale Services (later designated the School for Personnel Services) was established by the War Department as the Army Special Services branch on July 22, 1940. The first Recreational Officer School opened at Fort Mead, Maryland, on April 1, 1942, with a mission to support the troops by enhancing morale and providing entertainment by Army personnel, as well as by engaging outside, often local, talent. It was also one of the few racially integrated Army units during World War II. The headquarters moved from Fort Meade to Washington and Lee, and the first classes in Lexington began on December 7, 1942, exactly one year after the attack on Pearl Harbor.

Gaines continued to explore educational opportunities with the Navy, but he happily notified the trustees that he had signed a contract on November 28, 1942, with the US government to move the Army School to the campus. The Army unit would have "exclusive use" of the dormitories, the dining hall,

Tucker Hall, the basement of the Student Union, and one large room in the basement of McCormick Library, with provisions for "occasional use" of four other classrooms, the gymnasium, one athletic field, and "a few minor facilities." Renewable annually at the discretion of the government, the contract ran to June 30, 1943. While not as generous as Gaines had hoped, the compensation to the university was ninety-five cents per day per man—fifty cents for lodging and forty-five for facilities—or about $346 annually for each student. W&L decided not to undertake "messing" the men, which would have generated more revenue but also extra costs. The government agreed to pay for altering and expanding the dining hall.[21] Gaines had essentially leased a good part of the campus to a unit of the US Army, and there were about four hundred individuals per class, mostly commissioned officers. W&L had no control over the selection of students or instructors, nor did the university oversee their discipline or social relations among themselves or with the campus. (This administrative distance would prove to Gaines to be something of a blessing.) But the university had been saved from serious financial difficulty. As Gaines reported to the trustees in May 1943 a "slight surplus" in the budget, he noted that without "the Army School for Special Service, we should probably run a deficit of between $50,000 and $70,000."[22]

Recurrent fears that the Army School would be reconfigured or moved to military bases were never realized. The program remained on campus until it was closed in January 1946 with exercises in Lee Chapel. The unit—initially under the command of Col. Leon T. David and after March 1943 of Col. William H. Quarterman—graduated 25,000 students and left an indelible stamp on the wartime experience and atmosphere at W&L and Lexington. Organized into two departments—Orientation and Education, and Athletics and Recreation—officers trained to organize, manage, and staff Army Exchanges, educational activities, and recreational facilities—including theatrical shows, music, and handicrafts. The training often involved organized games on the playing fields, physical exercise and conditioning, and dances, movies, and sports offered for students and local residents. In April 1944, the Army Post Exchange School was moved from Princeton University to W&L and became part of the overall Army program. In addition to regular Army personnel, the trainees involved officers from the Navy, Women's Army Corps (WAC), Women Accepted for Volunteer Emergency Service (WAVES), and Marine Corps Women's Reserve.

Norman Lord, a student and instructor in the Army School who subsequently spent thirty-eight years at W&L as a coach and physical education teacher, described his wartime experience as helping to prepare officers to convey "a little hunk of home" to troops in the field. "Every person that went through the school," he recalled, "had to learn a little bit about athletics and the arts, music and drama and crafts, public affairs—everything related to taking care of people—morale. We [were] taught how to teach games to the people. We improvised games, all kinds of games, like dodgeball, tug-of-war, hide-and-go-seek, everything. If it was fun for kids, we turned the old guys into kids. We had them learn how to play, because we knew that they had to teach soldiers to do it when they left Lexington."[23]

A post exchange and headquarters were located in the dormitories, and an Army bookstore was set up in Payne Hall and a dispensary in the basement of the Student Union Building. The Kappa Alpha house was transformed into an officer's club, utilizing the garden for an outdoor dance floor, while the enlisted men established the Cadre Club in the Student Union. A lounge was provided in Reid Hall and a film library and projection room in the basement of Tucker Hall. The quartermaster's office was located in a building on Nelson Street. Most of the fraternity houses were occupied by Army personnel and were reimbursed after the war by the government, with extra compensation from the university, if necessary, to cover operating costs.

Some W&L administrators and faculty members had specific roles in the Army School. Dean Frank J. Gilliam, a veteran of World War I, was commissioned with the rank of major and served for a time as the student personnel officer, while Rupert Latture took over Gilliam's responsibilities as W&L dean of students. History professor Allen W. Moger was chief of the Tests and Measurement Department of the School for Personnel Services, and C. Harold Lauck provided printing services to the Army School, as well as the university. Earl Mattingly, the university treasurer, worked closely with the commandant on an array of administrative matters.

This unique military educational program was a financial godsend for W&L and a lively and patriotic asset during a dreary and uncertain time. As Professor Sid Coulling noted, "the community warmly embraced the newcomers, welcoming them into their homes for the most festive parties and dinners wartime rationing would permit. After all, these attractive young men were recognizably like the husbands, sons, and students who had been called to serve their country, so nothing was too good for them." The Army School even came to the attention of W&L students serving far away. Charles Didier, '42, recalled watching a movie in a driving rain in the Russell Islands and seeing newsreel footage from W&L. "I could not believ⟨

personnel playing drop the handkerchief on W

Earl Mattingly, who responded, "Charles, we ⟨

The Army School also brought to campus ⟨

have been there—including women, African⟨

ment and sports personalities. The comedi⟨

Douglas and Ephraim Zimbalist Jr. walked ⟨…

as did golfer Ben Hogan and baseball power hitter Hank ⟨

Price Daniel, former speaker of the Texas House of Representatives and ⟨

governor and US senator, was on the faculty. Those regularly enrolled students
who were unable to serve in the military, as well as a number of townspeople,
were frequently engaged as actors in plays put on by Army School professionals or as critics in the audience. Frank Gaines's son Edwin remembered that
"these people all had talent, and every church that wanted a performance or a
play, or more often [those who] liked the comedians, they were always here. I
remember the folks gave a reception for each group that came through, and my
father made some very good friends." The time Skelton appeared at a reception
with a local woman of questionable reputation was especially memorable: "My
father broke out laughing, and my mother was about to cry."[25]

The presence of African Americans on campus did not escape notice. US
senator Carter Glass, a "progressive" on some economic issues who had worked
closely with Woodrow Wilson, was publisher of the *Lynchburg News* and a
staunch opponent of changes to the South's traditional racial system. In February 1943, he penned an editorial condemning the presence of blacks at W&L
under any auspices. Board member James R. Caskie, also from Lynchburg,
recounted to Gaines his conversations with Glass on the matter, in which he
explained to Glass that the university had no control over admissions to the
Army School and that it would "send down to Lexington only the best class of
officers, rather than take the chance of having some other school much less
desirable forced on us with the students probably composed of a conglomera-
tion and mixture of all kinds." But, Caskie wrote Gaines, "Mr. Glass is rabid
on the negro question and my suggestions had no effect on him whatsoever,
since he stated that to his mind the larger question of the social system of the
South and the mixture of the races transcended all other consideration."[26]

US representative Clifton A. Woodrum of Roanoke wrote with similar concerns on February 16. Gaines responded that W&L had rented space to the US
Army and had no control over its admissions or its program, but he assured

that these students "were unusually high type men, all officers and men for their qualities of leadership." The first group of students consisted of about three hundred officers, but the second group of 450 students contained fourteen WACS and three African Americans. He further explained that he had kept the trustees fully informed and that the Army School was the only one of its kind in the country. He noted, "The Negro units in our fighting forces need the same kind of morale leadership in the hands of trained specialists as our white forces need." The Lexington community understood the situation, he wrote, including "the simple justice of having the best training for those Negro men who risk their lives for our country," and "there has not been locally a single chirp of criticism, so far as I know."[27]

Gaines was also obligated to respond to Robert R. Hobson, an attorney and alumnus from Louisville, Kentucky, who alleged that the Army School "is the worst hotbed of communism in this country." Gaines replied, "your letter is the first hint I have heard that the School champions communism," and went on at length to defend the lineage and patriotism of the school's leaders and faculty.[28]

In unanticipated ways, the Army School brought something of the outside world to W&L and Lexington. While temporary, the influx of new people with different backgrounds and experiences hinted at the diversity of the nation and presaged the challenges and opportunities the university would face in the decades following the war.

———

AS OF OCTOBER 1, 1943—some nine months after Pearl Harbor—the university recorded 2,405 enlistments of W&L men in the armed forces, including more than five hundred students who had interrupted their education to serve. At that time, twenty-two were confirmed killed, twelve were listed as missing in action, and seven were prisoners of war. By the end of the war, W&L students or alumni had served in every branch of the military and in every theater of combat, and 137 had died. Their names are inscribed, alongside those killed in World War I, on the Memorial Gate at the university's front entrance.

By 1944, after the invasion in Normandy, the German defeat in Russia, the grueling Pacific Islands campaign, and the beginning of raids on Japan, the ultimate victory of the Allies was in sight. Thoughts turned, at first tentatively and then in earnest, to family, education, and career, to a life beyond the war. Most veterans were all too happy to shed their uniforms, stow their wartime gear, and try to forget the searing moments of their wartime experience. Some were eager to take up where they had left off, while others had new and different aspirations. Washington and Lee did its best to accommodate those veterans who sought to enroll or re-enroll—which turned out to be as challenging in many ways as coping with wartime uncertainties.

As early as fall 1943, President Gaines shared with the trustees his uncertainty about the state of things once the war was over. In such uncertain times, how would Washington and Lee "continue its task of serving youth, the Nation, and our God"? Would students return to their studies after the conflict? "What will be the participation of the Federal Government in a broad educational program as part of the huge demobilization problem? What new emphases will be demanded by the temper of the Nation—more science for re-building, more history and international relations for the broad perspective, more attention to citizenship? Will the National Government require or even encourage a universal military training for physically fit youth? Will there be a place for the truly liberal or humanitarian education?"[29] Indeed, the cumulative effect of economic depression followed by global conflict challenged understanding and hardly provided a clear notion of the future.

TOTAL COLLEGE ATTENDANCE in the United States plummeted during the war years, but fall enrollment in 1949–50 reached nearly 2.5 million, almost two-thirds more than the roughly 1.5 million registered at the beginning of the decade. The increase at W&L over the same period was 33 percent, which did not reflect the extreme volatility between 1941 and 1948. The university's attention shifted suddenly from scrambling to keep the campus open and make financial ends meet to coping with unprecedented enrollment pressures from returning veterans eager to restart their lives and regular students no longer haunted by the possibility of military service or the woes of a poor economy. Gaines noted in February 1947 that this period "has been without parallel in my experience, or in the experience of anybody since the time of General Lee, for confusion, difficulty, and the unbelievable volume of work upon administrative officers." W&L "had to be reconverted from a 10% operating agency back to maximum, . . . then had to be expanded 20% beyond any maximum known before; then had the unprecedented task of housing 250 student families. All of these things had to be done at a time of fantastic prices and of unparalleled scarcities" of labor, equipment, textbooks, faculty, and housing.[30]

After the war, the US government provided a range of economic benefits to veterans, from no-down-payment, low-cost mortgages, to loans for starting businesses, to payment of tuition and living expenses so that veterans could continue or begin their education. The Servicemen's Readjustment Act of June 1944, or GI Bill, was a milestone in federal policy that not only stimulated huge college enrollments but also provided continued financial stimulus for the national economy. Among the most significant pieces of legislation in the twentieth century, the bill established a solid foundation for the dramatic demographic changes and economic expansion that transformed higher education, reshaped housing patterns and entire metropolitan areas, fueled social mobility, and undergirded the rise of the modern middle class. By 1956, 7.8 million, or almost half of all veterans of World War II, had received education benefits under the GI Bill.

The years after 1945 released a flood of opportunities, aspirations, and enthusiasm. The nation was not so much intent on restoring normality as on making something new and better, and this spirit and energy permeated all realms of higher education. As Gaines put it in 1948, "the current of our academic life . . . has been at flood-tide." Indeed, the foundations were being laid for a surge in college attendance, as well as for the framework of higher education in the remainder of the century. University leaders were generally well aware of the changes and challenges underway, and many institutions experienced the dramatic effects.

Washington and Lee counted only 144 students at the end of the spring term in 1944 and only 54 (with no students at all in the law school) by the end of the summer session, the lowest enrollment since the end of the Civil War. The number crept up in 1944–45 and ascended rapidly thereafter. Growth continued unabated before easing to 1,256 in 1949–50. The rapid increase in applications and attendance was welcome after the wartime anxiety and austerity, but it posed arguably more serious challenges and certainly more reflection about W&L's future and its role in higher education. By 1946, approximately twenty applications were received for every vacancy. The *New York Times* grouped W&L among other "highly selective" colleges, such as Amherst, Dartmouth, Lehigh, Colgate, Harvard, Princeton, and Union, and pointed out the positive influence of this surfeit of applications on rates of academic success and student retention.[31]

In a report to the trustees in May 1946, Gaines addressed the immediate postwar challenges for the university and the decisions that would have to be made. How would W&L accommodate the demand and how large should the enrollment be? How could the university ensure key elements of the traditional student experience and campus life when three-quarters of the student body were older veterans and as many as 250 to 300 of them were married? How would they secure enough quality faculty members to serve the greater numbers of students and still maintain academic standards? Where would they find the money to pay rapidly rising salaries? Where exactly were all these additional students—especially those with families—and newer faculty and staff going to live in a small town like Lexington? Would changes in the curriculum be necessary?

Amid swelling enrollment, W&L again pondered the size of the institution. The faculty had voted to increase the overall student body during "the period of this emergency," but opinion varied about the size of the increase. The arguments to expand W&L included the national need to accommodate the huge demand for college placement, the fact that larger enrollments brought increased revenues (especially since veterans on the GI Bill paid full tuition and fees), and the need to derail the rumored possibility that if existing colleges and universities could not accommodate the rising demand, the government might convert "abandoned army camps" into "G.I. Universities," with inevitable damage to educational standards.[32]

As for faculty, the university was faced with "a shrinking trickle of available teachers." More than thirty faculty members were still away on wartime service, and about a third of these did not return to the university. Even compared with the tribulations of wartime, Gaines averred that he had "never known such a confused situation." In May 1946, fifteen or twenty former professors had not yet returned, and rising enrollments required at least a dozen additional faculty. To make the challenge even greater, postwar inflation fueled rising costs and salaries. The Commonwealth of Virginia, for example, approved raises for faculty at public institutions of from 6 to 24 percent, and public and private universities nationwide were engaged in a bidding war for qualified, experienced instructional staff. Gaines favored an across-the-board raise, with additional amounts from a presidential fund for superior performance or for meeting competing job offers. Raising tuition and increasing enrollment were potential sources of funds for faculty salaries, but Gaines resisted doing both at once.

The need for higher salaries was significant and immediate. The administration calculated that the cost of living in Lexington in 1947 had almost doubled since 1940–41, whereas faculty compensation had risen about 20 percent over the same period, and the university no longer offered additional summer school compensation. One full professor reportedly exclaimed that after "eighteen happy years at Washington and Lee I am confronted for the first time with the prospect of impoverishment."

In October 1948, Gaines made the case for an increase in tuition that could provide more money for faculty salaries. Whereas W&L's salary range for full professors was $4,400 to $5,240, salaries at the University of Virginia, Virginia Polytechnic Institute, William and Mary, and neighboring VMI were higher. A newly minted PhD with some experience now demanded at least $4,000, and the resulting salary compression disadvantaged long-serving faculty members, even in the higher ranks (a classic challenge in higher education during times of rising salaries generally).[33] And W&L's $350 tuition ranked well below the charge at "comparable schools"—including Duke, Vanderbilt, Virginia, Tulane, Amherst, Hamilton, and Southwestern.

Gaines suggested raising tuition to $425 per year, which would generate approximately $90,000 in additional revenue, of which $72,000 could be allocated to salaries. The remainder could be applied to general maintenance or to meet higher costs, including those for treating students at the local hospital. The salary increases in September 1946 and January 1947 were salutary, as was the university decision to increase to 7.5 percent the institutional contribution to the retirement plan. Yet it was not clear that these steps would address all the issues and keep up with the cost of living.

Housing was perhaps the most intractable problem because the housing stock in Lexington and the surrounding area was fixed and not easily expanded. Married couples took twice the space required by single students and also directly competed with new faculty members in the residential housing market. "It was probably your humble servant," Gaines wrote, "who was asleep at the switch while these developments happened: the married students . . . swept into town and secured almost all the available houses and apartments, including those usually taken by the junior members of our faculty; the OPA [Office of Price Administration, a New Deal agency], which still operates in Lexington, doesn't want us to disposses [sic] outside families living in University houses—rented to them while our own people were away; building restrictions have been slapped on practically everything."[34]

Several trustees responded to Gaines's memorandum. John W. Davis concurred that a maximum enrollment of one thousand was preferable but that under the circumstances the university "should take all that we can teach and all we can house." He also agreed that salaries were too low and had "been too low for years." Furthermore, if he had a million dollars he "would want to see the entire proceeds go to salaries, instead of bricks and mortar."[35] In comments that would resonate in later discussion of W&L's size, William McChesney Martin warned against significant increases in enrollment beyond one thousand, lest "we would lose our distinctive touch in which there is so much tradition and become a big mechanical organization like so many of the large universities."[36] He concurred with the need for salary increases, suggesting an across-the-board raise of 10 to 14 percent. He also advised that the main focus of the university should be its welfare and maintaining its independence, rather than trying to meet national needs. Neither Davis nor Martin offered any solutions for the housing crisis.

W&L pondered increasing the density in the dormitories and fraternity houses, signed a contract for fifty new "government houses," and was allocated forty-eight more that were eventually built. These new dwellings would accommodate many married students and some faculty members for decades. The university also took over two remaining Army barracks as "auxiliary dormitories." James Ballengee, who was later university rector, recalled living after the war in the new housing units, which were designed to meet short-term needs but also provided a community environment for young families. "Everybody was trying to play catch-up, and we went constantly. I took a few days off, we got married in June of '47, and we moved out in what was then Hillside Terrace. A great many people started their married life there. They were prefab, three units in a building. You had an icebox. You had to put the sign up for the ice man to come and deliver. You only paid $50 a month. It was for GIs. You had no money, but nobody else did, either, and lots of work to do, and yet in a wonderful atmosphere, compared to what we'd just been through in the war, particularly."[37]

The university, which had been emphasizing first- and second-year coursework and specialized offerings for the military, now focused again on offering a full curriculum. A new group of integrated courses in the humanities—outside of regular departmental majors and in a variety of subjects from languages to philosophy—was added in 1946. At the same time, the faculty raised the percentage requirements of letter grades in recognition of the large number of As and Bs being awarded. Even so, students' academic performance was notable—"at a much higher level than in the pre-war years," especially among the returning veterans—according to Dean Tucker.

*   *   *

THE LAW SCHOOL virtually started over from scratch, operating temporarily in Payne Hall and opening in the fall of 1944 with only two students, one full-time professor, and two part-time instructors. Ramping up a full-scale curriculum with a full array of advanced courses was a challenge made even more serious by the passing of Dean W. H. Moreland, who died at home of a heart attack in March 1944, at the age of sixty-five. Professor Clayton E. Williams became dean, and more faculty members were hired. To cope with the influx of students, the law school implemented an "accelerated" program of three fifteen-week terms, each the equivalent of a semester, thus permitting completion of degree studies in two calendar years. Work on the *Law Review* resumed, with the first postwar issues appearing in March 1947. During the war, the Association of American Law Schools and the American Bar Association (ABA) had given special permission for the W&L School of Law to retain its membership status and accreditation even though it did not meet some of the usual standards, including size of enrollment. But in 1945, the difficulty with enrollment shifted to one of accommodating a rapidly rising number of students. With returning faculty and new hires, the challenge was met; according to Dean Williams, W&L enjoyed in 1947 "the fullest curriculum that has ever been offered by the Law School" and the largest enrollment in its history. The accelerated program, with its considerable demands on faculty time, was ended by the fall of 1948. The graduating class at the end of the last summer term numbered forty, the largest since the new Tucker Hall was opened.

Pressures on the law school from the ABA also quickly resumed, primarily concerning suspected shortcomings in the library and in faculty salaries. The size and characteristics of the law library had long been a matter of concern. Dean Williams noted in May 1947 that W&L's roughly 14,000 volumes could hardly compare with the 80,000 at Duke, 65,000 at Virginia, or 51,000 at Chapel Hill. Noting specific deficiencies in treatises, statutes, codes, reports, and digests, he remarked, "It would seem that on any basis of comparison, our showing is far below what it should be." He also attached a reminder from the ABA that the association's policy "considers it undesirable for university administration to appropriate to other than law school use income derived from law school tuition and fees." Williams observed that with current enrollment, tuition revenues should be sufficient to address the library's needs.[38]

In September 1948, Williams received a patronizing letter from John G. Hervey, an Adviser for the ABA Section of Legal Education and Admissions to the Bar, asking, "Is it possible that the salary scale in your school is as low as it appears to be?" Could W&L manage salaries closer to $7,500, or about half that paid by the larger law schools for "first class" faculty members? "In truth, we do not see how you can secure and retain such teachers at your present salary scale and have continuity in your law school program." The letter also questioned whether W&L "makes any salary deferential [*sic*] in favor of the teachers in the professional schools," a common practice "in all good schools." It would appear, Hervey continued, that W&L was "out of step with what prevails generally" and the salary issue should be brought to the attention of the administration.[39] In a letter to John W. Davis, Gaines defended the qualifications and distinction of the law faculty but admitted that our "whole salary scale is far too low." He also noted that "one of the happiest factors about Washington and Lee" is that no salary differential was established between faculty in the law school and those in the College, and that law school faculty members participated fully in all university committees and activities: "We have thus maintained singular unity in the whole school." Gaines also suggested, "The matter smacks to me a little bit of academic unionism." His response to Mr. Harvey (with copies to the full ABA council) defended the qualifications of the faculty and noted the 5 percent salary increase to be effective on July 1, 1949; the payment by the university of 7.5 percent of salary toward an annuity; the low cost of living in Lexington; and other support provided to the law school. He defended the common salary scale across academic units at W&L: "There is no factor that more certainly makes for faculty unhappiness than this differential."[40] Still, the salary of Dean Williams was only slightly above $7,000, and the other faculty received less than that.

The School of Commerce and Administration also experienced a "virtual suspension" of its programs during the war, with only a handful of majors and the majority of its faculty in national service of one sort or another. As did other universities, W&L attempted to "clarify and redefine the purposes and objectives of a school of business administration" in the postwar period. Dean Glover D. Hancock, who retired at the end of 1948, explained that the "modern economy is complex, and is rapidly changing. It is closely interwoven with government controls; and government itself is a vast network of economic enterprises and regulatory bodies." Preparing students through the study of economics, political science, and administration—with both technical skill and a solid liberal arts foundation—"is the major job of the collegiate school of business administration."[41] But until a full complement of faculty was available, providing instruction for the anticipated surge in students would be problematic. Still, in 1946–47, the School of Commerce accounted for about 29 percent of total undergraduate enrollment, which exceeded the prewar proportion.

In less volatile times, the university's bicentennial in 1949 would have been a major event on the calendar and a primary focus of administrative time and energy. The university leadership had long been aware of this impending opportunity for celebration and national recognition, but the uncertainties of war precluded thorough planning, and the war's immediate aftermath was marked by unsettled conditions and competing demands on public attention. Washington and Lee was nevertheless determined to make the best of the two-hundredth anniversary of the founding of one of America's oldest colleges, and officials and committees were appointed to organize and implement a celebration.

The convocation in September 1948 featured an address by US Supreme Court chief justice Fred M. Vinson, father of a member of the class of 1948. A series of bicentennial presentations followed during the year, including those by Henry R. Luce at the O.D.K. Assembly, Douglas Southall Freeman on Washington's birthday, and John W. Davis to inaugurate the John Randolph Tucker Lectures and celebrate the law school centennial. President Harold W. Dodds of Princeton addressed a special "academic celebration" on April 12 in conjunction with the annual meeting of the Southern University Conference, which brought to campus representatives from 150 colleges and more than twenty-five foundations and organizations. The National Bicentennial convocation, held on campus on June 16–18, 1949, attracted 1,200 alumni to Lexington and featured an address by James F. Byrnes—who, despite not having attended high school or college, was a former US senator, justice of the US Supreme Court, secretary of state under President Truman, and governor of South Carolina. (Byrnes and President Gaines were long-time friends and frequent correspondents.) Scholars, jurists, and notable alumni received special honorary degrees on three occasions in the spring. And the US Post Office issued the first commemorative stamp honoring a higher-education institution, featuring the Colonnade flanked by portraits of Washington and Lee.

The bicentennial celebration set a fund-raising goal of $3 million (the equivalent today of more than $30 million) for scholarships in memory of the W&L men who had died in wartime service, as well as for increased endowment and "plant additions and modernization." A bicentennial office was established in September 1946, and within a few months committees had been organized for soliciting donations in 115 regions, with a target completion date of January 1, 1948. The university distributed leaflets, pamphlets, Christmas calendars, questionnaires, and extra copies of the *Alumni Magazine,* and it sent representatives to twenty-one alumni meetings in fourteen cities. By September 15, pre-campaign contributions of more than $550,000 had been received. By 1948, the deadline for completed solicitations for the "Toward Our Third Century" campaign was extended by a year. President Gaines spoke to special meetings in twenty-five cities and other faculty and staff in eighteen more, an exhausting schedule. By August 31, 1949, the total raised, including pledges, had risen to around $1.8 million, about half of which was undesignated (that is, could be allocated at the university's discretion). This amount fell significantly short of the $3 million goal. Gaines deemed the campaign "reasonably successful in raising permanent funds" but lamented that it provided little for capital projects.[42]

The Alumni Office, now led by Harry K. "Cy" Young, worked closely with the bicentennial effort, including providing support for a narrated color motion picture entitled "Two Centuries of Service," completed in 1947 and made available to alumni chapters. The Alumni Fund had continued to grow even during the war, totaling $23,053 in gifts from 1,742 individuals in 1944–45. The average amount of gifts was less in 1945–46, but the number of donors rose, and a new record in both categories was set in 1947, even with "competing" solicitations for the bicentennial. The Victory Reunion Finals in 1946 generated record alumni attendance, and visits by university officials to local chapters resumed in earnest. The annual Alumni Fund drive was merged with the bicentennial campaign solicitation during 1947–48 and had its greatest success to date—1,137 individuals contributing $26,124, about 60 percent of which was designated for bicentennial projects.

As the bicentennial campaign neared its close, Gaines moved to focus the trustees' attention on future needs for well-organized and vigorous fund-raising. He predicted, despite the welcome and unobtrusive financial benefit to W&L of the GI Bill, that an "enormous increase of tax funds" would flow into public higher education and that "government agencies which furnish funds will expect some form of dominion over institutions that spend those funds." The independent universities must thus renew efforts to secure new resources, and W&L had "a lovelier story to tell" than most.[43] Independence from outside groups—governmental, religious, or otherwise—was deeply engrained in Washington and Lee's history and thinking, and his rather overwrought assessment of the politics of the time led Gaines to reiterate the virtues of self-determination. In July 1950, he shared with the trustees his fear that "publicly controlled institutions must be aligned with current political expediency."[44]

Gaines reported in 1947 that the total assets of the university were approximately $7.5 million and that "not one penny of this sum has come from any public agency or tax source, and not one penny has come from a donation of [an] organized religious group."[45] In June 1948, the endowment, which had begun with George Washington's $20,000 gift and included the major Robert P. Doremus bequest, stood at slightly under $3 million. Despite falling short of the $3 million bicentennial campaign goal, that effort—coupled with the annual Alumni Fund, high enrollment, and special gifts in the last half of the decade, had been salutary for Washington and Lee, which boasted a financial surplus at the end of 1949–50 and total assets of almost $10 million (counting anticipated gifts) and an endowment of almost $5.5 million.

LIFE AT W&L in the immediate postwar era was shaped by the extraordinary demographic profile of the student body. Three-quarters of all students in 1946 and 1947 were veterans, who, along with 250 to 300 student families, brought a new and distinctive dimension to the classroom, extracurricular activities, and campus life in general. The average age of freshmen in 1944–45 was 18, and almost 20 for all undergraduates. Only a year later, these averages were almost 22 and 23, respectively, declining slightly in 1947–48 to 19 and 22. The same pattern existed in the law school, with an average age for first-year students of over 24 in 1945–46 and over 25 in the following two years. Many students were not only older but also bore the experiences of wartime, having served with others from different backgrounds, traveled throughout the country and overseas, and faced the adversity and struggles of combat.

As at other universities, veterans received academic credit for appropriate courses taken as part of their military training, which accelerated progress toward a degree. Administrators, faculty, and students all commented on the dedication and sense of purpose displayed by veterans who were eager to make up for lost time and to get on with their lives and careers. Dean Lucius J. Desha commended the "seriousness of purpose" and high academic performance they brought to campus, as well as the "keen desire" of returning students to restore extracurricular activities and campus traditions—especially a commitment to the Honor System. This enthusiasm for all aspects of campus life led Desha to worry that, as more mature students gave way to younger ones, there could be "increasing danger of over emphasis on campus activities, to the point where a student's academic career may be impaired or jeopardized."[46] The veterans were able to keep their studies and activities in balance. As James Ballengee recalled, "Everybody was very serious that we had lost three years out of our lives and we had to play catch-up, and so we got married and we started having children and we got a professional degree and got in the world to make money and we were thankful we'd survived when so many had not. I think maybe we studied and worked harder than they had in the years right before the war."[47]

Fraternities resumed their activities in April 1946, but the houses, which needed renovations and "reconditioning," were not ready for occupancy until September. Extracurricular activities reappeared, including varsity teams in basketball and track, the Glee Club, the *Ring-tum Phi*, and dances. Visiting speakers opined on a variety of topics. Even with the unusual postwar student mix, the rhythms of traditional college life resumed. Returning also were the usual questions about intercollegiate athletics, especially football, and how the university should proceed after the wartime hiatus. Gaines lamented that "this question indeed seems always with us, like the poor of the Biblical affirmation."[48]

At war's end the university sent a questionnaire to alumni seeking their opinions on the preferred model for intercollegiate athletics, particularly the resumption of football. The choices were to eliminate intercollegiate football, play nonsubsidized football against smaller colleges, or resume football against "our traditional foes with a moderate and honest program of help for the athletes." Gaines expressed surprise at the large number of responses (more than three thousand), as well as at the fact that almost three-quarters supported the third option, not the answer he'd wanted. He would grow increasingly concerned about whether W&L could sustain a competitive, subsidized intercollegiate athletic program, given the university's size, mounting costs, and the problem of coping with rising tensions between alumni enthusiasm and faculty skepticism and resistance.

The university also had to contend with the danger of losing financial support for the journalism program from the Southern Newspaper Publisher's Association (SNPA). The publishers had been proud of their endowment for the "Lee School" of Journalism, but the program had been reduced in importance over the years and was no longer a separate school, which the SNPA perceived as the result of a lack of progress or attention from the university. Gaines assured the SNPA leadership that W&L still highly valued the journalism program and planned to expand and strengthen it (with their help, of course). He noted that during the wartime years, all "non-technical" programs at the university had suffered but that courses had been offered in journalism throughout the conflict, even though the number of students was very small. He offered his "personal assurance of appreciation for the importance of this program. Freedom of the press and power of the program seem to me more urgent and more significant today than ever before." This was accompanied by requests for an additional faculty member, equipment for the journalism laboratory, funds for "practical journalists" to come to campus as visiting lecturers, additional scholarships, and resumption of the Southern Interscholastic Press Conference on the campus. The SNPA responded favorably.[49]

Faculty and staff members moved in and out of the university during the 1940s for wartime service as well as to pursue opportunities in Lexington or new positions elsewhere. Membership on the board of trustees remained relatively stable. Davis and Martin stepped off the board in 1949 after twenty-eight and twenty-one years of service, respectively. New appointments filled out all board vacancies, and Herbert Fitzpatrick became rector in 1940.

Some notable names appeared on the faculty roster during the decade—including William A. Jenks, Charles W. Turner, Carlyle Westbrook Barritt, Linton Lomas Barrett, Marion Junkin, and Marshall Fishwick. After the war, Professor Ollinger Crenshaw embarked on a year's leave, later extended for a second year, to begin work on the history of the university that would eventually be published as *General Lee's College* in 1969. Lewis W. Adams was named dean of the School of Commerce and Administration in 1949, succeeding Glover Hancock, who retired after almost thirty years of service. Robert H. Tucker, who had served as acting president of the university in 1930 and dean of the university since 1932, retired to a faculty appointment as lecturer in economics. Professor Desha succeeded him for one year, after which a new permanent dean arrived in Lexington from his appointment as professor of sociology at Yale University—James Graham Leyburn, who would make his mark on W&L.

Washington and Lee has enjoyed the favor of important benefactors without previous connection to the university, but few have contributed so substantially to it over many years, maintaining such a close personal relationship with the president and his family, as Jessie Ball duPont, who gave millions of dollars to W&L and served as the first female trustee. Born in Northumberland County, Virginia, in January 1884, Jessie Dew Ball began teaching school at the age of eighteen and moved with her family to San Diego in 1909. A member of an old Virginia family and descendent of Mary Ball (George Washington's mother), she had met Alfred I. duPont when he visited her family property in Virginia to hunt. She was then fourteen; he was thirty-four. He made other visits, and they kept up a correspondence over the years. After the death of his second wife in 1920, Alfred and Jessie began a courtship, married in January 1921, and moved into the seventy-seven-room, 47,000 square-foot Nemours Mansion in Wilmington, Delaware. By that time, Alfred was no longer involved with the duPont de Nemours Company and had suffered recent business setbacks. Furthermore, he had lost an eye (in a hunting accident) and most of his hearing. Jessie ran the mansion and served as a helpmate and assistant in her husband's business dealings. In 1926, they moved to Florida, where they built a new home, Epping Forest, and he opened an office in Jacksonville. Jessie's brother, Edward Ball, joined Alfred in the business, which included the Florida National Bank, railroads, and real estate.[50]

When Alfred died in 1935 his estate totaled, after taxes, $26 million, and Jessie was the primary trustee, as well as president of the Nemours Foundation, established to care for crippled children and the elderly. She was also president of the Alfred I. duPont Foundation; chairman of the board of directors of the St. Joe Paper Company, which had vast land holdings in the Florida Panhandle; and member of the board of managers of the Alfred I. duPont Institute. Jessie was no stranger to business; she began investing in stocks and real estate as a young girl and worked closely with Alfred and his business interests. After his death, she divided her time between Wilmington and Jacksonville, and focused on the philanthropic and educational aspects of his legacy. She left most of the business dealings to her tight-fisted, ultra-conservative, hard-nosed brother Edward, who became one of the most powerful men in the state and a leader of the "Pork Chop Gang" of north Florida politicians.

While her brother was battling unions, acquiring banks, and shaping a growing railroad and real-estate empire, Jessie pursued her long-standing interests in education, health, and historic preservation—though also from a traditional, conservative perspective. She was a founding member of the Virginia Museum of Fine Arts in Richmond and, in 1929, one of the incorporators of the Robert E. Lee Memorial Foundation. From her offices in Wilmington and Jacksonville, she presided over her philanthropic projects, large and small. She sent hundreds of young men and women to college (meeting personally with as many as possible), contributed to capital projects, constructed a hospital on the grounds of Nemours in 1941, and in the same year established the Alfred I. duPont Radio Awards in recognition of the importance of this powerful medium. Her long, productive life included a special relationship with W&L

and with Frank and Sadie Gaines. Before her death in 1970, she had received thirteen honorary degrees and was the first female member of the Board of Control of Florida's higher-education system. One of those honorary degrees was awarded by W&L, and she was the first woman to serve on the university's board of trustees in 1950.

Jessie duPont's connections with the Gaines family were warm and intimate. Their letters to her were addressed "Dear Miss Jessie" and signed "As ever" and "With all my love"; her letters to them were addressed "My dear Sadie duVergne and Frank" and "My Dear Little Girl" and signed "Your devoted friend" and "Affectionately yours." Frank shared with her details of his various health challenges (carbuncles, ulcers, psoriasis, allergies) that he rarely shared with others, even in the family. Jessie often visited Lexington and appeared in New York and elsewhere when Frank was speaking. The Gaineses visited her in Delaware and Florida, especially at Epping Forest, and were guests on her yachts. She regularly sent gifts to them and their children, and flowers and other items to the president's home for special occasions. She provided their son Pendleton a scholarship to Germany and financial gifts to help in the purchase of an off-campus house for the Gaineses. Gifts of stock were made to both Frank and Sadie in 1937 and 1938 "for payment against the purchase of your estate" and "to be sold when the market is better and the proceeds apply against the purchase of the 'Gaines' Chateau' alias farm." (This would be Penrobin, south of Lexington along US 11 in Glasgow; the name was derived from the names of the Gaineses' three sons—Francis Pendleton, Robert, and Edwin.) Each gift was slightly under the $5,000 limit for personal gifts without tax and included shares of Paramount Pictures, General Motors, Bethlehem Steel, General Electric, and American Locomotive.[51] Frank Gaines was reportedly one of only two men whom Jessie duPont addressed by their first names.[52]

Jessie duPont invited Frank and Sadie to accompany her to the coronation of King Edward VI in 1937, providing passage, hotels, and seats in the front row of the viewing stand outside Westminster Abbey, secured by the Countess of Kingston. After seeking and receiving permission from the trustees, the Gaineses began their preparations. "I don't know when anything in our whole lives," Frank wrote to his friend, "gave us such an ecstasy, I might say a frenzy, of anticipation. You are, as [his son] Edwin would say, 'the goodest thing in the world' and we can never tell you how much we appreciate this grand idea that occurred to you." They all sailed on the *Berengaria* on May 4 and stayed at Claridge's Hotel in London. Frank and Sadie returned from Cherbourg (after a visit to Paris) on the *Hamburg*, arriving in New York on June 4 in time to attend graduation exercises in Lexington. Decked out in the proper attire, they had a favored view of the coronation proceedings and enjoyed British formality: "the proper attire for gentlemen in the grandstand . . . is a morning coat (cut-away) and top hat. Long tails and white ties will be essential for all dinner parties or evening affairs where ladies are present."[53]

Jessie also paid for transportation and lodging for the Gaineses to vacation with her in Canada in August of 1944 and 1945, and in the Mediterranean in 1952. She was godmother to their son Edwin and to his grandson Pendleton III, and through gifts of stock she provided significant financial support for the education of the Gaineses' grandchildren. In response to this latter gift, Gaines wrote "My dear, sweet friend" in 1950, "What bothers me now is to find the words of appreciation for one of the loveliest and most gracious things I have ever heard of."[54]

Her generosity to educational and charitable organizations was, of course, especially appreciated in the Depression and wartime years, and her personal warmth for Lexington was doubtless an advantage for Washington and Lee. She contributed, in one of her earliest gifts to the university, two hundred shares of duPont de Nemours Company stock to establish the Alfred I. duPont Scholarship Fund, a gift acknowledged by the board in February 1941 and further enhanced by another hundred shares later in the same year. In the fall 1946, she gave three hundred shares of stock (then worth $55,000), in honor of her father, to enhance faculty salaries. The board decided to establish five Thomas Ball Professorships, each drawing one-fifth of the income generated by the gift, but not to exceed $500 a year. In August 1954, she established an endowment—the Jessie Ball duPont–Francis P. Gaines Fund—with $254,112 of du-Pont, General Motors, and other corporate stock, to be used equally for faculty salaries and student scholarships. She designated this gift for "training youth to be intellectual, Christian, moral and Godly leaders. . . . in these terrible times when Satanic forces have been released, attempting the destruction of Christian civilization." The benefits were also to accrue only to members of the "WHITE race." In November 1952, she expressed surprise when she was notified that, up to that point, she had contributed over $1 million to Washington and Lee. "I had no idea that they would amount to anywhere near that figure."[55]

Jessie duPont's family connection to Washington, her reverence for Lee, and her deep interests in higher education and Virginia naturally inclined her toward W&L. But her warm personal relationship with the Gaineses was also a key factor in her beneficence toward the institution. According to Gaines's son Edwin, who had served as president of Converse College in South Carolina, Mrs. duPont relied increasingly on his father's advice. "She put my father on the board [of the St. Joe Paper Company]," Edwin recalled, "because he was the only one that [sic] could control Mr. Ball."[56] During her lifetime, Jessie Ball duPont gave $100 million to many universities and charities, and her relationship with Washington and Lee left a significant imprint on the institution.

BY 1950, FRANK GAINES had served as president for two decades. He enjoyed the trust and support of the trustees and an expanded network of national connections and responsibilities. Still highly sought after as a public speaker, he was able to accept only a handful of the invitations he received. Despite his protests to the contrary, he obviously enjoyed speaking before diverse audiences throughout the country, but he was also sensitive to concerns among the trustees or his colleagues that he might be distracted from his primary responsibilities. "I confess," he wrote the board in July 1950, "that the pressure on me to make speeches continues to be one of my problems. It is a phase of what seems to me the chief function of a college president—to try to say No without making people mad. I have adopted a fairly rigid policy, which I hope this Board endorses of not making speeches unless there is at least a remote promise of advantage to Washington and Lee."[57]

Gaines continued to be approached by other universities seeking to woo him away, including Rice Institute in 1944. He was understandably flattered by this attention and usually pointed out that these offers "might carry larger monetary interests." But he also strongly expressed his loyalty to W&L and the "inspiration from this University that I could not find elsewhere," statements confirmed by his long tenure in Lexington.[58] An especially tempting possibility arose at Vanderbilt University in late 1945, where the board narrowed a list of twenty-five candidates down to four, including Gaines. The search was not resolved until the following August, some months after Gaines had withdrawn his name from consideration.[59] A Nashville physician, Marvin M. Cullom, had encouraged Gaines, after twenty years in Lexington, to move on to "larger fields and greater usefulness." Gaines acknowledged the compliment, but reflected that the leader of a university is not merely doing a job but is a "custodian of a trust."[60] In February 1947, friends approached him concerning the presidency of Louisiana State University in Baton Rouge. Again, he demurred. He noted that he was engaged in a major fund-raising campaign and that he had a deep commitment to his institution: "I stood before the statue of General Lee and lifted up my right hand and swore that I would be faithful to a trust."[61]

Gaines was encouraged on several occasions to run for governor of Virginia. Douglas Southall Freeman, editor of the *Richmond News Leader,* assured him in April 1945, that Harry Byrd held him in high regard and that "you can be elected if you will declare yourself." Gaines always declined these political entreaties, averring that his "best chance for usefulness lies in the field of education."[62] But he enjoyed and cultivated business and political associations. Among other things, through the influence of Ben McKelway, who was editor of the *Washington Star* and whose two sons attended W&L, Gaines became a member of the Alfalfa Club of notables in Washington, established in 1913 to honor Robert E. Lee's birthday, and was elected its president.

Frank Gaines was an experienced leader whose ambition and confidence were always partly, and intentionally, obscured behind a veil of studied humility. He enjoyed being sought out, he relished his time at the podium, and he welcomed the accolades, but his dedication to Washington and Lee was genuine. Like all modern university presidents, he was always treading his way carefully through the competing views and interests of various constituencies (especially in athletics), attempting to avoid controversial political topics (at least in his correspondence), but he spoke out for key principles whenever necessary. Washington and Lee emerged from economic depression, world war, and national recovery as larger, stronger, and better prepared for the challenges of the coming decade.

⤚⥤

CHAPTER THREE

LIFE AT
MIDCENTURY

THE 1950S HARDLY FIT the stereotype of those years as dull, somnolent, or untroubled. The decade witnessed conflict in Korea early on, then rising Cold War tensions, domestic anti-communism, burgeoning suburbs and the reconfiguration of cities, steps forward in civil rights, and major changes in popular culture. Higher education, like many other sectors of American life, began to reposition itself, to consolidate the transformations brought about by global conflict, economic recovery, expanded government, and rising expectations, and to lay the foundations for a more prosperous and stable future. But the future would bring more dramatic social and political change than anyone imagined.

The decade opened with a haunting specter of war, calling to mind the disruptions, uncertainties, and sacrifices of less than a decade before. North Korea's invasion of South Korea in June 1950 challenged a partition of the country established in World War II, and it unleashed the anxieties of the Cold War. Thanks partly to a boycott of United Nations (UN) proceedings by the Soviet Union, the United States was able to secure UN backing for a "police action" to repel the invaders. The United States supplied most of the troops for this international coalition, drawing them initially from occupation forces in Japan and later from a military draft. Suffering huge losses, the North Koreans were driven back almost to the border with the People's Republic of China, which—with Soviet backing—entered the hostilities in October. This full-scale conflict ended with an armistice in July 1953, establishing a demilitarized zone roughly along the initial partition line. There had been over 33,000 US combat deaths (and more than 8,000 servicemen missing in action); many more combat deaths among the South Korean, North Korean, and Chinese forces; and millions of civilian casualties.

These events revivified the painful memories of World War II. Some Washington and Lee students were called up, and others enlisted so they could select their branch of service. The return of uncertainty—"will I be able to complete my education?"—and the possibility of a broader conflict jeopardized the recent surge in enrollments and revenues. Frank Gaines had long maintained that W&L needed military training opportunities for students who would otherwise be drawn elsewhere. The Korean conflict heightened these concerns. On August 29, 1950, Gaines reported to the trustees that sixteen "non-military colleges in our district have already applied for ROTC" and that students and their parents "are deeply anxious and making numerous inquiries." A poll of the faculty revealed "unanimous desire for some unit consistent with our academic purposes." The trustees endorsed his request to apply for a Reserve Officers' Training Corps (ROTC) unit, except for Herbert Fitzpatrick, who questioned the urgency and suggested that the matter be discussed fully by the executive committee or the board.[1]

In November 1950, Gaines requested help from Harry F. Byrd, US senator from Virginia, member of the Armed Services Committee, and soon-to-be W&L trustee. Byrd responded that he had made the necessary contacts with Gen. Matthew Ridgway and others. On January 9, 1951, Gaines notified the board that W&L had been awarded a Transportation Corps ROTC unit: "This is a matter of utmost importance to us. Dean Gilliam advises me that more than fifty percent of our applicants have been gravely concerned. Without this unit the prospects for a freshman class would have been slim."[2] In February, Gaines also submitted an application for a unit of the Air Force ROTC. He received notice in April that the application had been denied; 450 institutions had applied and only 62 were selected, confirming that W&L was not alone in seeking military training as part of its curriculum.[3]

The ROTC unit at VMI was designated as the initial sponsor for the W&L Army unit, and the first head and professor of military science and tactics—Lt. Col. Richard W. Jones Jr.—arrived in 1951 and served for five years. In 1954, faced with a surplus of officers in the Transportation Corps, the Army asked W&L to shift its curriculum from transportation to general military science, which would open up a larger available number of military commissions. W&L agreed, and the new curriculum was instituted in the 1954–55 academic year.[4]

Colonel Jones was succeeded by Lt. Col. Charles E. Coates Jr. in 1955 and by Maj. Edward J. Roxbury in 1959.

Accommodating ROTC at W&L was no simple matter. As Gaines predicted, large numbers of students joined the program—fully 80 percent of all freshmen and sophomores in the first two years it was available—and created a demand for suitable classroom and drill space. (In addition, 120 students commuted weekly to Fishersville to participate in the O-1 Naval Reserve unit there, and 40 others participated in an O-2 unit.) By December 1952, a majority of students were already in ROTC and enrolled in eight freshman sections, six sophomore sections, and five junior sections—with five sections scheduled for seniors in the following year—a total of twenty-four new classes as of September 1954. A new building was needed for classrooms, a pre-engineering laboratory, and offices.[5]

The fears of catastrophic enrollment decline turned out to be unfounded, but the initial concerns were not. Student morale improved after a fairly liberal national Selective Service policy was adopted, and the new ROTC unit helped maintain enrollment. Hostilities in Korea did not lead to major national mobilization, and W&L's enrollment gradually returned to nearly prewar levels and composition, in accordance with a desire to maintain a smaller size and intimate academic and campus environment. Other institutions were not as fortunate. Sewanee, for example, experienced "a disastrous loss of students" in the fall term of 1950 and closed two temporary buildings and a dining room.[6]

The thirty years after 1945 have been called the golden age of American higher education. Enrollment soared by over 80 percent between 1940 and 1950, with most of that occurring in the last half of the decade. Between 1945 and 1975, enrollment rose dramatically—from 1.7 to 11.2 million—signaling fundamental changes in how higher education was perceived and pursued in the United States. In 1945, 10 percent of the US population between the ages of eighteen and twenty-four was enrolled in college; in 1975 it was over 40 percent.[7] No longer solely for the well-to-do and those preparing for professions, college was increasingly considered necessary for a good job, and the degree a ticket to a good life. Rising aspirations and postwar economic prosperity, the GI Bill, and major government subsidies—at the federal and state levels—supported the enrollment surge for institutions and for student financial aid. In mid-twentieth-century America, college education was also regarded as a public good, a bulwark of economic development, national security, and effective citizenship—indeed, worthy of national investment.

Wartime mobilization had helped forge a closer connection between government and higher education. Science played a crucial role in manufacturing, communications, and modern weapons (including radar, code-breaking, and, most dramatically, the atomic bomb). Colleges helped develop military and civilian expertise and leadership during the war years, and the need to continue these national assets became even more intense in the Cold War, the pressures of which would sustain the greatest advances of higher education, technology, and scientific innovation thus far in the nation's history.

During the 1950s, W&L added more students and faculty members, pondered its identity and size, and made some changes in its curriculum, but it remained much as it had been a generation earlier. Most of the expansion in higher education occurred in the public sector, especially in large state universities and comprehensive institutions (mostly former teachers' colleges) that swelled with new enrollment demands and ample government support. New junior and community colleges were also established to provide vocational education and awarding two-year associate degrees as paths to further studies. The classic private liberal arts colleges were influenced by these trends and developments but accounted for an increasingly smaller share of total higher-education enrollment, leading to concerns that they might be bypassed by the desire for occupational training and cut off from new sources of financial support.

THE ENROLLMENT OF 1,171 students at W&L in 1950–51 was more than twelve percent below the 1,332 registered in 1947–48, the high point thus far in the university's long history. Things were returning to standards more typical of peacetime. Total enrollment rose and fell slightly over the decade, reaching a low of 1,025 in 1953–54 and a high of 1,158 by 1959–60. Law school registrations began the decade at 218, fell to 103 in 1955–56, and stood at 133 in 1958–59.

The student body remained overwhelmingly Protestant in religious affiliation at the outset of the 1950s, with Presbyterians, Episcopalians, and Methodists constituting 63 percent of the whole. Seven percent were Roman Catholic and 6 percent Jewish. Fifty-seven percent hailed from the southern states (including Texas and West Virginia), 26 percent from the Northeast (including Maryland), and 14 percent from the Midwest. Fifty-six percent of processed applications by the June deadline came from applicants in the South in 1953, rising to 74 percent in 1956 and to 70 percent in 1958 and 1959. The figures remained generally the same throughout the decade, and not much different from what they had been thirty years before—if anything, the geographic diversity was less and the predominant religious denominations were even more so.

Following the previous decade's enrollment volatility, the university again pondered its "ideal size." A subcommittee of five administrators and faculty members studied the matter and reported its findings in June 1957. W&L's average increase in enrollment since 1925 was substantially less than that at Amherst, Bowdoin, Hamilton, Swarthmore, and Williams. In the years between 1940 and 1955, W&L averaged slightly less than a 1 percent annual increase, whereas the other institutions had grown much more—from 1.36 percent a year at Bowdoin to 2.43 percent at Swarthmore. The subcommittee found that even with an increase in applications and the assumption that admitted students were more academically qualified, the overall retention rate remained essentially the same. Only about 60 percent of W&L students graduated in four years, and of the remainder, approximately 15 to 18 percent were not reinstated after having fallen under the Automatic Rule for inadequate academic performance. The initial conclusion was that W&L could begin increasing its freshman class at an annual rate of up to 2 percent and still improve quality without additional operating or capital expense beyond the additional tuition income. By 1960, the estimated cost of annual attendance was $1,750, including $300 a semester for tuition, plus average dormitory charges, board in Evans Dining Hall, books and supplies, and laundry. Other expenses—for travel, fraternity membership, and incidentals—easily pushed this annual figure above $2,000.

Ensuring academic ability at the time of admission was important for enhancing student retention. Washington and Lee was the first men's college in the South to require the College Entrance Examination Board aptitude test of all applicants, beginning with the class entering in September 1950. The principal reason for this decision, however, was to boost the "advancement in academic rating of the University in the eyes of the educational world."[8] Though some potential applicants may have been deterred, the number of applications continued to rise. By June 1952, 583 applications had been completed for the 300 places available in the Class of 1952.[9] Overcrowding in the dormitories led to the reduction of the 1953 entering class to 285 (out of 672 completed applications). The number of applications increased from 700 for 1954 to 1,112 for 1959 (the first year of the nonrefundable fee) and 1,186 for 1960. Entering student performance on the College Board examination also rose during the decade, from an average of 450 (out of 800) in 1951 to 528 in 1958. Even with stiffer competition, the university still accepted any member of an alumni family "who qualifies personally" and "gives clear promise" of ability to succeed, even if other applicants were better qualified. The Class of 1958 contained the sons of thirty-eight alumni, a record number entering in a single year.

Dean Frank Gilliam also reported in 1952 that James D. Farrar, '49 (and son of James M. Farrar, '14), had completed his second tour of duty with the Marine Corps and was appointed assistant to the dean of students (and assistant dean of students in 1953, and later associate dean), bringing "enthusiasm, energy, friendliness, and intelligent activity" to the position. He was the primary university liaison to the fraternities and also worked with many of the preparatory schools. He was named director of Student Financial Aid and Scholarships in 1960.

FRANK J. GILLIAM WAS among the best-known and highly regarded university administrators of the twentieth century. He served for many years as dean of students and director of admissions, and uniquely personified what it meant to be a gentleman, advisor, and stalwart friend. He provided an unforgettable personal and enduring university connection for former students, and it is impossible to imagine or understand W&L admissions or student life in the '30s, '40s, and '50s without him.

A 1917 graduate, Frank Gilliam returned to W&L to teach English in 1926 after service as an infantry officer in World War I and later as a Presbyterian missionary in the Congo. He became dean of students in 1931, serving in that position until 1962. Even though the formal title of director of admissions was not bestowed until 1951, Gilliam oversaw that function for many years. He also taught English composition and took up a major's commission during World War II to serve as principal university liaison to the Army School of Special Services. Made dean emeritus upon his retirement in 1963, after thirty-seven years of service and after suffering a serious heart attack in 1962, he continued to work in Washington Hall with alumni and donors. He died at eighty years of age on March 19, 1976.

A young and vigorous Frank Gilliam evolved into a beloved, avuncular figure in a "big, broad-rimmed slouch hat," known for his distinctive walk and a "sonorous, sometimes booming voice" that rendered superfluous his intercom connection to his long-time, devoted secretary, Mildred Brownlee. His warmth, charm, and uncanny ability to remember names were coupled with a genuine personal interest in students. He and his wife Louise frequently invited students to breakfasts, lunches, and dinners at "Belfield," the home and garden they built near the campus in the late 1920s. (It is now lovingly restored for university guests and events.) He wrote notes on every student grade slip, sent each semester to parents, and notes also to students (and alumni) about a variety of matters, including perhaps a gentle upbraiding for some unfortunate infliction upon the English language. A note delivered in class asking a student to "drop by" Dean Gilliam's office might elicit anxiety, but the meeting often ended with a pat on the back or an encouraging nudge to do better. All of this made Frank Gilliam a W&L icon. He was usually the first person on campus sought out by returning alumni.[10]

Gilliam was not simply accessible and charming, he was an innovative, extremely effective administrator and one of the most respected admissions officers in the region. Primarily responsible for W&L's decision to require that all applicants take the College Board examination, he was also the first member from a southern institution to serve on the College Entrance Examination Board executive committee. He crafted the university's recruiting strategy, sending representatives to public and private high schools and distributing information about the institution. He tirelessly supported requiring all first-year students to live in dormitories, a shared experience under the guidance of faculty advisors and student counselors, instituted long before "freshman experience" programs became widespread. He also favored residence halls for upperclassmen and dining facilities that could serve most students, the latter need finally realized with the opening of the Letitia Pate Evans Dining Hall in 1959. He worked closely with the new dean of the university, James Graham Leyburn, to encourage a focus on academic achievement and intellectual endeavor rather than on social life and intercollegiate athletics, and to provide alternatives for students not affiliated with fraternities. (Indeed, he first brought Leyburn, then a Yale faculty member, to the attention of President Gaines.) For years, Gilliam was the university's liaison to the fraternities, and he hoped that the student-led Interfraternity Council could mitigate the worst abuses of fraternity life. He always regarded this effort as a work in progress. More fulfilling was his work with and support of student government, especially the Honor System. He established Freshman Camp in 1928 as a healthy introduction to life at W&L. While only a few students attended at first, by the time of his retirement at least 90 percent of the entering class participated. He was also a prominent civic leader. As a member of the biracial Lexington Council on Human Relations, he was a clear voice advocating for the admission of black students in the early 1960s.

In his persistent, low-key, sensible way, Frank Gilliam was a steady hand and advisor to Gaines, Leyburn, and other academic leaders. He was a central cog in whatever mechanism the university selected to convey its message to students, parents, and alumni. Even when focused on individual students or particular projects, he was always able to see things from a larger, longer perspective. He was well aware of the common alumni preference that W&L always remain the way it was when they were students, but he also knew that the university must adapt to new needs and circumstances in a changing society and in the competition for students and greater institutional recognition. In the throes of student activism in 1970, he shared his conviction that W&L would never lose "its essential distinction of excellence," and advised alumni that while there may be many things they might not like, if the institution did not change "most of you would be ashamed of it."

CHANGES IN THE UNIVERSITY'S leadership were largely incremental, but some new appointments would especially affect W&L's future course. Herbert Fitzpatrick was succeeded as rector by James R. Caskie of Lynchburg, first elected to the board in 1924. New trustees included Christopher T. Chenery of New York City (1950), an engineer and utility executive who later became famous as the owner of the Virginia stable that produced the racehorse Secretariat; Harry Flood Byrd (1951), a former governor of Virginia and US senator whose political machine dominated Virginia politics for decades and who later mounted the "massive resistance" campaign against school desegregation; John Minor Wisdom of New Orleans (1957), a Republican whose support of Dwight Eisenhower's election as president led to his appointment to the US Fifth Circuit Court of Appeals and his notable efforts to assure equal treatment of the laws and adherence to the Supreme Court decisions on civil rights; and the first woman to serve on the W&L board, Mrs. Alfred I. duPont (1960). All trustees but Byrd and duPont were alumni. The administration now included James D. Farrar, appointed assistant dean of students in 1952, Edwin P. (Cy) Twombly as director of Athletics (1954), and Frank A. Parsons as director of Publicity (1954). David W. Sprunt was appointed director of Religious Activities in 1953 and remained as a professor of religion after this specific administrative position was eliminated. In 1956, Leon F. Sensabaugh, formerly at Birmingham Southern College, was appointed dean of the College, succeeding Leyburn, who had assumed the position in 1947 and now returned to the faculty.

By 1960, W&L listed four emeritus professors and ninety active, ranked faculty members (forty-five professors, twenty-three associate professors, and twenty-two assistant professors), fourteen instructors, and three lecturers. These included seven faculty members in the law school (four professors, two associate professors, and one lecturer), and seven in military science. Since 1945, the problem of faculty salaries had been made even more urgent by postwar inflation. The board periodically provided raises for faculty and staff and, by 1960, offered a competitive range of health and retirement benefits. Faculty compensation was a particular issue in the law school, where the accrediting agencies pointed to inadequate salaries and less than desirable resources in the law library. In 1953, the university also made significant efforts to improve and update its development operations.

The Alumni Office made steady progress in the Annual Fund drive, more than doubling the number of contributors and increasing the average gift by over 50 percent between 1951 and 1958. The efforts of class and regional agents, an expanded list of local chapters, class reunions, focused mailings, and a variety of other Alumni Association activities helped W&L weather the storm occasioned by an athletic scandal at mid-decade. This was, of course, partly due to the indefatigable efforts of "Cy" Young, whose retirement in June 1958 was greeted with regret and praise by alumni groups throughout the country.[11]

The annual alumni fund drive was a critical component of fund-raising at all universities, but it was only one component of development planning. A modern, comprehensive, systematic, ongoing development effort was first initiated at W&L in September 1953, with the establishment of the Office of University Development, headed by its first director, Donald E. Smith, formerly secretary-treasurer of the Worcester Polytechnic Institute Alumni Association. This was "conceived as a continuing, long-range program designed to determine and to satisfy as fully as possible the University's present and future needs."[12] Its purpose and activities would be entirely familiar to university leaders today. Committees were established to identify needs, gather information to establish priorities, and determine the "optimum" undergraduate enrollment, class size, and faculty teaching load, as well as new capital projects. These reports were consolidated and modified by a new steering committee for university development and submitted to the trustees in 1954. Two additional committees—on campus planning and faculty housing—submitted reports to the board in June 1955. Two years later, Smith outlined, and the trustees approved, a new Capital Funds Campaign to begin in 1958–59.

The effort to collect data on potential funding sources and donors—such as financial capacity, giving history, and connection to the university—was painstaking work, starting virtually from scratch and without the aid of modern electronic data searching or processing. Gradually, files were created that, along with the plans and committees, laid a foundation for future fund-raising. But this work and the campaign plans were unsettled when Smith resigned in October 1957 to become director of University Relations at the University of Rochester, a move the trustees received "with deep regret." In his last meeting with the board, in January 1958, Smith presented a final report and plan for the Capital Fund Campaign, which the board approved in general.[13]

Don Smith was succeeded on April 1 by James Whitehead, in the redefined position of director of University Relations. Unfortunately, and unaccountably, the new development initiative was essentially given up, much of the organizational structure was eliminated, and the information collection effort largely abandoned.[14] A development office with its own director would not be revived until a decade later. The alumni annual fund continued to be the major W&L fund-raising activity, but some specific campaigns for new projects and buildings were disappointing. All this occurred at the same time that state governments were pouring more and more money into the rapid growth of public institutions, permitting low tuition rates. Correspondingly, the need for greater support for independent institutions by foundations and individuals became even more acute.

W&L confronted substantial needs for funding to support student life and new classroom facilities. The most important additions to the infrastructure during the decade were the Jessie Ball duPont Hall in 1954, to house the art department among other things, and the Evans Dining Hall in 1959. The plans for duPont Hall, according to Mary Coulling, who worked with Don Smith in the Development Office, "had to be cut back, and back, and back. It ended up not being a terribly attractive building, but . . . there just wasn't the money. And then, I guess, we had the campaign also—the beginning of the campaign—for Parmly Hall . . . it didn't meet its goal."[15]

———

ALEXANDER VANCE, '31, first met James Leyburn at summer camp in Montreat, North Carolina. Later, in the summer of 1924 when Leyburn was a graduate student at Princeton, the two friends bicycled more than 1,600 miles through England and Scotland. After Leyburn joined the faculty at Yale, Vance mentioned him to Frank Gilliam, who then brought him to the attention of Frank Gaines. Leyburn and Gaines first met at the Pierre Hotel in New York, probably in 1946.[16] Leyburn had never lived in Lexington, but his deep

Washington and Lee roots, stellar academic credentials, and solid Presbyterian background greatly impressed Gilliam and Gaines. On June 4, 1946, Gaines offered Leyburn a full professorship and appointment as dean of the university. Leyburn accepted but asked that his arrival in Lexington be delayed until the fall of 1947.[17] Thus began the tenure of one of W&L's most notable and influential faculty members, his legacy measured not so much by dramatic changes or new policies as by his devotion to the life of the mind, aspirations for the university, respect for students, and his personal example. He was also a prolific and articulate commentator on W&L's condition, culture, and possibilities.

Leyburn's W&L lineage was impeccable. His great-grandfather, Dr. Alfred Leyburn, was a trustee during Lee's presidency and later served as rector. His grandfather attended W&L and his father, Edward R. Leyburn, was an 1887 graduate and Presbyterian minister. Known to family and friends as "Jimmy" Leyburn, he was born in Hedgeville, West Virginia, in 1902. The family moved later that year to Durham, North Carolina, when his father took up ministry at a new church. His collegiate studies began at Trinity College (later Duke University), leading to BA and MA degrees in Economics and Political Science, followed by an additional MA in Economics and Social Institutions at Princeton University in 1922. He taught at Hollins College for two years before returning to Princeton for further graduate work. He was not entirely comfortable at Princeton or with the study of economics, which seemed to him a rather detached and purely analytical field. A visit to Yale University convinced him to continue his studies there, but in anthropology and sociology, and he earned a PhD in 1927, with his dissertation, "The Frontier Family."

Leyburn remained in New Haven, rising from the position of instructor in the "Science of Society" in 1927 to professor of sociology in 1946. Along the way, he served as acting chair of the Sociology Department and director of undergraduate studies. In 1943 and 1944, he was principal mission officer of the US Lend-Lease Administration in the Union of South Africa, with an office in Johannesburg. This experience tested his administrative skills, stimulated his academic curiosity, and made a deep impression on him.

Leyburn was a prolific scholar, publishing books and articles dealing with folkways, race, and ethnicity. His best-known, prize-winning work was *The Haitian People* (1941), which was translated into Spanish and French. Prior to that, he had published the *Handbook of Ethnography* (1931) and *Frontier Folkways* (1935). His numerous articles and essays appeared in influential periodicals, including *Social Forces* (where he was a contributing editor), the *American So-*

ciological Review, and the *Journal of Negro History.* He also contributed essays to Presbyterian publications and continued to write in various areas of scholarly interest after coming to W&L, most notably his 1962 volume, *The Scotch-Irish: A Social History,* which stemmed from a course he was teaching and from exploring his own Scotch-Irish family roots in western Virginia. It remains the standard work on the subject.

Leyburn was a handsome, courtly bachelor with white hair and an almost military bearing. His manner was gentle and intense, and could be a bit intimidating. He lived a well-disciplined life, built around teaching, scholarship, and a love of music. (He was an accomplished pianist and organist.) A passionate and dedicated teacher, he offered an array of courses in sociology, history, and anthropology. His lecture on the death of Socrates was perhaps the most anticipated and remembered in the university's history. Another of his famous lectures—on the Greek striving for *arête,* or excellence in all things admirable—stressed the pursuit of a worthy, meaningful life and not only academic achievement. He was famously exact: student papers were invariably returned, with marginal commentary, by the next class meeting, and he always arrived precisely on time for meetings or for class—students were expected to do likewise. In an unpublished 1953 essay, Virginius Dabney, editor of the *Richmond Times-Dispatch,* referred to Leyburn as "something close to a genius," who created "a cosmopolitan atmosphere wherever he happens to be."[18]

Leyburn believed that while Washington and Lee exemplified essential values, it had greater potential than it either realized or had pursued. His work on the curriculum and raising academic standards for students and faculty was modeled on his own rich but rather ascetic life. He lived in a faculty house just off the Colonnade (now housing the Reeves Collection), with usually one or two student boarders, and no television set. His office door was always open, and his interactions with students were sincere, direct, and supportive. He regarded his colleagues and students as his responsibilities, his challenges, and even his family. He also regularly reminded the relatively privileged students of W&L of the precepts of noblesse oblige: of those who had much, much was expected. This idea was a reminder of the important elements of a meaningful individual life, not an endorsement of a hierarchical social structure. Inevitably, students associated him with the classical verities mirrored in his erudition and dignified mien. On the front door of his house was a brass plaque, given to him by a student, which read "Mount Olympus." As another of W&L's great professors, Sidney Coulling, noted in a presentation to the trustees in 1993,

Leyburn "had for the University the highest of aspirations, urging it to pursue excellence in all that was admirable, and at the same time holding up before it the challenge of noblesse oblige."[19]

When he arrived on campus in the fall of 1947, at the age of forty-five, after some twenty-three years in teaching, Leyburn approached his new duties as dean of the university with characteristic seriousness. As he recalled much later, "At Yale I was merely one faculty member among many; but one of my first discoveries at W&L was that, simply because I was Dean of the University and second in authority only to President Gaines, I was definitely *not* 'one among many.' I learned from the first week that I could not possibly have any faculty 'intimates' or any professor with whom I could casually chat about university affairs. If I wanted *friends,* they must be townspeople." This sense of difference may well have been exaggerated and compounded by his arrival in a new academic environment and community. It doubtless also contributed to the appearance of aloofness that some colleagues noticed and even characterized as arrogance. Students, however, recalled him differently. For whatever reason, Leyburn was highly sensitive to the close-knit relationships and varying expectations among the small faculty at W&L, and he maintained some social distance from his colleagues. He believed he "was regarded as almost a different species."[20]

The spirit and momentum of Leyburn's leadership was apparent in his formal accounting to the president after his first year. He reported in 1948 the "general attitude of students" as one of "serious application, tempered always by that laudable pursuit of a well-rounded life characteristic of Washington and Lee men." He noted that less than 10 percent of the freshmen were veterans, a situation signaling an end to the hectic enrollment patterns immediately following the war. He judged the work of the faculty to have "been strenuous and devoted," but he noted their "lack of free time" and urged the establishment of a sabbatical program "devoted to creative research," in addition to higher faculty salaries (to be derived from a tuition increase). "Our faculty," he wrote, "is exceptional in its quality, its loyalty, and its sheer virtuosity."

He was pleased "to record the fact that Washington and Lee has never deserted the ideal of a broad liberal education for all of its students," and he reported on the curricular changes that he and the faculty had been working on. These included new courses in mathematics, offered at different levels to serve specific student needs; the encouragement of independent majors and interdisciplinary work; new interdepartmental majors among geology, economics and social sciences; the separation of philosophy and religion into two separate departments; periodic meetings of the fourteen faculty members in the natural sciences to discuss "problems and programs of mutual interest"; the growth of the fine arts with the appointment of "a director of dramatics" and the offering of musical concerts in Lee Chapel; and the inauguration of "voluntary comprehensive examinations and senior theses, and required integrative courses for seniors." He also promised new faculty appointments in philosophy, painting, and music. (The new appointments would include Marion Junkin in Art, Edward D. Myers in Philosophy, and Marshall Fishwick in American Studies.) "It is my hope that we shall take the leadership among Southern institutions in the cultivation of interdepartmental majors, and in our successful inspiration of students with a love for the excitement of intellectual activity." Furthermore, Washington and Lee should "lead not only its students, but the people of this region, to an insatiable delight in the pleasures of the mind and spirit."[21]

These changes and others that followed were ambitious extensions of W&L's liberal arts tradition, labeled by a writer for the *Ring-Tum Phi* as the "Leyburn Plan," suggesting a grand design on the order of the "Marshall Plan" then being implemented in Europe. Leyburn never claimed to have any such grand design in mind when he arrived in Lexington, but he did strive to strengthen the academic program, break down barriers between departments and disciplines, and better enable students to pursue their individual intellectual interests independently and with fewer restrictions. He also sought to inspire the faculty and intensify their focus on serious intellectual work.

Only a few months after assuming his deanship, Leyburn laid out his thinking in an address to the Faculty Discussion Group on November 20, 1947.[22] "My purpose this evening," he began, "is to initiate a discussion of education at Washington and Lee." He recognized that his main role as dean was "to carry out what the faculty has agreed upon as wise." But he also declared his intention "to speak frankly and candidly." His beginning assumption set the stage for his remarks: "Every one of us wishes [W&L] to be known not only throughout the South but all over the nation as one of the two or three really great institutions of higher learning." Competition with the great research universities was unrealistic, but favorable comparison with Williams, Amherst, Dartmouth, and Oberlin was, he suggested, a reasonable goal. Why did students choose to come to Washington and Lee? Leyburn suggested three primary attractions—"the association with Lee; the social life of the university; and the prominence of its alumni in civic enterprise." These were all good reasons but not the "best" ones: "one rarely hears the claim that Washington and Lee is best known nationally for its outstanding scholarship, its high academic standards, the scholars on its faculty and those it produces among undergraduates." To realize this goal, or any worthy ambition, a university must look to its faculty, its students, and its curriculum.

He began, a bit uncomfortably, by discussing the faculty and the matter of performance incentives for tenured professors. "What," he asked, "keeps men on permanent appointment out of a rut?" The weight of academic pressure was reduced because "life in Lexington is pleasant," the university did not demand much in the way of research, and resting "on one's laurels is probably no less here than in any other comfortable place." While "the very human kindness of this institution" reduced the pressure on junior faculty, the university would "never achieve our object of making Washington and Lee famous in the academic field unless every man on permanent appointment is either a productive research scholar or a great teacher." While he appreciated the faculty's dedication and qualifications, "I think we have a right to ask every member of our group to achieve pre-eminence."

W&L students, Leyburn declared, "seem to be average." There were excellent students, of course, but only by raising standards could the university assure itself of a greater share of such students. Given the large number of applications received by higher-education institutions across the country, he suggested that the time "was never more auspicious" to be more selective in admissions, and he believed this improvement could be achieved without reducing enrollment or revenue. By widely broadcasting W&L's higher standards and its expectations of academic work based on those standards, the applicant pool of highly qualified students would increase, as had occurred in leading professional schools. In his view, "we should make every promising Southerner and Easterner think *first* of Washington and Lee." He could not help but note an irony: Why was it "that large numbers of our ten thousand alumni plead very tellingly for football scholarships, while remaining apparently only tepidly interested in Washington and Lee's intellectual triumphs?"

The best students would also be attracted to a better course of study. W&L already had a robust but fairly standard liberal arts curriculum, with a prescribed selection of courses in the first year, followed by courses chosen from various disciplines in subsequent years. Student choice was delimited by numbers of credit hours within specific disciplines, with the largest requirement for courses in the student's major. Leyburn wanted to take a fresh look at this model, based on the intellectual potential of the best students. "The generalization is this," he told his colleagues, "the only education which is permanently valuable for any student is that which he gets for himself, on his own initiative, to satisfy his own consuming curiosity." Thus, "the role of the faculty member is to arouse the first interest, to plant the seeds which will burgeon into the quest for knowledge, and the role of the curriculum is to encourage the student to learn for himself." The current curriculum, divided into semesters, credit hours, and courses "artfully designed to be unrelated to the courses of any other department" simply defeated this objective. "The implication is that we wish to keep everyone in line, not that we shall reward men for having initiative enough to get out of line." Beyond that, too many courses were "devoted to the retelling of facts, and too little calculated to stir the minds of our men to consider ideas." Was such a curriculum even "liberal" in the broadest sense of the term? "Is there anything in our procedure," he asked, "which will suggest to the student the implications of one of his subjects or courses for another? Is there anything to make him feel that he is building upon the work of his earlier years, or that there is a necessary interrelationship in all this knowledge? Is it ever insisted to him that life is a whole, and that the purpose of education is to help him achieve a synthesis of the individual parts?" A curriculum fragmented into isolated "majors" might not be the answer to such questions.

Leyburn realized that he was "yielding to the optimistic delusion that a majority of our men will be fired with the zeal for pursuing knowledge for its own sweet sake. Let me return to realism." The curriculum at least ought to carry more emphasis on "reflective" and "creative" thinking. This could be achieved, in part, by requiring comprehensive examinations at the end of the senior year, as well as a senior thesis. He also suggested that W&L offer two kinds of baccalaureate degrees—the pass degree ("we shall continue to have average men for a while") and the honors degree, requiring a senior thesis and successful completion of a "distinguished comprehensive examination in his subject."

He also pointed to academic areas that should be bolstered if W&L was to achieve preeminence among liberal arts institutions—especially philosophy and fine arts. He regarded philosophy as less a distinct discipline than a context for interdisciplinary thinking, "the integrating factor of the whole curriculum." And with only two courses in the fine arts, the university was failing to provide students access to architecture, sculpture, painting, and music, indeed to the creative and aesthetic dimensions of human culture.

He noted that the "number of other points on which I might express an opinion is legion"—from "the encroachment of athletics upon school work" to the class

schedules and "our addiction to committee work." But he reiterated his aspirations for the university and appealed for faculty support: "Washington and Lee
can be whatever we, the members of the faculty, decide it should be. My hope
is that we shall determine that it should become first the outstanding educational institution in the South, and then the outstanding teaching university
in the country. This means a better curriculum; better teaching; more interest
in research—not for itself, but for what it does for our liveliness of mind; and
a better student body. If we can improve the first three (curriculum, teaching,
research), the last will inevitably follow."

Leyburn then offered ten specific suggestions for faculty consideration. The
first would lead to some alumni discontent; "the primary goal of college life is
intellectual stimulation and achievement," and W&L's reputation should not
rest "upon the achievement of its football team, the success of its Fancy Dress
balls, or the luxury of its fraternity houses." The curriculum should be made
more flexible and accommodating to the serious student, "making him feel
that the university exists for him, not that he is a freak to be tolerated." He
hoped "to see a few *adults* graduated from Washington and Lee who had never
had to master the complexities of quality credits, grade-point ratios, and the
requirements for distribution and concentration." Leyburn also called for more
informal faculty-student contact. What many alumni now cherish as one of the
university's defining qualities—meaningful relationships between faculty and
students—was apparently not always so evident, and it led to complaints over
the years. Leyburn recounted his surprise that few faculty members met with
students outside of class and that students were so little inclined to regard the
ideas and opinions of the faculty. He therefore suggested that each department
encourage such informal meetings; "more can be done for the cause of intellectual awakening by one hour of excited man-to-man conversation than in ten
hours of class work."

He concluded, "I wish I could promise you all higher salaries, sabbatical
leaves, luxurious offices, and secretarial assistance. I *can* promise you that I
shall leave no stone unturned to help you make this university what you want
it to be: the one institution in this country which no faculty member would
think of leaving."

One can imagine the range of faculty reactions to this call to greatness that
challenged the usual way of doing things (especially departmental prerogatives) and pointed out deficiencies in faculty, students, curriculum, and even
traditions. The new dean of the university was a man of quiet eloquence and

perfect professional decorum but also something of a radical, who valued intellectual work above all else and resisted any structures and mechanisms that contained or constricted it. Students should have the greatest possible range of choice in their studies, and academic departments should be combined or the barriers between them minimized. Traditions were to be honored but sometimes also broken. Leyburn's students would come quickly to appreciate these characteristics. He was known for many things, but he was never thought of as a "fuddy-duddy."

The "ideal" or "best" student that Leyburn described was a far cry from the student most W&L faculty actually encountered in the classroom and was probably, for that matter, uncommon even at Amherst or Swarthmore. In that sense, his "plan" was a construction designed to make a point. While Gaines and Gilliam agreed that the university could be more selective in admissions, they were also aware that the attractions of social life, athletics, and the tradition of the "Gentleman's C" were very much a part of the W&L tradition and culture. The notion of W&L students engaging in "bull sessions" in the dormitory on "the nature of being" or "the interrelationships of natural science and politics" must have seemed unlikely, even bizarre, to many faculty members. But they could also grasp that this was due, in part, to peer expectations that frowned on too much of such things. Leyburn would always be a staunch advocate for the iconoclast, for the student who cut against the grain, who cultivated the life of the mind. He wanted students to be "well rounded" in the Greek sense, developing body and mind, mental skills and social skills, but he looked down on boorish behavior in the fraternities and especially the hoopla surrounding subsidized, spectator sports. His ideas resonated with many on the faculty, and who among them could take issue with great ambitions for institutional preeminence based on academic excellence?

Nevertheless, many faculty members opposed new innovations such as eliminating certain curricular requirements and undermining traditional academic departments, and some probably resented the aloof outsider who proposed such things. Professor Ollinger Crenshaw, then just beginning work on his university history, celebrated Leyburn's "masterful appointment, perhaps the best in years," and continued to support his approach to athletics, but he resisted the curricular innovations Leyburn and his faculty supporters proposed that seemed to exalt art, philosophy, and ancient literature over modern literature and disciplines like history. Crenshaw simply thought that most things were pretty good as they were, and he lamented new required courses in vaguely defined "pseudo humanities." He suspected that Leyburn "had very little use for history" and the "moss-back staff members," such as himself. "The fact is," Crenshaw confided to a former student, "I doubt very much if some or all of us would be retained here at all, but for the fact that we have tenure, and they *can't* get rid of us!" He suspected that "as time marches along, the game will be entirely in the hands of these ivory-tower people."[23]

In any event, the work began, and changes followed. The Committee on Courses and Degrees brought some general requirements, propositions, and guidelines to a special meeting of the Faculty Discussion Group on the evening of January 22, 1948.[24] The committee sought to ensure that all W&L students acquired the essentials of a liberal education. They logically organized these essentials, providing a solid foundation in the freshman year and treating the freshman and sophomore years as "a unit," or foundation for the selection of a major. Requirements in history, English literature, a foreign language, natural science, physical science, and mathematics should be undertaken in the freshman year, and requirements in fine arts, philosophy, religion, economics, political science, psychology, or sociology should be pursued only in the subsequent years. The requirement for graduation remained 122 semester hours. In his remarks introducing these proposals, Leyburn noted the purpose of encouraging "more of a sense of unity among under-classmen before they separate into their various schools and specialties," and deemphasizing the categorization of freshmen and sophomores into pre-professional groups (pre-medicine, pre-engineering, pre-commerce). Since some disciplines would be less favored than others in this reorganization, he asked faculty to take a larger view and compromise as much as possible in the deliberations.

The Faculty Discussion Group pondered the results of a survey of curricular requirements at fifteen institutions—including Amherst, Duke, Emory, Haverford, Oberlin, Swarthmore, Vanderbilt, Virginia, Wesleyan, and Williams. Proposed new copy for the W&L catalog laid out the curricular focus for each of a student's four years, with each succeeding year offering greater flexibility and choice, and more focus on subjects of special interest (the major). It also included provisions for independent work and departmental honors for students who wrote a senior thesis and took a comprehensive examination. Beginning in 1950, all seniors were to select a course "whose purpose is that of synthesis"—such as "Methods of Thinking," "American Society and Culture," or "The Conclusions of Science."

Some but not all of these changes were approved. Greater flexibility was provided in the junior and senior years; also available were bridges across disciplines and opportunities for intellectual attainment for superior students. Interdepartmental majors were offered for the first time in 1950 in nine fields, including American Studies, General Humanities, Geology-Economics, Modern Humanities, and Physics-Engineering, as well as a Major in Interdepartmental Work that an individual student could devise and present for faculty approval. The majors offered in nineteen departments were also bolstered to require coursework in cognate fields, further breaching strictly disciplinary barriers. And opportunities for honors work were emphasized and expanded. In 1951–52, flexible fifth-year programs of study after graduation that could lead to a second bachelor's degree were introduced. There were no required "synthesis" courses in the senior year, though, and the lines of departmental authority remained largely intact.

These proposed changes reflected Leyburn's desire to break down the compartmentalization of knowledge, but they maintained the basic building blocks of courses, credit hours, and distribution requirements, which he disliked. The standardization of these elements in American higher education appealed to accrediting agencies, state legislatures, and the public, however, and Leyburn (like many subsequent educational reformers) could not devise a suitable alternative.

Washington and Lee was pondering and reshaping its role in the postwar era. Where did it "fit" among liberal arts institutions? How large should it be? How should it compete for students and recognition in a time of rapidly rising costs and faculty salaries? What had it learned from its wartime experience in terms of curriculum and student demand? How could it best meet the challenges for independent institutions when new trends in government support clearly favored public colleges and universities? This was indeed a propitious time for Leyburn, who liked to deal with fundamental questions. His high expectations for colleagues and students were inspiring but also perhaps a bit naive. In a collegial but purposeful way, he drove changes forward because he had such strong convictions and could express them eloquently and coherently. In truth, many of his concepts (instituting a tutorial system) and specific ideas (minimizing disciplinary boundaries and traditional departments) were casualties of inertia, faculty opposition, and departmental prerogatives, and never implemented. But his focus on the preeminence of scholarship and the life of the mind remained compelling and a context for academic aspiration and planning at Washington and Lee.

Shortly after his arrival in Lexington, Leyburn was elected a member of the board of trustees of Mary Baldwin College in Staunton, Virginia. In an address to an open meeting of the Mary Baldwin Honor Society in February 1948—in the midst of the curriculum deliberations at W&L—he discussed "A Plan for an Ideal College."[25] In a biting commentary, he observed that college attendance was becoming "a normal part of American life" but that colleges had not "done a very good job of attaining their expressed ideals." College graduates were just as likely as others to have few books at home, to rely on book clubs for the books they did have, and to mostly read popular magazines like *Life* or *Readers' Digest*. "Is this what college has been for," he asked, "to train us in the liberal arts and the exercise of our minds, so that we can look at picture magazines and read pre-digested squibs?" This was evidence of mediocrity. "I contend that our college programs are illogical in plan, limited in perspective, and positively disruptive in final effect. I suggest that they make perpetual children of students, and actually put obstacles in the way of their becoming adults." Curricula were jumbles of disconnected courses, he reiterated, "as if study were a series of right-about turns on a parade ground, and not a steady and continuous advance into an undiscovered country, where each step led to a further step, and each corner revealed a wider view."

The "ideal college" would thus aim to "make all its students feel the positively exhilarating excitement of using their minds," fight against "the fragmentation of knowledge," and "encourage its students to become adults and to achieve a vivifying sense of magnanimity and responsibility." Freshmen would pursue a common curriculum, sophomores would take additional interdisciplinary courses, and students would plan their own junior and senior years, with advice and encouragement from the faculty and without the usual examinations. Leyburn also introduced a remarkable idea for the senior year that went beyond what he ever recommended in Lexington. Every student would take a final senior examination—"the first since sophomore year"—that would include three days of written and three days of oral examination, "with the public invited." The "ideal college," as Leyburn described it, represented a significant break from almost all college curricula, including W&L's. Ultimately, Leyburn's lasting contribution would not be reflected so much in the curriculum as in his passionate affirmation of the life of the mind and his conviction that all students were capable of sharing it.

Individual departments and schools made changes and adjustments in the curriculum through the 1950s, though the basic structure of academic requirements remained as the foundation. As did some other liberal arts colleges, Washington and Lee entered into cooperative agreements with Rensselaer Polytechnic Institute and Carnegie Institute of Technology in 1950, allowing students to complete three years of undergraduate work at W&L, followed by two years of study at the cooperating institution, leading to both a bachelor's degree from W&L and an engineering degree. A year later Columbia University entered into the same arrangement. In his final annual report as dean, in 1956, Leyburn argued for allowing academically advanced freshmen with a strong secondary-school background to pursue some elective work in the first year and not be limited to choices from five specified fields; Leyburn also urged the faculty to encourage more seniors to pursue honors work.

The spirit of these changes was reflected also in the professional schools. During 1957–58 the School of Commerce and Administration continued its trend of loosening strict requirements for the Bachelor of Science degree. In 1930 the degree had permitted six hours of electives in the final three years of study for majors in the school; now, it allowed thirty-three to forty-five hours of electives (or over a third of the curriculum in those ninety hours). Dean L. W. Adams observed that from "the most restrictive course of study on the campus, we have moved to the point where our students have more freedom of choice than those in any other major." While some students would inevitably "make their choice on a basis other than a well-rounded education," he added, "this is a small price to pay for the freedom from which others will gain immeasurably."[26] This statement Leyburn could heartily endorse.

W&L'S CURRICULUM CHANGES were introduced on the cusp of a difficult decade, marked not only by the scourge of domestic paranoia fueled by the Cold War but also by a fierce Southern backlash against the movement for racial equality and the 1954 US Supreme Court decision on school desegregation in *Brown v. Board of Education.* As in other periods of American history marked by confusion, uncertainty, and challenges to the cultural status quo, opposition to forces for social change erupted in the 1960s and were exacerbated by the conflict in Southeast Asia.

The fear of communism as a global conspiracy—exhibited in the calls for loyalty oaths and the hearings conducted by Sen. Joseph McCarthy of Wisconsin and the House Un-American Activities Committee—became more frenzied after the Soviet Union's successful testing of nuclear weapons, including a hydrogen bomb, and the launching of Sputnik, the first space satellite. Intellectuals, artists, leaders in the entertainment industry, and government officials (especially those involved with foreign policy) were pursued for expressing leftist sympathies and having political associations with labor organizations and the civil rights movement. College professors were frequent targets because of their diverse views, activities, and published writings. Faculty members at many universities—including Vanderbilt and Tulane in the South—were questioned and publicly harassed. In the worst cases, professors were fired in response to public pressure.

Such scrutiny was rare at Washington and Lee, and controversy virtually nonexistent. The university received complaints in 1946 concerning an economics text, one version of which was used in the Army School during the war and another in regular W&L classes afterward. *Economics, Principles and Problems,* by Paul F. Gimmell and Ralph H. Blodgett, reportedly advocated high taxes on the wealthy and a stiff inheritance tax to preclude the passing down of estates over more than three or four generations. As part of an organized campaign against the book, letters from the American Taxpayer's Association, the Colonial Dames of America, and a number of individuals fulminated and took the university to task. The Colonial Dames asked if W&L was "sympathetic with the communist philosophy and does it promote it?" Or perhaps the administration was not aware that such a book was being used, since methods "of infiltration of communist dogma in governmental and private agencies have been reduced to a fine art." Gaines responded variously to these letters, generally defending the need for students to know about all ideas while at the same time declaring the university's disagreement with "theories which are hostile to the fundamental conceptions of American democracy and Christian character."[27] In writing to senior faculty, he supported their right to chose textbooks, but he gently raised "a little question about our use of a text book that seems to present a social theory that would undoubtedly be repugnant to the majority of our alumni."[28]

The most obvious reason that W&L avoided any significant investigation or anticommunist allegations in this era was because it was a mostly conservative institution with a small, intimate academic environment and no outspoken faculty. Whatever their ideas, individual faculty members tended to be circumspect in their public comments or classroom behavior, lest they undermine the tightly knit college community or draw unfavorable attention from the administration, the trustees, or local politicians. In most cases, we can only speculate about the opinions of current events shared privately over coffee or drinks, but we do know that the faculty held varied opinions. In his unpublished and very frank memoir, "Hacking It," Professor O.W. Riegel expressed both strong opinions and a reticence about speaking plainly.

Riegel came to W&L in 1930 after working as a journalist in Paris and New York and teaching for three years at Dartmouth. His book, *Mobilizing for Chaos: The Story of the New Propaganda*, published in 1934, helped establish his reputation as a leading expert on the subject. He was one of the first W&L faculty members called to service in World War II, as the principal propaganda analyst with the Office of War Information in Washington. He returned to W&L after the war and eventually retired in 1973 after thirty-four years on the faculty.[29] He traveled widely in Europe in the interwar years, visited the Soviet Union in the 1930s, and maintained extensive contacts abroad. He maintained a cosmopolitan view of human affairs and a hard-edged intolerance for simplistic politicians and political categories. While he saw himself as "a non-ideological pragmatist," his views, amid what he termed the "conservative, traditionalist environment of Lexington and Washington and Lee University," were definitely liberal and unconventional, and he did not share most of these opinions with his students and colleagues. He regarded the rampant anti-communist obsession in the United States with contempt, and its advocates "as witting or unwitting servants of infamy." He disdained religion as "irrational fantasizing." He disliked the military, "militarized patriotism," and the "mindless patriotic slogans of duty to God and country." He listened quietly to Gaines's paeans to Robert E. Lee but concluded that he would have found Lee "personally an insufferable, self-righteous martinet." Even though not opposed to capitalism, Riegel "viewed the mercantile, industrial and banking worlds generally with cynicism and distrust" and knew that his was not "an endearing attitude for a professor in a university that depended for its means on the good will and benefactions of rich businessmen or their widows." In other words, given his views, he knew he was "vulnerable."[30]

As he himself put it, Riegel "resorted to concealment, half-truths and sly stratagems of evasion." At VMI parades he went without a hat to escape having to doff it "when the flag passed by." He avoided the Baccalaureate sermon and contracted "instant sore throat" during hymns and recitations of the Lord's Prayer. In the classroom he aimed "for neutrality in my presentations on controversial issues, tacitly inviting my students to draw their own conclusions." He handled "the ticklish matter of the anti-Communist obsession" by balancing classroom attention to anti-communist and Communist propaganda. His classroom stratagems, he believed, led students to regard him "as a man of mystery who taught them how to think." He resorted to irony and sarcasm, most of which he believed "bounced harmlessly off the prejudices of my patriotic young Americans." These were all examples "of the complexities of leading a double life" necessitated by the local and academic environment. But he retained his reverence for Whitman, Jefferson, and Emerson, and among his best friends were Christians, Republicans, and members of the military. "The university was tolerant, our colleagues and neighbors civil and kindly, and the setting idyllic. . . . I showed respect for the traditions and tranquility of the community and served the university as I believed it desired to the limit of my energy." But he found that leading "a subversive, covert life . . . was fun, partly because I enjoyed play-acting and partly because the contrast between my views and conventional ones presented amusing paradoxes, and sometimes provoked fresh ideas."

Riegel was one of W&L's most influential and successful teachers, and the leading light behind the Southern Intercollegiate Press Association and other outreach endeavors. He had little reverence for authority but worked effectively with the administration. The red-baiters would obviously have condemned him, as would many of his acquaintances, had he expressed his views publicly. Riegel survived, by his own account, through "sly acts of sabotage against authority and orthodoxy." Probably few other W&L faculty in this era harbored views as different from the prevailing culture as Riegel's, but many doubtless kept their opinions to themselves in this small, hospitable academic and local setting. As a consequence, the university was almost completely bypassed by the frantic anti-communist paranoia of the time.

STUDENT LIFE AT Washington and Lee between 1945 and 1960 continued many of the customs, traditions, and formal elements of the 1920s and 1930s, but these were clearly shifting and loosening with the approach of dramatic changes in the 1960s and 1970s. The rhythms of the school year were measured by fraternity rush and pledging in the beginning; the three major dances held in the fall (Openings), winter (Fancy Dress), and spring (Finals); fraternity parties; and the trips "down the road" to nearby women's colleges every weekend and especially toward the end of each semester. Activities were ordered according to academic regulations such as limited class absences and the Automatic

Rule. Other regulations, formal and informal, governed student conduct—most notably the Honor System but also expectations for conventional dress and adherence to the "speaking tradition." The campus was hardly cloistered, but it harbored a special community set apart from many aspects of work, career, family, and adult responsibility. These conditions inspired loyalty, shared cultural experience, and adherence to certain values but also resulted in social isolation for those students who did not entirely conform.

University life in the era has been chronicled in several fictional accounts. The setting for part of *The Hero* (1949) by Millard Lampell, who attended West Virginia University on a football scholarship and later became a prolific screenwriter, is loosely based on Washington and Lee. Its leading character is an outstanding football player recruited from New Jersey to "Jackson University" in Virginia. Ultimately exploited by the institution and ostracized by fellow students, he drops out of school and abandons his promising athletic career. The book was made into a 1951 movie, *Saturday's Hero,* starring John Derek and Donna Reed. While college football, and subsidized athletics generally, was popular in the 1950s, the novel only tangentially concerns things as they were in Lexington. Much closer to showing student life as it was is *A Sound of Voices Dying* (1954), written by Glenn Scott when he was a W&L student. This largely autobiographical account of a freshman year around 1950 describes fraternity rush and dating; student discussions of history, religion, and art; and an affair with a married woman six or seven years older than the narrator.[31]

The most noted fictional portrayal of the university is Philippe Labro's *The Foreign Student,* originally published in 1986 in France—where it resided for thirty weeks on the best-seller list and at the top of the list for sixteen weeks— as *l'Etudiant etranger*. It is still in print. Labro was a Fulbright exchange student at Washington and Lee from 1954 until his return to France in 1956. While never mentioning W&L by name, many of the landmarks are specifically noted, as well as the environs of the "green and white" Shenandoah Valley. It is mostly a fond account of two life-changing years in what was, for Labro, a most exotic institution and locale. While fictional, the book addresses some of the main features of life at W&L in the mid-1950s—dating, road trips, social life, and relationships with faculty—and of national life, especially the strict southern system of racial segregation. The main character has a clandestine relationship with a young black woman from Lexington and also pursues an unhappy and rebellious society girl from Sweet Briar College. His travel to Charlottesville to attend a lecture by William Faulkner reflects a real experience of Labro's.

Labro stated that he based the novel's journalism faculty mentor, Old Zack, on Riegel, though Professor William Pusey believed the character to be more "a curious mixture" of Riegel and Deans Gilliam and Leyburn. Labro went on to a distinguished career as a journalist, commentator, and film producer in France, and he wrote other best-selling novels. He received an honorary degree from W&L in 1988 and returned to campus in the early 1990s to observe the production of a (not very successful) movie based on his book.

Intramural sports were popular, but intercollegiate competition was increasingly dominant, especially in football. W&L's wider athletic universe and participation in the Southern Conference against large university opponents in big-city stadiums overshadowed the intimate campus environment of Wilson Field. The Generals' 1951 appearance in its first (and last) postseason game—against Wyoming in the Gator Bowl in Jacksonville, Florida—stoked the enthusiasm for "big-time" football. Students also attended other sports games, however, and the national collegiate culture of popular athletes and the incorporation of sports into the social scene were much in evidence at Washington and Lee.

Other student organizations flourished. The Troubadours provided credible and sometimes notable theater performances throughout the period. The Concert Guild brought musical productions to campus. A group of students organized the Friends of the Library to raise funds to supplement the university's appropriation. The new Department of Fine Arts established in 1949 brought exhibits and speakers to Lexington. The principal student publications, supported by activity fees—the *Ring-Tum Phi, Calyx,* and the *Southern Collegian*—continued their roles on campus, while a new literary magazine—*Shenandoah*—organized in 1949 by a small group of faculty members and students—including Tom Wolfe and William Hoffman—achieved considerable success without university financial support. With student editors and a faculty advisory committee, the first issues of *Shenandoah* appeared in 1950, printed on campus by the Journalism Laboratory Press. Among the early contributors and reviewers were William Faulkner, Ezra Pound, Wallace Stevens, and Ray Bradbury.[32] The *Southern Collegian* was already associated with off-color jokes and other rather racy content for the time. The Publications Board disciplined the editor in May 1950, following two issues of especially questionable content, and the faculty suspended two issues from publication in 1952 for the same reason.

One student activity that transfixed the campus in 1953–54 was the Radio Quiz Bowl that pitted the four-member W&L team against those representing other premier institutions. With an enthusiastic audience listening in Lexington, the W&L men defeated, in succession, Smith, Chicago, Princeton, Barnard, and Pittsburgh, finally losing to Syracuse. They won $2,500 in prize money and also drew favorable national attention.

Religious activities—largely speakers and conferences, charity work, small group meetings, and prayer services in the dormitory—involved a modest number of students under the auspices of the Christian Council, with guidance from a director of Religious Work. Partly in an effort to avoid becoming "a rather obscure religious club," the council sponsored discussion groups with broader topics of interest to students and faculty. The first meeting addressed the question, "Is There a Basic Problem at Washington and Lee?" The group consensus lamented "a distressing lack of community between students and faculty members, and between students and their fellows."[33]

The law school featured its own student activities, including the *Law Review* (first published in 1939–40); the W&L chapter of the Order of the Coif honorary society, which inducted its first students in 1950; and the Student Bar Association, organized in 1951–52. While law students were older, and some were married with children, campus social and cultural life was available to them. They participated in it to varying degrees, depending on their inclinations and perhaps on whether they had attended W&L as undergraduates.

World War II had raised fundamental questions about life, government, and even survival, throwing millions of ordinary Americans into far-flung places and encounters with unfamiliar cultures and languages. Peacetime brought not only renewed attention to careers and family but also heightened curiosity and interest in education, literature, philosophy, travel, and world events. While Washington and Lee had long enjoyed lectures and presentations from notable authors, politicians, officials, and assorted professors and clergymen—often visiting Lexington for the first time—such occasions drew some especially distinguished individuals to campus in the postwar era, including William Faulkner, Arnold Toynbee, Katherine Ann Porter, and Edward Albee.

The British historian Arnold J. Toynbee was something of an academic celebrity. His face had graced the cover of *Time* magazine in 1947, and his sweeping multivolume account of the rise and fall of civilizations, *The Study of History,* had sold more than seven thousand sets of the ten-volume edition in the United States by 1955. Given the enormous ambition of this undertaking, it is not surprising that scholars picked apart a number of his assertions and conclusions. His emphasis on religion and purely spiritual aspects of civilization earned him a popular audience (especially in the United States), as well as the skepticism of many professional historians. His visit to W&L for the spring semester of 1958 was his first extended stay on an American campus. The sixty-eight-year-old author and his wife Veronica, also a historian, lived at "Mulberry Hill" overlooking the campus. He delivered a series of lectures, followed by questions and discussion, on Friday afternoons in Lee Chapel under the general rubric "A Changing World in the Light of History." At the first lecture, on February 7, President Gaines presented him with an honorary degree. Tickets were in high demand, and the 550 seats of the chapel were filled with students and faculty from W&L and VMI, alumni, and local citizens; the audience members unable to find a seat in the chapel could watch a closed-circuit television broadcast in the McCormick Library. Encyclopedia Britannica Films recorded the entire series. During the semester the Toynbees were often entertained in Lexington, and he gave lectures at a number of other Virginia colleges.[34]

A year later the Texas-born essayist and short-story writer Katherine Ann Porter was appointed Writer-in-Residence for the spring semester of 1959 and thus became the first, albeit temporary, female faculty member at W&L. She had spent similar stints at Stanford, Michigan, and Texas, where she was popular with students. Her only novel, *Ship of Fools* (1962) was a great success, and she received the Pulitzer Prize in 1966. The noted playwright Edward Albee also visited Lexington, leading to (unconfirmed) rumors that part of his drama "Who's Afraid of Virginia Wolfe" was based on his time at Washington and Lee.

William Faulkner was already an iconic literary figure by the time he served as Writer-in-Residence at the University of Virginia in Charlottesville during the spring semester of 1958 and later in 1959. He had already published *The Sound and the Fury* (1929), *As I Lay Dying* (1930), *Light in August* (1932), and *Absalom, Absalom!* (1936), and was the 1949 Nobel Laureate in Literature. Many W&L students traveled to Charlottesville to attend his public lectures, which were often as enigmatic and demanding as his published prose. Faulkner was invited to Lexington for the last Seminar in Literature of the academic year and appeared before an audience of six hundred people in Lee Chapel on May 15, 1958. He read from his latest book, *The Town*, and answered questions about his work and the writer's life. "You never get it done," he said, "that's why it's the best vocation of all."[35]

Along with welcoming these famous lecturers and writers, the university continued to benefit from scores of visitors whose presentations covered diverse fields including politics, art, literature, film, and musical performance.

For the most part, these presentations were well attended—though the *Ring-tum Phi* periodically lamented the passivity of the student body—and many of the visitors were also invited to appear in the classroom or at fraternity house receptions.

BY THE TIME THE Mock Convention rolled around in 1948—again featuring the Republicans—the W&L event had registered, since its beginning in 1908, five correct predictions of the eventual party nominee and three incorrect ones, including the predictions in 1936 and 1940.[36] A returning veteran and senior law student from Roanoke, Beverly T. Fitzpatrick, was general chairman of the 1948 convention, appointed by Fred M. Vinson Jr., student body president and son of the chief justice of the US. Supreme Court. US representative Clarence R. Brown of Ohio, chairman of the Executive Committee of the Republican National Committee and W&L alumnus, delivered the keynote address. A full complement of the regional and national press attended, including newsreel photographers from Paramount and MGM. The traditional parade down Main Street drew thousands of spectators, and traffic on US Highway 11 was diverted; nevertheless "uncounted hundreds of tourists parked to watch what appeared to be a Roman holiday." Among the scores of floats, a chief feature was the live elephant provided by the Dales Circus, thanks to the efforts of Lea Booth, W&L's director of public relations. The convention itself was dramatic, with student delegations tightly packed in Doremus Gymnasium and in close contact with party representatives in their respective states. "To the accompaniment of exploding flashbulbs, steady whirring of movie cameras, and the unbroken clacking of typewriters, students cast ballot after ballot during the second day. Dewey and Taft rapidly outdistanced the field and moved into an anticipated deadlock." A last-minute vote switch of the Texas delegation precipitated a move to Arthur Vandenburg, who the delegates once again predicted to be the nominee. But just as in 1936, this turned out to be an incorrect choice, with Thomas E. Dewey eventually nominated to challenge President Harry S. Truman.

The Republicans returned as the focus of the Mock Convention in 1952; this election would finally bring the long Democratic grip on the White House to an end and also restore the W&L students' winning record. The convention chair was Townsend Oast from Portsmouth, Virginia, who, despite his political sympathies, was fully committed to the traditional role of the W&L event. Writing to Republican friends in Roanoke he admitted, "You are probably surprised to find out that I am a Republican. I suppose that adds to the mock flavor of our convention. Never-the-less we are trying our best to make this as much a Republican convention as possible."[37] The keynote speaker was US senator James H. Duff of Pennsylvania, a supporter of Dwight Eisenhower, who won the nomination both at W&L and at the real Republican convention. The parade and other festivities followed in the usual vein—with a mile-long array of musical groups and floats from forty-eight states and five territories. It was covered by an unprecedented number of newspaper, radio, and national television reporters. For the first time, elements of the Mock Convention were televised. A three-man crew from the CBS network filmed parts of the parade, and convention proceedings were carried on Edward R. Murrow's *See It Now* broadcast the following Sunday afternoon.

The convention in April 1956 turned out to be the most dramatic in the history of this major student activity, even though the election itself—a rematch of the 1952 presidential contest—was not. After five ballots, W&L correctly picked Adlai Stevenson as the Democratic nominee. He eventually lost to President Eisenhower, who garnered more than 57 percent of the popular vote. The Mock Convention chair, Carl Swanson of Kansas City, presided over the usual elaborate preparations, including appointments to all the state and territorial delegations, posters and banners all over Lexington, and the parade with more than ninety floats, marching units, bands, and drill teams.

The keynote speaker was US senator Alben Barkley of Kentucky, a leading Democrat who had served as temporary and permanent chairman of his party's national convention and delivered the keynote addresses in 1932, 1936, and 1948. After fourteen years in the US House of Representatives, he was elected to the US Senate in 1927 and served as majority leader from 1937 to 1947 and as minority leader until he was selected as Harry S. Truman's running mate in 1948. After an unsuccessful run at the presidential nomination in 1952 (key constituencies refused to support him because he was seventy-four years old at the time), he was again elected to the US Senate in 1954. A graduate of Emory University and the University of Virginia Law School, he was in some surveys the most popular Democrat in the nation and, among other honors, received the Congressional Gold Medal in 1950.

Having turned down a number of other invitations, Barkley accepted the opportunity to keynote the W&L Mock Convention. He and his wife attended a lunch at the President's House for about forty people, including Virginia governor Thomas B. Stanley, US representative Burr P. Harrison, the superintendant of VMI, and the presidents of Hampden-Sydney and Sweet Briar. Barkley rode with President Gaines in the parade's lead car and sat with him on the lawn of the President's House as the remainder of the procession passed on the way to Doremus Gymnasium. While they were in the car, Barkley turned to Gaines and said, "I have had some recognitions but you have had the real rewards. You have had the privilege of living with youth."[38]

Barkley declined an opportunity to rest a bit before his address and launched into this familiar task with the usual vigor. It was an appropriately rip-roaring recitation of Democratic progress from Jefferson onward and a condemnation of the Republicans. After about fifteen minutes, he offered a brief summary of his political experience and offices leading to his current status as the junior senator from Kentucky. "And I am willing to be a junior," he intoned. "I'm glad to sit on the back row. For I would rather be a servant in the House of the Lord than to sit in the seats of the mighty." With that, he took a step backward and fell heavily to the floor, within a few feet of his wife. Amid shocked silence in the hall, those on the stage moved curtains and chairs aside and called for a doctor. Later examination suggested that Barkley, aged seventy-eight, was virtually dead when he hit the platform. Hardin Marion, secretary of the convention (and future W&L trustee), put his hand under Barkley's head: "he wheezed three times, and he was dead."[39]

The student reporters on the scene suddenly found themselves covering a "real" news event, working alongside and assisting their professional counterparts from the wire services, newspapers, and radio stations. The convention was immediately adjourned, and Doremus Gym stood forlorn and empty but for scattered chairs and placards. The governor ordered a state trooper to drive the Barkley car and Mrs. Barkley, accompanied by Mrs. Gaines, back to Washington. Philippe Labro was on the scene and immediately relayed news of Barkley's death to a wire service in Richmond over the telephone in his thick French accent. His account of these events made it into many newspapers across the country the next day.

Carl Swanson and three other Mock Convention leaders represented W&L at Barkley's funeral service in Washington. With Mrs. Barkley's blessing—indeed, insistence—Doremus Gym was redecorated, and the convention reopened a week later and completed its business. Unfortunately, a formal complaint made to Gaines by the professional news photographers association alleged that W&L students and staff had interfered with their ability to discharge their responsibility to keep the public informed. Apparently, a photographer near the podium was prevented from photographing the stricken senator just after he had fallen, and other photographers were kept from filming him as he was carried away from the hall. Gaines replied that these actions were not intended to interfere with a free press but were an attempt to protect the senator's privacy and to respect Mrs. Barkley's plea, "Please, no photographs." He could have added that similar actions would have been taken by any self-respecting W&L student, then or since.

GREEK ORGANIZATIONS usually involved a minority of students at large universities. At W&L, however, the great majority of students have belonged to fraternities, which has had significant implications for student culture, social activity, student government elections, and housing and board for much of the student body. Fraternity affiliation influenced personal friendships and social life, especially in the first two years, overshadowing relationships established through freshman dormitory life, classes, and other student organizations. Fraternities were, quite simply, an essential, defining feature of student life at Washington and Lee, a reinforcement of the loyalty and conformity the institution itself fostered, and a source of camaraderie and fond alumni recollection, as well as, increasingly, intemperate, loutish, and even illegal behavior.

For many Washington and Lee men in the first half of the twentieth century, fraternity life was a positive aspect of their college years, marked by languid weekend afternoons in the living room with the "brothers," bountiful meals in the dining room; late-night bull sessions talking about movies, sports, and women; wild parties in the basement; road trips; and social escapades. In the era of housemothers (and even the occasional butler), the fraternity houses did indeed have an aura of home, with certain formalities and trappings, not to mention rules against entertaining women above the first floor. Even though they lost many of these characteristics after the mid-1960s, fraternities served as crucibles for leadership and provided small-group affinities, friendships, and identity for many members. But their overall role and influence was hardly benign.

Established in the nineteenth century as secret societies to rival student literary clubs, which they eventually displaced, collegiate social fraternities (the first appeared at Union College in 1825) provided a way for students to resist the tight control of faculty and administrators, engage in forbidden pursuits and entertainments, and celebrate the ideals of "masculinity." Consisting almost entirely of well-to-do, white, Protestant men (initially in the Northeast), fraternities reinforced social status for their members and provided access to social and business networks of "brothers" from chapters throughout the country. Fraternities accepted as members only those who met certain standards of "manliness," manners, social and economic standing, and "whiteness," and rejected those who did not. A fraternity man was ultimately defined by "the company he keeps." Toward the end of the nineteenth century, athletic ability was an especially important criterion for membership, as intercollegiate athletics came to dominate the interests of students and alumni. A too-fervent devotion to study was increasingly frowned upon, and an emphasis on conformity—in dress, behavior, habits, and even ideas—became more pronounced over time.[40]

These tendencies were enhanced by the use of fraternity houses not only for meetings but also as exclusive dining halls and residences. The first such structure was built at the University of California, Berkeley, in 1876, and similar houses proliferated throughout the country with the help of alumni and university approval. Houses strengthened the sense of "camaraderie" among brothers but also further separated them from the rest of the campus community. By the 1920s, "fraternity men" were prominent symbols of college life in the national media, and, collectively, they could dominate student elections and secure the favored positions in other student organizations. This was especially true at institutions with a proportionally high Greek membership, such as W&L.

In the twentieth century, "manliness" was defined increasingly by athletic ability, virility, and sexual conquest rather than by extracurricular activities and the ideal of the well-rounded gentleman. The term *gentleman* had a special meaning at W&L because of its association with the Honor System and personal integrity, but it could, and did, have other connotations in college fraternity life generally. As Nicholas Styrett observed, "Fraternity brothers cultivated a reputation as a moneyed elite on college campuses, as gentlemen. By calling themselves gentlemen, what they meant was that they had sophisticated tastes and manners suited to their station as sons of the upper classes. This emphasis upon gentlemanliness did not, however, preclude drunken sprees and debauched weekends in the city. In some sense, they used their status as self-proclaimed gentlemen to justify their less savory antics. The public image of the gentleman was used as a shield to protect their other behaviors."[41] Greek organizations thus sustained their sense of social standing and entitlement in part by engaging in rough and offensive behavior.

Tendencies toward excessive drinking and greater sexual freedom in the "Roaring '20s" were accentuated in fraternity life ever after—ranging from lively parties to binge drinking, vandalism, and sexual violence. By the 1950s, Styrett writes, "fraternities found themselves in an odd predicament. They publicly advocated for the societal status quo and were almost uniformly conservative in their political leanings and social and career ambitions." But they also "broke rules with abandon," especially those regarding alcohol, illegal parties, the destruction of property, hazing, and rushing.[42] By the 1960s, fraternities measured "manliness" primarily by sharing stories of sexual exploits, as well as by excessive drinking; this boasting tended to treat women as sexual targets and reinforced tendencies toward misogyny and homophobia. Though a caricature, the movie *Animal House* was based loosely on fraternity life at Dartmouth College, a rural all-male institution of about two thousand students.

Beginning in the nineteenth century, college administrations throughout the country attempted to ban fraternities because they were disruptive and undermined institutional control and campus discipline. Influential alumni organizations mostly blunted efforts to eliminate fraternities entirely. A notable exception was Princeton University, which banned Greek organizations in 1875, although the exclusive "eating clubs" that then arose were in many ways similar to fraternities. While there were defenders of Greek life in university administrations, a suspicion of fraternities and recognition of their negative impact on campus culture persisted. A 1913 survey of 151 college presidents revealed near unanimity of opinion: "fraternities were snobbish and undemocratic; they tended to lower scholarship; they monopolized other activities; they established 'unjustified artificial social relations'; and they were extravagant and populated by the wealthy to the exclusion of poorer students."[43]

Washington and Lee recognized the strength of fraternities in campus life, politics, and tradition—and their important role in providing living and eating facilities for many students—but was faced with the turbulence and disturbances these organizations created. The university took various approaches to regulating rush and pledging, mostly limiting the duration of these activities and pushing the whole process later into the academic year, if not into the second year entirely. These reforms would be long in coming. To fashion a sense of campus community, all freshmen should ideally live together in a single dormitory, and upperclassman residence halls and a campus-wide dining facility were proposed to limit the effect of social fraternities on the overall university experience. The university also recognized that "independent" students who were not invited or chose not to join a fraternity were at a pronounced social disadvantage and were among those most likely to transfer elsewhere.

In April 1949, Deans Leyburn and Gilliam asked President Gaines to support the purchase of a "club-house for non-fraternity men" so that this portion of the student body would have opportunities for social life. The lack of such opportunities was a problem, they wrote, in that it lowered "morale" and resulted "in loss of enrollment, in [damage to] public relations, and in subtle but very real ethical considerations. Ours is, for better or worse, a fraternity campus: all social life, most elections to important offices, and the leading of a normal life depend upon membership in a fraternity." The new club could offer bids at the end of rush to those not selected for a fraternity, which could "ease the heart-ache and disappointment which have driven many students away from the university." Dues for the club would be low, offering a "partial rebuttal to the repeated charge that the university is becoming only a 'rich man's school,'" a claim accentuated by the recent $100 tuition increase. Such clubs already existed at Williams and Wesleyan and were under consideration elsewhere. A separate structure or clubhouse was never constructed, but a nonfraternity union was established in Lexington.[44]

Fraternity house life at W&L in the 1930s and into the 1960s was still marked by the formalities of conventional dress, housemothers, dining rooms, occasional receptions for visiting speakers and dignitaries in the living rooms, and parties downstairs. The weekends could be chaotic, but classes, exams, and visits to downtown movie houses and beer joints dominated weekdays. Some houses gave special attention to academic achievement and faring well in the report W&L issued each semester, showing average grade point averages by fraternity. Compared with fraternity life in the tumultuous late 1960s, '70s, and after, this attention to academics now seems relatively civilized. But student drinking, carousing, and misbehavior remained challenges for the faculty and administration. The membership of the seventeen fraternities on campus in 1950 accounted for 80 percent of the student body.

THE PROBLEM OF ALCOHOL—its use and misuse—also has had a long history in American higher education. For the most part, it was banned from university buildings, dormitories, and off-campus dwellings like fraternity houses well into the twentieth century. Such restrictions had minimal effect: alcohol and drinking was an integral part of the college scene during the 1920s, even during Prohibition. By 1950 at W&L, Dean Leyburn was persuaded that the matter was serious enough to demand special attention. Writing to School of Commerce dean Lewis Adams in September, he noted that the "amount of open drinking, and of public disturbance as a result of drinking, reached such proportions during the past year that several of our faculty committees have had to consider" how to deal with the problem. Leyburn proposed a meeting of faculty and student representatives to discuss what might be done, but he discouraged treating the matter as a "moral issue," which the students would resent as "preaching." At the same time, he hoped all could agree that the matter posed a problem for the university's public relations: "open drinking in the stands at track meets, baseball games, and other events; a beer party in Red Square that lasted from early Sunday afternoon until after midnight; the reports that go back to preparatory schools (one of the strongest schools in the South now sends us almost no students because the parents fear the drinking here); the widespread reputation in the South of this university as a 'drinking school'; the large number of house parties in both semesters; the distressing amount of space given to the topic of drinking in the Ring-tum Phi, Calyx, and Southern Collegian."[45]

In December 1952, student body president I. M. Sheffield called a special student assembly in Lee Chapel to deal with recent and disturbing trends in the university's social life. "We must maintain a proper balance between good times and moderation," he implored. While many social activities were "graced by dignity, moderation, and an element of refinement," recent (unspecified) tendencies were not.[46] Evidence suggests that these entreaties had little effect on student behavior.

The Interfraternity Council (IFC) petitioned the board of trustees in 1949–50 to repeal its ban on bars in fraternity houses after several had been installed following World War II with the help of alumni and friends. Since the faculty, which bore responsibility for student affairs, rendered no opinion, the trustees refused to act on the matter. After a meeting of students and faculty, the request was again brought to the board. The petition recognized "that alcoholic beverages are used on the Washington and Lee campus," a situation "which has prevailed in the past, is prevalent in the present, and will continue into the future." Indeed, no one "could honestly believe that drinking does not go on" at W&L or any other college in the country. The presence of bars in fraternity houses would not produce more drinking, the petition asserted, but would allow it to be "centralized" in one place rather than occurring throughout the house. Furthermore, the ban "is a direct violation of the free traditions of Washington and Lee and the principles of society and higher education to-day."[47] Leyburn called another meeting of faculty and student representatives for March 27, 1951. The board ultimately failed to approve the IFC petition.

The faculty and administration assumed more authority over student conduct as the major changes of the 1960s approached. The W&L tradition of student self-control and governance, which the IFC frequently invoked, was deemed less and less effective by university authorities, but they were also uncomfortable with providing a suffocating supervision of student social life or a strict imposition of in loco parentis. Leyburn took a pragmatic view, reinforced by his desire to treat students as individuals and adults. Thus, the bars in fraternity houses seemed a means of isolating activity that would otherwise be occurring elsewhere. Leyburn believed the proposal was actually "most persuasive . . . as a means of limiting the amount of drinking." And he questioned the long-standing prohibition on faculty members drinking with students. He asked if "faculty-student relationships are to be close, is it wise to forbid faculty members to drink with students?"[48] Undoubtedly, he imagined lengthy academic discussions over sherry. But to Frank Gaines and many others, allowing faculty and students to drink together seemed a path to mischief and impossible to explain to conservative parents.

In July 1955, Leyburn wrote the members of the executive committee seeking a meeting to discuss the faculty regulation regarding "intoxicants." It reiterated a board expectation that the faculty would "take cognizance, supervision, and control of the habits and conduct of the students and of their organizations," and it deemed "drinking, gambling, and immorality" to be "explicitly forbidden." Intoxication, in particular, was a "grave offense . . . meriting temporary or permanent withdrawal from the institution." Leyburn was troubled that no objective definition of intoxication, gambling, and immorality was provided or understood: "I should not like to contemplate the condition of the university if all the students guilty of any of the three were dismissed." With widespread alcohol consumption and intoxication as a routine part of student life—and especially fraternity life—how could the university ever enforce this regulation? Furthermore, if President Gaines believed, as he frequently stated, that faculty should not drink with students, should "this rule not be specifically included?"[49]

In response to student behavior during the 1957–58 session which had "done harm to the name of Washington and Lee University" and "created grave concern on the part of the Faculty Administration," the rule regarding intoxication, gambling, and immorality was explicitly reaffirmed by the faculty in a special meeting on May 19, 1958. New rules recommended by a special faculty committee appointed by President Gaines were implemented in the subsequent fall semester. The "recent events" (apparently particularly objectionable offenses by W&L students at one of the women's colleges) required that the faculty more clearly define those offenses of "ungentlemanly behavior" that were unacceptable and to introduce new rules. In addition to restrictions on "public drinking," which had "always been considered a grave offense," rules prohibited women guests in fraternity houses above the first floor and required that women leave the houses by 2 a.m. "except on weekends of University Dances when the hour shall be 3 a.m." In addition to existing IFC regulations governing the number and scheduling of house parties, the university demanded adherence to all rules of conduct and maintained that students living independently in off-campus lodging should "conduct themselves in such manner as not to disturb the peace or the sensibilities of the community." Paid musical entertainment in fraternity houses was permitted only at specified times on designated weekends and was prohibited on Sundays. The rules were to be enforced by the dean of students, who also had authority to enforce "the rules applicable to fraternities" and was charged to periodically check the Lexington court records to detect any incidents involving W&L students. The dean of the university was required to report monthly to the faculty on any enforcement actions. Finally, the position of university proctor was established; the proctor was a nonuniformed officer with authority to uphold university regulations and to help ensure the safety of all students. The first appointee to this post, on January 2, 1959, was a World War II veteran and former Lexington police officer—the now legendary Charles F. Murray, soon known to all students as "Murph."[50]

A FUNDAMENTAL IRONY at Washington and Lee was that many of the deeply embedded traditions, and much alumni loyalty, was a consequence of social conformity that continually undermined social and intellectual diversity. To be a nonconformist at W&L required courage and stamina. Most students came from similar socioeconomic backgrounds, and the high participation rate in fraternities naturally reinforced accepted behaviors and social expectations. In addition, the institution itself—largely through student leadership—encouraged conformity through the traditions of "conventional dress" (coat and tie at all times on campus) and speaking to others. The Assimilation Committee of the student government was charged with enforcing these conventions. In a 1964 letter to fellow students, written when some of these conventions were eroding, the committee chairman emphasized that attending W&L entailed responsibility not only to university regulations but also to the Honor System, the speaking tradition, and conventional dress: "This spirit of Washington and Lee in which this well-rounded gentleman is envisioned can exist only so long as our time-honored traditions continue." To encourage the speaking tradition, freshmen would wear nametags rather than beanies (out of fashion in the mid-1960s). If necessary, the committee would resort to "fining the flagrant violators."[51] The protagonist in Labro's *The Foreign Student* was called before the Assimilation Committee in his first semester and gently but firmly upbraided for not following the speaking tradition. His offense was not always smiling when extending or acknowledging greetings. He found this bewildering.

This tension between tradition/conformity and intellectual diversity was certainly not limited to W&L, but it had long troubled James Leyburn and other members of the faculty and administration, and it was certainly noted by some students. Leyburn retained a 1952 term paper written by one of his students (on the condition that the author's name not be revealed), entitled "A Sociological Study of the Washington & Lee Student Body." In the paper, the anonymous writer asserted that the Honor System was admirable and widely supported among the student body, even though the implementation was not entirely impartial. (The executive committee "is judge, jury, and police force combined.") The Assimilation Committee, the author noted, was the most overt formal effort to shape new students into the mold of the W&L "gentleman," and fraternities (the importance of which "cannot be overestimated") not only reinforced these social expectations but also dominated campus politics and social life, with at least the tacit approval of the administration. The writer also observed, "Athletics [intra-mural and inter-collegiate] have the allegiance of the student body more than any other phase of student life except social events." He claimed that sexual relations between students and "local girls" were "common." The place of the nonconforming student (or "deviant") in W&L life was ambiguous and often solitary. Such a student could easily participate in literary societies, the International Relations Club, and the Non-fraternity Union, and offices in such organizations were open because they were not significant in campus life and were below the notice of the fraternities. The author concluded that the most important and prized element of campus activity was "social life and social achievement, supported by every institution and tradition on the campus, and buttressed by a favorable faculty and administration attitude."[52] The term paper provides no documentation in support of any of these observations or conclusions, but they clearly resonated with Leyburn, whose views on the matter were no secret.

Leyburn voiced his concerns directly in his 1952 annual dean's report. He pointed to "three aspects of student life" that were "potentially harmful to the best interests of the students and of the university," and observed that they are "interestingly enough, outgrowths of some of our most admirable traditions." First, student government, "by its very effectiveness, enforces a conformity of behavior." Requirements for conventional dress and friendly greetings were all to the good, "but it seems also to result in another kind of uniformity that is less worthy—that of mind, opinion, and personal affairs." The overall environment engendered pressures to conform, as in the case of students "gifted in the fine arts," those who attempted mealtime conversations that delved "below the surface," those who led a "deeply religious life," or those who offered less conventional political opinions. "I deplore," he wrote, "the steady decrease of individuality among our students." Second, he lamented the rise of "cliques," accentuated by fraternities that divided freshmen within the first week into "seventeen different groups" and then combined to form larger cliques that controlled student elections and led to student indifference as well as fragmentation. Finally, he noted that the ideal of the W&L "gentleman" harbored "a strong tendency to confuse those qualities that indisputably belong to gentlemanliness—honesty, rectitude, courtesy, for example—with superficial qualities that can be positively deleterious," such as "drinking like a gentleman" or "making a gentleman's C." The true gentlemanly ideal, he averred, was to be unique, rather than a "type."[53] There is no record of any response by the administration or the board of trustees to these observations.

Some students challenged the dominant political system in the spring of 1953 by proposing an amendment to the student body constitution that would have eliminated the control of offices by any one party. Though the amendment failed to get majority support, Leyburn applauded this effort at "reform" and noted that it at least had the effect of generating greater interest in student politics. He was also encouraged that the trustees had adopted the idea of a "Freshman Commons," initially raised by Frank Gilliam and supported by some student leaders, where first-year students would all take their meals (rather than in separate fraternity houses) and where upperclassmen could live upstairs. The commons would help correct the absence at W&L of any

dining facility or housing beyond the freshman year. The lack of these facilities affected all students, including fraternity members, who typically lived in
fraternity houses for their sophomore year and then occupied rental properties
scattered in and around town.[54]

Details would change over time, and conformity was certainly challenged
in the social upheavals of the 1960s and 1970s. By the end of the 1950s, the
days of conventional dress were already numbered, and the speaking tradition—though not general campus courtesy—gradually faded after the end of
the Assimilation Committee. But the tension between adherence to tradition
and open intellectual and personal experimentation would remain.

FRANK AND SADIE GAINES moved into the President's House in 1930 when
he was thirty-eight years old and entering his second university presidency.
Whether or not he anticipated remaining at Washington and Lee for three
decades, he completed the second longest presidential term in the university's
history, turning down other job offers and possibilities along the way. Guiding the institution through economic depression, a world war, the turbulent
adjustments to peacetime, and the challenges to higher education at midcentury (including a major athletic scandal), Gaines left an indelible and positive
imprint on the institution. He succeeded through an effective blend of personal
opinion and vision, close attention to institutional needs, a desire to serve the
wishes and interests of all major constituencies (especially the trustees), and
sound political instincts. His long tenure was also attributable to his desire
to shepherd the university along rather than impose his own personal vision
and ideas. His success over time was enhanced by his growing national reputation as a speaker and higher-education leader; his network of well-placed
politicians, authors, and influential friends; and his ability to engender support for W&L through these personal contacts. In addition to his offices and
memberships in many organizations, he received ten honorary degrees from,
among others, Duke, Columbia, Rollins, Baylor, Furman, Hampden-Sydney,
Richmond, and—in 1963—from Washington and Lee.

The Gaineses raised three children in Lexington, entertained countless students and visiting dignitaries, and coped with various health issues and mishaps
that occasioned leaves of absence. Frank Gaines was granted six months leave
in 1951 "to recapture some strength" after "ten years of strain," and he took
another three weeks in the spring of 1953 for medical treatment in Saratoga
Springs, apparently for penicillin poisoning. In June 1957, he broke several bones

in his hands just days before Sadie fell and broke her wrist. They always managed these challenges with medical treatment, convalescence, and good wishes from friends and family, though the health problems became more difficult over time and led to a discernable decline in Frank's energy and proficiency.

Gaines had begun his career during a time of relative national innocence, with social customs and expectations not too dissimilar from those decades earlier. He retired after the country had emerged as a world power, humanity was rendered vulnerable to nuclear holocaust, and social patterns were shifting and on the cusp of major change. Over this period he had become for thousands of students, parents, alumni, and the general public the personification of Washington and Lee University. When he notified the trustees in 1958 that he wished to retire, they knew that his decision signaled the end of an era.

When he retired in 1959, he was honored by the board with the title of chancellor (not conferred before or since), which assisted Gaines in his continuing work on behalf of the university. He delivered his last speech to the ODK Assembly on December 17, 1963. Introduced by his successor, he proceeded confidently and with ebullient good humor to reminisce about his life and to offer advice to the assembled student body. He said a great deal about leadership and the key characteristics of good leaders—breadth of interests, dedication to principle, and a desire to learn—and he referenced as an excellent resource *Profiles in Courage*, written by the young president, John F. Kennedy, who had been tragically assassinated only a month before. Gaines ended his address by citing his favorite epitaph, that of the British historian John Richard Green: "He died learning."[55] Gaines received a rousing ovation. He died at his home two weeks later, on New Year's Eve, and was buried in Stonewall Jackson Cemetery. Sadie continued to reside in Lexington, enjoying regular social contact with contemporaries and young faculty members and administrators. She died in 1974 and was buried alongside her husband.

President Francis P. Gaines, widely noted for his oratory

President Gaines leading academic procession, followed by
Dean of the University James G. Leyburn, 1949

The morning after the fire: Tucker Hall, December 17, 1934

Students gathered in downtown Lexington in 1943 before boarding buses
to begin their military service in World War II

Personnel in the Army School for Special Services
(later School for Personnel Services), October 1944

Jessie Ball duPont and President Gaines

The Mock Convention in 1956, with former vice president Alben W. Barkley
at the podium just before his collapse

Freshman Camp at Natural Bridge, addressed by football coach Lee McLaughlin,
with Dean Frank Gilliam in the first row, 1956

James G. Leyburn performing in Lee Chapel

Coach Lee McLaughlin and the 1960 football team, declared national small college champions by the Washington DC Touchdown Club and featured in *Sports Illustrated*

President Fred C. Cole

W&L History Department in 1965: *l to r, standing,* Ollinger Crenshaw,
Jefferson Davis Futch, *seated,* visiting instructor Anthony Wood, Alan W. Moger,
H. Marshall Jarrett, Charles W. Turner, William A. Jenks

Football without subsidy: W&L v. Southwestern on Wilson Field, 1967

Dean Emeritus Frank J. Gilliam, 1968

Frank A. Parsons and Professor O. W. Riegel

Student demonstrators picketing along the Colonnade, May 1970

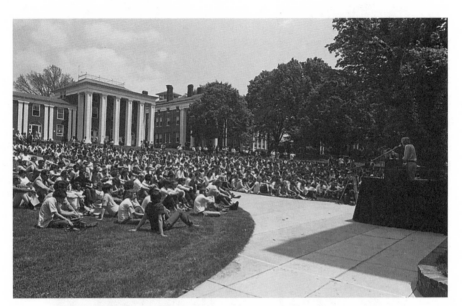

Executive Committee president Marvin C. "Swede" Henberg addressing
the student body during the "Eight Days in May," 1970

President Huntley observing student demonstration from
the doorway of Washington Hall, May 1970

~~~

CHAPTER FOUR

ATHLETICS AND THE UNIVERSITY

BY THE FOURTH QUARTER, Washington and Lee trailed Coach Bowden Wyatt's University of Wyoming Cowboys 20–0. This was the sixth annual Gator Bowl game in Jacksonville, Florida, in 1951, and W&L was ranked fifteenth in the nation and making its first bowl appearance, as the host team. The Generals finally scored, but it was not enough. The potent split T formation that had averaged thirty points a game during the regular season and chewed up 252 rushing yards against the Cowboys failed to penetrate the opponent's goal line. A pass interception, a fumble, a twenty-yard punt, and a pass interference call eventually undid Coach George Barclay's team. Quarterback Gil Bocetti's father had died only a few days before, and the Generals' star player—fullback, leading scorer, and future NFL All-Pro linebacker and head coach Walt Michaels—was out, recovering from a Christmas Eve attack of appendicitis. But the bowl trip capped a great 8–2 season with a Southern Conference championship; close losses only to Virginia, in the Tobacco Bowl in Richmond before more than twenty thousand people, and to Top Ten powerhouse Tennessee; and a season-closing 67–6 victory over Richmond.[1] Even after the Wyoming loss, W&L, a college with fewer than a thousand students, ended up ranked eighteenth in the nation.

A sunny New Year's Day with north Florida temperatures in the mid-fifties made an ideal setting for the 10,834 spectators in the stands. The Jacksonville W&L alumni chapter hosted a Christmas party at the Seminole Club for the team and a "lunch-brunch" at the Roosevelt Hotel on New Year's Day—presided over by President Gaines, alumni secretary Cy Young, and local chapter president Rhydon Latham, '28—for many of the two thousand students, alumni, and friends gathered for the game. The Generals wore all-blue uniforms with white stripes and numbers. W&L student Steve Miles (a future rector of the university) served as the prince consort to the Gator Bowl Queen from Wyoming during the halftime ceremonies. The whole scene was festive and colorful. Virtually all the elements that sustained and drove interest in intercollegiate football were there, from the "Washington and Lee Swing" fight song to the gladiatorial combat on the gridiron.[2]

Perhaps this was a taste of things to come—the large crowds, national publicity, and alumni gatherings amid all the trappings of a big game. W&L had arrived. Despite the loss on the field, the important thing was to be there at all. But even after a stunning win over Virginia in the 1951 season—which some remembered as the greatest of all W&L football victories—the trip to the Gator Bowl would turn out to be, in fact, the high point of "big time" intercollegiate athletics at General Lee's college. In less than five years, the football squad would be decimated by an unprecedented cheating scandal, an entire season would be cancelled, the future of football and other sports would be set upon a different path, and the university's character and purpose would be more indelibly defined.

EDUCATION AND SPORT have long been associated, from the Greek ideal of developing both mind and body simultaneously, to the nineteenth- and twentieth-century pairing of individual athletic achievements with participation in limited team sports in preparatory schools and universities in Europe and England. In the United States, sports became an integral part of collegiate life, initially as intramural competition and then between colleges (at first mostly in rowing and baseball). By the late nineteenth century, athletic contests between university rivals were already notable events on the collegiate calendar and included associated social occasions like party weekends and road trips. Athletics and fraternities tended to reinforce each other: both fostered elitism and masculine conquest, and together tended to dominate campus politics and social life. As did fraternities, football from the beginning presented a challenge for university administrators.

Football became by far the most popular intercollegiate sport, especially in the South, where the ideals of honor, courage, and manliness were readily expressed through martial contests.[3] In its earliest years football was barely organized and particularly violent, producing serious injuries and even deaths.

Players wore little padding and either flimsy leather helmets or none at all. Coaches were paid by alumni or from gate receipts, and the biggest issue of player eligibility was whether the player was a student at all rather than a local steelworker or stevedore. Avowed football fan Theodore Roosevelt was concerned for the future of the sport, and in 1905 the president called for action that led to the founding in 1910 of what became the National Collegiate Athletic Association (NCAA). Among other things, this organization helped institutionalize a major trend of American higher education in the twentieth century—the rapid growth of intercollegiate football and, later, basketball as public spectacle (vastly magnified by television), and the concomitant efforts to guide college sports' imperatives and curtail the worst excesses.

While some changes were made as the game of football matured, developing elaborate rules and more-or-less regular schedules, the competitive juices still combined with institutional loyalties to promote victory on the gridiron as the highest collegiate priority, especially for many students and alumni. Certain contests evolved into traditional rivalries, generating stories and taunts. Especially during the prosperous 1920s, football attendance soared, generating funding for higher salaries for coaches, scholarships for players, and the construction of new stadiums and other sports facilities. Even then, things seemed to be getting out of hand. (Hardly just an issue for our own time, the problem of how overemphasis on sports competition fit with the notion of amateur sports or the ideal of the "student athlete" dates back more than a hundred years. To a remarkable degree, the basic issues and dilemmas have remained essentially the same.) In 1929, the Carnegie Foundation for the Advancement of Teaching issued a report, *American College Athletics*, which condemned the increasing professionalization of college athletics, particularly football. Virtually every one of the 130 institutions surveyed were subsidizing athletes to some degree. Whether and to what degree student athletes should be recruited and supported to play sports remains at the heart of efforts to regulate and direct intercollegiate competition today.

Unlike most university activities—and to an unprecedented degree for higher education throughout the world—intercollegiate football games were public spectacles that engaged the attention of far-flung alumni and enhanced their loyalty and generosity. As dramatic expressions of success and failure, games were acclaimed or lamented out of all proportion to their intrinsic importance. The idealized Greek virtues of sport were quickly swept aside by the desire to win, to prevail against rivals, to uphold "honor" and avoid "humiliation." To win required attracting the most talented players, which in turn required recruiting specifically for athletes, offering scholarships, and hiring the best coach at a competitive salary, as well as building new facilities and playing fields. The most successful and best-supported programs set the standard for others, and vocal alumni expected their alma mater to keep up with the best, thus creating powerful pressures on university administrators and college budgets, and putting smaller universities at a substantial financial disadvantage that increased over time. The result was an enormously popular spectacle—built around student athletes and swamped with money and outside pressures—that became unquestionably the most corrupting influence on colleges and universities in the past century. Americans are now so accustomed to the excesses of college football that they consider them part of the fabric of the national character.

INDIVIDUAL AND TEAM SPORTS were as popular at W&L as they were at colleges elsewhere in the country. In the earliest years, teams were often assembled informally. In *General Lee's College,* Ollinger Crenshaw reports a baseball game in December 1866 between the "Beechenbrooks" from W&L and the Cadet Club at VMI, certainly one of the university's earliest intercollegiate contests, although without official sanction or organization. In 1871, the W&L "Shoo Fly" team traveled to Charlottesville to play "Monticello." Boat races were among the most popular collegiate sports events in nineteenth-century America, and teams from W&L competed against each other as early as 1869. Students formed the Athletic Association in 1872, mostly for track and field activities, and in 1878 a W&L pitcher, George Augustus Sykes, struck out sixteen batters in succession in Charlottesville, employing the first curve ball thrown in an intercollegiate game.[4] Interest in organized team sports derived increasingly from high school athletic experience, and the strong fraternity system also led to intramural and organized club competition.

Football is the oldest intercollegiate team sport at W&L, dating from 1873, when a contest with VMI may have been the first football game ever played in the South. Though few details were recorded, it likely involved large numbers of players on both sides, with few rules and not a few injuries. The first "official" intercollegiate football season on record was in 1890. (W&L's team lost both games played that year.) The first university records for other intercollegiate sports include basketball from 1906, track and baseball in 1907, tennis in 1919, and swimming, cross country, and wrestling in 1920 and 1921. Other sports were added later, such as golf in 1927 and lacrosse and soccer in 1947. The university responded to the growing student interest by constructing a gymnasium and athletic field.

W&L had its share of great athletes but none as notable as Harry K. "Cy" Young (1913–17), who was an outstanding player and team leader in football, basketball, baseball, and track, earning sixteen varsity letters during his collegiate career and recognition as an All-American in football and basketball. He also ran the one-hundred-yard dash in 9.8 seconds and lost only one race as a member of the track team. President of the senior class and president of Finals, Young was the quintessential "big man on campus." He continued his contributions to W&L as coach of the basketball team from 1933 to 1939, winning two Southern Conference championships in the process, and was an enormously popular W&L alumni secretary until his retirement in 1958. Among the legacies he left his alma mater was his habit of giving a rip-roaring oration before every game against the University of Virginia. As Jim Wamsley, '50, recalled, Young "heaped scorn on ridicule, contempt upon insult. Shouting hoarsely, his creased, tanned face gleaming with sweat, he built to his crescendo, stomping and kicking on the aged platform until it bounced, demanding from his spellbound audience a pledge of undying hatred for all Wahoos. 'Beat 'em,' he croaked, 'beat those damned Wahoos.' Then the chant came back at him in a roar from hundreds of young throats."[5]

Athletics were guided and nurtured by a number of notable leaders, including Edwin Parker "Cy" Twombly, who also arrived in Lexington in 1921. He was head coach of the swimming team for forty years, led the golf program for forty-seven years from 1927 on, and served as director of athletics from 1956 to 1969. Richard A. Smith, better known as "Cap'n Dick," returned to W&L as "graduate manager" (athletic director) in 1921 and remained until he retired in 1954. During that time, he was head coach of basketball for five seasons and of baseball for thirty years, winning a Southern Conference championship in 1935. Archie Mathis began coaching W&L wrestling in 1925 and had more than eight unbeaten records and four conference championships over seventeen years. And another student superstar—Leigh Williams—appeared in the late 1920s, also winning sixteen letters in the same four sports played by Cy Young.

Frank Gaines encountered football and its influence soon after his arrival in 1930. To a remarkable degree, the familiar issues pertaining to this intercollegiate sport today were already much in evidence then. In 1914 the undefeated Generals were declared South Atlantic Conference champions and were already playing an eight or nine game schedule against mostly larger schools. In 1921, W&L became a founding member of the new Southern Conference, along with Alabama, Auburn, Clemson, Georgia, Georgia Tech, Kentucky, Maryland, Mississippi State, North Carolina, North Carolina State, Tennessee, Virginia, and Virginia Tech (then Virginia Polytechnic Institute). Joining the conference was exhilarating for a small college in the Shenandoah Valley but reflected aspirations that would be difficult to sustain. Another conference re-sorting occurred in 1932, when thirteen of the larger schools (and Sewanee) left to found the new Southeastern Conference (SEC).

W&L managed to hold its own in the still-competitive Southern Conference, winning a number of championships in the 1930s and 1940s in track, swimming, wrestling, basketball, and golf. The football team boasted championships in 1934 and 1950, and finished as regular season champs on three other occasions. Contests with state rivals Virginia and Virginia Tech were especially memorable, and alumni were thrilled to see their Generals battling on the gridiron against larger schools in urban arenas. One New York alumnus and trustee wrote in 1933, "That old spirit which I used to foster when I was young and the many hurts and scars I nursed and retain, always revive an interest in athletics. I am proud of the football team.[6]"

One recurring issue was the unusual demand on student football players' time and attention, especially for "away" games. In a time of strict rules for class attendance and Saturday classes, the faculty were reluctant to grant excuses—especially when others in the student body also desired time off to attend the games. The executive committee of the faculty regularly considered the matter, setting an eight-day limit on excused absences for athletic participation. Occasionally, as in November 1933, the committee had to exceed even this limit, at the same time admonishing "the athletic authorities" to "arrange athletic schedules in accordance with faculty requirements." Overwhelmed with the "excellent conduct" of the student body at the 1931 Homecoming game, however, the committee declared a day's holiday permitting students to attend a game in Roanoke. If similarly good conduct was displayed, the committee announced, it would consider yet another holiday prior to the game with Princeton.[7]

This unusual allowance perhaps suggests how rare "excellent conduct" on the part of the student audience actually was. Football games were wonderful occasions for picnics and family activities on bright, brisk fall afternoons. But game days also featured student carousing, inebriation, and roisterous behavior, often with little attention paid to the game itself. Drinking that started well before the game often continued through the evening. Spectator sports did not create such behavior or in themselves encourage drinking, but they were certainly large public gatherings infused with holiday atmosphere and partisan enthusiasm. The university was compelled from time to time to issue warnings and devise stricter policies, but the tendency for rowdy behavior and drinking to get out of hand was largely characteristic of student life nationwide. This situation led to tension between alumni (and, to some extent, students) and faculty members, with administrators caught in the middle. For many alumni, the Generals represented the very best of alma mater. For the faculty, football was a growing distraction that threatened the underlying principles and priorities of the academy.

As far as athletics were concerned, there was a constant and rising pressure—within and outside the university—to win. Speaking to an alumni banquet in Richmond on October 29, 1937, "Cap'n Dick" Smith, with the new title of director of intercollegiate athletics, called for major changes in W&L's approach to football: "We are now going down the middle of the road, and I for one, am tired of it." He contrasted institutions like W&L, whose provisions for athletes were limited to giving some of them work opportunities on campus, with larger schools that provided up to sixty students with room, board, and tuition in return for playing football. "If we continue to play schools like Duke, Kentucky, and West Virginia, we must resort to open subsidization." Gate receipts from games against larger schools had actually declined on several recent occasions. "Unless we can give these larger schools competition, there is no advantage in playing them. People don't go to see one-sided games."[8] The bigger issues may have been the growing dissatisfaction among W&L supporters with the one-sided losses and the growing effect on athletic budgets of expenses versus revenue generated by football.

Alumni were more likely to weigh in on football than on virtually any other university activity. The Lynchburg chapter of the Alumni Association was particularly vocal during the 1930s, in one instance calling for the hiring of a new football coach because of the poor performance of the 1938 team (4–4–1); it wanted W&L "to compete on an equal basis with other universities." These alumni were unhappy about the decision to extend Coach W. E. "Tex" Tilson's contract by two years, and they joined with other alumni chapters to form an "alumni council" to work directly with university athletic officials.[9] This degree of alumni interest was clearly disturbing to the administration, which feared that the intrusion into university decisions could lead to mischief. Coach Tilson's teams fared even worse in 1939 (3–4–1) and 1940 (2–7–1).

Whether or not to "subsidize" or provide direct financial support for students to play sports was a challenge for W&L and many other institutions, especially in view of NCAA efforts to curtail potential abuses. As remains the case today, the flow of money into college sports undermines the amateur student-athlete ideal, as well as the concept of the academic community, not to mention enhancing prospects for both student favoritism and abuse. The dilemma over subsidizing student athletes is only part of a long and tangled story at W&L that ultimately centered on a moment when heartfelt but conflicting opinions and aspirations clashed. It is important to explore this moment at length and in depth because, like other pivotal moments in the university's history, it helped define the institution and shape its future.

WASHINGTON AND LEE was reluctant to provide financial support or admission for students primarily because of athletic ability. This refusal to favor athletes would ultimately prove to be a losing battle, at least with respect to criteria for admission; by the end of the twentieth century, even the most selective small colleges and Ivy League schools were considering athletic ability—along with other extracurricular accomplishments—among the factors "diversifying" and "rounding out" an entering class. But athletic scholarships were another matter.

The South's most prominent higher-education leader, Frank Porter Graham of the University of North Carolina, launched a major effort in 1935 to end the abuses stemming from financial payments to students for athletic performance. He even persuaded the new Southern Conference to adopt, by a 6–4 vote in February 1936, stringent new rules that required athletes to report all sources of income (to detect under-the-table payments from alumni) and satisfactorily complete one full year of college before they were eligible to play. The new plan immediately encountered a firestorm of protest, even from UNC alumni and boosters. By December, the Southern Conference weakened the rules by adopting changes suggested by the University of Virginia. No serious efforts to curtail subsidization of athletes would occur again until after World War II. By the time of his death in 1972, Graham would see that his worst fears had come to pass.[10]

President Gaines was always alert to athletic officials' efforts to tweak the admissions process to favor talented athletes, especially football players. In a pointed 1934 letter to athletic director Dick Smith, Gaines reiterated the purpose of "Presidential Scholarships" and the university policy that they should be awarded by administrative officials without regard to athletic skill: "It is distinctly understood that the Athletic Association (funded by alumni contributions) is not to pay tuition charges for any student, that it will not act as agent for any outside contributions to this end, and that this policy governs all officials of the Association." The athletic department could, however, give preference to athletes for paid work around the campus "immediately associated" with athletics.[11] A year later, Gaines reiterated these same instructions in a memorandum to Smith, Tilson, and Young. Referring to a letter sent to selected alumni soliciting support for tuition payments for several football players, Gaines wrote, "I must urgently insist that no such appeal shall be put out by members of our staff. The University becomes immediately and totally responsible for the act of any one of its agents."[12]

While the institution was not supposed to provide, orchestrate, or manage such financial aid, the actions of alumni and "boosters" were increasingly difficult to control. Alumni who wished to provide private "gifts" to encourage talented local boys to attend and play football for their alma maters posed a challenge for administrators, even if it delighted coaches and some athletic directors. This "unofficial" and "off-the-books" subsidization held great potential to undermine institutional control and still does today.

Such financial assistance by local alumni was especially difficult to detect. University policy required that financial aid flow through the institution, but there was some question as to whether W&L could legally prohibit financial gifts from one individual to another. The day before the Homecoming Game in 1937, Gaines met with two members of a committee of the Alumni Association who proposed to address the situation through semiformal means. They reported "that various alumni felt intense dissatisfaction over the current record of our football team; that this discontent would crystallize in the Home-Coming crowd; [and] that something would certainly be done by these individuals—the inference being that contributions would be forthcoming to be used to pay the expenses of students of football ability." They proposed that such gifts could be made to the alumni committee, which would make the awards only to students who had gone through the regular admissions process. Everything would be open and above-board, no university officials would be involved, and the money would be channeled in a "responsible" manner. Gaines explained that he was opposed to subsidization by alumni and thought it might be unfortunate for coaches because the "paying alumni" would then "surely demand victories as a return on investment." But he also knew that earlier efforts by the Southern Conference to bar all support of this kind had failed, and he suspected that other institutions were moving ahead to satisfy determined alumni. He concluded "that if the alumni are resolved to give support of this nature to athletes, this plan seemed to me the best I had heard." Early the next morning, however, he had second thoughts and, after consulting with Frank Gilliam, asked the Alumni Association to defer the entire matter.[13]

This proposal also lacked complete support of the Alumni Association leadership. Clarence L. Sager, a New York attorney and association president, vigorously protested the implementation of any such plan, which had been discussed at a board of directors meeting he was unable to attend. Complaining to Young that an athletic scholarship is a "contradiction in terms" and that he was "mortified beyond words that such action should have been taken by the Alumni Board during my term of office," Sager declared that he would "fight this thing with every legitimate and fair means at my disposal."[14] A day later he wrote Gaines, threatening to pull his support from solicitations for the annual Alumni Fund until the "athletic scholarship business" had been resolved. He wondered why W&L did not focus on the "larger purpose" of the university: "Were we all together to be engrossed in pursuing that larger purpose, all this fuss and bickering about whether we would play Duke or Johns Hopkins at football would seem so silly and inconsequential, as of course it is, and such statements as attributed to Dick Smith in the *Ring-tum Phi* of November 2nd [following his meeting with the Richmond alumni chapter] under big headlines on the front page, with picture and everything, would be met with the laughter and ridicule that it so much deserves."[15] Though Sager was likely in the minority among alumni, his opposition, and the administration's ambivalence and reluctance, ended consideration of the alumni athletic-subsidy plan.

Occasionally, Gaines admitted his frustration at being caught in the middle. In a confidential letter on December 16, 1937, he noted that his "first concern" was protecting the "good name of the University." At the same time, however, "I have the very difficult task to try to prevent as far as I can a division of alumni sentiment which might work great damage to the institution itself." He disapproved of the practice at some institutions of "raising large 'war chests' to purchase at the highest bid their gridiron warriors."[16]

One approach was to require students who received outside aid to report it to the institution. This was part of the initial Southern Conference strategy that was ultimately rejected. Sager wondered why this would not work at W&L: "If our honor system has any meaning whatever, a student receiving such support would be bound in honor to report it." An invocation of the Honor System was surely to raise any issue at W&L to a higher level of concern. As Gaines was quick to respond, though without directly addressing the aid issue, "I hope you will believe me that under no circumstances will we permit—to say nothing of endorsing—any program or project that might constitute a hazard to the Honor System."[17]

Then, as now, the compensation of coaches was an expense that attracted attention. "It seems almost ridiculous," Gaines admitted to trustee Herbert Fitzpatrick in 1935, "that a coach should receive more money than one of the most valued professors. . . . This matter is governed, however, by the law of supply and demand and our quarrel must be with that law."[18] He noted that when he arrived in 1930 the football coach received $6,000 a year and that he thought $5,000 should now be the top amount. Some institutions in the conference were reportedly paying coaches as much as $12,000 per year, even in the depths of the Depression.

Athletic personnel were often assigned multiple tasks and sometimes paid from sources outside the regular university budget. Cy Young's compensation in 1937 was for coaching football and basketball, serving as alumni secretary, and recruiting students (including football players) during the summer. The Athletic Department drew on funding from student fees, gifts made by the Athletic Association, football gate receipts and contracts, and proceeds from the dining hall.

Nevertheless, balancing the athletic budget was a chronic challenge for most universities playing intercollegiate football without a large alumni base and not fielding strong, popular teams. Accurately predicting revenues and costs—and thus potential deficits—was especially difficult. In May 1942, Smith shared with Gaines estimates of income and expenses for athletics for the year following September 1, 1941, and a projection for 1942–43. Total receipts, amounting to $26,014, included proceeds from the "campus tax" (student fees), concessions, and football receipts of nearly $15,000. Total salaries came to $17,380, which along with other expenses resulted in an approximate deficit of $2,763. Only $1,000 had been paid toward a loan of $7,000 taken in the summer of 1941, and Smith noted that another $3,000 loan would be required the following summer. Already, the war was beginning to affect the overall economy, with gas and tire shortages cutting into game attendance. Smith noted "that our salary budget is entirely too high for our present income," necessitating "drastic cuts for the coming year." Budget estimates for 1942–43 were based on projections of fee income from only six hundred students and $12,000 from football, which turned out to be optimistic. The budget slashed salaries by over 65 percent.[19] A short time later all intercollegiate sports at W&L would be suspended during the wartime emergency.

THE DISLOCATIONS AND DISTRACTIONS of the war years created an opportunity for the university to reconsider its intercollegiate athletic policies and posture, and important conversations and decisions occurred in the summer and fall of 1945. President Gaines's reservations about subsidized athletics were well known, leading to fear in some quarters that W&L would back away from its prewar aspirations. Some alumni were certain that if W&L deemphasized football and competed at a lesser level, it would suffer in reputation, future enrollment, and funding. "If W. & L. contents itself with intramural sports or contents itself to play such schools as Sewanee, Davidson, and Southwestern at Memphis," wrote one Chattanooga alumnus, "I make the prediction, because of our restricted curriculum, that about five or six years after the war is over, Washington & Lee's prestige will slip considerably and the authorities will find it difficult to maintain a student body of 1,000 in number." Trustee James R. Caskie of Lynchburg replied that the board and administration were "in a quandary" and begged for understanding: "We have ardent advocates for both big time football and for withdrawing from big time football and for limited interscholastic activities and effective and efficient intramural programs." He noted the dilemma posed by inevitably escalating competition; if W&L aspired to compete with Virginia, the latter would aspire to compete with North Carolina, which would set its sights on Duke, which would aspire to be in the Rose Bowl. And so it would go. Whatever the decision, it would arouse the ire of some alumni.[20]

Even though "big time" football was not nearly as dominant and all-consuming as it is today, it was still difficult to imagine W&L—with its rural location and small student population—competing with larger schools on an equal basis. But many were willing to try. One alumnus suggested that probably $50,000 a year would be required for W&L to remain competitive as a "quasi-professional college team" until such time as it could become self-sustaining through big games and larger attendance. Without such a commitment, the university was likely to disappear from public attention altogether. "A casual glance at any metropolitan newspaper or national magazine," one alumnus wrote, "will show that a large proportion of its space is devoted to college athletics."[21]

The board—despite its misgivings and reservations—had already started to move in this direction and adopted a resolution at its meeting on October 12, 1945: "Intercollegiate football on an openly admitted basis of aid to an extent that would permit us to compete with traditional rivals such as Virginia, V.P.I., Maryland, Kentucky and West Virginia. The plan should be set up, however, that any socalled [sic] athletic students should be of character and ability to be readily assimilated into the student body. That the plan should be openly and frankly admitted and carried out without subterfuge or hypocrisy."[22]

A few days before, the University Athletic Committee, including Frank Gilliam and Dick Smith, unanimously approved a statement calling for definitive decisions for the future. The committee declared that the "so-called middle-of-the-road policy, which largely governed the operation of pre-war athletics, will have to be abandoned." Recognizing that the problem applied solely to football, the university should determine whether to shift to a strong intramural program; continue intercollegiate football with "like-minded" colleges, such as Sewanee and Hampden-Sydney, and without subsidization; or to compete at the highest level, against institutions like Virginia and Virginia Tech, with subsidization and the necessary financial commitments.[23] These were the choices to be made before the 1946 season.

Gaines sent a questionnaire to all alumni in November 1945. He chose not to mention the various opinions already communicated to the administration about "big time football," nor did he discuss the financial and public relations implications of different options. Rather, he simply promised to retain an inclusive program of sports, including as many "minor" intercollegiate sports as possible, and to "safeguard all standards of the student body" with respect to admission and academic performance. He then laid out the three basic "suggestions" for postwar intercollegiate football at W&L and asked alumni whether they wanted to (A) "abolish it entirely," (B) continue it "on a strictly amateur basis" and compete only with universities with a similar policy, or (C) compete with "traditional rivals" and provide financial assistance to "students of athletic ability" who also met the regular admission and academic standards.[24]

Washington and Lee was not alone in wrestling with such choices, and the presidents of other universities were interested in the results of Gaines's survey. Likewise, W&L was watching its peers and their struggles with athletics even before the war. Sewanee was a small liberal arts institution that appeared especially rabid about football and even joined larger and more prominent intercollegiate teams in forming the Southeastern Conference in 1932. When the SEC announced in 1935 that subsidization of athletes by its members would be permitted, Sewanee was caught between its desire to compete at the highest level and its oft-stated claim that its athletic teams and spirit were "pure" and committed to the best principles of amateur sport. As at W&L, some alumni were convinced that without football "the university certainly would soon go bankrupt because students would abandon the institution in droves."[25] Charles Diehl, president of another small school, Southwestern in Memphis, feared that without football "a certain vitality would be lost from the campus, and that the student body would not be quite normal."

Alexander Guerry, appointed vice chancellor at Sewanee in 1938, was committed to abandoning "big time" football and continuing the sport on a fully amateur basis, and he became a national spokesman for amateurism. Writing to Gaines in December 1945, Guerry inquired about the results of W&L's alumni survey. "I think Sewanee and Southwestern are ready to attempt a program of intercollegiate football without subsidization, if five or six other colleges will join with us. It would be very fine if Washington and Lee were of the same mind." A few days later, Gaines received a letter from the president of Davidson College, J. R. Cunningham, reporting on the results of a recent alumni survey by that institution. After many meetings with various groups and committees, Cunningham wrote, "We are about to conclude that our policy will be to limit our schedules to institutions of our general size and type and stay in the field of amateur football." But there was clearly still some confusion on the matter, for he also stated that as far as athletes were concerned, "we will likely continue as we have done before, giving some limited scholarship assistance which will be administered by our regular Faculty Scholarship Committee."[26]

Gaines was unhappy with the outcome of the more than three thousand responses to the W&L alumni survey. As he reported in January 1946 to his colleagues at Sewanee and Southwestern: "Come weal, come woe, Our status is quo." He confessed that he had maintained "a faint hope, but very faint, that strong opinion might be registered in a kind of constructive mandate." He was "surprised" by the high rate of response—"perhaps a third of our living alumni" answered the survey—and by the fact that "almost nobody voted to abolish intercollegiate football." About a fourth of the respondents favored competing on a amateur basis with like-minded institutions, but fully three-fourths "wanted us to recognize football ability as one of the legitimate grounds for financial aid, and thus prepare to resume contests with our traditional rivals—meaning the University of Virginia and a group of similar colleges—all larger than we are, by the way." He reiterated the university's commitment to a solid intramural program and the maintenance of high admission standards, and speculated—inaccurately—that no alumnus aspired "to achieve the dubious glory of any kind of bowl." Despite his disappointment with the survey result, he had partly eased the way for it by reassuring alumni at the outset that the university would, in any case, maintain its academic and admissions standards.

On a personal note, Gaines declared himself ready to "bequeath the whole football program to my successor, whoever he may be and whenever he may appear." He also voiced the frustrations of most university presidents. "Of all the problems that I have dealt with in the nearly 19 years of administrative work," he wrote, "this problem has been the most absorbing, most irritating—and the labor I have spent in attempted solution has been least fruitful. I cherish a lingering faith, largely because I have nothing else in this domain to cherish, that professional football may one day take some of the pressure off colleges."[27]

Guerry was disappointed that Davidson and W&L had decided to provide some financial support for athletes. He lamented the sway of the "big boys" over football and the failure to fight against subsidization. "The public has been let down by the colleges which ought to enlighten the public. The public hears no voice raised against subsidized athletics and sees no program of reputable colleges based on any other plan."[28] It is hard to say how Guerry was able to lead a dramatic change in direction at Sewanee, where the campus community worried even more about its fate because of small size and isolation, while Frank Gaines struggled with contending forces and opinions in Lexington. Every institution is different, but there was apparently stronger "football fever" at W&L and less of an inclination to resist it, which led to a continuing—and ultimately elusive—search for an acceptable middle ground.

After considering the alumni survey results, the W&L trustees authorized the president to state that the university would offer aid "to worthy students who are good athletes and who stand in need of financial assistance," but asserted that neither entrance requirements nor academic standards would be modified to attract or retain student athletes. While the athletic director might make recommendations, any award of financial assistance "shall be granted only by the regular University Committee on Scholarships and Student Help."

W&L pursued this middle way, holding on to subsidization while declaring its commitment to the pure amateur athletic ideal.

The NCAA endeavored, with limited success, to implement new rules and restrictions. Subsidization—the direct payment of tuition and other scholarship aid to students in exchange for their athletic participation—appeared to undermine the very concept of amateur athletics. In 1948–49, the NCAA launched its first concerted effort to curtail violations. The so-called Purity Code or Sanity Code, adopted in January 1948, required—among other restrictions—minimum academic standards for participation, financial aid only for "need," and scholarship payments beyond tuition limited to on-campus work activities open to all students. They also reinforced the expectation that institutions exercise direct control over the athletic program and that all students be admitted on the same basis. While a great majority of universities signed on to this "code," it was clear that many were half-hearted about it or interpreted it selectively and liberally. Eventually, many universities—especially the larger football schools—simply declared that they would do otherwise, and, in 1951, the code failed.[29]

The NCAA effort began with a questionnaire sent to all members. W&L's responses—submitted on November 12, 1948—were perhaps typical of smaller institutions with high athletic ambitions but limited abilities to provide support for athletes under the new rules. Gaines noted that "athletic ability" was a factor in awarding financial aid at W&L but that the maximum grant was $950 a session, including $350 in tuition and the rest for room, board, books, and incidental fees. On-campus work was paid only for services rendered, rather than as disguised direct payments. Athletic officials did not grant financial aid to students, though they could advise the admissions committee. To the question of aid given to athletes by alumni or outside groups and not administered by the university, Gaines responded, "Not to my knowledge." W&L reported forty-seven students on financial aid for "athletic ability." Of the thirty-four upperclassmen, fifteen received a full $950 commitment. Only seven had a "B" average or better in their coursework, and thirteen were below a "C" average. Among the thirteen freshmen, eleven received aid at the $950 level; only three ranked in the top quarter of their high-school class, and five were in the bottom half. In view of the NCAA rule on campus work assignments for any aid beyond tuition, Gaines offered that, as a member of the Southern Conference, W&L "follows the custom of direct aid, rather than attempting to create so-called jobs. The average football player cannot in justice to himself carry his studies, participate in that sport, and then do much in the way of outside toil."[30]

The new NCAA code posed real challenges for institutions reluctant to embrace full subsidization but hesitant to deemphasize football or put themselves at a competitive disadvantage. Presidents of Virginia institutions agonized together about how to respond. William and Mary's president, John E. Pomfret, reported in April 1949 on a meeting in Savannah where he and the presidents of Davidson and Richmond had met with members of the NCAA Compliance Committee, chaired by Clarence P. Houston of Tufts University. Houston pointed to the 250 (of 280) members who had already signed the code and declared that those who had not signed "would be given until September first to get into line." Failure to sign could lead to expulsion from the NCAA. On behalf of his Virginia colleagues, Pomfret argued that the code "was unworkable and unenforceable" and that many institutions were still not in compliance. Particularly challenging were requirements that students receiving aid beyond tuition have a "B" average, that "needy" athletes be forced to work for room and board, and that only one meal a day could be provided for athletes at the "training table." The committee was not particularly sympathetic, leaving institutions with few options. Pomfret concluded by suggesting the possibility that all southern NCAA institutions drop out of the organization "and erect a code that all could honorably subscribe to"—an option never seriously pursued.[31]

The W&L Athletic Committee had notified Gaines in June that the university would abide by the code but also continue to provide full support to those athletes still eligible. The committee noted that the cost of football at W&L was then $85,960 (almost $862,000 in today's dollars), while the receipts amounted to only $65,000.[32] On June 20, 1949, Gaines wrote the chair of the NCAA Compliance Committee, affirming that the W&L board of trustees "instructed me to advise you that this institution will comply with full authority with the code of the N.C.A.A."[33] The board also limited the number of any awards permitted by the "Sanity Code" at one time to a maximum of fifty students.

Only a few months later, the NCAA sent Gaines a "frank letter" and a second questionnaire. The letter reported "a disturbing and serious situation": while virtually all members had accepted the new code, and only seven members rejected it, "there appear to be widespread contentions that the Code is being flagrantly violated and that although members have stated their intention to comply with it, the intention is not being carried out with sincerity." The questionnaire was sent to "certain institutions" because of unspecified requests for information or complaints. The questionnaire focused on support provided by outside groups, payments for jobs not performed, and athletes receiving aid after

January 1948. Gaines again responded that the university was unaware of any outside support but did confirm that the fourteen football players with on-campus
jobs (waiting in the dining hall, clerking in the university store, assisting in the
gym and training room, and helping on the athletic field) did not perform any
duties during the football season, and that eight students, mostly in the class
of 1953 but entering after January 1948, continued to receive aid.[34]

The NCAA's efforts failed because institutions and conferences simply refused to support them. All of this seems familiar today: the pressures from
alumni and, to some degree students, on university administrations to field
competitive football teams were relentless, if often hidden. Administrations
were also caught between alumni and faculty members, who generally favored
de-emphasizing subsidized intercollegiate sports. Smaller or less successful institutions received inadequate revenues from football and had to subsidize the
program from student fees and outside gifts, as well as schedule the teams of
larger schools for a share of more lucrative gate receipts (which Gaines termed
"suicide games"). The NCAA passed rules and regulations intended to preserve
the ideals of amateur competition and the "student athlete" in the midst of an
environment rife with institutional lip service, widespread rule breaking, and
outside money and influence, all of which was later enormously expanded by
television and its revenues.

While efforts to curtail subsidized athletics were usually overwhelmed at
larger institutions with powerful alumni and larger budgets, some presidents—
like Guerry at Sewanee—did take a firm and principled stand. President Colgate Darden of the University of Virginia, who corresponded often with Gaines
and other Virginia college leaders, refused to allow his team to accept an invitation to the Cotton Bowl following the 1951 season, a ban on postseason play
that established a long-standing precedent at UVA. But Darden's opposition to
joining the new Atlantic Coast Conference (ACC) in 1953 was overridden by
the UVA Board of Visitors. At W&L, Gaines wrote the trustees in June 1949,
"Sentiment in our University family is confused and probably divided, but it
may be that the time has come when we should say that four years of subsidized
football have not been successful, financially or statistically, and we shall adopt,
at least for a few years, another plan."[35]

During W&L's championship season of 1950 and after its Gator Bowl appearance in 1951, university officials continued to wrestle with financial challenges in football, efforts to meet the terms of the NCAA "Sanity Code," and
persistent faculty objections to the growing emphasis on the sport. The bowl

appearance accentuated the arguments on all sides. How to ultimately satisfy all the constituencies and adhere to the university's academic and communal values was not at all clear, but certain realities were hard to ignore. In closely held conversations, the board was becoming more and more convinced that continuing along the present path was unsustainable.

Clayton Williams, dean of the law school and chairman of the university's Committee on Intercollegiate Athletics, reported in May 1950 that more money would be needed. "In the light of our experience it seems apparent that strictly football receipts will not meet the total cost of the other varied athletic activities." He observed that revenues from the university store and the dining hall had been intended to support the athletic program and that the full cost of scholarships was not supposed to be borne entirely by athletics, but neither of these commitments had been fulfilled. In any event, the cost of football was estimated at $104,320, and the actual gate receipts were $70,000. A special "alumni fund" that would permit direct gifts to athletics seemed to be the only way to generate sufficient additional revenue.[36]

The following fall, the trustees formally adopted a new plan hashed out in a joint meeting of the Williams committee, the Board of Trustees Committee on Intercollegiate Athletics, and alumni representatives; the plan was to take effect on July 1, 1951. The budget for 1951–52 no longer included receipts from the university store or scholarships, which were transferred to a new "Generals' Fund" for alumni contributions and were no longer part of the athletic budget. Revenues were projected at $91,000, including $72,000 in gate receipts and $15,000 in student fees, and expenditures at $80,100. It was also happily noted that the NCAA was no longer pursuing adherence to the "Sanity Code." "This action," Williams wrote, "has removed a number of our problems."[37]

The W&L football team enjoyed a winning season (6–4) in 1951, with wins over West Virginia, Virginia Tech, and—most notably—the Virginia Cavaliers in a 42 to 14 victory that some recalled as the greatest game W&L ever played and that was Virginia's only loss that year. The university was able to retain Coach George Barclay for the 1951 season, after he was named the 1950 Southern Conference and Virginia Coach of the Year. Gaines notified the board's Athletic Committee in December 1950 that Barclay had received a favorable offer from an unnamed institution and the University Athletic Committee had recommended a salary increase to $7,500. While the amount did not meet the other offer, "it is the maximum we can give to stay within a policy which might be roughly defined as not paying the coach more than a professor has made, or could make for twelve months of work." Gaines considered Barclay "the best coach that has ever been associated with me" and endorsed the increase.[38] But Barclay departed at the end of the season for his alma mater, the University of North Carolina at Chapel Hill, where he produced a mediocre record over the next three years as the head coach. His principal assistant, Carl Wise, succeeded him at W&L but had dreary seasons in 1952 and 1953 (a combined 7–13 record), and later became an assistant coach at Clemson University. After the successes of the Barclay years, W&L fans were not pleased.

Growing alumni enthusiasm for football was accompanied by concerns among the faculty and administration that the sport—and its penumbra of activities and imperatives—was undermining academic priorities and even the culture and character of the institution. While football players met the minimum requirements for admission, they were often less academically prepared and less comfortable with a demanding curriculum, and they faced more stringent demands on their time than most other students. Football players also tended to be less affluent than other students and thus were often entirely dependent on grants-in-aid. They received "unofficial bonuses" that included funds for clothing (to keep up with the coat-and-tie dress requirements on campus) and even cash payments from coaches for certain outstanding plays on the field. As Frank Parsons later commented, "They were more at home in the pool room on the corner with some of the local townspeople than with other Washington and Lee students. They created their own isolation." And there was an increasingly corrosive distinction been "major" and "minor" sports and the athletes who played them: "We had second-class athletes," Parsons observed.[39]

The W&L Board of Trustees both sympathized with alumni enthusiasms and fretted over their potential consequences. The Southern Conference wrestled with issues of freshmen participation in varsity competition, out-of-season practices and training, and postseason games—all of which distracted from academic priorities and responsibilities. University presidents were increasingly involved in these decisions. Gaines wrote in January 1952 that the trustees "are disturbed by all forms of out-of-season schedule of any sport, and they are troubled greatly by the subsidization plan as now operated."[40] They looked hopefully to solutions worked out with peers.

The athletic situation stimulated comment from many sources. In October 1951, Richmond attorney (and later US Supreme Court justice) Lewis F. Powell Jr. observed to Gaines that drawing a line "at a reasonable place" between giving up the sport entirely or permitting athletic scholarships was desirable but difficult. Powell suggested that perhaps the "big six" universities in Virginia could leave the Southern Conference and start one of their own that would prohibit athletic scholarships. Gaines responded that two of the thorniest issues were direct alumni contributions to the educational expenses of student athletes outside the purview of faculty control, and the overall costs of the program, some of which—like up-to-date equipment and facilities—would continue even if "professionalization" and its revenues was abandoned.[41]

A group of Richmond alumni wanted to continue the current football program and maintain W&L's character or principles. This middle way included offering athletic grants-in-aid. "We would prefer, under ideal conditions, a policy which does not relate financial assistance to athletic ability. But we recognize that 'ideal conditions' do not exist." Financial support would be necessary to "compete with other comparable schools" in Virginia and in the Southern Conference. Eliminating football entirely would also eliminate the "source of revenue which, in major part, supports the entire athletic program of the University." And it would make W&L far less attractive to the "very best type of young men," who "will simply not go to a college which fails to give proper recognition to this [football] tradition." In their view, the alumni had not applied undue pressure for "big time" football and supported the administration's commitment to high academic standards. Intended as a measured and sensible approach, this justification of the status quo, as Gaines well knew, depended on holding to delicate balances that would be very difficult to maintain given financial realities and alumni enthusiasms.[42]

The Faculty Discussion Group devoted most of its November 1951 regular meeting to athletics. Gaines and athletic administrators were invited to attend, and the turnout was unusually large. As Gaines reported to the board's Committee on Athletics, two points were particularly emphasized. The first was that about half of the athletic deficit could be attributed to tuition given to athletes, which was not so much a cost as "money which the University does not receive" (i.e., money that the university pays itself). The other half was for costs the university would incur in any event if football continued "on the same basis." The second major point was that "our athletes are regular students." Professor A. R. Coleman of the School of Commerce and member of the University Athletic Committee provided "convincing" information on graduation rates, grade point ratios, and distribution "throughout the curriculum," demonstrating that "we have no snap courses or soft spots." Gaines was pleased with the tone of the meeting but confessed that "we have an energetic group—I do not know how large—vigorously opposed to the present program. I take it that these gentlemen would not abolish athletics as such but would insist upon the purely amateur status, and as a consequence playing only such colleges as would agree upon a similar plan."[43]

The faculty took a formal vote on the options for intercollegiate football at a regular meeting on December 3 and asked Gaines to share the results with the trustees. A scattering of faculty voted to abandon intercollegiate football entirely (5), continue the current policy (7), expand the current program with more athletic grants-in-aid (1), and continue the current policy but with "substantial reductions" in grants-in-aid (9). But the great majority (31, or almost 60 percent of the votes cast) favored continuation of intercollegiate football, with no athletic grants-in-aid and scheduling games with schools with similar policies.[44] The Executive Committee of the Faculty also asked Dean Leyburn to remind the athletic director of the university about rules concerning student leaves of absence for athletic participation. In a December 15 letter to Dick Smith, Leyburn included the university policy restricting such absences to no more than eight days, noted specific instances where the limit had been exceeded, and reminded the athletic director that the restriction applied to an entire session and not to each semester. The letter was signed, "Yours cordially."[45]

Later that month, Gaines wrote to an alumnus about "the perplexing question of athletics." He reported that, on issues of football, most of the Southern Conference presidents "are in great difficulty." Most W&L alumni "are in favor of continuing the football program we have had since the war. Our faculties are overwhelmingly opposed to it, and many thoughtful alumni—including some trustees—strongly object. Placed in the middle position, the presidents would like to save football as a college sport, and as a focus for alumni and student enthusiasm; but we recognize trends that we think would probably destroy football."[46] Another alumnus, attorney Beverly A. Davis of Rocky Mount, Virginia, agreed that most alumni supported the current football program, but except for the law school, "all faculty members I have come in contact with have but one thought in mind and that is, the subjects which they teach. It is my feeling that the majority of the faculty members, again excluding those in the School of Law, have little respect for each others [sic] courses. In other words, each faculty member wants his own assignments met with little or no consideration of the amount of work given by other members of the faculty, or the students." On the whole, he concluded, "they are a selfish lot."[47] Such comments only reinforced disagreements in the university community on the matter of football and the degree to which alumni and faculty could be pitted against one another—to the administration's great distress.

W&L, and most other Southern Conference schools, were concerned about expanding the scope of football and adding further to the demands on students and their academic work—especially postseason football games, spring practice, and the "platoon system," which permitted unlimited substitutions and favored larger squads and player specialization for offense and defense. A meeting of Southern Conference presidents in Chapel Hill in September 1951 agreed to deny permission for any member to accept a bowl bid at the end of that season. (President Gaines was ill and absent from campus during the summer of 1951 and March of 1952, and for a time Dean Leyburn served as acting president. Gaines later explained that while W&L abstained from voting at the Chapel Hill meeting, he would have voted with the majority had he attended.) Even after the Gator Bowl excitement, Gaines told H. C. Byrd, president of the University of Maryland, that the W&L board had taken "a position against Bowl games" and, in fact, opposed "all out-of-season practice or playing of a given sport." The main objections were "the excessive demand upon students' time," the "transfer of emphasis" from competition within the conference with similar institutions "to one national spectacle as the culmination of the season's endeavor," and the "increasing financial involvements which conceivably could constitute peril in the direction of scandals such as have developed in other sports at the time of the national spectacles."[48] It seems the president and the board had very different expectations than many alumni.

While the board and administration took comfort in the fact that athletes were admitted according to the same criteria as other students and that the curriculum had not been adjusted with athletes in mind (no offering "crip" courses or a major in physical education), the financial issues surrounding intercollegiate football became increasingly problematic and undergirded discussions of more abstract matters. Gaines reported to an alumnus in April 1952 that "our Board has been ready for at least a year to take certain drastic steps in the direction of what we call de-emphasis, but has waited patiently, hoping that our sister institutions would join us." He was confident that reforms would be accomplished "to bring athletics more nearly into line with the central purposes of the University."[49] Later that month, Dean Clayton Williams reported to Gaines and the trustees that even though alumni had contributed the $20,000 "allotted to them" (the Generals Fund) and the overall budget had been met, an additional amount of $10,000 would be needed by the end of the year to cover grants-in-aid. His committee also recommended that Carl E. Wise be appointed the new football coach for two years, with a telling proviso: "that if football is discontinued, the contract would be void."[50]

Gaines became increasingly active and vocal, mostly behind the scenes, on the issue of subsidization, especially since the trustees seemed more receptive. He reported to the board Athletic Committee in May 1952 on the recent meeting of Southern Conference presidents in Richmond, which this time also including faculty representatives, athletic directors (in Gaines's view "merely coaches under another title"), and "a panel of active and alert newspaper reporters." The main topic of business was a report on athletics by the American Council on Education, suggesting that athletic ability should be one, but never the only, factor considered for purposes of admission and that athletes should "meet the same standards of academic performance and economic need" required of all students. A Southern Conference committee had recommended that the language be modified to read "academic ability and/or economic need." Gaines rose in the meeting to question this point, with the obvious implication concerning academic requirements for admission, and was joined by several others (representing Richmond, Davidson, VMI, and Virginia Tech) in recommending that the language be referred back to the committee. But the majority agreed to adopt the new language, indicating to Gaines that the conference would "not take any steps toward reducing subsidization in any way, shape, or form" and, indeed, had given "a big green light" to the larger institutions to "do the same thing and more of it than we do now." Gaines asked the trustees for instructions. Should he write to the other dissidents and also to President Darden of the University of Virginia ("who is greatly perturbed") to discuss further steps?[51]

The faculty proposed that Gaines appoint a committee to "explore the possibility of making a scheduling arrangement with institutions of high academic standards who are willing to compete on a purely amateur basis." In October 1952, the committee sent letters and a questionnaire to the presidents of eighteen "medium-sized colleges of high academic standing which are located close enough to the Eastern seaboard to avoid transportation problems," including Amherst, Davidson, Georgetown, Sewanee, Richmond, Virginia, and Princeton.[52] While the responses to these letters are not available, the effort itself reveals that W&L was actively seeking an alternative path for its football program, even while the excitement of the Gator Bowl appearance was still fresh and many alumni were calling for more of the same.

President Gaines and the trustees were moving forward in tandem. In a letter to three other presidents in December 1952, Gaines revealed that the executive committee of the board had recommended that "we cease recruiting and subsidizing—except for present commitments—as of now." He also mentioned that he had been asked to identify and "work with a group of colleges, somewhat our size, comparable in academic purposes, trustworthy in integrity." He shared the difficulties of making such a change when the following year's schedule was fixed and normal recruiting would already be underway. He knew these moves would be controversial. "If any one of you spills a single one of these particular beans, you will thereby sentence me to 90 days of doing nothing but answering letters of agitated friends, and 90 nights of telephone conversation with sports writers."[53]

At the same time, Dean Frank Gilliam weighed in to support retaining intercollegiate football but eliminating subsidization and restructuring the program and the schedule. W&L's policy, he wrote, should be "that athletics, emphatically including football . . . should be planned and conducted with the single aim of contributing to the welfare and happiness of the boys who normally come to us for their education." Football should not be regarded "a legitimate end in itself." By 1954, "a drastic re-shuffling of schedule should be completely possible," perhaps reducing the number of games to seven, adding some "smaller colleges," and retaining one or two "traditional games" with rivals, "even with little hope of winning." A leader for the new program should be fully in agreement with these principles and objectives. Remaining in the Southern Conference would prove difficult under these circumstances, Gilliam observed, and new affiliations should be sought immediately. The new schedule would reduce revenue, and grant-in-aid commitments already made would need to be continued, rendering "the immediate financial situation worse instead of better." Hopefully, he wrote, members of the Generals Club and other alumni would "rally behind the program." And it should be made clear that the new policy was "consistent with Washington and Lee's ideals, and not a move presented as a retreat or an apology."[54] He attached a proposal for an agreement among W&L, Davidson, and Furman that embodied these principles.

Alumni continued to share their views, mostly in favor of making a better showing on the gridiron. One was "chagrined and perturbed" about the athletic situation. "We don't like to see our team a door mat for the big powers" simply because of a financial problem. What could the alumni do to help? A group of Louisville alumni sought a program "which would enable us to compete on substantially equal terms with our natural rivals" and even pledged $1,000 a year to help achieve this goal. But another alumnus complained bitterly about a recent solicitation for the Generals Fund. How could Washington and Lee, "with its high standards and lofty ideals," permit "such a fund for the hiring of athletes," which is "entirely foreign to its nature"? Gaines replied dutifully to all. He noted the migration of some Southern Conference members to the new ACC, those institutions' high ambitions and financial commitments to football, and the difficulties of keeping up while still adhering to high academic standards. He also shared one of his rising concerns: "We do not want to have two classes of men on this campus—students and athletes."[55]

In the fall of 1953, Coach Carl Wise submitted a plaintive report on the athletic situation, particularly football, which had reached "a critical stage." Wise attributed much of W&L's recent success (1950–51) to the fact that many of its rivals "had permitted their football programs to reach an embarrassing low point." In those circumstances, with a "good team" W&L could still win by forty or sixty points. But significant improvements at the university's five in-state rivals now left W&L woefully "undermanned." Thirty-two W&L students were receiving aid for the varsity and twelve for the freshman team. (Four scholarships were for basketball.) A minimum of fifty varsity players was necessary to be competitive. Other schools came far closer to meeting or exceeding this number: Richmond (48), Virginia (40), Virginia Tech (50 or 60), and VMI (40). The numbers were equally troubling for the freshman squad. W&L's efforts to attract nonscholarship athletes to the football team suffered from a lack of student commitment and the demands of the academic schedule, including compulsory physical education every morning, an hour of daily military drill in ROTC, and afternoon laboratory work. "It is difficult to get a man to work for you without compensation and football is work. He must leave a summer job and report here about two weeks early as well as take part in four weeks of spring football." W&L's College Board examination requirement was also an impediment, since athletes were often identified and recruited before they could be scheduled for the exam. The recruiting budget (for travel to interview and entertain prospective players) was also inadequate. The Generals Club had raised $10,000 to $13,000 annually for this purpose, but now those contributions were used for scholarships, and the remaining budget of $2,000 for recruiting was "ridiculously small" in comparison with other schools like Virginia Tech ($23,000) and Virginia ($14,000). Even the food was inadequate: "This is a daily complaint, has been for years. . . . Football players consume more food than the non-athlete." While Coach Wise's complaints were self-serving (contrasting his record with that of his predecessor), his perception of needs was largely accurate. More money and addressing the needs of the football team was required for success—indeed, to avoid future embarrassment—against W&L's traditional rivals. "I would rather drop football," Wise concluded, "than to see us go deeper into the rut."[56]

A detailed financial analysis of actual and projected revenues and expenditures framed the challenges and options ahead. Revenue estimates for 1953–54 included $48,000 in gate receipts, $18,000 from the Generals Fund, and $19,000 from student athletic fees. Grants-in-aid (exclusive of tuition) were projected at $36,000 for football and $5,000 for basketball, with another $33,000 and $5,000 in tuition grants by the university. Given the projected expenses of $99,000 for coach's salaries, equipment, and other sports, the overall deficit in 1953–54 would run about $52,000. The projected revenues revealed the university's dependence on two or three "money games"—$10,000 for the Maryland game, $15,000 for the North Carolina contest, and $7,000 for playing Virginia—altogether comprising two-thirds of total gate receipts. Without the revenues from "money games" and the Generals' Fund, the athletic deficit would be much greater.[57] While fashioned as an argument to continue competing at a high level in football, these calculations, along with other concerns about the numbers and comparative skills of W&L football players, raised significant questions about sustainability for the future. The trustees reluctantly decided in 1953 to continue to try subsidization for one more year.[58]

⟶

ON JUNE 1, 1954, a visibly shaken William M. Bailey, an intermediate law student and president of the student body, rose before a packed special student assembly in Lee Chapel. Few people in the audience knew about the greatest challenge to the Honor System in the university's history; nor could they envision its profound and lasting consequences. Bailey laid out the facts. Nearly identical geology quiz papers turned in by two football players and reported to the Student Executive Committee had led to its investigations, which revealed an organized effort—or, as Bailey termed it, "a syndicate"—to steal and distribute test information and alter some already-submitted exams. With the help of a student wife who worked in the office where tests were duplicated and stored, and a bribed night watchman, the group acquired master keys providing access to the test facility, the office where all keys were kept, and faculty offices in Robinson, Washington, Payne, Newcomb, and Reid Halls. Copies of tests and examinations were made, and some already-submitted exams altered. The Student Executive Committee met almost constantly in grueling sessions over almost four days. When presented with the evidence, fifteen students (fourteen athletes, twelve of them football players) signed affidavits admitting their guilt and withdrew from the university rather than proceed with a trial before the committee. The night watchman was fired. At the end of the presentation, Bailey and his fellow executive committee members received a prolonged standing ovation. The extent and audacity of the violations against the central pillar of the university's identity clearly called for extraordinary action, and the consequences for athletics at W&L were dramatic.[59]

The June 1954 *Alumni Magazine* carried a brief announcement of the details of the incident, which had been widely reported in newspapers. It summarized Bailey's presentation to the university community, as well as President Gaines's statement in support of the Student Executive Committee and his pledge that the administration would work "to remove any existing factors of whatever nature that might make a recurrence of this story possible."[60] Clearly distressed, Gaines confided on June 5, "this has been the worst experience of my administrative life. It is all over now but I still feel the effects."[61] In the annual report, issued that fall, he referred to it as "the most startling and devastating discipline problem in the annals of Washington and Lee."[62] The full consequences were only beginning to develop.

A football program that had always struggled to maintain a squad large enough to be competitive was suddenly in dire straits. Of the thirty-eight veterans and fifteen scholarship freshmen expected for the 1954 season, nine had flunked out and twelve had withdrawn because of the cheating scandal. The coaches realized that they could count on only "32 players with whom to meet a nine-game schedule that included West Virginia, Vanderbilt, Virginia, and Pennsylvania." On June 15, Gaines alerted the trustees to the possible need to cancel the 1954 football season and called a meeting of the board's executive and athletic committees for July 7.[63]

Three hours of discussion, closed to the press, also included the alumni and faculty representatives on the athletic committee, as well as Carl Wise, Dick Smith, Cy Twombly, the president of the Alumni Association, the president of the Generals Club, and other members of the administration. The trustees then retired to an executive session in the living room of Penrobin, Gaines's home outside Lexington, and subsequently issued a statement. They had been as-sured by athletic staff that W&L could meet its obligations to the 1954 football schedule and, on that basis, reiterated a commitment to the schedule—though one perhaps "modified" by replacing some "powerful teams" with other oppo-nents. They also believed "that football of some sort or another is an important factor in the life of college boys and should be continued," but they agreed "to recommend to the full Board that subsidization as such be stopped as soon as possible and that campus sports on this campus be placed on a amateur basis." The official press release alluded to a gradual de-emphasis of subsidization. These orderly new arrangements would prove impossible to sustain.

In a July 10 letter to Gaines, Coach Wise recommended that the 1954 sched-ule be honored because of the difficulty of making changes at such a late date. He also observed that it would be impossible to do so "under the conditions as agreed upon by the members of the athletic committee of the Board of Trustees." Thirty-seven football players would be far less than "the usual fifty, a bare minimum in the past under normal circumstances." Furthermore, the announcement of moving to nonsubsidized football "has almost wrecked the chances of getting a large portion of the boys with athletic ability to enroll here." In short, "it would be suicide without the maximum number of boys and a little cooperation [i.e., subsidy]." He observed that the situation "of be-ing placed between the alumni and the faculty during a period of adjustment from the Gator Bowl team to complete amateurism, will be at the best, a very unpleasant one for the football coach." He asked to be relieved of his contract and followed up on July 14 with a formal letter of resignation, to be effective in September.[64] In addition to Wise, all football coaches (except one assistant) resigned rather than attempt a season with a depleted team. On July 15, Gaines wrote again to the trustees, informing them of the resignations, and called a special board meeting for July 23 in Washington, DC.

The trustees were now confronted with an even more serious situation. As Caskie explained, the board was requested to provide "enough athletic schol-arships (in addition to those to which we were already committed) to bring the total of such awards to fifty. In effect the executive committee was asked to rescind its decision of July 7 and to grant perhaps an additional seventeen scholarship awards to which the University would be committed for the next four years, or for so long as the recipients remained in school."[65] Faced with these new circumstances, the board decided to suspend intercollegiate football and cancel all scheduled games. Other sports activities and games, including intramural football, would continue, and the possibility of reestablishing intercollegiate football on an amateur basis competing against "like minded" schools would be explored. The university would issue no athletic scholarships beyond those already committed but would expand the overall intercollegiate and intramural sports program to encourage the widest possible student participation.

These decisions made the front pages of most Virginia newspapers on July 24 and initially elicited a negative reaction from sports columnists and some alumni. But editorials endorsing the decision appeared in many newspapers, including the *Richmond Times-Dispatch, Atlanta Constitution, Lynchburg News, Newport News Times-Herald,* and the *Roanoke World-News.* Critical articles written by sportswriters and letters to the editor from disgruntled alumni began to appear almost immediately. W. E. "Tex" Tilson of Lexington, W&L's football coach from 1933 to 1940 and president of the Alumni Association, took exception to the *Richmond Times-Dispatch* editorial support of the decision. "The only way so-called 'professional' athletics in colleges ever will end," he wrote, "will be through the abolition of all intercollegiate athletics." While not condoning the worst abuses of big-time football, Tilson, who had turned his 780-acre Broadview Farm outside Lexington into a popular summer "ranch" camp for boys, argued for the benefit of athletic scholarships to many young men and the value of intercollegiate football. "Speaking as a W&L alumnus and for myself only, I am ashamed and heartsick."[66]

President Gaines and the trustees were inundated with letters and telegrams. To respond to these and also alert other universities—especially those in the now canceled football schedule—about the decision, Gaines prepared a two-page form letter covering the basic elements. He pointed out that the football squad now had too few players to compete, and the board had ruled out new subsidization. Nor was this the first time the board had wrestled with the issue. "It has been apparent for some time," he noted, "that subsidized football is inconsistent with our academic purpose." Athletes were increasingly isolated in a program with different demands and expectations from those pertaining to other students. "Where there is this strain, something is apt to give." Intercollegiate football also placed "a severe strain on the University's financial resources." He revealed that the deficit at the end of 1952–53 had been $8,000 and about $25,000 at the end of the next year, with prospects for a greater deficit if things had continued as they were—even with scheduling several games a year with "teams entirely out of our class" and only two or three games in Lexington. But he promised to improve all sports on campus and to return to intercollegiate football on a nonsubsidized basis as soon as possible.[67]

On August 18, Gaines sent a memorandum to "My Fellow Presidents of the Late Football Schedule," a personal letter "not for publication." He thanked them for their indulgence and understanding of W&L's decision, and he reported that while his mail had been heavy, it was "overwhelmingly favorable." He also noted that "our Board had already decided that in one way or another subsidization must be discontinued. The sudden paucity of players—which could only be remedied with a significant investment—essentially determined the timing of the inevitable."[68]

Protests from alumni ranged from wanting to keep things as they were to wanting some middle ground in subsidization that would allow the university to continue competing against traditional rivals. Not surprisingly, the shift in just a few years from going to the Gator Bowl to dropping the football schedule for an entire season seemed abrupt and even inexplicable. But many favorable comments also came from alumni and others who opposed subsidized athletics and "big time" football. The university continued its efforts to address alumni concerns through articles in the *Alumni Magazine,* including a detailed piece from Caskie in the December 1954 issue. He outlined six major "underlying conditions" that prompted the board's decision: (1) efforts to recruit talented athletes had led to the admission of academically underqualified students, many of whom left under the Automatic Rule; (2) the recent Honor System violations pointed out the stresses on students, admitted as "calculated academic risks," who were expected to meet the substantial time demands of football; (3) football at W&L "had come to be a sport played only by those who were subsidized to do so"; (4) students could rarely even be spectators since, for financial reasons, only two or three games were played each year in Lexington; (5) financial aid had come to be more generous for athletes than for other students; and (6) accurate budgeting for athletics had become impossible, since the final cost was unknown until the end of the year, when the university was obligated to cover whatever deficit remained.[69] The emphasis in the university's communications shifted gradually from defending the decision and how it was made to pointing out the advantages of broader athletic participation, the continuation of intercollegiate football on an "amateur" basis, additional scholarships available to all students, and the many examples of the healthy relationship between the university and its alumni. It also became clear that the athletic scandal had accelerated—and made more compelling—decisions that would have had to be made soon in any case.

EVERY CRITICAL JUNCTURE has engendered reflections upon the true character and significance of Washington and Lee: the way things were, the way things are, and the way things should be. The decision on football in 1954 was one of those occasions, bringing forth, focusing, and concentrating ideas and concerns that had been brewing for some time. One concern often expressed, in different ways and with varying urgency, was essentially the question of whether the ideal W&L student was an aspiring scholar or a "well-rounded" gentleman. In one sense, these were merely images or types that shaped memories of alma mater, but they also represented different visions for the university's future.

Thirty-nine cosigners of a letter to the president of the Baltimore chapter of the Alumni Association opposed the board's action and raised questions about faculty motivations and decisions concerning financial aid and curriculum. The main point was whether the W&L faculty was "discriminating" against athletes and whether "certain professors are raising their standards beyond the capacity of the well-rounded student." If W&L was de-emphasizing athletics, would "it discourage well-rounded men from attempting to enter the school?" Why not raise tuition to permit the award of more athletic scholarships to "fine well-rounded boys" who could not otherwise afford to attend W&L? What about the future of the Generals Fund? And "What relationship does the Alumni have with the school in setting policies for the University to follow?" Much of the concern centered on the chapter's activities in helping to recruit high school athletes to W&L and how these would be affected by "these recent happenings and rumors."[70]

In his response, Gaines admitted that while many faculty members opposed subsidized athletics, they would not mistreat any individual student. He did not apologize for W&L's academic standards and observed that the percentage of students failing due to the Automatic Rule had varied little during his twenty-four years at the helm. He did confide that "all of the subsidized athletes who went out in the cheating episode" blamed their actions on "the system" that required so much work (for games and practice) beyond that expected of regular students, and he had long been concerned about this difference and could offer some sympathy. As to finances, Gaines pointed out that there had never been an official connection between the university and the Generals' Fund, "which is entirely alumni sponsored and alumni-controlled." The university did provide $62,000 for all sports, yet it still had to deal with an "unbudgeted and unexpected" deficit of around $25,000 for the past year. W&L was actively seeking to raise money for scholarships available to all students, but "there is a generally accepted idea among students, certainly of the Southern Conference, that football . . . is a paid job," and players were not willing to put in the extra time and energy unless they received "compensation." Gaines also noted a growing concern—even in the mid-1950s—of those falling behind in what would later be termed the athletic "arms race." W&L hoped to resume football but did not expect that the team would have "financial success." He observed, quite presciently, that with "television entering prominently into public entertainment, I expect that no football teams, except the most widely publicized 'power-houses,' will have much financial success. We have not had such success with our limited program of subsidization."[71]

The Alumni Association received many communications as part of its inquiry into the football situation. US Army captain Paul J. B. Murphy Jr., '49, who had been president of the Interfraternity Council (and would be a major leader of W&L's Fraternity Renaissance Program in the 1980s), reported that in his undergraduate years "I first became aware of the possibility of W & L changing her personality" and basic principles. Along with student body president Fred Vinson and fellow student Addison Lanier, he had met with Dean Leyburn "to discuss our fears." While Leyburn denied any intention to "make basic changes at W & L," Murphy recalled, "politically speaking, there is within the Faculty a pro-Leyburn group and anti-Leyburn group plus the usual coalitions among the various departments." A "fine balance between the 'art of living' and the 'art of learning' has been upset with a continuous shifting of emphasis to the 'art of learning.' 'Good ole boys' have been supplanted with arty intellectuals among the student body. Football is gone." This was, in his view, the result of a "studied effort on the part of Dean Leyburn to change the personality of Washington and Lee." These were not new concerns: "I have spent many hours at alumni gatherings warning about this situation and I have not been alone." But nothing drew the attention of "older alumni" to the situation more than the football decision. For Murphy, W&L was "more than an institution of learning: it is (or was) a way of life." The mission of W&L was "that of turning out good solid citizens, men who would go back to their respective communities, serve on the town council, the PTA, etc. and make up the honest hard working men who direct the grass roots of the nation. It didn't seem important to turn out our future senators, scientists, governors, musicians, and presidents of corporations (although we certainly have our share); we weren't interested in big names, we wanted to give a good education, teaching the gracious way of life, and stoutly imbue with integrity and love of country the average boy who comes to Lexington." Such men were of far more value to society than intellectuals "divorced from reality."[72]

Murphy's concerns were neither typical nor a paean to mediocrity, but they did eloquently express a widespread belief that W&L primarily fashioned men of character and responsibility, who manifested "graceful living," patriotism, and other solid virtues. The term most commonly used was "well-rounded," a description often applied to the "W&L gentleman" ideal. Men of this sort were not "artsy" or closeted intellectuals. These classifications were unfortunate stereotypes, but they did reflect different perceptions of the university, and they help explain why the alumni backlash against the elimination of subsidized football quickly cast primary blame on the university's emphasis on scholarship and focused on James Leyburn and his efforts to raise W&L's academic profile.

Many other early protests also implied that something untoward was happening in Lexington, especially in the dean's office. One letter in the *Richmond Times-Dispatch* alleged that higher admission requirements had reduced opportunities for the "rounded-out" student. "In other words, your Phi Beta Kappa might be a wonderful college professor, but check over the old list and see which of your alumni are going places and doing things in the business world." The writer threatened to end future gifts to the university "until there is a change made in the policies of the dean's office and the university." Another letter observed, "Since 1948 there has been a growing effort among certain members of the faculty to change Washington and Lee. They want to make something else out of it."[73] Such missives reflected a degree of anti-intellectualism, particularly in the context of mid-1950s America, when elected officials and others often vigorously associated intellectuals and creative artists with elitist progressives (or worse), especially when they were pitted against that most all-American of pursuits—football.

Randolph W. Rouse, '39, president of the Generals' Fund (which still actively engaged in raising alumni support for athletic scholarships) was among the most vocal critics of the football decision. He pointed directly at Leyburn and "pseudo-intellectuals" among the faculty and accused them of campaigning to "change the complexion" of the school "in a direction that precludes a healthy intercollegiate sports program."[74] Leyburn, taken aback by these allegations, shared his distress with Twombly, recently appointed director of athletics, who was at the time vacationing in Maine. "All of us here," Leyburn wrote, "are extremely anxious to resume intercollegiate football in the fall of 1955," though on an unsubsidized basis. He pledged his assistance in bringing all coaches onto the physical education faculty and even proposed that "all of our freshmen and sophomores be required, as a part of their work in physical education, to go out for *one* varsity sport. They would have ten to choose among." Twombly responded that he had been thinking along the same lines. "We have an opportunity now," he wrote, "to manage our own house and reaffirm our amateur ideals" and "to make athletics a part of a wholesome experience for every student at W & L."[75] Appearing before a meeting of the Richmond alumni chapter, Leyburn said he was "amazed" at being so prominently mentioned in connection with the athletic decision. He affirmed his opposition to subsidization but thought football should actually have greater student participation in the future. Answering a question from the floor, he claimed that "finances were a very minor part" of the decision and that the university had been heading toward ending subsidization for some time.[76]

Ollinger Crenshaw, unhappy with many of Leyburn's academic proposals, was pleased by the trustee's decision to end subsidization and cancel the football season. As the former W&L tennis coach explained to a former student, "If by 'Leyburnism,' Mr. Rouse means opposition to subsidized athletics, and if by that term he means an increased emphasis on intellectual stimulation, real scholarship here, and on 'the academic,' then I must admit to the impeachment of being a 'Leyburnite.' I go along with Dean Leyburn in what has been done in adding courses in art and music to the curriculum." He was relieved that "the board came around at long last, and at the end of a long string of compelling circumstances, to the position which I and a number of other faculty members have held for years—viz., that intercollegiate athletics should be played by bona fide students and unsubsidized students who play the games for their own sake." As for the admission of average students, "the young men sitting before me in my classes" suggest that new academic standards have made little difference; in fact, some of the Leyburn-inspired "amorphous" interdisciplinary courses might actually be, in Crenshaw's view at least, less academically demanding.[77]

The Jacksonville alumni chapter passed and widely distributed a resolution questioning "the soundness of the character of learning now afforded at the University which precludes the teaching of a healthy competitive spirit which can only be obtained adequately through participation . . . in intercollegiate athletics" and supporting the awarding of athletic scholarships.[78] In a letter to Leyburn, the chapter president expressed his admiration for efforts to enhance academic life at W&L but remarked that such efforts should not be at the expense of "the further development of character," especially "competitive spirit, fair play, and leadership ability." Scholarships should be awarded to students for athletic as well as "mental" ability, and W&L should continue to strive to make "superior men out of average men." Leyburn replied that he very much favored character development and that football would continue—along with all the other intercollegiate sports at W&L—to engage the competitive spirit on an amateur basis. "I am an ardent football fan," he exclaimed. "Many alumni have been persuaded that higher academic standards caused the Board to make its decision; this is simply not the case." In fact, "everyone of us in the Washington and Lee community believes in intercollegiate athletics, in the value of competitive sports, and in the encouragement of the average man."[79]

A great many alumni supported the board's decision. The Birmingham chapter, for example, held a special meeting on December 1, 1954, and decided to "approve and commend the action of the Board of Trustees whereby Washington and Lee will continue to play football on a non-subsidized basis."[80] Some alumni had long been opposed to subsidized athletics, others were persuaded by pragmatic considerations of cost and capacity, and some discerned a direct threat to the university's integrity and its core values. Edgar F. Shannon Jr., '39, who grew up in Lexington (his father was a professor of English) and would later become president of the University of Virginia and a member of the W&L Board of Trustees, wrote in the *Richmond Times-Dispatch* that subsidized football "inculcates cynicism in both players and student body at a time when their ideals should be encouraged and solidified." The athletes dismissed from the university were warped in their moral judgment "by a regime that puts football before everything else and demands that they stay eligible in order to retain their room and board." During his college years, Shannon observed, "the honor system was Washington and Lee's most cherished tradition." But subsidization "has brought the most vicious, organized and extensive assault on the honor system that Washington and Lee has ever known." In his view, many of the alumni who had written harsh letters of protest against the football decision—and pledged not to give money or send their sons to the university—had attended W&L at a time before subsidized football had become so corrosive. And he concluded pointedly, "Washington and Lee can well do without the sons of alumni who put subsidized football before honor."[81]

The cries of protest were partly due to the suddenness of the board's action. The university recognized the wisdom of ending subsidization but would obviously have preferred a more gradual process to minimize hard feelings. On the other hand, any perceived threat to the Honor System would justify a strong university response and elicit the support of most alumni. The circumstances provided perhaps the best opportunity for the administration and the board to take an action they knew would be controversial: the scandal mitigated the chief barrier to such changes—deeply embedded alumni support for football. The vigorous exchange of views—in the newspapers, among alumni, and with the board and administration—eventually settled down, and the university was able to quash rumors that intercollegiate football was the victim of an emphasis on academic excellence. Some alumni would continue, for years, to lament W&L's absence from major southern football playing fields, but most either favored the decision or rallied around the university in spite of it.

In the early stages of the controversy, the alumni board of trustees came under unusual pressure, and its members met on several occasions with university trustees, beginning with a luncheon in Washington on October 16, 1954. Many were upset that the alumni leadership had not been alerted or consulted about the football decision. After its "inquiry" the alumni board reported to all W&L alumni that decisions had been made and new arrangements put in place, for reasons enumerated in the *Alumni Magazine,* and encouraged continued support for the university, regardless of individual opinions concerning athletic policy. "The Alumni Board," they wrote, "has the same unlimited faith in this administration, the faculty, and the University Board of Trustees as it has in present-day students and in the alumni body."[82] These sentiments did not, however, erase an underlying concern among many that the university was changing.

THE PATH TO RECOVERY was confusing. Some alumni remained angry, rumors persisted, and new efforts were made to find a middle way. Getting a football team back on the field in 1955 to demonstrate that the sport would continue, albeit without athletic scholarships, was an early necessity. Officially, the university had no team in 1954, but the forty-five or so football players still remaining (mostly freshmen and sophomores, with a few scholarship athletes) competed in four games against junior-varsity college teams and the Hargrave Military Academy. Boyd Williams, a local insurance man and former assistant coach at VMI and Richmond, stepped in as interim coach to hold things together.[83] One of his players, Uncas McThenia (later on the law school faculty) considers Williams "the unsung hero of the football rebirth." In February 1955, Bill Chipley, a 1949 alumnus and former Clemson and W&L football player who had approached Gaines to offer his services, was named the new head football coach.

Gaines communicated with leaders of other colleges that had ceased subsidization or were moving in that direction. He met with the presidents of Davidson and Furman in Charlotte in November 1954 and had favorable contacts with others, including President Walter A. Groves of Centre College in Kentucky. Edward McCrady, the vice-chancellor of Sewanee, which had now pulled out of the Southeastern Conference, wrote, "Nothing pleases me more than the prospect of renewing our athletic rivalry with Washington and Lee."[84] A seven-game schedule was established for 1955, to be played between October 8 and November 19, with three games in Lexington. The opponents were Centre College, Davidson, Southwestern at Memphis, Washington University of St. Louis, Hampden-Sydney, Sewanee, and West Virginia Tech.

W&L football was back, but without great success on the field. The Generals lost every game in 1955 by a total score of 198 to 26, managing only four touchdowns and, in one contest, only three total yards. The 1956 schedule of eight games against the same opponents, with the addition of Wabash College in Indiana, had much the same result: W&L defeated Sewanee but finished the season 1–7. Of course, this record did nothing to allay the concerns of alumni who thought ending athletic scholarships was a bad idea.

The Departments of Intercollegiate Athletics and Physical Education were combined in a new Department of Athletics, Physical Education, and Recreation under Cy Twombly's direction, and all its members were given faculty rank and status. Twombly was instructed to carry out an "integrated and co-ordinated" program emphasizing student participation. In the 1955–56 *President's Report*, containing the first separate "Report of Director of Athletics and Physical Education," Twombly noted that 345 different students had participated in thirteen varsity and five junior-varsity intercollegiate sports that year, as well as 842 in intramurals, and that his new combined department was dedicated to making athletics "a part of the educational experience of all students."[85]

The University Committee on Intercollegiate Athletics reported in the spring of 1955 that the trustees' resolutions were being faithfully implemented. The categories of "major" and "minor" sports were eliminated, and all were now offered on the same basis, including funding for travel and meals, the services of a trainer, and access to the equipment room. All basketball games were played in Doremus Gymnasium. Over a hundred different students (including some from the law school) had participated in varsity and junior varsity sports in the fall and winter, and 229 in the spring, thereby justifying a request for an additional playing field. A "maximum" budget was submitted for 1955–56, with $24,669 in net costs. Football remained the most expensive budget item but generated far less income than previously. Estimated revenue from the student activity fee (and the "breakage fund") still stood at $18,000. According to the committee, "the next school year is a 'make or break' as far as the student body attitude toward football is concerned." Coach Chipley was given permission to begin varsity football practice on September 7, attracting about fifty boys, in order to prepare for facing opponents with "more experienced squads."[86]

After winning only one game in two seasons and calling to recruit better players and weaken the schedule, Chipley's contract was not renewed for the 1957 season. Lee M. McLaughlin, coach and athletic director at Episcopal High School in Alexandria and a graduate of the University of Virginia, agreed to take the reins at W&L. Over eleven seasons, he would turn the football program around under the new athletic policies and finally put to rest—except for a few remaining die-hards—the notion that "big-time" football should return to General Lee's college. Another new addition was Eugene F. "Gene" Corrigan, who played lacrosse at Duke and coached lacrosse and soccer at W&L for three seasons, beginning in 1956. He moved on to become athletic director at the University of Virginia and then Notre Dame (and very briefly at W&L in 1969), and was appointed commissioner of the ACC.

In June 1958, W&L withdrew from the Southern Conference, of which it had been a founding member thirty-one years before. Though the university still benefitted from the competition and tournaments organized by the conference in golf, tennis, wrestling, and swimming, the new conference policy that prohibited freshman from varsity football was a big disadvantage. While the conference had at one time allowed freshmen to play on varsity squads as a means of allowing institutions like W&L to deploy an adequate number of players, the recent change in this policy "more than offsets the advantages of Conference membership."[87] Washington and Lee elected to compete henceforth at the small-college level in all sports except lacrosse.

Some continued to yearn for the football days of yore. One hundred and twenty students signed a petition calling for a reexamination of the university's policy on nonsubsidization. This prompted the student government executive committee, in January 1956, to appoint a seven-member "fact-finding board" (consisting of the presidents of the four undergraduate classes and three law-school classes) led by senior law-school class president Jack Osborne, a former varsity basketball player. Beginning its work in February, the group met with Gaines and Twombly, examined athletic financial statements, and devised a two-page questionnaire for all W&L students and those faculty members who wished to respond. The questionnaire contained the usual preferences for sub-sidized or nonsubsidized athletics and varying levels of competition for football. It also contained two questions specifically related to basketball.[88]

President Gaines and Deans Frank Gilliam and Leon Sensabaugh spoke at an open forum in Lee Chapel held by the Student Executive Committee on November 28, 1956, along with an alumnus and two students. The vice president of the student body announced the results of the student poll. All but about 150 students responded to the survey. Of the responses, 88 percent favored "some form of subsidization for football." In a joint memorandum in December to President Gaines, the president of the student body and the president of the IFC reported on the student poll responses, as well as opinions and proposals from the fraternities and from alumni chapters that had been polled by "Tex" Tilson, who was still drumming up support for a return to sub-sidized football.[89] Fourteen of the seventeen fraternities agreed to offer board or its equivalent to one athlete per year to help offset the university's cost. Of twenty-four alumni chapters, the overwhelming majority supported the student proposal that aid be offered to a "limited number of students that show athletic ability," not to exceed fifty, and without any "special considerations" in admission. The memorandum concluded that while the decision to abolish athletic scholarships "was proper and necessary," it had led over the subsequent period of three years to "a general weakening in school spirit as well as a loss of enthusiasm in the intercollegiate athletic program of the University." Compet-ing with W&L's "natural rivals on a more equal basis in all sports and raising to a higher level the contributions of athletics, Washington and Lee will afford its students a more well-rounded program." It was almost as if the 1954 crisis had never happened.

Individual alumni and alumni chapters—traditionally involved in helping to recruit local students to W&L—continued to seek ways to provide financial support for talented athletes. Even Professor William Hinton, who chaired the university athletic committee, wrote Gaines in April 1957, suggesting that the university provide more guidance in this regard, as well as greater flexibility in the degree to which athletic ability could be considered. Hinton reiterated the belief that W&L could not "field representative athletic teams with the boys who merely come to us" (except perhaps in swimming, golf, tennis, and "with the cooperation of the Baltimore alumni, lacrosse"). He suggested "an admissions policy which is sensitive to qualities and abilities over and above academic aptitude and which makes use of the personnel of the athletic staff in recruiting activities," such as reportedly occurred in the Ivy League schools. Hinton noted that he was writing "as an alumnus and faculty member," rather than necessarily reflecting the views of his committee, and insisted that he was not seeking to change the policy on subsidization but wanted to help the university deal more realistically with "the development of a satisfactory athletic program." Commenting to Gaines a few days later on Hinton's memorandum, Gilliam observed that the admissions committee was "going just as far as we possibly can" in considering extracurricular accomplishments of all types. "We have definitely recognized athletic prowess to the extent that there have been a fair number of votes in the Committee against such awards approved by the majority of the Committee." Setting up a separate alumni fund to be "used exclusively for boys of athletic ability," even if they were otherwise fully qualified for admission, "would thereby open the door to a return to the old policy that we followed under the Generals' Fund."[90]

In January 1958, trustee J. Morrison Hutcheson, who had served on the board since 1935, responded to an alumnus who had written a number of board members in support of awarding a "limited number of scholarships" for athletes so that W&L could compete against its "natural rivals." Hutcheson noted, "our oldest rivals are Virginia and V.P.I.," which "are now about four times our size, can and do take and keep almost any kind of student, and their financial outlay for athletic scholarships is much larger than we could ever attain." Alumni were welcome to send "as many athletes as they desire to W&L," but the university was unwilling to devote funds "to boys whose principle qualification is athletic ability." He reiterated the basis of the board's position: that athletics is "not a job to be compensated" and that "an institution dedicated to education is not obligated to furnish a public spectacle and the devotion of its funds for that purpose is wrong."[91]

Gaines had long enjoyed a friendship and amicable correspondence with Lewis F. Powell Jr. of Richmond, who agreed with the concerns expressed by other alumni who hated to see their alma mater at a competitive disadvantage. While he supported the move away from "professionalized" football, Powell regretted "the decision thereafter made to resume strictly amateur football for the simple reason that there are virtually no truly amateur football teams among comparable universities and colleges. Indeed, judging from our disastrous recent experience [on the gridiron], it seems evident that few of the small, relatively unknown colleges have amateur teams." He could not "recall a single Washington and Lee alumnus or student who has expressed approval of the current policy in my presence," and he believed that continuing the policy "will inevitably result in the deterioration of the quality of the student body (in terms of well-rounded, typical American boys), and will accelerate the obvious deterioration in the interest and devotion of many alumni." He saw "nothing whatever to be gained from continuing the present policy." Why not simply abandon football entirely "without further temporizing?" Basketball would possibly provide a successful and popular alternative, but the current policy "is forcing basketball . . . to the same apologetic state as football." While education should always be paramount, "a well-rounded college experience should embrace a variety of activities," including "wholesome and fiercely competitive intercollegiate athletics."[92]

Gaines responded at length, disagreeing that opposition to the university's policy was universal. He had received about a thousand letters, almost all from alumni, about 80 percent supporting the decision. He wanted Powell to know that a scholarship athlete nowadays faced great demands and pressures, becoming in many institutions "the hired man of the coach who is trying to make a famous record so that he may get a better job." Increasingly, universities had to provide a separate educational experience for subsidized athletes. He also argued that subsidizing even one student would "invite pressure unlimited." While Powell was thinking of "only one sport and one small venture . . . I can assure you that the majority of our alumni who want subsidized athletics have no such modest ambition." The Southeastern Conference had decided to allow 140 athletic scholarships for football alone, and a football coach had recently been appointed at Texas A&M University for an annual salary of $60,000. "These items are straws in the swiftly blowing winds of athletic subsidy."[93]

Powell was not fully convinced. He responded that while he admired Gaines's effective defense of the university's position, he continued to believe that it was "unwholesome and incompatible with the American competitive system, for young men to participate in games (or any other competitive activity) without desiring and expecting to win." Such competition was "an essential function of education," going far beyond the athletic field. The "most meaningful competition in the world today," Powell wrote, "is between Communism as an ideology and the Christian-Democratic philosophy." So W&L "should not sponsor any sport . . . on a basis which accepts the status of 'door mat' for all opponents. This 'de-emphasis' of winning and of fierce competition is a very demoralizing thing, and will not train leaders." In a handwritten note beneath his signature, he assured Gaines, "I am still very proud of W&L—and always will be."[94] For Powell and many other alumni, football was not only a sport but a reflection of life, and winning was extremely important.

In January 1958, a committee of the Washington alumni appeared before the board to argue for a resumption of athletic subsidies, and at the same time Gaines presented the student petition in support of such a move. The board declined to change its position. Gaines was still sufficiently concerned that he sent a "confidential and urgent" memorandum to the trustees, alerting them to the efforts of "a small group in Washington," which was seeking alumni support for a pledge to "make no contribution of any kind to this University until we have subsidized athletics." And "the Lexington agitators" were encouraging students to "write letters of discontent to their parents" to generate further pressure. While the financial effect of such efforts would probably be small, the "total distortion of the facts . . . might be damaging." He sought trustee concurrence for an article in the *Alumni Magazine* from the president and the rector, providing, yet again, the major reasons for current university policy.[95] Seven trustees responded, and all supported the issuance of such a statement. Gaines consulted with Sensabaugh and Gilliam. No one was apparently pleased with his first attempt, which he submitted to Caskie for review and suggestions on February 12.

The final version of the statement appeared in the February issue of the magazine and was mailed as a letter to the parents of all W&L students. In less than two pages, it presented the essential elements of the university's argument, honed in statement after statement and letter after letter over the past several years. It was intended to put matters to rest—not because of financial necessity—but to support academic integrity and the historical legacy of the university. Caskie and Gaines based W&L's athletic policy squarely on "principle" and lamented that, in the modern athletic environment, students "on athletic scholarships are compelled to make sports their primary interest," leading to "many academic tragedies, of which our campus has had its share." Subsidized athletes had to be provided "with an entirely different type of educational training, with lowered admission requirements, easier modes of instruction, evasion of the strong disciplines." At the same time, this approach discouraged nonsubsidized students from participating in sports, and an initial commitment immediately after World War II to twenty athletic grants-in-aid had led only a few years later to a request for eighty: "Subsidization is, in the phrase of the poet, 'ever climbing up the ever climbing wave.'" Alumni who had benefitted from athletic scholarships must realize, they wrote, that times had changed; the demands were much greater and dictated by a raging arms race to stay competitive and generate revenue. W&L was committed to a broad-based sports program and boasted thirteen intercollegiate sports and higher student participation than ever before. Schedules were being finalized with schools "of comparable amateurism." The university "welcomes the good athlete who can maintain his academic standing and who can graduate." Alumni were encouraged to identify such students and direct them to W&L, where they would be considered for regular scholarships. "No boy, however, will be compensated for athletic performance and no boy will be compelled to play a sport." The statement concluded with grandiloquent phrases obviously fashioned by Gaines—a plea to focus on larger matters related to "human destiny" and "expanding the power inherent in knowledge," rather than subordinate these to "to exciting athletic rivalries." Conscious of its history and purpose, "this institution elects steadfastly to put its precious privilege of education first and dominant always."[96]

Calling upon all his skills, Gaines maneuvered through these rough waters with increasing certainty and seriousness. He and other university officials faced pointed questions in meetings with alumni and even from students on campus. At the Founder's Day assembly in January 1958, Gaines announced that the trustees had decided not to award athletic scholarships in basketball (Dom Flora's highly successful program) either. As Sid Coulling recalls, there "had been rumors on campus—all of us heard them—that there would be some kind of noisy protest by the students at this required assembly." Gaines, "who had a genius for sensing an audience, skirted around it until the very end when he announced the Board's decision, and before there was any chance for there to be a reaction, he said, 'Now let us stand in silent prayer.' Everybody stood. You can't boo the Almighty."[97]

As students who had known the glory days of W&L football and basketball graduated, and as these and other sports competed routinely against a new array of opponents, the new athletic arrangements were accepted and even applauded—despite the persisting hopes from some alumni that after Gaines's retirement in 1959 a new president might bring back subsidized football. Notably, however, alumni contributions to W&L had never wavered throughout the controversy and had even increased. Though most teams had mixed success on the field, Twombly's swimmers were undefeated in their nine matches in 1959–60, and the football team under Lee McLaughlin went 8–0–1 in 1960, were undefeated in 1961, and were declared small-college national champions by the Washington, DC, Touchdown Club.

The lead article in the November 6, 1961, issue of *Sports Illustrated* featured W&L's football success, highlighted the university's decision to end athletic scholarships, and deemed it a national model. In "A Sport for Gentlemen," Walter Bingham reviewed the painful experience of dropping subsidized football but claimed that W&L had enjoyed more success than other institutions—like the University of Chicago and Johns Hopkins—that had done the same. In an essay illustrated by photos of the Colonnade and Wilson Field, Bingham remarked on the deep southern traditions that enveloped the campus, including the customs of conventional dress and gentlemanly behavior. McLaughlin—"a solidly built man in his late 30s with a grin as wide as his shoulders"—was celebrated as a fine teacher, perfectly comfortable in the new athletic environment, who recruited from prep schools and the W&L student body. An outstanding center, Jerry Hyatt, had never played football before, and the standout for the 1960 and 1961 squads was Terry Fohs, a 145-pound linebacker. The article was a panegyric to a successful small-university athletic program that had everything in perspective, explicitly contrasted with the growing number of athletic scandals that would continue to plague larger schools committed to "big-time" sports.[98] Needless to say, the seven copies of the magazine on sale at Doc's disappeared quickly.

As much as anything else, the *Sports Illustrated* essay laid to rest any serious pressures for W&L to return to the glory days of the Gator Bowl. Other incentives to stay on the new path, of course, were success, the passage of time, and perhaps the growing realization of the genuine extravagance and corruption of "big-time" intercollegiate football. Students with athletic skill now went out for the team, and game attendance rose, whatever the opponent. In 1962, W&L joined with Centre College, Southwestern, and Sewanee to found the College Athletic Conference (joined later that year by Washington University in St. Louis), with strict provisions against any athletic scholarships. "The success of the [athletic] program," the university asserted, "is judged not by the number of victories in a particular sport, nor the won-lost record of all sports in a given year. Success is measured by the broad application of all phases of the athletic program to the physical development and improvement of the students themselves."[99] The football Generals went 8–1 that season and won the first conference title.

Financially, Washington and Lee continued to support athletics without the revenue generated from football gate receipts. While individual athletes were not subsidized, athletics certainly was, without stinting on costs for equipment and travel. The funds supported a broad-based athletic program with significant student participation, and members of the athletic department were treated the same as other university faculty and staff. W&L's total expenses were substantially lower than those of its erstwhile gridiron opponents that had kept up with the athletics arms race. In 1972, W&L's total athletic budget of $370,000 (for intercollegiate sports, physical education, and intramurals) was less than Virginia Tech spent on football coaches' salaries and players' scholarships. W&L allocated $6,600 for recruiting athletes in all sports, whereas Virginia Tech expended $65,000 on football recruiting alone.[100] Academically, outstanding athletes who met the entrance requirements could receive recognition for their "special skills" from the admissions committee, but their entrance examination test scores and their overall grade point averages were, as reported by admissions director James D. Farrar in 1972, very similar to those of all W&L students. Financial aid was granted solely on academic achievement or need, and football and other sports were not permitted to interfere with academic demands, even in programs like pre-med that required many extra laboratory sessions per week. The traditional image of the college football hero—with monogrammed sweater and special privileges—no longer held sway on campus and would, in fact, receive "a certain amount of jeering," according to journalism professor Paxton Davis.[101]

Football fortunes were less favorable under coaches Buck Leslie from 1968 to 1972 (16–28–1) and Bill McHenry from 1973 to 1977 (12–36–2), but this was mostly taken in stride. New excitement arose for lacrosse, which W&L moved to the new NCAA University Division in 1972 (which became Division I the following year), especially the teams under Dick Szlasa from 1968 to 1972 (33–23) and Jack Emmer from 1973 to 1983 (108–47), who took the Generals to seven NCAA tournaments. Eventually, the demands of the athletic "arms race" caught up with lacrosse, too. By the mid-1980s, without benefit of athletic scholarships, W&L could no longer compete with the likes of Johns Hopkins, Virginia, Maryland, and North Carolina. After the 1986 season, the university moved from NCAA Division I to Division III, where it has competed very successfully.

Athletics at Washington and Lee continued to attract skilled athletes and wide participation across many sports, and the program produced many academic All-Americans, conference championships, and a national championship in tennis. The first five honorees inducted by the Athletic Hall of Fame, established in 1987 by the Alumni Association, included Walt Michaels, Bob Spessard, and Cy Young. By 1989, women student athletes began to enter the university's record books.[102] By all accounts, sports had assumed a role in university life—finding the balance with academics and other extracurricular activities that James Leyburn, Frank Gilliam, and many trustees and alumni had advocated, and that Frank Gaines had guided, often painfully and fitfully, into place. Given the enormous pressures of money and publicity that soon came to dominate, indeed overwhelm, college sports and to some degree all of American higher education, W&L's abandonment of "big-time" sports may have been inevitable, but it was not fated to be successful. Much discussion and many decisions defined the response to a change initiated by the crisis that provided an opportunity for the institution to ponder and reassert its core values and character. As the twenty-nine-year Gaines presidency ended, the university was beginning to settle rather comfortably into the new, post-1954 athletic era, as confirmed by the remarks of the new president, Fred C. Cole, in his 1960 inaugural address: "When athletics become apart from—rather than a part of—a college's educational program, then the threat of loss of integrity is very real indeed." Washington and Lee still had collegiate athletics, and it also had an honorable and sustainable future.

CHAPTER FIVE

REPOSITIONING FOR
NEW GENERATIONS

UPON HIS RETIREMENT, Francis Pendleton Gaines was feted by alumni chapters praising the number of degrees he had awarded to students, the fourteen honorary degrees he had received, the money he had raised, and the significant increases in institutional assets and endowment he had gained for Washington and Lee over his twenty-nine years at the helm. He was lauded by editorial writers throughout the Commonwealth and beyond, many noting the other university presidencies and political offices he had turned down or chosen not to pursue. He and Sadie decided to remain in Lexington, retiring to Penrobin and a small house in town during the winters.[1]

With Gaines stepping down, Washington and Lee had to embark on a task it had not undertaken in three decades—searching for a new president. This effort provided another opportunity to take stock and look ahead, ponder new challenges, and adjust to changing circumstances, and the university proceeded very cautiously. The board appointed six of its members to a presidential search committee chaired by Christopher T. Chenery. At its first meeting, on October 30, 1958, at the Mayflower Hotel in Washington, the committee selected a three-person advisory committee—a faculty member, an alumnus, and a "friend" of the university—and also asked the faculty to appoint five of their number to a serve as consultants.

The usual first step in an academic search is to assess institutional needs and determine the sort of person best suited to address those needs. At the search committee's second meeting, in Lexington on November 21, the first item of business was a discussion of the qualifications of a new president. This exercise was typically pro forma, to provide all the constituencies with a voice in the process. But to an unusual and surprising degree, this part of this search process was structured—indeed dominated—by a letter written three decades earlier by John W. Davis in connection with the search that resulted in Gaines's appointment. By adhering to Davis's ideas, the search committee signaled that it did not believe the circumstances in higher education had changed much since 1930 or that they should pursue new directions.

In his December 1928 letter, Davis had affirmed a traditional notion of the university and offered sensible, rather modest advice concerning a new president. He had supported a continued emphasis on the liberal arts and the humanities, with a curriculum that was "intensive rather than extensive," and advised that W&L should strive to be the "leading college of the South," while remaining a size that would maintain close contact between students and faculty. As for a new president, Davis had expressed a preference for someone "in early middle life with his future before rather than behind him," someone with "educational experience" but with "administrative ability rather than deep scholarship." The president should have a "pleasing personality" and be able to represent the university in public and effectively in fund-raising. In Davis's view, the president "should be a southern man or a man of southern affiliations," all other things being equal. "I hope I have no prejudice against the clergy," he wrote, "but it is not in their ranks that I would make my first search." Even so, the president "should have some definite religious affiliation," with the denomination less significant. "In short," he concluded, "my ideal is an upstanding, robust, courageous man, with no frills, fads or fancies on the one hand or traditional inhibitions on the other," and "able to inspire students and make an impact in the broader educational community."[2]

The search committee organized its discussions according to the points laid out in Davis's letter, with a keen awareness of the personality and qualifications of Frank Gaines. The committee generally concurred about the age and qualifications of the next president. While not essential that the successful candidate be born in the South, Rector James Caskie thought that he "should have an appreciation of the southern viewpoint." He put this more strongly in a letter to Huston St. Clair, noting that Davis's last legal case had been waged against racial desegregation. John Thomas preferred the appointment of "an active Christian," since Christianity "was the principal bulwark against communism." The committee also gave a nod to potential candidates among the faculty and provided for a "special committee" to bring suitable names forward for consideration.[3]

A faculty subcommittee took the opportunity to comment on the character and needs of the institution, drafting a three-page statement entitled "The Future of Washington and Lee." This document reiterated long-standing faculty concerns but called for no significant changes. The current organization and emphasis of the university should be retained, from the "cultural" bent of the curriculum to the more practical concerns of the Schools of Commerce and Law. New physical facilities were required, but "the greatest need is for additional competent instructors to give Washington and Lee the reputation we covet, costly though they would be." New course offerings and facilities in the sciences were necessary to "keep abreast of changing conditions," but additions to the curriculum should be authorized cautiously. Perhaps the most important step, the faculty group suggested, would be to raise the "caliber of the whole student body," currently derived from "the lower ranks of Eastern preparatory schools" and composed of too many young men who "have been (or are now) monotonously posted each session as below 'C'—not making progress toward graduation. Unless this situation is remedied, it appears futile to talk about real intellectual development at Washington and Lee." A new president would ideally share these viewpoints and have previous experience in higher education ("candidates from the business world should be carefully examined") but otherwise have the qualities set forth by John W. Davis.[4] An apparent consensus among the major constituencies was that while Washington and Lee University, on the cusp of the 1960s, could benefit from better students and more resources, it was essentially in good shape and on the correct course.

At its meeting on January 17, 1959—with Frank Gaines attending by invitation—the committee reviewed the fifty candidates suggested, selecting fifteen for serious consideration.[5] One name was Fred C. Cole, the executive vice president of Tulane University, who was nominated by several individuals, including Ann Pannell of Sweet Briar College, who called him "the ablest man in Southern education." Judge John Minor Wisdom of the US Fifth Judicial Circuit in New Orleans, who had joined the W&L Board in 1957, reported that friends at Tulane "tell me that for several years Fred has virtually run the university." He noted especially Cole's administrative abilities and access to the foundations, and described him as "personable, popular, and [someone who] would unquestionably fit in at Washington and Lee."

Ollinger Crenshaw had recently seen Gaines and "was again shocked by his appearance. How he will get through the current session I don't know. And his successor will have thorny problems, football (the students are bitter and virtually unanimously opposed to the board's policy of unsubsidized football), student conduct, finances, etc." Like others, perhaps, Crenshaw was also worried about efforts to extend the "existing dynasty" since Gaines's sons were both in college administration and his brother-in-law was president of Hampden-Sydney.[6] Crenshaw knew Cole personally and wrote to Joseph Lanier on the search committee, vouching for his fellow historian and recounting their associations through the Southern Historical Association and other organizations.[7]

The search was narrowed to three candidates and, on June 3, unanimously settled on Fred Cole, who was invited to meet with the committee as soon as possible at the Mayflower Hotel in Washington. The meeting was held at 4:30 the next afternoon, lasted for two hours, and ended with a decision in executive session to offer Cole the job. After consulting with his wife, Cole accepted the appointment as the seventeenth president of Washington and Lee University.[8]

Born in Franklin, Texas, Fred Carrington Cole studied at Louisiana State University as an undergraduate and earned a PhD in US history there in 1941. After Navy service during the war, he worked as a university teacher and administrator. Though he published articles dealing with agricultural history and the history of the New South, he demonstrated an early penchant for editorial work and university administration. He joined the faculty first at LSU and then at Tulane in 1946, becoming dean of the College of Arts and Sciences in 1947 and vice president of Academic Affairs in 1953. He served as editorial assistant and later managing editor of the *Journal of Southern History*, history editor of the LSU Press, and associate editor of the *Mississippi Valley Historical Review* (now the *Journal of American History*). He also had a long-standing interest in international affairs and education, served as chair of the foreign affairs committee of the Southern Regional Education Board, and wrote *The Teaching of International Relations in Institutions of Higher Education in the South* for the American Council on Education. Of particular interest to the W&L search committee was his work on the planning and administrative staff of the Ford Foundation in 1954 and 1955, helping to formulate plans for grants to private colleges and the establishment of the National Merit Scholarship Corporation and the National Council on Library Resources.

Cole had been involved in virtually every aspect of academic administration at Tulane, including two involving controversy. While Dean of Arts and Sciences, and in response to the heated anti-communist political fervor and outside pressures of the times, he conducted and summarized a survey in 1952–53 of departmental attitudes about academic freedom, with a view toward reaching consensus on faculty rights and responsibilities. In 1954, he moved approval of a statement before the graduate faculty that "steps be taken to clarify the policy of admission to the Graduate School in order that admission of Negroes may be facilitated." The statement received virtually unanimous faculty support but was neither welcomed nor endorsed by the Tulane board of administration, which promised only further study of the matter. Cole was also very much aware, from his senior administrative position, of the ongoing conflict in the late 1950s between the Arts and Sciences faculty and the athletic department (and some key board members) over curriculum changes favoring athletes, particularly football players.[9] His administrative abilities were forged under the strong leadership of Tulane president Rufus C. Harris, who resisted local attacks on faculty opinion, favored an end to racial segregation, and lamented the sway of intercollegiate football—all while dealing with a highly conservative, opinionated, and unusually intrusive group of trustees.

Six feet tall and slightly more than 180 pounds, forty-eight years old, with hair graying at the temples and a pleasant but reserved demeanor, Fred Cole appeared every bit the scholar and midcareer senior academic administrator that he was. Rarely without a cigarette in hand or close by, he enjoyed midday handball games whenever he could manage the time. He lacked the avuncular ebullience and florid oratory of Frank Gaines, but he brought to W&L a wealth of experience. He had dealt at Tulane with a volatile political environment, accentuated by its major-city location and intense media scrutiny. He brought to Lexington his wife, the former Lois Ferguson of Arkadelphia, Arkansas, whom he had met at LSU and married in 1937, and their four children—Caroline, then 21 and a senior at Newcomb College; Fred Jr., 17 and a student at Episcopal High School in Alexandria; Robert Grey, 14; and Taylor Morris, 7. The family moved into the renovated Lee House just days before his inauguration on May 7, 1960.

The new president was wisely reluctant to make grand pronouncements or propose new directions before learning more about the institution and its people—especially following a long-serving and popular campus leader and appointment by trustees who were not seeking significant changes. Cole communicated his belief in the "strong faculty" system: "I don't think the president of an institution is in the best position to suggest changes to a highly qualified faculty." He also voiced skepticism about educational "gadgetry" and experimentation, and affirmed his commitment to keep a balance among the humanities, social sciences, and sciences.[10]

The inaugural ceremonies were scheduled on the same weekend as the alumni reunion, which ensured a large attendance and a premium on local hotel rooms. May 7 was a bright, sunny, spring day. The formal academic procession, led by Cole and Rector Caskie, filed down the path from the Colonnade toward the outdoor ceremonies, which were followed by a luncheon for all attendees. The convocation itself was highlighted by a ringing endorsement of the liberal arts, an address entitled "What Makes a College Good?" by Nathan Marsh Pusey, president of Harvard, and by Cole's remarks, "The Indispensable Element of Greatness."

The new W&L president paid obligatory homage in his remarks to Washington, Lee, Gaines, and other university leaders, and shared some of his insights on higher education. He noted the unfortunate influence—even within universities—of utilitarian goals that increasingly overshadowed "the achievement of a liberal education as an end, or even as a means, in itself." While many praised the liberal arts, he noted, they tended to value only those elements that supported a narrower professional or practical interest. He praised the commitment in Virginia to "liberalizing studies" and cited Thomas Jefferson as the country's foremost exemplar of "universal" scholarship. He called attention to the need, arising from the changes in the world since the war, to educate individuals in the context of larger communities, with no inherent conflicts between the liberal arts and the sciences.

He argued that the most important objective for educational institutions "may be expressed in the word *integrity*," or "the state or quality of being complete, undivided, or unbroken" and free from "corrupting influence." One general threat to integrity was the demand "to fill immediate and specific needs," rather than focus on broader educational goals. He offered two specific examples of other challenges to integrity: athletics and sponsored research. Athletic events were increasingly a form of "public entertainment," and maintaining athletic prominence once it was achieved could be especially corrupting, leading to compromises in "admissions standards, the curriculum, and the needs of some academic departments." Cole observed that when "athletics become apart from—rather than a part of—a college's educational program, then the loss of integrity is very real indeed." Research and scholarship, he also noted, were always important in higher education, but the rise after the war of research for specific purposes— generously funded by governments, corporations, and foundations—could potentially corrupt the priorities of faculty members and their institutions. "Research should be undertaken," he said, "according to the motivation and qualification of the investigator and the judgment of his colleagues rather than the availability of a sponsor." Finally, Cole emphasized the value of a strong faculty. "It is the faculty, more than any other element, that gives a college or university its character and quality."[11]

Cole elaborated on these ideas in many speeches and articles over the course of his presidency. In the *Journal of Medical Education,* he extended his discussion about research and recalled his experience at Tulane, contrasting that institution with Washington and Lee. He lamented any occasion when research undermined teaching, especially as research became the "prestige function" in universities. Faculty members should be encouraged and valued for teaching, which should never be subordinate to research.[12] In his 1962 Founder's Day remarks, Cole addressed the compatibility of the humanities and the sciences, and the proper balance to strike between them (as popularized in C. P. Snow's much talked-about book, *The Two Cultures and the Scientific Revolution*). He likened the challenge of the current moment to that faced by President Lee, citing the same need in those different times to provide liberal education and also the proper array of practical skills.[13]

Cole consistently supported academic accomplishment as the single most important characteristic for students and the university's future. In one of his earliest speeches, delivered to alumni in October 1959, Cole noted that "scholarship is exalted as never before in our history." Nowadays, "we no longer hear boys called grinds or bookworms because they happen to go to the library on an afternoon and make a few grades of A. The employers' representatives who flock to campus want to see the seniors with the highest grades, and such things as associations and activities are secondary." In his view, this shift had actually resulted in more rather than fewer campus activities, cultural and otherwise. Independent colleges such as W&L had "to provide something noticeably superior" to what was available at far less cost in public institutions, which also freed them to "serve the transcendent needs of our civilization rather than yield to the pressures for mediocrity." A "faculty of the first rank" and a highly qualified student body were thus essential in preparing future leaders.[14] These aspirations extended an emphasis already underway and inspired continuous academic planning through the rest of the decade. Under Cole's leadership, the institutional self-assessment and redesign that occurred on his watch helped reposition Washington and Lee for the many challenges and opportunities to come.

THE 1960S WERE notably turbulent. Social, cultural, and economic changes proliferated and accelerated. Young people born during and especially just after World War II—the baby boomers—comprised the bulk of college attendees, fostering a youth culture that questioned the traditions, customs, and habits of the previous generation, adopted new forms of music and fashion, and engaged the major issues of the time, especially the battle for civil rights and opposition to the Vietnam War and military conscription. Despite its small size, rural location, and respect for tradition, Washington and Lee was not unaffected by these powerful social currents. And even apart from everything else, the 1960s were an important time for major changes in the structure of American higher education.

The surge in higher-education enrollment fueled by the GI bill and postwar recovery continued to wash over the United States during the 1960s. Virtually every statistic was dramatically higher at the end of the decade. Total college enrollment had more than doubled from 1960 to 1970, rising to more than 8 million, as did the number of bachelor's degrees awarded, reaching almost 800,000. The percentage of the total population aged eighteen to twenty-four enrolled in college rose from 23.8 in 1959 to 35 in 1969.[15] The period from 1945 to 1975 is often termed the Golden Age of higher education in the United States.

Much of the growth occurred in the public sector, driven by significant government funding. State governments recognized higher education as essential to expanding a well-educated citizenry that would hold better jobs, pay higher taxes, and be less dependent on public services, while also spawning innovation and ideas, creating new enterprises, and contributing to national security in the wake of the Soviet Union's launch of the first artificial satellite in 1957. States provided major portions of public college budgets and went to great lengths to keep tuition as low as possible. The "Sputnik effect," the fear that Russia had attained scientific and technological superiority, inspired major US government scholarship programs in all fields of higher education—such as the National Defense Education Act of 1958—and substantial support for large research projects through the National Science Foundation (NSF) and other government agencies. This effort was in effect a national mobilization of the nation's intellectual and technical resources to meet the needs of the Cold War and advance America's role and competitive position in the world.

The emphasis on research reshaped state and land-grant universities, adding to their large undergraduate enrollments an array of advanced degree programs, larger faculties, and new facilities and infrastructure to carry out an ambitious research agenda driven by governments and foundations—and by perceptions within the academy that accorded the most prestige and conferred the greatest rewards on these individuals and institutions. Higher education was widely considered, indeed promoted, as an investment in the nation's future, with each degree awarded returning economic and social benefits worth many times the original cost. Universities were seen as essential centers of learning in a complex world defined and driven by knowledge and new ideas. This broader "contract" bound public universities to the public interest and an expanded democracy in return for strong state subsidy, an arrangement that created the world's greatest system of higher education and would last, albeit with declining public support, for most of the twentieth century.

These developments alarmed smaller, independent institutions that feared they would be swamped, and even rendered anachronistic, by the surge in the public sector. Survival seemed to rest on tapping into these new funding sources—including student financial aid and sponsored research—which posed serious questions for institutions, like W&L, that were traditionally committed to maintaining their independence from outside control. The money was welcome but not the strings that were almost invariably attached. As the social and political landscape, and even the bedrock of behavioral norms and unquestioned traditions, began to shift, Washington and Lee endeavored to remain relevant.

A SIGNIFICANT NEW COTERIE of campus leaders was arriving to greet the turbulent decade and lay the groundwork for the challenges to come. New appointees to the board of trustees during President Cole's tenure included Jessie Ball duPont in 1960, future US Supreme Court justice Lewis F. Powell Jr. (1961), Joseph T. Lykes Jr. of New Orleans (1964), John Millard Stemmons of Dallas (1965), and Rosser Lynn Malone Jr. of New York (1967). All but duPont were W&L graduates. Trustee retirements included long-serving members Walter Lapsley Carson (after thirty-three years), Joseph T. Lykes (twenty-three years), James M. Hutcheson (twenty years), and James R. Caskie in 1967 after 43 years as board member and rector.

In the senior administration, Leon Sensabaugh resigned as dean of the university to assume full-time service on the history faculty. With trustee approval, Cole selected Sensabaugh's successor and also redefined the duties and scope of the position. William W. Pusey III, Thomas Ball Professor of German, who first joined the faculty in 1939 and had served as department head since 1947, became dean of the College in September 1960. He would, Cole explained, be

W&L's "principal academic officer" and act for the president in his absence but would no longer exercise oversight of the Schools of Commerce and Law. All deans would now report directly to the president. In Cole's view, the new arrangement would result in "greater efficiency" and be less awkward.[16]

In the spring of 1962, Dean Frank Gilliam, the beloved mainstay of the administration for decades, suffered an incapacitating heart attack at the most critical time of the admissions cycle, and Jim Farrar stepped in to do the job. Gilliam recovered and was back at work by midsummer, but he decided to focus on his tasks as director of Admissions and relinquish his other duties in student administration. Edward C. Atwood, who had served as associate professor of economics before taking an eighteen-month leave to consult with the General Electric Company, returned to campus as professor and dean of students. In June 1963, Gilliam retired with the title of dean emeritus at the age of sixty-eight, after serving his alma mater in various capacities for thirty-seven years. Assistant Dean Farrar was named associate dean of students and director of Admissions, and twenty-six-year-old Lewis G. John, '58, was appointed assistant dean and then dean of students in 1969. James W. Whitehead, director of University Relations, was given the additional title of assistant to the president for administration, and in 1966 succeeded Earl Mattingly as treasurer. Law professor Robert E. R. Huntley, appointed by Cole as W&L's legal advisor, succeeded Whitehead as secretary to the board of trustees.

Earl Stansbury Mattingly was something of an institutional legend, having served the university for forty-nine years. With a well-earned reputation for fiscal prudence and administrative efficiency (he insisted that the lights in Washington Hall be turned off between classes), he was also known for his personal dedication and keen sense of fairness. He worked part-time in the treasurer's office and was appointed W&L's registrar in 1920, while he was still a student. In 1940 he became the university's first full-time treasurer and secretary, and he helped shepherd W&L through the war years and the postwar expansion. His habit of memorizing student names, faces, and hometowns further endeared him to the campus community, and his service on multiple local boards and activities made him a familiar face around Lexington. Frank Parsons recalled a bit of doggerel that appeared in the *Southern Collegian:*

> The Earl of Stansbury knows your name,
> Where you came from and when you came.
> Frank J. Gilliam, equally knowing,
> Knows when you're leaving and why you're going.[17]

Mattingly died only months after his retirement and left his annuity to W&L to establish an endowment to be used for the general expenses of the university, noting, "My job has been my life."[18]

Other key changes included the appointment in 1963 of Clayton E. Williams as dean of the law school, succeeding Charles P. Light, and Robert E. R. Huntley's accession to the same post in 1967. Following his appointment as president of W&L in 1968, Huntley was succeeded as dean by Roy Lee Steinheimer, recruited from the faculty of the University of Michigan. Frank Parsons, assistant to the president for Institutional Research and director of Information Services, became assistant to the president in 1967, and a year later Farris P. Hotchkiss was appointed director of development. Cy Twombly's fifteen years of service as director of athletics ended in 1969, when Eugene F. Corrigan was appointed to the post. In 1968, Maurice D. Leach Jr. succeeded Henry E. Coleman (who had served in the position since 1948) as librarian. By 1970, as one indication of the growing size and complexity of the institution, the list of administrative officers had grown to thirty-seven, an 85 percent increase in ten years.

A new generation of faculty arrived during the great national expansion in higher education. Changes within the professorate included some notable retirements, including Rupert N. Latture from Political Science in 1962 and William Gleason Bean from History in 1963. Premature death took two pillars of the faculty. Fitzgerald "Fitz" Flournoy, '21, W&L's second Rhodes Scholar and beloved English professor and devotee of Shakespeare, died in January 1964, at the age of sixty-five, following a stroke. Another major loss was Ollinger Crenshaw, '25, whose death on March 17, 1970, ended forty-four years of faculty service and came only a year after the publication of his major work, *General Lee's College*. He had entered the university as a student in 1922, coached the tennis team for many years, and died in his sleep, also at the age of sixty-five. The university also suffered the sudden and untimely death of Coach Lee McLaughlin, the head football coach since 1957, who had guided the Generals to great success, with pride and without subsidization. He was fifty-one years old.

THE QUALITY OF THE FACULTY was central to the university's aspirations, especially as student qualifications rose and competition increased among liberal arts colleges, regionally and nationally, for recognition and financial support. Teaching and close faculty-student contacts were at the core of the university's reputation and what nowadays would be called the institution's "brand." Washington and Lee took pride in its faculty salaries and benefits—including favorable housing loans and a generous educational benefit for faculty children—and its comfortable academic environment, but it was also keenly aware that higher education was expanding much more rapidly than the pool of highly qualified professors. It was a heady time for aspiring academics, as graduate school applications soared, and young people set their sights on joining the professoriate. This eventually resulted in an oversupply of PhDs in many fields, but in the 1960s the number of academic job openings expanded dramatically. Most universities raised salaries during the decade and also offered lower teaching loads, "start-up" funds, and support for research and travel. The rapidly growing public universities threatened to squeeze out some segments of private education. Dean Pusey wrote in 1963, "fifteen years ago there were five people standing in line for any vacancy at Washington and Lee. The coin is now reversed: there appear to be five other institutions interested in securing the services of each man we wish to appoint." Also, "the location of an educational institution in the South, with attendant problems, does not make hiring of new faculty members easier." Retaining faculty that W&L had groomed and cultivated and that were then actively recruited by other universities was another challenge. "The only solutions," Pusey continued, "seem to be higher salaries, aggressive and imaginative location of the new man we want, and the continued encouragement of current faculty members through reduced teaching loads (when justified), grants of professional development, and an atmosphere of intellectual challenge. Otherwise it will not be only *old* deans (to quote the popular joke) who 'lose their faculties.'"[19]

The university's efforts to recruit and develop its faculty met with considerable success. The faculty expanded at a faster pace than enrollment but in line with W&L's aspirations. The number of active, full-time regular faculty rose by over 50 percent during the decade, from 86 to 131. The number of faculty members holding the PhD or its equivalent rose over the same period from 58 to 78, and many of the newcomers in the swelling ranks of instructors and assistant professors had just acquired or were nearing completion of requirements for the doctorate.

Salaries were important in attracting qualified teachers to the small town of Lexington, to an institution without major funded research programs, and in a national "buyer's market." If anything, W&L had to stretch a bit on salaries and amenities. Faculty salaries in general were rising faster than inflation, and health care and retirement plans were more generous than ever. While inflation rose roughly 30 percent during the 1960s, in many years W&L was able to allocate a 10 percent increase for faculty compensation, awarded on a merit basis. The American Association of University Professors (AAUP) ranked W&L sixty-fourth out of all American colleges and universities in 1969 in its average faculty compensation (outranked in the Commonwealth only by the University of Virginia). Total W&L faculty compensation (including fringe benefits of 12 to 14 percent of salary) rose during the decade by more than two-thirds, to an average of $20,247 for full professors, $14,530 for associate professors, $12,129 for assistant professors, and $10,301 for instructors. Through regular increases, the university mitigated the inevitable salary compression in the senior ranks that occurs in any active job market, while also competing favorably at the entry level. Some attractive fringe benefits were not included in these num-bers—subsidized low-interest loans for housing (running about 4 percent) and generous support for payment of college tuition for faculty children. Overall, W&L stood in a solid position concerning faculty compensation. By 1969–70, the average pay for full professors was equivalent to over $120,000 in today's dollars, and to over $72,000 (again, in today's dollars) for assistant professors.

Early in his administration, President Cole initiated a systematic effort to assess, support, and reward scholarship and creative activity. In March 1960, he asked all faculty members over the rank of instructor to submit a five-year plan "for research or other creative activities, broadly interpreted," including new course offerings and plans for further study, and laying out the library resources, equipment, funding, and leaves of absence that would be required. A new University Council on Leaves and Research would use this information to identify funding sources (including university funds), coordinate requests for leaves of absence, assess and provide recognition for scholarship underway but not yet completed or published, and ensure that research complemented rather than undermined "the basic University function of teaching."[20] Cole was pleased that the submitted reports were "thoughtful and realistic," reflecting "a very healthy attitude of the faculty toward continuing scholarship and profes-sional self-improvement." Significantly, "in virtually every case the program outlined is related to improving the individual's ability as a teacher on the undergraduate level."[21] Though he may have been averse to some aspects of ex-ternally sponsored research, Cole believed that faculty research was essential.

Cole also introduced a new policy on merit-based salaries and promotions, which the trustees accepted in January 1961. While all faculty members were expected to be "good academic citizens," possessed of "intellectual integrity" and appropriate credentials, salary increases and promotions were to be based primarily on "teaching ability and intellectual achievement." These could not be calculated by a "mathematical formula" but rather must be assessed both qualitatively and quantitatively. The policy included sixteen general criteria for such judgments, eight for teaching and eight for scholarship. In addition to the usual considerations (expertise in the subject matter, enthusiasm in the classroom, and publications), the teaching criteria included "a sense of balance (humor)" and, for intellectual achievement, "stimulation of the work of colleagues" and "Summer study or teaching." At the same time, the trustees also approved a new policy on faculty leaves of absence, subject to the availability of funds "to supplement outside grants" and the approval of the executive committee of the board.[22]

These measures confirmed the value now given to the full range of faculty activities. They also conveyed high expectations for faculty performance and development, with a continuing stress on teaching but increased emphasis on scholarship and intellectual achievement. Seniority, acceptable performance of routine responsibilities, and good "citizenship" were no longer in themselves sufficient for monetary reward or professional advancement. These new steps may have caused some anxiety in faculty ranks, but such policies were being adopted and strengthened at most universities and were coupled with a greater array of faculty incentives and rewards.

Grants to support research increased. The Glenn Grant-in-Aid Program, established in 1951, provided small awards to individual faculty members ($6,000 was awarded in 1963), and a book-publication fund helped underwrite the cost of publishing scholarly monographs. The Glenn program was, in fact, partly reimbursed from royalties on published projects it helped support. The new Robert E. Lee Research Fund, implemented in 1960–61, focused on student work, often in the research areas of faculty mentors. A $250,000, five-year grant to the university in 1967 from the Sloan Foundation to enhance science teaching was coupled with $197,300 from the NSF in 1968, permitting study leaves and other support for faculty in the sciences and social sciences. A $60,000 matching grant in 1968 from the Ford Foundation provided comparable support for teaching in the humanities.

WASHINGTON AND LEE's enrollment gradually rose during the 1960s, due to increases in the university's capacity to provide for more students (expanded faculty, curriculum, and housing), and also in part to greater retention. While freshman class size remained around 320, total enrollment rose at an annual rate of about 3.5 percent, to a record high of 1,461 in 1967–68, falling to 1,432 in 1969–70. Law school enrollment rose dramatically over the decade, more than doubling from 97 in 1957–58 to a record high of 216 in 1967–68, and then declining (after the removal of military draft deferments for graduate students) to 178 in 1969–70.[23]

With a rising pool of undergraduate applicants nationwide, W&L could afford to be more selective. The university's attention was explicitly focused on quality rather than quantity and enjoyed solid enrollments even though new requirements had been added to the admissions process and new, tougher standards had been applied to the Automatic Rule. Beginning in September 1962, W&L was the first southern men's college to require completion by all applicants of three College Board achievement tests, in addition to the usual aptitude test. The faculty voted in 1960 to require that all students demonstrate progress toward graduation by achieving a designated cumulative grade point average, as well as maintaining a satisfactory semester average. After the new requirements went into effect in 1961, the numbers of students withdrawn under the Automatic Rule actually decreased. The trends remained positive: the numbers of applications continued to increase along with average SAT scores, and fewer students flunked out—a sign, in Dean Gilliam's words, of the greater "holding power" of the university. Beginning in September 1965, a new early-decision plan was implemented, aimed at attracting the most qualified students and permitting applicants with excellent credentials and whose first choice was Washington and Lee to receive notice of admission by November 1.

Better qualified, and perhaps more committed, students helped ease the rate of attrition, which had long been too high, a concern for financial reasons and the university's reputation. In 1955, only 37 percent of W&L undergraduates received a degree within four years after admission. By 1969–70, in a dramatic turn-around, 69 percent of those who had entered in 1965 received their baccalaureate degrees. Some students continued to leave, the most frequently stated reasons being "geographic location" or a preference to attend a coeducational institution. (There was little to be done about the former, but the latter certainly caught the attention of university officials.) Dean Pusey also noted "lack of fraternity affiliation" as a common and long-standing cause of transfers to other institutions, and lamented that "energetic efforts" to enhance nonfraternity life and to attract transfer students from other universities had not been more successful.[24] Fraternities still dominated social life and student politics at W&L, but 23 percent of the student population was not affiliated with a fraternity at the end of 1969–70.

Following President Cole's remarks to the alumni about the importance of academic qualifications, Dean Gilliam also noted "a clearly recognizable trend toward a heightened increase in scholarship and interest" in academics among the majority of students. "It has been marked by pride and a recognition of the primary purpose of an academic community." Ed Atwood, the new dean of students, observed that the biggest change over the two years of his absence from campus "has been the increased interest in, and emphasis upon, the academic aspects of life at Washington and Lee"—a movement the university would try to "aid and abet."[25]

Though academic performance and potential received greater emphasis, a variety of criteria for admission were still considered. As Gilliam asked, "Is there any wiser procedure than that of studying all factors as the probable quality of the school attended, the grades and rank in class, tests scores on a national basis, the statements of those who knew the boy best as to his character, seriousness of purpose, maturity, and real desire for the essential of the type of education that Washington and Lee offers, and then awarding the places to the boys who seem to deserve them?"

The review of applications became more rigorous. The Committee on Admissions considered 1,599 final candidates for the September 1965 class, the largest number of applicants in the university's history (which dropped back to 1,250 in 1970). The average SAT scores had risen to a high in 1966 of 608 (verbal) and 643 (math), which compared favorably with the scores of entering freshmen at Davidson, Emory, and the University of Virginia. But the general demographics of prospective students remained much the same. The majority of applicants and new students continued to come from the South and claimed affiliation with Protestant denominations, especially Presbyterian and Episcopalian. For some time, a slight majority of entering students had attended public rather than private schools (generally around 55 and 45 percent, respectively), but the proportion from public schools rose to a high of 70 percent in 1966 and 1970.[26] The children of alumni continued to receive close attention and were admitted if they demonstrated the capability to be successful at W&L.

The university was reasonably successful in growing its endowment, but tuition was an increasingly important foundation for the operating budget, rising from 39 percent of total revenue in 1960–61 to 48 percent in 1968–69. Over the same period, endowment income—which increased by more than half—dropped from 27 to 16 percent of total revenue. Tuition rose during the decade more than two and a half times, and total estimated expenses by more than 80 percent, though the numbers need to be viewed in the context of over 30 percent inflation. Total estimated annual expenses to attend W&L were $1,750 in 1960 and $3,225 in 1971.

A goal of virtually all highly selective academic institutions is to admit the most qualified individuals regardless of financial need. About two hundred W&L undergraduates, or 20 percent of the total, received some financial aid in 1959–60, when the student-aid program was broadened to include not only endowed scholarship funds but also university loans and campus employment. The formula implemented in 1960 provided for loans to comprise an increasing share of aid during a student's career—from 25 percent of the total in the first year to 100 percent in the senior year.[27] While providing new options to help students finance their education, this did not meet the needs of men from low-income families, and it placed larger financial burdens on students as they advanced through their academic programs, as well as saddling them with greater postgraduation debt. By 1970, nearly a quarter of W&L undergraduates together shared over $450,000 in assistance of all types. By this point, the university was seeking to provide some assistance to 30 percent of its students, with roughly 10 percent receiving full grant support to meet economic need or to attract those most academically meritorious. The goal was to provide "greater economic and social diversity" in the student body, as well as to "be assured of a significant percentage of students from middle-income families" and the university's capacity "to offer special incentives to students with outstanding academic ability."[28] Despite these efforts, however, the student body remained highly homogeneous, as did the perception that only the relatively well-to-do enrolled—and not necessarily those with the highest academic aspirations or promise.

Endowed scholarship funds were the foundation for the financial aid program. The Thomas Ball Scholarship Aid Fund, the largest single gift for scholarships in the university's history, was established by a trust fund of $600,000 transferred to W&L in 1960 by Mrs. Jessie Ball duPont, who also provided other funds to support students and faculty members. Other endowed funds included the Letitia Pate Evans Scholarships, the Robert E. Lee Scholarships (supported by a $300,000 endowment from Dr. Gustavus B. Capito of Charleston, West Virginia), and the J. W. Warner Scholarship Fund to support students pursuing premedical studies. W&L was also among twelve liberal arts colleges in the country to award scholarships from the George F. Baker Trust of New York. The Baker Scholarships, awarded by the board of trustees, were restricted to favor students from the southern and border states who were interested in business careers. By 1970, the university listed sixty-one endowed scholarship funds and an additional nineteen Memorial Scholarships to honor W&L men who had died in World War II.

Increasing financial aid did not always ensure academic success to graduation. Even the highly selective Baker and Lee scholarship programs had their problems; as many as a third of the recipients either failed to maintain academic eligibility, fell under the Automatic Rule, or transferred to other institutions.[29] In the competition for the "best and brightest," W&L joined many other institutions in exploring the awarding of financial aid for academic merit rather than need.[30] Such support was particularly expensive, however, and W&L's financial aid programs continued to focus primarily on economic need and to struggle in the competition with its academic peers.

With passage of the US Higher Education Act in 1965, the federal government became a major player in providing financial aid directly to students. This development was welcomed by higher education generally, and especially by the rapidly expanding public sector, but it gave pause to some at W&L, where institutional independence from outside control was a tradition and a principle, though not a written policy. The university had accepted direct assistance from the federal government in various ways since the 1930s—the Army School, the surplus property program, wartime prefabricated housing, indirect student support through the GI Bill, and direct grants for research and equipment. In 1962, the board approved a proposal by Edward Turner, head of the Physics Department, to the NSF for a matching grant of $25,000 for instructional equipment. After much discussion, the proposal was approved because it was for "cooperation in the National Defense" and for a specific purpose, and it could be returned "should any effort at influence or control appear."[31] Government funding was becoming increasingly pervasive in higher education and was critical in the sciences.

A special committee to address the benefits and potential dangers from outside funding, established by the trustees and chaired by Joseph L. Lanier, held its first meeting in September 1965. The discussion centered on the conundrum of how to accept outside funding without giving up independence; as Lanier summarized it, "How can we participate and not be controlled?" Recognizing that times had changed, the committee asked Cole and Huntley to draw up a resolution regarding "principles and policy" on government and foundation funding for the October meeting of the trustees. In its report, the special committee advised that it was not "violative of the traditional policy of independence of Washington and Lee" to participate in federal government programs that benefited faculty and students (including student financial aid) as long as they did not "entail long-term or continuing obligations." Outside funding for permanent capital projects should be assessed case by case. The same principles should apply to assistance from private foundations, which had assumed an importance even greater than individual donors within higher education.[32] In January 1966, the board was informed that W&L had been granted a National Defense Education Act (NDEA) Institute of French and an NSF Earth Science Institute for the summer, and that the university would participate in three federal financial aid programs—Educational Opportunity Grants, College Work-Study, and the Federal Insured Loan Program.[33]

Major assets for student life, which Frank Gilliam and his colleagues had long desired, were the new Evans Dining Hall, completed in 1959, and the Newton D. Baker and John W. Davis Dormitories. For the first time, all freshmen could eat together (indeed, they were required to do so), and a reasonable amount of living space could be made available to upperclassmen. The fraternities adjusted to the new situation, and the university could now work on shaping and strengthening each entering class during the critical first year. A new Freshman Dormitory (later designated Gilliam Residence Hall) opened in September 1962 with accommodations for ninety students, including counselors, enabling the university to admit about twenty additional students each year. A fifteen-bed student infirmary on the lower level greatly improved these facilities on campus, though seriously ill students were still sent to a reserved section of the Stonewall Jackson Hospital. By 1970, a total of 466 students (including 365 freshmen) lived in university dormitories, and 900 lived off campus, including 255 in fraternity houses and 48 in married student housing.

A special April 1970 meeting of the board of trustees in Washington, DC, reviewed the overall circumstances and direction of the university, its growth and development during the previous decade, and its future plans. These projections—buoyed by increased enrollment and revenues—included an expansion of law school enrollment to 350 and a possible undergraduate student body of 1,700. Support for expansion was stimulated by the dramatic growth in higher education across the country, but how—and if—it could be done at W&L was not clear. Answers to these questions had changed over the decade because circumstances had changed. The materials the administration prepared for the board's consideration in 1970 raised a critical issue: "There is reason to believe that it would be very difficult for us to increase enrollment through the admission of additional freshmen without a decrease in the academic qualifications of the class as a whole." They also broached a matter that would intrigue and roil the university community for the following two decades. If W&L decided to expand its enrollment, "then it would appear that the best way to achieve this growth is by the admission of women."[34]

DURING HIS FIRST FEW YEARS in office, Fred Cole surveyed the risks, challenges, and opportunities for Washington and Lee. He explored ways in which the small liberal arts institution, which he perceived to be on the cusp of financial security, could achieve its maximum potential and make a larger contribution to American higher education. He brought to W&L the fresh perspective of a new generation of academic leaders, with skills gained and honed in the postwar era. His predecessor, Frank Gaines, had guided the university through multiple challenges, including war and the football scandal, with aplomb and charisma. Cole brought a less flamboyant and less easily approachable style to the president's office, as well as a more scholarly demeanor and the skills and experience gained in multiple academic capacities at a much larger, more comprehensive institution. He was acutely aware of the many changes in the educational environment of the 1950s and 1960s and what they might portend for a small men's college in the Shenandoah Valley. While he understood and respected W&L's history and traditions, he was concerned that the university might not fare well in the future without adopting innovations that could expand its reach. He also knew that change would not necessarily be welcomed.

The vast expansion of higher education framed all future expectations—whether fearful or hopeful—and especially brought to the fore issues of size, scale, and dimension. A proliferation of new graduate programs in established and aspiring research universities (many of which had been founded as teachers' colleges) became a measure of academic role, credibility, and prestige. At the same time, community colleges were assuming more responsibility for introductory work to prepare students for advanced study in large universities. Where in all this change did a traditional liberal arts college fit? How did W&L fit?

Cole envisioned a day when the university's financial problems would be solved. "It would appear," he wrote the trustees in May 1961, that "with the addition of approximately $30,000,000 to the endowment of the University, as it is now organized, its financial security for the future would be established." After that, the main question would be what W&L would contribute to the advancement "of this country and others." He praised the university's location (sometimes seen as an obstacle to growth) and described a future "center of scholarship and learning," which such a location made possible. "As one looks back from Washington and Lee to House Mountain, one sees locations for homes and buildings and grounds for natural scientists, social scientists, humanists, theologians, and mathematicians." On land the university already owned, a new intellectual community could be created: "Through working together and living together and sharing ideas and thoughts and plans, such association could advance solutions of problems and extend our knowledge and its synthesis in an incomparable manner." The project could start with a group of scholars in the arts and another in the physical sciences and mathematics, joined later by all major disciplines, including law. "Fortunately," he concluded, "the problems faced are only those of finance," and he sought permission to begin the planning for an ambitious venture that would take many years to develop.[35]

In July 1964, the trustees received, in the context of long-range planning, a description and schematic drawings of what would come to be known as the "companion college" or "Lee College" plan.[36] Cole's address to the opening assembly in the fall of 1964 proposed a "discussion topic" that still awaited board approval. He reiterated that most of the university's problems would be largely solved "in the foreseeable future." What then? How could W&L fulfill its responsibility to the future? How could it serve the excellent students who would be turned away because of limited space and capacity? In short, "if it should be determined that this University should play a larger role in American higher education, how can this be done without disrupting a good situation?"

How could the current academic environment—the student-teacher ratio and relationship, the availability of services and physical facilities, the intimate campus atmosphere—be preserved while the university also doubled its current enrollment of 1,300 students? The general answer Cole proffered was the construction of a new college, tentatively called "Lee College," on the same model as the existing one (which he proposed be labeled "Washington College"), on lands the university already owned beyond Wilson Field and around the Liberty Hall ruins. The new, companion college would essentially duplicate the first two years of the curriculum, with the same student-teacher ratio and the same basic facilities, including the library. Athletic facilities, the auditorium, the infirmary, the little theater, and perhaps the dining hall might be shared and the law school, the School of Commerce, and offerings in journalism and communications would not be duplicated. Advanced classes in the new college could be somewhat distinctive and offer additional opportunities that could be shared with students from the other college. The duplication would be so complete that neither college would be more desirable or prestigious than the other. One notable difference would be the requirement that "Lee College" students live in facilities on campus, though they also could join fraternities.

This near doubling of the university's undergraduate enrollment and physical footprint would, of course, require substantial new funding and pose a plethora of practical and abstract problems for an institution so firmly rooted in its past and traditions. The trustees did agree once again to consider the issue of the university's proper size, as well as its role and options in a new and challenging environment. The proposal for "Lee College" was accepted in this context as a "work sheet" for planning and as part of the preparations for the institutional self-study that President Cole hoped would help provide "guidelines and directions that will help determine, with wisdom and foresight, the future course of this University."[37]

Perhaps not surprisingly, the conservative board of trustees was never inclined to endorse or proceed with such dramatic changes to the small, intimate campus they knew, and they were perhaps less sanguine than Cole about the possibility of raising all the necessary funding. Indeed, the needs of the endowment were greater than Cole envisioned, and attracting that many qualified students would be challenging. Instead, W&L chose to continue to grow modestly and incrementally, while adding facilities—mostly athletic fields but also a new law school building—that stretched the campus across Woods Creek. The proposal of a more ambitious expansion did, however, help define the possible options that might be pursued in the context of a rapidly expanding higher-education sector in the United States, as well as some of the key elements of a much more controversial issue—coeducation.

COLE'S VISION OF a new "companion" college remained mostly that—a vision—but the curriculum was a reality that touched every student and faculty member. The Committee on Courses and Degrees routinely made minor adjustments, even in cases of individual students. More substantial revisions and fundamental issues were considered from time to time, especially in times of change in the broader society. General degree requirements that had remained basically stable for thirty years, despite proposals in the "Leyburn Plan," received attention during the 1960s.

Washington and Lee's general degree requirements never contained a mandated interdisciplinary "core" course or set of courses—usually separate and extradepartmental—around which all else revolved, as was the case at Columbia University since 1919, at Harvard University beginning in 1945 (introduced in the *General Education in a Free Society* faculty report) and revised and expanded in the Core of the 1970s, or in the "Great Books" program introduced by Robert Hutchins and Mortimer Adler at the University of Chicago.[38] Rather, W&L's model followed along the lines of the more common model of required study in departmental courses distributed among broad general areas of knowledge, such as humanities and science. But the same basic concerns and questions applied regardless of the model. What common academic background should all W&L students share? What was unique about a W&L degree? What basic knowledge and skills should an "educated person" have? These questions were even more pertinent at a time when higher education, the role of the liberal arts, and the post–World War II world generally were in flux.

The distinction between general and professional education that had been blurred earlier in the century was rendered much more sharply in the greatly expanded higher-education system in the years after World War II. A proliferation of postgraduate degree programs accompanied the rising educational requirements for entry into many professional fields, and undergraduate study in fields such as business became increasingly popular. Early in the decade, Dean Pusey expressed his skepticism of the general direction of higher education and fretted about W&L's place in the new firmament. Mostly, he was concerned about the future of the liberal arts and the notion that the bachelor's degree was becoming not a worthy end in itself but only a stepping-stone to graduate work. But "the first-rate undergraduate college with a carefully selected and skillfully taught student body is one of the best routes to successful graduate study." He estimated that about 45 percent of W&L graduates went on to further graduate or professional education.

The faculty at Washington and Lee, as at other institutions, regarded the curriculum both in the abstract—considering what would be essential to the "educated person"—and in the particular, such as determining what value the curriculum attached to specific disciplines and bodies of knowledge. Professors were especially concerned with whether the curriculum recognized their own disciplines and departments. Faculty disputations on the curriculum seemed obtuse or incomprehensible to outsiders, but what students were expected to learn rested, theoretically at least, at the core of what the university was about.

The general degree requirements in W&L's liberal arts curriculum for the first one or two years of study prevailed in the College and assumed a somewhat more applied and professional emphasis in the School of Commerce and Administration. The variations in academic requirements between the two major undergraduate divisions were never conceived in isolation from one another or from the broader academic goals of the institution. Even the School of Law, given its small size and high standards, evolved in a liberal arts context. Nevertheless, tension persisted between W&L colleges and even departments.

W&L had been fully accredited by the American Association of Collegiate Schools of Business since 1927 and was the smallest institution and one of a few purely undergraduate programs to be so recognized. The School of Commerce had long shared the same basic first-year requirements with the College and had always retained many other features of a liberal arts approach to undergraduate education, including offering a number of elective courses. Its disciplines were not confined to management, accounting, and finance, as was recognized by the new name adopted in 1969: the School of Commerce, Politics, and Economics. It was perhaps best regarded as an extension of the liberal arts program, with greater emphasis on business (leading to the BS degree) and political science and economics (the BA). Upperclassmen in the School of Commerce, Politics, and Economics increased as a proportion of total enrollment from 12.7 percent in 1957 to slightly over 17 percent in 1969, surging in the early years of the decade (to 21.4 percent in 1962) and then falling back.

Upon his arrival in 1959, President Cole called for a new reassessment of the undergraduate curriculum, and in March 1960 the Committee on Courses and Degrees began meeting as the Curriculum Committee. In September, the committee, now with Pusey serving as chair, held fourteen additional meetings, hearing from faculty members who discussed general objectives and specific courses in the careful and tedious deliberation typical of such endeavors. Members from different academic disciplines, subdisciplines, departments, and groups worked to reach a general consensus on the "basic subjects" that should be required of all students—and also to protect disciplinary "territory" and influence. James Leyburn was a persistent contributor to these discussions, always emphasizing the importance of elective courses and individual student work in the first year and beyond, an emphasis that would gain ground with each new review. The work demanded considerable faculty attention, undertaken with varying degrees of enthusiasm. Ollinger Crenshaw complained in December 1961 about serving on a committee "charged with drawing up a new, revised, up-to-date curriculum which will show the world that W&L 'keeps up,' is not apathetic and lethargic, and is ready to emulate in whatever way it can, the 'Ivy League' ideas on higher education. Perhaps my age and my conservatism," he added, "are responsible for my thinking so, but I feel our curriculum is pretty good and our degrees quite respectable as they are!"[39]

The result of these deliberations was a preliminary draft of a BA curriculum, presented to the full faculty on March 1, 1962. The draft required that freshmen attain "an elementary proficiency in a large number of basic subjects" and gave them "considerable freedom" to elect specific courses from designated groups. It also required a student beyond the first year to select "a major concentration," with "as many free electives as possible to pursue his interests outside his major field." General agreement on the concept of a new BA curriculum was accompanied by doubts about some of the details. Finally, on April 15, the committee presented yet another revised version to the faculty, which was defeated thirty-one to twenty-four.[40] Pusey recalled that William James termed the faculty "a ruminating animal," a description that could also "characterize the Curriculum Committee."[41]

Nevertheless, the process proceeded, and the faculty continued to meet as a committee. Some modest revisions were made and approved in September 1963. A new major in Sociology, with supporting courses, was added in 1962–63, as well as a new major in Contemporary Civilization in the History Department. Course offerings in mathematics were strengthened, with calculus now included in the required freshman course. Courses in certain areas of study were still required in the first year to lay the groundwork in the liberal arts, but now students could choose to defer one field of study until the sophomore year, when they were better prepared academically, and to substitute a course in an area of special interest. The faculty also expanded—from twelve to nineteen—the number of academic credits that could be awarded for passage of Advanced Placement tests, allowing students to skip introductory courses if they could demonstrate proficiency in the subject matter. These modest changes were hardly earthshaking, but they laid the groundwork for bigger changes to come.

Just as the arts had required attention and development in the late 1940s, and would be expanded again later in the century, the most compelling academic needs in the late 1950s and 1960s—the era of Sputnik and the Cold

War—were in the fields of science and technology. Washington and Lee had not neglected the sciences, but the necessary classrooms and laboratories were inadequate. Construction began in the spring of 1960 on a new building (later named Parmly Hall) to house the departments of Physics and Biology. Howe Hall was significantly remodeled to better accommodate Chemistry and Geology. These new facilities were completed and opened in the fall of 1962, the same year the university's first computer, the first model of its kind in Virginia (an IBM 1620), was installed. Interested students took advantage of the opportunity for noncredit instruction on this machine, but the full impact of computer technology lay decades in the future.

Washington and Lee did become an early leader in encouraging research by undergraduate students. The Robert E. Lee Research Program, introduced in September 1960, provided funds for students to pursue independent research under the supervision of faculty members in the sciences, humanities, social sciences, and the law school. In the first year, about twenty-five students participated; three years later, in the spring of 1963, seventy-one students involved in fifty-five different projects made oral reports of their work at a series of dinner meetings. Some presented papers to the annual meeting of the Virginia Academy of Science. Faculty members also benefited because many of the projects were related to their own research interests. At a time of rapidly expanding graduate programs, this emphasis at the undergraduate level took advantage of W&L's strength and received favorable attention in educational publications and in the *New York Times*. The university also participated in the NSF Undergraduate Science Education Program, with some fifteen students engaged during the summer of 1963.

INSTITUTIONAL ACCREDITATION conferred a "seal of approval" on universities to reassure the public that at least minimal standards were being met in an increasingly complex and confusing higher education system. Even more important for the institutions, accreditation validated their eligibility to receive federal funds. This process emerged in its modern form at midcentury and was implemented by regional accrediting agencies licensed by the federal government, but it was governed by the educational institutions themselves, following the principle and practice of decentralization and peer review that undergirded quality control in American higher education. The Southern Association of Colleges and Schools (SACS) headquartered in Atlanta was the regional accrediting body for W&L. Major reviews to reaffirm institutional accreditation were normally conducted every ten years and involved a self-study prepared by the institution, based on a manual of SACS procedures and standards, and a culminating visit to campus by an outside team of professors and administrators. This review could be a lengthy, detailed, and bureaucratic exercise, especially numbing to faculty members. But the SACS review of W&L in 1966 was a highly consequential and influential undertaking, both in approach and outcome.

W&L began the long process in 1964. The Self-Study Committee, essentially the President's Advisory Committee with Professor William M. Hinton added as chair, presided over a campus-wide, two-year review charged with examining every aspect of university operations. It involved seventy-five or eighty meetings, numerous subcommittees, and the efforts of virtually all faculty and staff members (and some students). The university elected to develop its own plan rather than follow precisely the approach laid out in SACS self-study guidelines, though all prescribed standards still had to be addressed. Fred Cole had decided that this effort should have the greatest possible benefit to W&L and provide the opportunity for a searching examination of university circumstances, issues, and plans. W&L thus decided to carry out much more than a reaccreditation exercise, and the ramifications were reflected in the university's policies, organization, and curriculum for many years to come.

One required element of the self-study was a formal statement on the "Philosophy of the University." The two "basic purposes" expressed in W&L's new document were fostering students' development of "the capacity and desire to learn" and understand, and creating a climate of learning that "stresses the importance of the individual, his personal honor and integrity, his harmonious relationship with his fellowman [sic], and his responsibility to serve society through the productivity of his training and talent." These goals were elaborated upon in several additional pages, stressing, among other things, the importance of the university's independence, the primary role of teaching, selective admissions without "other discriminatory barriers," the importance of the "Christian ideal" in shaping the institution, and the absence of "arbitrary limitations" on the size of the student body or the educational program. This was actually the first time such a statement had been formally devised. Its principal drafter, Frank Parsons, wanted to be sure that "with the exception of admitting women to Washington and Lee, we should not have any other impediments to change here."[42]

Another unusual feature of W&L's approach was the hiring of an outside professional consultant. The firm of Booz, Allen and Hamilton was engaged to assist in the review, especially related to trustee and organizational matters. Their participation—and emphasis on clarity of objectives and efficiency in execution—brought a definite corporate cast to portions of the report. The board committed to long-range planning and "increased responsibility for developing the University's financial base," improved communication with faculty and staff, and better utilization of non–board members on special projects and activities. The university administration implemented a number of changes before the report was completed, and determined to continue the Office of Institutional Research that coordinated the self-study "as a center for continuing self-evaluation." Perhaps most important, the administration decided to reestablish the Office of University Development. The concept of a "companion college" was included in the report as one "possible direction" for future development, even though it was still in need of "exhaustive study and questioning."[43]

A joint meeting of the trustees and the Self-Study Committee reviewed and discussed each section of the draft during a board meeting at The Homestead in Hot Springs, Virginia, on August 14–16, 1966.[44] Copies of the 460-page final report, with almost three hundred recommendations, were distributed to board members, faculty, and staff, as well as to the ten members of the SACS Visiting Committee, chaired by Cecil Abernathy, president of Birmingham-Southern College.

The Visiting Committee spent November 6–9, 1966, on campus, reviewing documents and files, verifying information, conducting interviews, and preparing a preliminary version of its report. The final report contained only two "recommendations" and five "suggestions," a favorable assessment that would lead to W&L's reaccreditation.[45]

W&L'S SELF-STUDY collected more information, extended the discussions about general education, and prompted a new effort to make changes. Dean Pusey, as acting president, initiated yet another comprehensive curriculum review in 1967. Once again, a committee convened and debated, proposed and disposed, pondering great ideas and delving into minuscule details. It was a different exercise this time, partly because the recently concluded self-study provided context and inspiration but also because times had changed since the current basic curriculum had been installed thirty years earlier and even, to some degree, since the 1963 revisions. Among other things, high schools had shifted from an eleven-year to a twelve-year system and now taught subjects like psychology and economics. Students were better prepared and arrived with different expectations. And the social and political changes underway by the late 1960s accentuated new expectations and further undermined the tolerance for regimented programs and institutions. Were the "best and brightest" students now being attracted elsewhere? A new Student Curriculum Committee functioned separately from the faculty, discussed a full range of curricular issues, and made a number of suggestions—such as increasing the number of accepted Advanced Placement courses.

The faculty committee continued to debate the breadth and depth of students' exposure to various disciplines and bodies of knowledge, the relationships among fields, and the development of critical thinking through independent study, as well as to explore how these matters were reflected in the curricula of thirteen other colleges and universities, including Sewanee, Davidson, Amherst, Haverford, Swarthmore, and Williams.[46] The many alternatives were eventually distilled into two options contained in majority and minority reports shared with the faculty during a month of weekly meetings of the Faculty Discussion Club during 1968–69. On May 1, 1969, after defeating three substitute motions, the faculty approved the majority report, along with a proposal for a new academic calendar of two long terms followed by a short term.[47]

The result, implemented in the fall of 1970, was a reshaping of undergraduate degree requirements and a dramatic change in the academic calendar. Academic credit based on time in class (the traditional "credit hour") was redefined as "credit," determined by the faculty based on the course content and what a student learned, a more flexible approach that would become essential in the still far-in-the-future Internet age. The sixty-eight hours of work required of every W&L student was reduced to thirty-six credits. Students could now choose courses from among four major groupings, or clusters of subjects and disciplines, with no fewer than six and no more than twelve credits from any one grouping. The goal was still fairly traditional—a distribution of departmental courses designed to ensure a broad liberal arts foundation—but with greater choice than before.[48]

The academic calendar of two fifteen-week semesters had been in place so long as to seem sacrosanct. But did it further the goals of a more flexible and innovative curriculum likely to attract the best students? The new calendar featured three terms—two terms of twelve weeks each (fall and winter) and one spring term of six weeks beginning in mid-April and ending in late May. A normal student load would be four courses in the long terms and one or two courses in the new spring term. A definite benefit was the conclusion of the fall term—and final examinations—before the Christmas break. Other colleges had implemented "short terms," but W&L was among the first to adopt a term of six weeks, rather than three or four, and to place it at the end rather than at the beginning or midpoint of the academic year. "There was nearly unanimous agreement," a Curriculum Committee leader wrote, "that we should try a three-term calendar in hopes that we might stimulate more independent work in the university during the short term."[49] The new arrangement posed special challenges for departments and programs, since existing courses had to be modified and new courses devised. For the inaugural spring term in 1971, faculty proposed intensive seminars and courses built around field trips and study abroad. In fact, the total number of undergraduate courses increased over the decade by almost a third, from 363 to 470, all thoroughly vetted by the Committee on Courses and Degrees. In spite of uncertainty in the beginning, and continued protests by faculty in some disciplines that twelve weeks was insufficient time to cover all the necessary material or deal properly with writing assignments, the new calendar turned out to be a persistent feature of the W&L educational experience, though with some modifications.

A need for greater exposure to global history and culture was noted in the self-study and included in the 1970 curriculum changes, though international education initiatives at W&L were modest. Each year, the university awarded scholarships to a few foreign students, who lived in fraternity houses and whose room and board were covered by grants from the Interfraternity Council. Students won Fulbright scholarships to study abroad, along with the occasional Rhodes Scholarship. The advent of the new six-week spring term provided an excellent opportunity for foreign travel and language study, and student enthusiasm for such opportunities was very high. A questionnaire returned by 42 percent of the freshmen and sophomores in the fall of 1969 revealed that more than 95 percent wanted W&L to offer its own study-abroad programs. More than 40 percent favored year-long programs, and almost 35 percent wanted programs lasting at least a semester. Almost 80 percent of the respondents expressed the desire to "stay over" and travel on their own. More than 98 percent believed that such programs would be "in the spirit of the new curriculum." Perhaps most surprisingly, 68 percent were willing to commit to "the total and exclusive use of a foreign language from beginning to end of the program," and more than 90 percent favored including more countries and areas in addition to those covered by the languages of French, German, and Spanish (ranked in order of preference: Britain, Italy, the Middle East, Africa, and the Far East). These responses may well have been overly exuberant, even naive, but they certainly conveyed strong and genuine interest. The new curriculum and calendar provided a new opportunity beyond the "standard" junior-year-abroad option then noted in the catalog.[50]

THE LAW SCHOOL retained its goal of preparing well-rounded, liberally educated practitioners. It had never sought to cover every aspect of legal education; rather, as Dean Light observed, "the faculty adheres to the view that the principal mission of basic legal education for the LL.B. degree is to develop the reasoning power of students and to train them in legal fundamentals."[51] Given its modest size, the law school offered a solid, basic legal curriculum, as well as an array of special programs, and expanded the curriculum to meet new needs and demands to the extent that the size of its faculty would allow. The number of faculty members had grown steadily since the end of the war, increasing by seven new professors between 1948 and 1963, and reaching a total of thirteen regular faculty positions and two visiting appointees in 1970.

In 1959, Professor Charles V. Laughlin reported the responses of W&L School of Law graduates to questionnaires seeking their views on the curriculum in light of their experience in practice. He also compared the W&L curriculum to those in other law schools—Virginia, North Carolina, Wake Forest, Duke, West Virginia, and Kentucky. Drake University in Iowa was also included because it was comparable in size to W&L and in a different part of the country. The comparison revealed that the W&L curriculum was very much in line with the others and did not require more than periodic reexamination and minimal change.[52]

New, specialized courses were added, including a number in the 1960s, covering Labor Law, International Law, Admiralty Law, International Law, Employee Rights and Criminal Procedure, Jurisprudence and American Legal History, and seminars in International Business Transactions and Taxation. The seminar format was difficult to implement (the enrollment in International Business Transactions was initially too large), but it nevertheless played a larger role in the curriculum, along with more emphasis on independent study and research.

The issues of most concern to the law school in mid-decade were the status and future of the "combination degree," and the need to choose between the

LLB (bachelor of laws) and the JD (*juris doctor,* or doctor of law) as the terminal law degree. For some time, W&L undergraduates who had completed three years of work toward a BA or BS in Commerce could, after submission of acceptable Law School Admissions Test (LSAT) scores, be admitted to the law school. After successful completion of the first year, they would receive the undergraduate degree and then continue work toward the law degree. As many as a third of first-year students in the early 1950s were pursuing this combined program, but the numbers had declined over a decade to no more than five or six a year. Since these, however, were often among the best students, the combination degree was retained.[53] The law school also bridged academic boundaries by offering a course in business law in the School of Commerce and allowing W&L undergraduates to enroll in law-school courses in constitutional law and administrative law as political science courses.

The controversy over the LLB and JD was prompted by a rising belief that a law school degree was a postgraduate credential rather than the bachelor's degree that it had traditionally been in the United States and remains today in most of the world. In the early twentieth century, students could enter law school directly from high school or after only a year or two of college work. Eventually, as national educational reforms separated undergraduate from advanced professional study, accredited law schools began to require a minimum of three years of college work or a baccalaureate degree prior to admission. It thus became a national issue, prompted by the decision of the University of Chicago, followed by about a third of other law schools, to award the JD. The W&L faculty was still reluctant to make any change and wrestled with the dilemma in the SACS self-study. But the trend already underway would continue, the JD became the accepted standard credential; previous graduates were able to exchange their old diploma for a new one.

The W&L School of Law offered an array of special programs that complemented the curriculum and honed skills for legal practice. The annual Tucker Law Lectures brought noted jurists to campus. The Student Bar Association fostered a variety of extracurricular programs, including the biannual publication of the *Washington and Lee Lawyer,* which focused on activities in the law school, professional practice, and life in the legal community. The Student Bar Association operated the Moot Court Program, which required all first-year students to hone their skills in oral argument and upperclassmen to engage in competition with other teams. The Legal Research Program, established in 1965 and limited to second- and third-year students, provided opportunities to investigate problems submitted by practicing attorneys. Research efforts were prominently emphasized in the W&L *Law Review*, established in 1939–40, which was also recognized for its usefulness for practicing attorneys. Three legal fraternities provided opportunities for professional association and recognition, as did the Law School Association of graduates and former students, faculty members, and members of the third-year class. Placement services operated by the dean's office helped students find employment after graduation, though not all students were entirely satisfied with the results. Finally, the wives of law students formed an "auxiliary" to serve as volunteers, help with official functions, and sponsor social activities.

The performance of graduates on the state bar examination was a key interest of all law schools. W&L graduates generally fared well in comparison with other major schools in and around Virginia—like the University of Richmond, the University of Virginia, William and Mary, Georgetown, and George Washington University—but the pass rates varied from year to year. An unusually poor performance of the twenty-eight W&L graduates taking the exam in December 1965 (only eighteen passed) was redeemed in June 1966, when 80 percent were successful.[54]

The Association of American Law Schools (AALS) placed increasing emphasis on the importance of faculty and student research, and on policies that encouraged and recognized "creative scholarship." Such scholarship was difficult in a professional school with heavy regular teaching responsibilities. An informal visit in March 1964 by a two-man AALS team suggested that W&L was not doing enough to further this activity, though they also advised that such research efforts not be coerced and praised the availability of Robert E. Lee Research grants for students interested in working with faculty members on specific projects. They noted that heavy faculty teaching loads were a major impediment to research. But the team also applauded the law school for "an easily recognizable, unique quality," a "well rounded and balanced" curriculum, "close relations" with the undergraduate colleges, and the ample attention and support it received from the administration. The law library also impressed the AALS team, which declared it well suited "for a private law school whose modest enrollment is composed of students who represent twenty-five states."[55] Trustee Homer "Rocky" Holt welcomed the complimentary report but questioned the emphasis on scholarship: "I am rather inclined to think that there is already too much purposeless writing."[56]

The law school ended the decade with applications rising by 65 percent between 1968 and 1970, which allowed the selection of an entering class of seventy from some five hundred aspirants. Curriculum changes and a larger faculty made enrollment expansion both feasible and desirable, and the new law school building then on the drawing board was designed for a total enrollment of 350. The 1970s would mark a new beginning for W&L's oldest professional school, as the university moved ahead under a new administration headed by an alumnus and former law-school dean.

MCCORMICK LIBRARY remained a centerpiece of campus life. The steadily growing collection numbered almost 180,000 volumes in 1960, more than 185,000 in 1962, and 278,258 (including 1,104 serials) in 1966–67. The university increased the library's $16,000 total operating budget—including funds for books and periodicals—in 1960 by 36 percent. An external review of library operations that year recommended further increases to the budget and rollover of unexpended funds to the following year, the provision of faculty "studies" or carrels, faculty use of interlibrary loan, and location of the university archives in the library. This report resulted in additional increases to the budget and the purchase of additional equipment. The library, like other aspects of university operations, experienced the effects of an inflation rate of more than 31 percent during the decade, as well as a lack of space, and was increasingly unable to meet the needs of growing academic programs.

W&L's library resources compared reasonably well with other selective liberal arts colleges with similar undergraduate enrollment but still lagged behind Bowdoin, Swarthmore, Williams, Amherst, and even Davidson in key areas such as total budget, number of staff, new acquisitions, periodicals, and hours when librarians were available to assist students.[57] Despite the addition of a new reading room with capacity for sixty students, overcrowding was increasingly common, especially during examination periods. The McCormick Library remained a small-scale operation. Open until midnight during the week, it's weekend hours were less reliable and depended largely on available staff. After faculty members raised complaints in 1964, the librarian, Henry Coleman, explained to President Cole that he closed the library on Saturday afternoons when there were home football games because he wanted to attend and "assumed that most normal persons would prefer to encourage our splendid amateur athletes by attending these games."[58] He compensated by keeping the library open longer at other times. Some faculty members remained unpersuaded.

A new head librarian, Maurice D. Leach Jr., assumed his duties in July 1968 and quickly identified a number of areas for improvement. Leach had chaired the Department of Library Science at the University of Kentucky and, most recently, had served as a consultant to the Ford Foundation. A glaring short-coming at W&L, he noted, was the "appalling" number of library staff, which trailed far behind most comparable institutions. The university had some "out-standing resources" in chemistry, Civil War history, romance languages, clas-sics, and humanities—due less to planning and budgeting than to the efforts of individual departments and faculty members. Less unique to W&L were problems caused by inflation and rapidly rising costs, especially for periodicals, which challenged the acquisition budgets of all libraries and forced the cull-ing of existing resources to make way for more. W&L did provide more money for the collection and staffing, and McCormick remained open for even more hours than many of its peers, but some of the library's most serious problems were structural and logistical.

An architect evaluated the existing library even before Leach's arrival on campus and concluded that it would be better to build a new structure than to invest money in renovations. (Just to rewire and replumb the building would require $750,000.) He and Leach worked together to identify problems and propose solutions. They knew that McCormick was running out of storage space for books and that it lacked adequate seating; all four hundred seats were almost continually occupied during exam periods. The building had fixed walls, some three-feet thick, that limited flexibility and impeded efficient use, forcing users into a confusing warren of rooms and spaces. Four offices for faculty had been added, but the number was inadequate. Even though funding had not been raised or committed, Leach was already formulating general plans for a new library with far more space, student carrels spread throughout each floor, enclosed study spaces for faculty and honor students, a room for rare books and special collections, a one-hundred-seat auditorium, and wiring for the latest audiovisual and electronic equipment, such as microfilm readers.[59]

A similar situation existed in the Law Library, which had for decades strug-gled to keep up with the minimum number of volumes required by the AALS for a school of W&L's size. By 1965 the main problem was a lack of space for the growing collection of 35,000 volumes and 249 periodicals, with about 1,500 new volumes being added each year. A large reading room could accommodate about sixty students, but extra storage for books was available only under the Davis Dormitory and the new Freshman Dormitory. The head librarian of the

University of Virginia Law School was commissioned to do a study of W&L's current and future needs, and the board of trustees approved the development of plans for a much-needed addition to Tucker Hall. As in the case of the undergraduate library, the solution lay in alumni beneficence and the building of a new structure.

Major improvements to the university's libraries were among many significant projects that relied on more energetic efforts to raise money. At a time when public higher education was carried on a rising tide of federal and state government financing, and before the full impact of the Higher Education Act of 1965 and its direct support to individual students, independent universities like Washington and Lee continued to rely almost solely on tuition and gifts from individuals and foundations. The endowment was also, of course, a key measure of capability in the competition with other selective institutions for students and faculty.

During the 1960s, Washington and Lee's endowment grew by 53 percent to a market value exceeding $20 million (ranking sixty-second in the country), in addition to income from special trust funds. Alumni giving increased more than five fold, from $47,075 in 1960–61 (when it resumed after a hiatus during the capital campaign) to a record $300,000 in 1968–69.

A $2 million capital campaign, initially dubbed the "University Development Program" and later designated "The Vision of Greatness" campaign, proposed in 1957 by then director of development Donald E. Smith as a $7 million two-phase effort, was launched in 1958–59 to raise money for much-needed facilities in the sciences and journalism. By 1961, the campaign had registered almost $2,190,000 in gifts and pledges from 4,135 contributors, with more than $1.5 million designated for the sciences. Construction of the new Science Building (later named Parmly Hall) and the expansion of Howe Hall began in 1961, at a cost of $1.5 million, and provided new and renovated space for Biology, Physics, Chemistry, and Geology. The expansion provided an office and small laboratory for each faculty member and included labs for student work, a greenhouse, an observatory, departmental libraries, and new equipment. The renovation transformed Howe Hall from an "architectural incongruity" into a more fitting companion to the Colonnade and other buildings.[60] The space in Reid Hall vacated by Physics was renovated primarily for the Department of Journalism and Communications, including the Journalism Laboratory Press and a studio for radio station WLUR-FM.

Four projects completed at the beginning of the decade, together costing almost $1.4 million, had an enormous positive effect on student life. The new Letitia Evans Dining Hall, with a capacity of 650, enabled all freshmen and some upperclassmen to dine together and provided excellent space for social functions, such as Fancy Dress. Two new dormitories, named for former trustees Newton D. Baker and John W. Davis, together housed eighty-three upperclassmen and law students, and Gilliam Dormitory accommodated ninety-one freshmen and counselors, as well as the university medical center and infirmary. A new wing for what was officially called the Student Union Building, added as part of the Evans Dining Hall construction, accommodated the University Supply Store and Book Store. In 1969, the Student Union Building was completely renovated, with an added connecting wing to Evans Dining Hall, designated the Early-Fielding Memorial University Center. Most dramatic was a $3 million, 100,000-square foot addition to Doremus Gymnasium (which had been basically unchanged for fifty years) that included a new swimming pool, a basketball court, locker rooms, and offices. Construction of the new facility began in February 1970 and was completed in 1971, giving W&L a head start in the national race to satisfy rising student expectations for campus athletic and fitness facilities.

Extensive renovation began on Lee Chapel in 1962, supported by $370,000 from the Ford Motor Company. Allen W. Merrell, Ford Company vice president, formally presented the first installment at the 1961 commencement. Merrell saluted Lee's "courage, his integrity, and the lofty dignity of his character that caused him to rise above bitterness [and] inspire all of us." The painstaking work restored the chapel to its appearance in 1883, when the addition to house the Valentine statue and the Lee family mausoleum on the lower level was completed. The chapel's masonry was generally sound, but some interior beams and structural elements were replaced and strengthened, the walls were refinished, and modern lighting, heating, air-conditioning, and dehumidifying systems were installed. The portraits gracing the chapel's walls were placed in storage or relocated to the McCormick Library. The modest chapel was lovingly restored as an iconic campus symbol and National Historic Landmark.

Other projects included the remodeling of the President's Home ($65,833), completed for occupancy by President Cole in 1960; construction of the University Maintenance Center in 1965; installation of a prefabricated building for use by ROTC and the Buildings and Grounds Department in 1967; remodeling of the Troubadour Theater in 1969; and the conversion of a former faculty residence, once occupied by "Fitz" Flournoy and located just below duPont

Hall, into the Alumni House, supported by $80,428 in alumni contributions and opened for reunions in Spring 1966.

As the 1970s ended, a campus master plan included a variety of future projects that would enable the university to accommodate a larger student body of 1,700 undergraduates and 350 in the law school. Chief among them was a new 100,000-square-foot library, sited directly behind the Colonnade; a new law school building, projected near the old tennis courts and Wilson Field, on the other side of the Woods Creek Ravine; the conversion of the McCormick Library to serve as the new home of the growing School of Commerce, Economics, and Politics; and renovations to Newcomb and Tucker Halls, the first for History, Religion, and Philosophy, and the second for Foreign Languages. Other needs included an athletic field house; upperclassmen dormitories to provide more housing on campus and a "better sense of academic community"; improvements to landscaping, roads, and infrastructure; a proposed $1.1 million "restoration" of the historic Colonnade and adjacent faculty houses; and conversion of the campus heating system from coal to gas. Another project on the list was restoration of Col Alto, the pre–Civil War Lexington mansion on Nelson Avenue—a bequest to the university by Mrs. Rosa Tucker Mason, who died in 1961, for a presidential house, conference center, and guest residence. Lastly, plans for up to fifty new units for married student housing, convenient to the new law school building, meant the end of Hillside Terrace, the collection of New Deal Era student dwellings west of campus—equally famous for thin walls and surprising persistence—that had long been inexpensive homes to newly married couples and their children and pets.[61]

The estimated cost of all these projects, not including the Doremus addition, exceeded $16 million. They represented an increasingly ambitious and confident vision of what the university could achieve, shaped both by the largely successful developments of the 1960s and the pressures of competition among institutions for the most up-do-date facilities and amenities. The new campus would take W&L into the twenty-first century.

The university's fund-raising organization and operations had, by some accounts, been weakened by the dissolution of the Development Office after Donald E. Smith's departure in February 1958 and the transfer of its responsibilities to a new director of University Relations. Fred Cole, when he was appointed president in June 1959, retained the new arrangement. Efforts to fund some projects faltered, but the capital campaign was completed successfully, and the growth in annual alumni giving and the endowment was impressive.

But a modern fund-raising infrastructure—built on a long-range plan and extensive information about potential donors, their preferences, and financial capacity—was badly needed. The university's endowment was called upon to fund an increasing proportion of the operating budget, the list of needed facilities continued to grow, and local-bank bridge loans were sometimes required in the summer to cover expenses until tuition payments were received. Moreover, the university's fund-raising efforts fell behind its needs and its aspirations.

Cole was quite attuned to the importance of support from private foundations and the federal government. He led the effort to upgrade the university's science facilities and stressed the importance of new funding to secure the university's future. He did not, however, enjoy the grueling work of fund-raising—the personal cultivation of individual donors and the travel, speeches, and cocktail parties necessary in any campaign. He had the temperament and highly developed skills of a scholar and administrator but not the chummy conviviality so often essential in securing major gifts and alumni goodwill. Under the leadership of Frank Parsons and, shortly thereafter, Farris Hotchkiss, a development office was restored in 1967.

THE SACS SELF-STUDY discussions led to major changes in the composition and organization of W&L's governing body. The board of trustees had always been self-perpetuating; members served for life and elected new members. This concept, dating back to colonial times and intended to ensure stability in leadership and continuity in policy, resulted in lengthy terms of service, terminated only by resignation or death. In 1960, eight of the fifteen trustees had served for fifteen years or longer, and the rector, James R. Caskie, had been on the board for thirty-six years. Walter L. Carson died in 1959, after thirty-three years of service. By 1966, the senior voting trustee (Caskie) had served for forty-two years. This arrangement tended to perpetuate a similar worldview, insulate the board from external influences, neglect new talent, and reinforce prevailing values, priorities, and prejudices. Not surprisingly, new board members closely resembled the older ones: white, male, alumni, and southern.

W&L's board was perhaps not overly sclerotic in comparison to many other private institutions, but it seemed unprepared to bring energy and fresh perspectives to address the multiple challenges of the time. James Whitehead remembers that his tasks during board meetings were to keep Rector Caskie awake (he had very poor eyesight and would often fall asleep during meetings) and to interpret for James M. Hutcheson, who was hard of hearing.[62] Frank

Parsons—who was a "general-purpose assistant" to Fred Cole and who, along with Bob Huntley, drew up the details of the new board reorganization plan—recalled a moment after one board meeting in the president's outer office on a rainy, gloomy day. Walking around the room, smoking one cigarette after another, Cole was clearly distressed. "I've never seen him more discouraged," Parsons said. Caskie, then eighty-two, had just resigned, but they had replaced him with Hutcheson, then eighty-four.[63] The board's discussions and decisions in this period tended to be dominated by "younger" trustees, especially the energetic and forceful Homer "Rocky" Holt, who was sixty-eight years old in 1966. He had already been on the board for twenty-six years.

Governing boards composed of outside "lay" members were a particular characteristic of American higher education, an organizational device with many strengths—and weaknesses. Such boards were intended to ensure accountability to the larger community and a broader perspective untainted by pecuniary interests, specialized academic expertise, or internal institutional politics. In the independent sector, members were typically graduates of the institution, major donors, or notable citizens; in the public sector, they were usually political appointees, though with most of the same characteristics. Ideally, boards provided broad, strategic oversight of the institution and focused on matters of planning, policy, and the appointment of the institution's president and other senior administrators. Ideally, board members were solely concerned for the best interests of the institution rather than by the needs of any particular constituency. On the other hand, there were few constraints on board actions, which could greatly magnify the weaknesses of this system. Boards were susceptible (as a group or as individuals) to becoming significantly involved in the day-to-day business of the institution, thereby undermining the authority of the administration. Their ideas and actions could be deeply flawed and based on purely personal predilection and narrow interests. A few strong members could dominate board operations and act beyond the control of fellow members, the administration, or any constituency. Board members also were usually unfamiliar with the peculiar patterns of academic culture—academic freedom, the key role of the faculty and shared governance, and the deliberate pace of decision making—and were likely to draw on their own experience and think in terms of other nonprofit organizations or businesses and law firms.

In times of change, boards could be bulwarks against dangerous tendencies or fashions, but they could also be impediments to progress and necessary adjustments to changing realities. Any weaknesses were greatly magnified by the self-perpetuation that ensured that many board members were firmly tied to the outlook and prejudices of previous generations. This danger was fully illustrated in the response of southern university boards of trustees to racial integration.

With the advice and guidance of Booz, Allen and Hamilton, the W&L board examined the "best practices" in the country in pondering their own organization. This matter was already under consideration by the administration, and the self-study provided an excellent opportunity to examine it in the context of a comprehensive institutional review. From his experience at Tulane, Fred Cole was well aware of the deleterious impact of an opinionated and intrusive board, and he quietly encouraged these discussions. A special meeting of the executive committee, including Cole and the lead consultant, met on March 28, 1966, to consider the proposed changes. Their recommendations were approved by the full board in executive session on May 14.[64] Among other things, the trustees established new standing committees and accepted increased responsibility for setting institutional objectives, overseeing comprehensive planning, and developing financial resources.[65]

The board acknowledged that it had given "more attention to individual qualifications" than to "compositional requirements" in selecting new board members, and also that it should consider areas of particular experience and expertise. Trustees should be recruited "from a broader geographic area." These and other recommendations by the consultants were referred to the Nominating Committee for review and not included in the self-study report. Finally, on May 18, 1968, with continued support from Bob Huntley, W&L's new president, the trustees approved expanding the board to twenty-one members and electing a member nominated by the Alumni Association on a rotating basis. In October, it adopted further provisions, including a preference for at least one or two non-alumni trustees, "a conscious effort to diversify the membership of the Board in terms of occupations, geographical location, and age," and to declare vacant the position of any trustee who failed to attend board meetings for more than a year. Finally, at its meeting on May 17, the board adopted recommendations of the Nominating Committee by a vote of ten to two (with trustees Rocky Holt and John Hendon opposed) and made appropriate changes in the by-laws.[66]

The changes, fully implemented in January 1970, were significant. The board continued to select new members, but its size was increased from sixteen to nineteen (rather than the twenty-one proposed earlier). Members were elected to six-year terms (eligible for reelection to one additional term, after which they were ineligible for reelection for one year) and were forced to retire once they reached the age of seventy (except for currently sitting board members). Beginning in 1970 and every two years thereafter, the board would consider for membership at least one nominee by the Alumni Association. The university president continued as an ex-officio member. A retiring board member could be elected trustee emeritus, able to attend and participate in future board meetings but not to vote.

The procedures implementing these changes were incorporated in amendments to the by-laws. Current active members with the greatest seniority (even those over the age of seventy) would serve initial two-year terms, and members with less seniority would begin terms of four years. Upon reaching seventy years of age, they would be ineligible for reappointment. If less than seventy, they could stand for election to new six-year terms, or terms of shorter duration, but they would have to retire upon reaching the mandatory age limit. New and very recent appointees would begin six-year terms. These changes in the board, begun when Cole was president and completed early in the Huntley administration, were designed to ensure greater turnover among the trustees, fresher perspectives (especially from younger members), regular participation, and incorporation of the organized alumni in some formal way into the leadership of the university.

The self-study also led to changes in administrative organization and staffing, primarily to reduce the number of people reporting directly to the president, achieve more logical distribution of responsibilities among senior administrators, and strengthen functions that were relatively neglected. The new organizational chart included assignment of institutional research to a presidential assistant, assignment to the treasurer of responsibility for "all business and development services" (and a new Office of University Services), and creation of a new position of assistant dean in the College.

Functions identified as "not well provided for" in the current framework received particular attention. A new Office of University Development, with its own director, was created to oversee fund-raising activities. This new office was an institutional successor to the effort led by Don E. Smith until his departure in February 1958. The new office would not report directly to the president but to James Whitehead in his expanded position as assistant to the president and treasurer.[67] The board approved the appointment of Frank Parsons as director of development and Farris P. Hotchkiss as associate director in January 1967.

Hotchkiss became director when Parsons was named assistant to the president in the fall of 1968. Even though designated leadership for development had been restored, the special committees and organizational activity of a decade earlier were long gone.

IN MAY 1967, President Fred Cole submitted his resignation, effective September 1. He had accepted the presidency of the Council of Library Resources in Washington, DC, an organization he had helped establish as a consultant with the Ford Foundation in 1954–55. The Trustees accepted his resignation "with profound regret," a sentiment also expressed by many faculty members. Now fifty-five years of age, Cole departed after eight years of growth and adjustment for W&L and a number of professional accomplishments and accolades. He had chaired the board of trustees of the College Entrance Examination Board and the Advisory Council on Research of the Office of Education, served for three years as president of the Virginia Foundation for Independent Colleges, and chaired the nominating committee for national Phi Beta Kappa.[68] The trustees began preparations for a presidential search and appointed professor of German and College dean William Webb Pusey III as acting president.

Soon after Cole's departure, Bill Pusey wrote him with news of the campus and reassurance that "many of the things you began are gradually being implemented." Less than three months later, Pusey wrote to celebrate the election as president of a man Cole had brought into the administration as legal adviser to the university, secretary of the board, and dean of the law school. Indeed, Cole had helped groom Robert E. R. Huntley to be his successor. Pusey wrote, "I think Bob is top-flight and will do a good job." He also reported the trustees' approval to admit "a few Mary Baldwin girls . . . to advanced physics courses" through a new exchange program. The beginning of a new presidency in challenging times had obvious significance for Washington and Lee. Along with the erosion of campus traditions, student unrest, and financial uncertainty, the subject of women in W&L classes would become a major controversy.[69]

During Cole's tenure—brief only in comparison with his predecessor's lengthy time in office—he guided W&L successfully through a challenging transition, bringing to bear his knowledge of academic culture and administrative operations. He assembled a capable administration, instituted more up-to-date administrative practices, sought consensus for decisions, patiently steered intense and routine conversations, offered ideas, put more emphasis on support for faculty research and new science facilities, and instituted new merit-based criteria and procedures for faculty rewards and promotion that lasted long after he left. He presided over significant increases in the number of faculty and in faculty salaries, new incentives for scholarship and research, an expansion of campus buildings and facilities (especially in the sciences), increases in financial aid, stronger standards for admission, the installation of the university's first computer, and the renovations to Lee Chapel. He also strongly embraced the university's new direction in intercollegiate athletics. Eliminating the development office did not end gifts to the university, but it was nevertheless a step backward from modern fund-raising that had to be reversed later. But Cole did more than any president before him to emphasize academic achievement as W&L's highest priority, the core of its aspirations and reputation. Using the SACS self-study, he encouraged and sustained a broader conversation about the principal issues facing the university and helped bring about significant, and overdue, changes in the curriculum and in the organization of the board. He worked closely—and often behind the scenes, assisted by Bob Huntley and Frank Gilliam—with the faculty and the board to guide discussions on controversial topics, such as changing student habits and traditions, as well as options for meeting future challenges, ranging from funding to the future shape of the institution. He made clear to reluctant trustees the necessity for racial integration and took steps to implement it. He brought strong new people to the board and also positioned and groomed the man who would be his successor.

In a 1989 address in Lee Chapel, Huntley said that Cole "brought a great inner strength to Washington and Lee at a time when its traditional strengths were showing signs of decay and erosion." Working with the trustees, Cole "refought the battle of free inquiry and free speech on the campus, the admission of black students, and the role of the faculty." He helped lay the foundations "that we are still building on." Fred Cole, Huntley observed, "was a shy man who never got the credit he deserved. I admired him greatly; to the degree that I could live up to it, he was my exemplar."[70]

Cole had speculated that eight years was about the right tenure for any president, having by then achieved many of his goals but also having faced backlash and the prospect of limited future effectiveness.[71] In this context, his timing was probably right. Despite considerable contributions over most of a challenging decade, Cole was not perfectly suited to the role of a small-college president. He was not a good public speaker, nor did he enjoy large cocktail parties, small talk, and the fervid bonhomie of alumni gatherings. He disliked noisy, unruly, inattentive behavior by students or alumni. He was always a perfect gentleman, though also personally reserved and even reticent, in contrast to the open warmth of Frank Gaines.[72] He arrived at an awkward time, in the middle of a capital campaign requiring many commitments away from campus, usually at podiums before alumni groups. He was patient with the trustees but had to sometimes nudge them in unwelcome directions, and he became less sure of his ability to influence them in the future.[73] He doubtless knew that Huntley, an alumnus with a sharp analytical legal mind and a knack for working and negotiating with trustees and alumni, would be better suited to tackle the challenges ahead—especially a major fund-raising campaign. Cole clearly found leadership of a foundation or the national library association to be a more comfortable assignment, but he left a significant and positive mark on Washington and Lee, having repositioned it for a new time and the challenges that lay ahead, and having laid essential foundations for the good work of his successors.

CHAPTER SIX

ISSUES OF RACE AND THE CIVIL RIGHTS REVOLUTION

RACE IS A BROAD VEIN coursing through the bedrock of American history, exposed most nakedly on the cultural landscape of the South. The introduction of chattel slavery in the New World shaped human action, defined human relationships, and contradicted the finest declarations of freedom and equality in the emerging United States. Throughout most of American history, many white Americans believed, in varying degrees, that "primitive peoples" but especially African Americans were innately inferior to whites. These notions were deeply embedded in the South and were employed to justify institutionalized racial inequality, first under slavery and later through the structures of racial segregation.

Racial segregation was a comprehensive and pervasive system of social control, implemented through "Jim Crow" laws that arose to govern race relations after Emancipation and Reconstruction. Blacks and whites were strictly separated in almost all areas of activity and commerce, including in schools, courtrooms, hotels, waiting rooms, public transportation, and toilets. Even drinking fountains were separate. Segregation was an omnipresent daily reminder of the supposed "natural order of things," which reinforced the social legitimacy of prejudice. It also sabotaged the democratic process by the disenfranchisement of blacks through poll taxes, arbitrarily administered voter registration "tests," violence, and intimidation. The Southern racial system was nevertheless complex and multilayered, because contacts between whites and blacks were also prevalent and routine, even though strictly controlled. Relationships did exist among the races, but formal segregation prohibited anything that might imply racial equality. The journalist Harry Golden, editor of the *Carolina Israelite*, famously quipped that blacks and whites were welcome to interact with each other as long as they didn't sit down.

Many whites, however benevolent they considered their feelings for individual blacks, came to believe that their southern "way of life" was dependent on the preservation of racial inequality. They could hardly imagine their society surviving without it.

AS A WHITE, CONSERVATIVE, southern university—and one with historic Confederate associations—Washington and Lee was hardly a bastion of social reform or racial progress. One dramatic flare-up in the 1920s revealed the state of race relations and athletics in the South and at W&L. The football team made an appearance in Little Washington, Pennsylvania, in October 1923, to play Washington and Jefferson University, which had a black halfback, Charles West, on the roster. Following the standard practice for southern institutions at the time, W&L reached—or thought it had reached—a "gentleman's agreement" (not stated in the contract between the two schools but nonetheless a condition for W&L's participation) that West would be held out of the game. Several days before the game, W&L's graduate manager (the equivalent of the latter-day athletic director), Richard A. "Cap'n Dick" Smith, reminded his counterpart at Washington and Jefferson about this matter, which they had already discussed. "The faculty here would not allow us to schedule this game if they knew that we would play against him. We realize the feeling here is different than at your school and of course hate to bring the matter up on that account and are leaving the matter in your hands to handle as you see fit."[1] As it turned out, the Washington and Jefferson coach refused to abide by the informal agreement and kept West in the starting lineup. On the orders of Henry D. Campbell, dean of the university, the W&L team refused to compete and left the field, causing a furor. A parade of Washington and Jefferson students reportedly "changed into a mob and many of the townsmen joined them," tearing down W&L pennants and pelting the visitors with rotten fruit.[2] The Washington and Jefferson graduate manager denied having ever committed to such an agreement in the first place. The coach in question was John Heisman, who was at Washington and Jefferson for only that one year, after having served as head coach at other institutions, including Auburn, Clemson, Georgia Tech, and Pennsylvania, and the man whose name the New York Athletic Club affixed in 1936 to its trophy for the outstanding collegiate football player in the nation.

Governor W. A. MacCorkle of West Virginia asked W&L president Henry Louis Smith for particulars. Smith responded that W&L had done all it could to avoid the situation, sending Coach James DeHart to Washington and Jefferson to work out suitable arrangements (similar to those worked out with Rutgers University several years before). But when the W&L team arrived, they were "both surprised and horrified at the strange and unjustifiable stand taken" by the new Washington and Jefferson head coach, presumably because West was the son of "one of the leading citizens" of the community. Smith reported that the W&L team "was attacked by the mob, the policemen, several of whom were negroes, not only allowing but encouraging the riot." To another correspondent, the education director of the Brooklyn YMCA who had inquired about the incident, Smith wrote, "I am sure you are totally unaware of the absolute social cleavage between the two races" in the South.

> There is no single sentiment in the whole South which so nearly amounts to a universal and passionate religion as the fixed determination that the whites of the South shall not amalgamate with the blacks but that the two races shall be free from admixture. Practically all Southerners whose land is swarming with negroes, constituting from thirty to sixty per cent of their community, believe that if amalgamation were allowed to begin we would become a land of half-breeds in a very few generations like Santo Domingo, Cuba, and Haiti. No farmer with a hundred registered Jerseys on which his living depends could be more determined to avoid amalgamation with hopeless half-wild scrub stock than the Anglo-Saxon communities of the South.

Allowing "one of negro blood" to play on a southern team "or attend a Southern social function is just about as unthinkable as it would be, for example, for young women of high social standing to attend a Northern social function with no clothes on."[3]

Though shocking and offensive to modern ears, this statement was an accurate reflection of the racial arrangements—and anxieties—in the South at the time. The decision to leave the field at Washington and Jefferson was quickly and unanimously endorsed at W&L by the executive committee of the student body and apparently enjoyed wide support among the faculty. The issue of race in intersectional athletic competition continued to arise—at W&L and most other universities in the South—well into the 1950s. In December 1937, for example, President Frank Gaines wrote to Smith concerning a scheduled basketball game with Long Island University, a team with a "colored youth." Recalling the unfortunate 1923 fiasco, Gaines reiterated the university's position—if Long Island University could not guarantee, in writing, "that this colored boy will not be played as a member of the regular team or as a substitute under any circumstances," then the game should be canceled.[4]

With the passage of time, W&L's desire for national prominence (in athletics and otherwise) increasingly conflicted with sentiment in the rest of country regarding racial segregation. W&L trustees were not all of one mind on the issue. In November 1949, Gaines sought individual trustee opinions about scheduling northern teams with black players. Specifically, he pointed to possible football games with Lafayette and Yale, both of which had black players, and noted that the unwritten "gentlemen's agreement" used in the past would no longer be honored by any northern school. He also noted that the University of Virginia had played a game against a Harvard team with a black player in 1948 and that playing such games only on the home fields of the other schools, "even if temporarily possible, could not be permanent and would not settle the issue."[5]

Rector Herbert Fitzpatrick urged adherence to standing—though unwritten—policy. "Taking into consideration our entire situation," he wrote, "the history of the institution, the type of boy which Washington and Lee wants in its student body, the section from which we expect, in the main, to draw, I do not believe that the school can afford to meet teams in intercollegiate sports which 'accept players who are not white.' If this means not scheduling any college, it cannot be avoided." But future rector James Caskie responded, "I am thoroughly convinced that it is a question of time, and probably a short time now, when such games will be scheduled by all southern schools. However, so far as Washington & Lee is concerned, I think it is yet a little too early, as we have a special and peculiar situation." Huston St. Clair declared, "It is better that we play a school that has one or more Negro players than to refuse to play the school solely because it does have." J. Morrison Hutcheson of Richmond concurred that "the arguments for, out weigh those against" and offered his support. John Newton Thomas, a member of the theology department at the Union Theological Seminary in Richmond, was especially supportive of scheduling teams with black players: "I might even go so far as to say that this would, in my judgment, mark a real advance for us." And John W. Davis, who weighed in as a trustee emeritus, wrote to say he "would not balk at the presence of a Negro on their team if they want him." In a handwritten comment, he added, perhaps in jest, "Such an encounter might re-activate our team."[6]

Trustee Clarence R. Avery of Chattanooga admitted that "this race question is getting pretty serious and I personally don't know the answer." He would leave the decision on scheduling northern teams up to Gaines. He also shared Gaines's inquiry with fellow Chattanooga alumnus Edward E. Brown and forwarded Brown's response to Gaines. Brown—who had complained in 1945 that W&L would lose enrollment if it failed to schedule larger schools in football—stated that he had no objection to W&L playing any teams with black players, even in Lexington. "I am further of the opinion," he wrote, "that where the school admits negroes to its student body that these negroes should not be denied the privilege of competing for places on the school's athletic teams. It seems to me that we have reached the place in this country where economic and athletic opportunity must not be denied the negro, but this does not mean that I favor social equality or the FEPC [Fair Employment Practices Commission]."[7] How to make necessary accommodations without embracing "social equality" was a conundrum.

By January 1950, W&L had still not decided on its scheduled game with Lafayette. Gaines wrote to the Lafayette president, Ralph C. Hutchison, expressing the "highest respect for Lafayette" and never mentioning the issue of the black player on their football squad. Rather, he noted the "present disposition" to "play more teams in our immediate vicinity, notably the Southern Conference to which we belong," and expressed his general frustration with the several committees and other complexities of scheduling. "Off the record, but in dead earnest," he wrote, "when you have been in this business as long as I have, you will be rather glad to have some other agency to take over athletics; if you do not have such agency, you will not have much time for anything else. It has comforted me on many occasions to be able to say that I am not responsible in any way, except a remote veto power, for this scheduling business."[8] It would not get any easier.

Prior to 1950, racial controversy rarely impinged on the routine operations of the university. Complaints surrounding a handful of African Americans at the Army School during the war years were largely confined to a few zealous individuals and were successfully fended off by the administration, which pleaded helplessness to do anything about it. As the old racial system, framed by segregation, began to buckle in the 1950s and 1960s, the fears and animus of southern whites were heightened, leading to violent excesses often quietly sanctioned by the authorities and to the government-sponsored campaigns of resistance to racial integration in Virginia and elsewhere. For some whites, however, the events of these years revealed the old system and its underlying assumptions to be unsustainable, and they recoiled from the vicious racism that signified spiritual poverty and led to social disorder. In general, W&L proceeded carefully and fitfully through the civil rights maelstrom, wishing neither to upset the traditionalists nor to support ignorance and violence.

SOCIAL TRANSFORMATION swept the nation in the postwar years. In 1947, Jackie Robinson joined the Brooklyn Dodgers, and in 1948, President Harry S. Truman's executive order ended segregation in the Armed Forces. The most far-reaching changes, however, arose from a series of legal decisions. The US Supreme Court's rulings invalidated provisions in Virginia for segregating interstate buses (1946), prohibited the University of Oklahoma Law School from denying admission to anyone based on color (1948), declared racially restrictive covenants unconstitutional (1948), outlawed differential treatment on racial grounds by public institutions of higher education (1950), and abolished racial segregation in railroad dining cars (1950). By court order, an African American student was admitted to the University of Virginia law school in 1950. A federal district court ordered separate but equal schools in South Carolina in 1952 (a case argued for the state by John W. Davis), which the US Supreme Court agreed to hear as part of the landmark *Brown v. Board of Education of Topeka, Kans.* This sweeping case, decided in 1954 and reaffirmed in 1955, overturned the "separate but equal" doctrine laid out in *Plessy v. Ferguson* and declared racially segregated schools throughout the country to be unconstitutional. The decision was a clear and definitive message that the old order was doomed.

Undermining the legal framework for segregation was only the beginning of the battle against deep-seated prejudice and custom, and the hearts and minds of many in the country were still reluctant to change. Southern cities and state legislatures struck back with a variety of measures intended to delay, impede, or prevent efforts to integrate the schools, firing teachers and principals who obeyed court orders, shifting public funds to private white academies, and even closing public schools altogether. State laws declared the school desegregation decision—and in one case, even the Thirteenth and Fourteenth Amendments to the US Constitution—illegal, following the pre–Civil War doctrine of state's rights and "nullification" of federal law.

Though not a Deep South state, Virginia was in the forefront of the fight to maintain existing racial customs. United States senator Harry Flood Byrd, the courtly but powerful leader of the political organization that for decades dominated state politics through county courthouses—and at the time a W&L trustee—announced on February 24, 1956, a campaign of "Massive Resistance" to school desegregation. A series of laws passed by the General Assembly employed virtually every major stratagem to deflect integration, the most notable —and notorious—of which authorized the governor to close any school that integrated. By 1958, the NAACP had won court orders to integrate schools in several jurisdictions, including Charlottesville and Norfolk. Governor J. Lindsay Almond Jr. responded by closing those schools. Local and state government continued to fight efforts to reopen the schools, even after successful lawsuits filed by parents of white children who were denied public education. The Norfolk schools reopened in February 1959, but the disruption of education in some other areas did not end, and private, all-white, "segregation academies" essentially funded by the state persisted until the 1960s and beyond. The most egregious and destructive example of this approach was in Prince Edward County, which shut down its entire public school system from 1958 to 1964; its white academy did not admit black students until 1986. Even when Massive Resistance ended, Virginia employed a "Freedom of Choice" approach that allowed students to pick the schools they attended—helping to sustain segregation and leading to court-ordered busing in the late 1960s and 1970s.

Court decisions continued to dismantle segregation in public transportation, education, restaurants, and other public places, but their enforcement was spotty and often fiercely resisted. In the end, direct challenges had to be launched against local customs that were supported by armed authorities. New organizations—like the Southern Christian Leadership Conference (SCLC)— sprang up, putting African American churches in the center of the protests and championing the doctrine of civil disobedience and the tactic of nonviolence. The first SCLC chairman, Dr. Martin Luther King Jr., emerged as an eloquent spokesman for the movement. Whether organized or impromptu, nonviolent challenges to racial discrimination placed the established order on the defensive. But the sacrifices were considerable. Blacks and sympathetic whites were intimidated, insulted, beaten, and even killed while local authorities either looked the other way or actually perpetrated the violence. Federal judges received vicious phone calls, death threats, and cross-burnings at their homes, and they often had to be placed under special protection.

The black children who first integrated the all-white high school in Little Rock, Arkansas, in 1957, under the protection of the National Guard called out by President Dwight Eisenhower, were subjected to jeers, obscenities, and harassment from white onlookers. Similar scenes played out elsewhere as court decisions on school integration were implemented. Blacks seeking service at segregated lunch counters were ignored by the staff and surrounded by bellicose white crowds who taunted and spit on them. This "sit-in" movement, which began in Oklahoma City in 1958, grew larger and spread to Greensboro, North Carolina, and Richmond, Virginia, in early 1960, and later to Atlanta, where King was among those arrested.

Courts had decided that segregated interstate public transportation was illegal, but local communities refused to obey or enforce the decisions. "Freedom Riders," groups of courageous blacks and whites, boarded Greyhound buses in the North and rode into the Deep South. The bus of the first group was burned outside Anniston, Alabama, in May 1961. They continued on another bus to Birmingham, where they were attacked and beaten in the city's bus terminal by an outraged white mob facilitated by local police. Traveling on under escort from state troopers, provided at the insistence of the federal government, they were arrested in Jackson, Mississippi, and spent months in the notorious Parchman State Prison. The severe and even life-threatening beatings inflicted on nonviolent protesters in public bus stations revealed that authorities in the South were determined to uphold the existing system at all costs and—as the protesters hoped—cast in high relief the moral issues involved. The United States was now suffering serious damage to its image abroad.[9]

The national momentum for change grew in the pivotal year of 1963. The new governor of Alabama, George C. Wallace, promised in his January inauguration to uphold "segregation forever." In the spring, King targeted the industrial city of Birmingham as a site for nonviolent demonstrations. The effort to overwhelm the city's jails with arrested protesters was unsuccessful, until a spontaneous outpouring of black youth, much to the distress of many parents, left their schools to join the movement in the streets. Met by police dogs, blasts from fire hoses that threw them in the air like rag dolls, and mass arrests, the protestors did indeed flood the jails. The dramatic photographs of these events were transmitted around the world. White business leaders, who stayed out of the public fray but who had long empowered racist elements in the city government and police to resist change and ensure "public order," finally intervened when it became apparent that the city's image and business prospects were seriously threatened. Department stores were desegregated, and other modest reforms followed, but Birmingham had become an example and a rallying cry. In August, as part of the March on Washington, King delivered the "I Have a Dream" speech, which was all the more dramatic and effective because of the backdrop of Birmingham. In September, a bomb at the Sixteenth Street Baptist Church there killed four young black girls, an event that aroused further national outrage and helped pave the way for national action.[10]

At colleges and universities, integration proceeded more or less smoothly, except in the Deep South. The 1956 arrival on campus of Arthurine Lucy, the first black student at the University of Alabama, was accompanied by days of riots, and she was eventually expelled. That institution was not integrated until June 1963, after Governor Wallace theatrically stood in the doorway. James Meredith was barred from entering the University of Mississippi in September, and his admission under protection of National Guard troops was accompanied by days of riots, leading to some deaths. On the other hand, some southern law schools had been successfully integrated during the 1950s, and the first black undergraduate student at the University of Virginia graduated in June 1962.

The civil rights movement extended through the remainder of the decade, as did the resistance it encountered. The "Mississippi Freedom Summer" of 1964 brought thousands of college students and other volunteers to register black voters and work for local civil rights organizations. Alabama state troopers attacked nonviolent protesters on the Edmund Pettus Bridge in Selma, Alabama, on a march to the state capital in Montgomery on March 7, 1965. After "Bloody Sunday," as it became known, the National Guard was again federalized to protect a march that grew even larger.

One of the most shocking and painfully memorable events of the time was the assassination of President John F. Kennedy in Dallas, Texas, on November 22, 1963. Afterward, his successor, former vice president Lyndon B. Johnson of Texas, implemented key portions of Kennedy's legislative agenda and also brought to bear his own personal commitment to racial equality. Two of these laws are among the most significant in American history: the Civil Rights Act of July 1964 and the Voting Rights Act of August 1965. The accumulated court decisions and the courage of federal judges in the South to enforce them; the specter of hatred, fear, and injustice that convinced the country that change was essential; and new legislation to advance equal rights and guarantee the right of blacks and other minorities to vote—with dramatic impact on local governments in the South—were all important in bringing about fundamental change.

Despite the significant advances in civil rights, the political climate was hardly stable, and the country's future uncertain. The assassinations of Martin Luther King Jr. in April 1968 in Memphis, Tennessee, and Robert F. Kennedy in June in Los Angeles, California, threw a pall over the national mood. At the raucous Democratic National Convention in Chicago that summer, police attacked demonstrators and even some delegates in the streets, signaling further challenges ahead. By this time, new and perhaps even more difficult issues of race, such as economic inequality and denial of opportunity, were highlighted in major urban riots (including in Los Angeles in 1965 to protest police brutality and economic conditions in the black "ghetto" of Watts) and coupled with the rising resistance to American involvement in Vietnam; these issues were expanding the agenda for change. Student sit-ins and demonstrations in 1969—at Brandeis, Wisconsin, Duke, and Cornell, among others—indicated that change and conflict were coming to higher education and would shape the character and style of the next decade.

WASHINGTON AND LEE shared the prevailing ideas, customs, and political environment of the American South at midcentury and, as a conservative institution, was not particularly eager for change driven by outside pressures. Many students and alumni were from outside the South, but the majority lived and worked in southern communities, and some held very strong allegiances to the existing social system. As with other southern private universities aspiring to national recognition, W&L hoped that the issue of race could be approached gradually and under the control of "responsible" members of the white commercial-civic elite who understood the ways of the South and could avoid violence and controversy. But avoiding conflict had become impossible by the late 1950s. "While tensions had been growing between regional leadership and national prominence since the end of World War II," historian Melissa Kean wrote, "only now did these paths come to seem incompatible. Simply put, there was no longer any way for these schools to please both the white South and the rest of the country."[11]

The building legal momentum to secure civil rights during the 1950s was, not surprisingly, recognized and discussed in the nation's law schools, and those in the South came under increasing pressure from their peers outside the region to accept students regardless of color. The law schools became "lightning rods for challenges to the racial status quo."[12] An especially serious and recurrent challenge was the opposition to racial discrimination by the Association of American Law Schools. In the fall of 1950, a resolution introduced by Yale Law School, and proposed for consideration at the annual AALS meeting in Chicago in late December, provided that any law school with racially restrictive admissions be expelled from the organization. President Gaines received a letter in early November from A. G. Lively, an alumnus, judge, and attorney in Lebanon,

Virginia. Lively lamented the "extent to which many organizations have gone and are going to try to dictate to the white people of the South social and political policies," and suggested "aggressive opposition" to such dictates. Gaines responded that W&L had heard nothing about the matter but would look into it. (In fact, the proposed resolution had been circulated to the membership in early October.) "Of course I share exactly your sentiments," Gaines wrote. "The extreme steps now being taken have disturbed me, but I have reached a point at which nothing surprises me. But don't worry about your Alma Mater."[13]

W&L joined most other southern law schools in opposing the Yale resolution at the annual AALS meeting, on the grounds that factors such as race, gender, and other "personal characteristics" should play no role in considerations for admission. (Ironically, of course, this was precisely the position of those opposed to racial segregation.) The "Yale amendment" failed, but a committee was appointed to consider the future adoption of such a proposal, and the AALS Articles of Association were amended to declare nondiscrimination on the basis of race as an objective to be pursued (voluntarily) by all member schools. The AALS Special Committee on Racial Discrimination was established in 1951 to promote and monitor progress toward this objective.

In a 1954 interim report, the committee identified southern institutions that had complied with the standard, including all AALS-member law schools in Arkansas, the District of Columbia, Kentucky, Maryland, Missouri, Oklahoma, and Texas. Only sixteen member schools still refused to comply, including W&L and two other private institutions in Virginia. The University of Virginia had modified its admissions requirements and was in compliance. In its final report for 1954, the committee recommended that pressure continue on noncomplying members and pointed to the steady increase in the number of schools in voluntary compliance and to the potential impact of the Supreme Court's *Brown v. Board of Education* decision.[14] In February 1955, Gaines received a letter from the committee chairman summarizing these actions, confirming his belief "that the current year may witness the ending of racial discrimination in admission to the study of law in most, if not all, of the sixteen member law schools which still discriminate on racial groups."[15] Gaines had reported in a confidential letter to Rector Caskie and trustee Homer Holt on December 5, 1955, that fifteen of the thirty southern AALS law schools were already admitting or planned soon to admit African Americans and that a concerted fight by the presidents of southern universities against a nondiscrimination resolution would be ill advised.[16]

In a prepared statement to the AALS, Gaines reviewed the history of W&L and argued that universities themselves should determine standards of admission and that, in any event, private institutions should not have to follow requirements that applied to public universities. Furthermore, he questioned nondiscrimination requirements on the basis of race while such requirements were not mandated for gender or religion. "What of possible limiting of Jews and others on racial or religious grounds?" he asked. "After all, should not an independent school be allowed to determine the type of school and character of the student body it desires?" Why shouldn't independent institutions "conduct an all male school or an all white school if it may be legally done?"[17] Gaines must have been aware that this was a rear-guard action against a challenge that would soon have to be addressed. But the W&L School of Law did not comply until the institution affirmed a nondiscrimination admissions policy in 1963. It would be among the last AALS holdouts.

In February 1956, Gaines sent a confidential letter to Caskie and Holt, seeking their advice. W&L law students belonged to an association of law schools in the region, and they expected that a W&L student would be elected president of the group and that Lexington would be the site of the annual meeting in the spring of 1957. At least several black students would almost certainly attend. "There will be no social features that involve the mixing of the races with the possible exception of a convention banquet," Gaines speculated. Since previous conferences at Duke and the University of South Carolina had included black students without provoking an incident, he was "inclined to think that I should give these boys the green light." He also noted what was becoming increasingly obvious: "If we are to withdraw ourselves from relations with other colleges which admit Negroes, we shall soon be in a rather isolated spot so far as all intercollegiate contacts are concerned." Caskie concurred, with regret, and expressed a hope that the "social features" would be kept to a minimum and the banquet held somewhere off campus. "We mix with negroes in many places now of necessity, and I think it would be a mistake to make an issue of a situation" like the student convention. Holt responded that W&L should not isolate itself from other law schools, and he was "sure the program will move along without any unpleasant incidents."[18] It did.

BOARDS OF TRUSTEES of private institutions throughout the South were composed largely of alumni from the region or surrounding locality, usually prominent businessmen, professionals, community leaders, and donors. Though not all of one mind, they tended to be middle-aged or older, and financially and emotionally invested in the status quo and the traditional values and assumptions of their education and upbringing. If they realized the injustice of strict racial segregation or at least the need for change, they also tended to believe that any action should be careful and incremental, in order to preserve the social fabric and protect vested interests, and, of course, that people like themselves should direct that change. Not surprisingly, they looked askance at the civil-rights lawsuits and demonstrations that provided momentum and took out of their hands the timing of the changes, as well as the leadership. Control often shifted to outsiders—frequently referred to as agitators, communists, and socialists—who did not understand the South and its customs. When confronted with urgent necessity, they mostly did what had to be done but rarely acted with much sympathy or enthusiasm, and they were increasingly at odds with their administrations and with faculty and students.[19]

The situation at Washington and Lee was similar but not identical to that at other southern universities. Trustees were almost all alumni from the South, but some were relatively moderate on racial issues or recognized the inevitability of integration. As a group, they were unsympathetic to the pace and character of the changes advocated by the civil rights movement in the region and in their communities. Some members harbored strong opinions on the issue but maintained at least the appearance of comity. While the most ardent opponents of change tended to be the loudest, there was little recorded dissension in the trustee meeting minutes and none in public. This mirrored a familiar pattern in white business and civic leadership groups throughout the South, with moderates not wishing to appear to favor the civil rights movement or to expose themselves to criticism and harassment in the communities where they lived and worked.

Two alumni serving on the W&L board during this challenging time were among or about to become the most distinguished jurists in the country. John Minor Wisdom of Louisiana and Lewis F. Powell of Virginia were variously involved in legal issues across a wide spectrum but particularly concerning race, civil rights, and social justice in and after the 1950s. Their work and influence extended well beyond the affairs of the university, but both men brought their judgment and experience to bear in service to their alma mater.

Wisdom graduated from W&L in 1925, received a law degree from Tulane in 1929, and served as a lieutenant colonel in the US Army during World War II. He was arguably the most important judicial figure of the time in advancing the civil rights of African Americans in the South. From an aristocratic family in

New Orleans, his father was a cotton broker, an 1873 graduate and later trustee of Washington and Lee, and a pallbearer at Robert E. Lee's funeral. John's older and younger brothers were also W&L alumni. He was a serious, eager student, avoiding fraternity life and throwing himself into the curriculum. He reportedly took every English class the university offered and also pursued interests in history, philosophy, and Greek and Irish mythology.[20] These interests were reflected in his legal opinions, which were impeccably written, precise, and replete with literary allusions and historical references. As a young lawyer in New Orleans, he opposed Huey Long's machine politics, worked to strengthen the moribund Republican Party in Louisiana (then ruled by a handful of Old Guard Republicans), and supported Eisenhower for president in 1952. The new president returned the favor by appointing Wisdom to the US Court of Appeals for the Fifth Circuit in 1957.

Part of the New Orleans social and civic establishment, Wisdom was no political radical. According to his biographer, Joel William Friedman, this "tradition-laden son of the Old South" never thought of himself as a reformer and was an active member of the elite in his home city and state. "But as a public man, he held dear two fundamental beliefs." First, "his mother had instilled in him an unshakable commitment to the notion that everyone was entitled to be treated fairly and with respect," and second, he believed that "the full blessings of democracy could not be enjoyed in the absence of a political system marked by two viable and energetic political parties."[21] His years on the Fifth Circuit bench—the court's jurisdiction included all the Deep South states—guaranteed that he would be cast into the legal fray of civil rights. His commitment to fairness would be inscribed in eloquent legal decisions that helped forever change the region and the country.

Wisdom's decisions advanced the racial integration of schools and universities, ensured black voting rights, undid the effects of past discrimination, blocked state and local actions restricting civil rights, and ensured that Supreme Court judgments were obeyed in resistant states and localities. His judgments also expanded the rights of other disadvantaged groups, such as Mexican Americans and the mentally ill. He confronted recalcitrant politicians and other judges who issued stays against government action and generally dragged their feet on embracing change. Wisdom was well mannered and self-effacing, but he never backed down from a necessary fight. If appealed, his opinions were almost always sustained by the Supreme Court, which often based its decisions on Wisdom's arguments. Perhaps his greatest decision was in an Alabama case, *U.S. v. Jefferson County Board of Education* (1966), which brought forceful impetus to the implementation of school integration in the face of determined opposition and legal stalling tactics. This was, according to Friedman, "the single most influential non-Supreme Court decision in the era of school desegregation." Wisdom did all this work in the face of great local resistance and threats to himself and his family; obscene phone calls were made to his home at all hours, his dogs were poisoned, and rattlesnakes were placed in his yard. But he was never intimidated and kept an active social life in his New Orleans club among his wide circle of friends.

Serving on the W&L board from 1957 to 1978, Wisdom was present for many of the key meetings in which the trustees contended with racial issues. His participation in these discussions was almost always in the privacy of board meetings, but he clearly favored changing the university's policies. Though he retired from active service in 1977, Wisdom continued to maintain a full judicial caseload well into his eighties. He was awarded the Presidential Medal of Freedom by Bill Clinton in 1993, and the US Congress named the Federal courthouse in New Orleans in his honor in 1994. In 1998 he received an honorary Doctor of Laws degree from Washington and Lee. He died in 1999, two days shy of his ninety-ninth birthday.

Lewis F. Powell Jr. arrived in Lexington the fall after Wisdom graduated. While a student at W&L, he was president of his fraternity, managing editor of the *Ring-tum Phi*, member of Phi Beta Kappa and ODK, and president of the student body. He graduated first in his law class in 1931 and spent an additional year at Harvard Law School, where he encountered professors like Felix Frankfurter and an approach to the law very different from the more traditional thinking he had absorbed at W&L. After rising to the rank of colonel in military intelligence during World War II, he settled in Richmond (turning down a generous offer from John W. Davis to come to New York) and developed a leading corporate law practice and solid standing in the community. Powell possessed qualities of both ambition and reticence, polished with impeccable manners, a combination that led to great success in his relationships with others and won him a reputation for integrity, competence, and leadership. No one embodied the principles of the Honor System more fully than he did. As John C. Jeffries Jr. noted in his excellent biography, "Lewis Powell was by instinct a team player. As a boy and as a man, he worked to position himself within the conventions of the system." He "first adapted himself to the environment, then tried to adapt the environment to suit him."[22]

Powell had long maintained an interest in the affairs of his alma mater. His frequent letters to Frank Gaines covered many subjects, especially intercollegiate football. (He understood the problems of subsidized athletics, but his strong dislike of mediocrity extended to W&L's showing on the gridiron.) By the time he joined the W&L board in 1961, Powell's clients included Colonial Williamsburg, the Chesapeake Corporation, Miller & Rhodes, and the State Planter's Bank. He added Philip Morris as a client and became a member of its board in 1963. (Powell tried to take up smoking, but as Jeffries noted, he "never learned to inhale.") He was elected president of the American Bar Association in 1964–65, and in 1971 President Richard Nixon nominated him to serve on the US Supreme Court. He remained a W&L trustee until 1978.

Like Wisdom, Powell had supported Eisenhower's presidential candidacy but had done so in line with the political wishes of the "Byrd Machine," which shunned the Democratic nominee. Powell was a strict, "establishment" conservative on most issues and was a long-standing supporter of Senator Byrd. He was especially concerned about the military threat posed by the Soviet Union, as well as attacks on free enterprise by communists and socialists. He feared that the United States was losing the global contest with the Soviets for the hearts and minds of developing countries and, at one time, even advocated "constant surveillance" of textbooks, television, journals, and all places where left-wing opinions might be expressed.

Powell served as chair of the Richmond School Board from 1952 to 1961, a period encompassing the days of Massive Resistance to desegregation, including the state's assumption of control over local school-attendance policies. Governor Almond appointed him to the State Board of Education in 1961, at a time when public schools were wrestling with implementing school desegregation. Powell's election as a W&L trustee that same year placed him in the midst of key board discussions involving race, though he was unable to attend some important meetings.

Powell was taken aback by court decisions that could fundamentally change the society in which he grew up, but he recognized the strength and direction of those decisions and was prepared to accept desegregation. He was not, however, prepared to be an advocate for change or to assume a leading role in bringing it about. He publically supported Senator Byrd but privately opposed Massive Resistance and the denial of education to any child. Much of his work on the State Board of Education supported improving educational standards and preventing the closing of any public school. During eighteen years in public office, he carefully avoided public comments on integration, desegregation, or racial matters. He never commented on his reasons for not speaking out, but his biographer concludes that one reason was doubtless his dislike of public disputes, and discussions of race were almost always awkward and potentially volatile. It was also a calculated strategy to preserve his position and professional standing while taking deliberate steps, behind the scenes, toward inevitable change. According to Jeffries, Powell "was supremely tolerant of the status quo." He "was reluctant to speak out in a way that would impair the influence of the natural ruling class. Even when he wanted change, he worked only from within."[23]

One major pillar of Powell's life was a commitment to the law, which led him to oppose, and even misinterpret, civil disobedience. In a 1966 lecture at W&L, "A Lawyer Looks at Civil Disobedience" (the substance of which was later published in *US News & World Report*), Powell associated civil disobedience with "organized lawlessness and even rebellion," and he pointed to Martin Luther King's "Letter from a Birmingham Jail." The doctrine of civil disobedience, of course, entailed the full acceptance of penalties for breaking the law and was not an attack on the legitimacy of law itself. Characteristically, Powell crafted a scholarly elaboration, published in the *Washington and Lee Law Review,* that allowed exceptions without really admitting any error in his argument. He also avoided any further mention of King.[24]

During his time on the Supreme Court (1972–87), Powell played an important role in many decisions, often operating as a "swing vote" between the conservative and liberal factions. He remained among the conservatives, albeit with a reputation for moderation, and he now recognized the justice of racial integration, even to the extent of revising his own recollections. In the early 1970s, he insisted that he had always been a supporter of *Brown,* even when the decision was supremely unpopular in Virginia. To the dismay of many friends, he wrote, "I have honestly believed in the advantages, in our pluralistic society, of the children of all races and creeds being brought together in public education." This view was in fact a radical departure from his position in 1954. As Jeffries observes, "By this time, he honestly believed in the value of integration, and it seemed inconceivable to him that he had ever endorsed or tolerated the regime of segregation."[25] This was doubtless true of other southern white community leaders who were moving forward in a new reality.

Lewis Powell—whose papers now reside at W&L—and John Minor Wisdom were both members of the establishment in cities and states that resisted change. Powell most clearly personified many of the characteristics of W&L's trustees and of many alumni at the time—conservative in temperament, resistant to rapid change, and affiliated with established local leadership but also offended by violence, illegality, and instability. Prepared to accept and adapt as change became inevitable, these men shared a pronounced desire not to talk about it. Because of his judicial role on the Fifth Circuit Court and his temperament, Wisdom was a more forthright challenger of the status quo. His legal opinions, though not delivered from the Supreme Court bench, were also more influential than Powell's—certainly on matters of race and social justice—in the course of American history.

WHILE W&L WAS a conservative institution and slow to change, its dedication to the liberal arts, student independence, and the virtues of honor and integrity produced accomplished graduates in virtually every field. They held a variety of personal convictions and political opinions; some resisted the tide of social change, especially on matters of race, while others embraced change and actively pursued it. World War I veteran and Rhodes Scholar Francis Pickens Miller, an alumnus descended from Presbyterian ministers, was a leading Democratic opponent of the Byrd organization in Virginia. He ran unsuccessfully for governor in 1949 and, in 1952, against Byrd himself in the primary for the US Senate. A vocal internationalist, Miller was an early critic of Adolph Hitler and supporter of American aid to Britain. He advocated what today would be termed "progressive" policies, including support for civil rights. John Maguire, '53, had a particularly remarkable life and career. A native of Montgomery, Alabama, he ventured north to Virginia for his college education. During his time at W&L, he attended seminary in 1951 and shared a room with another young student—Martin Luther King Jr.—that led to a lasting friendship. In 1968, Maguire became founding board chairman of the MLK Center for Nonviolent Social Change, and he founded the Institute for Democratic Renewal in 1998. Much of his life was devoted to teaching and university administration. In May 1961, age twenty-eight and a professor of religion at Wesleyan University, Maguire rode on the third bus sent into Alabama to challenge racial segregation. On the way from the Greyhound terminal in Atlanta to his hometown of Montgomery, Maguire and another Freedom Rider, thirty-six-year-old social activist and Yale University chaplain William Sloane Coffin Jr., reportedly sat together and attributed their presence on the journey to the influence that James G. Leyburn had had on their lives.[26]

Finally, it should be noted that embracing change—or at least making the best of the inevitable—was the prevailing sentiment in the W&L administration and faculty. Many students were also less invested in the status quo than their elders, and they approached civil rights and other issues with a relatively open mind. W&L's experience differed from that of larger private universities in the region because it was not located in a large city like New Orleans or Nashville, and the campus was relatively free of the intense political discussion fueled by major newspapers and organized groups, as well as the need to accommodate black visitors and interracial groups. Even though on-campus discussions of racial issues were conducted with a pronounced degree of decorum, the trustees as a group were out of step with the administration, faculty, and, increasingly, many students. The law school had some faculty and students who supported desegregation, but it was not a declared leader for change and was among the last of southern law schools to desegregate. Moreover, W&L had no formal religious affiliation and no school of theology to push forward a moral agenda. It did, however, encourage religious work and awareness, and the faculty and students involved in religious organizations and issues on campus took a lead role in encouraging desegregation.

The student executive committee of the University Christian Association—descended from the original campus YMCA and supported by student fees—sought to invite the Rev. Martin Luther King Jr. to speak to the Seminars in Religion Program. It was early October 1961, the year of the Freedom Rides. King had been arrested a year earlier during a sit-in at Rich's Department Store in Atlanta, sent to state prison, and eventually released on bond after the intervention of US attorney general Robert Kennedy. King had risen from his role as a young pastor in Montgomery during the bus boycott in 1955 to become the most prominent civil rights leader and spokesman for nonviolence. Asked for its advice on this student proposal, the Faculty Committee on Christian Work—chaired by E. C. Griffith and including among its members James Leyburn, Marshall Fishwick, David Sprunt, William Watt, James Farrar, and Earl Mattingly—voted 7–2 to extend the invitation but advised President Fred Cole that the board of trustees should be notified. The board was not usually involved in approving invitations to campus speakers, but it decided at its meeting on October 13 to decline the request to invite King "as not being in the best interests of the University." Judge Wisdom was present for the discussion, but no vote was recorded. Lewis Powell did not attend the meeting until the following day, when he took the oath of office as a new trustee.[27]

After President Cole reported the board's decision in November, the faculty adopted a resolution expressing "genuine regret" at an action that "seriously limits the freedom of inquiry that should prevail in an institution of higher learning, and denies to students the opportunity to learn and judge for themselves, even upon issues of controversy." The faculty also directed that the resolution be made public. In his opaque response, Rector James Caskie did not address the reasons for the decision but affirmed the board's commitment to "act in what it considers the best interests of Washington and Lee University. In this case, there exists an honest difference of opinion as to what course of action best serves the interests of the University. It is good that such a difference of opinion can take place in an atmosphere of mutual respect. It is wholesome that the avenues of communication between the Faculty and the Board remain free and open." This response was also reported to the press.

An editorial entitled "Snug Harbor at Lexington" appeared in the *Richmond News-Leader* and was picked up by several other newspapers. It noted that northern universities "regularly invite Southern spokesmen to their campuses," though they are usually outnumbered by "liberals." Universities in the South lagged behind in tolerating "conflicting points of view." Whatever individual opinions about King and other leading civil rights spokesmen, "they are eminently qualified to discuss the Negroes' position on one of the great social issues of our time." Echoing the faculty's resolution, the editorial concluded that an "institutional policy that seeks to shelter students from conflicting winds of doctrine in the end is self-defeating." The *Virginian-Pilot* observed on November 24 that the "faculty's attitude is so clearly in conformity with the great traditions of university freedom, of the virtues of free inquiry, and of the rights of men to examine ideas in the competition of the market-place that it is surprising that a university faculty has to recall these fundamentals of American life." Rather, "the trustees have struck a serious blow at the spirit of free inquiry, and in doing so they have damaged the good name of the university for whose interests they have responsibility."

Andrew W. McThenia Jr., president of the student body (and later a member of the law school faculty) wrote to the trustees, requesting that they reconsider their decision. At its meeting on January 20, 1962—attended by both Wisdom and Powell—the board discussed the request and "declined to reconsider its action." (Again, the board's minutes referred to "a speaker" without mentioning King's name.) The trustees also acknowledged the faculty resolution and declared their "full support of freedom of discussion and opinion, and their conviction that it is appropriate and desirable—especially on a college campus—to afford an opportunity for the honest presentation of differing or diverging views by speakers of character and competency." The trustees also resolved that the faculty and administration "shall endeavor (first) to bring to Washington and Lee University speakers of the highest quality and competence, and (second) to maintain such balance of both speakers and subject matter as will best promote the traditional objectives of Washington and Lee University."[28] It clearly implied that an appearance by Martin Luther King Jr. did not meet these criteria. In 1961 he was not yet an iconic figure and was often regarded, even among the educated elite in the South, as a disruptive troublemaker, "outside agitator," or—even worse—a communist. Whatever the private discussions of this matter within the board, the decision was unambiguous.

On February 12, the faculty approved an amendment to the *Faculty Rules and Regulations*, requiring that all proposals for speakers on campus from student or faculty groups (except for ODK, Phi Beta Kappa, and the Tucker lectures) be submitted to the Committee on Lectures "for approval or for recommendation to the President." The committee would assist in bringing "suitable" speakers to campus and approve "all expenditures for the same." The fifteen-member committee, chaired by Professor Allen W. Moger of the Department of History, included Deans Lewis W. Adams, Edward Atwood, Charles Light, and William Pusey, a student representative, and other faculty members (including J. Paxton Davis, John M. Gunn, David W. Sprunt, Robert Stewart, and William J. Watt).

The new arrangements led to some loosening of the restrictions on invited speakers. An invitation was extended to Ralph Ellison, noted author of *The Invisible Man*, who spoke on American literature in Lee Chapel on November 15, 1963. Students and faculty gathered to meet the African American author at a reception in the Student Union following the lecture. (Among the visitors to campus for this event was the young southern writer Reynolds Price.) Ellison's appearance was welcomed by the editors of the Tuesday edition of the *Ring-tum Phi* (the "liberal" edition of the student paper) but was greeted skeptically by the "conservative" Friday edition. One commentator hoped the talk would be strictly academic and not an "appeal for sympathy, money, or anything else which would have advanced the cause of the Negro."[29] The Committee on Lectures approved a number of speakers who spoke on major issues of the day. The first CONTACT Symposium in the spring of 1965, initiated and conducted by the Interfraternity Council, featured James Silver of the University of Mississippi and author of *Mississippi: The Closed Society*, *New York Times* columnist

Tom Wicker, and W&L alumnus Francis Pickens Miller. Efforts to bring controversial speakers to campus continued to be handled gingerly.

In September 1966, the student executive committee of the University Christian Association (UCA) was still trying to bring topical and newsworthy speakers to campus. A poll asked for student preferences among six specific speakers who ranged across the political spectrum. It attracted three hundred responses and resulted in the following order of preference: (1) Stokely Carmichael, head of the Student Non-Violent Coordinating Committee (SNCC); (2) Dr. Martin Luther King Jr.; (3) Robert Welch, head of the ultra-conservative John Birch Society; (4) Gus Hall, head of the Communist Party of the United States; (5) Harvey Cox, the liberal activist and Harvard theologian; and (6) James Farmer, head of the Congress of Racial Equality (CORE). James Awad, president of the UCA, appeared before the Faculty Committee on Christian Work on October 6 and requested permission to invite "one or more" of these speakers (now also including Malcolm Boyd, a white clergyman and Freedom Rider) to campus. Awad also requested a broader application of the committee's requirement that speakers under its auspices "have credentials in the field of religion." The speakers on his proposed list were "issue-makers of the times" who represented various aspects of challenges facing the country, from the civil rights struggle to "nazi-like white supremacist attitudes" and the "death of God" movement." W&L students should hear directly from the leaders of these movements as part of the university's educational mission.[30]

The faculty committee, doubtless thinking of the board's inclination, approved King, Cox, and Boyd for UCA sponsorship but not the others, whom they deemed to lack "religious credentials." The University Lecture Committee unanimously approved the recommendation for invitations to the three speakers. In response to one letter protesting these invitations, committee chair Allen Moger pointed out that students, "even the conservatives among them," wanted to be aware of current events and controversies and to hear a wide variety of viewpoints. To deny them such opportunities would "dangerously lower their opinion of Washington and Lee."[31]

King never spoke at W&L, but the way had been paved for a greater array of official and unofficial speakers, invited by a variety of campus groups and representing a variety of views, to keep the university aware of the currents of the turbulent 1960s and early 1970s. Whatever their views, students were clearly interested in a wide range of opinions and perspectives, particularly controversial ones. The trustees, after three hours of private discussion at their

October 1966 meeting at the Homestead, decided to take no further action to control outside speakers on campus and to leave such matters to the discretion of the faculty and its committees. According to Moger, one trustee described the decision as "a great victory for Fred Cole—a victory won because of Cole's tact, persistence, and 'keeping his head.'"[32]

THE W&L BOARD had made an even more important decision two years earlier. As at other southern colleges and universities, the administration, faculty, and some students had pressed for change while the board resisted. W&L was notable primarily because the decision to admit black students was so long deferred and because the trustees who made the decision were then so reluctant to discuss it or even acknowledge it. Historian Melissa Kean has written of trustees at other private southern universities: "Forced to swallow the camel, they strained mightily at the gnat."[33]

Racial integration at southern and border-state university professional schools had occurred even before the 1954 *Brown* decision, and the momentum was building by the early 1960s on a solid legal framework. Resistance had by no means ended, as demonstrated by the turmoil at the Universities of Alabama and Mississippi, but change continued nevertheless. Public institutions faced the prospect of legal action and federal enforcement, but private colleges and institutions were also under pressure. The passage of the Civil Rights Act in the summer of 1964, with its Title VI prohibiting federal funding to any institution practicing racial discrimination, made the consequences for resisting change obvious. Furthermore, national foundations and granting agencies increasingly demanded the end of racial restrictions in admissions as a condition of support, as did the standards of regional and professional accrediting organizations. Faculty members—and perhaps some students—were increasingly reluctant to join or remain at segregated institutions. Washington and Lee also faced a ten-year review of its SACS institutional accreditation in 1966, with the self-study to begin in 1964, including admissions policy as a prominent component.

The prevailing trend seemed all but inevitable. The University of Virginia had admitted an African American student to its law school in 1950, graduated its first black PhD in 1953, and its first graduate from the College of Arts and Sciences in June 1962. Sewanee opened its School of Theology to applications from African Americans in 1953, extended the policy to the rest of the university in 1961, and admitted the first black students to the College in 1963. Vanderbilt admitted two black applicants to its law school in 1956. The year 1961 was a major turning point for virtually all schools. The boards at Duke, Tulane, and Emory had voted to admit blacks, and Emory and Vanderbilt were desegregated at the undergraduate level by 1962. The same decision was reached by 1963 at Sweet Briar College and Randolph-Macon Woman's College.[34]

The boards of the leading private universities of the South wrestled with the dilemma. "Their trustees had dodged demands for racial justice since the end of World War II," writes Kean, "but by the early 1960s only a single choice remained: they could go along with the federal government, the national foundations, and the professors and thrive, or they could defy them and wither. Their power to control events had evaporated—their right to make decisions for everyone else—was gone. In the end they capitulated, but not with particular grace."[35] W&L still waited, and the longer it waited, the greater the consequences would be. It had already become something of an outlier.

W&L was not in turmoil over the issue, and discussions proceeded with remarkable decorum, but the momentum for change accelerated. Convinced that failure to act would severely harm the university and erase many of the gains it had made in national recognition, President Cole and the administration applied respectful but steady pressure behind the scenes. Among other things, Cole attempted to establish links with black colleges in the Commonwealth. He was also, according to Frank Parsons, "appalled at what was going on in Prince Edward County," where the public schools were closed to avoid integration.[36] Cole sent W&L faculty members there to offer moral support and encouragement to students and teachers, but he knew that the board would not authorize anything formal or commit university resources.

Most faculty members, as best can be determined, favored a change in W&L's admissions policy and were increasingly inclined to speak out. Students, both liberal and conservative, either favored integration or at least appreciated the difficulties of standing firm against the tide of events. All were aware of the board's 1961 decision to deny an invitation to Martin Luther King Jr. and were frustrated by the board's reluctance to address the issue of integration in any way.[37]

As at other institutions, bringing African Americans to campus brought a real and personal dimension to otherwise abstract debating points. The Robert E. Lee Episcopal Church invited Hampton Institute chaplain Rev. Walter D. Dennis, history professor Virginius Thornton, and five Hampton students to visit Lexington during the weekend of February 7–9, 1964, as part of a "racial cultural exchange." The university gave permission for the group to attend W&L classes if the instructors approved. (They all did.) The visiting delegation stayed in the homes of church members, attended evening discussions with W&L faculty members and students in private homes, and met for lunch at the Robert E. Lee Hotel. Naturally, W&L's position on racial integration was the main topic of discussion. According to Roger Paine, editor-in-chief of the *Ring-tum Phi* Tuesday edition, the two W&L faculty members attending the Saturday evening discussion at the home of the Rev. John Fletcher attempted to explain the university's stance on integration. History professor William A. Jenks "explained that it was impossible to arrive at any solid conclusions as to W&L's position. As far as he knew, no definite statement had ever been made by the Board of Trustees." Jenks "expressed his own personal surprise that three schools which he thought Washington and Lee would lead in the problem of integration—Mercer, Stetson, and Wake Forest—had already made the advance, leaving W&L as one of the few leading southern colleges remaining segregated." He feared that even a positive decision by the trustees at this point might be regarded as "tokenism." Dr. Edward L. Pinney of Political Science observed that, according to the administration, no African American had applied for admission; perhaps an application by a qualified student could serve as "a catalyst to decision." The Hampton delegation pointed out the difficulty of placing responsibility for resolving this issue on the applicants, especially because W&L had made no effort to recruit blacks or provide information to predominately black high schools. Nor did most students desire to be the first African American on a small all-white campus. One of the W&L students added that "W&L's silence on the integration issue speaks louder than any words—until W&L makes an actual statement of policy, saying that it will not discriminate against applicants on the basis of race, no qualified Negroes can be expected to apply."[38]

In the same February 11 issue, a *Ring-tum Phi* editorial, likely written by Paine and titled "We Shall Overcome," called for an immediate decision by the board of trustees "for or against the rights of the Negro" and in the best interest of students who would participate in the real world rather than an isolated outpost of the past. "With each passing month W&L's silence is looking more antiquated, more bigoted, and more embarrassing. While we have long since lost our chance to be the South's first champion of the rights of all men, let us at least prevent ourselves from looking like the South's last sewer of prejudice."[39] The *Ring-tum Phi* Friday edition took a predictably different tack—not overtly in favor of segregation but rather pointing out that no black student would want to attend W&L because he would not enjoy "any favorable degree of social acceptance."[40] All parties were aware that the board would deliberate the matter during the coming summer.

On July 2, 1964, in the wake of the passage of the Civil Rights Act, Fred Cole was invited by President Lyndon Johnson to join the new national Citizens Committee for Human Relations, composed of 450 leaders throughout the country, for the purpose of "resolving racial disputes and tensions through reason, persuasion, and conciliation." The other seven members from Virginia included Lewis Powell (then president of the American Bar Association). Cole responded that he would be "privileged" to serve. Some trustees were not happy. Rector James Caskie wrote to convey his distress that he was not consulted prior to Cole's decision. While he held him in high personal regard and recognized that he was acting as an individual, Cole's membership on "the enforcement commission" gave an "unfortunate" impression. As a lawyer, Caskie declared, "I am thoroughly convinced that the Civil Rights Act is under any fair interpretation unconstitutional." Caskie feared that alumni and the public would now perceive the board as favoring the act, as well as think the board was "on the side of integration of private institutions and private property rights," an impression that in his view the "great majority" of the trustees would not appreciate. Caskie further offered that he had almost reached the conclusion to decide to support admission without regard to race but that Cole's action had led him to reconsider. "I feel now I am placed in the position where, to maintain my integrity, I shall probably feel forced to vote against any integration at Washington and Lee." He also confided that he had long hoped that "we could keep out of the mess entirely." Cole remained a member of the Citizens Committee and attended its first meeting in Washington in August, which was addressed by President Johnson and Attorney General Robert F. Kennedy.[41]

On July 14, 1964, after lengthy discussion, the board of trustees approved an official statement reaffirming that admissions decisions were left to the faculty. The statement noted that no board resolution or provision existed that "established a policy of discrimination among qualified applicants for admission" and that the faculty had traditionally decided on qualifications for applicants. "The Board of Trustees," the statement concluded, "has no cause to doubt the appropriateness of this delegation of authority to the Faculty and has no cause to doubt the collective wisdom of the Faculty in discharging the concomitant responsibility."[42] The statement's purpose and implications were intentionally obscured and even its public distribution was curtailed, but its wording and tone suggested what was doubtless the case: the trustees faced a looming necessity that most of them did not welcome and would have preferred to deal with in their own time and manner. This was, for the moment, as far as they were prepared to go. Of the eleven trustees voting (John Minor Wisdom among them; Lewis Powell was absent), eight were in favor and three were opposed: James R. Caskie, J. Morrison Hutcheson, and John F. Hendon of Birmingham, who wanted the record to show specifically that he was opposed because he did not wish to admit blacks to Washington and Lee.[43] President Cole had reportedly asked Robert E. R. Huntley, then legal adviser to the president, to help persuade the trustees to address the issue of race and admissions. Huntley confided in a later interview that he had engaged the assistance of long-time trustee and former West Virginia governor Homer "Rocky" Holt—a dominant force on the board—to persuade his fellow trustees to take this important step, though there is little elsewhere in the historical record to indicate that Holt was enthusiastic about such a change (though he did vote for the decision).[44]

In response to faculty inquiries, President Cole reported the board's decision at the first faculty meeting in October, but he made no announcement to the students. The editors of the *Ring-tum Phi*, Stephen P. Smith and L. Shannon Jung, asked President Cole if the trustees had taken any action on admissions, and he responded to them—as he had been instructed by the board—not as individuals but as representatives of the student press. The editors then requested that the board issue a public announcement at its October meeting and give them something they could print. In a show of great deference, these student journalists promised not to comment or speculate on the board's decision. Cole communicated their request to the board, which approved an official release on October 24, only for distribution to the *Ring-tum Phi*. The statement "reaffirmed the university faculty's responsibility in determining standards of admission for qualified applicants" and quoted from President Cole along the lines of the original board resolution: "no provision of the Charter, no provision of the By-Laws and no resolution of the Board has established a policy of discrimination among qualified applicants for admission." The statement named all thirteen members of the Committee on Admissions chaired by Dean Atwood, and it noted that the same authority had been delegated to the law school faculty. The board authorized no other statement to any other outlet.

The *Ring-tum Phi* issue of October 27, delayed by a printing problem, appeared on the morning of October 28. It carried the board's entire statement, along with an editorial comment and a story on a scheduled discussion of the "integration statement" by the ODK Forum. The paper referred to "the announcement made today by President Fred C. Cole that Washington and Lee will lower racial barriers in admissions policy." Inquiries from other news sources, even the *Lexington News-Gazette*, were rejected because the board had insisted that university officials make no further elaboration on the statement. The result, of course, was that the *Ring-tum Phi* story and one other story for the *Richmond News-Leader* by a senior journalism student became the basis for the Associated Press wire story and the stories that appeared in most state newspapers and many national outlets, among them the *Stars and Stripes*, CBS News, and NBC News. A typical headline, in the October 29 issue of the *Providence Journal* in Rhode Island, read "Washington & Lee, 215 Yrs. Old, Drops Negro Barrier." In every case, the stories focused on changes in the university's policy on racial integration.

The board had insisted that its statement not refer to "integration" or "Negro" or "race," but by refusing to elaborate it had effectively relinquished its ability to explain, in its own words, the meaning and implications of its decision. This approach was a mistake, doubtless due to the unhappiness of many board members with the decision, perhaps especially because its necessity was driven by outside pressure. The less said about it the better.

At the trustees' meeting, Judge Wisdom spoke against the statement, which he reluctantly voted for, because it was so obtuse: "I feel that the statement is not as responsive as it should be to such a serious inquiry." The statement ought more clearly to recognize that the board accepted its responsibility for the admissions policy even though, as in most universities, decisions were delegated to the faculty. His affirmative vote was cast "on the assumption that the reference in the statement to the absence of any discriminatory policy in our Charter and Bylaws is intended to clarify the fact that the University's admissions policy now permits the admission of qualified applicants, regardless of race or color." Holt asked that the record show "that he does not agree in full with Judge Wisdom's statements and assumptions."[45]

In November, after the decision on admissions had been extensively reported, the trustees received a request from the alumni board that the next issue of the *Alumni Magazine* carry a full report of the decision and explain the circumstances behind it. Frank Parsons, managing editor of the magazine, set to work on "A Matter of Admissions . . . ," an article of ten typewritten pages. Offering the background, rationale, and implications of the board's decision, the article was intended to be the first full "authorized" explanation of the matter.[46] The draft made clear that the decision dealt with race. "The [Board's] statement," Parsons wrote, "made no mention of the words 'Negro,' 'race,' 'integration,' or 'desegregation,' yet the issue it dealt with for Washington and Lee is related to the larger, national social issue that is associated with these terms." Recognizing "the absence of any stated policy of discrimination" at W&L, the statement meant that no policy of de facto discrimination would be imposed against "fully qualified applicants for admission." The article reviewed the history of the discussion and the media coverage, the racial integration of "virtually all good colleges and universities in the South and elsewhere in the nation," the variety of reasons why a clarification of admissions policy was necessary—including faculty recruitment and government and foundation funding—and possible future implications for the composition of the student body. The key question was, "Should a young man, fully qualified in all respects to meet Washington and Lee's exacting standards of admission and performance, be denied the opportunity of the University's influence and education solely because of his racial origin?" Significantly, Parsons noted another major issue the university had to address: simply waiting for applications was not sufficient. In light of the intense national competition for qualified African American students, W&L must continue its "visitation and other promotional programs at high schools and preparatory schools" that had provided good students in the past and must seek out black applicants.

Parsons submitted a draft of his article for review by the trustees. Lewis Powell, who had not been able to attend the recent board meetings, thought the statement was "well written and informative," but he also found it too "defensive" and apologetic. He preferred something more succinct, stating that the board had clarified that the university's policy was in line with policies at most universities in the country. Powell, following his own proclivity to keep public discussion of such matters to a minimum, preferred to present the decision as routine rather than to address its merits. But he deferred to Cole's and Parsons's judgment in the matter.[47] Other trustees must have reacted much more strongly. An article entitled "The Matter of Admissions . . ." did appear in the fall 1964 issue of the *Alumni Magazine*, but it bore no resemblance to Parsons's earlier draft. In one page, it repeated the statement given to the *Ring-tum Phi*. It noted that the statement was released only to the student editors and offered the additional clarification "that the Board would impose no *de facto* policy of discrimination against fully qualified applicants for admission." But it contained no reference to "integration," "desegregation," or "Negroes."[48] The board thus continued to maintain its policy of silence on this issue, neglecting to deploy even the usual euphemisms and frustrating the desire of the faculty and administration to communicate what the university had done.

The board's decision on admissions—conveyed and explained largely by the press—was lamented by some and celebrated by others. Parsons said that letters to President Cole ran about three to one in favor.[49] Editorial comments in the press were almost entirely favorable. The *Washington Post* concluded that the decision "honored the memory of both great Virginians" gracing the name of the institution. It noted Lee's criticisms of slavery, as it did his commitment to national reconciliation after the war. "Lee gave his gifts to help build a new South. . . . Certainly he would have applauded his school's decision to conform with American practice by dropping racial bars."[50] The board of trustees could have said as much.

For the university, reaching a decision on admissions was easier than giving it practical effect. Desegregation was not integration. The administration and the Committee on Admissions were well aware that, because of W&L's size, location, history, and campus social environment, active recruiting was essential to attract black students. These problems had been noted in earlier discussions and in the unpublished draft of Parsons's article, and it would require mention and elaboration in the self-study report for SACS. Even then, the board was not inclined to endorse or even acknowledge any such effort.

The trustees and the Self-Study Committee of faculty and administrators met jointly at the Homestead resort in Hot Springs in August 1966 to review a draft of the report before it was submitted to SACS and its review team. Dozens of committees and scores of individuals had been working on the document for two years, and it now awaited approval by the board. Most aspects of the report provoked little comment, but a very tense discussion ensued on the recommendation that "the University's recruitment program be broadened, particularly aimed at attracting qualified Negro applicants to Washington and Lee." (The university had already extended invitations to three African American applicants, and two were scheduled to enroll in September.) Detailed minutes of these discussions were taken, probably to help the authors of the self-study respond to any trustee concerns and suggestions. The minutes provide a rare look into conversations that were almost always private and usually unreported, and they perhaps cast some light on earlier board discussions.[51]

The self-study report draft recommended not preferential admission but rather special efforts to identify academically qualified blacks and attract them to the all-white, rural institution. Educators understood that simply opening admissions would not achieve the objective and that considerable thought, planning, and adjustment were needed. The visiting SACS team would expect all of this to be addressed in the self-study. The university had traditionally targeted its recruitment efforts at different groups of students, including sons of alumni and talented athletes. Now "Rocky" Holt strongly objected to any attempt to "recruit on any basis." Dean William Pusey pointed out that the "majority of faculty feels that it would be desirable and necessary if we have several Negroes in our student body." Holt responded that he would not object if Negroes were given an opportunity to apply, or even if "up to 50" enrolled, but "we should not go out and hunt them up." James Caskie concurred: "We have never recruited on account of race and it is not a proper time to start now." A lengthy discussion followed, with faculty and administration pressing the trustees to allow a more active implementation of the admissions decision.

Professor William Hinton explained that, while there was not complete agreement on the matter even among members of the Self-Study Committee, discussions with the faculty and students supported such a recommendation. Many younger faculty members from outside the South "cannot quite understand why we don't have a few qualified Negroes in the student body" and see this as "a fundamental matter" in attracting new faculty. "Most feel that this is a statement that should be made." The faculty "have been living with this and we see it in a somewhat different way than you have seen it." Professor Allen Moger stressed the importance of extending a welcome to black students. "Those of us who live on campus," he observed, "reading student columns and editorials, listening to new faculty members express surprise and alarm—to us this kind of thing would have a great effect and help in being able to answer enthusiastic students who question." Admission, he added, should be based on merit: "We are at a peculiar stage of our history. Dozens of schools in America have had to do this merely to remove the impression that they don't want a Negro. The whole atmosphere at UVA is different. The Negro doesn't think he is welcome at W&L. Letting him know that he is welcome if he measures up will help to put us in step with the rest of the country." Dean Edward Atwood immediately added that while the board had made a statement about admissions, there was still a problem—"a feeling among students and faculty that we don't really mean the statement. They think it is something we did because we had to do it." W&L should not sit back and wait for applications, because the best black students were being heavily recruited throughout the country.

The trustees were still not swayed. Joseph Lanier declared that a more active approach was discriminatory. He understood the situation, he said, but "we have more than faculty, students, and alumni involved—we have the long-time traditions," and there "should not be discrimination of one group against the other." He then asked what role the trustees had in the self-study. President Cole responded that the board had ultimate responsibility, but if the trustees disagreed, it "will be hoped that after this careful and thoughtful study that this document would be accepted as a representative report of this University." Lanier and Holt then moved to strike the offending recommendation. Dean Pusey noted, "This leaves the committee in a spot." Moger asked Holt, "Would you be implying that the hundreds of schools in America that are trying to get Negro students are wrong and we are right?" Holt again objected: "You are going out to hunt Negro students with more enthusiasm than other groups." Professor John Gunn weighed in: "Students have questioned the sincerity of the University in the admissions statement. As long as this impression is abroad the University is disadvantaged."

Professor Hinton suggested that perhaps the recommendation could be stated differently without eliminating it entirely. Exasperated, Holt exclaimed, "I have been on this Board since 1940. If I am not here for any purpose, why should I be here. If the Board of Trustees don't amount to anything, why are we meeting here for two days. I never have been a figurehead and I am too old to begin now." President Cole made yet another effort to reach an agreement. "We are here," he said, "to have frank and open discussions on something that is a healthy need for the future. I hope we can discuss it. The committee feels very strongly that this should be stated in the best interest of the University. . . . There is no desire on the part of anyone to take a position that is not an honest one." In response to another query from Lanier, he said, "If this is to be put into effect, it would need the action of the Board of Trustees. It is nevertheless the position of this committee that it reflect the view set forth." Moger suggested that maybe the term "Negroes" could be left out. Holt suggested that members of the board "step out of the room" to discuss the matter among themselves. Caskie noted that two black students had been already been accepted and that "this action speaks louder than words." Lewis John returned to the basic problem: nondiscrimination in admissions and efforts to encourage applications from certain students were two different, and not inconsistent, things.

Holt continued to object, and other trustees began to weigh in. John Stemmons noted that the recommendation was obviously not acceptable to the board and that it would be better if the committee revised the statement on its own rather than have the board reject it. Huston St. Clair observed that this was a "temporary problem" and should not be part of a "long-time report," and Joseph T. Lykes, Jr. agreed. The board was obviously not dealing with the real question at issue, and President Cole suggested, "We could state facts as they now exist. This would be an affirmation of a policy that Negroes would not be discriminated against. And the committee could review the facts that now exist—" Holt interrupted: "I am opposed to discussing Negroes in this report." Cole persisted: "It would be helpful if this could be revised, pointing out the action and making a statement that would be in keeping with the times and with what is the policy of the University." Holt responded that it would be enough to say that the board would leave admissions to the Admissions Committee. The offending statement—including any specific mention of "Negroes"—was stricken from the report.

WASHINGTON AND LEE would continue to wrestle with the opportunities and demands of the new era that began with the enrollment of its first two African American students in the fall of 1966: Dennis Haston and Leslie Smith. The university had made few preparations for this step, but Dean of Admissions James D. Farrar and others had obviously been thinking about it. The challenge was to identify and attract black students who could succeed both academically—no small matter at a time when black students received separate but distinctly unequal elementary and secondary educations—and socially. They had to be prepared to confront a social environment that was often uncomfortable if not downright forbidding, even to white students whose background, interests, or behavior were unconventional. Being the first black students at an all-white, generally conservative, fraternity-dominated university would have been daunting for anyone, especially in light of the controversy leading up to the admissions decision, the lingering and skeptical references to academic qualifications and social acceptance, and the fact that some students and faculty members were not happy with integration. In fact, however, W&L had a much greater need for black student enrollment, acceptance, and success than blacks had for the university.

Dennis Alan Haston—eighteen years old and a June 1966 graduate of Lexington High School—enrolled with the freshman class in September. As a resident of Rockbridge County, he could pay lower fees and live at home rather than on campus, avoiding the issue of integrating the dormitories. Dean Farrar, who knew Haston's family and believed that Dennis's good academic record and familiarity with W&L would prepare him to meet the challenge, actively recruited him after the regular application deadline had passed. Haston chose W&L over Morgan State University in Baltimore, noting that "the price was excellent and I would be only a few blocks away from home." He was also interested in helping to remove racial barriers.[52]

At the same time, Leslie D. Smith Jr. from Chuckatuck, Virginia, enrolled in the School of Law. He was a graduate of Saint Paul's College, an all-black school in Lawrenceville, Virginia, that had earlier sought assistance from W&L to enhance its educational programs, a request that Fred Cole accepted.[53] The president of Saint Paul's, Earl H. McClenney, personally recommended Smith for admission to the law school (which had extended an offer the previous year to another African American who chose not to attend).[54] Smith received financial assistance and resided in Davis Hall, the law school dormitory, taking his meals at Evans Dining Hall.

Haston attended freshman orientation at Natural Bridge and roomed with a white student, but he elected not to participate in fraternity rush. The fraternity system that enabled a single member to reject a potential new pledge was not truly open to him in any event, and some fraternities had racially exclusive clauses in their charters. Nevertheless, Haston made friends in his second semester, attended several dances, and joined the track team. He reported little overt racial hostility during his time at W&L; his most serious encounter with discrimination occurred when he was denied service in a restaurant in Tennessee while traveling with the team, which moved to another restaurant where every member could be served. The coursework was demanding, and, despite faculty efforts to get him to stay, Haston decided to transfer at the end of his first year at W&L to Bluefield State College.

Leslie Smith also experienced the challenges of being in a white educational and living environment for the first time. With a gentle nature and good sense of humor, he made friends, participated in law school activities, and belonged to the Order of the Coif. He was befriended by faculty members, especially Bob Huntley and Charles McDowell, whose home he frequently visited for dinner. He struggled with the law curriculum, and faculty members provided him with tutors and extra reading assignments. Huntley developed a reading list of important works of literature, philosophy, and history that Smith had never encountered in his undergraduate studies. His grades steadily improved, and Smith graduated with his class in June 1969. He had worked during the summers in Washington, DC, on Capitol Hill and in a high-profile law firm. After graduation he joined the US Department of Justice and worked in the Civil Rights Division, facilitating compliance of southern school boards with court orders for racial integration. Smith was murdered in Washington in 1971. The crime was never solved.[55]

In 1968, six black students applied for admission to W&L. Four were accepted, and two enrolled: Walter Blake and his friend Linwood Smothers. A graduate of Lexington High School, Blake had admired the university since childhood. A national semifinalist in the National Achievement Scholarship Program, he was heavily recruited by universities including Harvard, but he followed in the footsteps of his friend Dennis Haston. Blake participated in fraternity rush, became a member of Zeta Beta Tau (as did Smothers), majored in economics and engineering, and by all accounts had a full student experience at W&L. He was better prepared academically than Haston and the other black students admitted thus far, and he was also determined "to prove that a black student could come here and withstand whatever this institution threw at him and make it out."[56] Blake and Smothers graduated in 1972.

In 1969 all five blacks applicants were accepted, but none enrolled. In 1970 the number of applications from African Americans rose to thirty-six, and fifteen new black students enrolled at W&L. By 1983 the alumni rolls included about a hundred black graduates. The presence and role of African American students, faculty, and staff at W&L would evolve with the university. Their importance would always exceed their numbers, which would remain relatively small. But an important threshold had, though belatedly and somewhat awkwardly, been crossed. Despite continuing challenges and failures, the W&L of 1970 had come a vast distance from the overt racism of the 1920s and the football debacle at Washington and Jefferson. The university was more open to the future and many more changes to come.

CHAPTER SEVEN

STUDENT LIFE AND CULTURE

From Buttoned Down to Loosened Up

THE 1960S WAS a time of social and political upheaval in the United States and much of the rest of the world. A host of domestic issues, coupled with an assertive youth culture and an unpopular war, roiled traditional politics and led to new initiatives and priorities. The movement for racial equality provoked new demands for economic justice, and nonviolent civil disobedience was increasingly accompanied by assertions of African American pride and black power. The nation's cities harbored yawning gaps between wealth and poverty that inspired both reform and racial violence, including riots in Harlem in the summer of 1964 and in the Watts area of Los Angeles in 1965. The "War on Poverty" launched by the Johnson administration in 1964 responded to many of these issues in a manner reminiscent of the New Deal, but it engendered many controversies at the local level. Changes that eroded old customs and assumptions led to relief for some, unrealistic expectations for others, and a conservative backlash that churned the political waters even more.

One authority has argued that the "sixties" did not really begin until 1965, when the nation seemed to lurch from experiencing a booming economy and a number of major policy achievements in civil rights, education, and health care to facing a more contentious and problematic social and political landscape.[1] The most corrosive element was US military entanglement in Southeast Asia. President Johnson escalated US involvement from providing small numbers of military advisers to bombing North Vietnam and sending US ground troops. This action almost immediately inspired protests and campus sit-ins, which proliferated as the conflict grew in intensity and the American commitment increased. Much of this protest was fueled—especially on campuses—by the conscription of citizens to fight in a controversial war; the draft seemed to fall hardest on minorities and the poor who were less able to secure educational or other deferments. Vietnam seemed, in fact, to bring together and intensify all other major currents of political and cultural disaffection with authority.

While most young people followed conventional educational paths, a grow-ing counterculture movement, led by intellectuals, writers, and musicians in San Francisco and other large cities, gained momentum from a rising youth culture stressing independence and new ideas. The Beats of the 1950s were joined by young people of the 1960s who sought to "drop out" of conventional society and experiment with new styles of living—exemplified in different dress, music, behavior, and even vocabulary—all intended as rejections of traditional authority. Sexual freedom and the recreational use of drugs, psy-chedelic and otherwise, were part of the new "lifestyle." While this followed a long tradition of idealistic nonconformity in US history, it came as a dramatic and wrenching challenge to Cold War America. It seemed to many a direct assault on traditional American values and institutions, as well as evidence of a moral decline. To many young people, even those who remained mostly on the sidelines, it was exciting and tantalizing.

One W&L graduate was a major chronicler of these cultural phenomena and a key, if somewhat unlikely, figure of the era himself. Tom Wolfe hailed from Richmond, where he was a student leader, editor of the newspaper, and tal-ented baseball player at St. Christopher's School. At W&L he was sports editor of the *Ring-tum Phi* and helped start the new literary magazine, *Shenandoah*. He was especially influenced by Professor Marshall Fishwick's broader, multidisci-plinary view of society and culture, and following his graduation in 1951, Wolfe followed in Fishwick's footsteps to the doctoral program in American Studies at Yale. Wolfe pitched for the W&L baseball team and played semiprofessional ball, and tried out (unsuccessfully) for the New York Giants in 1952. But his future was not secured through academia or sports but by a new approach to understanding and explaining cultural phenomena, a new way of reporting that he called the "New Journalism," which applied literary techniques and anthropological observation and insight to news reporting. His first book, a collection of essays entitled *The Kandy-Kolored Tangerine-Flake Streamline Baby* (1965), reflected his new, flamboyant take on the times.

Wolfe's next effort established his role as an observer and interpreter of the counterculture. *The Electric Kool-Aid Acid Test* (1968) recounted the travels and psychedelic escapades of Ken Kesey and the Merry Pranksters, who embodied the bold challenge to traditional life and mores. Derived from the author's many weeks of immersion with its subjects, the book was as experimental as the famous counterculture group itself, mirroring and accentuating the provocation of tradition in style and even punctuation. Wolfe went on to write many commentaries and best-selling novels, and his signature white suit (which he began wearing in 1962) further enhanced his status as a cultural celebrity. Despite his flamboyance, Wolfe was conservative in his politics and tastes. He maintained close ties with his alma mater and in October 1984 was sworn in as a member of the W&L Board of Trustees.

The counterculture was largely nonpolitical in the beginning (the purpose, after all, was to "drop out" by "tuning in"), but its cultural trappings—especially music, clothes, and behavior—attracted millions of young people and, inevitably, became politicized by the social and economic injustices of the urban crisis and especially by the Vietnam War and the military draft. It contributed to the growing political volatility of the country over the decade, brought to a dramatic intensity in 1968 with the Tet Offensive in Vietnam, the assassinations of Martin Luther King Jr. and Robert F. Kennedy, and the turmoil of the Democratic National Convention in Chicago.

These changes seem even more rapid and stark in retrospect. Young people born just before or during World War II tended on the whole to be more conventional in behavior and outlook than those born after the war—the large cohort of baby boomers that exhibited greater readiness to strike out on new paths and to defy authority. On university campuses, the change was clearly discernible. And it was a worldwide phenomenon, as much in evidence in Europe as in the United States.

The European historian Tony Judt recalled his time at King's College, Oxford: "We were past the midpoint of the 1960s—the Mods had come and gone and the Beatles were about to record Sgt. Pepper—but the King's into which I was matriculated was still strikingly traditional. Dinner in Hall was formal, begowned—and required. Undergraduates took their seats, awaited the arrival of the Fellows, then rose to watch a long line of elderly gentlemen shuffle past them on their way to High Table." Yet, he added, "we were a path-breaking cohort. By the time we graduated, gowns, caps, gate hours, and a whole rulebook of minor regulations—all of them in place when we arrived—were the object of amused nostalgia."[2]

*   *   *

The quiet and seemingly cloistered campus of Washington and Lee University was neither unaware nor untouched by the changes of the 1960s. Rather, with traditions perhaps more embedded in campus life than elsewhere in the United States, change was all the more noticeable. Fred Cole reassured the trustees in January 1965 that the "restlessness which seems to exist on other campuses does not now exist at Washington and Lee."[3] Within seven months, however, he was admonishing the student body for neglecting university traditions, and five years later the campus was caught up in national political protest.

These changes followed broader national shifts in fashion and expectation. Most college students did not, after all, adhere to so formal a dress code, and few people would argue that informal dress precluded one from getting a good education. Mandated civility was certainly not the norm. At the University of Virginia, in fact, routine greetings among students were considered unfashionable. But W&L had its traditions, and their gradual erosion was a matter of concern, especially to alumni.

At the beginning of the decade, freshmen still wore blue beanies on campus, confirming their low rank in the student pecking order. Traditions were explained at length during orientation at Natural Bridge. Conventional dress still meant a proper jacket, dress shirt, and tie, and all students were expected to greet each other in passing. These conventions were enforced through the student-run Assimilation Committee. However rambunctious the fraternity parties, the student body and its leaders were generally deferential to the faculty and administration and to long-standing rules. Ten years later, the beanies were gone, conventional dress was literally fraying, the speaking tradition continued as part of university culture but was voluntary and less pervasive, and the idea of assimilation was out of vogue. The student government had taken away the committee's authority to levy fines, though it could still encourage traditional dress and behavior. Academic rules were eased, and a new curriculum with more flexibility had been introduced. Notably, the Honor System remained intact and still revered, along with the legacies of George Washington and Robert E. Lee, and students continued to play a significant role in university governance.

Even in 1962 or 1963, subtle changes were occurring in conventional dress. Some ties were loosened, and ski jackets and other outerwear substituted for proper blazers or coats. By 1965 many students carried rather than wore their jackets, went sockless, and left collars unbuttoned and shirttails dangling. The overall impression was of studied, some would say slovenly, indifference. The alumni reaction was predictable, and its insistence and urgency suggested that for them conventional dress represented the many other traditions that seemed threatened. The Alumni Board adopted a resolution in June 1962 lamenting the apparent "disregard on the part of present students at Washington and Lee of the tried and revered traditions of the University and a sharp decline in their *esprit de corps*," and it recommended that the university administration and student government "take all appropriate measures and actions within their jurisdiction to assure a more complete and dedicated adherence to those principles." These concerns were discussed at length as part of the two-year SACS self-study in the mid-1960s. Student leaders said that they were concerned about these tendencies, even as the Student Executive Committee was reducing the authority of the Assimilation Committee. James Kulp, a law student and president of the student body, suggested that some guidance or policy from the university would be helpful. In response, President Cole devoted his remarks at the opening assembly in fall 1965 to the topic.[4]

The assembly gathered on an unusually hot day in a stuffy Evans Hall. Professors sweltered in their academic robes, and virtually all students removed their jackets. Some were dozing. President Cole began by noting the many changes and adjustments W&L had made in its long history: "The University has changed, does change, and will continue to change with the times and the demands of the times." But "certain values and certain attitudes" are "unchanging to the degree that all Washington and Lee men can share these values and attitudes." While all students are treated as individuals," he noted, "certain traditions help bind the community—of students, faculty, and alumni—together," including "the shared experience of pride in your University." But, he asked, "I wonder how many of you share this pride. I wonder, because there is reason to believe that some of you do not." Some students did not speak to each other on campus walks, and if current trends continued, especially with warm weather in the spring, "the freshmen quickly will feel that his expenditures on jackets and ties could have been invested more wisely in other ways." Cole pointed particularly to the reactions of alumni: "I have had voluminous correspondence with many, and long conversations with others. They simply don't understand why you would allow to be weakened those concepts and practices in which they took such pride as students, and in which they still take pride as alumni."

The Self-Study Committee had concluded that "gentlemanly dress" could contribute to a sense of self-respect and discipline that might positively influence academic performance, but it was also agreed that this was a matter for the students themselves to decide. A strict dress code mandated by the administration was not the answer. Cole appealed to the assembled students to "ponder your right to destroy and maim that which many others before you sustained with pride and dignity" and to "decide if you are going to hold in contempt or in apathetic indifference this bond of fellowship." He hoped they would do the right thing and wished them well in the coming year. He had never before addressed the student body in such an insistent and didactic manner, and they gave him a standing ovation.[5]

A full report and discussion of the status of conventional dress appeared in the fall 1965 issue of the alumni magazine, along with a copy of Cole's speech to the student body.[6] Written in his usual vivid style by Frank Parsons, '54, the essay on conventional dress was an unvarnished report relating the various arguments and options. Parsons touched on the "virtually vanished" speaking tradition that so concerned alumni, and he described in detail the current appearance of many students on campus: "A multitude of shirt sins, previously hidden by coats, became visible—ragged sleeves, flapping shirt tails, ink-stained breast pockets. Some students appeared to own only one shirt for classroom wear. In a word, students looked grubby." He noted that Cole's remarks had seemed to stimulate more proper attire, at least the donning of jackets, in the weeks following the assembly, but he also explained to his fellow alumni that a trend toward more casual dress was evident throughout society and was already completely dominant off-campus. Students seemed to understand the importance of symbols in the ongoing life of the university, but "tradition for tradition's sake appears to have little appeal to students of the mid-1960s." In a student body "essentially conservative in its political, economic, and social attitudes," Parsons wrote, "many seem to feel they should be rebellious one way or another. Some will choose to attack conventional dress. After all, it's easier and safer to hate your coat than a Communist or a Bircher or whatever." In other words, modern student dress should not be taken too seriously. The fear was that this erosion of traditions might extend to something more sacrosanct—like the Honor System.

An unusual three-day conference for alumni chapter representatives in early October 1967 revealed continuing concern. A luncheon session in Evans Dining Hall included the delegates and thirty students—but no faculty members or administrators—presided over by student body president Richard Nash. At this point, 5 to 10 percent of students were not wearing coats and ties, and the great majority of the other students supported their right to ignore the tradition.

"This issue of dress," the alumni magazine reported, "produced perhaps more vehemence than any other topic discussed during the conference."[7] Alumni suggested that willingness to adhere to university traditions like conventional dress be a part of the admissions interview and that on-campus observance be enforced. Alumni secretary Bill Washburn pointed out that conventional dress was not an administrative mandate but a student-enforced tradition and that most "students no longer enforce their opinions or morality on a minority. They just will not do it." Even more pointedly, Severn P. C. Duvall, head of the English Department, observed that "Washington and Lee is not a finishing school, and the faculty are no substitutes for parents." A good faculty, he argued, "will encourage the student to *reconsider* the old familiar *patterns*" and to "encourage them to *scrutinize* unexamined presuppositions of their selves and their world." Duvall characterized education "as a radical act in the rudimentary sense of the word."[8] In this context, wearing a coat and tie was not so important.

As far as "preppy" dress—or for that matter, any prescribed code—was concerned, the early 1970s carried the erosion of the tradition even further. Some alumni still deeply regretted the loss of sartorial propriety. Tom Wolfe admitted his own stylistic challenges to the usual dress during his student days (white ties with black shirts), but he regretted the lapse of the tradition. "It's a constant reminder that you're something special, that you're maintaining standards that other of your contemporaries are not maintaining, and that something more is expected, and that you expect more of other people."[9] But the practice did not survive. Many years later, a 2012 *Ring-tum Phi* front-page story reported a decision by the faculty to issue warnings and even impose small fines on students who attended class in pajamas. Could this be true? Indeed, no. Informal dress had become the "new conventional," and to ban it was so seemingly preposterous that it was the lead story in the April Fool's issue of the paper.

WASHINGTON AND LEE was known for the active social life of its students well before national surveys of the country's best "party schools." The campus social scene included the usual seasonal dance sets—with the Fancy Dress Ball held in the new Evans Dining Hall for the first time in 1962—but increasingly revolved around weekend fraternity parties and some off-campus venues. The entertainment—from top-billing performers to fraternity party "regular" bands or "combos"—was by the 1960s almost exclusively African American. The music was largely rhythm and blues–inflected rock and roll. In these early days, some iconic performers in American popular music appeared together in concerts or even in individual fraternity houses. Their performances brought to campus a plethora of musical riches, attuned to the spirit of the times.

The combined Homecoming-Openings Weekend in mid-October 1961, for example, brought "old grads and young girls" to Lexington, including over four hundred alumni. The festivities began with an afternoon cocktail party in the Mayflower Hotel on Friday the thirteenth, with music by the Clovers and the Dukes of Rhythm, followed by a pep rally before the football contest with Randolph-Macon College the next day. An evening concert in Doremus Gymnasium featured Hank Ballard and the Midnighters, the Isley Brothers, and the Edsels, followed by open parties lasting until 2 a.m. in five fraternity houses. One of the most popular groups at W&L throughout this era appeared at Phi Gamma Delta: Doug Clark and the Hot Nuts from Chapel Hill, North Carolina. Following the football game on Saturday, in addition to a more sedate schedule of alumni activities (including a coffee hour with President Cole), were combo parties at nine fraternities, featuring the Tams at SAE, Jo-Jo and the Wailing Frets at Phi Gam, the Screamers at Sigma Nu, and the Hi-Los at Phi Psi. Joe Tex and the Dukes of Rhythm appeared at the Moose Lodge on Sunday afternoon (BYOL). As the *Ring-tum Phi* added: "Later—down the road."[10]

The same weekend the following year included a cocktail party featuring the Del Vikings and a "formal dance" in Doremus with music by Clyde McPhatter and his orchestra. The Saturday evening concert ("conventional dress required") featured the Shirelles, the Coasters, and King Curtis and his orchestra. Sixteen fraternities held parties over the weekend (three of them—featuring the Del Vikings, Coasters, and Shirelles—restricted to members only), with entertainment also provided by many other groups, including the Delcardos, the Prophets, Huey Piano Smith, the Zodiacs, and the Clovers. One group was notably absent from the schedule. The Hot Nuts had been banned in 1961 from any function on or off campus, an edict handed down by Assistant Dean of Students James Farrar. This action was a response to complaints received from some faculty and alumni following the band's Phi Gamma Delta performance. The Interfraternity Council had considered such a ban after the group "was the focal point of a near riotous fraternity party which had to be quelled by Lexington Police" in 1958 but instead recommended that each fraternity exercise "discretion" in hiring the group. Critics objected to "off-color songs," which were, of course, the reason for the group's popularity among students. Decades later, Doug Clark and the Hot Nuts were invited to an alumni reunion, where everyone reminisced about the good old days. By then, their signature song seemed rather tame.

Fraternity houses were the locations of most weekend entertainment. Rules governed how many houses—and which houses—could hold open parties, and they were not supposed to conflict with regular dance sets. The bands often performed in house basements, and the parties themselves were typically jammed with students and their dates, with loud music, dense tobacco smoke, and dance floors awash in spilled beer. These parties were part of the "work hard–play hard" male student culture of the time and are a source of fond alumni memories. Avid partying continued in subsequent decades and remained a characteristic of Washington and Lee, but with the decline of fraternities and the rise of recreational drugs and binge-drinking, the "informal" party scene held off-campus became more prevalent—along the Maury River in rented student houses, in fraternity "country houses" passed down to new student generations, or at other off-campus sites, such as Zollman's Pavilion.

One of the most memorable concerts during the decade was the appearance of the young James Brown and his Famous Flames before a packed audience in Doremus Gym in the spring of 1965. W&L even spawned its own rock and roll combo during this era. The Sabers—all W&L students—performed from 1961 to 1965 in high schools and colleges as far north as Johns Hopkins University in Baltimore and as far south as Sea Island, Georgia, sometimes traveling and appearing with the Sensations, a group of four local black men from Lexington. African American culture shaped the era's popular music, which penetrated deeply even into conservative W&L.

Fraternities were the center of social life at Washington and Lee for the 80 percent or more of the undergraduates who belonged, and they fed one-half and housed one-third or more of the student body. Their dominance on campus effectively isolated from key aspects of student life the 20 percent of undergraduates who did not belong. These eighteen organizations were also a continuing source of concern to the university administration and faculty. Fraternities that had housemothers (and in some cases even butlers and houseboys), reasonably maintained facilities, fully staffed kitchens, and more-or-less balanced books in 1960 had become very different places by 1970. Financially strapped, with declining memberships, some houses went under. By the end of the 1960s, Kappa Sigma and Kappa Alpha had folded, and Sigma Phi Epsilon operated as a lodge in a private apartment.

Before 1970 the university required fraternities to have housemothers. These women were employees of the fraternities, had apartments in the houses, and usually supervised the kitchen, prepared menus, and acted as hostesses whenever guests (especially females) were present. In 1970, in light of declining revenues, housemothers became optional, and then they virtually disappeared from campus. Each fraternity also had an adviser, almost always a faculty member (and sometimes an alumni board), to assist with preparation and review of the financial balance sheets submitted to the dean of students each month, and to make the mortgage payments and pay other expenses. In almost all cases, the university held the mortgage on the fraternity house, offered at below commercial rates. Fraternity officers controlled all other expenditures, and members paid dues and special assessments. Since freshmen were required to live on campus, most fraternities required sophomores to live in the house.

All fraternities were represented on the Interfraternity Council. The IFC held regular meetings and imposed regulations on individual fraternity operations (interpreted and enforced by its judicial board). Regulations included restrictions on social functions: party weekends were limited to the four dance sets and seven other "combo weekends," and no more than nine fraternities could hold house parties at the same time except on dance or football weekends, and these were by invitation only. No event could be scheduled on Sundays or during official university functions. With the administration's urging, the IFC engaged in civic projects, provided room and board for three foreign students, sponsored activities like the CONTACT symposium, and conducted its own self-study. There were also signs that the IFC was becoming less dominated by "student machine" politics; for the first time it elected an Independent Party candidate, E. Ross Kyger, as IFC president.

Fraternity rush, held in the fall before students attended their first classes, was a frenzied period, bewildering and exciting, that set the tone and context for life at W&L for new students. Men interested in joining a fraternity were required to make short visits to a minimum number of houses over several days and then declare their top three choices. A student-faculty committee matched up preferences with fraternity bids. Deferred rush began two weeks after Rush Week ended and could continue for the remainder of the academic year. Hazing was much less of a problem than it had been. "Hell Week" was abolished in May 1962, and while sometimes things got out of hand, pledging activities were now restricted to the Lexington city limits and to things like "physical exercising, constructive jobs around the houses, a certain amount of waiting on upperclassmen, and an occasional scavenger hunt."[11]

Individual fraternities determined their own budgets and varied in their ability to manage finances and the support they received from alumni. They depended on dues, room-and-board fees, and on keeping the house fully occupied. In general, dealing with fraternity finances was problematic, especially since advisers varied in their attention to details and it was hard for the dean of students to keep up with eighteen budgets and balance sheets.

Dean of Students Ed Atwood reported to the trustees in July 1965 on the issues of social fraternities.[12] He began by repeating the quixotic hope, long expressed by academic authorities, for "changes that will de-emphasize the undergraduate social atmosphere, and put greater stress upon the academic aspects of undergraduate life." He conceded the importance of these organizations in feeding and housing many students and providing—for the 80 percent of undergraduates who were members—physical facilities, entertainment, and "alcoholic refreshments" for the weekend parties, as well as "experience in small-group living and training in self-government and leadership." Leadership of the houses often devolved on lowerclassmen (especially the sophomores living in the house) and "socially-oriented" upperclassmen rather than on the more responsible juniors and seniors, who usually lived outside the houses and only attended parties or took meals there. (Private apartments—not subject to university restrictions on female guests—were increasingly popular among students.) Fraternities were much more likely to be "social clubs," competing with one another to mount the biggest parties, often at considerable expense. Fewer faculty members were willing to counsel fraternities on their finances and social activities. A long-standing issue had been the early induction of freshmen into fraternity life before they adjusted to university life or even attended their first classes. Delaying rush until later in the freshman year was an option, but delay into the sophomore year would be difficult given the prevailing pattern of fraternity housing and finance. Eventually, in 1970—along with the adoption of the new curriculum and academic calendar—fraternity rush was pushed to the middle of the term.

More than two hundred students, or 20 percent of undergraduates, were not affiliated with fraternities and had no access to comparable social and recreational facilities. About half chose to remain independent, and the others had been either turned down by all eighteen fraternities or the bids they'd received failed to match their preferences. In the fall of 1959, 18 percent of freshmen did not receive bids, and the proportion in the early 1960s remained as high as 24 percent.[13] (Some men pledged fraternities during deferred rush.)

Proposals for "100 percent rush" and "open membership"—providing access to fraternity membership to any student—were rejected as impractical because such arrangements were not acceptable to many national fraternities.

Atwood observed, "This group of students is, for practical purposes, deprived of a normal undergraduate social life," a situation that accounted for the large proportion of students who transferred to other institutions. Altering the operation and membership policies of the houses seemed impractical, and the focus remained on enhancing the social lives of independent students. Atwood mentioned improvements to the Student Union, such as new recreational facilities (billiards, ping pong, and bowling) and a pub selling low-alcohol beer.

Fraternities also posed obvious challenges for racial integration. Some national fraternities maintained restrictive clauses in their charters, barring blacks from membership. Herman B. Wells, chancellor of Indiana University, and also vice-regent of the Sigma Nu fraternity, wrote to Fred Cole on November 3, 1966 (and to other presidents), expressing his dismay at the recent narrow defeat by the fraternity's national convention of a provision allowing local chapters to exempt themselves from these restrictions (a "waiver with honor"). He sought Cole's opinion of the decision's effect on the university and the fraternity. Cole responded, "I have for years had a negative reaction toward discrimination of any nature that was based upon such factors as race, religion, color, and national origin. But, as I am sure you will understand, those of us who have spent our lives primarily in the South are not quite sure when we came to hold the views that now seem to be so obviously correct. In any case, at this time in history I do not believe that any educational institution, or an institution that is associated with education, can justify arbitrary discrimination based solely on race." He also believed—perhaps with W&L's recent decision on admissions in mind—that fraternities should move "at the earliest date possible" because "a decision for non-discrimination related to race is inevitable," and "the longer a delay is permitted the greater the problem in justifying such a delay becomes." Because blacks had attended W&L for such a brief time, he observed, the issues "had not been as sharply drawn here as they may have been at some other institutions." He also drew a distinction between "the University public on-campus and that composed of alumni and others who have a deep interest in the welfare of the institution. It is my opinion that the latter group would probably oppose drastic changes in the traditional character of fraternities whereas the on-campus group would, on the whole, support action toward racial non-discrimination." Dean Atwood confirmed that the Student

Affairs Committee was investigating the matter and might ask fraternities to seek exemptions from such restrictions.[14]

President Robert E. R. Huntley wrote to the national executive secretary of Sigma Chi Fraternity in May 1968 that "three Negro and two Oriental students" would enroll in the fall and that they should "be given full consideration for membership by all eighteen of the national fraternities" at W&L. He inquired about Sigma Chi's policy and how racial restrictions could be waived. He added, "Effective action in these matters is best accomplished when not accompanied by public proclamations, and, therefore, we would prefer to make the appropriate arrangements quietly and without undue publicity."[15] As it turned out, fraternities were not as large a problem as anticipated, due largely to the more tolerant policies of one group—Zeta Beta Tau. The two black students who joined the freshman class in 1968 both pledged ZBT, and in the following decade a larger African American student contingent worked to form a new black fraternity.

One serious matter had been looming for some time: the care and maintenance of fraternity houses. These structures suffered substantial wear and tear and were largely unoccupied during the summer months. Maintenance was easily put off, and needs for repairs grew increasingly serious. At an April 1968 meeting, fraternity faculty advisers projected that the total needed for work on all houses was $600,000, and some suggested that the needs were even greater. They proposed the continued extension of loans to fraternities below the commercial rate but also wanted to charge a 3 percent minimum maintenance fee, collected by the university, that would provide funds for current and future repairs. Some advisers wondered if fraternity members might take even less care of the houses if they knew that maintenance funds were available. Would members who caused damage be required to pay for repairs if funds were otherwise available? Such concerns only underlined the nature and severity of the problem.[16]

The SACS self-study included a lengthy discussion of fraternities and their influence on student life; it argued that fraternities were less effective than they had been even fifteen or twenty years earlier at indoctrinating and orienting new students to campus traditions (like conventional dress). Furthermore, fraternities encouraged attitudes and social life that undermined academic work and university ideals, and they posed issues of financial management and maintenance of facilities. The role of housemothers was valuable but "often a precarious one," and "the type of older woman who makes a good housemother seems to be vanishing." (One housemother was rumored to have locked herself in her apartment on weekends.) Self-study recommendations urged giving "immediate attention to the social problems of non-fraternity students," with expanded facilities in the Student Union; bringing housemothers "into closer connection with the University"; expanding a continuous self-study by the IFC; setting standards and goals for fraternities; requiring periodic assessment; and eliminating "all practices that perpetuate religious and racial discrimination."

The most dramatic option was eliminating fraternities entirely. Apart from being virtually unthinkable to alumni, implementing such a decision—or even significantly reducing the proportion of fraternity membership—would immediately pose a large burden on the university to provide room, board, and entertainment for much of the student body. The living and dining facilities could be self-sustaining, but it did "not seem feasible to turn 1,300 students loose on the City of Lexington and the surrounding area in a search for recreation. If the fraternities were removed, and comparable campus facilities were not substituted, the ramifications could be disastrous since Lexington is probably not a large enough city to absorb the recreational activities of Washington and Lee students." Nevertheless, the Self-Study Subcommittee noted such a possibility: "If after trying the proposed approaches to reform and improvement, the fraternity situation did not become more satisfactory, it seemed probable that Washington and Lee would have to face up to the problem by the abolition of fraternities and the substitution of something else in their places."[17]

WASHINGTON AND LEE'S long touted reliance on students to govern and even discipline themselves became especially relevant as expectations that the university act in loco parentis faded. The Student Executive Committee, the apex of student governance, was composed of twelve members: the president, vice president, and secretary elected at large by the student body, and representatives (and officers) elected by each class, including two from the law school. (A 1965 constitutional amendment retained the law school as an integral part of overall student government but decreased the number of its representatives from three to two and increased representation of the sophomore class.) Standing committees of the executive committee selected their membership through a process of applications and interviews each year. A student-government operating fund was derived from student fees and regularly audited.

To the extent the university permitted, student discipline was a responsibility of student government and the fraternity system. The Assimilation Committee sought to indoctrinate new students and encourage their continued observance of university traditions. The Cold Check Committee penalized students who wrote bad checks in the community, and the Student Library Committee monitored use of that facility. The Student Control Committee was established to transfer to students the routine regulation of student behavior on campus and in Lexington and surrounding areas. The Judicial Committee of the Interfraternity Council dealt with student disciplinary matters within the fraternity system. Overall authority for student discipline was centralized in a new Student Affairs Committee in November 1965, as recommended by the Self-Study Committee and approved by the faculty. This new group was composed of the three deans of student affairs, three faculty members, and four students—the presidents of the student body, the IFC, the Student Bar Association, and the Student Control Committee. Together, they reviewed decisions by the Student Control Committee and the Judicial Committee of the IFC. Discipline in the dormitories was the responsibility of dormitory counselors and the administration. In 1970, in light of the student unrest on many campuses, including Washington and Lee, the University Council—of twelve students, the student body president, twelve faculty members, and five administrators—was established as a forum to exchange ideas on a variety of issues.

The role of the university proctor, former Lexington police officer C. F. Murphy, was extremely important to student discipline. Affectionately known by the students as "Murph," he reported directly to the dean of students. He was in a position to ensure adherence to university policy, but he focused less on the enforcement of rules than on the prevention of misbehavior. The SACS Self-Study noted his "phenomenal knowledge of names, faces, and automobiles" and his "uncanny knack of being in the right place at the right time." His excellent rapport with students and the fraternities helped prevent trouble and doubtless greatly reduced the number of discipline cases.[18]

For many years, fraternity cliques dominated student politics. Candidates selected by the largest coalition usually won, leaving only lesser offices to genuine competition. By the mid-1960s this system had become more open, and independent candidates were elected to some important positions, though proposals in 1965 to create open nominating conventions failed to win a required majority of the total student body. The SACS Self-Study did not recommend changes in student government but did endorse conventional dress and the speaking tradition, and asked for faculty cooperation in efforts to sustain these traditions.

Implementing the Honor System was the most consequential responsibility of student government. This aspect of the university had long ago ceased to be merely part of student activity. Never a formal set of rules, it has shaped the institution's ethos, a shared set of values traced to the founders, spanning generations and setting standards for individual character and life long after graduation. It is as much an idea as a program. To a degree, it is also a "brand" W&L employs to distinguish itself from other universities, a very real and palpable part of campus life, a shared commitment of mutual trust that grows stronger with time and memory.

Evidence suggests that a code of honor existed at Washington College before 1865. But the Honor System is most directly traced to Robert E. Lee's declaration soon after he became president: "There is but one rule here, and it is that every student must be a gentleman." Students' lives and behavior would thus be based on honesty and integrity, so well exemplified by Lee himself, without itemization or elaboration. It is not entirely clear how this expectation was initially implemented, though some students were expelled for violations. The modern Honor System is a function of student government first formally recognized in 1905.

The Honor System has, of course, changed over the decades, becoming more formal and procedural as the larger society has grown more litigious. Its essential elements have remained remarkably intact; simply put, the system expects students not to lie, cheat, or steal. Students pledge on all class assignments that they have neither given nor received assistance (except under specific guidelines from the instructor that allow for collaboration with others). Examinations are not proctored. Those accused of violating the honor code are judged solely by fellow students and, if found guilty by two-thirds of the executive committee of the student body, are subject to a single sanction: immediate expulsion from the university.

The basic elements of the system at midcentury are similar to those in place today. The mechanics of the process were straightforward and dramatic.[19] The Student Executive Committee heard the charges in secret. The accused was notified of the charge, usually no more than a few hours before the hearing. Witnesses were called and questioned by the committee and by the accused, who could be present during the entire hearing. The accused could also appeal to the student body in an open public hearing that had some trappings of a formal court proceeding—a student jury, rules of evidence, and two student advisers to represent the accused. The verdict of the student jury was considered final. Open hearings were rarely requested, and students sometimes withdrew rather than subject themselves to even the executive committee review.

A student who left the community under these circumstances withdrew from the university with a notation that he had been accused of an honor violation. If he was found not guilty, all evidence and records of the trial were destroyed and the matter held in strictest confidence. If the student was found guilty, all records of the proceeding were maintained, also in confidence, and the student was forced to withdraw from the university and leave the community immediately, his belongings gathered and sent to him later. The harshness of such a judgment was somewhat mitigated by the notation "Withdrew without securing official permission" on his transcript. Professors could provide academic recommendations for the student's admission to study elsewhere, and with the permission of the student and his parents, the dean of students could send a letter concerning the withdrawal to other schools. In fact, most of the expelled students were admitted to other colleges.

The cheating "syndicate" that led to the withdrawal of fifteen students in 1954 was the most notorious challenge to the Honor System. The number, extent, and nature of the violations were unprecedented and placed inordinate demands on the executive committee, which conducted weeks of investigation and met in almost continuous hearings. The Honor System prevailed—the executive committee rose to the occasion with wholehearted support from the student body. Though there were many other reasons, financial and otherwise, behind the trustees' decision to abolish subsidized football, the affront to the Honor System was unquestionably the most compelling.

The Honor System was never an oppressive set of regulations prescribing particular behavior. Professor John M. Gunn once pointed out that it focused on "the most central elements of good moral character, and of good scholarship, . . . honesty and rectitude."[20] It sustained an environment of freedom and trust on campus, but it was always a work in progress. Despite considerable efforts to educate all students about the requirements of the Honor System, some ran afoul of scholarly rules of attribution and were found guilty of plagiarism, and some were accused of violations that were inadvertent. The Honor System had to function in the real world, and doubtless one reason it has endured, according to Gunn, was that it "confined the boundaries of enforceable behavior to that core that students are willing to enforce upon each other." As the executive committee itself explained, the system was "concerned solely with those offenses which are considered as dishonorable by the student generation involved." Insincere professions of affection to women and misrepresentations of age to purchase alcohol did not fall under the purview of the Honor System. As Gunn wrote of this "undoubted chink" in the system, "it seems to be part of the culture that a 19-year-old's fundamental right to buy beer, even though it is illegal, transcends his obligation to tell the truth about his age." This attitude was probably itself a deeply embedded tradition at Washington and Lee.

The Honor System evolved over time and adapted to new generations, but the adjustments were not easy. The social changes underway throughout the country, beginning especially in the 1960s, included declining respect for authority and tradition, as well as greater attention to legalistic solutions and concepts of due process and social justice. Inevitably, questions about the single sanction and the possibility of graduated penalties arose. (Should the severity of the penalty fit the specific nature of the offense?) Students and faculty members required more detailed guidance about what was permitted in various sorts of assignments (take-home tests, homework, required reading) and what academic work should be "pledged." Plagiarism was especially troublesome because of the complexities of scholarly attribution. Some faculty members were apparently skeptical about the Honor System itself. In short, General Lee's brief description of gentlemanly behavior seemed one hundred years later to be vague and even anachronistic, especially when it was increasingly codified, parsed, and applied to new times.

The executive committee conducted twelve hearings for honor violations in 1964–1965, leading to three withdrawals. Fifteen hearings the following academic year led to four withdrawals. That all accusations did not result in hearings tends to support the conclusion that the process proceeded carefully, with due attention to the rights of the accused.[21] Still, all hearings were serious matters, and all withdrawals painful.

In March 1962, a student reported three others for rifling the candy machines in the freshman dormitory. The executive committee proceedings the next evening ran until 6 a.m. the following morning. One student chose to withdraw, but the other two opted for a hearing. Both were found guilty. All three were taken to the Mayflower Hotel, where they met just after the trial with the dean of students, who encouraged them to contact their parents. Dean Atwood reported to Cole that the students were surprised at the severity of the penalty, and one father "was bitter that a student could be expelled for such a 'minor offense.'" All the parents apparently accepted the verdicts and focused on finding other colleges for their sons. Atwood discussed the options for enrollment in another school: "I explained that we would be as helpful as possible if another school asked for an explanation." More troubling was Atwood's report that the student who reported the honor violation was "being subjected to a considerable amount of abuse in the freshman dorm. There seems to be considerable feeling among the freshmen that he should not have reported the incident." At the request of student body president Andrew Mc-Thenia, Atwood arranged for a meeting of all first-year students so that "the Executive Committee could re-explain the Honor System."[22] Even students recently exposed to a full explanation of the Honor System during freshman orientation believed that expulsion was excessive and the obligation to report violations unreasonable.

Some faculty members also were not entirely persuaded that the penalty was just. Faculty and administrators who were graduates of the university had a special understanding of long-standing traditions and customs. As the faculty grew larger in the 1950s and 1960s, and was recruited from a national pool, at least some were skeptical of the operation of the Honor System, in particular the single sanction and the lack of what they perceived as appropriate due process. Frank Gilliam expressed "a feeling of disturbance" about this to Fred Cole. In an undated memorandum entitled "The Honor System and New Faculty Members," he suggested that just as no student should accept admission to W&L unless he also accepted the standards of the Honor System, so also should faculty members teach at the university only if they shared the same conviction. "It seems rather clear" he wrote, "that such implicit acceptance of the Honor System has not been shared by some of the newer and younger members of the faculty." He asked why the university could not "determine that no member of the faculty is engaged who does not accept full commitment to the Honor System just as it exists, almost uniquely, on this campus?"[23] This concern persisted when some faculty members tried to deal with student dishonesty themselves, rather than report it to the executive committee. Some disagreed with obliging students to inform on one another. But full acceptance of all aspects of the Honor System had never been a criterion or requirement of employment.[24]

The number and type of academic assignments subject to the Honor System proliferated, requiring explanation to students and faculty. A two-page statement by the Student Executive Committee in November 1970, "Recommended Faculty Guidelines for the Honor System," covered homework, reading, tests, open note tests, and independent examinations. On the one hand, the more detailed the requirements became, the less effective the Honor System might be; on the other hand, "translating" the system's purpose and requireme[nts] new generations in more detail helped them to endure.

The SACS Self-Study in 1966 identified the Honor System as "the mos[t] significant aspect of student life" and supported by an "overwhelming consensus." Its long-term effectiveness "is to be found in its absolute nature" and in its "control entirely by students." The self-study recommended no significant changes.[25] John Gunn attributed the persistence of the Honor System to three things: its management by students rather than the faculty or administration; the "very force of the tradition, enhanced by the exemplary character of Robert E. Lee"; and "the consistency of the single penalty for offense."[26] Its periodic changes and adaptations were also doubtless responsible for it lasting.

At the same time, doubts persisted. The authority and role of the executive committee came into question when two open trials were held in the later years of the decade. According to Neil Kessler, Friday editor of the *Ring-tum Phi,* these hearings "caused considerable anxiety, consternation, and alarm, and possibly a lack of confidence in the Executive Committee."[27] He also noted that a survey of juniors and seniors in three fraternities, taken in 1966, revealed inconsistencies in the system. Only about a third stated that they would report a fraternity brother for an honor violation, and three-quarters admitted to having committed or witnessed violations of the "letter of the law." How could an honor system survive in a time when the "century-old norms" of social conduct no longer pertained? In response, Jay Passavant, president of the student body, appointed two committees to study the Honor System, one to examine the jurisdictional limits of its application and a second to study procedures and seek ways to assure due process. These reviews came at a time of student unrest and the reexamination of many traditional assumptions and social norms, when honor codes at many universities had become embroiled in politics and dissent. How W&L's Honor System fared would say much about both the times and the institution.

THE MOCK CONVENTIONS in 1960, 1964, and 1968 reflected to some degree the political volatility of the decade but were generally civil and festive affairs. While primaries became increasingly influential, the party conventions were still important and—for the party out of the White House—difficult to predict, with plenty of maneuvering involved. W&L's Mock Convention continued to stand out among scores of other collegiate efforts for its accuracy, and it garnered significant media attention. The campus conventions correctly predicted

and the general flavor of the national party conven-
in the '60s.

onvention featured the Democrats, with former
the keynoter and US senator Henry M. "Scoop"
ate as a principal speaker. Truman was in full cam-
ugh his remarks were fairly sedate. Smiling and affable, he
de Fred Cole at the front of the traditional parade, featuring the usual
array of floats and personalities—including Miss America, Linda Lee Meade.
Truman rode down Main Street and then observed the rest of the procession
to Doremus Gymnasium from a reviewing stand on the lawn of the President's
House. At one point, the Florida delegation let loose from their float a barrage
of oranges directed at the seated dignitaries, some hitting but not harming the
former president. (Truman later joined student body president J. Frank Surface
in dedicating a plaque honoring Sen. Alben Barkley, who died at the Mock
Convention podium in 1956.) The question for the convention was whether the
Democrats would again nominate Adlai Stevenson, turn to US Senate majority
leader Lyndon Johnson, or choose a newcomer, US senator John F. Kennedy.
Stevenson led on the fourth ballot, but Kennedy finally prevailed on the sixth.
Senator Jackson was selected as the vice-presidential nominee. Kennedy was
at the moment deeply engaged in a tight race in a key primary election in West
Virginia, and the selection of this young Roman Catholic was far from certain
at the time, adding luster to the W&L result.

After Kennedy's assassination in November 1963 and his replacement by
Vice President Johnson, the Democratic nominee in 1964 was never in doubt.
Attention shifted to the Republicans. Former president Dwight D. Eisenhower
declined an invitation to attend, and the May 1964 Mock Convention keynote
speaker was former US representative Walter Judd of Minnesota, who had been
the keynoter for the 1960 GOP convention. The opening speaker was Virginia
congressman Richard H. Poff, and the student chairman was senior law student
Philip D. Sharp Jr. The parade—led by Judd and Fred Cole in an open black
Duesenberg—featured more than fifty floats, twelve bands, six beauty queens
(including Miss America and Miss Virginia), and two elephants. While Henry
Cabot Lodge of Massachusetts was selected by many other college conventions,
with support also for Nelson Rockefeller, Richard Nixon, and Pennsylvania
governor William Scranton, the W&L students detected a strong surge in the
party for the candidacy of Arizona senator Barry Goldwater, whose deeply conservative and straightforward message was also personally appealing to many

W&L students and attracted many young supporters who had little previous political experience. To an unusual degree, the W&L convention provided some of these key supporters with an opportunity for a "dry run" of the upcoming convention itself. John Grenier, chair of the Alabama Republican Party, headed up Goldwater's effort in the South (which would play a significant role in his nomination). Grenier had no convention experience, but he was intimately familiar with the Goldwater vote-gathering effort throughout the country. He spoke at W&L in advance of the Mock Convention and was on campus during the entire event, mostly ensconced with the Alabama delegation in its headquarters on the top floor of the Robert E. Lee Hotel. He kept a tally of the votes and worked the phones to other campaign leaders as balloting began on May 3. Goldwater narrowly missed nomination on the first ballot but won overwhelmingly on the second. Scranton—supported by an enthusiastic Pennsylvania delegation—was selected for the second spot on the ticket. Goldwater accepted his nomination immediately by telephone, with the call broadcast over the public address system. Some pundits suspected that personal student enthusiasms had gotten the better of them and had produced a flawed result. But, once again, they had chosen correctly.

Many of the themes and currents stirred by Goldwater in 1964 persisted in the GOP convention of 1968, particularly in its reaction to the Johnson administration's "Great Society" policies on civil rights and economic justice. The Democrats, following President Johnson's withdrawal from the race, were in disarray, accentuated further by Robert Kennedy's assassination in June following his victory in the California primary. A number of party luminaries—including Senate minority leader Everett Dirkson and Senators Charles Percy and Jacob Javits—turned down invitations to be the keynote speaker in Lexington. Florida governor Claude R. Kirk Jr. accepted, and US representative William E. Brock III, '53, of Tennessee was the parade grand marshal. Other notable Republicans visited campus in the months prior to the convention, including Nixon, Goldwater, and Senator Strom Thurmond, who spoke in Lee Chapel on March 21. Dean William W. Pusey, then acting president, privately confided his lack of enthusiasm to former President Cole on February 1: "Mr. Nixon came and went. I could not gracefully get out of introducing him. If you saw a picture of us together, he had his arm around me, and not vice versa! Actually, the students seemed to get a big kick out of seeing him and all the TV cameras and newsmen. Next Barry Goldwater and Strom Thurmond. It is *not* a big year for democrats at Washington and Lee."[28] The parade had the usual array of floats, though some were a bit skimpy. (The Hawaii delegation entry consisted of a tractor towing a toy red wagon with a single small plastic pineapple.) Regrettably, none of the three elephants scheduled for the parade appeared; one stubbed his toe before shipment, and a truck carrying the two others broke down en route. Shortly after Governor Kirk's speech, a bomb threat cleared Doremus Gym, but activities soon resumed. Nixon won on the third ballot and made his acceptance speech by telephone. The state votes in the balloting were remarkably similar to those at the actual convention some months later. Senator Charles Percy was nominated for vice president. One new element in this Mock Convention was an effort to draft and adopt a party platform, based entirely on student opinions. (In a sign of the times, after a tense forty-five-minute debate, an amendment to abolish the draft was adopted 694 to 634.)

One element of the Mock Convention tradition was the students' boorish behavior, usually fueled by alcohol. Though their behavior never got completely out of hand, the possibilities inspired anxiety among convention planners. The 1968 chair, Steven R. Saunders, wrote Richard Nash, president of the Student Executive Committee, that he had met with the IFC to warn that serious misconduct might threaten the continuation of Mock Conventions altogether. Saunders hoped the Student Control Committee could punish by "social probation" or by "a stiff schedule of fines" actions such as "drunk and disorderly conduct, creating a public disturbance, public drunkenness," and so on.[29] Disorderly behavior during Mock Conventions probably did not exceed that occurring during any big party weekend, but there were certainly more members of the general public and many outsiders and media representatives to witness it.

In addition to athletics and the Mock Conventions, the variety of on-campus activities at Washington and Lee that complement the academic program has helped secure its place as a leading liberal arts institution. For some students, participation in extracurricular opportunities was deeply memorable and important. The three official student publications—The Calyx (the yearbook), the Ring-tum Phi, and the Southern Collegian—fell under the authority of the Publications Board, composed of students, an alumnus, and a faculty member, that was responsible to the executive committee of the student body. During the 1960s, the Ring-tum Phi was published in two separate editions, with different staffs, twice a week (Tuesdays and Fridays) during the academic year. Beginning in 1970, it appeared only once a week. The university, though potentially legally liable for its content, exercised no censorship of any kind, though the dean of students often reminded the editors of their responsibilities to observe high journalistic standards. The *Southern Collegian* magazine appeared four times a year, on the major dance weekends. Devoted to short commentary and humor, its content became increasingly raucous and even obscene, often to the delight of many students and the consternation of offended alumni and the administration, which withdrew university financial support and effectively stopped the magazine's publication in 1966. A new independent student literary and arts magazine—*Ariel*—began publication in 1962 without university funding; its editors would not agree to come under the authority of the Publications Board. Law students edited the *Washington and Lee Law Review,* operated the Legal Aid Association and the Legal Research Association, and represented the university in moot court competitions.

Other university-sponsored cultural and artistic activities included the music program directed by Robert Stewart, which in mid-decade attracted about sixty-five student participants to the Glee Club and its ten concerts a year; the Brass Choir, which often performed with the Glee Club; and the Concert Guild, a mostly student organization that sponsored with university funds about a half-dozen campus performances a year by well-known artists. The new Student Concert Society was created in 1963 to present students from W&L and other colleges in recital. The student a cappella group, the Sazeracs, performed frequently on and off campus. Professor William W. Chaffin directed the strong debate programs at W&L. The fifty or so students on the Intercollegiate Debate Team participated in some eighteen tournaments a year, in addition to a number of on-campus debates. The Troubadours staged three plays a year with an all-student cast and crew, working in the inadequate facilities of the Troubadour Theater. A relatively new program was "Radio Washington and Lee," supervised by the Journalism and Communications Department and involving about thirty-five students. A music show and brief news program were broadcast over the Lexington commercial station, and efforts were already underway for the university to hold its own license for FM broadcasting.

Many students participated in various religious organizations on campus and attended local churches. The Young Republicans, the Young Democrats, the Conservative Society, and a newly established chapter of Young Americans for Freedom provided access to political activities, including guest speakers. Some literary clubs and discussion groups—such as the Civil War Roundtable—were active to various degrees, and the University Dance Board sponsored the four major dance weekends each year through ticket sales and an annual budget of around $25,000. Various other social clubs and secret societies—Sigma, the "13" Club, the White Friars, and the Mongolian Minks had no particular or known function, other than giving parties. Cadaver, a secret society, painted its symbol (a skull with a "C") around campus and occasionally donated to university projects. The administration considered many of these groups' initiation rituals "juvenile" and even harmful (such as the branding of each Sigma member and the occasional defacement of campus structures).

The university continued to draw a number of speakers to campus, sometimes in response to student demands to hear from people who generated headlines and stirred controversy, regardless of political persuasion. The long established Tucker Lectures in the law school annually featured a major attorney, jurist, or scholar. The CONTACT symposium was entirely shaped and implemented by students under the aegis of the IFC in 1964–65, and it has continued in one form or another ever since. Most lectures occurred outside a regular program or series. In 1960–61, for instance, thirty-five visitors held forth on topics from history and classics to geology and world affairs. Arnold J. Toynbee returned to campus in March for a lecture called "Does History Make Sense?" The Seminars in Literature program, running since 1952, brought four speakers to Lexington, and the Glasgow Endowment sponsored a symposium on writing. The Tucker lecturer that year was alumnus and future trustee Ross L. Malone. Student attendance at lectures, when not required as part of class work, was often disappointing—a complaint echoed on many other campuses and often attributed to the distractions of student life. But many students were involved, and lively discussions with visiting speakers often extended well after the formal presentation had concluded, continuing at receptions held at fraternity houses or faculty homes. Through the classroom, clubs, organizations, and visiting lectures—and despite their conservative leanings and seeming absorption in social activities—W&L students stayed well aware of varied opinions, global events, and national politics.

President Cole reported, with some relief, to the trustees on October 22, 1965, that a poster appearing on the Colonnade just before Homecoming Weekend, calling for two hours of picketing against the Vietnam War in front of Evans Dining Hall, had elicited no response whatsoever, perhaps indicating that the call did not come from "within the student body."[30] Even so, while protest of any sort was exceedingly rare at W&L, changes in many aspects of collegiate life throughout the country—even at W&L—were underway.

"Black Ball" in Evans Hall, sponsored by Student Association for Black Unity, 1975

Band Performing in Red Square, Homecoming, 1975

Fancy Dress Ball in Evans Hall, 1977, without period costumes but revived with more formal attire from a hiatus earlier in the decade

A new, less formal tradition: Fancy Dress Weekend at Zollman's Pavilion, 1976

Farris Hotchkiss

Law school dean Roy Steinheimer

Groundbreaking for Lewis Hall; including, *l to r,* Frances Lewis,
Dean Roy Steinheimer, Sydney Lewis, John M. Stemmons, D. E. "Pat" Brady,
Rector John Newton Thomas, and President Huntley (pointing)

A national contender in lacrosse: W&L v. the University of
North Carolina on Wilson Field, c. 1976

President John D. Wilson

President Wilson congratulating his predecessor and honorary
degree recipient Robert E. R. Huntley, 1984

Professor Sidney M. B. Coulling

Professor, Dean, and Interim President William Webb Pusey III, 1983

Former rector James M. Ballengee, 1996

Professor Pamela Simpson

Freshman Orientation for the first coeducational class, September 1985

Sorority Bid Night, 1989

W&L Women Cross-country Runners, 1991

Philippe Labro and Tom Wolfe

Farris Hotchkiss with Gerry Lenfest (*center*) and Tom Touchton, chair and co-chair
of the "On the Shoulders of Giants" campaign launched in February 1992

John Elrod, John Wilson, and Bob Huntley, 1995

CHAPTER EIGHT

AN ALUMNUS
TAKES OVER

A GRADUATE OF Washington and Lee had not served as its president since before the Civil War. Yet when the presidential search committee, appointed after Fred Cole's resignation in 1967, settled on thirty-eight-year-old alumnus Robert Edward Royall Huntley, their choice seemed inevitable. A native of Winston-Salem, North Carolina, a young Huntley had first met Francis and Sadie Gaines when they were guests at his family's cottage at Virginia Beach. Gaines was then serving as president of Wake Forest College. "I remember him sitting on the front porch of the cottage reading dime novels and enjoying his vacation," Huntley recalled in 1989. After Gaines moved to Lexington, "It was he, and my knowledge of him, that caused me to decide very early that Washington and Lee was where I would come. My brother came here for the same reason and I never considered any other school, either then or later." Huntley found the Gaineses "to be among the most magnetic people I have ever met. . . . They had what, in a later day, we learned to call charisma."[1]

Huntley received a bachelor's degree in English in 1950, served for three years in the US Navy, and in 1957 earned the LLB degree summa cum laude. He was elected to Phi Beta Kappa, the Order of the Coif, and Omicron Delta Kappa. As an undergraduate, he shared a room with classmate, fraternity brother, and future CBS TV newscaster, Roger Mudd, and he studied with some of W&L's leading professors, a number of whom were still on the faculty when he became president. While he studied law, he and his wife Evelyn (originally from Virginia Beach and a William and Mary graduate) lived in "the paper huts of Hillside Terrace" on Myers Street. After a year of practice with an Alexandria,

Virginia, law firm, he was appointed in 1958 as assistant professor of law and only a year later advanced to the rank of associate professor. After a year at Harvard, resulting in an LLM degree in 1962, he returned to the faculty of his alma mater as professor of law. Gaines and Cole appreciated Huntley's considerable leadership potential, and Cole appointed him the university's legal adviser and then secretary to the board. As Frank Parsons recalled, "Fred Cole recognized early the qualities that Bob Huntley had in terms of the brilliance of his mind, his reasoning powers, his powers of persuasion. He made Bob the University's legal counsel, and in order to bring Bob in contact in the best possible ways with members of the Board of Trustees, he made him the secretary of the board so he'd be at all the meetings. Bob was very persuasive with certain members of the board to lessen their stiffness on this matter of racial integration, so he played a very key role in that transition."[2] When Dean Charles P. Light Jr. retired in 1967, the trustees asked Huntley to leave the room while they agreed unanimously to appoint him as Light's successor. He had served as dean for less than a semester before he was elected president of the university. Remarkably, Huntley had risen from new assistant professor to president in ten years.

Huntley was one of a number of thirty-something college chief executives appointed around the same time, chosen not so much because of the rising youth culture of the period as out of a desire for fresh, energetic leadership—or at least the appearance of it. While Huntley was young in years, his demeanor was that of a confident, seasoned, careful leader, politically astute and skilled in interactions with board members, the faculty, and other major constituencies. His oratory was low-key, modest, and usually brief, more like Cole's than Gaines's. He generally projected an air of gregarious informality, warmth, and good humor in personal relations, a demeanor perfectly appropriate to the prevailing culture of his alma mater, while not diminishing the authority of his office. He was straightforward in dealing with problems and impatient with pomposity and posturing. Colleagues often described him as "brilliant." He could also be abrupt and gruff at times. Like Cole, he was rarely without a cigarette in hand. (Once, in his early professorial days, Huntley managed to set his lecture notes on fire.) The president's house was now occupied by the Huntleys and their three daughters, Martha (9), Catherine (7), and Jane (19 months).

Huntley was inaugurated in front of 1,200 guests in Doremus Gymnasium on a gray and rainy October day in 1968. Official delegates, twenty-three of them presidents, came from ninety colleges and universities, and included Huntley's fellow W&L alumnus Edgar F. Shannon of the University of Virginia.

Cole was there on behalf of Louisiana State University and the Council on Library Resources. A concert the night before, a reception in Evans Dining Hall, and the Homecoming game the following day completed the inaugural festivities. W&L and Hampden-Sydney played to a tie on a muddy Wilson Field.[3]

The convocation address was delivered by William C. Friday, president of the University of North Carolina, a native of Rockbridge County and already acknowledged as the foremost higher education leader in the South. Friday's remarks focused on the more demanding and complex duties of university presidents in the late 1960s, particularly coping with "the efforts of some segments of this student generation to find a more direct role in bringing about a substantial change in our society." While such efforts "are often lost in the extremism of a small number of highly vocal students who resort to abusive language and illegal acts," he said, the larger desire for greater involvement is constructive, and the expression of all views on campus must be protected.[4] These observations would prove to be especially prescient.

Huntley's inaugural address affirmed W&L's basic strengths and values (the liberal arts, the Honor System, the substantial student role in governance), reassured alumni that a fading adherence to conventional dress and the speaking tradition were not signs of general institutional decline, and noted critical needs, especially in new capital projects. He also called for a university that did not "cater to any particular ethnic or economic group, but which seeks a diverse student body and faculty where members may share in common only the ability and the conviction to learn from each other." He alluded briefly to the challenges reflected in the tumultuous events of the preceding spring and summer (the King and Kennedy assassinations, urban riots, and the turbulent Democratic national convention in Chicago), and the general mood of the times by quoting from Gaines: it was "a time when man's sharpened awareness of the inequities in his midst is coupled with a growing frustration and bitterness, a time when concepts of order become confused with suppression and concepts of justice with anarchy." Even in these times, as Gaines had said, "the search for truth and understanding from which eventually may grow the kind of wisdom that brings fullness to life" would assure that W&L remained truly relevant.[5]

THE LATE 1960S and the 1970s witnessed a leveling off of the surge in higher education fueled by returning veterans and economic prosperity, but new momentum came from the demographic wave of the "baby boomers" and increased flow of federal and state money into research grants, instructional programs, economic development, and direct student support. Higher education in the United States was now the most dynamic in the world, and the much higher proportion of college graduates in the US population reflected the national push toward the greater good of access to education. But with success and maturity came other problems.

The increasing number and size of institutions led to greater competition for enrollment and financial support. The infusion of public funds into state colleges and universities—providing unprecedented access, as well as modern facilities, new programs, and low rates of tuition—posed direct challenges to those outside the public sector. About half of all students were enrolled in private institutions at midcentury but only slightly more than a quarter by 1975—and liberal arts colleges were an increasingly small segment among the independents. These challenges were made even more severe by a weak economy and significant monetary inflation, with consumer prices more than doubling during the 1970s. Furthermore, the number of young people was declining, with obvious implications for future college enrollments: the US birth rate had fallen since the early 1950s, and the enrollment of recent high school graduates in higher education flattened out and remained fairly steady for eighteen years after 1965.[6] The larger number of nontraditional students and those first in their family to attend college confirmed the greater access afforded by American higher education, but many were also less prepared for college study. This situation led to new remedial courses for first-year students in many universities and raised concerns about potentially smaller pools of eligible applicants for selective liberal arts colleges.

While the substantial number of new PhDs minted during the 1960s and 1970s strengthened faculties, the professoriate was more professionally mobile than ever and held rising expectations for higher compensation, lower teaching loads, and additional perks. Beginning in the early 1970s, the prospects for mobility declined as the numbers of job seekers greatly exceeded the number of open faculty positions, but the competition among selective institutions for the best scholars and teachers remained intense. The changing student culture brought altered expectations as well, with students desiring more independence and individual autonomy, as well as greater participation in university affairs. Some began to display attitudes that would grow into what would be termed "academic consumerism," and some student behavior tested the bounds of institutional authority.

Administrators and trustees alike—at W&L and elsewhere—knew that the higher-education firmament was shifting. Persisting down the wrong path could undermine an institution's future for generations to come. The years of Bob Huntley's presidency were thus largely dominated by rising to these major challenges while preserving the essential character of the university. His agenda was taken up with attracting and sustaining sufficient numbers of qualified students, implementing the new curriculum and academic calendar, maintaining a committed teaching faculty of serious scholars often sought by other institutions, updating and greatly expanding the university's facilities, and raising the money necessary to significantly increase the endowment, support major capital improvements, and lessen W&L's reliance on tuition increases to cover operating costs—all in a time of considerable economic inflation. Along the way, important and controversial issues had to be addressed, including the size of the university, the potential enrollment of women, the pursuit of greater diversity in the student body, the increasingly serious problems in the fraternity system, and how to cope with changes in American youth culture, including sex and drugs.

THIS ARRAY OF CHALLENGES confronted the new administration and (as envisioned in the 1967 SACS self-study) an expanded board of trustees—increased from sixteen to nineteen in 1969 and then to twenty-two in 1972. Board members held fixed and limited terms, faced a mandatory retirement age of seventy, and were now expected to actively help generate new resources. The nineteen trustees in 1970 included new faces: John W. Warner, then serving as assistant secretary of the Navy in Washington (1968) and E. Marshall Nuckols Jr. of Newtown, Pennsylvania, a lawyer, senior executive of the Campbell Soup Company, and former president of the Alumni Association (1969). Nuckols succeeded Huston St. Clair, who retired in 1971, as rector. The new membership policies led to the first phases of regular turnover. Newly elected members during the decade included Jonathan (Jack) Warner of Tuscaloosa, Alabama, CEO of the Gulf States Paper Corporation and an avid art collector; Sydney Lewis, CEO of Best Products in Richmond; and Edgar F. Shannon, who grew up on the W&L campus and, as president, led the University of Virginia through racial integration, coeducation, and opposition to the Vietnam War. Beginning in 1972, the presidents of the student body and the Alumni Association also attended all board meetings, except for executive sessions.

The university administration and faculty also expanded. The ranks of administrative officers had grown to forty in 1975, with the most additions in the middle ranks of associate and assistant deans and administrative personnel. As administrative challenges and responsibilities proliferated, James White-head, Frank Parsons, and Farris Hotchkiss, '58, were among the key individuals charged with a variety of tasks. Significant academic leadership appointments included Roy Steinheimer, from the University of Michigan, as dean of the School of Law in 1968; Edward C. Atwood as Dean of the College of Com-merce, Economics, and Politics; Lewis G. John, '58, as dean of students in 1969; and William Joseph Watt as dean of the College in 1971. The size of the faculty and the greater number and variety of courses in the new curriculum increased, along with the gradually expanding student body—particularly in the law school. The regular faculty (professor, associate professor, and assistant professor) numbered 141 in 1970, with 70 at the rank of professor.

The university's total enrollment fluctuated during the period—from a low of 1,432 in 1969 to 1,742 in 1978.[7] The enrollment of 1,533 in 1970–71 (including a record 97 in law) was the first time W&L's student population exceeded 1,500, but it would be surpassed in all subsequent years. Enrollment was driven by many factors, of course, especially the size of newly admitted classes and their rate of persistence to graduation. The size of freshman classes rose, and the percentage of students who graduated four years later began to regularly exceed 60 percent, a far better number than the less than 50 percent rates recorded during the 1950s. The 60 percent "persistence rate" threshold was cracked for the first time by the class of 1964. More than 85 percent of first-year students returned for their second year, a crucial indicator of both student satisfaction and academic success.[8] Student attrition during the academic term was inevi-table and attributable to an array of reasons (including family circumstances, academic difficulties, social life, and cost), but it tended to be relatively small. Keeping most members of each class together as a strong cohort was, as other institutions had discovered, quite beneficial not only in immediate tuition revenues but in subsequent alumni fundraising.

Recruiting sufficient numbers of students who could succeed academically and pay W&L's tuition was critical; it was an art that Dean Frank Gilliam had practiced, largely by intuition and experience, for decades. By the 1970s the whole process had become more complex and challenging—especially since total applications to many private universities declined during the decade. A particularly serious problem, according to the 1978 *Self-Study Report,* was "the rapidly eroding level of knowledge, skills, abilities, and motivation" of entering freshmen, an "alarming year-by-year deterioration" reflected in declining SAT and achievement test scores; also, fewer members in the top fifth of their high school class were choosing to attend W&L. Faculty members were "hard put to deal with the deficiencies of less qualified students" and began to call for more financial aid based on academic merit.[9] James D. Farrar Sr., '49, appointed director of admissions in 1962, was at the center of W&L's student-recruiting efforts during this era. He played a crucial role in shaping the university's overall strategies to achieve a more diverse student body, rather than one determined only by the ability to pay, and he was especially involved in bringing the first African American students to W&L. Succeeded as admissions director by William H. Hartog in 1978, Farrar was appointed coordinator of the newly created Alumni Admissions Program in the same year.

A large applicant pool was critical for any selective institution, and W&L could generally rely on receiving about four applications for each place in the freshman class. How many acceptances to grant and the subsequent yield of actual enrollment (not too few, not too many) were the key numbers. For the entering class in 1974, for instance, W&L received 1,235 applications (down slightly from the previous year), issued 809 acceptances, and enrolled 366 students. In 1975, applications rose to 1,399, of which 819 were accepted, and 373 enrolled. W&L had always accepted a high percentage of "legacies," or children of alumni, which continues in some degree to the present day. In 1974, for example, eighty-seven alumni sons applied and seventy-three were accepted; the rate usually averaged about two-thirds.

The increasingly competitive market for students qualified both academically and financially required new recruitment strategies: four-color brochures, regular mailings to selected potential applicants, greater involvement of alumni at the local level, more extensive visits by admissions officers to public and private secondary schools, and participation in "college fairs" involving many other institutions. This was mundane work, akin to marketing any retail product, but it was crucial in generating an entering class that would help define the university itself at a time when student interests and expectations were changing. W&L's greatest recruiting advantages were its long history and positive reputation for excellent teaching, small class sizes, and exciting campus social life, but its strongly traditional reputation and all-male character deterred some highly qualified students.

The enrollment of highly qualified students also depended, more than ever, on financial aid for those who lacked the family resources to pay W&L's tuition costs and who had opportunities to attend high-quality, but far less expensive, public institutions with a greater array of program offerings. The university had generally provided aid to about a quarter of those enrolled, but most of this funding was modest and weighted toward loans rather than grants. Going head-to-head with universities that were prepared to cover all or most of an outstanding student's financial needs—or award such help solely on the basis of academic merit—was a bracing reminder of the importance of student scholarships and grants-in-aid.

The enrollment problem, exacerbated by the declining numbers of college-age students, continued into the next decade. W&L celebrated the admissions outcome in 1980, marked by 1,413 applications and a first-year enrollment of 343, including eleven National Merit Scholars (almost double the record number set the year before). But Director of Admissions William Hartog cautioned that such success was far from guaranteed in the years to come. Institutions like Washington and Lee—"private, undergraduate colleges, with high academic standards, comparatively high tuition, and geographic, academic and economic bases that are narrow in some degree—are the most vulnerable to that decline in the sheer numbers of students of college age." Unlike many other institutions, W&L "cannot generate substantial income through auxiliary programs such as continuing education or part-time undergraduate programs." He offered a concrete example of the problem: of 524,895 high school seniors in W&L's principal ten-state recruiting area, only 9,241 were real prospects: those who took the SAT with a sufficiently high score, ranked in the top 40 percent of their class, were male, and "came from families with an income sufficient to pay Washington and Lee's tuition." Universities throughout the country also recruited these prospects. W&L's efforts by 1980 included visiting about five hundred secondary schools in thirty-three states, establishing alumni admissions programs in fifty cities, and admitting students and awarding financial aid on a "rolling" basis (i.e., not waiting until April 1 each year to announce acceptances).[10]

The university encountered particular difficulties in attracting students from outside the traditional pathways to admission. This was especially true for African Americans, who were likely to find W&L's history, social life, and small-town setting off-putting or at least quite insular. Despite some trustees' objections to targeted recruiting, by the late 1960s W&L was engaged in special efforts to attract African Americans and to ease and promote their assimilation into the student body. American higher education was already moving toward the goal of "diversity" in the student population as a critical component of the educational experience for all students, and W&L struggled not to lag behind. By 1977, the twenty-five African American students accounted for less than 2 percent of total enrollment. W&L had also created the position of assistant dean of students and coordinator of minority affairs to work with individual black students and the Student Association for Black Unity (SABU), as well as to advise the admissions office on recruiting. The law school, where African American students comprised about 5 percent of total enrollment, established an explicit "affirmative action program for racial minority applicants," in which applications were "considered separately and objective criteria are not as critical to the admission decision as with other applicants." The university made every effort to also provide financial aid.[11]

W&L had always recruited from public high schools, whose graduates accounted over the years for from 40 to 60 percent of entering W&L classes (and this proportion would continue to grow), but most of these schools had, obviously, only recently integrated. Sticking with the familiar recruiting "pipelines" fashioned by old associations and academic and financial requirements would almost certainly result in the continuation of a white, male, economically privileged student body. Addressing this problem was a major activity of selective institutions (private and public) throughout the country, and certainly in W&L's case it would require significant new recruiting strategies and sources of financial aid in order to attract and sustain minority students and those from less favored socioeconomic backgrounds. The challenge was even greater for W&L because (except for a time during the Depression years) the university offered financial aid solely from endowment and other funds designated for scholarships. In 1980, for instance, some 175 students sought financial aid, but only 135 could be helped.

FOLLOWING THE 1967 SACS self-study discussions, the faculty approved major changes to the curriculum and academic schedule that were implemented in 1970 and 1971. Students had more choice than before, and the new spring term, first available in 1971, presented a range of special topics and stimulated a significant increase (about a third over the decade) in the number of courses on offer. A reduction in the number of required courses led to lower enrollments in English, history, and foreign languages, as well as in sociology and art, but the natural sciences remained at about the same level. After some initial decline, mathematics rebounded with new requirements in commerce (including statistics). Psychology, accounting, and business administration experienced a steady rise in student interest. These changes led to some modest shifts in faculty assignments. Departments added courses, especially for the spring term, including a new course in directed individual study or research. These changes were the university's response to curricular trends nationwide and part of a continuing effort to put a further special stamp on a W&L education. While faculty opinion of the new curriculum and calendar remained generally positive, a quarter to a third disapproved of various elements—especially the lack of an English requirement and the 115 credits required for graduation.[12] How to support student choice among a broad array of courses taught by a small, though gradually increasing, faculty was a continuing challenge.

Former dean and interim president William Pusey initiated and nurtured a new major in East Asian Studies. A professor of German, Pusey recognized the long-term implications of new US relations with China, highlighted by President Richard Nixon's historic visit to that country in 1972, and the rising importance of East Asia, especially Japan, Taiwan, and Hong Kong. Pusey began work on the program just as the new curriculum and academic schedule provided opportunities for new courses and study abroad possibilities, and shortly after the university received the extensive Reeves Collection of Chinese export porcelain in 1967. I-Hsiung Ju was appointed artist-in-residence in 1968, and other new faculty members with expertise in East Asia were hired in politics, religion, and history. By 1977 the major included more than two dozen courses, as well as those in Chinese and Japanese language. The university also benefited from the generosity of the Taiwanese government, which was making efforts to sustain its relationship with the United States. Other opportunities included a program of student exchange with a division of the University of Hong Kong and participation in the Henry A. Luce Foundation fellowship program. And the university's first full-credit summer study-abroad program, directed by the new East Asian Studies Program director, Dr. Harold C. Hill, took students for ten weeks to Taiwan.[13]

That the fine arts had remained relatively undeveloped (some would say neglected) at W&L was perhaps typical of smaller men's colleges, where studies tended toward careers in business, law, and medicine. But James Leyburn's arrival in the 1940s signaled a greater emphasis thereafter on study of the arts, which he saw as an essential mark of an educated individual. The first full-time faculty member in the arts, Marion M. Junkin, joined the faculty in 1949 (and served into the mid-1970s). By 1965–66, five faculty members (three in art and one each in music and drama) taught over seven hundred students in a limited curriculum with few majors, and in 1970 Fine Arts was split into a Department of Art and a Department of Music and Drama. In 1973, the University Council Committee on the Arts formally asked the trustees to devote more attention to the needs of these disciplines.[14]

Since 1965, Fine Arts course enrollment had more than doubled, reaching 1,524 in 1972–73, even though the number of faculty had only grown from five to eight. Much of this growth occurred after the introduction of the new curriculum and academic calendar that permitted more freshmen to take arts courses. The new spring term allowed the "total theater" courses that became very popular and provided study-abroad opportunities like the English Drama course offered in the United Kingdom. The number of arts majors remained small—around six or ten a year in art and three to six in drama (music offered no major)—but the arts were securing a place in the liberal arts curriculum.

Costs for the fine arts were generally high due to the need for expensive equipment and dedicated space. The Troubadour Theater at the corner of Main and Henry Streets became the University Theater in 1972, and while the number of productions had increased in both number and ambition (there was even talk of a regular summer stock program) the theater rehearsal and performance space was still far from ideal.[15] The University Committee on the Arts now recommended that the art, drama, and music components be reunited into one administrative unit, so "this large department would speak with a unified voice for the arts" and perhaps "permit the re-introduction of the broad major in all the fine arts." The departments were again combined in one Department of Fine Arts, and Dr. Albert C. Gordon of the University of Toledo was named department head and instructor in drama in 1974, bringing the full-time faculty to ten. Class sizes were reduced to no more than forty in art history sections (except for the large history of theater course) and fewer than that in most others, thus virtually eliminating student complaints about crowded classes.

The board toured the existing fine arts facilities during its regular meeting on May 24, 1974. The following day, Huntley reported that while university fund-raising would address many of the needs of the fine arts, plans did not include "an adequate theatre facility." He questioned "whether the University should commit itself to the long range plans for a single Fine Arts Center." But in a show of support for the fine arts, the trustees resolved that its executive committee conduct further study of facilities and be "empowered to proceed with a study on costs, sites and other related matters for a Little Theater, a

Little Theater and Concert Hall, and a Total Fine Arts Center."[16] The next two decades would witness significant advances in both curriculum and facilities for the fine arts.

The advent of the computer age was important for both the curriculum and university operations. W&L had purchased its first mainframe computer, an IBM-1620, in 1960 and had replaced it with more advanced models from IBM in 1968 and DEC in 1970. The science departments—especially physics, chemistry, and astronomy—were the principal academic users of these machines. Other areas, especially Political Science, also found the computer important for complex statistical calculations. A computer committee, with representatives from all areas using the machines, determined in 1975 that there was more academic demand than the current equipment could fulfill—especially in order to give students adequate hands-on experience. With help from the National Science Foundation to develop applications, including some for computer-based instruction, the university purchased a machine that supported distributed terminals, greater time-sharing and processing options, and seven programming languages. The university thus joined the demanding and expensive race to keep up with the seemingly insatiable interest in computers and the desire for more powerful and sophisticated applications. It was still quite early in the "computer revolution": the new Harris S-125 machine boasted only 365K bytes of virtual memory.[17]

ADMINISTRATION AND FACULTY at W&L had debated coeducation as early as the 1890s, partly in response to a steady enrollment decline. While faculty sentiment was divided on the matter, the trustees voted in 1896 to table any further discussion of admitting women.[18] The university's all-male enrollment was a serious challenge during World War II, but while some women were allowed to take courses, a move toward coeducation was explicitly avoided. A declining pool of qualified students prompted the resurrection of the issue in the 1970s, when many other previously all-male institutions had already admitted women or were on the cusp of doing so. Unlike the awkward and muted consideration of racial integration, discussions of coeducation were often public, exhaustive, and sometimes heated. This was an especially hot-button issue at W&L.

Along with many other issues, coeducation had been discussed within the committees of the 1966 SACS self-study. While admitting women was not

among any of the recommendations, it nevertheless enjoyed the support of
some key faculty members and the generally open-minded, if skeptical, President Huntley. Religion professor Louis Hodges, an outspoken advocate of racial
integration, also assumed a leadership role on this issue. In February 1969, he
submitted to Huntley the results of a poll and petition of regular faculty taken
over the previous three weeks. The petition stated four reasons for advocating
the admission of women: to "broaden intellectual perspective in our classes,"
to gain the educational benefits of "in-class competition between men and
women," to maintain "a high quality student body," and to help in recruiting
men. (Another supposed benefit was that if women were on campus, then cars
would become less important, and thus a less expensive social life would be
possible; in retrospect, this thinking was completely inaccurate.) Out of 114
faculty members, 90 "were in favor of the admission of women for in-residence
study." While some declined to sign the petition because they wanted to study
the matter further, others demurred because the statement was not sufficiently
unequivocal in support of coeducation. A number suggested that "some type
of exchange program" might be a sensible intermediate step toward full coeducation. Only fourteen faculty members were opposed. Hodges concluded
that the faculty were "overwhelmingly in favor of the admission of women to
Washington and Lee."[19]

The new president seemed receptive to further consideration of coeducation
but also apprehensive about possible reactions to such a move, especially from
alumni. In private conversations and public meetings, he frequently expressed
his concerns about the growing challenges to small, selective, private institutions like Washington and Lee. Yet he also believed that W&L possessed a
unique character and appeal that put it in a relatively better position than many
of its peers and transcended the issue of coeducation. Because it was widely
discussed on campus, coeducation naturally came up in Huntley's meetings
with alumni groups, and he reassured them that—whatever happened—W&L
was a special institution that could sustain its quality and traditional character
even with new competition in changing times. He was ambivalent: What if
coeducation was necessary to preserve its "basic purpose"? As Huntley put it,
"I am convinced that we are better off dead than mediocre."[20] He also sensed
that W&L must soon decide the issue, one way or the other. In March 1970, he
wrote to a major donor that the "thorny problem" of coeducation "will need to
be resolved before very much longer" but that the university was proceeding
deliberately. It was impossible to say what the consequences of any decision

might be, but "in the next two years no more than approximately eight all-male institutions of even mediocre quality" will remain in the United States. And he noted the possibility that some male students would "shun completely any non-male institution."[21]

In April 1969, Huntley appointed a faculty committee, chaired by Hodges, to study the matter. The committee, which first met on April 14, consisted of seven faculty and administrators—including Dean William Watt, the new athletic director Gene Corrigan, the new dean of students Lewis John, and the new head of the Department of Commerce, John F. Devogt—as well as two senior students.[22] At the same time, Huntley appointed a Study Committee on the Size of the University, chaired by Professor John M. Gunn. These committees functioned separately, but size and coeducation were clearly related. Many trustees and alumni opposed any significant increase in the size of the student body, and Huntley himself told the trustees that if women were admitted, W&L would be "unable to live with the decision to reduce the number of men."[23]

Huntley initiated discussions of a student exchange program with surrounding women's and men's colleges that would permit women to attend classes and earn academic credit at W&L, with a reciprocal opportunity for W&L men. In a meeting with Texas alumni in July 1968, he noted that cooperation with surrounding women's colleges was under consideration, though "we have no plans to consolidate and nothing is in the planning now to become coeducational." But he did not rule it out: "We just don't know now, but the question has been raised from time to time." He mentioned the program beginning that fall for Mary Baldwin students to take physics classes at W&L. "There are many young ladies," he affirmed, "who are equally qualified to take advantage of the educational opportunity we offer."[24] He introduced the plan for an exchange program to the trustees in October 1969 (several raised reservations about the concept) before referring it to the faculty for review and approval. In January 1970 the board approved W&L's participation in an exchange program with four women's colleges—Hollins, Randolph-Macon Woman's College, Mary Baldwin, and Sweet Briar—as well as with Davidson, Hampden-Sydney, and Randolph-Macon. The stated reasons were to "provide a more diverse campus environment," explore the possibilities of such cooperative ventures, and "broaden the educational opportunities" of students. The program was never very large: twenty-six women attended classes at W&L as part of the exchange program in 1971, but there were only twelve in 1975–76.[25]

The Committee on Coeducation completed work on January 21, 1970, and its report, with conclusions and recommendations, was among the documents provided to the trustees at their special meeting in Washington, DC, on April 4–5. Huntley then shared it (without the recommendations) with deans and department chairs on April 13. In the winter issue of the 1970 *Alumni Magazine*, Louis Hodges assured alumni that his committee had been charged only to gather information, not to determine policy, and he laid out its approach to assessing the impacts of possible options: establishing a "coordinate" adjacent women's campus, expanding the exchange program with women's colleges, or deciding to remain all male. The committee selected two general models for detailed examination—one in which females replaced 40 percent of males in a W&L with its current enrollment, and one where eight hundred women are added for an overall enrollment of about two thousand. Hodges noted some practical questions—such as demands for new residence halls and renovations to campus facilities—but the main considerations had to do with "the anticipated shift within the curriculum," based on the assumption that women would pursue different majors, such as the fine arts. The optimum ratio of men to women was another important issue. The research and experiences of other all-male institutions that had admitted women (among them Princeton, Franklin and Marshall, Sewanee, Trinity, and Yale) were major sources of information for the W&L committee. The usual ratio of men to women in these cases was between 70/30 and 50/50. Hodges referred to raw data from the Princeton study that 80 percent of the seniors surveyed (male and female) in the upper two-fifths of their preparatory school classes expressed a strong preference for attending a coeducational institution. He also included striking data from a recent W&L survey: of the 305 men (out of 406) who did *not* accept offers of admission, 36 percent said they preferred a coeducational college. This was "the second most frequently checked response," falling only below geographical location. Furthermore, those 36 percent had average SAT scores two points higher than the actually admitted class. Photographs of attractive, well-dressed women striding along the Colonnade or sitting in class alongside men accompanied Hodges's article.[26]

The committee report itself was more detailed and more declarative in its findings. The opening section on admissions went straight to perhaps the major concern—the decline in the quantity and quality of students applying for admission. The report noted that between 1966 and 1969, the percentage of students offered admission increased from 48 to 66 percent of total applicants, and the number of those accepted who chose to attend another college rose from 46 to 53 percent. Also, student credentials (standardized test scores and class ranking) were declining. "This rather dismal admissions picture," the report observed, was due to a number of factors, including the declining size of "the college-going population," the rising relative cost of private higher education, "and the expressed preferences of many students for large universities and for urban locations." Predictions of "a sharp drop in the percentage of increase of first-time male students entering four-year degree-granting colleges" were especially relevant. (The director of admissions, James Farrar, predicted that over the next five years it would be difficult to expand the size of the entering class, while "at the same time maintaining the present academic qualifications of entering students.")[27] Citing a Princeton University study, the committee concluded, "the admission of women would tend to upgrade the quality and increase the number of male applicants." Princeton and Yale had noted a doubling of total applications following the decisions to admit women, with more than 60 percent increases in the number of applications from men. These and other schools moving to coeducation had also reported no difficulties in attracting a significant pool of qualified women applicants; Sewanee had twice the number of anticipated female applicants, and those applying to Franklin and Marshall were academically superior to the male applicants.[28]

The Committee on Coeducation commented that in institutions similar to W&L in type and size, the proportion of women usually ranged from 40 to 50 percent of total enrollment, and concluded that whatever the precise ratio, "the number of women should be large enough so that the women would not feel in the distinct minority." Impact on the curriculum was difficult to assess, but the report noted that college women tended to gravitate toward liberal arts and sciences like languages, biology, English, sociology-anthropology, and fine arts, and less toward "vocational" areas, except for education, where they were dominant. The committee surmised that coeducation would not undermine or distort the traditional W&L curriculum, though special arrangements might have to be made for practicum training for those seeking to be teachers—though it was "unanimously opposed" to establishing a department of education. Coeducation would also create a greater need to bring more women onto the faculty, rendering W&L "generally more attractive to faculty personnel whom we would wish to recruit."

The report concluded that women in the classroom would contribute additional perspective and provide healthy "competition" for men, rather than serving as distractions. Women should also bring "greater interest" in cultural activities and contribute to a healthier on-campus social life, with presumably less emphasis on the male bravado of the fraternities and weekend road trips to women's colleges. Many practical questions remained, especially the provision of residence halls for women, who otherwise would be left to fend for themselves beyond the freshman year in the crowded Lexington housing market. Another issue was whether "parietal rules" would require restrictions on women that did not apply to men. The committee concluded that despite parental preferences, the same rules should apply at W&L to both men and women, avoiding "employment of a double standard in any form." Dormitories could be locked in the evenings, but students should be able to come and go as they wished at any hour.

The report claimed that coeducation would have no major impact on physical education, because the new gymnasium facility would be adequate and had been planned with such provisions in mind. If women did not displace men in the overall enrollment, the intercollegiate athletic program would actually benefit. Fraternities would not be hurt by coeducation as long as the current enrollment of men was maintained. The committee did share concerns, expressed by others, that "additional strains would be placed on the honor system" by increasing enrollment to two thousand and that the reporting of violations would perhaps be affected by more "complicated" student relationships.

Attempting to evaluate the financial effect of coeducation, the report used the different models the committee had devised at the outset: adding 800 women to the present size of the University (model 1) or adding 500 women while maintaining the total enrollment at 1,250 (model 2), using the "present structure and operation of the University" as a benchmark. They estimated the costs for each model of instruction, administration, general operations, and amortized capital needs for student housing and dining. Income estimates included tuition and fees as well as grants, annual giving, and endowment. Operating expenses were far easier to estimate than the effect of coeducation on alumni giving. Adding students would increase costs—for operations and facilities—but also generate additional revenue from tuition and possibly greater support for capital projects. The latter was crucial, because however calculated, coeducation posed financial challenges for the university that were difficult to predict, and greater outside support—especially from alumni and friends—would be essential. The report noted that W&L was in the midst of raising money for major new capital projects and renovations—and that either coeducation model would create even more demands that, in the absence of federal aid, would require long-term commercial financing, probably at the prevailing 8.5 percent interest rate.

The committee added four specific "Conclusions and Recommendations" to the report sent to the trustees for the April 1970 special meeting. The committee predicted that "a decision to admit women would result in a greatly strengthened student body," would require only "minor changes" to the curriculum, and would be both "possible and desirable." Adding women to the student body would "enrich the life of the entire university community," even if women displaced men. Coeducation would require more money (a minimum additional annual cost of around $780,000). Under the heading "Special Recommendations and Commentary," the committee expressed its strong preference for adding women, while maintaining a minimum of one thousand male undergraduates, and providing residence hall space for three-quarters of women students. It included one bracing caveat: "The change we recommend is feasible only if additional funds, in large amounts, can be found." This brought into crisp focus the importance of support for any decision by all university constituencies, especially the alumni whose opinions on the matter had not been sought in any systematic way.

The committee's assessments of financial impact were suggestive but inadequate, and its report was not informed by opinions from major university constituencies—especially alumni—and left many large questions unresolved. But the report addressed every key issue and was a remarkably thoughtful and comprehensive first step in the university's consideration of coeducation. And it was probably the easiest step. The fate of coeducation truly lay in the details—and in the hearts and minds of the university's graduates and major donors.

Coeducation remained a topic of conversation, especially after the first female participants in the new exchange program arrived on campus and attended regular classes. Even before the issue was taken seriously by the administration and the key constituencies, the notion of women students at W&L carried a certain novel fascination, reflected in periodic commentary in student publications and the *Alumni Magazine,* often accompanied by photographs of females on campus with books in hand. Already, coeducation was thought virtually inevitable in some quarters on campus, while in others it was considered unthinkable.

The students who planned the sixth annual CONTACT symposium, held in the spring of 1970, brought to campus an array of notable speakers (the theme was modern communications). This time the symposium was also part of "Coeducation Week" and attracted about 120 women from nearby colleges. Pink and yellow handbills were posted throughout campus announcing "The Girls is [sic] Coming," and the event gave ample opportunity for the university to contemplate what coeducation might be like. The *Alumni Magazine* was quite giddy about the event, observing, "The miniskirts came to General Lee's College the second week of February," as if young women had never set foot on campus before. Coeducation Week

> was to some a lark, to others a dark foreboding. It was the feminine point of view and logic in the classroom, lively male-female *tete-a-tetes* over coffee at the Co-op or a draft at the University Center, self-conscious small-talk before dinners in honor of the coeds at the fraternity houses, voluntary intellectual seminars in the afternoons attended by the women, not as well by men, evening addresses by the likes of [former U.S. Attorney General] Ramsey Clark and [NBC News correspondent] Robert Goralski attended well by all. It was a taste of springtime during an otherwise dreary February. It was the talk of the town. Even traditionalists opposed to coeducation could scarcely deny that Coeducation Week enlivened the environs.

Both the Tuesday and Friday editions of the *Ring-tum Phi* were favorably impressed, though the more conservative Friday edition noted that one week was hardly a fair test of coeducation. But the experiment showed promise: "Class attendance has increased, and everybody seems to be dressing a lot better than is normally the case." One W&L student, afraid that women in class would be distracting, discovered that "they're just as distracting when they're not here." The women were quite enthusiastic on the whole and pleased to be treated as something other than "social objects." Some faculty members apparently had to cut down on their usual lusty jokes, and one Sweet Briar student commented that one professor, seeing women in the room, declared, "Well, we won't talk about fertility today after all."[29]

Coeducation remained a popular subject for student media. The *Ring-tum Phi* observed on March 1, 1972, "Since Christmas, coed-mania has swept this campus like an infectious plague. Every winter contemplation of this utopia seems to be relapsing as the principal indoor sport." Endorsed by the Student Executive Committee, the University Council, and the Committee on Coeducation, the admission of women was to be on the ballot for student vote during the upcoming Big Five Elections. The paper went on record as opposed to coeducation, and it reminded readers that whatever their opinions, students were not likely to have much influence: "The lesson to be learned here is that students are virtually powerless concerning coeducation."[30]

In May 1973, Dean Lewis John discussed coeducation with the board, joined by the president-elect of the student body, Douglas R. Schwartz, who listed coeducation as among the major issues of the Student Executive Committee. At the October trustee meeting, Schwartz pressed the issue and asked that coeducation be on the board agenda at the winter meeting.[31] In January 1974, Huntley noted rising "attention on Co-Education by students and to a lesser degree by the faculty" and asked if the board "wished the [trustee] Executive Committee to give attention to procedural questions relating to these matters." The board approved further study of both issues and asked for recommendations by the May meeting.[32] The Executive Committee, chaired by Huntley, recommended in May that the board "appoint a Committee to study the matter in detail and report to the Board at the earliest convenient time during the next academic year." The trustees authorized the rector to appoint such a group but insisted that "the Committee's responsibility would be fact-finding and that the study was not to be interpreted as pro or con on the feeling of the Board of Trustees in connection with Co-Education."[33] The trustees were both reluctant to make a decision on the matter and determined to have more of an active role in its future consideration. Up to this point there was simply insufficient board support to make a change.

The first meeting of the new board Coeducation Study Committee (also later referred to as the Trustee Study Committee on Coeducation) met in Lexington on December 7, 1974. Chaired by Frank Brooks of Baltimore, the committee included four other trustees, including the rector, and a number of university officials, including Huntley and the deans. The committee assigned areas for specific investigation to four task forces and selected for "intensive" study some universities that had made the transition to coeducation. The committee also decided that while "no general solicitation of opinion on the merits of co-education" should be made among students and alumni, samples of opinion from leaders of these constituencies would be sought and the faculty asked to provide written statements on "the pedagogical consequences of co-education."[34]

In January 1975, Associate Dean Robert W. McAhren asked the faculty to submit written statements concerning coeducation at W&L. By April 16, the committee had received only twenty replies—a low number that disappointed the proponents of coeducation and was interpreted by opponents as a sign of faculty disapproval or indifference. Of the twenty, fifteen supported the admission of women, four were opposed, and one was undecided. McAhren summarized these opinions for the committee and provided copies of the letters. On April 21, at Huntley's request, he distributed to the faculty a summary (without the letters and the names of the respondents) and asked for additional reactions and opinions. The second request provoked six responses, of which four were generally favorable to coeducation, one was undecided, and one was negative (from the same individual who had responded negatively to the original request).[35]

Faculty favoring coeducation focused on the rising status of women in American society, the unique perspectives women could bring to the classroom (especially in discussions of social and moral issues), the disadvantages of an "unhealthy" all-male environment that inculcated "exploitative" attitudes toward women and failed to prepare men for life in the "real" world, and the appeal of students who would be more likely than men to prepare for class on a regular basis. One commented that W&L men had a "distorted, narrow and nearly immoral view of women," because their interaction with females was largely only as "weekend dates or road-trip targets." Another, who was at Princeton during its transition to coeducation, stated that men would be "more teachable" with women on campus. His male students, he observed, spend "a good half of some weeks chasing skirts all over the Eastern seaboard." Pamela H. Simpson of Art, one of the first females on the faculty, believed that it was W&L's "duty" to offer opportunities to women.[36]

Some reasons for favoring coeducation reflected prevailing gender stereotypes that would later become less readily accepted as women moved successfully into business and the professions, while others mostly noted the unwelcome aspects of an all-male environment. But there were sharp differences among pro-coeducation faculty about how to implement it. Most were willing to accept a larger enrollment in order to accommodate the addition of women students. One professor was adamant that the university's small size was a great asset and that the total enrollment should remain the same. Along with several others, he was most concerned by the decline in intellectual ability of the current student body; in his view, the admission of women would "get rid [of] the weak third of the freshman class."

The major burden of opposition to coeducation fell on one faculty member, who responded fulsomely to both requests for opinion. A popular lecturer, he was already known for outspoken commentary on an array of social and political issues. Even by the standards of the mid-1970s, his thoughts about the role of women in American society were extremely conservative. Coeducation, he declared, was a passing fad that violated the traditions of Western Civilization and was "typical rather of Soviet Russian and Red Chinese societies." Women were likely to "dwell on pseudo-philosophical and . . . moralistic aspects of historical problems" and were "unwilling to deal with tangible elements in historical situations." In "Western countries," he claimed, "nothing much is at stake in education for women beyond high school." And he would find teaching them to be "exceptionally difficult and painful." Pleased to see that that so few positive comments had been generated by the first request for opinion, he claimed that the "silent majority" could "be assumed almost always to be content with the status quo." He accused colleagues who favored coeducation of recourse to jargon, morality, and fads, and lamented their failure to clearly delineate the allegedly disastrous consequences of remaining all male.

Louis Hodges was also distressed by how few responses the committee received, and he called for continued formal and informal discussions of the matter. Astounded by the comments made by this one faculty member, Hodges asked that the names of all respondents be released. Two law-school junior faculty in the law school submitted a lengthy response to the second request, which noted that the 1970–71 poll of faculty had produced an 85 percent endorsement of coeducation and that the law school now admitted women. They also pointed to the changing role of women in US society (only 3 percent of attorneys in the country were female, but women already accounted for more than 30 percent of law-school enrollments) and argued that by remaining all male Washington and Lee might "become an enclave of the good old boys sitting around discussing a world which no longer exists."[37]

Farris Hotchkiss, then deeply involved in the capital campaign, talked to development officers at other formerly all-male institutions that had become coeducational. None reported a negative effect on fund-raising, and some even suggested that development efforts had played no role in their institution's decision to admit women. Hotchkiss guessed that remaining all male would neither hurt nor help fund-raising, but admitting undergraduate women might result in some "diminution in our ability to raise funds for a short period of time," especially for capital projects. This would be especially true if the number of male students was reduced to make way for women. His concerns were borne out by the reactions of those few alumni and parents who offered opinions on the matter. By April 15, letters had been received from members of the

Alumni Board and thirty-five men who had attended Special Alumni Conferences. Only six definitely favored coeducation, though most stated that they
would continue to support the university as long as it preserved its academic
excellence. Of the seventeen non-alumni parents who wrote, fourteen preferred that the university remain all male.[38]

The board's Study Committee on Coeducation met in San Antonio in January 1975 and in Lexington in April to begin drafting a report. Between these
two meetings, Deans Farrar, John, Watt, McAhren, and Atwood visited Randolph-Macon, Davidson, Sewanee, Dartmouth, and Williams and provided
written summaries of what they had learned. The committee also assembled
studies and reports from many institutions that had made the move to coeducation, including Princeton, Williams, Amherst, Dartmouth, Haverford, and
Notre Dame. The Princeton study, in particular, was a detailed and deeply
informative analysis by an outside consulting firm of the first three years of
coeducation at that institution.

The board Study Committee's report, submitted in October, was long and
detailed and reiterated most of the observations of the initial Committee on
Coeducation chaired by Hodges. It observed that only three all-male colleges
roughly similar to W&L remained in the United States: Hampden-Sydney, Wabash, and Wofford, and of these only Hampden-Sydney was a possible competi-
tor for students or faculty. The report noted the consideration of coeducation
by the Hodges committee six years earlier and the continuing relevance of the
options it identified. The new report also summarized the reasons given for
coeducation at other schools. The Ivy League institutions claimed that they
acted mostly because of the positive influence women would bring to the social environment and the classroom. Among most other schools, the major
reason was to increase the quantity and quality of applications for admission,
"a consideration that seemed particularly acute as applications to private colleges began to dwindle in the late 60s. This dwindling coincided in time with
the growing interest in women's rights."[39]

The admissions picture at W&L, discussed in some detail in the report, resembled that at many other institutions. Over the previous fifteen years, 1965
had been the peak year for applications (1,600). During the next decade, the
total fell to about 1,400, and the SAT scores of entering freshmen dropped by a
hundred points. While W&L's experience tracked a national pattern of decline
in private institutions generally, its total applications reached its low point in
1968 but then—unlike most similar institutions—moderately improved. The

report noted, however, that "one significant figure continued to deteriorate, the number of offers of admission which must be made in order to 'fill' the freshman class." Between 1968 and 1976 the number of offers required to achieve an entering class of 370 increased by more than 10 percent. In contrast, the application totals at Davidson, which "had reached alarmingly low levels" prior to its admission of women in 1973, dramatically increased thereafter. Similarly, total applications at Sewanee—at "near disaster levels in the late 60s"—more than doubled following coeducation. The report also included predictions that college-age populations for the next ten years would level off in the late 1970s and decline in the 1980s, reducing the potential pool from which to draw new students. The consequences of this trend were further compounded by a growing number of accepted students at W&L who chose to go elsewhere because it was not coeducational—the reason most frequently given for declining to enroll. The report concluded: "Washington and Lee could significantly increase the number and quality of its applicants, at least in the immediate future, if it should become coeducational *and* at the same time retain its attractive qualities of small size, strong faculty, and diverse program."

The report devoted one separate volume to letters and comments received from faculty, alumni, and parents. While not in any way representative of all members of these constituencies, the letters did present a range of opinions and preferences concerning coeducation at W&L and doubtless had some influence on the trustees' ultimate decision. Reviewing legal requirements, the report noted that if the university admitted women, they must be treated "in a completely non-discriminatory way—e.g., as to course enrollments, housing, and university services." Providing "reasonably equivalent" opportunities for women in athletics could prove challenging. The effect on the curriculum should be modest in the first five years but might grow larger after that. And while the law was not entirely clear, maintaining quotas on admission by gender was permitted in private colleges and apparently widely practiced. Finally, the committee provided a brief summary of the opinions it had received. At this stage of its deliberations, the committee had not addressed the practical matter of cost or proposed any alternative models, such as those offered in the 1970 faculty report. The goal was to determine what should be done before deciding how to do it.

The results of another faculty poll revealed a much closer margin of support for coeducation than previously reported: 53 in favor, 49 opposed, and 5 undecided. In a resolution adopted on October 6, 1975, the faculty endorsed coeducation and asked the board "to give favorable consideration to this opinion at its earliest convenience." On October 17, the board formally received the committee report and left it to the president and rector to determine if it merited further consideration. Over the next few months, the trustees pondered the issue and its implications. On January 31, 1976, the board unanimously approved a resolution: "After considering at length the Report of the Committee on Coeducation, the Board of Trustees concluded that Washington and Lee should remain all male at the undergraduate level with the exception of mutually agreeable exchanges or cooperative arrangements with our neighboring women's colleges."[40]

Huntley announced the decision at the faculty meeting on February 2. He acknowledged the strong opinions on the issue among the faculty and others in the university community: "But I can tell you," he said, "that in the time I have been associated with the Board I know of no matter which has received more careful, more thorough, more hard-headed attention." The *Alumni Magazine* reported the decision in its winter issue, focusing on the importance of the university's traditional character and the potential problems of admitting women as undergraduates, especially the almost certain necessity to significantly increase the size of the student body.[41]

No precise record of the trustee's discussions of coeducation was kept, but the major issues were clear. The most difficult barrier to coeducation was the consequence of increasing the small size of the student body, which many regarded as a major source of the university's appeal. Displacing hundreds of prospective male students by admitting women instead was even less desirable. Issues of the curriculum and provision of equal facilities and services to women were thought less important and were not examined in detail. The costs caused concern, especially since they would be substantial and were largely unknown. At the same time the trustees were pondering coeducation, they were acutely aware of the intensive fund-raising underway to provide essential facilities, in particular a new university library. New projects like residence halls would require even more money, and any threat to ongoing development efforts was serious. Hotchkiss, who favored coeducation, was concerned about potential initial setbacks in fund-raising, and he hoped any announcement to admit women would be delayed to minimize any negative effect on the development program, now moving toward its second phase. The trustees were aware that remaining all male would have a long-term impact in terms of the size and quantity of the admissions pool, but they were also less desperate than their counterparts at other institutions. W&L, after all, seemed to be holding its own, even if more admissions offers were required to fill an entering class. But the long list of institutions, including many prestigious ones, that had decided to admit women provided some cumulative proof of the consequences of remaining all male at the undergraduate level. If W&L was "unique," it was also now clearly an outlier.

Other institutions had wrestled with the same issues, with varying results. Randolph-Macon College in Ashland, also a member of the Eight College Exchange Program, sought to retain its all-male character but suffered plummeting enrollment in 1969 and 1970; entering class sizes dropped and the attrition rate in 1970–71 was 41 percent, leading to a budget deficit. Faculty and students pressed for coeducation, and while the board was reluctant to make such a momentous change, circumstances forced the issue quickly, and Randolph-Macon decided to admit women as undergraduates in 1971.[42] Declining applications were also a factor at Davidson College. A commission on coeducation—made up of trustees, faculty, students, and staff—reported favorably on admitting women in May 1969. After first seeking to enroll about thirty women students through the exchange program and then accepting as degree candidates the wives and daughters of full-time faculty and staff, the trustees accepted an April 1972 faculty recommendation (passed by a vote of 60–6) to admit women undergraduates, and Davidson became coeducational in 1974. "It was," according to one account, "the most dramatic change ever made in the nature of Davidson College, yet it seems impossible to treat it as dramatic, so natural and successful was the change and so calmly accepted. The decline in applications, noticeable in 1971, was halted abruptly."[43]

Washington and Lee had wrestled with admitting women undergraduates for almost a decade before deciding not to make a change—despite considerable evidence of a declining undergraduate admissions pool, the success of coeducation in the law school, substantial positive evidence for coeducation at many other colleges and universities, and support from the faculty and administration for change. In addition, the trustees were already planning for an overall enrollment of two thousand in connection with the development program. In 1976, thirty women were enrolled in the law school, and the first six, who entered in 1972, received their degrees in the spring, becoming the first female members of the W&L Alumni Association. According to Dean Roy Steinheimer, women "enriched the quality of our student body."[44] But the situation with regard to undergraduates was different. Rather than being "natural" and "calmly accepted," coeducation would in fact prove to be one of the most dramatic and controversial changes in the university's history, even more so than racial integration. Washington and Lee could perhaps afford to delay because its admissions still seemed relatively robust. The trustees' decision in 1976 to back away from a course already taken by almost all of the university's peers simply deferred the matter for a few more years, when all the compelling facts remained essentially the same and feelings ran even stronger. Coeducation would have to be taken up at great length all over again.

RISING COMPETITION, a predicted decline in the number of qualified applicants, greater emphasis on campus amenities, and academic programs with more variety and choice—all of these things demanded significantly more money. Although Fred Cole had said in 1961 that W&L would be financially secure with $30 million more in the endowment, a decade later Bob Huntley confronted a seemingly never-ending need for new buildings, higher faculty salaries, and more student financial aid—and without an adequate endowment.

The challenges revealed that W&L had not kept up. New demands, inadequate resources, and structural deficiencies in budgeting and fund-raising seemed to overshadow the incremental progress on many fronts. Earl Mattingly's frugality, secrecy, and tight control had kept expenses down, but at the cost of transparency and any real budgeting process connected to planning or development. The consequences were managed internally during Gaines's administration, which projected an image of a stable, prosperous university. But they became increasingly apparent after Cole's arrival and into the Huntley years.

According to Huntley, Cole struggled to discover how much money W&L actually had. The new president asked James Whitehead to work with Mattingly in order to learn as much as he could about the university's finances. A graduate of the University of Tampa, Whitehead was director of the Empire State Foundation in New York (a counterpart of the Virginia Foundation for Independent Colleges) when Frank Gaines brought him to W&L in 1958 to be director of university relations, which included responsibility for university development. Over a long W&L career, he served as treasurer, secretary to the board, and the key figure in the establishment of the Reeves Center. With little expertise in finance, Whitehead was—like Parsons and Hotchkiss—asked to do many things.

Deciphering the university's finances was not easy. Mattingly tended to think he reported directly to the board rather than to the president, and he was stingy with information and immersed himself in minuscule details.[45] Cole increased faculty salaries by consolidating funds in various accounts that Mattingly had squirreled away, and he shared with the board the rather discouraging outlines of the university financial situation. Important university initiatives had produced several years of budget deficits, covered with board approval from nondesignated endowment funds. The trustees were accustomed to working with—and being reassured by—Gaines and not attending very closely to the budget. Gaines had also been able to call upon Mrs. duPont to cover modest end-of-year shortfalls. But she was not, as many thought, the source of major, university-sustaining contributions to the operating budget.

When Huntley took over in 1968, the financial situation had become more apparent. "Not to put too fine a point on it," he later recalled, "but the school was broke." This was perhaps an exaggeration, but there was certainly a recurrent cash-flow problem, made worse by an inadequate endowment. On several occasions, he had to borrow money from local banks over the summer to pay salaries until fall semester tuition revenues kicked in. Huntley hired an accountant to determine which funds were dedicated for endowment and which were "quasi-endowment" that could be used for operations. The clarification confirmed that the endowment was inadequate for the university's current operations, much less its long-term aspirations.

Economic "stagflation"—high monetary inflation coupled with low economic growth—was the backdrop for everything during a decade marked by persistent unemployment and a lagging stock market. Efforts to mitigate inflation, including President Nixon's imposition of wage and price controls in August 1971, were overwhelmed by the rapid rise in oil prices stemming from production limits imposed by the Organization of Petroleum Exporting Countries (OPEC) in 1973. Inflation during the 1960s was slightly more than 30 percent; during the 1970s it was more than three times higher. The Consumer Price Index rose dramatically as the decade progressed—from 4.4 percent in 1970–71 to 13.5 percent in 1979. The index underestimated the real impact on educational institutions, where the "market basket" included high cost and specialized items like salaries of highly trained personnel, sophisticated facilities, and expensive equipment. Dramatic anti-inflation measures—especially double-digit interest rates—in the late 1970s and early 1980s ended the price spiral but brought forth a new array of economic challenges. Preparing annual budgets during the 1970s truly seemed like racing just to keep from falling behind.

Tuition accounted for about 60 percent of all W&L revenues throughout the decade, reflecting both contributions from other sources and the continuing dependence on student payments. Comprehensive tuition (a new calculation bundling tuition, fees, and other costs) was rising, adjusted by a few hundred dollars every year or two, from $2,200 in 1971–72 to $4,050 in 1980. The estimated cost of attendance in the first year rose in the same period from $3,225 to $6,250. These steep increases actually lagged behind the rate of inflation, but they resulted in rates that were very high compared with the heavily subsidized cost of attending public institutions. The law school noted in mid-decade that its tuition—the same as that for undergraduates—was on average at least twice as high as that in state-supported schools.

W&L offered financial aid in some form to about a quarter of the undergraduate student body, but the need—the number of eligible students who could not be assisted—grew continually. Faculty salaries were regularly adjusted, but raises were whittled away by inflation and challenged by comparable or greater increases at other institutions. The university reported in 1975 a decline in W&L's compensation in the AAUP annual salary survey. The Consumer Price Index "rose 10.6 per cent during the 1974–75 academic year, while average faculty compensation rose only 6.4 per cent." Especially troubling, according to the report, was that for "the first time in many years, Virginia Polytechnic Institute has a higher median salary, placing Washington and Lee third in the state behind the University of Virginia and VPI." On the positive side, faculty benefited from the relatively modest costs of living in Lexington and the university's low-cost housing loans, and W&L's undergraduate faculty compensation still ranked in the top 20 percent among colleges awarding only the bachelor's degree.[46]

Operating costs, especially for energy, soared during the decade and led to some annual budgets that included deficits to be made up with cuts or more revenues during the course of the year. Endowment earnings (which provided about 14 percent of the university's annual revenue at mid-decade and 10 percent in 1978–79) suffered from the national market decline. Space was an increasingly pressing problem, especially in the School of Commerce, Economics, and Politics. Every academic unit seemed to be awaiting relocation into more adequate accommodations. At the same time, student expectations for better facilities and amenities were rising.

The university was fortunate to escape the more dire, even desperate, circumstances that afflicted some other liberal arts colleges. Its admissions were still relatively stable in spite of rising tuition, though it granted more acceptances to build an entering class. Alumni loyalty remained strong, though the rate of annual giving was comparatively modest. But it was difficult to envision a successful future, built on academic excellence and student preference, without a larger endowment and rising revenues, an expanded pool of applicants, and renovating, replacing, or adding to the campus infrastructure. Money wasn't everything, but it was essential to realizing any worthy vision for Washington and Lee.

THE LAW SCHOOL had been an integral part of W&L for more than a century. Beginning in the 1920s, but especially in the 1960s and 1970s, legal education was transformed, perhaps even more than higher education generally. Whereas the study of law had once been essentially a professional apprenticeship at the undergraduate level—requiring little previous college work—it now was expanding and flourishing as a postgraduate program. The law degree was now required in most states to take the bar examination or to enter licensed legal practice, and it could lead to a wide variety of interesting and lucrative careers. The days of individuals "reading" law in an attorney's office or a few students sitting at the feet of a small faculty, studying a basic set of legal principles and precedents, was over. The balance that W&L had sustained between undergraduate study and a postgraduate professional program was also now challenged.

Professional education in most fields had raised academic standards, tightened requirements, expanded curriculum, increased practicum training, and raised stipulations for entry-level credentials for practice. Standards for law schools—concerning library size, faculty qualifications and compensation, student-teacher ratios, and curriculum—had been rising since the 1920s through a collaboration of the American Bar Association (ABA) and the American Association of Law Schools.[47] Following the example of the American Medical Association, the ABA and AALS raised the bar for legal training after 1945. By 1970, general acceptance of a national standard had been achieved: three years of study at an ABA-accredited school following four years of college was the required preparation for practice in a homogeneous and "intellectual" profession.[48]

These changes were accompanied by a surge in law-school enrollments, especially just after World War II. The number of persons taking the LSAT doubled between 1968–69 and 1971–72.[49] Any competitive program had to provide a larger curriculum with more offerings—including seminars and electives—taught by a larger faculty with specialized expertise, research opportunities, and nationally competitive salaries, in adequate space suitable for professional training. The LLB degree was superseded by a new, standard credential—the postgraduate Juris Doctor, or JD. New courses and additional faculty demanded more students and tuition revenues. At W&L, a substantial increase in office and classroom space, well beyond what was available in Tucker Hall, was crucial. The question became whether W&L could continue to sustain a first-rate law school, given these new demands and the size and character of the university.

President Huntley was well aware of these shortcoming and challenges, as well as the need to find someone to succeed him as dean. As he later recalled, the "law school . . . wasn't a drag then; it was probably a slight, modest plus financially, but if it was going to become what I knew it had to become to fulfill its destiny, it was going to be a drag. Could the school say grace over that?"[50] The new dean would be key in leading the law school toward fulfilling its "destiny" without imperiling or undermining the undergraduate programs. Huntley took an active role in the process from the beginning, calling colleagues throughout the country to stimulate interest and solicit nominations. A law professor at the University of Michigan, Roy Steinheimer, agreed to fly down and discuss the job. Steinheimer (a licensed pilot) and his wife set his Beechcraft Bonanza down on a primitive airstrip, little more than a cow pasture, outside of Lexington. He and Huntley hit it off right away, establishing a close personal and professional relationship that would transform the law school. After a second visit only weeks later, Steinheimer was appointed the new dean on September 1, 1968.[51]

The change was no easy decision for Steinheimer. He held a senior position in a highly regarded faculty in Ann Arbor, owned a sheep farm, and could travel far and wide in his own plane. He knew little about W&L, and what he discovered revealed the challenges ahead. But he was drawn to challenges. He and Huntley agreed completely on two of Steinheimer's conditions—that he could work to improve the diversity of the law school by recruiting both black students and women (though at that point the trustees were opposed to coeducation) and also that the law school had to have more space and increase its enrollment. As Steinheimer recalled, "I didn't have anything in my mind as to what our stature would be after I had been there for five years. I just knew it was a sick law school and it needed a lot of help. . . . I was going to make it better than it had been when I got it."[52] He and his wife sold their flock of sheep to a friend in northern Virginia and moved to Lexington.

Among the rising financial demands on the law school and its programs were the persistent assessments that faculty salaries were inadequate compared to national standards and that the faculty's scholarly productivity was too low. The former observation had been made consistently for decades, but the latter was relatively new. As legal education had fully assumed its postgraduate status, the expectation that faculty members conduct and publish original research had risen as well. Research support for faculty—including grants, leaves of absence, and faculty evaluation criteria—became standard expectations in accreditation reviews. (The tension between scholarship and practice, between the desire for law schools to become more than trade schools and the reality that most students aspired to be successful practicing lawyers, had long simmered in legal education and demanded attention.) These complaints persisted into the 1980s, even as W&L was taking measures to address them.[53] Without adequate space, however, more students, faculty, and courses would be impossible. Space, of course, depended on more money and would be among Huntley's top priorities. A new law school building would be among his greatest legacies.

The 1970s was a period of growth and change in the law school, greatly accentuated by the completion of a new building. The number of applications rose from about 300 in 1966 to almost 1,300 in 1977, on the way to a projected overall enrollment of 350 (with 240 students enrolling in 1975). Between 1968 and 1979, the percentage of women among law students in the United States rose from less than 10 percent to more than a third, and women drove much of the enrollment growth at W&L. The first six women who enrolled in 1972 were followed by thirty-nine in 1977 (over a third of the entering class), and the proportion of applications from women continued to increase. While W&L wrestled with the idea of undergraduate coeducation, circumstances thrust the law school—and Dean Steinheimer—into a pioneering role.

The true coeducation pioneers at W&L were the six female law students who arrived in the fall of 1972. The trustees approved coeducation of the law school rather abruptly in May 1971, a move dictated by civil rights law rather than by choice. Many trustees were not pleased. Steinheimer later reported that while he was not discouraged from seeking African American students, "I was absolutely not able to recruit women. The board wouldn't let me have them."[54] But the board was placed in an impossible position. As Steinheimer put it, the choice was "either wind up the law school operation or admit women." While existing single-sex undergraduate programs were permitted to continue under the Civil Rights Act of 1969, this exemption did not apply to postgraduate programs, which were required to admit students without regard to gender. This was also an accreditation requirement of the AALS.[55] The timing was fortuitous: female law-school enrollment was rising rapidly throughout the country while the W&L School of Law was in the process of increasing the size of its entering class.

Coeducation in the law school provided an indication of what such a transition might look like for the institution as a whole. The first six women students each had a connection to W&L (usually a father, brother, or uncle) and were quite aware of their pathbreaking role. They were also very good students. Steinheimer recalls meeting with them every several weeks to discuss issues and requests related to coeducation. One of the first issues they raised concerned the bathrooms in Tucker Hall; there was a restroom restricted to faculty, a larger facility for general use, and a small one for female employees. The dean informed the faculty that their facility was now designated for the women students—who redecorated it by placing a potted plant in the urinal.[56]

As Sally Wiant—one of the pioneering students and later member of the W&L law faculty—recalled, these first women had to be determined in order to survive the adjustments of a rather clueless campus. The women were restricted from using the pool much of the time because the men usually swam without bathing suits, and the women would have to go through the men's locker room to get to the pool. According to Wiant, "We had decided that were we permitted to swim, that we would simply wear suits and if the males chose not to wear suits, that was fine." They also pointed out that access to the pool could be achieved by the installation of a single door. Even so, they could not swim at the same time as undergraduate men because they might embarrass them. Wiant noted that the male law students tended to act as "big brothers" for the first small group of women, but as the number of women increased and the novelty wore off, these relationships became more difficult, with the male students and some of the faculty showing more evidence of an "offensive mentality" toward women.[57] The female law students initiated the first improvements in campus lighting and security, and they served on a number of committees charged with easing the way for female undergraduates.

The law school continued to develop curricular options that to some extent mirrored those of the undergraduate departments: more courses in more subjects with more choice. The forty courses offered in 1965–66 had increased to about seventy a decade later. Constitutional law was now two courses rather than one, and three courses were offered in torts. New areas were added to keep up with the law itself—covering copyright and intellectual property, employment practices, environmental regulation, psychiatry and the law, and urban law. The number of courses dealing with business organizations and corporate law had quadrupled, and those in the area of federal taxation had doubled. Clinical education—in addition to moot-court opportunities—was also improved, so students could learn about legal interviewing and counseling, negotiations, trial practice, and legal writing. The curriculum in the first year was laid out, but after that (except for the course Professional Responsibility, which was still required) courses were offered on an elective basis, many of them as seminars taught by faculty specializing in the topic. An independent research course was also available, as well as work in the new Frances Lewis Law Center, devoted to legal reform and study of the law in a broader societal context.[58] All of these steps were essential to remaining competitive, and the trends would continue to shape legal education at W&L and elsewhere for some time to come.

An AALS team returned to W&L in 1979–80 and noted considerable progress. Law students were now enrolled from thirty-nine states and forty-four undergraduate institutions; based on grade point averages and LSAT scores, they ranked in the top 15 percent of all students at accredited law schools. The law library contained 217,000 volumes and had been designated a federal document depository. The new Law Center hosted its first Frances Lewis Scholar in Residence, provided research grants to six faculty members, and conducted two conferences. Burks Scholars, third-year students chosen on the basis of academic achievement and ability in legal research and writing, served as teaching assistants to approximately twenty first-year students, and they supported the Burks Moot Court Competition for students at the end of their first year. Sixteen third- and fourth-year students provided legal counseling and assistance to female inmates of the Alderson Federal Penitentiary in West Virginia. Many more clinical programs would be established in the future. The *Washington and Lee Law Review* and the Student Bar Association continued their work, and W&L's chapter of the Black American Law Students Association (BALSA) hosted the Southeastern Regional Conference.[59]

Challenges remained: attracting minority students, hiring faculty in a competitive job market, maintaining coherence in a greatly expanded curriculum, attaining an optimum balance between legal scholarship and practical skills for practice, contending with the swirling array of social and political issues that demanded attention and response, and assuming a larger role within an undergraduate liberal arts institution. While some faculty and alumni questioned whether W&L truly appreciated its "jewel in the crown," the law school was by the early 1980s larger, stronger, and better positioned to make its own way in the dynamic national arena of legal education.

THE SACS SELF-STUDY had called for changes to the board of trustees and sustained institutional planning and fund-raising that regularly involved the trustees. These initiatives and pressing financial realities gave rise to the most ambitious development program thus far in the university's history, absorbing the energies of key leaders, some faculty members, and committed alumni.

Independent of both governmental control and religious affiliation, Washington and Lee was dependent on tuition and gifts for survival. Frank Gaines was especially adept at wooing new friends and support for the university, at least on an individual basis, and his personal connections helped sustain W&L through the throes of the Depression and well into the 1970s. W&L had brought the Alumni Association more closely into the university's operations in the 1930s and 1940s, and contributions rose steadily to the annual fund. In the 1950s, the university created a coordinated fund-raising operation tied to institutional planning and a designated development office under Donald E. Smith. He designed a nine-year, two-phase, nearly $7 million capital campaign—the largest thus far in W&L's history—focused on space and facilities for Biology, Geology, and Physics, as well as renovations in Reid Hall for Journalism and Pre-engineering. As chancellor, Gaines used his networks and notoriety to good effect, and immediately after becoming president, Fred Cole began an extensive tour of alumni chapters. More than $2 million was raised for "The Vision of Greatness" campaign by the summer of 1960, but the next phase's goal of almost $5 million for improvements including athletic facilities, a new auditorium, and a new dormitory was not realized. These projects would be prominent targets in the next major fund drive (beginning in 1970).[60]

The W&L board appointed trustees in part because of their ability to support the institution financially, but they were rarely drawn into the development enterprise. During the 1960s, the need for a more organized and energetic fund-raising effort became obvious. The basic structure and first steps of these changes occurred during the Cole administration, but development, campus planning, and new facilities would be the centerpieces of Bob Huntley's presidency. The board reorganization included the establishment of three new standing committees: Development, Investment, and New Trustees. In May 1966, the board also approved a Development Council, made up of major donors and others, to assist the Development Committee.[61] In January 1967, the trustees accepted the Development Committee's recommendations concerning the organization, direction, and leadership of a new planning and development effort, led by Frank Parsons and Farris Hotchkiss. Parsons, a W&L graduate who had first joined the university as director of publicity in 1954 after the football scandal, had served in many capacities—assistant to President Cole, director of information services, and coordinator of the SACS self-study—and was now director of development. A thin, balding man with a neatly clipped beard and a visage reminiscent of Shakespeare's Puck or folk singer Pete Seeger, Parsons was the ultimate multitasker, knowledgeable about many things, a quick learner and skilled writer. He was Bob Huntley's right-hand man and for some years presided over campus planning. He continued working in a variety of positions well into the 1990s. It was often his duty, he later recalled, to play devil's advocate and deliver the bad news—hoping the messenger would not be shot. Over the years he wrote and edited scores of speeches, announcements, and explanations of important and controversial events and decisions, and he ran the *Alumni Magazine*. Especially noted for his quick wit, candor, and excellent writing skills, he was also a wily poker player.[62]

Farris Hotchkiss, '58, had been a student leader—a member of ODK and an editor of the *Ring-tum Phi* and the *Calyx*—who returned to Lexington in 1966 as a two-year fill-in for his classmate, Assistant Dean of Students Lewis John, who took sabbatical leave for doctoral study. Like Parsons, Hotchkiss was adept at many tasks and quickly proved himself. Blessed with enormous energy and persistence, as well as a gift for persuasion, he seemed particularly suited to his new role as associate director of development. When Parsons was named assistant to Cole and then to Huntley to coordinate "immediate and long-range University planning," including the new master plan of buildings and facilities, Hotchkiss was appointed director. Through professional training and his own commitment and ability to work with others, Hotchkiss honed his fund-raising capabilities and became a key leader in the major capital campaigns and of alumni and development activities until 2001.[63] It would be difficult to imagine the university's planning, development, and communications efforts without Parsons and Hotchkiss.

John M. Stemmons, '31, was a major business and civic leader in Dallas, Texas, who joined the W&L board in 1965. His Industrial Properties Corporation developed the 1,300-acre Trinity Industrial District, which included the Dallas Market Center, and he served as director of many other corporations and participated in and often led virtually every key civic organization in the city. The Stemmons Freeway is standing recognition of his contributions and influence. Upon joining the W&L board, he quickly put his talents to use as chairman of the new Development Committee. In October 1967, the board approved the committee's recommendations to establish the Robert E. Lee Associates, a recognition of those who had contributed at least $1,000 in a single year to W&L. The board also authorized the administration to move forward "to provide at the earliest possible time a plan for the long-range development of the University in terms of enrollment growth, the physical development of future buildings, and budget projections for faculty expansion, support for the educational programs, and all other relevant matters." The study should assume that the university would continue its current educational program and increase its enrollment by 2 to 3 percent a year over ten to fifteen years, reaching a maximum of two thousand students.[64]

In May 1968, Stemmons, Huntley, Rector St. Clair, Henry L. Ravenhorst (professor of engineering and a certified architect), and Douglas E. Brady Jr. (superintendent of buildings and grounds at W&L and mayor of Lexington) toured the entire area to the north and west of the central campus to assess its suitability for major new buildings and other facilities. In June, Stemmons returned to Lexington with Marvin Springer of Dallas, who worked with him in a number of land development projects in Texas. In August, Huntley and the Development Committee discussed the production of a new campus master plan by Griswold, Winters, and Swain, landscape architects in Pittsburgh, Pennsylvania, who had initially been engaged by President Cole to consider improvements and beautification.[65]

Identifying and assessing needs was the first step. The deans and other administrators itemized program and physical requirements for review at a special two-day meeting of the board in April 1970. They included a building for the law school, an undergraduate library, and expanded space for the gym and for the School of Commerce, Economics, and Politics. The law school required additional faculty and courses to cover the demands of a modern curriculum, and the McCormick Library had been inadequate for years, in terms not only of accommodating books and staff but also of providing room for the university archives and study space for students, who were crammed into nooks and crannies during examination periods. The School of Commerce, facing rising numbers of majors and now offering courses to 90 percent of the undergraduate student body, was simply out of space in Newcomb Hall. Doremus Gymnasium remained essentially as it was when it was built and could no longer support the physical education curriculum and the rising array of intercollegiate and intramural sports; nor could it provide many of the amenities available at other universities.

W&L was never able to house the majority of its students on campus, even though doing so had long been a standing priority. Construction of new residential space was on the list of capital needs. While it was not at the top of the list, an auditorium or concert hall that could serve the entire student body for convocations or special functions was also included. The new campus master plan linked most of these projects in an expansion of the campus to the south and west. Everything depended on new funds. After reviewing the needs and options, the board authorized a development program to provide new buildings for the law school and the undergraduate library, construct new student housing, expand the gym, double the endowment, and bring annual giving up to a level sufficient to cover 12 percent of the educational and general budget.

On George Washington's birthday in 1972, at the Founder's Day Convocation, Huntley and Rector John Newton Thomas announced the inauguration of a development campaign with a ten-year goal of $56 million, with $36 million to be raised by 1976, the bicentennial of the nation's independence. The nineteen trustees had contributed $2.5 million of the more than $9 million that had already been raised. Huntley admitted that the goal was extremely ambitious, but he described it as "an objective we must *aspire* to . . . Washington and Lee's past and its commitment to the future require us to do so." Campus improvements accounted for $24,150,000 of the overall campaign goal; another $24 million was earmarked for endowment to support faculty salaries and student financial aid.[66]

Almost immediately, the campaign's prospects for success improved significantly with a large new gift. On December 10, 1971, Huntley and Steinheimer approached Sydney Lewis, '40 and '43L, a successful businessman from Richmond, and his wife Frances for a gift of $100,000. In 1957, the Lewises had founded Best Products, Inc., which became the nation's largest catalogue-showroom retail chain, with some 242 outlets in twenty-eight states. Sydney Lewis served as chairman and CEO, and Frances as executive vice president. Already known for their philanthropy in the arts and higher education, the Lewises seemed interested in making a far more generous gift than anyone at W&L anticipated. Huntley quickly followed up the next day with a letter focused on opportunities in the law school.[67] He summarized the concept they had discussed of a law center, which would, "by involving faculty and students in meaningful research activity, add an extra dimension to the educational processes of the law school" and, in effect, greatly expand the overall impact and reach of a school that was slated to employ twenty full-time professors and enroll 350 students. A new building, already in the advanced planning stages, was expected to cost $7 million. The Lewises wanted to accomplish that and more; they proposed a gift of $9 million, sufficient to meet most of W&L's goals for the law school. Huntley wrote, "It would be our intention, if satisfactory with you, to have this facility bear the name of Lewis Hall." Two million dollars of the gift would be placed in a special endowment for the Frances Lewis Law Center, and the university would move forward "with confidence over the next few years to raise the additional five million dollars required to complete the law program." Both Lewises were invited to serve on the board of trustees. (Sydney served from 1972 to 1983, and Frances from 1984 to 1989, followed by their daughter Susan.) By the time the gift was announced, Sydney Lewis had already become a trustee, and by April 1972 the total gift commitments had doubled, to $18,700,000, of which the trustees had given $11.5 million.

The campaign also got a boost from the university's commitment to proceed with construction of the addition to the gym, even though only part of the funding had been raised. The new 100,000-square-foot wing on the rear of the old gym almost tripled the size of Doremus and added a new swimming pool, a basketball arena that could accommodate up to 3,600 spectators, handball and squash courts, locker rooms, and areas for instruction and physical therapy. W&L finally had a modern athletic and recreational facility, to be further enhanced by new tennis courts and recreational fields on the emerging west campus. The $3.25 million addition was opened in February 1972, as a sign of more changes to come, though securing the full financing was still part of the new campaign.

More than ever, W&L involved the trustees and major donors in the fundraising program. Hotchkiss—who could, according to Huntley, "sell ice to Eskimos, or more appropriately, get blood from turnips"—headed the campaign staff and was almost constantly on the road stirring up enthusiasm and new potential donors.[68] He offered frequent reminders that solicitations had to be personal and persistent, with an intensity exceeding the usual casual collegiality that normally characterized relationships among W&L alumni. At a meeting of the Development Committee in Tuscaloosa, Alabama, in January 1974, Hotchkiss reported on the disappointing campaign progress to date. He attributed it to the poor national economy but also complained that the solicitors and the potential donors "apparently do not regard the objectives of the Development Program as particularly urgent or indispensable to the University's future academic quality." At the same meeting, the board ordered that further planning for the new library should cease until funding had been identified for the project.[69]

The belief among many alumni that W&L was a "wealthy school" was a persistent challenge. Having Mrs. duPont on the board merely confirmed this misconception, and Gaines did not publicize financial details that remained "deep, dark secrets." Cole did share details with the board, but the trustees still did not "appreciate" the full dimensions of the situation.[70] Everyone realized that new gifts to the university had to be focused on new initiatives and facilities; no one was eager to make a gift to cover a budget deficit or deferred maintenance.

By 1976, the end of the first phase was in sight. Hotchkiss reported to the board in late January that $31.5 million of the $36 million goal had been reached.[71] At this point, another major gift materialized. The will of John Lee Pratt, a businessman and philanthropist from Fredericksburg, Virginia, provided for division of his estate among ten colleges and universities, the largest shares (20 percent each) to go to Washington and Lee, the University of Virginia, and Virginia Tech. Other institutions—including the Johns Hopkins University and Randolph-Macon Woman's College—were to receive percentages ranging from 4 to 10 percent. If any of these bequests failed or were refused, they were to go to W&L. From this single act of generosity, W&L received $11 million, the largest donation the university had received since George Washington's gift.

The Pratt gift was yet another instance of exceptional generosity to W&L from a non-alumnus. Pratt had attended Randolph-Macon College in Ashland for one year and then transferred to the University of Virginia, where he received a civil engineering degree in 1905. He worked for DuPont and then for General Motors, where he served as a director until 1952. In 1955, he met

Frank Gaines at Mrs. duPont's home in Delaware, after which the two men struck up a lasting friendship. President and Mrs. Gaines visited Pratt's home, Chatham Manor, near Fredericksburg, and shortly thereafter Pratt sent a generous contribution that established the Robert E. Lee Scholarships. (Pratt asked that the contribution for the scholarships be anonymous, but his gift became known after his death.) President Cole also struck up a firm friendship with him. The will providing for a 20 percent portion to W&L was drafted in 1963. The trustees' resolution extolled the donor and noted his warm friendships with Gaines and Cole.[72]

Huntley celebrated the Pratt bequest but noted that its provisions did not directly affect the campaign goals. The Pratt funds were to be spent within twenty-five years and only on faculty salaries and student financial aid, not on bricks and mortar. The money would be especially useful in mitigating the effects of inflation on salaries and scholarships but could not be added to permanent endowment (which, despite $5 million in new funds, remained essentially at the same $20 million value it had in 1970) or further capital needs like the new undergraduate library, which was still only partially funded. But the Pratt gift was a welcome source of inspiration.

Phase I of the development program concluded on schedule in 1976, exceeding the $36 million goal by $1.5 million. But the challenges for the remaining portion of the campaign—Phase II, with a goal of $26 million, announced in New York City on October 17, 1978—were even more daunting. Most of the six- and seven-figure contributions had already been solicited, requiring a shift to a greater number of smaller donors. In addition, some of the capital projects already underway, or even completed, had not been fully paid for, and the highest-priority item—the new undergraduate library—remained on hold. The national economy remained difficult, and inflation was relentlessly increasing construction and other costs, while the endowment return could not keep up. (For planning purposes, the university assumed an annual inflation rate of 7 percent and an endowment yield of 5.2 percent.) John Stemmons retired from the board in 1977, and leadership of the Development Committee passed briefly to Jack Crist and then to S. L. Kopald, Jr., '43, a retired business executive and civic leader from Memphis, elected to the board in 1976.

The Annual Fund—the one consistent and growing element of giving to the university—was also critical. In 1968 it moved to the Development Office, and Jim Bierer, '40, became the first Alumni Fund Chairman in 1971. Despite its accomplishments, the fund drive needed to evaluate its operations and effectiveness, its relationship with the university, and its communications with alumni; it also needed to work on strengthening alumni chapters and assisting in recruiting students and fund-raising. In July 1974, Bill Washburn offered a frank assessment. Of thirty chapters, twelve were rated good, seventeen fair, and twenty-one poor. Washburn wondered if an aggressive focus on fund-raising might even be counterproductive: "I do not think the chapters have traditionally been thought of as vehicles to raise money on an annual basis. Certainly many are not organized with this in mind." Perhaps chapters that focused on fund-raising were "apt to scare the alumni away."[73] A year later, the Alumni Association study committee accepted the more active involvement of alumni in university fund-raising and made specific suggestions for improving communications and strengthening local chapters and the Alumni Association office.[74]

Royce Hough, chairman of the Annual Fund from 1977–79, reported that the participation rate remained steady and the gift total was ahead for the year. But problems remained. While the W&L constituency was generally "receptive" and "reasonably affluent," it was also scattered across the country, and many alumni "often perceive W&L as wealthy. The element of need is not adequately understood." Hotchkiss echoed Hough's concern that "the W&L constituency does not adequately understand what the University stands for and is attempting to accomplish."[75] Efforts continued, focusing especially on soliciting gifts in the $10,000 range and identifying new donors.

The Development Program ended on schedule and beyond expectations. Phase II exceeded its $26 million objective by $3.5 million. The entire ten-year effort, begun in January 1972 and concluded on December 31, 1981, raised $67 million, surpassing the goal of $62 million. (Not included in this figure, because of the terms of the gift, was the Pratt bequest, valued at $12 million in 1981.) Huntley announced the results at the Founders' Day convocation in January 1982, precisely ten years after the campaign's official launch. In a celebratory article in the *Alumni Magazine*, the university could boast of "the largest successful effort by a college or university of its size."[76] The $67 million consisted of $22.8 million for endowment, $30.8 million for new and renovated facilities, and $13.4 million from annual giving and other unrestricted gifts (including $1.5 million from business and industry through the Virginia Foundation for Independent Colleges). The physical campus was transformed, and gifts also supported seventy-two endowed scholarships, six professorships, three teaching funds, numerous special endowments, and the Frances A. Lewis Law Center. The largest single gift was the $9 million from Frances and Sydney

Lewis for the law school building. (They contributed an additional $1.5 million for other capital projects.) Seven other gifts exceeded $1 million, led by the $2 million gift Miss Ruth Parmly made in honor of her father. The William R. Kenan Jr. Charitable Trust established the Kenan Professorship, and the Kresge Foundation and Andrew W. Mellon Foundation made key gifts for the new library as well as to the School of Commerce, Economics, and Politics. Sixty-seven percent of contributions to the campaign had come from alumni, 8.5 percent from foundations, and 5.7 percent from corporations. Faculty and staff had given $200,000. In a decade, W&L more than doubled the value of its endowment and transformed its physical capacity and footprint. Hotchkiss reported that in 1981 W&L ranked higher in endowment per student ($22,239) than Brown University, the University of Richmond, Davidson, Hampden-Sydney, and Duke.[77]

In a postcampaign assessment, the Development Committee offered suggestions for the future, especially encouraging "upper bracket donors" to increase their gifts, improving the Annual Fund, and increasing participation rates. The committee also pointed to the rising significance of deferred giving, the need to keep major donors involved in the life of the university, and the importance of keeping track of future prospects. In May, Hotchkiss reported that more than $2 million in new annual and capital gifts had been received since December 31, which "indicated that W&L can continue vigorous fund raising for present and future needs on the heels of the completed Development Program."[78] The modern era of continuous, intensive fund-raising had arrived.

The details of university development—and especially of organizing and implementing a complex, modern fund-raising campaign over many years—might seem tedious to anyone but development specialists. But the significance of the ten-year Development Program for Washington and Lee can hardly be overestimated. It left a lasting mark on the programs and physical character of the university and signaled a new operational norm. Never before had such a campaign been conducted with such effort, intensity, and ambition, characteristics that became regular elements of university operations and outlook. The same trends were prevalent throughout higher education, becoming just as typical of public institutions after the decline in public support beginning in the late 1980s and 1990s. University presidents would come to think of virtually everything they did through the prism of friend-raising, fund-raising, networking, and continual development efforts. Frank Gaines would, in all likelihood, have fared well in this new environment, but the standard for organized, systematic fund-raising had been raised considerably. Inspirational oratory and social networking were no longer sufficient. Clearly, the Gaines era had given way to that of Robert Huntley and his successors.

—✒—

A MORE FULLY REALIZED west campus emerged from the Development Program. Even after expanding to the other side of the Woods Creek ravine and toward the ruins of Liberty Hall, W&L remained small in size, but it became notably larger in its capacities and physical footprint. In October 1982, Frank Parsons observed that for "the first time in fourteen years, there is no new construction on campus."[79]

The completion of new buildings opened up space in existing ones. The law school's move to the Lewis Hall in 1976 vacated Tucker Hall, which was then renovated for the Psychology Department and the Computer Center. The opening of the new library in January 1979 made McCormick available for renovations to accommodate the School of Commerce, Economics, and Politics, which triggered renovations in Newcomb to accommodate the faculties of History, Sociology, Philosophy, and Religion. New parking areas arose around the campus, along with access roads, walkways, a new plaza, improved lighting, two new athletic fields, eight all-weather tennis courts, assorted landscaping projects, and a new heating and cooling plant. New buildings were integrated with the old, and the emerging west campus with the iconic front campus and Colonnade (recognized as a National Historic Landmark in 1973). The addition to Doremus Gymnasium was completed in 1972 and named in honor of trustee Jack Warner in 1977. The overall cost of new construction, renovations, and improvements exceeded $30 million.

Several other important projects were not included in the Development Program. Among these were the construction of the Woods Creek Apartments in 1975, providing housing for married students and unmarried law students, and extensive renovations to the interior of the Graham-Lees freshman dormitory. In 1977, a gift was made to W&L of Skylark Farm on the Blue Ridge Parkway; the university turned it into a conference center. On the front campus, renovations and modifications transformed 30 University Place into the Reeves Center, completed in 1982. Also pending on the list of potential projects was Col Alto in Lexington, a historic house given to W&L for use as a presidential residence and conference center.

Sydney Lewis Hall was formally dedicated on May 7, 1977, attracting 1,500 guests over a weekend that coincided with Law Day, the John Randolph Tucker Lecture, and meetings of the W&L Alumni Association, the Law School Association, and the board of trustees. Built to accommodate an enrollment of 350, the $8-million, 121,600 square-foot building included study carrels for every student, a Moot Court Room, and the 50,500 square-foot Wilbur C. Hall Library, with capacity for more than 270,000 volumes and a media center connected by cables to every carrel and classroom. W&L's only postgraduate professional school had come a long way from its beginnings in 1869 and the Tucker Hall fire in 1934, and now occupied one of the most modern and impressive legal education buildings in the country.

Assembled on the lawn before the main entrance, dignitaries and guests heard remarks from Sydney and Frances Lewis, Rector Marshall Nuckols, Huntley, Dean Steinheimer, and US Supreme Court justice Lewis F. Powell Jr. The gathered throng reenacted (at least in part) the celebration of the opening of Washington Hall in 1824. At that earlier event, John "Jockey John" Robinson, an Irish immigrant and college benefactor, had generously supplied a forty-gallon barrel of fifteen-year-old whisky made on his Hart's Bottom estate near Buena Vista. Decorum quickly vanished, and even Jockey John was appalled at the resulting melee. Some faculty members smashed the keg with an axe to restore order. For the Lewis Hall celebration, Alex M. Harman, '44L, Justice of Virginia's Supreme Court of Appeals, arranged for forty-five gallons of malt whisky in the original keg to be sent from Scotland. Fulfilling a long-standing promise to Huntley by supplying the whisky, he even provided the tin cups from which to drink it. Many toasts were offered and much whisky consumed, but the celebration remained decorous, and this time no axe was required.[80]

The new undergraduate library was slow to reach fruition, primarily because of its high cost and the difficulty of securing major gifts. But it remained a major—even *the* major—priority of the Development Program. By 1976, more than $600,000 had been spent on plans for what, at 130,000 square feet, would be the largest building at the university, situated on the hillside directly behind the Colonnade. When initial efforts to fund the project stalled, the trustees sought bids to gain a more precise idea of the cost. The bids came in at a lower price than previous estimates and also suggested that further delay might put the university in a construction cost-spiral. The remaining work on the library—including furnishings and equipment—would amount to at least $8.5 million, and indebtedness on the gymnasium addition was $2.2 million. More than $5 million in unrestricted new bequests (including $3.8 million from the estate of Mariam Caperton McClure) brought the university's available resources to about $7 million. The board decided that the gap between funds in hand and those required was still too great to justify moving forward. However, a special board meeting on June 26 resulted in new pledges from the trustees themselves totaling $1,550,000 and approval of the library. The university then issued $7.6 million in construction contracts. The overall trustee contribution to the Development Program rose at that point to almost $14 million.[81]

In exploring every funding opportunity for the library, W&L even contemplated the possibility of federal assistance, always a last resort. The application called for an environmental impact assessment, including an estimate of any long-term effects of the project on animal populations and habitat diversity. Frank Parsons, delegated responsibility for yet another unusual task, responded that approximately 10–20 squirrels seemed to be living in the library site. Some trees "that now provide either homes or exercise areas for the squirrels will be removed, but there appear to be ample other trees to serve either or both of these purposes." The animals will likely "find no difficulty in adjusting to this intrusion . . . They have had no apparent difficulty in adjusting to relocations brought on by non-federally supported projects." As to whether any change in the squirrels' behavior would result, Parsons wrote, "It will be difficult to tell if they are unhappy about having to find new trees to live in and sport about." Within the ranks of the federal bureaucracy, Parsons became known as the "squirrel memo man" and President Huntley received a letter from a Health, Education, and Welfare Department official saluting the university and offering best wishes that the squirrels and W&L would "co-exist in harmony for many, many years." The *Wall Street Journal* congratulated all parties for their sense of humor.[82]

The library opened within the construction budget and ahead of schedule in early 1979. Maurice Leach, the university librarian, devised a unique way of conducting the move and also involving the entire community. A short distance separated the new building from McCormick, but some 250,000 volumes had to be transported from one location to the other. More than 1,600 people—students, faculty, alumni, and townspeople, with 320 freshmen and thirty dorm councilors leading the way—gathered on the morning of January 10 to physically carry paper bags filled with books to their new home, forming seemingly endless human lines flowing to and fro across campus. With 125 people directing deliveries to the proper areas, an effort expected to take seven hours was completed in less than half that time, and at 8 a.m. on January 11, the library was opened for business "on a limited basis." Afterward, more than three thousand people from on and off campus packed the spacious new main reading room for a celebratory party, fueled by forty kegs of beer and music by "Ace Weams and the Fat Boys" and the "Charlottesville Allstars." A bit taken aback by it all, Huntley declared it "one of the best occasions we've ever had at W&L." Parsons lamented only "that we ran out of books to carry."[83]

By October 1980, the renovated McCormick was complete and the library in full operation. Newcomb Hall's renovations were due for completion in the summer of 1981. About half the work had been completed on Tucker Hall. The broad plaza between the Colonnade and the new library, extending from McCormick Hall on one end to duPont Hall on the other, united all the major buildings on the "back campus" and was named in honor of trustee emeritus John Stemmons. Attention now shifted to projects not funded by the Development Program: planning for the renovation of 30 University Place, extensive renovations of Graham-Lees Dormitory, and preliminary planning for a new university theater. The university hired a well-known San Antonio architect, O'Neil Ford, to plan the theater project, and he had visited the campus and drawn initial schematics, but the necessary funding never materialized. The site chosen for the project was near the old railway station, approximately the area now occupied by the much more ambitious Lenfest Center.[84]

The university's footprint was expanding even beyond the campus. In June 1977, Leslie Cheek Jr. and his wife Mary Tyler Freeman Cheek offered to give W&L their Skylark Farm at Mile 25 of the Blue Ridge Parkway in Nelson County, with its 365 acres of land, three residential buildings, several outbuildings, and furnishings "for enjoyment by the personnel of the University." Mr. Cheek, former director of the Virginia Museum of Fine Arts in Richmond, was stricken with Parkinson's disease, and the family could no longer make full use of the property. Mrs. Cheek, the daughter of Douglas Southall Freeman, former editor of the *Richmond Times-Dispatch* and biographer of George Washington and Robert E. Lee, made the gift in his honor. Mrs. Cheek wrote privately to Huntley that giving Skylark to W&L "is the happiest possible solution of our problem."[85] On June 20, the university took ownership of the property, accepting the Cheeks' caveats that it retain its rural character, not be opened to the public, and not be subdivided, leased, or sold.[86]

"It is our intention and hope," Huntley wrote the Cheeks, "to use the property for various University-related purposes, such as special meetings or retreats. It is also our hope to make it useful to staff, faculty, and special friends of the University from time to time as a place for rest and renewal." The university would endeavor to comply with the Cheek's requests, he added, but "will have discretion to determine the kinds of circumstances which might justify or necessitate sale of the property at some future time."[87] Huntley provided the board with details of the gift, which would require university funds for maintenance and operation. Nonetheless, he wrote, "the sheer beauty and grace of the spot led me to accept."[88] In October 1977 the trustees formally received the gift of Skylark Farm, without legal restrictions on its use.[89] The university later presented the Cheeks with honorary degrees, and they remained in close touch with Huntley and his successor, John Wilson. The Skylark Farm Conference Center, less than an hour's travel from Lexington, would indeed be the site of many "special meetings and retreats."

Another major gift to the university was both unanticipated and unlikely. The W&L administrator who successfully guided the realization of the Reeves Center for Research and Exhibition of Porcelain and Paintings in 1982 was James W. Whitehead, who first came to W&L in 1958 as director of university relations and subsequently served as treasurer and secretary to the board of trustees. Nothing in Whitehead's background and experience had prepared him for the world of the decorative arts, but, like Parsons and Hotchkiss, he learned to do many things.

Whitehead received a postcard in the fall of 1963 from an alumnus in Providence, Rhode Island, who mentioned a possible gift of a "work of art" to the university. The sender, Euchlin Dalcho Reeves of Orangeburg, SC, was a 1927 law-school graduate. Intrigued and skeptical, Whitehead arrived in February 1964 at a modest home, where Reeves showed him an astounding array of plates, cups, bowls, saucers, and serving pieces, stacked densely throughout the house and in a crowded adjoining building that resembled a vault. Reeves and his wife, Louise Herreshoff Reeves—then in a nursing home—had been ardent collectors of old porcelain, much of it made in China and shipped to the United States and Europe in the late eighteenth century, bearing western coats of arms, national flags, designs, and even likenesses of famous people. They had also acquired notable pieces of furniture. Whitehead knew little about porcelain or furniture, and the mass of material he encountered and the manner in which it was stored led him to doubt its value. But when Reeves pointed out pieces that had been made by Paul Revere and others that belonged to George Washington, W&L's treasurer became determined to know more.[90]

In early 1941, Euc Reeves met Louise Herreshoff Eaton, a great-great-grand-daughter of the eighteenth-century Providence merchant and benefactor John Brown. They enjoyed each other's company, sharing an interest in collecting antiques, and—after three months—he proposed marriage. She readily accepted, but her family opposed the union, so the couple eloped on May 27, 1941. She was sixty-six years old and a widow; he was thirty-eight. The marriage continued through their silver anniversary and until their deaths in 1967. Euc died first, in January, of a stroke at age sixty-three, and Louise in May at ninety-one. Although Euc had made no such provision in his will, Louise—well aware of their shared wishes—made the gift of their porcelain and other antiques to Washington and Lee. The collection was enormous, with more than six thousand ceramic and glass objects from Europe, Asia, and the United States, including 1,800 pieces of Chinese export porcelain. Some two hundred crates were stored in the basement of the Student Union Building before being moved to the basement of the ROTC Building. Experts confirmed that it was one of the finest collections of Chinese export porcelain in the world.

The collection also came with a stunning surprise. Some crates from Providence, holding many "old wooden picture frames" and added to the shipment at the last minute, contained a hundred oil paintings and many additional drawings and watercolor pictures from the 1890s through the early 1920s in a variety of styles—Fauvist, Expressionist, Impressionist, Postimpressionist—and ranging from portraits to landscapes. Remarkable in their treatment of light and use of vivid color, they had clearly been produced by a gifted artist. As a young woman, Louise had been a skilled and acknowledged painter, especially of portraits, and she had spent most of the time between 1890 and 1902 living, studying, and painting in Paris, and then for almost a decade in New York City before returning to Providence in 1911. One of the few women painters in the United States at the time, Louise, at age twenty-three, had one of her works selected for exhibition in the 1900 Paris Salon of the Societe des Artistes Francaise. After her beloved aunt died in April 1927, Louise never painted again. Now her artistic legacy was entrusted to Washington and Lee.

W&L was a small institution, and its art treasures—the Charles Wilson Peale portrait of George Washington the most notable—were scattered about campus. Without an art museum or other suitable facility in which to display a world-class porcelain collection, or the financial resources to manage it, some faculty and others naturally wondered whether W&L should be the repository for this collection at all. Jim Whitehead's commitment to the collections and to the story and people behind them was critical. With the support of Presidents Cole, Pusey, and Huntley, he brought the art to W&L. The only question was where to put it.

Early on, the idea was for storage and display in rooms of Col Alto, but when it became obvious that it would be too expensive to renovate the house for the university's use, attention shifted to the main campus for a permanent home. Eventually, with a gift from Elizabeth and Floyd Gottwald, a former 1840s faculty house at 30 University Place on the Colonnade, once occupied by James Leyburn, was remodeled and expanded to house the porcelain and the Herreshoff paintings. Many items of Reeves furniture were moved to Lee House. Whitehead became the founding director and presided at the dedication of the Reeves Center for Research and Exhibition of Porcelain and Paintings in September 1982, an event scheduled to coincide with the annual meeting on campus of the 240 members of the Decorative Arts Trust. The center—along with additional acquisitions and the opening of the Watson Pavilion for Asian Arts in 1993—is now an integral part of the main campus.[91]

The university conducted another ten-year self-study for the Southern Association of Colleges and Schools in 1976–78. Delayed in order to include the results of Phase I of the Development Program, the report confirmed that W&L had not just taken the results of the 1964–66 self-study to heart but had essentially achieved all its recommendations and incorporated its multiple new procedures, goals, and assessments into the university's operations.[92] The self-study's recommendations for improvements fell within the current planning framework, moving in the direction set more than a decade earlier. Even the basic structure and character of the 1978 version were familiar; the editor of both was Frank Parsons.

Washington and Lee made substantial progress in the decade and a half after 1967. The university's finances were more secure, its buildings and facilities upgraded, and its programs expanded. It continued to attract academically qualified students, though concerns remained about the size of the pool from which new applicants could be drawn. The debate over coeducation, stretched over almost a decade, had in the end not produced a definitive or entirely satisfactory decision. The university had improved and was better positioned for the future. But W&L's responses to the challenges of the new era of higher education occurred against a backdrop of major transformations in university life nationwide, including changes in student expectations and behavior that mirrored broader social trends emerging in the late 1960s. Fund-raising for new buildings and facilities depended on the efforts of alumni who were often confused and even appalled by the most extreme tendencies. The challenge, as always, was to maintain the university's essential character and traditions while adjusting to new demands and expectations.

~~~

CHAPTER NINE

MAJOR ISSUES IN
TURBULENT TIMES

THE 1970S MAGNIFIED and consolidated social changes already underway. Protests were more assertive and grounded in a broader youth culture that challenged established authority, sought identity, and found expression in new forms of music, dress, and ways of living shaped by greater sexual freedom and recreational drugs. The civil rights struggle had moved beyond pursuing voting rights and desegregation to battling economic injustice and rooting out—and seeking compensation for—the deeply embedded racism that undergirded centuries of American history. A movement for greater roles and rights for women gained momentum with publication of Betty Friedan's *The Feminine Mystique* in 1963 and passage of the Civil Rights Act in 1964. Rising participation of women in the workforce focused attention on pay inequality and the constrictions of traditional societal roles, and led to greater political advocacy by organizations like the National Organization for Women (NOW) and the activism of the women's liberation movement. Though the Equal Rights Amendment, passed by Congress in 1972, failed to win adoption in the required two-thirds of the states, it received broad support across the political spectrum. The 1973 Supreme Court decision in *Roe v. Wade*, securing abortion rights and the availability of effective contraception ("the pill"), gave women unprecedented control over their own bodies. "Virtually all the social movements of the late 1960s and 1970s," historian Joshua B. Freeman observed, "involved not only sharpened conflict between particular communities and the larger society but also conflicts within communities about what goals to pursue and how to pursue them, conflicts between the young and old, traditionalists and modernists, militants and moderates, and separatists and assimilationists."[1]

Colleges and universities were at the center of many of these trends. The institutions were growing and proliferating, and new ideas resonated in their classrooms. By 1970, a third of all eighteen to twenty-four year olds was enrolled in college or graduate school. Increasingly, university administrations, established curricula, and in loco parentis were regarded as part of the "establishment" to be resisted. The dramatic arrest of nearly eight hundred student protesters in the Free Speech Movement at the University of California at Berkeley in 1964 and the violent removal of student protesters from buildings at Columbia University in April 1968 were atypical but paved the way for further campus unrest, especially as the Vietnam War dragged on and became a focus for virtually every protest group. The New Left movement led by organizations like Students for a Democratic Society (SDS) condemned many aspects of American life and veered toward radicalism, while at the same time a New Right coalesced around the Young Americans for Freedom (YAF) and the writings and presidential candidacy of Barry Goldwater. Higher education was increasingly caught in the middle of this generation gap between conservative legislatures, trustees, and alumni on one side and restive students and some faculty on the other. The curriculum and classroom discussions increasingly reflected the greater emphases on race, ethnicity, and gender in society and culture (in new courses and syllabi, assigned readings, essay topics, faculty lectures, and student questions), as well as perceived negative consequences of the projection of American power ("empire") in the world—all of which challenged authority and undermined traditional assumptions and scholarship. These disparate social, cultural, and behavioral trends coalesced in the popular imagination and were often channeled through political action.

Washington and Lee's students, though not unmoved by social injustice or unaffected by popular culture, were largely traditional and conventional, and the campus—apart from the social scene—remained relatively quiet. Student political organizations were as active toward the right as the left, and mock conventions were more social and educational than political events. Student rebellion was more likely reflected in dropping the coat and tie rather than "dropping out" altogether, and many alumni were astounded when protests eventually penetrated even the sedate, hidebound precincts of Lexington. But social justice, youthful autonomy, resistance to the war, and justifications for protest had been active topics at W&L over the previous decade—sustained through national and student media, in the classroom, and by visiting speakers. Largely from relatively privileged backgrounds and not prone to undermining the established order, W&L students were nevertheless aware of national and global events; attuned to the literature, music, dress, and trends of the time; and not averse to tweaking authority. And they were finally moved to action by dramatic events in early May 1970.

BY THE END OF the 1960s, no issue stirred campuses more than the Vietnam War. College-age students were subject to the military draft, and many saw the war itself as a symbol of misguided, traditional power and authority. The war was a powerful focus for youthful energies and discontents, but it also animated even those not overtly opposed to it. Students could adopt new fashions and music and seek greater autonomy—even challenge authority—without resisting the draft or joining a commune.

The Vietnam Moratorium, on October 15, 1969, was an early opportunity for national student protest against the war. On campuses across the country, professors and students dispensed with "business as usual," devoting regular class periods to discussions of the war, holding special meetings and discussions, and submitting petitions to administrations. At W&L, the Student Executive Committee resolved that each student could participate—or not—as they wished. On October 15, six speakers offered varying viewpoints in Lee Chapel—including a Presbyterian pastor, a VMI professor, a representative of the John Birch Society (who blamed the war on a conspiracy between the United States and the Soviet Union), and W&L professors Milton Colvin and James Loesel from Political Science and Harry J. Pemberton from Philosophy. The *Ring-tum Phi* estimated that about five hundred people were involved in Moratorium activities, and fifty to sixty students planned to attend an antiwar march to be held in Washington, DC, on November 15.[2]

As American involvement in Vietnam dragged on, conservatives called for decisive action to secure "victory," while liberals favored winding down US commitments and even withdrawing altogether. Almost no one was satisfied with things as they were. President Richard Nixon had pursued a plan of "Vietnamization"—a policy relying more on South Vietnamese forces and drawing down the number of American troops—and sought help from the Chinese and Russians to facilitate a negotiated, "honorable" end to the conflict. But outside help was not forthcoming, and the war continued to go badly for the United States. Nixon instituted a lottery system for the draft to ensure greater fairness, but this change also ended the system of deferments that had protected many enrolled students from military service, and it increased anxiety and tension on campus.

The president—faced with the same dilemmas that had consumed his predecessor—decided to strike at areas outside Vietnam that were used as supply lines and sanctuaries for enemy troops. Nixon launched a heavy bombing campaign of northern Laos in February 1970 and a joint US–South Vietnamese invasion of Cambodia in April. His announcement of the Cambodia "incursion" on April 30 provoked campus protests throughout the country. Expansion of a war already considered by many as unnecessary and even morally wrong unleashed new resistance to militarism, bureaucracy, racism, unresponsive government, and other social ills that had been building up over the previous decade. Students also rallied to protest violence against fellow students. Mobilized to control the peaceful demonstrations at Kent State University, the Ohio National Guard in the confusion opened fire on protesters with live ammunition, killing four unarmed students and wounding nine on May 4. After this, campus protests became a national conflagration. "Their sheer size," wrote Freeman, "stunned the White House, the nation, and the protesters themselves. Protests took place on more than 80 percent of the nation's nearly three thousand colleges and universities, with five hundred crippled by strikes. Some four million students and 350,000 faculty members took part in protest activity of one sort or another. On less than a week's notice, 100,000 people assembled at a rally in Washington, D.C." Demonstrations occurred at virtually every type of higher-education institution and involved students from every part of the socioeconomic spectrum, among them a number of Vietnam veterans. Some protests were unusually militant. "During May, over a hundred protesters were shot by law enforcement officers or guardsmen. Meanwhile, an epidemic of bombing and arson broke out on or near campuses. In the first week of May alone, thirty ROTC buildings were burned or bombed."[3]

In Lexington, four to five hundred students gathered on Tuesday evening, May 5, for a rally on the lawn in front of Lee Chapel. It opened with music by "Cancer," a student combo. Jeff Gringold, the student who led the meeting, called for shutting down the university, echoing a common refrain of protests on most other campuses. Two young instructors, Paul Corcoran in Political Science and Henry E. Sloss Jr. in English, also spoke. A student from the University of Virginia called for a strike of classes and invited everyone to Charlottesville the next day for a rally featuring the well-known activists Jerry Rubin and William Kunstler. An "unidentified member of the Black Panther organization" called for armed resistance. President Huntley, well aware of the mood on campuses nationwide, had earlier in the day called for "rational thought and demeanor at a time when it is easy to yield to irrational attitudes and behavior." He warned against allowing national divisions to fragment the W&L community: "I know that this kind of isolation already is growing among factions on this campus. I know also that it can become an epidemic and that the disease that accompanies it could be incurable." Corcoran—a one-year appointee—took issue with Huntley's statement and called for him to defend it. Twenty minutes later, Huntley left his law school class and in brief remarks to the assembled group "praised the orderliness of the rally" and warned against violence: "I call on you, from whatever faction you are in, to share your deep convictions with those who would ordinarily share theirs with you." His sole concern, he explained, was "this campus, its effectiveness, its spirit, and its community." He received standing ovations both before and after his remarks.[4] The rally concluded by 9:30. In a special meeting on the same evening, the Student Executive Committee endorsed a student petition to end the Cambodian invasion and adopted a resolution that called attention to activities scheduled for May 6, dubbed "Freedom Day."[5]

The next morning, between thirty and forty students picketed on the Colonnade for about two hours, urging a strike of classes, and then joined approximately two hundred W&L students to attend the rally in Charlottesville. The picketers did not interfere with students wishing to attend class (some who opposed the strike showed up in coats and ties), and a regular class schedule was maintained. The UVA rally offered inspiration for more dramatic action, and that evening the president-elect of the student body, Fran Lawrence, and Staman Ogilvie, a member of the executive committee, both of whom had been in Charlottesville, visited Marvin C. "Swede" Henberg, student body president. Henberg agreed to call a student assembly for Friday, May 8.

Several students, representing no group or organization but including some who had attended the UVA rally, met with Huntley on Thursday morning, May 7. They requested, in light of the extraordinary national events, some relief from their regular academic schedule to allow full participation in the student movement. Huntley then met with the Faculty Executive Committee and called a special meeting of the faculty for that evening. On that same afternoon and into the evening, about a hundred students gathered in the University Center tavern, the "Cockpit," for "rap sessions" on the war in Southeast Asia and the Kent State shootings. Conversations—often spontaneous and uncoordinated— occurred at the same time, not surprisingly leading to a good deal of confusion.

Henberg and Lawrence, the outgoing and incoming presidents of the student body, worked together during the student unrest. Henberg, from Laramie, Wyoming, tended to be cautious and reportedly saw his role as a liaison between the students and the administration. Lawrence was more actively involved with and supportive of the student opposition to the Cambodian invasion. Both saw the "Cockpit" discussions as an open forum and free exchange of ideas, some of which might be considered by the student body at a later time. In fact, the discussions resulted in a resolution to close the university by May 11, canceling classes and examinations in lieu of a "free university" format for wide-ranging discussions of national issues, especially the causes and consequences of the situation in Indochina. At the same time the faculty met—with Henberg and Lawrence attending—to discuss options for students who wished to miss classes and attend the protests in Washington. The faculty agreed to accommodate students "who feel strongly that they should not and cannot participate effectively in Washington and Lee's academic program during the balance of the current session because of the sense of immediate concern and fervor they feel about major national issues." The faculty also agreed that classes would not be suspended and "educational responsibilities abandoned." Any student who "as a matter of conscience" wished to leave campus for the remainder of the term but to remain enrolled could submit a request in writing to the Faculty Executive Committee, and receive an "I" (incomplete) grade until September 30, 1970, after which the "I" would revert to an "F" if the coursework was not completed.

The student body met as scheduled in front of Lee Chapel on Friday, May 8, at 1:00 p.m., with Henberg presiding. The approximately nine hundred students spread across the front campus included a number in shirts and ties. Henberg and Lawrence had decided to honor the "Cockpit" deliberations, which they had encouraged, by presenting and considering the resolution to close the university. Students spoke for and against the measure, and some wanted an immediate vote. But Henberg and apparently many others at the meeting agreed to postpone a ballot until the following Monday, May 11.

The *Ring-tum Phi* estimated that some three hundred students left Friday afternoon to attend the large demonstrations in Washington, DC. That weekend also happened to be reunion weekend, Law Day, and the annual meeting of the Alumni Association. Huntley recalled that the alumni encountered students "bare from the waist up and no shoes, and with tents pitched around the campus, growing scraggly old beards and long hair and so on."[6] Although the administration must have been apprehensive, it turned out to be salutary that all of these events coincided. At least some students who remained on campus engaged alumni in discussions about the war and the student protest, while alumni representatives praised the students for their restraint and expressed appreciation to Huntley for the manner in which the university had handled matters during the previous week. On Sunday morning, students held a memorial service in the University Center for the four students killed at Kent State; it was followed by a rally in the Freshman Dormitory quadrangle and a rare joint meeting of the outgoing and incoming Student Executive Committees, which endorsed the student proposal but "with the understanding that explicit in the resolution a respect for those students wishing to continue their course of study is affirmed." How these students might continue if the university was "closed" was not explained. "It is our feeling," the joint statement read, "that the United States is in a period of extreme difficulty and that our normal activities are no longer adequate to meet the challenges of the times." Debate continued into the evening, with student government leaders urging approval of the resolution and a group called "Keep W&L Open" urging its defeat.[7]

On Monday, May 11, the students voted. The resolution expressed concern about the war in Indochina and a desire "to join with our fellow students in this country by closing Washington and Lee as of May 11, 1970." Classes should be cancelled retroactive to May 6 until the fall, and the university and its facilities should be made available for free and open discussions "on the economic, political, philosophical, sociological, etc., ramifications of the Indochina war." The resolution provided that students arrange with professors for grades in current courses or receive a letter or P/F (pass/fail) grade for work completed as of May 6. Graduating seniors would "not be deemed to have completed their requirements for graduating until June 5, 1970." Over 96 percent (1,319) of the eligible voters had cast ballots, with 1,065 in favor of the resolution and 254 opposed. Seventy-eight percent of the student body had voted to cancel classes for the remainder of the term.

This result was not entirely surprising to those who had followed campus events and discussions over the previous week. At each juncture, the continuation of normal academic activities had seemed increasingly less possible. Events on other campuses were followed closely, adding to the sense of urgency and magnitude. Students at the University of Virginia held large rallies against the war, boycotted classes, set fires around campus, blocked traffic, and occupied the ROTC building. Many were arrested and transported to jail in moving vans (though the university remained open and relatively free of violence).

The student vote at W&L was decisive but not unanimous, and Henberg and Lawrence disagreed about its meaning and significance. Henberg later recounted the "incredible political push" for a student vote on a "confused, contradictory resolution—a fact which I was aware of all the time." He voted against it. Lawrence voted in favor of the resolution and believed it was an important expression of student opinion, but he admitted that it was poorly worded and continued to refer to the "closing" of the university even after it had been amended. Many students, Henberg observed, voted to send a symbolic message against the war and express solidarity with students elsewhere, knowing that the faculty would make the final decision. Some wanted mainly to extend the pass/fail option, and others perhaps to get a head start on summer jobs. Lawrence believed that the vote was really not to close the university but rather to encourage the faculty to broaden the discussion of national issues and events. Both agreed that better "communication" could have remedied some of the problems, and neither saw the vote as challenging or initiating a confrontation with the faculty. Most students who favored the resolution expected the faculty to take notice of this strong statement of student opinion—which did, in fact, refer to "closing" the university.

The faculty gathered in a second special meeting on Monday evening following the student vote. Henberg presented his views on the student resolution, and Huntley assessed the situation. The subsequent discussions revealed sympathy for the students' demands and motivations, and some faculty members were reportedly shaken by the overwhelming student support for the resolution and perhaps inclined to end the semester early. Frank Parsons later recalled that Huntley refused to allow this option to even be considered, because "he was under obligation to the Trustees and the University's charter to prevent the University from closing down under such conditions."[8] Huntley recalled that the faculty was never willing to give up their academic authority to the students or even to the board.[9] Eventually, it approved a motion to supplement the earlier faculty action on May 7, acknowledging the student referendum as "a significant and sincere expression of concern about major national issues" and pledging to "utilize all available resources to conduct seminars and hold discussions" of the issues the students had requested. The option for incomplete grades in all courses until September 30 was reiterated, though individual students were required to give notice of their intent by May 21. Regular classes would continue for students who wished to attend, but absence regulations were suspended from May 6 until the beginning of exams. Huntley called a student assembly for noon the next day.

Students congregating in Evans Dining Hall during the faculty meeting learned the gist of the motion just adopted, and many were not pleased. Faculty members who came to the dining hall to explain the action were shouted at. Taking over Washington Hall was reportedly considered, but the students settled on boycotting classes and holding an assembly on the front lawn the next morning, in advance of Huntley's noon meeting.

The students met at 8:45 on Tuesday, May 12, and heard a statement adopted by the Student Executive Committee the night before (which Henberg claimed was informal, because he was not present). It described the faculty motion "as an act of grave irresponsibility," condemned it" in the strongest terms possible" and asked that the decision be reconsidered. The statement also advised students to resist the faculty motion by boycotting classes, refusing to register or pay fees for next year's classes, attending student-run open seminars, and actively participating "in war concern activities." To temper the provocative rhetoric, the statement also asked "that the student body react to the faculty decision with the same rationality and constructive action which has typified the events of the last several days." Student leaders requested that Huntley receive a fair hearing at the noon assembly. Despite some conciliatory language, the situation had hardened into a test of wills between the administration and faculty on one side, and the student body on the other.

Before the assembly, Huntley issued a statement explaining that the faculty decision was not a rejection of the student resolution but instead expressed "deep concern" for student views, expanded the provisions of their May 7 motion, and accepted every request made by the student's save one. "That one would have cancelled all academic work outright for anybody for any reason. I believe that implementing that action would be tantamount to closing Washington and Lee University," a decision both "unfair and unwise." That was precisely what many students had demanded.

Huntley appeared before a crowd of students on the front lawn in front of Lee Chapel and met with a degree of open hostility that was typical of many other universities at the time but was exceptionally rare at Washington and Lee. The president remained calm and deliberate in his remarks and responses to questions. He insisted that the university was sympathetic to student concerns. "Do not confuse lack of agreement," he said, "with lack of concern." He emphasized the many elements of the faculty decision that were responsive to student requests, and he tried to convey the serious implications of closing the university and why he considered this unacceptable. "If a sense of betrayal has been created in you, it was unintentional—a matter of the head and not of the heart." He applauded the student's commitment and involvement: "I must say I believe you have succeeded in bringing this student body into a sense of community, a sense of willingness to talk, a sense of willingness to share deep conviction, a sense of dedication to something higher than self." But to be sustained, it must not "fall apart as soon as a responsible decision has to be made." In any event, the faculty decision was final.

Many students remained unsatisfied but also increasingly resigned to the situation. Both Lawrence and Henberg understood that a protest initially directed against events in Indochina and student deaths at Kent State was now being directed at Washington and Lee itself and, if continued, would only become more radical. After an intense week, the student leadership was tired. The executive committee reconvened and decided to direct students away from continued confrontations with the faculty. At yet another student assembly, at 5 p.m. on Tuesday—called by Lawrence and convened by senior Gates Shaw—Phil Thompson, vice president elect of the student body, declared that the "faculty can go no further in keeping with their responsibility to the University. We ask that no acts of ultimate irresponsibility result from this." After meeting with Huntley earlier that afternoon, Thompson had concluded that the committee had "gone as far as we could in a responsible manner" and could do no more "without jeopardizing the existence of the University." He urged students to focus their efforts on the "real issues" and participate in the Free University Forum beginning that evening with three seminars, including one on the Black Panthers.[10]

On May 13, Huntley sent a four-page letter to the parents of all W&L students, recounting the week's events since May 7, offering reassurance that despite the "deep feelings" no disorder or violence had occurred. He also provided details on the faculty decisions and the options available to students. The university "must follow a course that is consistent with its institutional integrity," and he asked for "understanding and forbearance in a time that is difficult for everyone involved." A student letter of May 14, also mailed to all parents, declared "our firm conviction that violence and coercive action exacerbate a situation and tend only to obliterate the real issues" and pledged a "desire to maintain the atmosphere of concern coupled with rational dialogue and responsible action."[11]

During the height of the nationwide protests, radical measures at some campuses included bombings of ROTC buildings and occupation of other structures. At W&L, some students quietly sought to protect the campus in case things got out of hand. One group spent a cool evening camping out on the porch of the President's House to ensure its safety, despite Mrs. Huntley's invitations that they come inside. Some students reportedly armed themselves and stood guard over the ROTC building, where items from the Reeves collection were stored in the basement as they were being unpacked and sorted. James Whitehead and others packed fifty barrels of the more precious items and took them by pick-up truck to a site off campus.[12] Such measures proved unnecessary, but the events in Lexington and nationwide were unprecedented and unpredictable, and some people wanted to be cautious.

The faculty rose to the occasion, though with mixed feelings. Many faculty members opposed to the Vietnam War and the Cambodian incursion were moved by the student's commitment but were also stunned by their degree of support for closing the university and even more surprised by the student anger directed at them personally when they refused. A letter signed by sixty-two faculty members, transmitted to the *Richmond Times-Dispatch* by Severn Duvall of the English Department, was published on May 28 under the heading, "Faculty, Officials at W&L Oppose War."[13] The letter was indeed a strong condemnation of the war, the incursion into Cambodia, and the policies of the Nixon administration. This letter inspired a number of responses, including one from law professor Charles V. Laughlin, questioning the propriety of the criticism and noting that the signers represented only about one-third of W&L faculty and administrators.[14] In a response to one unhappy alumnus, Duvall—a former US Marine—explained that the signers were acting as individuals and not as representatives of the university, but he clearly connected the sentiments to the events of early May. He lamented the perception that faculty and students were pitted against one another; "perhaps the most serious loss of all (though hopefully only temporary) was a student faith in the shared convictions and ideals of teacher and student." He disapproved of the student resolution to close the university, but he was "moved, and depressed, as students whom I know and respect told me in subsequent days how disappointed they were, how much they had counted on greater faculty sympathy and understanding."[15] When the unrest and confusion continued, even sympathetic faculty members grew impatient with the students' drama, intransigence, and unreasonable demands. In any event, the close relationship between student and teacher, a great strength of the university, was sorely tested.[16]

In time, an element of calm returned to campus, and 82 percent of students registered for the next academic year, but the aftereffects and repercussions of the "eight days in May" lingered. While many students continued to attend classes and take final examinations, 609 students elected to take incomplete grades in all or some of their courses. By the end of the term slightly fewer than four hundred students still had incomplete grades to make up. Students also took advantage of the open seminars and discussions available through the Free University Forum. The sessions featured readings from literature and poetry and a few musical performances, and topics included "Polarization as a Political Technique," "Strategy and Tactics for Campaign Work," "The Impact of the Indochina War on the Ecology of Vietnam," and "The Truth About Vietnam," led by two student members of the John Birch Society.[17]

On May 14, a group based at Brandeis University designated Washington and Lee the "Southern Regional Strike Headquarters." This unlikely identification suggested that the student activism would continue indefinitely, especially when the Student Executive Committee recognized it as a regular student organization with allocated space in the University Center. But this turned out to be a "headquarters" in name only—it did not receive any student-body funds, apparently involved only a handful of students, and soon moved to an apartment off campus. Otherwise, the usual end-of-year activities continued apace—including the senior banquet, sports awards barbecue, and commencement.

The graduation ceremonies took place on a bright, sunny June day. Sixty students took advantage of the option of not wearing caps and gowns, and they donated the money they would have spent on them to the Student War Memorial Scholarship Fund. The 301 graduates included 44 who received military commissions. Eight students failed to graduate because they chose the "I" option and had not completed all required coursework. Huntley's remarks cast recent events in a broader perspective. There was still much to mourn in the world, he noted—"the bitterness which pervades the soul of our nation" and the "moral isolation which seems to surround us." On the campus, "we could decry those pressures which seem to push us ever closer to a situation in which we might spend most of our time in reconciling power centers in our midst, a situation in which the quest for noble ideals could be supplanted by a struggle of opposing wills." The essential purposes of the university remained as valid and timeless as ever, unshaken by recent events.

What to make of all this? Were most students genuinely upset about the war and the drift of national politics or simply caught up in springtime campus frenzy? Were they interested in working in the political arena or heading early to Virginia Beach or home to summer jobs? How did events in Lexington stack up against happenings elsewhere? The *Roanoke Times* dispatched a team of reporters to chronicle the recent activism on Virginia campuses and devoted the third installment to W&L. They noted a dramatic campus turnaround—from eight hundred student signatures on a Young Republican petition in support of the Vietnam War in 1966 to the same organization's defeat of a resolution supporting the Cambodian invasion in 1970. Earlier there had been virtually no student radicalism at all; now some four hundred students had been actively involved in protest, "a larger percentage of the student body engage[d] in campus protests" than at any other institution in Virginia.[18]

The paper attributed the turnaround to students' greater awareness of national issues, a growing unhappiness with the war and the military draft, and even the influence of a "liberal faculty." Dean of Students Lew John noted that only a handful of W&L students had been involved in organizing open forums and circulating petitions, and even then they had done so in a low-key way. One such group called itself the "Lee-Hi Truck Stop Liberation Front." But news of the war and growing national discontent fueled a growing movement that, according to John, bridged the "fraternity-independent gap" and increasingly involved moderate students, some of whom became more active than the activists. The *Times* reported that a "football tri-captain and head dormitory counselor [had] been described as the chief architect of the student resolution calling for the closing of W&L," and that the campus campaign head for Nixon in 1968 and Gov. Linwood Holton in 1969 had become the public relations chief for the Regional Strike Headquarters. At the same time, many observers agreed that "roughly half" of the students who voted in favor of the class shutdown "did so because of genuine concern; the other half was on a lark." The article attributed the faculty opposition to canceling classes—despite considerable sympathy for the student cause—to growing concern about the drift of an antiwar and social justice student movement into something more militant "that pitted students against the W&L power structure." When the protest subsided, there "had been no destruction of private property. There had been no violence. There had been no police confrontation." But "there had been changes."

The student protests at W&L were similar to those at some other institutions and far more sedate than those on many campuses, especially larger public institutions like the University of Wisconsin at Madison. Closer to home, matters were more heated at UVA, where a previously scheduled visit by Jerry Rubin, one of the "Chicago Seven," and radical lawyer William Kunstler coincided with the Cambodia–Kent State protests. On May 6, following their presentation at University Hall (which some protesters from W&L attended), they accompanied about two thousand students to demonstrate at the president's residence. Though not requested by the university, the local commonwealth attorney invoked the Riot Act, and state police rushed a campus crowd that evening and even pursued students onto the lawn and into their rooms, arresting sixty-seven.[19] Like W&L, UVA did not cancel classes but allowed students to delay completion of coursework until the fall. In Blacksburg, students occupied Williams Hall at Virginia Tech, and over one hundred were arrested and jailed by the police when they refused to leave.

At Randolph-Macon in Ashland, students also favored a strike of classes and confronted the faculty in unprecedented fashion. "The raw emotion, verging on open hostility," observed a university historian, "made it exceptional, and perhaps unique in the twentieth century."[20] A similar compromise was reached, whereby students could take incomplete grades in some or all of their courses and make them up by the end of the following September. As at W&L, relatively few students actually took that option. Vanderbilt University also experienced "the most politically intense week" in its history, and for the first time "a clear majority of the students united in some protest activities."[21] The faculty refused to cancel classes or exams, but some professors did make accommodations for individual students. Princeton University closed for the remainder of the semester.

Campus administrations struggled to tamp down the emotions, protect public safety, and respect legitimate expressions of student opinion while also maintaining the support of boards, alumni, and major donors, most of whom opposed the protests. It was a delicate balance. On May 10, UVA president Edgar F. Shannon Jr., a W&L graduate and future trustee, spoke to a crowd of students and faculty from the steps of the Rotunda, where he expressed his personal opposition to the Cambodian invasion and initiated a message to be sent to Virginia's US senators, condemning the "unspeakable tragedy at Kent State." Nearly five thousand students and faculty signed the message within twenty-four hours. Some elected officials and alumni roundly criticized Shannon for taking a political position, but UVA remained open and relatively free of violence. (Shannon was supported by the board of visitors and received a standing ovation at Final Exercises.) Vanderbilt chancellor Alexander Heard was known to be opposed to the war in Indochina and sympathetic to student opinion, which may have mitigated some of the protests there.

At W&L, Bob Huntley maintained a consistent appeal to comity, rationality, and the right of free expression, and he bore up patiently under the anger and invective that greeted his appearance on May 12. But he was meticulously noncommittal on the issues giving rise to student discontent. Thus, he avoided the criticism of alumni and others opposed to the demonstrations. He did receive hundreds of letters and telegrams, expressing a wide range of opinion. Many complimented the university for its moderation and refusal to close. Some believed that no concessions should be made to "radicals" and that students or faculty who boycotted classes should be immediately dismissed, or that the university should "close indefinitely" to punish students by seriously interrupting their education. Some parents favored disciplinary action against their own sons. A few attributed the protests to a global communist conspiracy. Some conflated campus unrest with the fading of conventional dress and other traditions, and alluded to withholding future contributions. A 1967 graduate complained to Bill Washburn that on his recent visits to campus he had encountered sloppy attire, and his greetings were returned "by sullen, leering silence." Huntley responded to these communications, often using three or four standard paragraphs. His main goal was to diffuse anger and reassure alumni and others that the university had avoided violence, maintained a "basic sense of responsible commitment," and would make every effort to "keep Washington and Lee's ship on an even keel." One of these boilerplate paragraphs addressed concerns about the dress and appearance of students and some faculty members. Without expressing sympathy for this trend, Huntley noted, "even the male 'models' on Fifth Avenue look this way now."[22]

In a formal statement, the board of trustees commended "the administration and faculty of the University for the wise, firm, and courageous manner in which they dealt with the situation on our campus during the period of unrest." They also commended "the student body for its adherence to orderly procedures, in contrast with the coercion and even disorder on many campuses," and for accepting the judgment of the faculty "in good spirit and in a manner consistent with the best traditions of Washington and Lee."[23]

———✦———

THE STUDENT UNREST, along with apparent declines in campus dress and decorum, further whetted fears that W&L's traditions were in trouble. Even the student-run Honor System was reexamined in the late 1960s, prompted by a series of specific questions about rules and interpretations. Would a system of graduated penalties be fairer? Should punishment better fit the nature of the offense? Would a year's suspension have an equally deterrent effect? Should legal counsel be available to accused students on such an important matter? What should faculty members expect and what should they explain to students? In November 1970, the Student Executive Committee distributed to the faculty a list of suggestions and definitions of what class work was "pledged" and what was not, why students should be allowed to leave the room during exams but encouraged to "take alternate seats" to avoid even the appearance of cheating, how to interpret rules for "open book" and "open notebook" examinations, and why instructors should not give identical tests to different sections of the same class.[24] Was it an honor violation if a student talked with another about a test, even if the content of the test was not discussed? The more the Honor System was parsed and applied to myriad situations, the more it seemed somehow diminished.

Surveys revealed that many were confused or even ignorant about aspects of the Honor System. Students were more reluctant to report a friend or fraternity brother for a violation than to report people they disliked or did not know. A number admitted to violating the letter, if not the spirit, of the Honor System, and some questioned the fairness of the Student Executive Committee.

In 1968, the student body president, Jay Passavant, appointed two committees to look into different aspects of the Honor System—its jurisdictional limits and general procedures. As Neil Kessler, Friday editor of the *Ring-tum Phi*, noted in an article for the *Alumni Magazine,* "The Honor System is coming under its closest scrutiny in history."[25] In April 1970, the Student Executive Committee considered the possibility of introducing a one-year suspension as an alternative penalty to expulsion for less egregious violations of the Honor System. How, then, would W&L's most significant tradition fare after the unprecedented events of the "Eight Days in May"?

In May 1971, Student Body President Fran Lawrence read to the trustees a statement on the Honor System adopted by the Student Executive Committees of the current and upcoming year. The statement noted the need to reexamine this W&L tradition periodically but reaffirmed its central core and the single sanction: "Both in its nature and its function, the Honor System enjoins a way in which human beings relate to each other. That way of relating is premised on simple and mutual trust. We seek through the gentleman's code of honor to maintain a community based on trust, not on force nor on legal code. It is inherent in trust that no precise definition nor codification is possible. Clearly, however, trust entails the absence of suspicion, threat, and fear. It assumes respect for persons, and it acknowledges honesty and trustworthiness as the prerequisites of respect." The only written statement expressing the Honor System should be: "A Washington and Lee student is to conduct himself as a gentleman in matters of honor at all times; he is trusted and he assumes the obligation to be trustworthy."[26]

The trustees promptly endorsed the statement and expressed appreciation to the student leaders, including President-Elect Steve Robinson, who then read a letter affirming the Honor System that he planned to send to all incoming students. Huntley, in the *Ring-tum Phi*, also applauded the statement, adding that it "may be that such an atmosphere of trust and honor is rarer in the world today than ever before; if so, it is even more to be cherished and coveted among us here."

The Honor System would continue to be adjusted, in ways that seemed to some small and to others hypocritical. Perhaps in response to student surveys, the long-observed explicit obligation to report dishonorable behavior by fellow students (failure to do so was considered equally dishonorable) was eliminated by the student body in 1975. The applicability of the Honor System to W&L students at all times and in all places, even many miles away from campus, was now restricted to Rockbridge County during academic terms, greatly enhancing effective enforcement. Similar concerns led to many universities' abandonment or major modification of strict honor codes, but students adjusted the W&L Honor System to fit new realities and sustained the principle that honor was indivisible.

THE UNIVERSITY ATTEMPTED to keep alumni informed about changes in student attitudes and behavior, and to reassure them that their alma mater was not on a downhill slide. In November 1969, only six months before the May protests, Swede Henberg spoke to a Parents Weekend audience about student life at W&L, and his remarks were published in the February issue of the *Alumni Magazine*. He praised the openness and energy of the administration and the prospect of greater choice in the new curriculum. He also argued that student life should be largely in the hands of the students and that faculty acting as disciplinary agents was regrettable. He portrayed the university as a community where students were assuming a more equitable and appropriate place. He also mentioned, in passing, that he was in favor of coeducation.[27] In the same issue, Dean John offered his views in "Question: What Is Today's Student Like?" He noted that students were "not so willing to accept authority," they exhibited "a high degree of tolerance for individual differences" ("it is popular to let each person do his own thing"), and they were likely to "be more concerned, more aware, and more involved in issues transcending the campus." The majority would not impose conventional dress on the minority who chose to dress differently, and many students "can be characterized by their concern for others, by their idealism, by their greater involvement and participation, and by their desire to contribute."[28]

The *Alumni Magazine* also reprinted remarks delivered during the Homecoming-Fall Reunion Weekend in October 1972 by Professor Sidney M. B. Coulling, in which he pointed out that the university was always changing with generations and was never "what it used to be." Though expressed in different ways, the desire for knowledge "is our primary mission now just as it was in the days of William Graham, and Robert E. Lee, and Francis P. Gaines."[29] In the spring of 1974, three past presidents of the student body, the current president, and the president-elect, reflected on student life at W&L, and excerpts were published in the September issue of *W&L* magazine. They agreed, more or less, that things were improving, due partly to the greater variety of activities on campus and the work of the new Student Activities Board, which sponsored entertainment and breathed new life into Fancy Dress. The student apathy and indifference that Steve Robinson remembered from earlier in the decade seemed to be declining. They agreed that the administration was open and that faculty-student relationships were strong—except that "liberal-minded professors" seemed too reluctant to invite student participation in academic policies. Perhaps the students, lacking long-term perspective, were the least likely to understand the changes that were occurring, but they were certainly aware of them. Bob Brennan, president in 1972–73, tried to explain the transition: the students now beginning to come to W&L "are not the jacket-and-tie types, but . . . are dedicated to Washington and Lee and are involved in Washington and Lee in a different way than people used to be."[30] This was, for some alumni, perhaps not so reassuring.

The realities—and especially the pace of change—in student life were reflected in the university's evolving policies. Practices that were completely accepted in the late 1950s raised doubts in the early 1960s, and less than a decade later they seemed quaint and outmoded. Traditionally, university-sponsored social functions were governed by faculty rules and overseen by faculty chaperones, but a paper prepared for the Faculty Committee on Student Social Functions in 1961 by Professors John M. Gunn Jr. and Edward J. Roxbury charted the changes underway. Pointing to "progressive changes in the social habits" of W&L students that "have accelerated in very recent years" the paper noted the decreasing number of university-wide functions, "fewer dances and more concerts, less formality in dress, different styles of music and dance, and declining attendance at University dances" and more fraternity house "combo" parties. The authors asked "whether the University Faculty wish to acquiesce in these changes" or whether "in the interests of preserving traditions and a certain public image they wish to exercise greater control over the form of University-sponsored social functions?" How would the faculty insure that these functions maintained, as expressed in the faculty regulations of 1955, "accepted standards of social usage and good taste" when these too were changing? Should the faculty specify "minimum standards of dress" and prohibit "certain dance steps, e.g., the twist"? Should more of these decisions about arrangements, dress, and entertainment be delegated to the students?[31]

The faculty voted to establish the Student Control Committee of five student members in November 1961. Although the committee acted only as a "supplementary agency" for enforcing policies set by the faculty, its establishment signaled a shift in responsibility for student conduct and discipline to the students themselves. In 1962, the membership increased to seven, and court cases involving students were now included in its purview. A new Student Affairs Committee, composed of students and administrators, was created in 1965 to oversee the Student Control Committee, "assume jurisdiction over all student affairs not now covered by other committees," and advise the dean of student affairs. In November 1970, after the student unrest of the previous spring, the faculty voted to allow the Student Affairs Committee to "establish policy and approve regulations regarding the visitation in fraternity houses and University dormitories." At the same time, the Student and Faculty Executive Committees jointly proposed the University Council, which was established on December 7. Composed of twelve students, twelve faculty members, and designated senior administrators, including the president and deans, the new council assumed broad authority over student affairs (but not the Honor System and the curriculum). Meeting monthly, beginning on February 27, 1971, the council reviewed proposals and reports concerning student affairs from all sources, including the faculty and administration.[32]

Students at W&L and throughout American higher education increasingly demanded a greater voice in regulations, especially concerning life in the dormitories and fraternity houses (including parietal rules). The Student Control Committee received a specific disciplinary role over behavior in the dormitories in 1966, and the Student Affairs Committee plan for "the regulation of dormitory life" was approved by the faculty in 1969 and amended in 1970. The plan divided the dormitories, as much as possible, into "self-contained residential units" of forty to fifty students, each of which would set "standards of social responsibility" for submission to the Student Control Committee. These standards could include "social hours" for the weekends but permitted no overnight visitations. The Student Affairs Committee also approved similar new rules permitting women to visit the upper floors of fraternity houses. In 1970, the committee recommended, and the faculty approved, transferring authority to the Interfraternity Council for setting the number and hours of fraternity house parties. The faculty also approved a committee recommendation that use of illegal drugs be considered "a serious disciplinary offense" that could lead to suspension or expulsion from the university.

In 1974, the University Council adopted a statement, "Policy and Standards for Student Conduct and Discipline," outlining general principles for handling individual cases. In the midst of shifting standards and expectations, the council sought the "reasonably consistent and nonarbitrary handling of individual cases," while avoiding "the inherently undesirable and stultifying effects of drafting a detailed disciplinary code." The standards they noted would apply to students on campus, throughout Rockbridge County, and on other campuses during the academic year. With respect to students charged with criminal offenses, "the University is neither a shield nor a sword." Its own disciplinary procedures would defer to those of the state but would not be an investigative arm of the state.[33]

The faculty accepted more student involvement in curriculum matters and generally worked to promote open campus communication. The Faculty Executive Committee, meeting in March 1974, recommended that both the executive committee and the Committee on Courses and Degrees include two student voting representatives, and student representation could be considered for all other faculty committees. Upon request of any member of the University Council, a written summary of the faculty debate on any issue would be distributed within twenty-four hours of the meeting to the president of the student body, the editor of the *Ring-tum Phi*, the news director of WLUR, and the university's public relations officer."[34]

University policies evolved, students assumed more responsibility, and much of student life resumed a more conventional aspect as the intensity of May 1970 faded. But three challenges especially tested the campus community during the 1970s and into the 1980s: drugs and alcohol, fraternities, and race and campus diversity.

ALCOHOL HAS BEEN a part of university social life for generations. A bane of college administrators, and the subject of many efforts at "reform," drinking has also been closely associated with social fraternities. At least until the 1980s, patterns of campus alcohol use may not have changed significantly: some students did not drink, some drank heavily, and most fell in between. W&L's response was shaped by changing social patterns and fluctuating laws setting the legal age to purchase and consume alcohol. Some states set the age at twenty-one and others at eighteen. After passage of the 26th Amendment to the US Constitution in 1971, allowing eighteen year olds to vote, almost all states reduced the drinking age to eighteen. Even in this new environment, alcohol regulations throughout the country varied. In Virginia, the drinking age was lowered to eighteen from twenty-one (for beer and wine only) in 1974 and raised to nineteen in 1981 (for off-premises consumption) and for all beer in 1983. The National Minimum Drinking Age Act of 1984, passed primarily to curtail drunk driving, required states to raise the legal age to twenty-one for the purchase or possession of alcohol or else lose 10 percent of their federal highway funds. All states swiftly complied. The roller-coaster regulatory regime reflected the national ambivalence about alcohol and may have actually encouraged the rise of binge drinking.

A 1980 study of drinking habits at W&L commissioned by the Student Executive Committee, elicited from roughly half the student body (675 responses,). The results revealed that 7.6 percent of respondents did not drink at all, 11 percent consumed more than twenty-five drinks per week, and the "average student" reportedly consumed about nine beers or other drinks in a week. The results also suggested that students tended to follow the drinking habits of their parents, especially their fathers, and most said that their parents were "moderate" drinkers. Drinking was directly connected to social life. (Only a few students reported that they drank alone or in the mornings.) Abstainers were more than twice as likely as others to be dissatisfied with W&L social life, but of all respondents 13 percent said they would prefer soft drinks to alcohol if they were available. Sophomores, who were most likely to reside in fraternity houses, reported the highest impact of alcohol on their academic performance and grades. One-fifth of all respondents, and 40 percent of "heavy" drinkers, said they had missed a meeting or a class due to alcohol. Perhaps most disturbing, especially considering the winding, mountainous roads used on many trips to women's colleges: 12 percent of respondents frequently drove while drinking, and a third said they did so occasionally.[35]

Illegal drugs were a new phenomenon at W&L. Drugs such as marijuana and hashish were essentially absent from the campus scene as late as 1965 but were becoming more prevalent only a few years later. LSD was a hallucinogen associated with the counterculture and its emphasis on expanding the mind and exploring new sensations and states of consciousness. It, too, was present on campus at least by 1968. Estimates of drug use at W&L varied, but everyone—including Dean Atwood and the university psychologist—agreed that marijuana and hashish were common; some students had apparently been alarmed by "bad trips" while using LSD. All these substances were illegal, and state and local authorities generally regarded the use of them as a much more serious infraction than college students did.

Prompted by a rising level of concern, and with no specific agenda in mind, President Huntley called a special student assembly on December 4, 1968. He admitted that he was no expert on drugs or their role in society, but he knew that they were "seriously illegal" (however irrational some of the laws might be) and could have a "permanent harmful effect" on people who used them. With tobacco and alcohol already available, "it is particularly untimely to add another such vice as this." In his opinion," the use of marijuana on many users increases what I regard as the most counter-productive tendencies in our society, withdrawal introspection, the navel contemplation syndrome . . . which removes man from reality, allows him to escape the true problems he must face and indeed isolates each man from the other." To avoid immersing the campus in a serious problem, he appealed to the students' individual judgment: "I ask you then in the only way that I think we can, to spare us a prolonged preoccupation with an Indian weed."[36]

Drug use on the nation's campuses grew with greater social acceptance and the turmoil of political protest. Marijuana, especially prevalent at rock concerts, was often featured in books, movies, and on television. Many young people considered it less dangerous than tobacco. Though Virginia and some other states reduced the charge for marijuana possession from a felony to a misdemeanor, there were still heavy penalties for selling the drug and a lingering fear that use of entry-level drugs could lead to dependency on more serious ones like cocaine. The clash between growing social acceptance and legal reality—and the actions of ambitious prosecutors—was dramatically highlighted at W&L in the fall of 1972.

The local commonwealth attorney, John Reed, launched a yearlong investigation into local drug sales in Lexington and Rockbridge County, resulting in a number of arrests—including of students at W&L and VMI. Two undercover officers of the Virginia State Police, who had been working on and around campus during the investigation, testified to a special grand jury convened on November 14, 1972. The jury returned fifty-four indictments against nineteen people, thirteen of them current or former W&L students. The ten currently enrolled students were charged with thirty-six counts for the direct distribution of marijuana, hashish, and LSD. Legal proceedings continued through the year, and trials were set for April and June. Apart from the serious charges themselves and what they might mean for the campus community, the university faced decisions concerning policy and student discipline. Since the evidence would not be revealed until the trials, how should W&L proceed in the meantime?[37]

The Student Control Committee had jurisdiction over such matters, with decisions subject to review by the Student Affairs Committee, chaired by the dean of students and composed of students, faculty members, and administrators. Both groups agreed to defer action until the court cases were decided. Until then, the Faculty Executive Committee considered possible revisions of university policy, especially concerning the possibility of withholding degrees from students still under disciplinary review beyond their graduation date. In the first three court cases, decided in April 1973, the students entered guilty pleas, with sentencing deferred until June. The Student Control Committee proceeded to consider disciplinary action and decided in a split vote to take no action at the present time, a decision sustained by an 8–2 vote of the Student Affairs Committee. The faculty deliberations also resulted in no policy recommendations, but rather a decision to appoint an ad hoc faculty committee to begin a comprehensive policy review in the fall of 1973.

The reluctance to act reflected concerns that university actions might interfere or influence pending court cases and sentencing and that "degrees of criminality" should be addressed. The array of different individuals and cases indicated the complexities of the circumstances and issues. The Student Control Committee noted the lack of "widespread understanding among the student body that the University would feel the need to take action were cases such as these brought to light." But the alumni board of directors decided at its meeting on May 11 to express serious concern about the drug charges and "the whole University policy as it relates to the disciplining of students convicted of felonies." Once again, opinions differed across the generations, creating more challenges for the administration.

The trustees discussed student discipline at length on May 26 and approved the list of candidates for the May 31 graduation—including all the indicted students—pending final action by the faculty, which recommended granting degrees for eight of the nine indicted seniors. (One failed to meet the academic requirements for graduation.) University policy in such cases continued to be discussed well into the 1980s, with the faculty inclined to award degrees to individuals who had not yet been convicted of a crime, while the trustees tended toward withholding diplomas while charges were still pending.

The court decisions followed in due course. All ten of the indicted students entered guilty pleas, and all received probation. All were found guilty, and seven were sentenced to as many as thirty years in prison, reduced to jail terms of from sixty days to two years. Dean John visited several of those serving their sentences at the Bland Correctional Farm in southwest Virginia. In June 1975, one of the convicted students, who had served seven months in jail and subsequently enrolled and was first in his class at the William and Mary Law School, received a full pardon from Gov. Mills E. Godwin so that he could take the bar examination and practice law.

That the university took no disciplinary action in these cases surprised some people. But most acknowledged that W&L's policies on drug use—and the broader issue of disciplinary action for those convicted of crimes—should be reviewed. Even the Student Control Committee qualified its May 8 recommendation against disciplinary action with the statement that there were cases in which the committee "would very likely ask for suspension or even expulsion." The University Policy Statement on Drugs, adopted in May 1971, identified the institution's "prime responsibilities concerning drugs [as] education and counseling," and providing "an environment in which students may discuss drug problems openly and without fear of reprisal." In other words, the principal focus would be on encouraging student initiative to seek help for issues regarding drugs. But the policy also noted that "the campus is not a sanctuary from law enforcement agents" (which was certainly confirmed by the November 1972 indictments), and the university would not intervene to protect students from the law and "would not ignore violations which come to its attention." Penalties would be based on the specific circumstances.

Washington and Lee continued to rely primarily on student personal responsibility rather than punitive action, but this policy became more difficult after the felony indictments in 1972 and similar cases thereafter. W&L would again consider how to gauge discipline for students when criminal charges for drug offenses were pending. University policies regarding substance abuse—and the penalties involved—would in time become more extensive, specific, and targeted.

FRATERNITIES REMAINED the focus of social life at W&L and posed the usual problems: finances, maintenance, noise, questionable behavior, and lack of connection to the university's academic life. At the beginning of the 1970s, fraternity membership plummeted, and some houses went under. Toward the middle of the decade, a new equilibrium seemed in place, with lower membership but fewer, stronger organizations. In 1980, the university took over the routine maintenance of the houses and imposed new regulations and oversight to mitigate the serious deterioration in fraternity life and financial sustainability. Once again, W&L contemplated ending the fraternity system altogether.

Dean Atwood had complained in 1965 about the "lack of fraternity leadership" because upperclassmen attended parties but were unwilling to become fraternity officers. The houses, for the most part, were not kept in good repair.[38] In 1968, after an inspection revealed maintenance needs approaching or exceeding $600,000, the university imposed a monthly maintenance fee of 3 percent of the estimated value of each house, to be placed in a maintenance fund. The university also offered loans for the construction or renovation of fraternity properties at 4 percent, well below the commercial rate.

In August 1970, the *Alumni Magazine* alerted its readers to the many changes greeting students in that fall semester: "Fraternities, at one time a stalwart institution on campus, suddenly and dramatically have become a part of changing times." The article reported that two houses had folded, one had moved, and many others were "plagued with either manpower shortage, financial troubles, or both, and it could mean that several more houses will join those now gone in the upcoming months."[39] Only 58 percent of the 1970 freshman class pledged a fraternity. (In 1968, it was 81 percent.) The magazine observed, "today's is a generation of students who have been taught that they know more of the answers than anybody else ever knew; that it is a sign of weakness to give in; that nothing is nobler than to do one's own thing."[40]

The "for sale" sign on the front lawn of the Kappa Sigma house on South Main Street was an indicator of the changes afoot. At least twenty new pledges were needed in the fall of 1969 to support costs, and only two joined. Left with a membership of only eighteen, the brothers elected to disband and put the house up for sale. Even more dramatic was the loss of the Kappa Alpha Order, founded at W&L in 1865. When ten regular and five eating members (about a third of the membership) resigned, the finances were thrown in disarray, and the national charter was rescinded in April 1970. After the membership of Sigma Phi Epsilon dropped to fewer than thirty, the house was rented out to other students to cover costs, and the fraternity moved into a private apartment. In the previous year, Delta Upsilon was rocked with an internal dispute over marijuana, after which some members were asked to leave. Only seven underclassmen members remained.[41]

The *Roanoke Times* questioned the presidents of the surviving houses about their fraternities' financial positions, and the responses varied: "There was unanimous agreement, however, that fraternities were slipping." Among the "common replies," the paper reported, were that more "liberal" students tended to see fraternities as a "discredited element of the past," that fraternities had not "kept up with the times," and that the organizations had lost too many upperclassmen members. The high cost of membership was prohibitive for many students, and the completion of the new Student Union had made fraternities "less necessary." The "liberal" nature of W&L students was perhaps overstated, but the increasing tendency of upperclassmen to attend fraternity social functions and remain otherwise independent was not. Nor was the effect of new competition from the Early-Fielding Memorial Student Center, completed in the fall of 1969, with its TVs, game rooms, pool tables, movies, combo parties every Saturday night, and the "Cockpit" tavern, which served beer.[42] Dormitory visitation rules had also been liberalized along with those applying to the fraternity houses.

Some alumni were understandably upset by these developments, especially because they seemed to coincide with the student unrest in May. President Huntley, who maintained his appreciation for the positive aspects of fraternities, offered these alumni both reassurance and a realistic perspective. During the previous decade, he said, "fraternities here have become isolated from the University and from the community-at-large." Upperclassmen used fraternities as little more than restaurants and nightclubs, and an increasing number had deactivated. However, he wrote in a standard letter responding to individual inquiries, W&L "has definitely *not* become anti-fraternity, but it cannot attempt to insulate fraternities from the pressures that all of us feel." The university "must in various ways create a more realistic situation for fraternities—one in which they will survive on their own merits" and in "closer association" with W&L and its educational goals.[43]

By 1976, Psi Upsilon had closed its doors, but Kappa Alpha returned under a provisional charter, granted in 1975, and Sigma Phi Epsilon reoccupied its house on Preston Street. Still, the campus fraternity scene was changing. Only about half of the student body now belonged to fraternities, and the pledge rate among freshmen seemed stabilized at about 60 percent. The university continued to provide support through low-interest loans for construction and renovation. The IFC decided in 1975 that national affiliation would no longer be required for recognition at W&L, and Pi Kappa Alpha had already moved to become strictly local. Fraternities still provided a vigorous social life but were more like informal social clubs, with minimal interest in ritual. Administrators continued to hope that these changes would result in a healthier overall campus environment.[44]

A new University Council policy, adopted in February 1976, reiterated university support but also emphasized the responsibilities of fraternities to the university and the community. Houses must be maintained in their structural integrity and physical appearance, and members must "conform to standards of gentlemanly conduct." The IFC and the Student Affairs Committee would provide oversight, and the latter was charged to appoint a "fraternity inspection committee" to periodically review compliance.[45] Two years later, the Fraternity Committee of the board of trustees met with Dean John and other administrators and expressed "their belief that the fraternities have failed individually and collectively through the IFC, to meet the very minimum standards laid down by the University." They also endorsed the latest steps taken by the Student Affairs Committee to distribute monthly maintenance checklists for completion by each fraternity through the Inspection Committee, which would make spot checks in addition to the regular scheduled inspections. The board encouraged the Student Affairs Committee "to take quick action against any violations" and deal with them "harshly." Penalties could include social probation or worse. A mandatory meeting of all fraternity presidents was scheduled for May 1978 to emphasize the board's concern.[46]

In 1979, fraternity membership stood at 814 out of 1,328 (61 percent) of all students; 225 lived in the fraternity houses, and 550 took meals there. The faculty continued to express its hope that the University Council "devise a code of social and residential behavior in fraternity houses" that would, at a minimum, bar mid-week house parties, "hazing" of any kind, and excessive and inconsiderate noise levels. Definitions of hazing ranged from "paddling and verbal abuse" to "grossly undignified behavior." The faculty's main concern was its sense "that the quality of fraternity house life at the University has fallen, in some cases, to degrading levels inimical to the University's mission." The University Council adopted an IFC proposal that admitted that improvements were necessary but asked that the concept of self-government be preserved. The IFC also concurred with the prohibition on mid-week house parties, adherence to local noise ordinances, and elimination of anything posing "emotional or physical hazard" to students. The faculty approved a motion acknowledging the IFC efforts at "self-control," asked the University Council to submit a full report "on the implementation" of its new policy before January 7, 1980, and requested that the dean of students include in that report a listing of fraternity-related complaints and problems.[47]

A special report in 1980 concluded," Most fraternity houses are in such a state of physical deterioration as to require major renovation soon," at an average cost of $100,000 per house. It further noted that the fraternities could not survive without university financial assistance in some form." The university agreed to absorb some overhead costs but instituted a new annual fee of as much as $2,800 for each fraternity house (subject to later adjustment), hired two new employees in Buildings and Grounds, and assumed responsibility for maintaining the plumbing, heating, and electrical systems of all fifteen houses (which collectively held mortgages with the university exceeding $500,000). In addition, the university would closely review the financial statements of all seventeen social fraternities. In a letter to fraternity presidents, Huntley noted the university's continuing "commitment to a strong and healthy fraternity system." These actions addressed the immediate issues, but the long term was less clear. The committee's report outlined three possible "long-range models" for the fraternities: continuing and improving the current system, university ownership of all houses, or a more radical change to an on-campus complex of "social lodges," where members would live, dine, and socialize.[48] The report set the stage for further, and very necessary, actions later in the decade.

AT WASHINGTON AND LEE, adapting to social diversity and new cultural forces was a continuing challenge. The first African American undergraduate student at W&L, Dennis Haston, was from Lexington, enrolled in 1966, and transferred after his first year. The next two black undergraduate students, Lenwood Smothers and Walter Blake, also from Lexington, enrolled in 1968 and graduated in 1972. Leslie Devan Smith, also admitted in 1966, was the first African American law student and the first black graduate of W&L, with a law degree in 1969. He had been guided to W&L from St. Paul's College, a small black institution in Lawrenceville, Virginia, by Huntley and Cole. It was much more difficult to attract other black students, especially men with good academic records, who were being aggressively recruited by virtually every other university in the country. W&L had little or no experience in attracting a racially, ethnically, or even economically diverse student population, but Jim Farrar Sr. and his colleagues and successors knew that a larger minority enrollment was essential to a sustainable recruitment plan. Farrar, who had been deeply involved in these efforts from the beginning, assured Huntley in 1969 that faculty and staff would visit predominantly black schools in Philadelphia, Richmond, Norfolk, and Washington, DC; take advantage of national scholarship programs for minorities; and use "all available resources for identifying qualified black students."[49]

Because of the dismal state of segregated secondary schools, most black students—while intelligent and determined—were not academically prepared for Washington and Lee. Huntley said of Leslie Smith, who had graduated at the top of his class at St. Paul's: "He was untutored but he had plenty of sense and he wanted to succeed." Huntley and Smith discussed books from a list Huntley provided that helped to alleviate the "disadvantage he suffered in comparison with the other law students." Smith struggled in his first year, but "by his third year he was making A's and B's." Most faculty members were helpful without lowering academic standards. "They didn't cut [the African American students] slack"; Huntley recalled, "they didn't grade them differently; they just gave them more time, spent more time with them."[50] One of the members of the class of 1974, William Hill from Atlanta, recalled the "culture shock" of being surrounded by white students for the first time, and the academic challenges: "I found myself up at night reading to catch up, and for a lot of these guys, freshman year at W&L for them was review with very little new information. And they partied. They had a good time. They were out on weekends. I was in the library working my butt off just trying to make Cs. So the academic pressures were horrendous." By improving his study habits and gaining a better understanding of what a W&L education was all about, his academic performance improved: "Once I figured out that I wasn't preparing for a job, I was just trying to make myself better by trying to broaden my horizons, then all of a sudden things got better. Classes got easier. It started to make more sense because I enjoyed what I was doing." Hill graduated from the law school and later proudly sent his daughters to W&L.[51] As Walter Blake, who enrolled in 1968, said, "You had to be a survivor to make it through here."

Eugene Perry had studied with white students at Waynesboro High School and been recruited by colleges throughout the country—eighty-three by his count—and offered admission to many. He had applied to Washington and Lee, largely because of Robert E. Lee and his commitment to honor and civility. In fact, he admired both Lee and "Stonewall" Jackson, even though they had been "on the wrong side." Perry visited campus and talked with Farrar, a man Perry thought embodied Lee's spirit and values. Still, enrollment was not an easy decision. While Perry was visiting campus with other potential black applicants, some white students yelled offensive remarks and had to be reprimanded by older white students. Only three other African American students entered W&L with Perry in 1971. He realized that while he had attended school with whites, very few W&L students had ever had black classmates. Perry also remembered some faculty members who assumed he had a poor educational background and treated him in a condescending manner. But he accepted the challenge to succeed in a white-dominated environment and a highly traditional university, and sought to make the best of it. Despite warnings that he should not enroll in any classes taught by Jefferson Davis Futch, a very conservative professor and popular lecturer, Perry enrolled in several and found Futch to be a good teacher and fair grader. Perry graduated in 1975, kept in touch with his alma mater, and served on various alumni committees.[52]

As more African American students enrolled, the national climate and their expectations had changed. The victory over desegregation led inevitably to awareness of the many ways in which African Americans were disadvantaged in American society. The rights to vote, go to the same schools as whites, and eat at public lunch counters were important, but these advances did not alleviate poverty, poor schools, the lingering disdain often encountered from law enforcement and other authorities, and the still fresh memories of lynching and overt racism. The accumulated burden of mistreatment and discontent weighed heavily on the rising generation of African Americans and led to greater demands for economic parity and expanded roles in society and government.

Black university students across the country began demanding courses and programs in African American history and literature, and sported "Afro" hairstyles and African garb as signs of racial identity. They helped shape the national youth culture of the time, which emphasized more flamboyant dress, music with roots in black culture, and ethnic pride. Critics branded traditional notions of "assimilation" into the majority society as cultural suicide. African American students in predominantly white universities were thus especially sensitive to direct slights and a general lack of white awareness and under-standing. At W&L as elsewhere, too many white students bore the smug assur-ance of the majority and, obliviously or callously, continued to use racial slurs and references. The same was true of some faculty members.

The challenge for administrators was to guide the institution as a whole through these important social and cultural changes with a minimum of dis-ruption and with no diminution of institutional purpose. Rough spots along the way were inevitable. Early in his new presidency, Huntley emphasized that the university would seek qualified students from all races, (doubtless recalling the board sensitivity on the proposed targeted recruitment of minorities, which had quickly given way to necessity). The forty-five members of the Progressive Student Alliance (PSA), organized in 1969, addressed the need to diversify the student body and the faculty, through contacts with black colleges, focused re-cruitment in areas where minorities were likely to work and reside, and hiring more black teachers and admissions personnel.[53] As African American students established themselves on campus, they sought to expand their number.

In 1970, the twenty black students then enrolled at the university orga-nized the Student Association for Black Unity or SABU (later the Minority Student Association), and, with financial assistance from the admissions office, published their own recruitment pamphlet, "Brother to Brother." While not dismissing the difficulties, the pamphlet emphasized the advantages of being a trendsetter, educating whites about black culture, and the importance of learning to live in a complex society. "By coming to W&L, you can help bring men a little closer together."[54] In that year, the university received thirty-six applications from African Americans; it offered twenty-four acceptances, and fifteen students enrolled. In twenty-five years following racial integration, W&L accepted 67 percent of black applicants (the overall university acceptance rate was 30 percent) of whom 42 percent accepted.[55] SABU members also assisted the university's efforts by visiting high schools to discuss life in Lexington.

As W&L adapted to new patterns of race relations, there were lingering challenges. W&L students were admitted free of charge to Concert Guild pre-sentations in Lee Chapel, but in the early 1970s blacks were routinely asked to present student identification while whites entered without question. (President Huntley explained to black students that this was not intentional racial discrimination and to white students that this practice must stop.) Occasionally, a disparaging word was overheard from a white student. When African American students protested that the playing of "Dixie" at athletic events was offensive, and it stopped. While these occasions irritated blacks, they were also messages to whites that certain practices that had been accepted as routine must be reexamined and changed. Huntley later reflected that all the black students experienced, inevitably, "some degree of alienation," mitigated, he hoped, by "many hours of conversation" with him, Dean John, and others, and the institution's commitment to their success.[56]

The university's association with Robert E. Lee was not a cause for protest or concern for blacks at the time, and W&L experienced fewer problems concerning its association with the Confederacy than VMI. The annual celebration of the VMI cadets' participation in the Battle of New Market featured the Confederate flag (only introduced in the ceremony in the early 1950s), the playing of "Dixie," and a much closer association generally with the military aspects of the Civil War and the Confederacy. Cadets had to salute "Stonewall" Jackson's statue on their campus and when passing Lee Chapel, a custom deeply resented by black members of the corps. The VMI student government eliminated the practice in 1969, and the board of visitors finally stopped the playing of "Dixie" and removed the Confederate battle flag from the New Market ceremony by the end of the 1970s. At W&L, references to Lee focused on his character and bearing and his significant service as president of Washington College.[57]

Black students relied heavily on one another for support and friendship even as their numbers on campus increased. African Americans in the class of 1974 mostly lived, studied, and partied together. They encountered little resistance from other students and enjoyed friendships and associations with whites, but they stuck together through SABU and other channels, and raised complaints and offered suggestions to the administration. Financial aid had played a large role in expanding minority enrollment, but black students insisted that the university needed to do more to make black students an integral part of the campus.[58] Progress was slow, but ten black students graduated in the class of 1974.

As well as providing camaraderie and mutual support, SABU gave African American students an opportunity to explore and present "black culture" in the campus environment. While not a fraternity, the organization sponsored parties and other social events involving blacks at W&L and other area schools, and most members donned jean jackets with red, black, and green decals when walking on campus. SABU also celebrated Black Culture Week, observed nationally every February, by sponsoring a series of seminars and lectures by visiting speakers. In 1973, US representative Parren J. Mitchell of Maryland gave the Leslie D. Smith Memorial Lecture. Other events included a symposium called "On Being Black," concerts, and a Black Ball featuring music by "Black Rock."[59] In October 1975, SABU organized a march around the dormitories to protest the failure of the Student Executive Committee and Student Activities Board to respond to their call for more black entertainment on campus. Later that year, the members refused to help recruit black students to W&L because they believed they would feel unwelcome.

In 1975, a chapter of Alpha Phi Alpha, a historically black fraternity, was established on campus. The university made the vacant and unfurnished Sigma Phi Epsilon house available and provided a television, chairs, and tables. Unfortunately, the new chapter did not last, and a subsequent effort to reactivate in 1991 was also unsuccessful.

In January 1977, the Student Executive Committee convened to hear an accusation against an African American student for an honor violation, reportedly involving a research paper. Before the hearing on the merits of the case could begin, the accused said he would withdraw from the university because he could not get a fair hearing. On the morning of the following day, Dean John met with President Huntley, accompanied by two law students who had advised the accused student and Curtis Hubbard, an African American educator who had come earlier to W&L in 1976 from Hampton Institute to serve as assistant dean of students and advisor to minority students. Later, other black students and three officers of the student body joined the meeting.[60]

The black students demanded that the charges be dropped because of alleged procedural irregularities related to the Student Executive Committee hearing and asked that the student be reinstated. They also presented a number of other needs that needed to be addressed—the hiring of black faculty members (there were none at the time), the enrollment of additional black students (only two black freshmen enrolled in 1976), and the provision of greater financial aid. Huntley scheduled a meeting to discuss those issues with the black students the following day, and he consulted with the student body officers concerning how they wished to proceed with the Honor System hearing. (The accused student had decided not to withdraw.) The Student Executive Committee met that evening to consider whether to proceed to hear the case on its merits.

While these discussions were underway, eight to a dozen black students gathered in Huntley's outer office and later announced their intention to remain there to protest the specific Honor System case and in support of their other concerns. The news media were alerted to the "sit-in," which also drew the attention of local NAACP members. Civility prevailed (with the exceptions of loud music and disruption of normal business). Huntley explained to the students directly, and through Dean Hubbard, that he could not intervene in the Honor System. He also had no intention of forcibly removing them from his office, but constructive discussions were precluded by what he considered to be a "coercive gesture." The students left the president's office that evening. Around the same time, the Student Executive Committee decided to hear the Honor System case on Sunday afternoon, January 23. The accused student was found guilty and was withdrawn from the university.

Compared with events on other campuses, the "occupation" of the president's office at W&L was modest. But on this small campus, it made an impression. As the university struggled to achieve a healthy, diverse academic community, the pace of change lagged behind everyone's hopes and expectations, partly because every other university was seeking the same thing and partly because of W&L's unique character. The challenge was becoming more complicated: "diversity" now encompassed not only African Americans but other minority or underrepresented racial or ethnic groups, like Latinos and Asians. Like other universities, W&L needed to modify its concept and terminology.

In October 1982, W&L dedicated the new Minority Cultural Center in a former upperclassman dormitory that served as a residence for five undergraduate students and provided office space for SABU and the Black American Law Students Association. The center's main purpose, according to John L. White, the director of minority affairs, was "to promote a sense of community among the minority students" and serve as a site for informal meetings, mini-conferences, art exhibits, small concerts, and study sessions. Governed entirely by the minority students themselves, it was not intended to separate minorities from the rest of the campus community. Rather, White added, "the idea is to provide opportunities through which the students can promote better understanding with the entire University community by having certain events, both formal and informal, that will be interesting and valuable for all students." The new center, along with the three scholarship funds for minorities, became another means of attracting new minority students.[61]

The university's inability to recruit black faculty members was a continuing source of frustration. This problem pervaded all of higher education during the 1970s and the remainder of the century. It was largely a result of the poor educational opportunities available to African Americans before and after integration, and the rapidly expanding opportunities for blacks in business, law, medicine, and other lucrative careers. Only a small number of blacks pursued advanced degrees or scholarly careers. Institutions like the University of North Carolina at Chapel Hill diversified their faculties by hiring some senior professors from black universities, but this tactic fell under heavy criticism from the less well-funded black institutions that had long provided the bulk of higher education to African Americans. Some universities began cultivating promising black scholars as potential employees early in their graduate training. Each college and university competed with all others on the basis of prestige, salary, benefits, and location. The competition to hire from the limited pool of qualified African Americans could be brutal, and it did not end with the first appointment. In many cases, successful black faculty members were almost immediately hired away at a bigger salary. And the majority of blacks who received advanced degrees opted for far more lucrative careers outside the academy.

W&L sought black faculty who would be satisfied to live and work in a small, rural southern community with limited black civic or social life, teaching mostly upper-middle-class white students in a highly traditional setting. Furthermore, they had to be excellent teachers and contributing colleagues. A position at W&L might fade in comparison with generous job offers from Princeton, Yale, UNC, or the University of Michigan. And, for W&L, it was extremely important that minority hires succeed in their work. The result was that the addition of black faculty was painfully slow. The first appointment was Stephen Hobbs in the law school in 1981. Remarkably, Theodore DeLaney worked on the staff at W&L, graduated from the university in 1985, returned to the History Department as a fellow in 1991, and then joined the faculty after receiving his PhD.

Beginning in 1974, the university hired African Americans staff members who could be accessible to black students for counseling and guidance, usually in the role of assistant dean of students and director of minority affairs. Lutrelle Rainey, a local Baptist minister, served only a short time and was succeeded by Don Willis, a third-year law student. Curtis Hubbard arrived in 1976 and left the position soon after the protest in 1977. John L. White, '74, served part-time while he was a law student. But the first African American secretary,

Marjorie Poindexter, a great friend and informal advisor, provided perhaps the most important support for black students. Many W&L faculty and staff also provided assistance for black students during this difficult period of institutional transition—including Huntley, Farrar, John, the other deans, and many faculty members. They helped through regular counseling and academic advising, working with organizations like SABU, providing transportation to local colleges, and intervening when fellow students were unhelpful or insensitive. The university proctor, Charles Murray, known to all as "Murph," also played a crucial role. As Walter Blake recalled, "Murph was cool. Murph understood us. He watched out for us. He knew what was going on. . . . He either diffused situations before they happened or buffered us by keeping certain elements away from the campus that could have made things a bit dicier around here than they really were." Blake added, "If anyone, in my experience with the university, deserves to be an honorary alumnus to this institution, Murph is it."[62]

WHILE DEALING WITH these challenges, the university was also engaged in an extensive review of coeducation and in the most ambitious and successful fundraising campaign in its history. The new curriculum and academic calendar were largely a success, and the law school experienced unprecedented growth during this time. Students were engaged in the usual active social life and in extracurricular activities like the Mock Convention, the CONTACT symposium and other lectures, dramatic and musical presentations, and intramural and intercollegiate athletics. Campus life continued even while it was changing.

The 1970s provided dramatic issues for debate and discussion—Watergate and the Nixon resignation, the "Energy Crisis," the withdrawal from Vietnam, persistent counter-cultural and racial dissent, and the rise of Jimmy Carter and Ronald Reagan—and myriad opportunities for academic and extracurricular activities at W&L. The CONTACT Symposium continued bringing notable speakers to campus, including Truman Capote, George Plimpton, and the radical attorney William Kunstler in 1976.

The *Ring-tum Phi* remained the principal student journalistic voice and began appearing once rather than twice a week in the fall of 1970. University support for publication of the *Southern Collegian* had been terminated in 1966, but *Shenandoah,* initially designed as an outlet for serious student literary writing, was thriving as one of the nation's premier "little quarterlies." Edited by students and by James Boatwright, Dabney Stuart, and Stephen H. Goodwin in the English Department, *Shenandoah* attracted contributions from major writers and poets, including Flannery O'Connor, Reynolds Price, James Dickey, John Dos Passos, Ezra Pound, William Faulkner, Robert Lowell, and Tom Wolfe.[63] Philippe Labro's movie, "Tout Pent Arrirer," based on his experience as a foreign student at W&L in the 1950s and filmed partly on the W&L campus with French actors, had its world premier in Lexington on April 13, 1970.

The Fancy Dress Ball and weekend, long the centerpiece of the social calendar, went by the wayside in 1970 and 1971 as the student body focused on other concerns. It had a rebirth of sorts in February 1972, but in name only. Students attended in T-shirts and the band was Sha-na-na (not even a distant relation of the Glen Miller Orchestra). In 1973, no one showed up in a tuxedo or a gown. In 1974, the Fancy Dress Ball was revived in something like its traditional form, with a Mardi Gras theme and more traditional attire, but the bands were Daddy Rabbit and Billy Preston's group, and one young woman—dared by her date and thinking the young university president was a student—poured beer over Bob Huntley's head. More than thirteen hundred people attended Fancy Dress in 1975, when the theme was "A Salute to Hollywood," featuring the Jimmy Dorsey Orchestra and a more concerted effort to enforce a formal dress requirement. In the new spirit of the times, the ball itself followed a much less formal "grain party" at the off-campus Zollman's Pavilion, with entertainment by the Drifters. While Fancy Dress survived as a quaint tradition and an artifact of a previous era, it could never be the same. The era of formal dance sets and three-day weekends with three and four big bands was over. Even the combos of the 1960s were increasingly displaced by larger, more fiercely electronic rock bands, more often enjoyed in off-campus locations.

The Mock Convention persisted in much the traditional way but with political dramas as a backdrop. The sixteenth Mock Convention was held May 7 and 8, 1976, in the shadow of the Watergate scandal that led to Nixon's impeachment and resignation. The Democrats were invigorated by the chance to retake the White House by defeating the incumbent, Gerald Ford. Sen. William Proxmire of Wisconsin delivered the keynote address, and the platform speaker was senator and former governor Dale Bumpers of Arkansas. The assembled delegates chose the 1972 Mock Convention keynote speaker as their nominee: former Georgia governor Jimmy Carter. For the first time in Mock Convention history, delegates also correctly named the vice-presidential nominee, Sen. Walter Mondale of Minnesota. Even so, the Mock Convention's efforts to shape the platform remained more a reflection of student opinions and preferences than an accurate reflection of the national party platform. Meeting until 1:30 a.m., the delegates voted down most of the liberal planks, much to Senator Proxmire's chagrin. (He wondered aloud which party's convention this was supposed to be.)

In May 1980, it was again the Republicans' turn. Former senator and 1964 presidential candidate Barry Goldwater of Arizona received a warm reception as the keynote speaker, and Louisiana congressman Henson McMoore addressed the convention on the platform. Two W&L alumni were key participants: William E. Brock III of Tennessee, chairman of the Republican National Committee, provided the opening address at the third session, and Sen. John W. Warner of Virginia (then married to the actress Elizabeth Taylor) led the parade, which featured the Budweiser Clydesdales and an African elephant named "Jewel." The convention nominated Hollywood actor and former California governor Ronald Reagan on the first ballot, with 79 percent of the delegate votes, and James Baker of Tennessee for vice president.

Throughout an era of sociocultural change and political upheaval, athletics continued to engage student interest through participation in intramurals as well as a full range of intercollegiate sports. Despite continuing pressures from alumni, by this time nonsubsidized athletics were the rule. In September 1968, soon after Huntley's appointment as president, W&L mourned head football coach Lee McLaughlin's unexpected and untimely death at age fifty-one just weeks before he was to become athletic director. In an August 14 memorandum, Huntley reminded the trustees that it had been McLaughlin who rebuilt the football program following the end of subsidization in 1954: "he, more than any one person, has been responsible for the almost unbelievable success of that program in the years since." The man known as "Coach Mac," Huntley wrote, "was as beloved here by students and faculty and by the Lexington community as any person ever connected with this institution."[64]

Suddenly confronted with the need to appoint a new athletic director, the university offered the job to a promising administrator who had played lacrosse at Duke and coached the W&L soccer and lacrosse teams in 1955–58 before coaching those sports at the University of Virginia: Eugene F. "Gene" Corrigan. His time at W&L was brief. He returned to the University of Virginia as athletic director in January 1971 and subsequently served in the same post at the University of Notre Dame and then, for ten years, as commissioner of the Atlantic Coast Conference.

W&L turned next to a thirty-eight-year-old alumnus, William D. "Bill" McHenry, '54, then at Lebanon College in Pennsylvania. A football and lacrosse star in his college days, he was president of the U.S. Lacrosse Coaches Association, and his brother Bob, also a W&L alumnus, was head coach of the sport at Yale.[65] McHenry took over the football head-coaching duties from Buck Leslie in 1973, the same year that Jack Emmer began his enormously successful eleven seasons as head coach of the lacrosse team.

After the end of subsidization, W&L had tried to limit its schedule to competition against similar "peers," a task that continued into the 1970s and beyond. Alumni still complained that traditional rivals Virginia, Virginia Tech, and Davidson were no longer on the regular football and basketball schedules, which now included schools "no one ever heard of." In 1962, W&L competed in the NCAA Division III College Athletic Conference (CAC) and won a number of championships before becoming a charter member in 1976 of the Old Dominion Athletic Conference (ODAC), in which most W&L teams compete today. It was a long way from the Gator Bowl, but one W&L sport—lacrosse—continued at the Division I level, though without athletic scholarships.

The university's success in lacrosse gave W&L fans a lot to cheer about. In the glory years of the 1970s, W&L competed successfully at the highest level against much larger schools—including Virginia, North Carolina, Maryland, Johns Hopkins, and Navy—earning significant national recognition. The Generals played in the NCAA tournament in every year from 1973 to 1978 and again in 1980. After undefeated regular seasons, W&L advanced to the Final Four in 1973 and 1974, losing first in the semifinals to Maryland and a year later to Johns Hopkins. The Generals returned to the Final Four in 1975, taking revenge on Johns Hopkins by ending its twenty-seven-home-game winning streak but again losing in the semifinals.

It was increasingly difficult to field a competitive team against schools that subsidized individual athletes. W&L provided aid to athletes on the same basis as it did to all other students, often offering a combination of grants, loans, and work study not comparable to full athletic scholarships. Coach Emmer complained to Huntley in 1978, "Washington and Lee has not been competitive from a financial aid standpoint in recruiting the outstanding lacrosse player who meets our academic standards."[66] Other coaches, even those competing at the Division III level, shared his frustration and criticized the admissions office for turning down promising athletes—not for scholarships but for admission. Like many other liberal arts colleges, W&L did in fact extend preferences in admission to students with special abilities, including athletics.

Director of Admissions Bill Hartog shared his own frustrations with Bill McHenry. In a March 1982 memorandum, he laid out the details of admissions policies and procedures, noting that 765 of 1,600 applicants had been offered admission, and 200 had been placed on the wait list. The 765 averaged scores at the 82nd percentile on the SAT. Hartog noted that he had personally reviewed 125 applications of students identified as having athletic promise. Their test scores were notably lower than other students offered admission, and they ranked collectively in the 65th percentile of their classes. Nevertheless, he had agreed to admit 65 of these applicants. Others he placed on the wait list, mostly because "the athletics department" was interested in them rather than because of "any particular academic strength on their part." He reiterated his pledge to the coaches to "give priority to any athlete in whom they have an interest if that student's record is competitive." In his view, this was a "rather liberal policy" and probably more generous than an admissions committee might be. But "I am reaching the end of my rope." He could be more liberal in admissions but not "equally liberal" with scholarships.[67]

The president of Davidson appealed to Huntley in 1978 not to drop the college from W&L's football schedule. While remaining in NCCA Division IAA, Davidson did not subsidize students for athletic performance but did "make grants up to demonstrated need rather than require football players to take job and loan packages." They played many of the teams on W&L's schedule, like Hampden-Sydney, and would be willing to compete in other sports as well as football. Huntley responded that he would personally like to see athletic competition between Davidson and W&L but noted the difficulties. W&L did "not provide athletic scholarship assistance in any sport even to the extent permitted by Division III regulations," Huntley wrote: "Our aid packages for athletes are literally indistinguishable from the aid packages for non-athletes, are never conditioned on athletic ability or participation, and contain no additional grant component beyond that available to any student with similar need." He admitted that schools like Hampden-Sydney and Randolph-Macon maintained policies similar to Davidson's but that schools most similar to W&L were in the north and east. "At the moment, our policy is one of scheduling football with those schools in Virginia with which we have a chance of competing, even though their scholarship program is more extensive than ours, and at the same time try to find places on the schedules of the schools north of us which have programs similar to ours." This, he said, had led W&L to drop Davidson from the football schedule.[68]

In 1982, and after a 9–4 season, Jack Emmer reflected on whether W&L should remain at the Division I level in lacrosse. W&L competed successfully with a "Division III philosophy" against Division I programs, but "more colleges have upgraded their lacrosse programs with increased athletic scholarship monies," he wrote. More competitive admissions and decreasing financial aid made recruiting more difficult; indeed, five or six accepted but "needy" lacrosse players received no financial aid at W&L and decided to go elsewhere. Emmer thought the university should continue a Division I program, "as long as we have the raw talent to be competitive with the top teams in Division I but through such intangibles as tradition, dedication, campus enthusiasm, etc., we continued to be successful in 1982 with a 9–4 record." His players could not accept a "downgrade" of the program to Division III. McHenry endorsed this recommendation and added, "Jack Emmer and his coaching staff got more out of the talent that was available to them than at any time since I have been associated with Washington and Lee."[69] Huntley agreed. But in 1983 Emmer ended his final season at W&L at 5–7, his only losing record in Lexington. He spent the remaining twenty-one years of his head-coaching career at the US Military Academy and retired with the most wins of any lacrosse coach in NCAA history, having taken teams from three different colleges to the NCAA tournament. Dennis Daly succeeded him at W&L, posting losing seasons until 1987, when W&L moved to Division III and immediately recorded an 11–4 season and went again to the NCAA tournament.

As many as a third of W&L students participated in the twelve intercollegiate sports and more than two-thirds in intramural sports.[70] Even in the absence of athletic scholarships or Division I competition, many students made sports a major focus of their time at W&L. Significant improvements in athletic facilities resulting from the capital campaign were put to full use. From 1973 to 1977, McHenry took over the head-coaching duties in football, but the team struggled against strong conference competition until 1981, when they won the ODAC title under Gary Fallon. Verne Canfield's basketball Generals were more successful, winning at least half of their games in the previous ten seasons, going 19–7 in 1975. The wrestling squad won conference championships in three consecutive seasons (1976–79) under Gary Franke, and Dick Miller's cross-country team was also competitive. Win or lose, W&L offered sports opportunities that complemented rather than overshadowed the university's academic mission.

A DECADE USHERED IN by campus turmoil and marked by changes in student life and university policies settled into new patterns of greater student independence, institutional accountability, and resource demands. Many aspects of university life—the academic grind, social pressures and entertainments, and extracurricular activities (especially athletics)—persisted, though reshaped by changing styles and expectations. After 1970, Washington and Lee faced growing challenges as it tried to maintain an acceptable balance between tradition and transformation.

~~~

CHAPTER TEN

ON THE
THRESHOLD

BOB HUNTLEY WAS approaching the fifteenth year of his presidency, and while he knew that the trustees would welcome his continuation in the job, he also knew that he had already served beyond the typical time in office for college presidents and that President Gaines had perhaps stayed in the job too long. The big remaining tasks—especially the likely necessity of revisiting coeducation and tackling problems in the fraternity system—would demand at least five more years. After consulting with his wife Evelyn, he decided that fifteen years were enough. The major expansion of the campus, greater financial stability, growth of the endowment, and many other accomplishments made his a tough act to follow.

Bob Huntley received accolades as he stepped down, including many warm letters from faculty colleagues and even a poem—"Fare Thee Well, But Not Forever"—from Bill Pusey, who had once been his teacher. The board established, in his honor, the Robert Edward Royall Huntley Professorship, the first named chair in the law school. He accepted a senior executive position with Best Products, Inc., in Richmond, to continue his association with Sydney and Frances Lewis, and he remained a member of the Board of Philip Morris, Inc. He and Evelyn moved to Richmond but would eventually return to Lexington. Fred Cole wrote from his home in Chapel Hill: "I have much difficulty in thinking of Washington & Lee without you as President. . . . I am proud to be able to call you friend and former associate." Huntley replied, "I admit I have some difficulty in thinking of Washington and Lee without either you or me as President, but I remain convinced that the change at this time is a good move for me and for the school."[1]

A presidential search began, this time without an obvious successor in the wings. James Ballengee, the new rector, chaired the board's Presidential Search Committee and appointed Dean William Watt as chair of the fourteen-member Faculty Advisory Committee.[2] Ballengee shared the advisory committee's criteria—boilerplate typical of such searches—with the other trustees and appended a four-page statement written by alumnus and senior faculty member Sidney Coulling.

In addition to all the usual qualities—intelligence, vigor, and judgment—Coulling hoped the new president would possess "a sociable, outgoing personality" and moderation: "By moderateness I mean the realization that this is essentially a traditional, conservative institution where extreme views can be disruptive rather than helpful, and where effective change is made gradually." A new president should accept the role of students and faculty in university governance and respect W&L's traditional identity as an all-male institution but be "open-minded on the question of its becoming coeducational." His (a female president was at the time unthinkable) "primary responsibility" should be consolidating the "gains made in the past decade" as a foundation for moving forward, especially in three areas. The "number one priority" was dealing with "the problem of our decline in academic strength." Coulling believed, as did many other faculty members, that the student body was less qualified, more passive, and even "anti-intellectual." Secondly, even after the end of subsidization, the athletic program had grown "out of balance with the academic, as evidenced by enlarged coaching staffs, increased practice time for some athletic teams, and pressure on admissions to accept athletes." Thirdly, a new president should address W&L's "widespread reputation as a school of bourbon, fraternities, and parties." Among other issues, he noted an "obvious imbalance" between the College and the School of Commerce, which could be addressed by supporting the humanities, by "fostering the idea of college life as a time for intellectual inquiry," and by "encouraging attitudes that counteract the pragmatism of much of our present student body." An "obvious cleavage between the undergraduate body and the law school" would also demand the president's attention. At one point, Coulling noted that in many ways a new president would stand in Bob Huntley's shadow and should thus be satisfied with rewarding work that is "less visibly dramatic than in the past." But Coulling's own outline of the challenges suggested that the work might be very dramatic indeed.[3]

The search led—after sorting through almost a hundred names—to the election on September 1, 1982, of the fifty-one-year-old executive vice president and provost at Virginia Tech, John Delane Wilson, who accepted the new challenge in Lexington after a long and successful career spent mostly in public higher education. A native of Lapeer, Michigan, he excelled as a history major at Michigan State University and on the football field as a star defensive halfback for the Spartans, named national champions in 1952. President of his senior class and a member of the first Academic All-America Team ever chosen, he pursued graduate studies in English literature as a Rhodes Scholar at Oxford University, leading to his MA degree—and to his marriage in 1957 to Anne Veronica Yeomans, an English subject. After two years service as an intelligence officer with the Strategic Air Command, he returned to Michigan State, received his PhD in 1965, and directed the Honors College while teaching courses in Elizabethan literature, particularly Shakespeare. In 1968, he became president of Wells College, a women's institution in Aurora, New York. Seven years later he was named provost at Virginia Tech. While in Blacksburg, he was a trustee of Hollins College and chaired the Virginia Foundation for the Humanities and Public Policy. When he accepted the presidency of W&L, the Wilsons had four children ranging in age from fourteen to twenty-two.[4]

No one was more surprised by his appointment than John Wilson. He did not apply for the job, send in any information, or ask to be considered. He was invited to Lexington to meet with the selection committee for a day in June 1982. Three weeks later, W&L offered him the job. After consulting with his family and reflecting on this new opportunity—so different from Virginia Tech—he accepted. "I discovered," he recalled, "that my heart really was in those four undergraduate years." In the Jeffersonian ideal of an aristocracy of talent, he acknowledged, "I'm frankly an elitist."[5]

John Wilson's associations were mostly with public land-grant universities, though his own academic and cultural tastes inclined to the liberal arts. In addition to his studies in history and literature, he had a life-long love of music, drama, and the visual arts. Instead of filling his office with smoke, as his two predecessors had, Wilson filled his with music. A classical or operatic recording always played in the background, even during meetings, and at a particularly significant moment in a piece, Wilson would raise his hand to stop the conversation until the passage was finished and then signal when talk could resume. Culturally literate as he was, some people noticed that his polyester suits and sport coats didn't quite fit the W&L style, even after conventional dress was long gone. But John Wilson was acutely aware of the traditions and social environment of his new institution and how he could best find his place within them.

Wilson was installed as W&L's twenty-first president on the afternoon of May 19,

1983, before fourteen hundred people, including representatives of forty-six colleges. The weather was rainy, windy, and cold, and everything was moved from the front lawn to the gymnasium of the Warner Center. His friend Thomas A. Bartlett, the chancellor of the University of Alabama System and former president of Colgate University, introduced Wilson as "one of the most admired and respected people in American higher education."[6]

Already in office for just over four months, Wilson's inaugural remarks were perfectly attuned to the audience and the W&L gestalt. He began by recognizing many people in the audience—from special guests to trustees and members of the grounds crew and food service—and he acknowledged his debt to key figures in the university pantheon: Gaines, Leyburn, Gilliam, and Huntley. Leyburn had visited him in his office that morning and found a copy of his own 1947 address to the faculty on Wilson's desk—which the new president described as "a seminal document in our recent history" which "issued a call to Washington and Lee to be better still and to reach out still further and to aspire to be first among the great teaching institutions." These leaders and others, Wilson said, "form the base cleft of Washington and Lee; they provide the great undertones of the place, the musical foundation as it were." But "the treble cleft is no less important," describing "a pleasing harmony of purposes," including the grounds crew who mowed the grass around the academic buildings first so as not to disturb classes. And, perhaps wishfully as much as thankfully, Wilson acknowledged Rector Ballengee's assurance that the president's task was to express clearly the university's needs and that the trustees would "make certain that you and the faculty have the means to achieve those ends."[7]

Of course, Wilson acknowledged Lee, whose leadership had forever joined the liberal arts with "the legitimacy of applied knowledge" and structured professional studies firmly upon "broadly based work in the arts and sciences." In words that have even more relevance today, Wilson said that W&L had no aspirations to be "a highly polished, stainless steel model of cost efficiency designed chiefly to train persons for pre-defined places in the occupational complex of what is often called the real world." In his view, the "real world" is "marked profoundly by moral uncertainty, by nuance and ambiguity, by ideological stress, by confusion of choice and motive, by human passion, by suffering and pain, sometimes by hatred and also by happiness, by moments of joy and love." This is the world that students must be prepared for, not by imposing "a false clarity upon complexity and ambiguity" but by developing "a tolerance for ambiguity" and an appreciation for "vicarious experience"—the imagination, history, literature, philosophy, and the arts. "The process I describe," he continued, "will help students begin the lifelong task of understanding the cultural envelope in which they live and breathe" so that "they will one day stop asking what is wrong with Hamlet and will ask instead what is wrong with the Denmark it is Hamlet's misfortune to live in." Wilson's was a deeply felt plea for the importance of "cultural literacy." Much as Leyburn had said thirty-five years before, W&L should be not a place of conformity and stability but one with ample "room in it for idiosyncrasy, for delight in odd ideas," for "strange juxtapositions of seemingly disparate things, for contemplative moments, for the unrequired book or the unassigned symphony." When he concluded, the faculty must have been pleased—this was not bad for a star defensive halfback!

Wilson would need as much good will as any new president of a traditional institution propelled by strong winds for change in a fast-moving, competitive educational milieu. In January 1983, shortly after he had arrived, Wilson began a practice that continued throughout his presidency—sending regular (at least monthly) letters to trustees that were substantive, thoughtful, personal, informal, and often surprisingly frank. He wrote these missives in longhand on a legal pad, often on his kitchen table. In this way, he informed trustees about campus events and policies—and the man they had chosen to lead the university. In this first letter, he shared his plans to have all the seniors in groups of twenty over for dinner at Lee House and to meet individually over time with all members of the faculty. He began with a personal reflection, doubtless heartfelt but also carefully chosen: "I have now experienced that mild sense of euphoria you all have known in past years and which can only come to one who, in the early morning, walks along the colonnade, past those great white symbols of permanence and tradition, safe in the knowledge that it is 'his' place."[8]

The new president's style was different from that of his predecessor. Huntley was straightforward, a lawyer's lawyer, who preferred brevity and getting to the point. Wilson was, in comparison, downright literary. Law school faculty, accustomed to short memos from Huntley, were taken aback by one of Wilson's first communications that continued, as Sally Wiant recalled, "for a page and a half." Not only that, but he wrote "about what it was like to sit in his office and look out over the state of the university and see the sun setting on Liberty Hall," about "the peals of laughter and the cheers trickling over from the lacrosse game."[9] Lawyers didn't talk this way, but any fears they may have had were allayed by Wilson's commitment to what he called "the jewel in the crown."

⟶⟶

JOHN WILSON BECAME president of W&L after the post–World War II "golden age" of higher education had begun to fade. Greater access to college, the proliferation of new institutions, and the expansion of older ones marked an enormous growth in higher education that inspired even more ambitious plans. By the time Wilson was president, 8.65 million students were enrolled in more than 2,500 institutions, including a rapidly rising number of community colleges. Three-quarters of them were enrolled in public institutions in the 1970s. But as the economy faltered and enrollments leveled off, colleges and universities were often overextended—with inadequate endowments, bonded indebtedness for buildings not yet completed, and an array of degree programs and larger faculties premised on the expectation of continued rapid growth. "They were ill equipped," one historian observed, "to handle sustained declines in funding."[10] The anxiety only increased with the actual drop in overall higher education enrollment in 1975–76.

Helter-skelter growth also sowed confusion about the mission and role of individual institutions, most trying to serve as many constituencies as possible. Coordinating boards in many states pushed to curtail unnecessary program duplication, but the drive for prestige and greater funding was powerful. Confusion grew with the introduction of "portable" federal financial aid in 1972 (known as Pell Grants) that gave grants directly to students rather than to institutions, fueling a rampant for-profit higher-education industry that quickly became almost entirely dependent on this indirect government support.

As institutions touted their key roles in economic development and the rising earning power of their graduates, students turned to increasingly vocational degrees. Especially for families with little experience of college, the purpose of getting an education was, understandably, to land a high-paying job rather than to attain broad cultural literacy, critical thinking, and self-fulfillment. Using specific employment to gauge the value of a college degree became a burden—some would say a curse—haunting higher education into the twenty-first century. Beginning in the 1970s, students flooded programs in business, engineering, and pre-professional studies leading to law and medicine. Later, the demand shifted to the new field of computer science. A proliferation of undergraduate programs in criminal justice, social work, and a variety of allied health fields also highlighted the vocational emphasis. This shift resulted in a relative decline in the liberal arts that has continued, though most institutions have retained at least minimal requirements in general education as a foundation for vocational and specialized programs. These trends accelerated with the rise in consumerism, as students began to see themselves as consumers or customers and higher education as a commodity measured by its employment outcomes and status in the marketplace. Institutions began to think in the same way, developing extensive marketing campaigns and competitive strategies to increase "market share." Demand for more campus amenities—recreational facilities (including climbing walls and even water parks), intercollegiate athletics, dining halls and food courts, and residence halls that resembled hotels—was a measure of this competition, especially among less prestigious institutions. The rise of college rating systems in the 1990s essentially guaranteed the dominance of a consumer mentality. These trends became embedded in the higher-education landscape and were noted even at older, traditional liberal arts institutions like Washington and Lee, prompting Sid Coulling's lament to the presidential search committee about the overemphasis on athletics, social life, and "the pragmatism of much of our present student body."

Even as the economy recovered in the 1980s, public funding continued to decline, competition for private resources increased in both the public and independent sectors, expenditures on athletics and amenities escalated, and student expectations for access and amenities rose. But overall public confidence in higher education eroded, due to the confusing variety of institutions and missions, rising tuition costs, the excesses of some of the most prominent schools and the malfeasance of others (especially the for-profit sector), and the reality that even the best academic preparation could not guarantee lifetime prosperity or a job in times of economic recession. Unprecedented student access led to the perception of a college degree as an "essential" ticket to a good life, so higher education was held accountable for much that was well beyond any institution's control. In this environment, higher education became the focus of a continuing trend of increasing regulation and government demands for accountability, ranging from elaborate academic program approvals to financial accounting and regular reporting on virtually every activity. Ironically, the rapid growth in the numbers of administrators and middle management in virtually all institutions—so roundly criticized by government agencies as detracting from educational goals—was a direct outgrowth of increased regulation and accountability. Although American higher education had become the envy of the world, it was increasingly beleaguered by its success, especially in the public sector.

Even a small college in Lexington, Virginia—never the "ivory tower" envisioned by idealists or recalled by alumni—could be caught up in the social and cultural changes reverberating on college campuses. Race was only one of the elements that transformed traditional strictures and expectations. African Americans continued to demand equity, opportunity, and recognition of the grave damage wrought by centuries of slavery and oppression. Hispanics, Asians, and other groups also insisted on overdue rights and recognition, and they sometimes clashed with one another. Many women sought equal access to higher education and the professions, equity in compensation, and an end to the misogyny that riddled academia as well as other areas of American life. Homosexuals also began to break the shackles of prejudice in their own movement for civil rights, but they faced deep cultural resistance, often rooted in prejudice and religious belief.

The pressures to recognize these groups and causes and to rectify past injustices produced a fierce conservative backlash, with universities often caught in the middle. This was especially the case with "affirmative action" in college admissions, favoring students from groups that had long been underrepresented in higher education. These efforts to effect social change and better prepare students for the "real world" of the future were attacked by those who saw them as abandoning a commitment to academic merit and fostering "political correctness"—that is, as undermining free inquiry and freedom of speech by establishing intellectual orthodoxy in support of broadly political ends and selected individuals or groups. Faculties were accused of foisting immorality and political liberalism on their students. These "culture wars" and "identity politics" resonated throughout the country but were debated with special fervor in colleges and universities, which only added to growing public skepticism about higher education.

The expansion in higher education generated many new faculty jobs and a proliferation of graduate programs that produced—even overproduced—new PhDs. Faculties became less mobile after 1970, and curricula more diverse. The job market for newly minted PhDs collapsed in the early years of the decade, though competition for the best faculty in the most desirable fields was still fierce. With time, the job market recovered in some fields, but many public universities relied increasingly on part-time and non-tenure-track faculty to teach basic courses. Curricula now included new fields like computer science and various interdisciplinary degree programs in women's studies, urban studies, American studies, African American studies, Hispanic studies, and regional studies in Asia, Latin America, and the Middle East. These programs often contributed to intellectual ferment and new perspectives, but some were also criticized for watering down disciplinary content and rigor, and for fostering "political correctness."

Washington and Lee weathered these trends of the 1970s and entered the 1980s with positive momentum. The university was not so much over-extended as "under built" for a larger curriculum and student body. New re-sources were still a major challenge, and while W&L did not entirely overcome the problem, the university did address it. The economy posed the same prob-lems for all institutions, and keeping up with national standards and competi-tion in faculty salaries and facilities was W&L's primary intended use of new resources and a larger endowment. The curriculum reflected more variety and emphasis on area and interdisciplinary studies, but W&L—unlike many others, especially in the public sector—did not launch an array of new degree pro-grams or seek to serve all interests and purposes, and was thus able to maintain its identity and focus as a liberal arts institution. Even so, enrollments defi-nitely moved toward majors in commerce and preprofessional programs, and rising student expectations for facilities, services, and amenities heightened the competition with other institutions, as W&L sought to consolidate and apply its recent progress toward being among the very best of institutions of its type in the country. Reaching this goal meant successfully competing for the most talented and committed students. By 1983, national demographics suggested that retaining an all-male enrollment would make that task especially prob-lematic. And other serious threats to the health of university life—especially the fraternities—demanded immediate attention.

AS PROVOST AT a large public university, John Wilson was no stranger to these trends in higher education, but he approached his new responsibilities with enthusiasm. He assembled the principal university leadership (the Monday luncheon group originally organized by Bob Huntley as the nucleus) for a two-day retreat at Skylark Farm in late July 1983. While Wilson had been gathering information and sizing up the issues since January, this was his first opportu-nity to systematically address them with all the key players outside the usual press of campus business. It was also a chance to frame the issues to reflect his sense of priorities, his major concerns and ambitions, and what he had learned from his almost seven months living and working on campus. This would, in fact, be the first in a series of Skylark meetings he would call periodically to assess circumstances and progress, air different views, share information, and make sure every issue was on the table.

The meeting agenda contained eight major headings, beginning with the overall financial situation and budget forecast, and moving next to the closely related matters of admissions and student financial aid. Wilson introduced each section with a brief comment and some requests. The financial projections for the next decade, for example, should include "a parallel set of projections based upon an enrollment of 2,000 students." Under student financial aid, he noted the increasing offers of "no-need scholarships" to strong applicants by many top private institutions and the possibility that W&L's "loan/grant ratios . . . are becoming uncompetitive." Dealing with this problem could be critically important, he observed, in the "recruitment of superior students."[11]

The next three major items—fraternity life, residential life, and the admission of women—preceded issues of faculty development and the curriculum. Wilson was up-to-date on fraternity matters and recognized "the fact that fraternities . . . have a monopoly on social life (thus commanding recruitment advantages they haven't earned." He posed six specific questions for discussion, including questions about the role and purpose of fraternities, their costs and management, and how to "proceed to reform the anti-intellectual character of social life in the houses" and perhaps also "a social system that seems to be based inordinately upon unhealthy stereotyping." This discussion had a bearing on the general issue of residential life, as Wilson thought that a much higher proportion of the student population should reside in university housing. The current situation, he observed, "enervates our co-curricular programs, our esprit, our sense of ourselves as a community." W&L should also address housing needs for law students and foreign students, and consider increasing enrollment to 1,650 and admitting undergraduate women. The issue of coeducation was placed in the middle of this agenda, but its resolution was hovering over all other decisions. Wilson was working on a detailed analysis but wanted everyone to know "that I am aiming to resolve this matter one way or the other by May of next year." Quickly addressing the issue was important because it "is on everyone's mind here in Lexington and we must clear the air one way or the other as soon as we possibly can."

Many matters that had been discussed at length for years now demanded definitive decisions. Discussions were based on a ten-year projection assuming 6 percent annual inflation and a faculty salary pool for increases of 9 percent. Was this adequate to hire and retain the best faculty, especially since the salary averages might be even "further behind" in the law school? Under this agenda item, Wilson also mentioned teacher evaluation, visiting faculty, special leaves, basic research support in the sciences, more formality in the tenure and promotion process, expanding the administrative role of the department chairs, and whether or not W&L should "employ a 'star' system approach" in appointing a few key faculty.

W&L was still refining and developing its new curriculum and the calendar introduced in 1970, and this remained a work in progress during the dynamic 1980s and 1990s. Wilson had already decided to appoint an ad hoc task force to help establish a freestanding computer science major, inside or outside the Mathematics Department. He also wanted a fresh look at the physics/engineering program. He thought Russian Studies could be added to the list of area studies programs that already included Asian Studies.

If all this was not enough to engage those assembled at Skylark Farm, he added seventeen other brief items that could fill in "our idle moments." These included making operational changes for the board of trustees, recruiting minority faculty and better integrating minority students into campus life, considering options for the intercollegiate athletic program, and "bridging the psychological ravine between the Law School and the undergraduate programs." The Skylark agenda thus not only reflected Wilson's views and priorities but also brought the perspective of the latest higher-education best practices to W&L.

Two days were not sufficient to cover all these items. The important thing was the range and ambition of the agenda itself and the obvious and implied connections among all its components. Wilson wanted the board to know what he was thinking and doing, and he forwarded the Skylark agenda to the trustees in mid-August. The ultimate goal, he wrote, was to "create a strongly positive environment for young people," in which they could "rapidly grow in intellectual and in personal maturity"—a work always in progress and one to be pursued in smaller steps toward definable, achievable objectives. The "most important task over the next twelve months" for the board would "be to participate thoughtfully in the process of deciding what it is we must aim for if Washington and Lee is to be in the exclusive first rank of serious places in the year 1994."[12]

Washington and Lee had reached a new financial plateau in capacity, as well as in expectations, aspirations, and the strength of its competition. The future depended on robust enrollment and the continued support of its alumni and other key donors. Total endowment assets in June 1984 stood at almost $37 million, and the Pratt Fund at over $13 million. (Mr. Pratt's original gift of $12.5 million in 1976 was to be used for student financial aid and faculty salaries. He requested, but did not mandate, that the fund be expended within twenty-five years, but the board of trustees decided to preserve the principal and spend the proceeds according to his wishes.) Tuition revenue still accounted for over 50 percent of the university's budget (but less than it had been in previous years) and covered almost all expenditures for instruction. The Plant Fund for buildings and equipment held long-term debt of $11,770,000 from three loans through the Virginia College Building Authority's sale of tax-exempt bonds for capital projects, and $90,000 from a local bank for a data-processing and telecommunications system. Limiting the reliance on tuition, and thus tuition increases, and further increasing the endowment were ongoing challenges. W&L still required that all student financial aid be provided through government grants or private gifts, rather than drawn from operating revenues. The competition among top schools for the "best and brightest" students created strong pressures for more and larger "merit" scholarships, while need-based aid remained critical to diversifying the student body. A loan fund with assets of $2,681,000 held private gifts to assist students in financing their education; students could also get aid from the National Direct Student Loan Program (requiring a university commitment of one dollar for every ten granted by the government).[13]

RETIRING TRUSTEES joined a growing list of emeriti, replaced by new, and usually younger, faces. The larger number of trustees was more typical of other private institutions. The Development Program prepared the board as a group for more active involvement in direct fund-raising and generated greater expectations for individual generosity as part of an evolving "culture of philanthropy." Some stalwarts left active service in 1983—including Sydney Lewis and Jack Warner—and new trustees appointed in that year and in 1984 included Frances Lewis and the author Tom Wolfe. By 1990, new appointees included William B. Ogilvie Jr. and Virginia Rogers Holton (1986) and Harold F. Lenfest Jr. (1989). A. Stevens Miles Jr. of Louisville, Kentucky—who as a student represented W&L on the field at halftime of the Gator Bowl—succeeded James Ballengee as rector.

The growth of the university was also evident from the rolls of administrators and faculty. Thirty-eight administrative officers in 1980 included deans,

directors, and an expanding group of assistants, associates, supervisors, ac-
countants, and coordinators. More people were needed to manage a modern
university, as reflected in newer positions, such as university counseling psychologist, director of minority affairs, and university photographer. Nineteen
staff worked in the university library and fourteen in the law library. The athletic staff grew to sixteen full-time positions. Also important—especially as far
as the students were concerned—were the university proctor, Charles "Murph"
Murray, and the assistant proctor, William "Burr" Datz. Ten years later, the
number of administrative officers had risen to seventy-four, with even more
midlevel coordinator, associate, assistant, and other support positions, now
grouped into the conventional categories of academic administration, student
affairs, admissions and financial aid, finances and personnel, and university
relations. The list expanded to ninety-eight in 1995.

Some senior administrators, many of them W&L alumni, continued to serve
in the Wilson administration, joined by an infusion of new leadership from the
outside. Farris P. Hotchkiss remained director of development but was also
director of university relations in 1982, which included oversight of communications and alumni affairs; he became vice president of university relations in
1987. Frank Parsons was university editor in addition to his duties as executive
assistant to the president. James Whitehead carried the new title of curator
for his work with the Reeves Collection and remained secretary of the board,
but he relinquished his financial responsibilities in 1980 to a new treasurer,
Emmett Stewart Epley. Ed Atwood remained dean of the School of Commerce,
Economics and Politics. Lewis John continued as dean of students until 1990,
when he returned to full-time service on the faculty and was succeeded by
David L. Howison. Dean of the College William Watt retired in 1984, and in
1987 his successor, John William Elrod, was additionally named vice president
for academic affairs (now the standard designation for the chief academic officer and second-ranking university official). Originally from Georgia, and with
degrees in the philosophy of religion from Columbia University, Elrod taught
at Iowa State University for thirteen years before arriving at W&L. Larry C.
Peppers, a Vanderbilt PhD, left the faculty of Creighton University to become
dean of the School of Commerce in 1986.

A university alumnus (and future W&L president) with a PhD from Syracuse, Kenneth Ruscio, '76, was appointed assistant dean for freshmen and
residence life in 1987 and associate dean of the School of Commerce in 1991.
Richard B. Sessoms was named director of alumni programs and secretary in

1983. In 1987, James D. Farrar, '49, the long-time director of admissions who had led the way in integrating and diversifying W&L's student body, was appointed associate director of special programs. His wife, Anne S. Farrar, had been associate director of development since 1985. Their son, James D. Farrar, Jr., '74, who had literally grown up on the W&L campus and was a four-year letterman in lacrosse and football, was named associate director of alumni programs in 1988 after a time as teacher, coach, and administrator at the Episcopal High School in Alexandria, Virginia. Farrar moved on to succeed Sessoms in 1990 as director of alumni programs and executive secretary of the Alumni Association. Frank Parsons further embellished his jack-of-all-trades reputation, becoming coordinator of capital planning in 1989 (an activity in which he had long been engaged, without a title). Robert P. Fure, a faculty member in English, was designated director of special programs in 1981, a job that would grow to include extensive travel itineraries as well as year-round programs on campus, particularly popular with—but not limited to—alumni.

The faculty ranks also grew, with new appointees bringing a dedication to the classroom and excellent credentials from leading institutions. The 1980 course catalog listed 168 active ranked faculty members: eighty-three professors (including several visiting faculty members but not including the eleven emeriti), thirty-three associate professors, and fifty-two assistant professors. Five instructors, some of whom would be promoted to assistant professor, rounded out this core professoriate. The group of thirteen lecturers included visitors and other temporary teachers, eight of them in the law school. The total law faculty had now grown to twenty-eight—eleven professors, two associate professors, seven assistant professors, and the eight lecturers.

In his 1986 Founder's Day remarks, John Wilson described faculty recruitment as "renewing our primary resource," a task made more urgent in the face of so many anticipated retirements in the coming decade. The Long-Range Plan Steering Committee estimated in 1989 that during the next ten years almost a quarter of the full-time faculty would retire. Coupled with the need to expand the teaching force, these retirements could necessitate hiring sixty new faculty members. While a challenge, Wilson also noted that this situation presented an opportunity to increase "the number of women, African Americans, and internationally educated individuals who populate our campus."[14]

Even though a surplus of PhDs emerged in some liberal arts disciplines in the early 1970s and afterward, the total number of new doctoral graduates was falling in the 1990s. The competition for first-rate professors in history,

English, sociology, psychology, philosophy, and other fields actually intensi-fied but was most challenging in the sciences, engineering, and in business specialties like finance. In every area, Washington and Lee had unusually high expectations that all faculty be capable and dedicated teachers, willing to make work with students their highest priority. Scholarship was appreciated and expected, but it was to be done in support of work in the classroom, laboratory, and with individual students. Competitive salaries and fringe benefits were critical for attracting good faculty. University efforts in the 1960s and 1970s were aimed at bringing W&L's faculty salary scales in line with those at similar institutions throughout the country. According to the AAUP annual survey, the median total compensation of W&L faculty in 1972–73 was in the top quintile of similar institutions and exceeded those at Haverford, Gettysburg, Davidson, Swarthmore, Oberlin, Williams, and Amherst; in the Commonwealth, it was exceeded only by the University of Virginia (including its graduate schools). Huntley observed that in "only 13 years we have risen from a position of being merely average in this respect to a position of leadership."[15]

W&L remained competitive in a 1983–84 survey but with disciplinary varia-tions and a rising degree of salary compression.[16] Entry-level salaries for as-sistant professors were most sensitive to the market and rose most rapidly. But proven senior faculty members were also in high demand, and many a dean witnessed the hiring away of promising and carefully cultivated junior faculty just as they rose into the tenured ranks. While W&L was less attractive for faculty primarily interested in advanced research and the financial support and relief from teaching duties that many larger universities provided, it also had advantages for those interested in a traditional, intimate academic envi-ronment with the opportunity to work closely with good students and equally dedicated colleagues.

Average W&L faculty salaries rose over the 1960s by 77 percent for profes-sors (from C to B in the AAUP salary grades), 65 percent for associate profes-sors (from C to A), and 69 percent for assistant professors (B to A). Only the average salary for professors significantly exceeded inflation, reflecting the university's effort to address salary issues in that rank, especially as promotions added twenty professors over the decade. From 1974–75 to 1985–86, average salaries rose at an even faster clip: 144 percent for professors, 139 percent for associate professors, and 140 percent for assistant professors. In all but one year, the salary amounts were at the top AAUP grade, but these increases were virtually equal to the high rates of inflation during this fourteen-year period.[17]

W&L's efforts to maintain a single faculty salary scale across the institution be-gan to waver in the 1970s, with different market forces according to discipline, and especially with rising salaries in the law school.

Only a few classes enrolled over fifty students, and one history professor taught three of them. "Apparently," Wilson observed, "it has become neces-sary to the W&L experience to have at least one course with Jefferson Davis Futch—and his class enrollments are allowed to rise beyond anything we call 'normal' here."[18] The long-range plan noted that a quarter to a third of W&L classes enrolled more than twenty students, and around a hundred sections each held thirty or more. The plan called for a student-faculty ratio of ten to one—150 full-time faculty for fifteen hundred undergraduates—with an increase in women faculty from 10 to 20 percent over ten years and in African American instructors from 1 to 5 percent.[19]

Wilson and his colleagues compared W&L's efforts with the fund-raising and faculty salaries at peer universities. Looking at institutions like Davidson, Wilson wrote the trustees in 1989, "I worry that I am moving us too slowly, too conservatively, too cautiously. I sometimes wake at night wondering whether we will lose ground. I surely thought that we would gain three to five percent-age points this next year in terms of faculty salaries. But now I fear we will only be holding our own and will scarcely gain at all." Ironically, W&L's efforts to raise faculty salaries benefited from "affluent parents" that minimized the need for student financial aid. "We can be occasionally dismayed," he observed, "that we do not have a larger proportion of the middle or lower half of the 'middle class.' But you can be sure that we would have a very different financial profile if that were the case. I suppose this is another way of saying that a more diverse student body is not inexpensive."[20] Indeed, compared with their national peers, W&L's students benefited from significantly higher average parental incomes.[21]

Fair and equitable procedures for evaluation and advancement were also important faculty issues, and were taken up by the ad hoc Committee on Fac-ulty Evaluation. Initially chaired by Sid Coulling and then by geology professor Edgar Spencer, the committee met from 1985 to 1987. Fashioned after consider-ation in the Faculty Discussion Club, new guidelines for promotion and tenure were adopted for the *Faculty Handbook*. In 1986–87, the committee developed new procedures for carrying out those guidelines, approved unanimously by the advisory committee and the president and implemented in September. The new procedures—similar to those at other universities—made more formal and systematic the practices that had been generally followed in the past, with particular attention to protecting the interests of individual faculty and the institution.[22]

BY 1971, THE REVISED CURRICULUM and academic calendar had increased the total number of courses and expanded the flexibility available to students for meeting the "core" requirements. These changes, though primarily motivated by the spirit and demands of the late 1960s, followed James Leyburn's long-held view that students should be tied less to specific course requirements and encouraged to engage in more independent study. By the early 1980s, however, the W&L faculty, increasingly concerned about the inadequate preparation of entering students, voted to tighten up the general degree requirements in a more traditional configuration. Sid Coulling, chair of the ad hoc Committee on General Education, led a two-year reconsideration that led to faculty approval of new requirements, to be effective in the fall of 1984. As Coulling explained, such deliberations were always arduous because the curriculum was "the collective expression" of the faculty's "educational beliefs and a statement about the institution itself." The new requirements included twelve credits in the humanities and nine in the social sciences, and mandated courses in composition, foreign language, literature, mathematics, and the natural sciences. It also required at least one credit hour of physical education. The changes were necessary, Coulling explained, because, "generally speaking, students entering college today are not as well prepared in English as their counterparts once were; that particularly in an age of television and the computer they need an understanding of their own and of a foreign culture as it is conveyed in imaginative literature; and that in an increasingly complex and shrinking world they must have training in mathematics, science, and a foreign language in order to compete successfully." He also noted that the gap between the best and least prepared students was increasing, and thus provisions were made for demonstrating proficiency and for applying courses in the major to the general degree requirements.[23] But W&L was still "a fortress of the liberal arts," according to the *Richmond Times-Dispatch:* while almost a quarter of all bachelor's degrees awarded in Virginia were in business and management, these fields accounted for only 16 percent at W&L, where a third of degrees were awarded in the liberal arts. The recent curriculum revision further bolstered the liberal arts and accounted for almost a third of the courses required for a degree.[24]

W&L also moved to address the rising need and demand for international studies. The program in East Asian Studies had grown steadily around a core of courses in various departments dealing with China and Japan, encouraged by a 1973 grant from the Mary Reynolds Babcock Foundation. A formal major was introduced in 1978. By 1986, some forty courses were available, a new faculty member specializing in East Asian economics was on the way, and thirteen students were declared majors. Grant support from a number of foundations increased academic opportunities, and exchange relationships with foreign universities—Chung Chi College in Hong Kong and Rikkyo University and Kansai Gaidai in Japan—facilitated study abroad. An average of six exchange students from Japan and Hong Kong enrolled at W&L each year.[25]

Wilson sought to enhance the arts in the curriculum and throughout the university. The $10 million Lenfest Center for the Performing Arts, with 50,000 total square feet and two theaters, completed in 1991, was the most dramatic advance. Dedicated with great fanfare in May by a performance of *Evita,* a recital by Marilyn Horne, and a reception held in a replica of New York City's Sardi's Restaurant, the center met a long-standing need on campus for a major performance venue. The primary honored guests were Marguerite and Gerry Lenfest, '53, whose $3-million gift made the new facility possible.[26]

JOHN WILSON ARRIVED to find a more competitive and sustainable law school housed in new, excellent facilities. Its perceived role within the university was also changing. In May 1981, the *Alumni Magazine* addressed an issue heightened by the new physical distance between the law school and the undergraduate college. Entitled "The Woods Creek Gap: How Wide is the Separation Between the Law School and the Undergraduate School?" the magazine piece followed up on articles and editorials in the *Ring-tum Phi* and the *Law News,* anticipating that the alumni community might be drawn into the discussion.[27]

For most of its history, W&L had been able to balance the interests of undergraduate liberal arts and the postgraduate professional program. In the nineteenth century, the law school was small and virtually a component of the undergraduate curriculum. Later, the option to combine the senior year with the first year of legal studies provided a seamless transition for hundreds of W&L students. The relatively small number of law professors received the same levels of compensation and benefits as other professors. In the days before there was a dining hall on campus, many unmarried law students took their meals in fraternity houses and attended classes in Tucker Hall and elsewhere along the Colonnade. By the 1980s, W&L's responses to changes in legal education had created new opportunities but also challenges—including the "Woods Creek

Gap," differential tuition and faculty salaries, and views on student governance and the Honor System.

Roy Steinheimer concluded his transformative service as dean and his fruitful collaboration with Bob Huntley in 1983. His successor, Frederic Lee Kirgis Jr. came initially to W&L as director of the Frances Lewis Law Center in 1978 after private practice and faculty positions at the University of Colorado and UCLA. Randall P. Bezanson succeeded Kirgis in 1988, followed by Barry Sullivan in 1994. Bezanson came to W&L from the law faculty at the University of Iowa, where he served for five years as vice president for finance before arriving in Lexington. Sullivan took his law degree at the University of Chicago and clerked for Judge and W&L alumnus John Minor Wisdom in the US Court of Appeals for the Fifth Circuit before entering private practice and government service as an assistant solicitor general of the United States and as special assistant attorney general of Illinois.

Early in his deanship, Kirgis promised to address "the difficult situation" of the divide between the law school and undergraduate college, though most of his priorities concerned the needs of the law school: hiring more faculty, enhancing its reputation outside the South through more research and scholarship, offering more financial aid, and continuing the strong sense of community he detected throughout W&L.[28] Size and campus location were frequently cited as causes of the divide, but other factors were also involved. A declining proportion of law school students had been graduates of W&L with fraternity and other campus connections. Many were married and lived in houses and apartments on and off campus. Law students were understandably more focused on career and family than undergraduates and less likely to be part of fraternity and campus social life. They were also increasingly more diverse in socioeconomic background and political inclination. Few took their meals in university facilities. A growing number were women, while the College remained all male. Many law students participated in intramural sports and attended campus performances, but they inhabited a separate postgraduate professional culture. They began to press for greater independence from student government and either exemption from the Honor System (because the legal profession already embodied all those principles) or jurisdiction over their own honor system. W&L remained a small, intimate campus, and the "Woods Creek Gap" was a concern only relative to the way things used to be. The university and its law school were changing, and a highly regarded undergraduate college and a nationally ranked law school were not mutually incompatible.

When Kirgis decided to return to full-time faculty duties in 1987, John Wilson had his first opportunity to find a leader for the law school. Indeed, Wilson appointed himself to the search committee and personally called some of the leading candidates. He was particularly taken with Bezanson, then still at Iowa, who had clerked for a US Court of Appeals judge in the District of Columbia and for Justice Harry A. Blackmun of the US Supreme Court. His scholarship focused on constitutional law, mass communications, and administrative law, with a particular interest in libel law.

Bezanson's ideas on legal education and their potential for W&L were what most impressed Wilson. "I came early to recognize," Wilson wrote the trustees, "a deeply thoughtful approach to legal education and a conviction that it can and should be improved. Special emphasis upon legal writing, small intense seminars at various points along the way, a revised and animated third year and room in the curriculum for broad interdisciplinary topics of emerging legal significance became key points in our conversation. Overarching it all was a deeply held coincidence in the mutual relationship of teaching and scholarship and genuine affection for students and the life of the mind."[29] Wilson was sufficiently impressed that he promised Bezanson seven new faculty positions over the next five years, thereby reducing the student teacher ratio to ten-to-one, among the lowest of any law school in the country. Additional faculty members were also needed to implement the labor-intensive demands of supervising and evaluating intensive student writing.

Bezanson thought the W&L law school could achieve greater national recognition and even influence the development of American legal education. He believed that writing was a critical legal skill and a means of bringing discipline to thinking and analysis, and should be emphasized in all levels of the curriculum. Writing had already been integrated, in 1986, into small sections of the first-year torts and contracts course. In 1989, the faculty adopted changes that provided more emphasis on writing and research in small sections, and moved the moot-court program from the second semester to the second year. In 1990, the faculty adopted an upper-level writing requirement; every student had to complete a research and writing project under the direct supervision of a faculty member. (Bezanson had critiqued typical second- and third-year legal studies as needlessly repetitive and sought to enliven them with student research projects "in an active enterprise with faculty," through seminars and even clinical programs and problems involving complex litigation.) This new emphasis also provided a potential bridge over the "Woods Creek Gap." Research and writing should involve other disciplines, especially the social sciences, and numerous connections with the undergraduate liberal arts curriculum, and it was consistent with W&L's emphasis on small classes and close faculty-student contact.[30] The new dean also hoped to enhance computer technology in the law school, expand the diversity of students and faculty, and advance academic quality through admissions.

These changes and others were duly noted in the law school's 1993 self-study for reaccreditation. Since 1988–89, the size of the faculty had increased by almost 50 percent, from twenty-one to thirty-one. The number and stipends of summer research grants rose along with faculty size. Faculty evaluation and promotion procedures now included pre-tenure support committees for each probationary appointee, annual faculty reviews, and a more formal process for the award of tenure. The Frances Lewis Law Center expanded its activities and projects, including its scholar-in-residence, judge-in-residence, and lawyer-in-residence programs. The law library's collection of 305,000 volumes was still low compared to those of many other top law schools, but technology and electronic material helped remedy some deficiencies, and the library's range of media services in support of the academic program was among the best. New courses and seminars offered by regular faculty, visitors, and adjuncts expanded the curriculum, including offerings in bioethics, "elder law," sports and entertainment law, the abortion controversy, civil rights, and radical legal thought. A larger faculty supported a 30 percent increase in the number of small, advanced class sections. Old and new clinical programs, including the Legal Practice Clinic and the Prison Practicum embracing the work in the Alderson Prison, were now supervised by faculty and entered the "mainstream" of the curriculum. W&L ranked among the top 20 percent of all law schools in 1989 on the basis of median LSAT scores, and average GPA and LSAT scores rose steadily thereafter.[31] The admissions committee now considered a range of factors, including age, geographic location, economic status, and ethnic background, in an effort to diversify the student body. Financial aid had more than doubled since 1988, and about 60 percent of all law students received grants in 1993. Student placement remained good, and W&L students performed consistently above the average on the Virginia Bar Examination. All in all, this was a very positive self-assessment, endorsed by the Law Council of the School of Law Alumni Association.[32]

The law school student body was more ethnically diverse than the undergraduate population, though still less so than hoped for. In 1993, 16.2 percent were counted as "minority"—thirty-six African Americans, ten Asian Americans, nine Hispanic, and one Native American. Members of the latest entering class came from twenty-nine states and eighty-five undergraduate institutions, continuing a trend toward a more national student profile. Among them were only a handful of W&L graduates: in 1992, thirty applied, fourteen were admitted, and two enrolled. The rising qualifications of entering students included minorities, who had basically the same GPA/LSAT profile as other students admitted to W&L and were in the top 10 to 20 percent of minority applicants nationwide.[33] But the law school had only one African American faculty member, and recruiting efforts through visiting professorships were unsuccessful. Since 1988, five minority faculty visitors had taught at W&L, but none were offered a regular faculty appointment. Apparently, not all faculty members regarded this as a "serious problem," but most continued to pursue the goal of hiring more African American faculty, including new ways of screening faculty candidate qualifications, with perhaps greater emphasis on public service.

The changes from 1983, some underway and some driven by Bezanson's arrival in 1988, were considerable. The standard teaching load remained at twelve semester credit hours, but courses were re-sectioned with varying credits allocated to implement a new curricular focus that was, especially in light of the greater emphasis on scholarship, more labor intensive for faculty. Some faculty members readily adjusted to these changes, while others were less accepting. Discussion about "community" in the law school revealed differences about the term itself. But Wilson was delighted with the changes. He congratulated Bezanson in May 1989 on "an extraordinary year in the life of the Law School and my highest expectations have been exceeded, many times over."[34] Philanthropic giving to the law school was, however, a lingering challenge, and Bezanson mentioned fund-raising as a future priority in each his annual reports. The Law Council, the executive committee of the Law School Association, was expanded, especially with members in a position to be helpful. The Annual Fund did grow and total giving to the law school reached $2.5 million in 1990, buoyed by contributions to the project to house Justice Lewis F. Powell Jr.'s papers.[35]

Bezanson and Wilson were both inclined to communicate in long, conversational memoranda, a correspondence that further reveals a shared vision for the law school even amid the critical battering the school and the university took over issues of diversity and "political correctness." But these had been very eventful years. By 1994, the 360 law students (40 percent female and

16 percent minority) had attended 171 undergraduate schools and had come from forty states and Washington, DC. (37.8 percent came from Virginia) The entering class was highly qualified, and most recent graduates were successfully placed (60 percent in private practice and 23 percent in judicial clerkships). Law-school enrollments were projected to decline for the remainder of the 1990s, in line with broader demographic and employment market trends, but W&L seemed well positioned to hold its own. It had received high *U.S. News and World Report* rankings among all the nation's law schools. Both Wilson and Bezanson looked skeptically upon such rankings but agreed that they could not be ignored. To be the very best among the nation's premier law schools was still an aspiration, but a solid national reputation had been established, and Bezanson pointed out in 1992 "that we remain the only nationally recognized school that is unaffiliated with a major research university or with a Division I athletic program."[36]

Bezanson returned to the University of Iowa in 1994, leaving behind a considerable W&L legacy. He had in many respects extended and expanded the transformation initiated by Roy Steinheimer. His successor, Barry Sullivan, arrived with substantial experience as a litigator for a large Chicago law firm, a clerkship with John Minor Wisdom, and a stint in the US Department of Justice. His undergraduate degree in philosophy and political science from Middlebury College had prepared him for an institution such as Washington and Lee and for the writing-based curriculum and small sections in its law school. The "Woods Creek Gap" remained, but the major development on the west campus over the next two decades, including athletic facilities and new student housing, made Lewis Hall and its occupants seem less remote.

THE REVOLUTION in digital information and computer technology began reshaping higher education in the 1970s and quickly made an imprint at W&L. At first, computer use was confined to those, mostly in the sciences, who had mastered the arcane languages and code of a centrally located machine. Change came rapidly. In 1981, the university named a coordinator of academic computer applications. By 1990, additional positions appeared: an information systems coordinator, a computer lab director in the School of Commerce, and—perhaps most notably—a microcomputer coordinator and additional coordinators in the School of Commerce and the law school. Newer desktop machines, not to mention the first twenty-four-pound "portables," decentralized computing in the office as well as the classroom and vastly increased the number of machines on campus. The central mainframe was now mostly used for business and administrative support.

In the late 1980s, the W&L academic mainframe, a Prime 9955 minicomputer, was connected to about thirty offices and labs through sixty-four publicly available workstations. Washington and Lee also established a microcomputer laboratory in 1987 and provided microcomputers in faculty offices a year later. One hundred and eighty microcomputers were available throughout the campus, and the first network was installed as an editing lab in the Journalism Department. The university provided these resources freely, without fees or charge-backs, on a twenty-four-hour basis. Students could purchase microcomputers and supporting equipment at a discount through the university, and faculty could receive a three-year, interest-free loan for the same purpose.[37]

By 1995, the staff roster included fourteen positions devoted to computing, filled mostly with computer specialists, arranged in a new organizational framework. Powerful networks, soon to be connected through the Internet or World Wide Web, were managed and supported by seven new computing and network experts. Two "user support specialists" were required by the proliferation of machines and users. With more powerful and smaller devices, vastly greater storage, and more complex software and graphics capability, more equipment and personnel were needed. Universities were sorely pressed to keep up with the latest hardware and software, and every new breakthrough rendered some existing technology obsolete. Lewis Hall, for example, was constructed with state-of-the-art connectivity—cables leading to every classroom, faculty office, and library carrel—which would, of course, be superseded by the Internet, intranets, and Wi-Fi. Change would eventually even lead to a reassertion of centralized databases (banks of Internet servers and "the cloud") and a thorough decentralization of handheld devices that combined computing, data, and telecommunications.

In the fall of 1984, W&L established a Department of Computer Science and added the field to its list of majors, with fifteen new courses, leading to either a BA or BS degree. Though computing and "intelligent devices" would eventually become ubiquitous throughout higher education, Dean William Watt echoed the belief that "computer science is a discipline unto itself and deserves to be treated as such." The first department chair, Ted Sjoerdsma, left the same position at the University of Iowa to introduce the new program at W&L, with a particular interest in relating the new field to the liberal arts.[38] A new microcomputer laboratory opened to serve all students.[39] In 1992, the university boasted a "computerized classroom," with sixteen microcomputers connected to the instructor's computer as well as to the university mainframe, an electronic mail system, and "Annie," the computerized card catalog in the libraries, named for Annie R. White, the legendary former head of the library who also founded the Fancy Dress Ball.

Eventually, college students at W&L and elsewhere would be wedded to handheld smart phones and tablets. "Computing" became no longer a separate function but a foundation—a context—for communication and entertainment. Virtually instant digital access to enormous stores of information, and dramatic improvements in graphics and digital images reshaped—if not repurposed— virtually every discipline, from the basic sciences to the arts.

SOCIAL, ECONOMIC, RACIAL, and ethnic diversity in student bodies and faculties was a priority of American higher education in the last third of the twentieth century. Partly an effort to redress the effects of past discrimination, creating diverse educational environments was also crucial to preparing graduates who were capable of living, learning, and working with many different individuals and groups. Universities sought students from previously underrepresented groups, including African Americans, Hispanics, and other minorities; women; and "nontraditional students" who fell outside the age range of eighteen to twenty-two. For Washington and Lee—long defined as a traditional, small, white, male, relatively affluent institution, and among the least "diverse" in the country—pursuing greater diversity posed a considerable challenge. The *Long-Range Plan* in 1989 noted that the student body "remains too socially and economically homogeneous" and called for redoubling "efforts for diversity." The Admissions Office was already reaching out to seven thousand African American students by direct mail and reported an increase in the number of black applicants to sixty-six in 1988 (from only thirteen a decade earlier); enrollments had grown from two to eighteen.[40] Given the tenor of the times, W&L was also buffeted by the strong backlash to diversity measures, and especially "affirmative action," that racked all levels of higher education and many other segments of American society.

Compared with diversity initiatives at large public and private universities, W&L's progress seemed meager and slow, but changes did occur. A 1985 article in the *Alumni Magazine* focused on three currently nontraditional students.[41] Two were older white students—aged thirty-two and thirty-four—who were pursuing bachelor's degrees after working in a variety of jobs. At W&L, older students with life experience were underrepresented. One student was overheard asking another, "Did you see that guy in our class? Why, he's got to be *at least* 30 years old!" Whatever their age, however, white males provided little racial or ethnic diversity.

The third student, a junior, was older but African American, and had a unique history—and future—at Washington and Lee. Theodore "Ted" DeLaney was forty-one, married to Pat (then serving as Lexington's city treasurer), and the father of a seven-year-old son, Damien. A native of Lexington, DeLaney had declined a scholarship offer from Morehouse College in 1961 and had begun working at W&L in 1963, first as a janitor and then as a laboratory technician in the Biology Department, where for twenty years he assisted W&L students. He began taking courses part-time for credit in 1979 and, with the encouragement of his wife and others, enrolled as a full-time W&L student in 1982. While an undergraduate, he also served as president of the Lexington PTA and secretary of the Rockbridge County Board of Elections. Even after years of working in the biology lab, he was taken aback by the homogeneity in W&L classrooms: "Not only are they the same age and basically from the same socioeconomic background, but they all share the same points of view." DeLaney received a BA in 1985 and, with the encouragement of his professors, entered graduate school in history at the College of William and Mary. He returned to W&L in 1991 as an ABD ("all but dissertation") fellow, and joined the faculty after completing his PhD degree.[42] A teacher and adviser to many students, DeLaney has served on numerous committees and as department chair, and his son Damien is a graduate of the W&L School of Law.

The number of black students at W&L was never large. Rather than recruiting as many African Americans as possible, the university focused on recruiting those who had the greatest chance of success at W&L. When all of higher education was marshaling every effort to remedy the dearth of opportunities for African American students, and larger public universities were adding hundreds of black students to every entering class, the proportion of African Americans and other minorities at W&L appeared—and indeed was—relatively meager. Blacks comprised 2.8 percent of the student body in 1987–88 and 3.8 percent in 1991–92. The law school actively recruited African Americans, and the number of applications rose in the early 1980s to a high of seventy-five in 1984. Thirteen blacks actually enrolled in law school in 1985, but only four in 1984 and 1986.[43] W&L remained overwhelmingly white, and the university continued to contend with the racial insensitivity displayed by some white students and professors.

Race issues became embroiled in many aspects of campus life, including Fancy Dress. The 1988 event theme was "reconciliation" following the Civil War, which involved Civil War uniforms, symbols, and flags and celebrated the end of Reconstruction in the South. The Minority Student Association called for a boycott of the event. What most W&L students and alumni tended to regard as a worthy theme—the mollification of regional conflict—blacks recognized as the end of federal protection and a return to local racial oppression and the rise of Jim Crow. As Wilson recalled, "Several black couples attended but others did not and that was too bad." One alumnus expressed shock at the boycott: "This fine university is steeped in more than 200 years of Southern tradition, and blacks who come here know this. If they don't like it, why do they attend W&L? If they can't accept it, they should leave."[44]

A program sponsored by the Jessie Ball duPont Fund was designed to support minority recruitment at selected southern liberal arts institutions—including Washington and Lee, Davidson, Rhodes College, Sewanee, Furman University, and Lynchburg College. Washington and Lee's effort—the FUTURES program—identified potential black students in collaboration with the Fairfax County Public Schools, selecting ten each summer from those who had completed the tenth grade and had high academic potential or maintained "B" averages but were still considered academically at-risk. The students received assistance in course selection, SAT preparation, study and time-management guidance, and books for a home library, and they were also invited to attend the regular four-week Summer Scholars program on campus. Those eligible for admission to the program received a 50 percent reduction in tuition and room and board. A male and female African American student at W&L served as counselors and mentors.

The duPont Fund commissioned a report on these efforts by the Center for Assessment and Policy Development. The report, completed in March 1993, was the basis for a meeting of senior administrators from the participating institutions held in Atlanta that August.[45] John Wilson and John Elrod attended from W&L. The report, shared with the institutions in July, elicited some distressed comments. On the whole, the efforts of all the institutions were found wanting. The report declared that actions at W&L and most of the others to contact potential students were inadequate and that the on-campus experience was frequently off-putting: "The emphasis on 'tradition' and 'heritage' translates into an emphasis on racism from African American students' perspective." Black students believed they were too often treated as members of a category rather than as individuals. The biggest failing was the small number of black students on campus, resulting in part from a very small number of applicants, compounded by a "rigid definition of a liberal arts curriculum" and inadequate numbers of black faculty and staff members. The report was particularly adamant that efforts focused mainly on retention were "destined to fail"; retention is something the institution *does*, whereas "being diverse" is what the college *is*. The report's recommendations were sweeping. "An inclusive, comprehensive definition of diversity," it concluded, "will require a substantial change in the policies, activities and climates of these institutions in virtually all areas of operation." A comprehensive effort to "overcome the racism" that exists on campus was only part of a necessary institutional transformation. The applicant pools of African American students should be greatly expanded to substantially increase the number enrolled.

John Wilson's response criticized the report's conclusions and the appropriateness of its recommendations for these particular institutions. In his view, "the evaluators have views just short of contempt for what we are and what we aim for." The report seemed to recommend, he wrote, that duPont Fund resources should be redirected toward bringing "many hundreds or thousands of youngsters in large urban institutions to truly make an impact instead of fooling around with mere dozens in selective liberal arts colleges." Wilson reaffirmed W&L's commitment to recruiting only African American students with the academic preparation necessary to succeed—those who could participate "in this elitist effort to train leaders for the nation in the years to come and we certainly don't apologize for our concern with their retention and ultimate success here." He noted that 80 percent of black students at W&L "do succeed . . . even more if you add in the law students."[46] Some other college presidents reacted similarly, and even more pointedly.[47]

While the report reflected the national sense of urgency to greatly increase the proportion of blacks at American colleges and universities, the scale of expectations outlined for these liberal arts colleges did not fit their size or character. The reaction by Wilson and others may have been defensive, but ensuring that minority students could succeed and graduate at rates similar to those of other students was critical in the smaller and more intimate environs of institutions like W&L. Wilson's frustration might also have been due to the fact that many trustees were highly skeptical of the idea and usefulness of diversity in general.

Two months after the duPont Fund meeting in Atlanta, Sidney Coulling delivered to the trustees—at Wilson's request—a presentation on the university's mission statement, adopted in May 1988. At a dinner on October 21, Coulling reflected on the statement and, in the process, on the university's history and values.[48] He explained the statement paragraph by paragraph, calling particular attention to the one dealing with admissions. Specifically, that paragraph declared that the university "seeks to create a student body that is geographically, socially and economically diverse but unified as 'an aristocracy of talent.'" Coulling tied this statement directly to Lee's legacy. "How strange it is," he said, "that whereas Douglas Southall Freeman, writing in the 1930s, could praise Lee for starting a 'diversified' student body, to seek the same objectives today is to invite from some quarters criticism expressed in what has surely become the most hackneyed phrase of our time, as if one can no longer do the right thing for the right reason. But whatever criticism it may invite, or whatever problems it may pose, diversity must remain a crucial priority if we're to provide at Washington and Lee a climate in which students may genuinely mature." He also linked the need for diversity to James Leyburn's repeated lament about conformity among W&L students and the "fear aroused in them by any challenge to their narrow and comfortable notions." Students learn as much from each other as from the faculty, Coulling added, and "we do them a disservice if we don't create the opportunity for real intellectual growth that the class of young and active minds can provide." While Coulling never referred specifically to racial and ethnic diversity, his argument was perhaps more powerful because it permitted his audience to draw the obvious inference for themselves. Invoking Lee's legacy also helped move things along.

Wilson was delighted. He wrote Coulling a few days after the board meeting: "You exceeded all expectations on Thursday evening, and helped, enormously, a Board that was genuinely divided and confused on basic questions of institutional identity. Even on Saturday morning people were referencing their comments to paragraph four of the Mission Statement"—a paragraph that "had become the center of a true constitutional document and we now have fresh instructions to insure diversity of background in our community." Wilson was convinced that this would not have happened without Coulling's thirty-minute presentation. "People with the best will in the world fear change and shrink from participating in a decision that could weaken or divide an institution they love. They fear most of all being labeled 'politically correct.'" The board was not "nearly unified" on the issue: "The fear of balkanization, as one trustee put it, is still there but I trust it will soon fade."[49]

* * *

MANY BLACK STUDENTS at Washington and Lee were successful. Linwood Smothers, '72, completed a six-year cooperative program in physics and engineering that W&L offered in collaboration with Columbia University and became a project manager at Lockheed-Martin. William Hill, '74, '77L, became an attorney in Atlanta, president of the W&L Law Council, a justice of the Georgia Supreme Court, and father of two daughters who graduated from W&L. Thomas Penn, '74, became a Baptist pastor in Roanoke, and his son Courtney, '92, became a W&L admissions officer. Willard Dumas, '91, from New Orleans, served on the Student Executive Committee for four years and as president of the student body in 1990, going on to doctoral study at the University of Chicago. Mikel Parker, '99, from Atlanta, was elected president of the Interfraternity Council.

Beginning in 1988, a number of African American graduates returned to campus for the Minority Student/Alumni Conference, at which black alumni and current students met with minority high-school students who had applied to W&L. As James D. Farrar Jr., the associate alumni director, pointed out in 1990—when both William Hill and Thomas Penn participated—these conferences brought black alumni back to campus, reaffirmed current students, and helped attract more minority students to W&L.[50] Even the most successful African American graduates were quick to recall the continuing social isolation minority students encountered at W&L, exacerbated by the dominance of fraternities and the failure to establish a historically black fraternity on campus. (The Chavis House provided a meeting place for minority students, though it was hardly the equivalent of the fraternity social scene.) The IFC approved an effort to establish a colony of Alpha Phi Alpha in 1991, but it failed due to the low number of potential members. However, some W&L students were able to join all-black fraternities at George Mason University or the University of Virginia.[51] Minority students were involved in many other campus activities. The Minority Student Association organized the first Martin Luther King Jr. Memorial Lecture, held in Lee Chapel, in January 1990, part of a series of programs that also involved the Lexington community.

Hiring and retaining African American faculty members was a persistent and frustrating problem both for black students and the administration. One rising sophomore wrote John Wilson in 1986: "Where are our professors and why is there only one black administrator? Don't you believe as a young black student, I need positive role models? Where are they?" Most of the blacks on campus were janitors or cafeteria workers. A responsive university, she suggested, would immediately hire minority staff to identify and hire other black staff and faculty members and would appoint an African American to the board of trustees. She hoped that "it will get better and we won't always feel like 'polar bears in the middle of Africa.'" Only the president, she insisted, could initiate and carry out the necessary changes.[52]

Progress toward a remedy for the dearth of black faculty and senior administrators suffused all of higher education. Virtually every college and university implemented programs to succeed in this competition, and they employed every stratagem to meet institutional goals and public expectations. The main difficulty was supply and demand: too many jobs and too few African Americans enrolled in graduate programs. University presidents and deans were especially frustrated because the complexity of their explanation of the problem to students might seem evasive or defensive, especially when students tended to believe that plenty of qualified faculty were actually available and that the paucity of black professors was due simply to a lack of administrative effort or commitment.

John Wilson responded: "I know full well that we must do more than we have to attract and retain black faculty and staff." There had been recent specific efforts in hiring and retention but not for new undergraduate faculty. He picked up on the student's suggestion "to establish an exchange program" with black faculty at other institutions as a possible "good beginning point." He also expressed his disappointment with admissions for the class of 1990: "Never in our history had we so many fine black applicants and we were able to accept a very healthy percentage of those who applied." But the low number who accepted was "terribly discouraging." The competition from the Ivy League schools, as well as UVA and William and Mary, was very stiff.[53] In fact, one month after receiving the student's letter, Wilson wrote the deans and Hotchkiss that W&L should "put special emphasis in the years ahead on the identification of prospective faculty from the ranks of black scholars." He suggested a "visiting black scholar program" to assess potential permanent hires and also diversify the teaching force, and he reiterated two of his key principles: that "our white students need, beyond the normal measure, to come to know black professionals of the finest calibre," and that "mediocre appointments will be viciously counterproductive."[54]

In 1988, the university introduced two new programs to recruit minority faculty. One provided for visiting faculty to take leaves of absence from their home institutions to teach full-time at W&L for all or a portion of an academic year. Benjamin Daise, associate professor at Hobart and William Smith Colleges, was the inaugural participant in this arrangement. The "ABD" program was specifically aimed at recruiting regular full-time minority faculty members by attracting them to the campus before they completed their doctorates and entered the job market. Those who had completed all work toward the PhD except for the dissertation could work on that final requirement at W&L and receive a stipend, faculty office, and library study carrel while teaching only one class a semester. Joyce G. MacDonald, a doctoral candidate at Vanderbilt, was the first ABD fellow. Another fellow, Jarvis A. Hall, delivered the first Martin Luther King Jr. Memorial Lecture in 1990, on "Non-Violent Social Change." And, of course, there was Ted DeLaney.

The rationale—indeed, the very idea—of affirmative measures to remedy past racial discrimination, along with the educational imperatives of providing an ethnically diverse academic environment, encountered an intense conservative backlash that regarded such measures as discriminatory and a product of liberal pandering. Washington and Lee was perhaps especially vulnerable, with its high profile in Virginia and generally conservative alumni, who tended to regard special privileges extended on the basis of race to remedy past inequities as "reverse discrimination." These accusations often originated from the *Richmond Times-Dispatch,* which published a number of critical columns and editorials.

In an op-ed piece for the paper in 1991, Robert G. Holland, '63, a former member of the W&L journalism faculty, opposed diversity efforts throughout higher education, calling "diversity" "a code word for the use of racial or gender preferences to gerrymander the composition of student bodies or work forces." He singled out the annual report of W&L's law dean, Randy Bezanson, for "gushing" platitudes and offering a "puerile tribute" to diversity as an essential part of modern legal education, a view derived from "leftist fever swamps." (Holland further railed against the law school's ban on military recruiters and its upholding the American Association of Law School's policy against discrimination on the basis of sexual orientation, simply because it was "demanded by a rinky-dink accrediting outfit.") His basic point was that affirmative action and a commitment to diversity were inherently discriminatory and thus morally wrong, and he claimed that they were promoted as part of a broader effort to be "politically correct." As Holland put it, "While prattling mindlessly about the glories of diversity, college presidents deny the existence of a Thought Police to enforce the orthodoxy."[55]

Another attack on "political correctness" appeared in September, written by William S. Cogar, '51, '55L, a Richmond attorney. He lambasted the university's ban on military recruiting, even though it had been "suspended" at W&L, and Wilson's failure to visit Richmond to explain the decision to alumni. Cogar described diversity as an abandonment of academic standards in favor of flawed social policy and bemoaned "the heaps of political correctness" offered up in Dean Bezanson's report. He further warned, "these insidious institutional transformations" driven by "tenured liberals" were "germinating and metastasizing at Washington and Lee." Finally, he condemned the University's Confidential Review Committee, a body of faculty and students created in 1988 to deal with sensitive issues of campus sexual assault and offensive speech, for its policy on "anti-harassment" that banned offensive conduct and statements based on racial, ethnic, religious, or sexual grounds. This "draconian muzzle" was an offense to free speech and further indication of the political correctness trend.[56] In an earlier letter to Bezanson on the law school's adoption of the AALS policy, simultaneously published in the *Richmond News Leader,* Cogar had wondered if those faculty who voted in favor of it might be homosexuals, an allegation Wilson termed "an extraordinary assault upon the integrity of our Faculty."[57]

What Holland called a "rinky-dink accrediting outfit" was the organization which set standards and requirements for national law-school accreditation. The AALS adopted standards promoting ethnic and racial diversity and also prohibiting discrimination based on sexual orientation, which led to banning recruiters who discriminated against homosexuals. Bezanson's discussion of these matters was completely in line with AALS policy and the assessment criteria for accreditation. Of 126 law schools responding to a 1991 survey, 91 had discrimination policies that included sexual orientation, and 76 percent (including almost all of those to which W&L compared itself) applied those policies to placement procedures; only ten of those excluded the military.[58] But these policies inspired national controversy, and Bezanson and Wilson bore the brunt of it at W&L. The concerns "being visited upon higher education" were important and could not be avoided, Bezanson observed to Wilson, and "were subtle and complex, not given to simplistic overstatement. . . . It is tempting to succumb to simple solutions when the pressure is on, but if we fail to resist that temptation we will have failed in the very purposes for which this institution exists."[59] He was reassured that the Law Council "understood and respected" W&L's policy, was "dismissive" of the *Richmond Times-Dispatch* characterizations, and supported continued efforts toward both quality and diversity.[60]

However, Bezanson, along with many other W&L faculty members, was very concerned about any efforts to control speech. In his view, the experience of higher education in the previous four decades had led to "a fairly clear-minded idea of free expression in the academic community—a recognition that it needs to be robust, wide-open, and uninhibited, and even a recognition that it will be at times disruptive." Aspirations for a community based on "individual dignity and rational discourse" were noble and important, but the means of achieving such a community must be based on free and open discussion. The policy on harassment should, he recommended, include a distinction between speech and conduct expressing an idea—which should be protected—and that which inflicted actual physical harm. Bezanson also argued for a new university declaration of commitment to free speech.[61] W&L did make changes in the policy and the jurisdiction of the Confidential Review Committee, but the fact that these same issues persisted in higher education well into the twenty-first century confirms that achieving an appropriate balance between rationality, civility, and free expression was not a simple matter.

In the early 1990s, university presidents and administrations found themselves in a difficult situation, caught between their peers in higher education, the demands of minority and previously underrepresented groups, the rules of academic accrediting agencies, and the US Office of Civil Rights, on the one hand, and angry alumni and conservative media, on the other. Wilson lamented "the shrillness with which America now conducts its public policy conversations." "The paranoia is fog-think at the moment and I don't see any signs that it will soon lift."[62]

Wilson provided the trustees with responses to Cogar's specific allegations. He had waited for the faculty to change its original 11–9 vote in favor of the ban on military recruiting, and, when it did not, he suspended the policy, partly on the grounds that it unfairly isolated the Judge Advocate General corps. Indeed, a number of faculty and students opposed the ban and the inclusion of sexual orientation as part of a policy on discrimination. On October 7, 1991, the law faculty passed a resolution against adding sexual orientation to the AALS discrimination prohibitions and directed the dean to so inform AALS, which he did on October 8. Wilson thought the faculty directive reflected "plain old boorishness."[63] On diversity, Wilson explained to the trustees that Bezanson's report attempted to go beyond the "stereotypical view of diversity as an ethnic/quota code word and talk about the real nature of diversity in a professional school setting . . . diversity of age, of experience, of educational and geographical background, of sex and religion and ethnicity, of socio-economic status." Cogar and others were mistaken, he argued, in assuming that it meant quotas or in any way a lowering of academic standards. He admitted that the harassment policy needed revision; it had been adopted by the faculty six years earlier to deal with sexual misconduct and to meet federal government requirements for a harassment-free work place, but it was poorly written and was never intended to refer to speech. The deans were currently revising it, "with a clear statement of our fidelity to the free expression of ideas." Finally, he noted that he had already arranged to speak to the Richmond alumni on October 30.[64] A *Law News* editorial rose to the defense of diversity, noting the unfairness of basing all admissions decisions on test scores alone, invoking the US Supreme Court decision in the *Bakke* case, highlighting the importance of "increasing the effective participation of all sectors of society in the justice system," and deriding Holland's "screeching hyper-rhetoric."[65]

Criticism emerged on campus, frequently from the *Spectator*, a student publication. The cover of the "Alumni Weekend Issue" in May 1990 featured Wilson as Uncle Sam, proclaiming "I Want You to Teach, Minorities Encouraged to Apply (Ph.D. Not Necessary)." An article in the same issue opposed affirmative action in higher education generally and at W&L in particular. Wilson called the trustees' attention to inaccuracies in the story, especially an "invented" statement attributed to him, but he took consolation that "We are a civil community for the most part and we also have, I hope, a sense of humor." He was concerned about a "possible surfacing of strained racial feelings" on campus.[66]

American higher education struggled in the last two decades of the twentieth century, coping with the multiple challenges of greater size, rising and competing expectations, a less-favorable economic climate, and the turmoil of significant societal change. Though affected by this, Washington and Lee determined to maintain its core identity and character. Competing for students and faculty, fashioning the best possible academic program, responding to powerful demands for greater racial and ethnic diversity, and dealing with the potent backlash against these demands and responses pervaded the years of Wilson's presidency. And there were other continuing pressing issues—problems with the fraternities, student alcohol and drug abuse, and the need for greater financial resources for everything the university hoped to do. But at the outset of Wilson's arrival in Lexington, one issue more than any other demanded attention—an issue that seemed, to some, to pit the university's identity against its academic and financial future. The new president concluded that the question of coeducation must be decided, one way or the other, before anything else on his agenda could be fruitfully pursued.

—✦—

CHAPTER ELEVEN

MEN AND WOMEN TOGETHER

Expanding Old Foundations

TWENTY-TWO TRUSTEES gathered in Lexington on Friday, July 13, 1984, to wrestle with the seemingly interminable issue of coeducation. They would make the definitive decision the next morning.[1] Admitting women undergraduates had been studied before—twice between 1969 and 1975—without notable controversy or final resolution. But when the issue was formally taken up again for review in October 1983, it engendered far more debate. Each trustee received over a hundred letters from alumni and friends, many condemning the idea, and scores of articles and letters had appeared in newspapers and the *Alumni Magazine*. A recent poll revealed a majority of students opposed to coeducation, but faculty members were overwhelmingly and vocally in favor. A policy decision spurred by concerns of academic quality and enrollment had become a reflection across all constituencies on the very nature of the university itself. In 1984, W&L was only one of three nonmilitary all-male colleges in the country (along with Hampden-Sydney College and Wabash College in Indiana). Did that make it an even more unique and special place or an isolated anachronism? After 235 years as an all-male institution, would the admission of women corrode beloved traditions? Emotions were running high, the trustees were of different minds, and no one dared predict what the vote was going to be.

The board heard committee reports on Friday afternoon before adjourning to the Keydet-General Motor Inn for dinner and discussions lasting well into the evening. Several trustees spent restless nights, and one reported that he only made up his mind at 4 o'clock that morning. The rector, Jim Ballengee, heard him pacing in the next room. Board discussions had been serious and restrained, but usually noncommittal, and no vote had been taken. New trustee Frances Lewis feared that hers might be the only vote in favor. On July 14, the meeting convened in the library's Northen Auditorium at 8:30 a.m. (Some noted that it was Bastille Day in France.) Rather than going into a regular executive session, the board allowed the administrators—who had been embroiled in the issue for months—to attend the deliberations. The motion on coeducation came to the floor at 10:40 a.m.

—⋖

JOHN WILSON KNEW when he accepted the W&L presidency in September 1982 that coeducation was a persisting issue there, if for no other reason than that so few all-male colleges remained in the United States. Without much fanfare, the law school had enrolled a significant number of females since 1972, and a few women exchange students and nondegree "special students" had been attending regular classes since 1981. The issue was not resolved, but it didn't seem to be on the front burner either. Wilson was taken aback by how quickly it came to the fore. The first questioner at his first news conference asked about his intentions concerning coeducation, and he received letters on the issue before he even moved to Lexington.

In November 1982, Wilson received a letter from an alumnus asking why his daughter—or Wilson's—could attend Yale, Harvard, Princeton, and even West Point but not W&L. Did the board believe "that General Lee, if alive today, would discriminate against the admission of women to Washington and Lee"? Wilson responded with a long, thoughtful letter, declining "to speak clearly on the issue of coeducation . . . before I've had a chance to live and work in the community for awhile." Nevertheless, he expressed a series of thoughts that framed his approach to the matter. He "admired" the board's earlier decisions not to succumb to the "shabbily rationalized" conversions to coeducation that had swept the country. But coeducation was no longer a "fad," and only a few all-male institutions were left, each claiming to be "special." He noted that when his Oxford College (Exeter, founded in 1314) began admitting women in the late 1970s, "it became clear to me that something very important had happened in the Western World." The college for men, he observed, "assumed its character from the dominant shape and mores of society" which no longer prevailed. This did not negate the value of these institutions, but it "does impose upon them the burden of rationalizing their single-sex character when the social props have been kicked out from under them."

Wilson vastly underestimated the gravity and volatility of the issue he would encounter in his new post. He believed that W&L "is only half-hearted in its devotion to its single-sex character. I discover no militancy on the question." He admitted that practical issues would need to be resolved, such as residence hall space and athletics, but these "are not impediments." The W&L community, he too readily asserted, "is currently willing and able to take up a significant question of this sort without chasing false rabbits (e.g., will women support the annual fund?) and without all the posturing that occurred elsewhere back in the seventies. It can do so because it has the confidence that comes from centuries of successful service and because the place is healthy and under no current pressure from admissions or OCR [US Office of Civil Rights] to 'do something.' I'm also pretty confident that the alumni loyalty is so deeply grounded that one would not have to worry about widespread alienation."[2] While there were elements of truth in Wilson's remarks, they ultimately proved wishful thinking.

Wilson sent copies of this correspondence to Frank Parsons and trustees Jim Ballengee and Edgar Shannon on January 3, 1983, noting a bit sheepishly, "Perhaps I went too far in betraying my own lack of *total* conviction on the correctness of our current position." In order to continue the discussions and learn more, he shared the correspondence with members of the Monday Lunch Group of administrators that Huntley had established (soon to begin meeting over breakfast). After years of more or less quietly contemplating coeducation, they were taken aback by the new president's straightforward remarks.

Farris Hotchkiss responded with a tightly structured two-page memorandum distilling his thoughts from long experience dealing with coeducation, alumni relations, and fundraising. He suggested that perhaps "a certain inflexibility of thought has crept into our thinking about co-education," a reluctance to finally follow the trend. W&L should study the costs, facilities needs, curricular implications, experience of other schools, and opinions of alumni, especially those that "count the most." He raised a key question: Is it "possible that, in time, our all-maleness will be viewed not as independence of thought and steady mindedness but, rather, as anachronistic and lacking in courage and leadership?"[3] James Whitehead wrote, "Tradition alone cannot be our defense against accepting qualified female students," and failing to do so would be "incongruous with the times."[4] Commerce dean Ed Atwood was "personally ambivalent." One of his main concerns was that coeducation would require an increase in the size of the student body (and a probable decrease in the number of business majors). He was unenthusiastic about coeducation, failing to see the "long term benefit" but acknowledging that, if founded in 1983, W&L would certainly be coed. Atwood speculated that coeducation would not occur unless there was a financial problem, an admissions problem, or an unequivocal recommendation from the president. He also warned, correctly, that some board members might be "annoyed in the issue coming up once again."[5] Dean of the College William Watt was "sure that the overwhelming majority of faculty members would prefer to teach women in their classes," even though some studies found no "pedagogical advantage" to coeducation. But Watt was most concerned about the "practical questions." As to institutional size, in his twenty-eight years at W&L, the 50 percent increase in the number of students and faculty members had not undermined the institution's character.[6]

Bill Washburn, the alumni secretary, pointed to the "vast majority" of alumni that preferred remaining all male. He touched on a persistent concern, especially among older, graduates: "I do *not* think that our alumni want to see W&L become selective or so 'hung up' on the highly academically qualified students to the degree that the students they get are intellectually gifted *but* of one or certainly few dimensions." If the "so-called prestigious schools (such as the Harvard types) want to go after the 'gifted' student of poor balance, then let them go ahead." (Indeed, the "balanced student" represented to many the "ideal W&L man" but was also sometimes code for resistance to higher academic selectivity.) Washburn also believed that most alumni opposition to coeducation was because it would increase the size of the student body. However, if "clear and overriding reasons" for coeducation were presented, most alumni would support it, just as they had continued to support the university following the end of subsidized athletics in 1954.[7]

Wilson also turned to several professors for opinion and advice. He asked history professor Robert McAhren, who had been involved with the coeducation discussions in 1969–70, to look again at the Princeton report detailing that institution's experience. McAhren perceived two significant differences between Princeton and W&L: first, "the W&L alumni and friends are likely to be much more conservative and therefore more resistant to change than the Princeton alumni," and second, "Princeton became coeducational in an epoch friendlier to such moves than is our own." He speculated that the failure to ratify the Equal Rights Amendment by the extended deadline of June 1982 might have had some influence on alumni sentiment. Based on the Princeton experience, coeducation would almost certainly improve the size and quality of the applicant pool and perhaps also the "general quality of academic life." But he also referred to Alexander W. Astin's contention that single-sex (especially all-male) institutions offered better academic experiences, higher student self-esteem, and more overall satisfaction than coed ones. McAhren's earlier support for enlarging the student body to implement coeducation had now changed; it would be better, he wrote, to keep the same size because smaller classes and "the informal nature of student-faculty relationships" is "an essential ingredient of our appeal." His greatest concern with coeducation was the possibility of reduced alumni support and what he understood to be a generally lower rate of giving supposedly typical of female graduates. He warned that coeducation might improve the quality of the student body but perhaps might not raise academic performance, "an outcome completely contrary to the expectations of many faculty proponents."[8]

Wilson asked Pamela Simpson, associate dean of the College, about W&L's exchange program with other institutions, begun in 1969. During that period, she reported, 155 women students from Sweet Briar, Hollins, Randolph-Macon, and Mary Baldwin had been enrolled for at least a semester of regular classes at W&L, and 51 W&L undergraduates had enrolled in those colleges.[9] The program was providing limited opportunities for gender diversity, but it was not addressing the major issues.

Wilson found the W&L campus seemingly awash in curiosity and speculation about coeducation. It was a frequent topic of conversation at the dinners he held at Lee House for seniors and third-year law students (including, of course, some women). "We hardly got past salad when the question of coeducation invariably arose. I have never seen a community so intoxicated with the subject as the Washington and Lee community seemed to be when I arrived here last January."[10] Increasingly, Wilson perceived that coeducation was intertwined with, and even overshadowed, other important matters, from fraternities and social life to curriculum and on-campus housing. Could any of those issues be usefully addressed without first resolving what appeared to be the major concern?

At the Skylark Farm administrative retreat in July 1983, Wilson declared his intention to resolve the coeducation matter "one way or the other" by the following May, an intention he shared with the rector and a few other trustees. This was not general public knowledge until October, when the *Newport News Daily Press* ran a story headlined "W&L Considers Admitting Women as Undergraduates," based on an interview with Wilson conducted by a recent W&L graduate, Phil Murray, '83. The story described Wilson as W&L's "strong-willed new president" who intended to resolve the coeducation issue by a firm recommendation. The article went on to recount the changes that had occurred since 1975, discuss the demographics underlying the admissions concerns, and point to potentially high costs "that may be prohibitive."[11] The story was picked up by the Associated Press and appeared in the *Richmond Times-Dispatch*. In this story, Wilson supposedly had "set out to put his personal mark on the small, private, liberal arts school."[12] The story suggested that the new president was determined even before his arrival in Lexington to bring coeducation to W&L and that he was the principal moving force behind it.

Wilson acknowledged to the trustees on October 11 "that the question of the admission of women . . . swam back into the papers this past week," and he informed them that he hoped to present at the upcoming board meeting "my analysis of this question in as many of the dimensions as I have come to understand." No action was contemplated at this point, he wrote, but "I do hope it will be possible to structure our deliberations in a way that will position the Board and the University to deal intelligently with this important matter by May." While that was not a firm deadline, "I have been continuously drawn into conversations about it since I arrived ten months ago and I do not believe it would be healthy to leave it suspended for a lengthy period." To illustrate, he pointed to active and increasingly vocal student interest: "I am told that George Washington's statue is graced this morning with a sign reading 'No Marthas.' I think that is rather clever and am grateful (a) for the wit and (b) that the student who put it there got down in one piece."[13]

The widespread newspaper coverage in early October inspired a rash of letters to the *Ring-tum Phi* and the university, as well as banners across fraternity houses reading "Better Dead Than Coed" and bumper stickers with less decorous phrases like "Girls in the hay, but not all day." A CBS-TV news crew, with correspondent Lem Tucker, arrived on campus less than a week later to interview Wilson as part of a story on the few remaining all-male colleges. For whatever reasons, the debate on coeducation this time had more energy and intensity than before and was obviously building momentum. Wilson and the administration scrambled to get ahead of it.

In mid-October, 115 alumni arrived in Lexington for the three-day Alumni Leadership Conference, and the discussion on coeducation was in full flower.[14] Though not on the agenda, the attendees heard reports on demographics and academic and social life—all pointing to whether women undergraduates should be admitted and what this would mean for the size of the university and the persistence of revered traditions. They learned that SAT scores were dropping, more offers were now necessary to fill a freshman class, only 7 percent of recent applicants listed W&L as their first choice, the all-male character of the university was the main reason given by students who elected to go elsewhere, and W&L's principal competitors who drew away a number of admitted students—Virginia, William & Mary, and North Carolina—were all large, public, coeducational institutions.

Wilson decided to face the issue head-on with the constituency that was most likely to be opposed to change. In the final conference session, he addressed what he knew was a widespread, if unspoken, question: "Why is this stranger, especially from up there (Virginia Tech), why is he of all people taking up this cross?" Because, he said, the issue was waiting for him when he arrived and demanded attention. "It is not an ideological question," he pointed out, "because women were happily admitted to the law school some ten years ago, and that has worked out splendidly from all accounts. Undergraduate women come as exchange students and to participate in the undergraduate life without difficulty. It isn't because we are taking it up because of arrogance." Rather, he said, the issue arises "because we are worried about maintaining the quality of this place, which is its distinctive feature." It was not only a question of numbers. Coeducation addressed student quality in a declining applicant pool, promising to attract "a more diverse set of talents," create a "more stimulating academic environment," develop an improved social environment from the fraternities to "the whole sort of intense social system that we have with much going up and down the road," and prepare graduates for the future by giving them "the fullest possible sense of the contributions of their capable colleagues who happen to be women." Wilson was making the case while trying to walk a fine line.[15]

The board of trustees gathered in Lexington for its regular meeting on October 22. Both the presidents of the Alumni Association (Peter A. Agelasto III) and the student body (Robert C. Jenevein) also attended. Wilson acknowledged the "premature publicity concerning coeducation" and the necessity "to address the question of this serious matter in a serious way." The board agreed to leave any public announcements concerning the issue to the discretion of the rector and the president and his staff. The trustees asked the president "to reexamine the general question of coeducation in the undergraduate schools of the University," a reexamination "warranted, not by demographic projections alone, but by our desire to understand *all* of the options before us." They intended to move forward carefully and deliberately, keep all constituencies informed, and continue discussions at the February meeting.[16] A clear indication of the depth of feeling on the issue was the resignation at this point of trustee Jack W. Warner of Tuscaloosa, Alabama, president and chairman of the Gulf States Paper Company and a great benefactor of the university who had recently been elected to an additional term. Warner saw the issue coming, and wanted to be free to fully express his mind to his fellow alumni and others.[17] He became the most visible, vocal, and persistent opponent of admitting undergraduate women to W&L.

Wilson first presented his "analysis" of coeducation, setting out the issues and concerns as a basis for further discussion, in the form of a memorandum to the trustees.[18] The twenty-one-page document was widely distributed throughout the campus, as well as to alumni and friends, and was printed in the November issue of the *Alumni Magazine*. This significant and widely read and referenced document defined the broader conversation.

Writing in his characteristic informal, conversational style, Wilson summarized broader changes in American society and higher education, bringing them into the context of Washington and Lee. A transformation had occurred over the previous fifteen years, "a reflection of a profound and permanent change in the way we look at and think about each other, men and women alike, in this country." Rather than a "fad," the greater involvement of women in society and the workforce was a "permanent change in American society." This change, in his view, "had the curious effect of isolating Washington and Lee," which was now pressed to "justify itself" and its all-male status. In response, the university could note that all-male institutions had prevailed throughout much of American history and could point to the success of its graduates. And unique among other distinguished colleges, W&L enjoyed the "indelible mark" left by Robert E. Lee. But was such a response sufficient or persuasive?

Would coeducation undermine the "intangible spirit" of W&L? There "is an air about this place," Wilson suggested, "formed by and through a masculine society, with all its rough camaraderie and good spirit and mutual affection and trust. *That* is, finally, what people mean to say when they vaguely refer to 'tradition' or 'custom' as their main justification for arguing against change." Beyond these intangibles lay a "serious danger for the future health and usefulness of this venerable institution." The "unprecedented decline in college-age people" posed a challenge to all of higher education and could not be ignored. He noted that W&L was currently accepting slightly more than half of those who applied and had also suffered about a one-hundred-point decline in average SAT scores: "Can we continue to command our current share in the market for the next fifteen years?" The university as it stood, he stated flatly, "cannot survive a drop in enrollment of 25%." W&L would be forced to accept a larger and larger share of the total applicant pool, threatening both enrollment and quality and leading to "a very tight and difficult downward spiral."

Wilson proceeded to address other concerns: the academic environment, the social environment, and the capabilities of women. "Most members of the faculty," he stated, "including faculty who are alumni of Washington and Lee, favor the admission of women" because it would enhance the quality of academic work. The admissions staff believed that admitting women would open up two new pools of applicants—women and also men who did not apply because they preferred a coeducational environment. The faculty also believed that men should learn to treat women as colleagues "capable of serious intention or serious work," rather than as simply "attractive, pleasant companions on social occasions." Since 90 percent of W&L students shared precollege classrooms with women, this situation should pose no unusual "distractions" or difficulties. Wilson reminded older alumni in particular that current W&L social life was far different from in the past: "It is more intense, more extensive and far less subject to constraint." Trips "down the road" now occurred throughout the week, and the typical fraternity party was not confined to members and their dates. Rather, it often happened in an "open house where uninvited carloads of women arrive and join with other uninvited men." Fraternities competed to have the best entertainment and attract the largest crowds. Among other things, he observed, this led to "the unearned monopoly of social life by the fraternity system," with too much movement by car and too much alcohol. Women in the student body could provide more opportunities for social interaction apart from the big party scene and also contribute to a more residential university with greater co-curricular life. In addition, women were rising and achieving prominence in most professional fields, and now constituted a third of young lawyers and Rhodes Scholars. "The women of society do not, strictly speaking, need Washington and Lee. . . . But we must wonder if Washington and Lee, with its established tradition of producing significant leaders, does not need its fair share of achieving women." Alumni would appreciate these new opportunities for their daughters.

Remaining all male, Wilson wrote, would not provide a "clear choice" for future students because, as Bob Huntley once said, it was "a choice that no one seems to want." Fraternities ought to be able to survive after coeducation in a student population with about a thousand men remaining. Fraternities suffered mostly from their current weaknesses, attracting only about 65 percent of the student body. The career and subject interests of women were now much more closely aligned with those of men than they had been even ten years before, thus requiring few curriculum adjustments. The impact of coeducation at W&L on surrounding women's colleges would be limited, and "in terms of relative enrollments, would inevitably be small." Responding to one of the greatest stated concerns, the contemplated increase in size—about 1,000 men, 500 women undergraduates, and 350 in the law school—would ensure a necessary critical mass for athletics and other activities but not preclude small classes and a sense of intimacy, though it would require additional faculty and staff.

Wilson acknowledged that much of the apprehension about coeducation was due to the coincidence of his recent appointment and "a sharpened sense of anxiety about our future enrollments." He noted that the quality of the students who enrolled was most important: "In brief, what we are talking about is the level and application of the extended conversations we carry on here—and upon that, in turn, rests the morale of the faculty, the success of our graduates and the ultimate reputation of the University. Nothing we do will be more important than how we set about to insure the future quality of Washington and Lee."

Wilson had not made a recommendation to the board, and he still maintained that the issue required further study and would benefit from the opinions of students, faculty, and alumni. But his "summary paper" of October 1983 was clearly weighted toward a preference for coeducation and a concern that W&L, as one professor put it, was "now in danger of being congealed into an eccentricity."[19] A number of reasons were offered, but the argument, and the urgency, rested overwhelmingly on one: the future decline in college-age students and its impact on W&L. Wilson was clearly on a fast track to resolving the issue one way or the other.

The following months were filled with questions, accusations, complaints, and conflicting information, as many alumni learned of the seriousness of what seemed a sudden renewal of the coeducation issue. Beginning in September 1983, Wilson visited as many alumni chapters as possible, accompanied by the new alumni secretary, Dick Sessoms, and often by his wife Anne. Alumni opposition was intense, sometimes bordering on incivility, leading to stressful encounters that continued into the spring 1984 Alumni Reunion Weekend and in countless phone conversations. Wilson usually began his alumni presentations by stating the best case for W&L remaining all male and then pointing out that admitting undergraduate women was what the times and the university's future demanded.[20]

Letters and calls flowed into the president's office and to individual trustees. The *Ring-tum Phi* carried student opinions and published a special eleven-page "Front Lawn" supplement on November 3, containing an interview with Wilson; demographic data from the Admissions Office; a discussion of the possible effects on fraternities, athletics, and surrounding women's colleges; a report on the experience of other colleges; and comments from notable alumni Lewis Powell, Roger Mudd of CBS News, and Lloyd Dobyns of NBC News.[21] Justice Powell declined to speak publicly on the matter but said he had written a letter to Wilson. In the letter he appealed for "diversity" within higher education and enclosed a copy of his dissent in the US Supreme Court case overturning the single-sex policy at the public Mississippi College for Women. Mudd favored "retaining a few good all-male schools," and while Dobyns hoped W&L would not change simply for economic reasons, he also recognized that traditional attitudes toward women no longer prevailed. Wilson took the opportunity to again say that he didn't bring the coed question to W&L: "I probably turned out to be more of a catalyst than I realized to this whole process of self-examination. So I didn't bring the issue of coeducation to Washington and Lee, the Western World has brought it to all of us." When asked if his raising questions about coeducation, fraternities, and on-campus housing might alienate certain people, he replied that raising such questions was his job. He was also well aware of the danger lurking in all this talk of change: the story might begin to be about him instead of the university: "I only hope one thing and that is my motives are not suspect, that I am not thought to have some hidden ideological agenda."

In his regular monthly epistle to the trustees, on November 16, he shared his frustration that the conversation on coeducation had spread far and wide, often on the assumption that a decision had been made even before any formal studies were commissioned. "It still ought to be possible, in a rational world," he wrote wistfully, "to look at serious subjects, of crucial importance to the future of the University, in a calm and deliberate way. . . . I fear there are many who believe that now is the time to organize an active lobby on the issue."[22] In the meantime, he received a number of letters supporting coeducation. One recent Dallas alumnus admired Wilson's courage and reminded him that Lee "came to Lexington to invest in the future."[23] Kenneth Ruscio, a 1976 graduate and postdoctoral student at UCLA who had been assistant director of admissions at W&L, wrote to say that despite different opinions on coeducation, the loyalty and bond among the alumni would supersede them. Ruscio would return to W&L, eventually as president.[24] Wilson was most comforted by the confidential letter he received from Jim Ballengee on November 3. "I believe," the rector wrote, "that the Board of Trustees should develop a careful plan for the admission of women as degree candidates in the undergraduate college." Beyond the demographic data, it was simply "the right thing to do."[25]

Despite signs of support, the trustees were discomfited by the flurry of commentary—and open resistance—from various quarters. Farris Hotchkiss led an effort to fashion a public-relations strategy through the University Relations Group to better explain the university's position and channel the discussion in a more positive direction. The group consisted of university personnel dealing with alumni, athletics, and the news media, supplemented by volunteer consultants from corporations and other universities. Hotchkiss, Parsons, Sessoms, and six outside consultants met in Richmond on December 14 to devise recommendations and address widespread misconceptions. The focus, they decided, should be on the decision-making process and distributing factual information to alumni, and the issue should be quality rather than coeducation. The *Alumni Magazine* should provide opinion on both sides but avoid turning the discussion into a "pro and con battleground." The university should directly address the notion that the problem was somehow a failure of the admissions office, and the rector should be brought forward "into fuller view" at the same time that President Wilson was taken "off the spot." "As matters stand now," the group noted, "he is very vulnerable—unnecessarily so."[26]

One strategy was, as Parsons later explained, to reflect through the *Alumni Magazine* "our genuine effort to fairly represent the open nature of the Trustees' study, even to provide a forum wherein those who opposed coeducation could voice their sentiments."[27] The January issue was forthright on coeducation and contained a wealth of data on admissions, the demographics of the student population, and letters from Peter Agelasto, the alumni board president, and Jack Warner, an avowed coeducation opponent. An eleven-page article by Jeffrey Hanna, "The Admissions Race is On: As the Numbers Go Down, the Competition Heats Up," detailed how a total prospect pool of 67,000 was systematically whittled down to 1,500 or 1,600 applications and, eventually, an entering class of about 360. To achieve this, the university had to raise the number of offers. The projected decline in the number of eighteen-year-olds—and high school graduates—through 1992 would likely mean a significant reduction in either enrollment (maybe as much as 28 percent) or in student quality.[28]

To counter perceptions that student recruitment efforts were inadequate, Hanna's article detailed W&L's current process and the greatly increased resources marshaled to support it. The budget for the office of admissions rose from $75,000 to $340,000 in seven years, and Bill Hartog's staff now numbered five full-time professionals (three of them alumni) and three part-timers. In a "sort of marketing effort associated with major corporations," new tools like market research and direct mail assumed much larger roles than in the past and produced a much larger prospect pool (67,000, compared with 3,500 in the mid-1970s). The staff traveled hundreds of thousands of miles to visit individual prospects, went to 435 secondary schools, and attended 89 college nights. Prospect visits to W&L were also increasingly important; 84 percent of the entering class in 1983 had visited the campus. The recruiters stressed three main features of W&L: the depth and breadth of its academic offerings relative to its size, the Honor System, and the distinctiveness of its "all-maleness" ("coeducational on the weekends"). The Alumni Admissions Program, established in 1978–79, was an integral part of the effort, with committees in sixty-two cities in thirty-two states. Admission was not based solely on SAT scores but took into account other important characteristics, including athletic and other extracurricular interests. Still, the admissions staff encountered a rising number of potential students who were put off by the university's all-male character. Responding to a 1982 questionnaire, 34 percent of students offered admission listed this as a major reason for not attending W&L.

Agelasto assured readers that all alumni would have an opportunity to respond to a written survey before the trustees reached a final decision on coeducation, and he introduced former trustee Jack Warner's letter.[29] Warner declared that he was *totally against coeducation for W&L now and in the near future.* He questioned whether the admissions office had, in fact, done a good job of emphasizing W&L's distinctiveness, which was its major competitive advantage, especially against larger schools. He pointed to the university's past success, its recent high rating in *U.S. News and World Report,* and the relatively high number of applications received in 1983. "Why," he asked, "tamper with a good thing!" W&L "surely ought to be able to continue our strong Washington and Lee posture and enroll 400 or so students annually." He complained, on the whole correctly, "nothing new has been introduced that wasn't known in 1976, and yet this proposal is again before the Board."

On January 5, 1984, Wilson—looking ahead to the February board meeting—wrote Hotchkiss. He recognized that getting the board to agree to study the matter "probably requires very little," but persuading them to do so "under some time insistence requires us to add *urgency* to the general logic of examining coeducation." He did not want the discussion to drag on interminably. "A veritable mountain of information" should be made available to the board, but the presentations should be limited in number, emphasize the need for a decision by May or the summer, and focus on admissions and demographics, campus life, and financial "bottom line" implications.[30]

Studies and reports were collected during January and February—on admissions, student attrition, graduation rates, test scores, social life, and comparisons with other universities—and circulated within the administration and shared with the trustees.[31] Of the 178 letters the university received on coeducation, 58 percent were opposed (some adamantly), 29 percent were in favor, and 13 percent were ambivalent or willing to support the board's decision. Opposition to coeducation was more pronounced among those who graduated before 1950.[32] Professor Toni M. Massaro of the law school responded to Wilson's request for information about the potential effect of the Equal Rights Amendment, then still pending ratification. Massaro pointed out that existing law treated discrimination by gender far less strictly than by race and would almost certainly allow W&L to "correct" any gender imbalance that might result from a "gender blind" admissions policy.[33]

The board, meeting in Lexington, went into special session on the afternoon of February 3 to hear reports on the implications of coeducation. Bill Hartog presented on admissions, William Watt on academic and athletic space, Lew John on residential development, and Farris Hotchkiss on the potential impact on giving patterns. The trustees then announced that a "comprehensive study" would be undertaken on undergraduate coeducation by the board's standing committees, focusing on eleven specific elements, from the size of the university to intercollegiate athletics and the "intangibles" of the W&L experience. They hoped to discuss the results of these investigations at the regular board meeting in May and to make a final decision on the matter in a special meeting tentatively scheduled for July.[34] The following morning the board approved the formation of a new standing Committee on Campus Life, including housing, dining, fraternities, athletics, and other extracurricular activities. And the Board's Executive Committee, augmented by a few additional members, was charged with assessing the impact of coeducation on the important "intangibles"—the university's character, size, traditions, standards, and special attributes.[35]

The real possibility, even likelihood, of admitting undergraduate women to W&L was now fully revealed, and Wilson remained the focus of press reports and many alumni complaints. A February 5 story in the *Roanoke News* by Mary Bishop began with more than a little hyperbole: "John Wilson couldn't be at the center of more controversy if he suggested that Washington and Lee kick Robert E. Lee out of his vault in Lee Chapel, chop down all the white columns along the university's colonnade and join the community college system." Wilson was "the embodiment of the issue, a man accused by foes of coming in with a 'silent agenda' to turn the school coed, which he denies." He was "a Northerner who some see as a threat to one of the last great Southern gentlemen's universities." The "normally well-mannered school is in a feisty mood," the story continued, and students had taken to commenting on Wilson's "broad-striped ties" and synthetic fiber suits. On the other hand, Wilson enjoyed the support of faculty, who praised his courage, and some students.[36]

With few exceptions, the flood of reports and information confirmed or updated what had been collected a decade earlier, though the demographic projections and many other troublesome trends were either new or more serious than before. Hartog predicted, given all the factors—economic, demographic, and the current competitive position for students and admissions criteria—a 1996 class of no more than 265 students if W&L remained all male.[37] Reports were again assembled on the experience of other universities that had admitted women—Princeton, Columbia, Notre Dame, Amherst, Dartmouth, Haverford, and Williams—and one, Wabash College, which had not. Parsons provided the trustees with copies of W&L's earlier investigations on coeducation and distributed a summary volume of the 1975 study.

Hartog offered more detailed data on admissions—some of which was published in the January *Alumni Magazine* and presented to the board at the February meeting—that confirmed the higher number of offers, lower rate of acceptances, and "a steady erosion of the quality of those entering as freshmen," even though the number of students receiving financial aid had increased by 53 percent between 1979 and 1983. In 1965, of enrolled freshmen, 53 percent had graduated in the top fifth of their high-school class; by 1983, only 34 percent

had done so. Average combined SAT scores fell nationally over the same period by 65 points, and by 35 points at Davidson, 26 points at Duke, 61 points
at Richmond and the University of Virginia, and 65 points at Johns Hopkins.
At W&L the drop was 114 points. A greater dependence on direct mail had
produced a larger prospect pool but, in the midst of stiff national competition,
rendered the university especially vulnerable during economic downturns. And
the geographic origins of the freshman class had remained strikingly consistent
since 1961, with about 55 percent of students applying from Virginia, Maryland,
New Jersey, New York, Pennsylvania, and Texas. W&L's survey of secondary-
school counselors revealed especially troubling evidence of students actively
avoiding all-male institutions.[38]

At the same time, Wilson was working to shape the discussion. He com-
piled a list of fifteen "pros" for coeducation and ten "cons," and added seven
questions that were likely to be asked or that he could ask alumni groups.[39] He
also drafted guidelines and suggestions for the executive committee's study
of the "intangibles." One approach was to take as a model the "Statement of
Institutional Philosophy" initially prepared for the 1966 Southern Association
of Colleges and Schools (SACS) self-study and to test how coeducation might
influence each of its principles and objectives. Another approach "might usefully have the Committee set out the main outline of a defense of the all-male
undergraduate experience. I believe this to be imperative in any event, for we
need to know where we are, in philosophical and practical terms, before we can
sensibly contemplate altering our current condition. And, especially, we need
to have in hand a compelling rationalization of our all-male character if, in July,
we agree to remain as now we are." To this end, he provided a brief rationalization of ten major arguments for remaining all male at the undergraduate level.
Intentionally, he left out negative arguments and also—significantly—the issue
of academic quality: "We are, after all, engaged at this stage, in a somewhat
more abstract exercise." He asked trustees to suggest other positive arguments
before subjecting the overall argument "to a searching critique." He said he was
open to a decision either way but that remaining all male could not be simply
affirmed, as it had been on several previous occasions. Doing so would now
demand explicit agreement on specific arguments, which would serve as "a
fitting philosophical guide for the years to come."[40]

A Sociology Department survey showed a majority of students opposed to
coeducation and 80 percent of the faculty in support (fourteen said they would
not remain at W&L if it remained all male); over 80 percent of both groups

believed that coeducation was likely to be adopted "in the near future."[41] As the May board meeting approached, the letters continued to come in, and the pressures for the university to back down or delay consideration of coeducation increased. Meanwhile, Jack Warner's vocal campaign against coeducation ramped up. In an eight-page April 20 letter to "Selected Alumni and Friends" of W&L, including all current and emeritus trustees, Warner again laid out his arguments. He alleged that many alumni had been reassured during the development campaign that the coeducation issue had been tabled, and thus the new effort constituted a "violation of the trust provided in the recent past." The questionnaire sent to all alumni on March 30 provided an opportunity to express an opinion but, in Warner's view, reflected the bias of those favoring coeducation. And visits by the administration to alumni groups seemed part of the orchestrated campaign. "As the 'demographic scare' is the vehicle to bring about coeducation, coeducation may be a means to achieve very specific objectives." Warner was not very specific about what these "specific objectives" were. One of them, he wrote, might be about "who will be '*the force*' to guide the school's future." The only two groups in favor of coeducation, as far as he could tell, were "the faculty and the new administration." The Honor System standards followed by the students "appear to be lacking by other groups on the campus." The faculty was acting in direct self-interest; if the demographic projections were correct, there would be fewer students, and thus fewer faculty and opportunities for promotion. As he wrote Agelasto on January 26, the faculty were likely cowed by the subtle hint of administrative support for coeducation, and "'tenure review' is designed to stifle dissent." As for the administrators, their self-interest perhaps lay in achievements that would help them "move up the ladder" to larger universities. The trustees, Warner emphasized, should establish their authority over the campus rather than riding "the coattails of the new administration, letting it assume the leadership in moving to a pro-educational decision."

Warner's main points were that the university could not afford to lose the support of its alumni base and undermine its competitive position by abandoning its distinctiveness. The demographic projections were "Clap trap!" Most graduates, in his view, could not accept that such a storied and successful institution could now be so vulnerable. As Warner put it, "In a population of 230 million people, surely there are 400 highly qualified young men who can be attracted to Washington and Lee every year." Perhaps the failure lay, as he had asserted before, with an inadequate admissions office. Finally, he urged all alumni and friends, regardless of their position, to share their opinions with the board. The May board meeting was "when minds will be made up."[42]

On April 25, trustee emeritus E. Waller Dudley appealed to Ballengee to delay the vote on coeducation. The board was on the spot, he said, proponents on both sides were adamant, and "a loss of significant financial support would surely follow any decision to convert." John Wilson, in his view, was an "exceptional man," but if the matter "is allowed to come to a head at a time when the vote would almost surely go against him," it would seriously undermine his credibility. If the university lost Wilson, "it does not take much imagination to figure out how difficult it will be to attract an equally able successor." Dudley noted the board's own responsibility "for this state of affairs" by not putting the issue on the "back burner" until Wilson had fully established himself: "The problem now facing the board is that the merit of the question itself has been totally obscured by the anger of countless alumni who were only recently informed that the University has never been healthier, thanks to a brilliantly successful fund drive, a marvelous student body and a top notch faculty."[43] Dudley had a point. The development campaign results were heartily celebrated, and virtually all the information in support of coeducation had been known a decade earlier. Dudley recommended "a prolonged 'cooling off period.'"

Trustee A. Christian Compton, justice of the Supreme Court of Virginia, expressed a similar sentiment in view of the flood of letters he and fellow trustees were receiving: "I believe we must do something to defuse the coed controversy . . . The volume has risen so sharply in the last month that I no longer make any attempt to respond to each one." Regardless of the decision, he feared, "lasting and irreparable damage may be in store for Washington and Lee." He lost sleep over the matter because "the impact of the 1954 decision to discontinue subsidized athletics will be seen as insignificant when compared to the fallout from a decision now to embrace coeducation in the college."[44]

With the May meeting only a few weeks away, John Wilson received hate mail, and he and Anne suffered late-night phone calls to Lee House. "It's been a most difficult winter and spring," Wilson confided to his friend Marshall Fishwick. "I'm having to cope with a strong movement amongst conservative alumni to frustrate the coed talks by questioning my character. It is enervating," he complained, "as you can well imagine. I don't know how things will come out or, at this point, what my own future might be. It is easy, in this situation, to win, but lose, if you know what I mean." The trustees had already scheduled a July meeting to vote on the matter. "I've been urged not to take a position lest the Board find it impossible to support my recommendation and thus appear to repudiate me. Yet one must obey one's own inner-calling on things of this sort," Wilson wrote. He was not one to stand on the sidelines: "I am confused, as you can see. But otherwise happy enough."[45]

"I do not think," Farris Hotchkiss wrote Wilson on May 14, "that we should engage in temporizing, delays, grace periods, time-of-testing, or the like. I believe that you should report to the Board in July that (a) your senior staff unanimously recommends undergraduate coeducation; (b) some 85% of the faculty recommends that action; (c) the majority of the Alumni Board recommends that action; (d) some 40% of the students and alumni who responded to polls and surveys recommends that action, or would not oppose it; and that (e) you recommend that action." Wilson would be taking a personal risk in making a definite recommendation, but anything less "would be false and transparent." Hotchkiss was especially sorry that "Washington and Lee will have a longer period of anger and reprisal than has been reported by other formerly all-male schools." He attributed this to the long period of time the opposition had available to take public positions, the fact that W&L was among the last all-male schools to confront this decision, that so many alumni prized the university's "social impact" more than its academic aspects, the heavy influence of "conservative, Southern thinking," and the W&L "mystique" of being both unique and, in most alumni recollections, ideal. "Our financial support will be weakened for 3–4 years," Hotchkiss predicted. "We may lose some support permanently, some of it rather major in dimension," but the change was important and necessary: "Lee would be proud of us."[46]

Keenly aware of his exposure and vulnerability, Wilson attributed most of it to timing. As he wrote one deeply concerned Dallas alumnus, "I think the issue arose, after lying dormant for eight years, because (a) I was new in 1982–83 and (b) the faculty were more sharply aware than ever before of the tremendous strains we are now beginning to face in the recruitment of bright and able freshmen. I deeply regret," he added, "that my own motives, real or imagined, have been entangled in this issue." Rather than his coercing the faculty toward coeducation, as some suggested, "The faculty have been urging this change for over a decade here."[47]

Anticipating the May board meeting, Wilson reviewed his options in typical fashion—by organizing his thoughts in a list. Under the heading "Crude notions of one sort or another" he enumerated thirty-one pros and cons that might come up (or that he might bring up) in discussions. The "movement toward delay is growing," he wrote, and if he recommended change, he might be "repudiated" by the board. If he made no recommendation, he would "have failed faculty, staff & trustees." If the board delayed, the "Warner group will have 'won' and jeopardized future moves (whether by me or a successor)." At this point, "damage will result in moving both ways." Could he and the board accept a "coordinate college" in lieu of undergraduate coeducation?[48] Wilson could not predict what the final decision would be. Many individual trustees were doubtless working through a similar calculus.

When they convened for the unusual three-day meeting in May, board members knew that a final decision would not come before July. This allowed time for still further immersion in virtually every conceivable aspect of the issue. The trustees and their spouses enjoyed a reception and dinner in Evans Dining Hall, as guests of the Student Executive Committee, and a presentation on "Perceptions of Washington and Lee" by eight students representing all academic classes. The board met on Saturday for a full agenda of regular business. Charles D. Hurt Jr., president of the alumni board of directors, reported that the alumni had been given ample opportunity to express opinions on coeducation, and they had the "utmost confidence" that the trustees would make a "proper decision" in the matter. Ballengee announced that the board had made "significant progress" and that a decision on the issue was anticipated at the special board meeting on July 13 and 14.[49]

During May, mail continued to deluge the trustees. Mark B. Davis Jr., an attorney in Louisville, wrote each trustee on May 25, with Wilson's encouragement, appealing for favorable consideration of admitting women undergraduates. He received replies from almost everyone, mostly noncommittal. Some were "form" letters necessitated by the volume of mail the trustees were receiving.[50] Lewis Powell reiterated his "personal preference" for maintaining things as they were: "I think the rush to coeducation has become a sort of stampede." Edgar Shannon replied, "Since I have received a number of vehement letters on the other side of the question, it is gratifying to have your [Davis's] testimony." Thomas B. Branch III of Atlanta responded that he had already declared his support for coeducation and guessed that the board was currently "about evenly split" on the matter. Trustee emeritus and former rector John Newton Thomas acknowledged that he had received few letters in support of coeducation and enclosed a copy of his May 7 letter to Ballengee advocating a delay, perhaps indefinitely, because of the charged atmosphere. J. Thomas Touchton of Tampa sent a copy of a six-page typed letter that he had sent in reply to other letters, in which he particularly lamented the widespread misunderstandings, errors, and rumors surrounding the discussion.

The news media fueled and reflected the rising drama now that a decision was close at hand. A Roanoke television station covered the issue in depth. The *Washington Post* noted, "Both the controversy and the reasons behind it have attracted national attention, in part because the country's colleges and universities will face an uncomfortable fact: The baby boom is over." W&L especially drew attention because it was "a tradition-laden, academically respected institution nestled in once-aristocratic Virginia and carrying symbolic importance in the South."[51] The *Norfolk Virginian Pilot* described how the debate had roiled the campus: "Change has never come easily at W&L."[52]

AT LONG LAST, ON JULY 14, 1984, a motion to admit undergraduate women as degree students to Washington and Lee was put before the board of trustees. Representatives of the news media and others gathered outside the meeting room. Ballengee asked each trustee to stand and state his or her position on the issue, beginning with President Wilson. Going around the table for the next hour, some read prepared statements and others spoke extemporaneously. They agreed that without at least sixteen affirmative votes (two-thirds), the matter would automatically be reconsidered.[53] The question was called at 11:45 a.m. Secretary James Whitehead called the roll. The final ballot was seventeen in favor of coeducation and seven opposed.[54]

Almost an hour later, after a statement and press release had been prepared, four trustees appeared for a news conference in the School of Commerce. Dr. Edgar Shannon Jr. and Virginia Supreme Court justice A. Christian Compton flanked Ballengee and Wilson. Since the media almost filled the room, the conference was shown on screens set up in Reid Hall for the overflow crowd, and it was also broadcast live on WLUR-FM. The campus switchboard was swamped with calls for the next four hours.

Ballengee read the announcement: W&L would "admit qualified students, regardless of gender, to all its degree programs commencing in the Fall of 1985." He then read the supporting statement. The board had paid special attention to the opinions and advice of students, alumni, and faculty members, and "attempted to place those judgments in the larger context of continuing change in American society and in the widening responsibilities assumed by talented women in our time." In the end, "the Trustees found unmistakable common agreement that Washington and Lee's most precious assets are its reputation for excellence and its long and distinguished history of service to the Commonwealth and the nation." While opinions on the board were divided, "the Trustees are united in pledging their full commitment to the successful implementation of the University's new course." The Board Executive Committee was charged with overseeing the university's preparations.[55]

The floor was opened for questions, which quickly honed in on the importance of the demographic projections. Ballengee confirmed that this was a concern. The enrollment in all-male schools, he noted, had declined to about eight thousand. "That looks like a product that isn't very much in demand to many people." Wilson commented that demographics were by no means the sole issue; the university's future had to be shaped in the context of changes in the larger society, and he expected the entire university would benefit. Justice Compton reported that he had voted against the resolution because he believed that the university was doing a fine job in its current configuration, but he said the time had now come for all "who love and support Washington and Lee" to "work just as hard to make coeducation another positive factor as we worked against the proposal to coeducate." A new Committee on Coeducation composed of administrators, faculty members, and students, working closely with the Board Executive Committee, would work out the details of the next steps. Current plans, according to Wilson, were to admit about eighty women students in the fall of 1985 and to move slowly to increase the overall undergraduate enrollment from 1,350 to 1,500, including as many as 500 women, over ten years. He noted that this was only a modest expansion overall, bringing in about 150 additional students. He confirmed that these changes would mean enrolling fewer men. A new residence hall would be needed in any event, since the university had already been planning to house a higher proportion of its students on campus, and the gymnasium facilities also required renovation. Edgar Shannon pointed out that expansion of the athletic program due to coeducation at the University of Virginia had been substantial but "was a fairly minor aspect" in terms of cost. Wilson affirmed W&L's commitment to the fraternity system; any decline in the number of fraternities "would be only through natural attrition, not through policy." It would be up to the women, he added, as to whether sororities were established. Responding to a question, Wilson said he would rely on the incoming president of the student body, Cole Dawson of Houston, to help shape the student response.[56] Dawson had participated in the trustee's final deliberations and strongly supported coeducation, a position he reaffirmed in a letter to the *Ring-tum Phi*. The news conference ended after thirty minutes. The university breathed a sigh of relief and began to wrestle with the challenges ahead.

On Monday morning, July 16, four young women who had been touring colleges in the area learned of the trustee's decision and appeared for interviews in the admissions office. The university mailed five hundred letters to women who had previously inquired about applying to Washington and Lee. The admissions office had also purchased a list of 35,000 names of female high-school graduates to be contacted, and now the staff put it to use. Bill Hartog was especially relieved: he was so closely identified with the need for coeducation that he told Wilson shortly before the trustee vote that he would probably have to resign if it was not approved.[57] An alumnus from Richmond wrote, "My third child was born on June 24, 1984. Three children—three daughters. Please change my 'no' vote on the coeducation questionnaire to a 'yes.'"[58] The future had arrived.[59]

LETTERS WERE MAILED on Monday to every W&L graduate, class agents and alumni admissions representatives were primed to explain the new program, and a full report was scheduled for the next *Alumni Magazine*. Wilson wrote to the faculty and staff, reminding them that only fourteen months remained in which to plan for the arrival of the first female undergraduates.[60] He also wrote to all the area women's colleges, pledging his "commitment to work toward closer relationships," even though these relationships would now change: "But I see no reason why our students and faculties cannot cooperate in many useful ways, some, I hope, new and fresh to us." He explained the plan to admit no more than a hundred women students in the first year and promised to "severely limit transfer opportunities." He confided to his fellow presidents that, at the moment, "I want mainly to sit for a few days without thinking further about coeducation. I can't remember when I have felt quite so drained."[61]

The board's decision garnered praise in the news media. In a *Richmond Times-Dispatch* editorial headlined "W&L's Act of Evolution," Robert G. Holland compared the historic event with the French storming of the Bastille: "The [W&L] Board's decision was not an act of radical revolutionists determined to smite the status quo. It was an agonizing choice made by well-heeled corporate executives, investment bankers, businessmen, attorneys, and educators. . . . Few would quibble with a conclusion that the ending of the males-only tradition at Gen. Lee's College, surely one of the most conservative places in academe, says something profound about change not only at the nation's sixth oldest college but also in relations between the sexes generally." Holland recalled the university's previous controversial decisions to end subsidized football and to admit black students, both now regarded as "morally and pragmatically correct." Quoting W&L history professor Taylor Sanders on the high number of colleges that had failed because they could not adapt to changing times, and the transformative leadership provided by Lee after the Civil War, Holland declared, "Despite its reverence for history, Washington and Lee has never chained itself to the past." Holland ended with a comment by English professor Sidney Coulling: "I have no reluctance in believing that Robert E. Lee would have favored this change. This is one more change in our evolution."[62]

In early September, Wilson announced the formation of an ad hoc Coeducation Steering Committee, chaired by Associate Dean Pamela Simpson, with twelve members drawn from the student body, faculty, and administration.[63] The committee would deal with admissions policies and procedures, residential accommodations, health and counseling services, athletic programs, dining-hall operations, student organizations, faculty/staff appointments, security, and campus renovations. The first task was planning for a freshman class of about four hundred in 1985, with 80 women and 320 men. The initial planning period was ten years, with a target of 500 women undergraduates enrolled by 1995 within a total undergraduate enrollment of 1,500. (After 1995 W&L would pursue balanced enrollments of men and women.) Both men and women transfer applicants should be considered for the limited number of places available; on-campus residential capacity should be increased but not required beyond the freshman year; a "strong program" of athletics should be developed for women, along the lines of that available to men; sorority affiliation should be deferred until sufficient numbers of women are enrolled; and the university should continue to work on efforts already underway to improve the fraternity system. At the October board meeting, Simpson reported on the initial work of the committee—the formation of six subcommittees, general discussions of admissions policy, and discussions with students and faculty members who had experienced the coeducation transition at other institutions.[64] In his monthly letter to the board, Wilson reported an increase over the previous summer of 66 percent in on-campus admissions interviews, including a 39 percent increase in male prospects.[65]

In 1985, W&L enjoyed the "brightest admissions situation" it had experienced in a long time, with eight applicants for every place in the class of 1989. During the summer, the Davis, Gilliam, and Graham-Lees dormitories were rearranged in alternate floor and alternate wing configurations, assuring security and privacy for women students, though some single rooms were converted to doubles to increase capacity. Plans were accelerated for the construction of a new 240-bed residence hall for juniors, seniors, and law students.[66]

The task of nurturing, consoling, and reassuring alumni continued. The Alumni Office coordinated visits to alumni chapters by Wilson, faculty members, and student singing groups, such as Southern Comfort and the new University Chorus, which included first-year women. The students were housed in alumni homes, which brought alumni face-to-face with coeducation and the reassurance that these were impressive students who shared their affection for W&L.[67] Many alumni supported the change. In October, William E. Brock, '53, then US trade representative and former US senator from Tennessee, wrote, "I am deeply proud of our university for having taken what is both a courageous and a right decision. I do have a bit of regret, in that it occurred a bit late for my own daughter." He also passed along brief biographical information on two "remarkable young people" who would be great assets to the W&L community: Alston Parker (who had already applied for early admission) and her brother Stephen. "I find it particularly fascinating that you might begin our co-educational enterprise with a brother-sister team."[68]

Wilson wrote Marshall Fishwick in November, "A few alumni have already advised us that we should look to others for support." He was prepared for reduced contributions to the alumni fund for a few years, as other institutions had reported, but he was delighted with the admissions results. "We are sharply up in every category at this stage and look for a very reaffirming experience." One problem now was alienating the fathers of daughters who were denied admission.[69] As the academic year wore on, Wilson noted, the admissions data remained quite impressive—more applications, a lower acceptance rate, a rise of eighty points in test scores. "Of course," he confided to Fishwick, "the old guard won't find encouragement even in such numbers. They believe we should be enrolling 'good fellows' from 'good families' and think such persons cannot also be bright." On the other hand, Wilson reported that his "hate mail has considerably subsided, for all of that." The die-hards "still think I am a run-away intellectual bound to change the old place in deeply harmful ways. Maybe they will turn out to be right. I hope not."[70]

The results of the alumni survey had revealed more nuanced opinions and ambivalence about coeducation, and belied the notion that most graduates, especially older ones, were misogynistic "good ol' boys." While about 60 percent had opposed coeducation, all responding alumni had rated the all-male character of the university as only ninth in importance among thirteen specific institutional characteristics. The quality of faculty, small classes, the Honor System, academically selective admissions, and relatively small enrollment were deemed most important. About 30 percent had been in favor of admitting women undergraduates. While most respondents wanted W&L to make "every reasonable effort" to remain all male, less than a quarter favored this if it meant lowering admissions standards. Three-quarters also thought women would be equally attracted to the commerce, premed, prelaw, and journalism programs, and two-thirds of alumni respondents believed that coeducation would not undermine the Honor System. An overwhelming majority had read both Wilson's "Taking Thought on Coeducation" essay and Jack Warner's letter in the *Alumni Magazine*.[71]

Letters appeared in the *Alumni Magazine* on both sides of the issue, before and after the board's decision. Alumni who favored coeducation often pointed to the changing role of women in American society and the positive influence they would have on the university. "How can any student, male or female," asked a 1969 graduate, "receive the most balanced possible view of the human experience in an environment largely devoid of the opposite sex except on social occasions?" In the same issue, a member of the class of 1959 and former president of his local alumni chapter, declared that the university's all-male status was a definite deterrent to many worthy applicants and that in "the real world today, women have truly become our equal, with large numbers of them achieving great success and prominence in all fields of endeavor."[72] An alumnus from 1955 wrote, "If you see young ladies in the morning at breakfast or debate issues from a course . . . over a beer and a hamburger or run five miles through the autumn with one of them, you get a whole different, fuller perspective than if the near totality of your social contact consists of shouting at each other over the noise of some rock combo in a frat house cellar."[73] Of course, some reactions in the immediate aftermath of the decision were hostile. A very recent alumnus declared, "This is truly one of the saddest times of my life, for [the board's] vote has destroyed something which gave me foundations and ideals upon which I have based my life."[74]

THE FIRST UNDERGRADUATE "coeds" arrived on schedule for the fall semester in 1985. Move-in day on Sunday afternoon, September 8, seemed a threshold moment. An extra section of the *Roanoke Times and World-News* on September 1 covered the preparations.[75] Renovations to bathrooms, a new locker room in the gym, and lighter items on the dining hall menu were intended to make the former male bastion more inviting for women. The rooster wallpaper in the "Cockpit" was replaced, as was the name of the hangout itself. The hunt for chauvinistic symbols even considered the traditional fight song. The "Washington and Lee Swing" remained intact (since football was played solely by men), but the unauthorized substitution of "Sweet Briar" for "those Wahoos" in one verse was discouraged. New lighting was installed along campus pathways, and security officers wore informal uniforms and drove marked cars. Privacy was increased in campus heath services, and thanks to consultations with Davidson College, preparations were made to deal with women's health issues. Freshman orientation was expanded, with an optional weekend of mountain hiking. Fraternities invited all women students to rush parties. The initial women's sports—cross-country, tennis, golf, and swimming and diving—were expanded based on student interest, and a female assistant athletic director was appointed. Other changes were in the works, including plans for a mixed chorus and a new sexual-harassment policy. A variety of exhibits and presentations focused on women in the South and important women in the history of W&L.

The entering undergraduate class was excellent by almost any measure. They scored 65 points higher than the previous year's class on the SAT and included thirty National Merit Scholars, thirty-six students who ranked first or second in their high school class, seventy-seven who had been student government president or vice president, eighteen National Honor Society presidents, sixty-nine captains of varsity athletic teams, and—especially important—fifty-four children of alumni, thirty-seven more than the year before.[76] The 406 freshmen included 105 women. While the news media scurried about covering the occasion, the students themselves were mostly interested in settling into their dorm rooms, attending orientation, and registering for classes. History professor Taylor Sanders addressed them on the lawn adjacent to the Liberty Hall ruins, comparing the university's evolution to "a crusty old snake beside a stone wall . . . sloughing off old skin and emerging something new, yet basically the same. The core goes deeper than mere tradition." And Trustee Compton, who had voted against coeducation fourteen months earlier, spoke at a freshman class picnic about the university's special characteristics, especially the Honor System, and what the new students would gain from it.[77]

Not all undergraduate women were in the class of 1989. Kathleen Plante had already been on campus for a very successful year as an exchange student from Hollins College. (She was even chosen the W&L Homecoming Queen.) She transferred as a regular student to W&L in 1985 to major in East Asian Studies and serve as a dorm counselor for freshmen women, and was one of the first four women graduates in 1987. (Four more transfer students graduated in 1988).

The class of 1989 was the first class with women who had experienced four undergraduate years at W&L. Commencement was a happy occasion, and some women pointed to both their "pioneering spirit" and the frustrations they had encountered. Marie Dunne, former editor of the *Ring-tum Phi*, confessed, "it was rough," and speculated that every woman, at one point or another, had probably considered transferring. "We've been through a lot. But it's gotten to the point where we really are a class."[78] Amy Balfour, who would go on to be a leader in the law school, observed, "We've had a very special class. We've managed to stick together, get along and have a great time."[79] The *Roanoke Times and World News* surveyed the effect of four years of coeducation from a number of perspectives and concluded that undergraduate men were less "reckless" when women were classmates. Women excelled in the classroom, assumed leadership positions, and made a positive impact on the institution, even leading to "cultural reform": "The preppy, conservative school is getting more shadings of liberal thought, students say."[80] The *Washington Post* commented in 1990 on the school's reputation and persisting traditional notions about women: "Drawing strongly from the South, the university is something of a breeding ground for young, motivated, conservative students, 95 percent of whom are white. BMW's and Porsches are the cars of choice." But the article also quoted John Klinedinst, president of the Alumni Association: "Coeducation is the best thing that ever happened to W&L."[81] Perhaps the most encouraging sign at the 1989 commencement was that no official mention was made of the special nature of the graduating class. This was indeed intended to be the "new normal." The first three women to receive both undergraduate and law degrees from W&L graduated in 1993.

The incorporation of women undergraduates into the academic and cultural fabric of one of the nation's oldest colleges proceeded alongside, and as part of, major changes in American society and higher education generally. New standards of equity and student responsibility, as well as social pressures and economic realities, shaped university policies in an era also marked by unprecedented student diversity and access to higher education. Rather than follow a unique path, W&L had joined the mainstream of higher education as far as gender was concerned and would face the same rewards and difficulties as most other universities, public or private.

John Wilson now looked ahead and set goals and targets for the first ten years of coeducation, and in September 1993 he appointed a Coeducation Review Committee to assess progress and continuing challenges. Wilson asked this group of a dozen faculty members and students—co-chaired by Pamela Simpson and Bob Strong—to address two broad questions: (1) did the environment at W&L "promote the highest possibilities for the development of our students and faculty," and (2) did women have "a sense of ownership" in the W&L community that equaled that of men? The assessment therefore dealt with many evolving dimensions of university life not entirely connected to coeducation. The final committee report was submitted in September 1994.[82]

The committee's overall, and perhaps overly modest, conclusion was that coeducation was "proceeding well." An outsider might have judged it to be a roaring success, certainly on the basis of its original justifications. Between 1984 and 1993, total enrollment was up to 1,600; applications had more than doubled, to 3,318, and the acceptance rate had declined; average SAT scores for the entering class were almost a hundred points higher (at a time when national SAT averages were falling); and retention to graduation had risen from 81 to 90 percent. Even though the total number of men had declined, fraternity membership had increased from 63 to 82 percent, reaching a participation rate reminiscent of the early 1960s. The number of full-time faculty women had risen from six to eighteen. The endowment had almost tripled, to $147 million, with the annual fund growing significantly and women graduates contributing at a higher rate and in larger average amounts than men. Many other factors contributed to these results, of course, but coeducation was clearly not an impediment to progress. The work of Bill Hartog and his admissions staff had been validated in almost every respect. But John Wilson knew it was still a work in progress. "We are stumbling along as best we can, and I think are making fair progress," he wrote to another college president in 1987. "We won't be out of the woods for several years, minimally until the last two all-male classes graduate. One of these will leave us this June, and I'm only now hoping that the few bold male chauvinists among them will not choose commencement time for an ill-suited display of one sort of another."[83] (They did not.)

In certain ways, as some alumni initially feared, coeducation was too successful: women applicants on the whole were more academically qualified than men, and maintaining the prevailing 60/40 ratio of men to women required effectively discriminating against the many qualified females who heavily populated the admissions waitlist. Women were also consistently more successful in the classroom; their average GPA never fell below 3.0, whereas the average for men never rose above 2.9. As predicted, women made greater use of the student health service, and they enrolled more often in basic liberal arts courses—history, English, journalism, biology, and psychology—than in business or accounting. The commerce school recorded the greatest decline in majors over the decade, but four of the most popular majors for graduates (including Politics and Economics) remained in the top five. The athletic department accommodated the demand for women's sports and recreation with few difficulties, though some women complained that the campus community regarded their athletic teams and events with "less respect." Participation in women's intercollegiate sports actually declined somewhat toward the end of the first coeducation decade.

There were surprises. The assumption that women would be more inclined to live on campus was erroneous; in 1993, 37 percent of male students and fully half of the women lived off campus. The long-sought university goal of a more cohesive academic community continued but was not particularly advanced by the admission of women, who were also drawn to the independence of off-campus living. The need for even better university lighting and attention to campus security also exceeded expectations. And it was quickly evident that more laundry facilities were necessary in the dormitories, as women used them much more frequently.

The participation of women in campus social and political life proceeded more slowly than the administration and faculty had hoped because of the role and influence of fraternities. After the university-sponsored "renaissance," fraternities at W&L were arguably stronger than ever and continued to define student social life and politics. Women—and independent students—had no adequate social space of their own. If a female student invited a date from off campus, they had really nowhere to go on weekends unless they were invited to a fraternity party. Many women described this situation as being more like a "guest" at W&L than an integral part of it. According to a subcommittee report, "students do not share an interconnected social life. Instead, they share a common social structure: the fraternity system."[84] Sororities were one pos-

sible answer, and many women affiliated with these organizations as they began appearing on campus—with chapters of Chi Omega, Kappa Alpha Theta,
and Kappa Kappa Gamma—in 1988–89. With the addition of Phi Beta Pi in
1991–92, four sororities had over four hundred members, or 66 percent of total
female enrollment. But sororities were not the equivalent of fraternities; they
had no houses in the beginning and held meetings in rooms in the student
center and elsewhere on campus, and they had too many members—over one
hundred per chapter.

Fraternities had long influenced student politics; though dominance by the
"Red Square" clique was a thing of the past, bloc voting continued. In the first
decade of coeducation, women undergraduates were less likely to be elected to
student government offices or to be appointed to committees by the Student
Executive Committee. "Paradoxically," the subcommittee report observed, "the
Greek system provides a unity that depends on fragmentation which, consequently, has solidified its power." Therefore, "there is no mechanism to enable
a political structure that is independent of the social to develop." Student political opportunities were thus shaped by the lack of a physical place for students
to interact and a "multi-textured social fabric." Yet there were signs of progress.
Women held positions in the dorms; as editors of the *Ring-tum Phi*, the *Calyx*,
and *Trident*; and chaired a number of student committees, including Fancy
Dress. But committee appointments by the Student Executive Committee were
relatively few and spotty. Some women won elected positions. The first female
undergraduate elected to the Student Executive Committee, in 1988–89, was
Alston Parker—the young woman who had so impressed Bill Brock as a candidate for admission. The first female undergraduate member of the Student
Conduct Committee (Shannon Comer) was not elected until 1992–93. These
numbers were not representative of a group accounting for 40 percent of total
enrollment—and were especially inadequate for minority women.

Women continued to encounter sexist remarks in and out of the classroom,
even from a few professors, and some believed they received less extensive and
less helpful faculty advising than men. One complaint involved a sexual over-
ture by a faculty member,[85] and reports of sexual harassment from some faculty
members continued into the 1990s.[86] These irritating and frustrating instances
of misogynist behavior were certainly not in line with official university policy
or the W&L traditions of honor and comity, but they were, unfortunately, not
atypical of the broader culture as men were challenged to adjust to the rising
status and role of women in American society.

The admission of undergraduate women heightened institutional awareness of sexual harassment and sexual assault, though these issues were by no means due to coeducation. Such problems arose with alarming frequency throughout higher education. A series of annual surveys, focusing on first-year women, conducted by the associate dean of student life and university psychologist, Anne Schroer-Lamont, provided a sense of the dimensions of the problem at W&L. In the spring of 1990, 8 out of 108 freshmen women reported being sexually assaulted, and 7 said they were raped by a W&L acquaintance. Participation in the survey by other classes was much less, but the responses were still revealing. Eighteen percent of law-student respondents included twelve women who reported twenty-seven incidents of rape or sexual assault. Overall, fifty-five women reported eighty-six incidents, many of them at W&L during the 1989–90 academic year.[87] In 1992, twelve freshmen women reported being either sexually assaulted or raped, ten by W&L men, with seven incidents occurring in the freshman dorms. In the great majority of cases, alcohol use by one or both parties was also involved. Only two of the twelve women said they had reported the incidents to university officials. In 1991–92, the Student-Faculty Hearing Board heard four cases, only one of which resulted in a conviction. No cases at all were reviewed in 1993–94.

The university developed a sexual-harassment policy similar to those at many other institutions and conducted "Responsible Dating Seminars" during orientation and educational workshops throughout the year for both men and women, in coordination with the university health services and local law enforcement. Schroer-Lamont began regular weekly support group meetings, every Friday afternoon, for women who had experienced rape or sexual assault.[88] While W&L's policies and procedures generally paralleled those at other universities, the coeducation report observed that the various W&L committees were not well coordinated and the university lacked a single person or point of access for seeking redress.

The combination of the relative openness of residence halls, the widespread use of alcohol, and the presence on campus during the weekend of many students from surrounding colleges—including VMI—posed real challenges for university officials. Student attitudes were also important. A survey of Virginia college students, conducted by the Virginia State Task Force on Sexual Assault, revealed that men at W&L were three times more likely than the statewide average to believe that men accused of sexual assaults or rape were innocent.[89]

Gender diversity in the faculty and administration was a critical component of the university's coeducation strategy. Initial progress was slow: the first woman on the faculty was hired in 1973 and the second in 1975. But the pace increased after the decision on coeducation, and the administration actively encouraged departments to include women and minorities in all faculty applicant pools. The number of full-time female teaching faculty rose from six in 1984 (two tenured) to eighteen in 1993 (eleven tenured). Much of this progress was due to new faculty positions being added to accommodate the increased student enrollment (the existing faculty was heavily tenured with a high proportion of full professors) and to the fact that the number of women with advanced degrees and academic aspirations was rising rapidly. W&L adopted coeducation later than most formerly all-male institutions and still had eleven undergraduate departments without any female faculty in 1994. The number of women in the administration slowly increased, but no woman was in the top administrative ranks or among those who met regularly with and advised the president. As noted by the Coeducation Review Committee, women faculty registered lower satisfaction with their jobs than men; fewer believed they were "valued" or held equal "ownership" in the institution. Many women responding to a confidential survey also expressed a sense of marginalization and complained about the "chilly climate" in the institution toward female faculty and a lack of fairness in the tenure and promotion process. The survey also revealed that while the job satisfaction of male faculty members increased the longer they served at W&L, the reverse seemed to be true for women faculty members.[90]

The Women Faculty/Administrators Discussion Group offered suggestions to the Committee to Enhance Faculty Quality, as part of the long-range planning and reaccreditation process. The group acknowledged the university's "good faith effort" to address their concerns but pointed out additional needs to be addressed, particularly the need for a family-leave policy that covered all employees, not just faculty members, and support for child-care facilities: "It seems apparent that the entire community requires additional information in order to act responsibly in this matter."[91] Dean Larry Peppers, chair of the committee, responded that the university was committed to doubling the percentage of female faculty and was putting policies in place to "respond to the changing composition of our work force and to broader societal changes." The changes already in place were "just the first of many innovations" to be adopted in this "evolutionary process."[92] In a 1995 memo to Wilson, Schroer-Lamont observed that more women were participating in the Women's Faculty/

Administrative Discussion Group and also in a new organization for students, Women in Leadership.[93]

The final report of the Coeducation Review Committee, submitted in September 1994, was held over for a year so the new president could present it to the trustees. John Elrod brought it before the board and presented each recommendation on October 2, 1995, along with its justification and the "administration's disposition." All recommendations except one were accepted—including the construction of a true university commons and adequate social spaces for sororities, steps to better deal with alcohol use and sexual abuse on campus, and special efforts and incentives to recruit and retain female faculty members. Two decisions, especially, reflected how far W&L had come down the path of coeducation. The recommendation for a permanent committee on coeducation was rejected, because it "could serve to perpetuate coeducation as a unique and separate issue rather than weaving various coeducational concerns into the fabric of the University." And the committee's first recommendation, and long-sought goal, was eventually implemented: the end of the 60/40 enrollment quota that turned away so many qualified women undergraduates.[94] In May 1996, the board unanimously voted to raise total undergraduate enrollment to 1,675 over four years (920 males and 755 females) and eliminated quotas thereafter from admissions considerations, allowing "the gender pattern to evolve under the supervision of the administration."[95]

John Wilson reflected in 1994 on the continuing difficulties of achieving a gender balance in academic programs and departments, especially in keeping with enrollment. "My successor," he wrote, "will find it infinitely harder to keep things in line while maintaining a stable state in total faculty positions." But "I honestly do believe that we are still in transition."[96] As he looked back on the decade since 1985, he was grateful "the transition has gone as smoothly as it has." He was struck by "the generational changes that we have experienced along the way, changes that we have little control over. I am thinking about the evolution of the feminist movement(s), the alterations in sexual mores, the escalation in alcohol abuse by women as well as men (we've lost our monopoly!). I'm amazed that we have known as much success as we have."[97]

CHAPTER TWELVE

RAISING THE BAR

WITH COEDUCATION DECIDED, Washington and Lee focused on its implementation, as well as myriad other challenges. As usual, Wilson approached this "next phase" by posing broad questions about the institution and laying out options for the future. He wrote the trustees in October 1984 that amid all the preparations for coeducation, "we could lose sight of the larger intentions which must guide us." He began with broad strokes, outlining "the idea of the University." W&L, he suggested, "is a *nationally prominent, small yet comprehensive university of the first rank*" guided by values of "*integrity, honesty, courtesy and mutual respect.*" How to preserve and even expand upon that history and tradition would require careful, thoughtful planning and real achievement. The university's reputation "cannot, for long, be 'created' by public relations efforts." He underlined the importance of student quality and diversity, faculty development (especially in light of the impending retirement of "the great center of our most experienced and successful colleagues"), academic program development, and attention to annual giving and the endowment (to catch up with institutions like Amherst, Williams, and Swarthmore, which had "two to three times the endowment per student that we enjoy"). He also offered a long list of other matters requiring attention, ranging from student residential life to athletics, fraternities, and new capital improvements."[1]

Wilson periodically renewed his attention to the "big" questions and the need for thoughtful planning. In a memo to the Advisory Committee on April 1, 1985, he reiterated many of the same points, with more attention to campus life and cocurricular and extracurricular programs.[2] A longer memorandum went out on October 18 to the Advisory Committee and the central administrative staff that stressed "planning limits and definitions I want us to follow in thinking systematically about Washington and Lee's future."[3] A discussion of "conspicuous strengths and weaknesses" included needs for improved faculty salaries, especially in law, and competitive scholarship funds, as well as addressing the "deteriorating" fraternities, underfunded programs in the arts, and "a scattered and underdeveloped community life." He suggested three overall "strategic options": expanding the university ("Lee's grand conception," influenced by Jefferson) with several professional schools and degrees through the doctoral level; keeping the current scheme dominated by undergraduate studies but with some selective postbaccalaureate development; or embracing a commitment to undergraduate education with the sole exception of the law school. He quickly dispensed with the first option as unrealistic but found appeal in the second (perhaps they might offer the MBA in the commerce school), which would bring W&L closer in its offerings to William and Mary, Wake Forest, and Dartmouth. He settled on the third option, however, as "the most attractive and realistic." He worried about the law school's current sense of isolation but endorsed efforts to strengthen it and draw "the law and undergraduate faculties together more often and more usefully."

Through "a combination of historic accident and design," Wilson wrote, W&L was "poised to be in the top tier of peer institutions." Achieving this goal required a continuing concern for "comparative standings" and thus a more precise sense of where W&L stood in a wide variety of measures and what exactly its "peer" group was or should be. A first step would be collecting key data from twenty-two comparable undergraduate institutions and basic information about "regional rivals." In addition, W&L should gather as much comparative data as possible from other law schools, including Yale, Northwestern, Chicago, and Virginia. Regardless of comparative standing, Wilson observed, W&L should be more selective in undergraduate and law school admissions, enhance the university's "intangible qualities," beef up the faculty salary schedule (law school salaries for the most productive faculty were "some $5,000 to $7,000 behind our competitors"), and strengthen the curriculum in key fields.

Wilson arranged another "extended conversation on the future of the University" among members of the central staff at Skylark in September 1986. If the 2:1 ratio of 1,000 men and 500 women was reached by 1995, he asked, what would it mean for the admissions profile and enrollment in specific programs?[4] All the other key questions were then taken up, including faculty matters, academic program development, the quality of campus life (especially on-campus housing options), finances, and buildings and grounds.[5] The entire campus—including the board—was soon brought into these discussions with the inauguration of the next self-study for the decennial reaffirmation of institutional accreditation by the Southern Association of Colleges and Schools. Once again, this exercise was utilized to build a ten-year long-range plan as a basis for university policy and a major capital campaign. The new self-study steering committee, chaired by John Elrod, included veterans of past efforts, especially Frank Parsons, who had written the two previous documents. Wilson confirmed to the trustees that the "desired result will be a program to catapult Washington and Lee to the top tier of any list the list-makers put together in the next dozen years."[6]

Along with many of his colleagues, Wilson was not satisfied with the quality of campus life. "This broadly-based area," he wrote prior to the 1986 Skylark meeting, "may be the most important on our agenda insofar as it represents, in my opinion, some of our current, most conspicuous weaknesses. It may, also, be the hardest to move forward, requiring as it does, student participation and endorsement."[7] Fraternities and fraternity life were the sources of greatest concern.

UNIVERSITIES THROUGHOUT the country had experienced student misbehavior and interference with academic pursuits since the early nineteenth century. In faculty eyes, the two greatest distractions were subsidized intercollegiate athletics and social fraternities—both of which demanded student time and resources, required constant attention from the administration, and drew strong support from national organizations and powerful alumni.

At W&L, fraternity members accounted for up to 80 percent of the student body. Greek life suffered in the 1970s as student tastes veered away from traditional collegiate endeavors, and overall membership dropped to 58 percent in 1970. Three houses closed by 1971, and another moved from a house to an apartment. Eventually, membership rebounded, reaching over 60 percent in 1979, but the houses themselves had been stripped of whatever genteel features they may have had before, such as housemothers and proper living and dining accommodations. Throughout the decade, the administration insisted—with limited success—on a new code of fraternity behavior, better financial management, and proper upkeep of the properties. In 1980, exasperated by lack of progress, the university took over maintenance of the plumbing, heating, and electrical systems of all fifteen Greek houses. When John Wilson arrived in 1983, doing something about the fraternities—even in the fraternity-based culture at W&L—was widely seen as a necessity.

Less than four months after he arrived in Lexington, Wilson confided that his "secret longing" for W&L students to be gentlemen was "accompanied by a clear-eyed view of how wide the gap is, at any one time, between this ideal and life on Saturday night in the fraternities."[8] In his second board meeting, Wilson heard trustee Waller Dudley complain about deteriorating student conduct, the condition of the houses, the effect of midweek parties, and the prevalence of sophomores residing in the houses. Wilson promised that such problems would be "carefully addressed."[9] Over the summer, he had given much thought to the problem, dispatching Lew John and Dan Murphy to New England to learn about the fraternities at Amherst, Dartmouth, and Trinity. The Trinity faculty had voted to eliminate fraternities, but the trustees refused to do so. "The president," Wilson wrote in his monthly missive to the board, "has been suspended somewhere in the middle, an uncomfortable, but familiar spot." Amherst now required fraternities to admit women, but the decision had not had much effect on "modulating the intensity of social life." Dartmouth, most similar to W&L, had embarked on a plan to take over the ownership of houses on a volunteer basis and issued an "elaborate" code of minimum standards that might be difficult to enforce. Williams had begun to dissolve its fraternity system in 1962. Wilson observed that a "fundamental shift" had occurred over the previous fifteen years in the very nature of fraternity life. Rather than providing a "home" for students, fraternity houses were mainly now sites for open entertainment. Sophomores lived in the houses, and other members came there only for meals and parties. Whatever W&L decided to do, it could not turn its back on the "problem of aging, derelict physical spaces if not an aging, derelict way of life for undergraduate men."[10] In a letter to Fishwick, Wilson wrote that he was not very popular with the fraternities, "having told them how insipid most of what they do really is."[11]

The fraternities did little to alter these impressions. Houses continued to be abused and were often virtually vandalized as members left for the summer. Occasionally, a parent would witness the damage, including piles of trash and broken furniture suffused with the odor of dead animals lying somewhere underneath. Parties were often open to anyone, without invitation, whether or not they attended W&L, leading to further damage to the houses, as well as lamentable behavior for which the fraternities usually disclaimed responsibility. Wednesday night parties, which caused high student absences on Thursday mornings, were especially unpopular with the faculty. Active partying, in fact, seemed to be ongoing, in one place or another, throughout the week. Fraternity rush, held at the beginning of the school year, was also a continuing issue. New students were swept up in a social whirlwind for the first third of the semester, with each fraternity attempting to outdo the others with extravagant parties, celebrations (usually with alcohol) on "bid night" when offers for membership were issued, and parties again on "tear night" when the offers were accepted or rejected. Fraternities continued to dominate all social life at W&L for members and nonmembers.

In 1985, Wilson reported some progress, including new restrictions on rush to basically the two weeks of student orientation. "Our rush activities this year," he wrote the board, were largely dry, without guests, and usually over by the end of the first week of classes." He also reported new restrictions on the size of fraternity parties and hoped that the opening of the new student pavilion on the back campus would provide an alternative location: "We truly hope to give the fraternity houses a chance to breathe while we figure out the best way to start them back to physical health." He was "optimistic about the chances for improvement and will work, as quietly as possible, toward that end."[12] But a few months later, he again confided to Fishwick: "I'm up to my ears this year with these wretched fraternities. I don't know how they came to be so important around here or how they assumed their current form. But I hope we can figure out a way to make them better. In the meantime, the 'Hill' keeps getting scourged for its Neanderthal mentality. Can they possibly mean me? What a thing to squabble about in one's old age."[13]

The reform and reaffirmation of the fraternity system at W&L—an achievement perhaps second only to coeducation during Wilson's presidency—was known as the Fraternity Renaissance. In this case, Wilson rode the crest of fifteen years of alumni, trustee, and faculty concern about the deterioration of campus life and decorum, and a sustained and growing determination among all parties to do something about it. The usual mechanisms for supervising fraternity operations—the individual house corporations and faculty advisors—were not adequate to address a systemic set of problems. Wilson understood that the university could take no major action concerning the fraternities without support from the alumni, who often rose in defense of the system. For help, Wilson approached the Alumni Association Board and its committee on fraternities. The association in turn established, in 1985, the Alumni Fraternity Council to promote the "well-being of the fraternity system" at W&L, with

Col. Paul J. B. Murphy, '49, as its first chair. Wilson then appointed Murphy to also chair the Fraternity Housing Renovation Steering Committee. J. Thomas Touchton, '60, chaired the board's Campus Life Committee, created in part because of the board's unhappiness with social life on campus.[14] Wilson called upon all members of his administration for assistance but relied most directly on Dean of Students Lew John; Leroy C. "Buddy" Atkins, the associate dean of students directly responsible for fraternity affairs; and Parsons, who once again rose to the task of coordinating the construction and renovations.

Wilson wondered whether W&L should even retain fraternities. Several other selective institutions had abolished or were in the process of restricting their fraternity systems. Except among the W&L faculty—where such drastic measures may have been welcomed—and despite Wilson's frustrations over student behavior—ending fraternities at W&L was never seriously discussed. For one thing, these organizations were more deeply embedded in the history and campus life there than at virtually any other institution. And fraternities continued to feed and house a considerable number of students. Mostly, however, influential alumni and donors, especially in the wake of the decision to admit women, would have fiercely resisted any drastic measures. Without some action, though, it appeared that the fraternities might self-destruct.

Any effective intervention would have to address the physical deterioration of the chapter houses as well as the patterns of student life and behavior that caused the damage and also undermined the university's ideals and mission. The new policies evolved over several years, mostly from 1986 to 1988. A day-long symposium in October 1986, organized by the Alumni Fraternity Council, with almost 150 attendees—including fraternity members, faculty, and some national fraternity representatives—met in the Moot Courtroom of Lewis Hall to identify problems and explore solutions. John Wilson opened the meeting with upbeat remarks about "rethinking and optimistic restructuring" of the fraternity system, and he pointedly referred to the "golden age" of fraternity life, with housemothers, intellectual discussions in the living room, and occasional "elegant and elaborate parties." Whether or not this recollection was entirely accurate, it emphasized the degree to which fraternity life had fallen from the ideal. The meeting focused on how fraternities influenced the quality of life at W&L and brought forward issues that most chapter members had not thought about—such as legal liability and insurance, and how these were related to alcohol abuse and house maintenance. Many discussions concerned the deteriorating relations with the Lexington community. The overall message was that such problems were serious and required immediate attention from the students themselves.[15]

The Fraternity Renaissance itself began in earnest with the university promulgation in 1987 of "Standards for Fraternities," which laid out mandatory guidelines and expectations, as well as privileges and responsibilities, and set standards for the exterior and interior condition and appearance of the fraternity houses. The Fraternity Housing Renovation Steering Committee, chaired by Colonel Murphy, helped oversee this aspect of the Fraternity Renaissance, which would entail a substantial financial investment beyond the means of most individual chapters. The term *renaissance* to describe this effort was quite intentional and conveyed its scope, ambition, and purpose.

The reality of the changes to come was made clear. Touchton recalls speaking to freshmen and sophomore fraternity members in Lee Chapel. "We said, 'There are going to be changes made in the fraternity system, and if you don't like it, there's the door.'" He added that coeducation and the larger number of applications gave this ultimatum more credibility: "It was easier to be hardnosed in 1988, versus 1978, let's say." On the other hand, so soon after the coeducation decision, the board was inclined to move gradually and deliberately.[16]

These discussions and evolving policies occurred in the aftermath of a campus disaster: the Phi Gamma Delta house was destroyed by a fire—later deemed to be arson—on April 11, 1984, killing one student, Thomas John Fellin. The future of this fraternity at W&L seemed bleak, even nonexistent. But Ed Bishop, a 1968 Fiji (Phi Gamma Delta) alumnus, devised a complex but effective mechanism to address the challenge. He organized a limited partnership with five other alumni investors to purchase the house and land, pay for the extensive construction and renovations, and recoup the investment with rent receipts and some additional gifts. The exterior of the house was restored and the inside redesigned as a spacious, livable residence with a separate party room and an apartment for a housemother. The deal came with clear and strict rules governing occupant behavior: large fines (and possible expulsion) for property damage, immediate expulsion for drug use, a dress code for the dining room, and a housemother. A gleaming new Phi Gamma Delta house was completed by early 1986.[17] Not long afterward, the board's Campus Life Committee toured the facility and were impressed by both the means used and the results attained.

Discussions focused increasingly on how extensive renovations to the fraternity houses would be financed. The Fijis had wrested success from disaster, but similar results for the entire system would require a major university financial commitment, with commensurate control over the investment—control that could only be achieved by university ownership of the fraternity houses. This raised many practical considerations and potential difficulties, including the provisions of actual university ownership, alumni reactions, the mandatory participation of all fraternities, the tax deductibility of any gifts to the program, the impact of Lexington zoning regulations and reviews, and especially the total financial cost and how it might be recovered. The momentum behind the effort pushed changes forward, but many questions and particulars remained unresolved. John Wilson regarded the Fraternity Renaissance as part of an overall university-housing strategy, while others saw it as targeted on fixing specific problems. Even recalcitrant students concerned about independent student governance could discern that W&L was committed to a more sustainable system of social fraternities—and was ready to put university money on the line.

Touchton and his committee estimated in February 1987 that completely renovating the fraternity houses could cost as much as $5 to $6 million. In May the board authorized the first phase of a professional feasibility study by VMDO Architects of Charlottesville, which inspected all seventeen houses during the summer. In early 1988, Colonel Murphy wrote all fraternity and house corporation presidents concerning the implications of the new standards and the preliminary report from VMDO Architects; he emphasized that compliance with all the standards (except physical renovations) must be achieved by September 1, 1988, or the chapters would be subject to probation and even the withdrawal of university recognition.[18]

The heavy use and expected longevity of renovated fraternity houses mandated higher standards for materials and construction, and thus a higher total cost—estimated at just under $10 million. Ballengee appointed a Fraternity Financing Options Committee, composed of key trustees and headed by F. Fox Benton Jr., chair of the board's Investment Committee. Construction could begin on the first several houses by the summer of 1989. John Wilson again reminded the board of the critical importance of the Fraternity Renaissance Program, characterizing it as "a leading indicator of overall institutional progress" and nothing less than an effort "to produce a model fraternity system in all respects."[19]

Greek behavior continued to validate the necessity for change. After the 1987–88 academic year, the houses were left in unacceptable condition.

Buddy Atkins wrote the chapter presidents on June 30, two months before the deadline for compliance with the new standards: "You, gentlemen, really have a chore ahead of you. We are talking about a *renaissance* not a *renovation* program. Following the house inspections in late May and my own visits to the houses since you left, I am struck by how few chapters showed an improvement in their treatment of the house. . . . There must be a drastic change in attitude soon, because you are running out of time. If the property which you have is not respected, cared for and improved, neither the University nor the alumni are about to spend a cent to renovate or replace the property." A renaissance must indeed precede any renovations. "Unless," Atkins added, "you can generate that rebirth of values throughout all levels of your chapter, you may well enjoy the dubious distinction of being its last president." In a letter to the trustees, Wilson advocated "a very tough line" to change these persisting patterns: "I am more than ever convinced that we simply must take this difficult problem, head on. We cannot meet out fiduciary responsibility and bequeath these derelict houses to the next generation."[20]

When the board convened on October 21, 1988, Wilson had already begun his semester's sabbatical at Oxford University. But he left behind a September 5 memorandum recommending that trustees approve the Fraternity Renaissance program, with a $10 million university investment and provisions for university ownership of the chapter houses. Many details remained uncertain, including the exact costs and amounts to be recovered through rents and gifts. The Fraternity Financing Options Committee's report of October 5 "refined" Wilson's recommendations by presenting more specific plans. All participating fraternity-house titles would be deeded to W&L (with forgiveness of any existing indebtedness to the university), thirty-year leases with annually adjusted rents would be charged through the individual house corporations, and resident managers were required in each house, along with full compliance with the Renaissance Standards. The university would assume responsibility for maintenance, property insurance, and ad valorem taxes. Participation in the financing program was voluntary; chapters could seek other means of raising the necessary money (as Phi Gamma Delta had done). But compliance with the standards was mandatory and noncompliance at any time could lead to termination of the lease. A resident manager, with specific responsibilities, was also part of the arrangement, and houses had to establish reserve funds for furniture and equipment. Some financial data was still missing. A general estimate of $5 million to be recovered from gifts and another $5 million collected from the fraternities in rents might or might not be accurate. In the end, the need outweighed the doubts. Despite matters still to be decided, but with a desire to get the renovations underway as soon as possible, the trustees voted unanimously in favor of the Fraternity Renaissance Program on October 22.[21] In a January 1989 letter to "Friends of Washington and Lee," John Wilson reported, "For the first time in a long time, the entire community is united behind the determination to restore the houses to top physical condition and to achieve new standards of behavior in the houses."[22]

By the spring of 1989, the first four fraternities had been approved for participation in the Renaissance Program: Pi Kappa Alpha, Sigma Alpha Epsilon, Beta Theta Pi, and Sigma Nu. Concerns lingered over the costs, especially when they exceeded the estimates for the first renovations. Since each house was different in size and layout, and the renovations were extensive and over a period of years, cost containment was a challenge. In his June letter to the board, Wilson agreed that "we must do some hard thinking (as a staff) on what principles should be followed in determining the appropriate level of funding for each house scheduled for renovation," since the physical standards set a minimum but not a maximum. "Our system-wide approach has many advantages but it doesn't provide an incentive for the house corporation to hold down its expectations."[23] He sought to reiterate the importance of the effort and perhaps also to reassure some who doubted whether such a total commitment of the university was necessary. "It is my conviction," he wrote in January 1990, "that we must see this renovation through . . . that we must not leave to the next generation a horrendous problem involving both the safety and well-being of our students. At the same time," he added, "I recognize that a vote for the fraternity renaissance program appears to be a vote for the present system, warts and all. In the eyes of some, even many, the warts have grown so large that the whole system has been jeopardized and is no longer worth saving."[24]

Renovations were underway on six chapter houses by the summer of 1990 and scheduled for completion in January, when work would shift to five more (including the former Zeta Beta Tau house, now to be the new home of Kappa Sigma). Chi Psi and Delta Tau Delta did not require extensive work, which could be done over one or two summers. Kappa Alpha and Sigma Phi Epsilon had yet to sign up for the program but did so later. The Sig Ep house, like Sigma Chi's, required extensive renovation or new construction and even relocation. Each participating fraternity worked with the architects, but every individual renovation included certain basic features, including a large sound-proofed party room in the basement (to which parties would be restricted) with concrete floors with drains, living rooms that looked more like hotel lobbies, dining rooms large enough to accommodate all upperclassmen members, adequate off-street parking for house residents, and an apartment for a nonstudent resident manager.[25] The construction itself largely preserved the appearance of the exteriors but was extensive on the inside, tearing out walls and reconfiguring spaces, in addition to installing sprinkler systems and updating plumbing and wiring.

Fraternity misbehavior continued even during the renovations. Two members of Phi Psi and one from SAE were suspended for the remainder of the winter term in 1991 for throwing bottles through Phi Psi house windows and the housemother's suite at SAE. The penalty was considered far too harsh by many students but defended as justified by the administration, which wanted to address reckless vandalism that undermined the Renaissance program. In 1992, the Student Affairs Committee suspended Delta Tau Delta from campus for five years because of "systematic" vandalism to the chapter house over a ten-week period. Members broke windows, toppled walls, destroyed a brick bar, and removed ceiling tiles before leaving the house for the 1991 Christmas break. Renovations of the house were scheduled to begin in January. Taylor Cole, '75, former president Fred Cole's son and the president of Delt's house corporation, did not defend the members' behavior but noted that fraternities were now "in a new era" and that penalties would send a message to others. "If it commits acts of vandalism or destruction, a fraternity will be held accountable, and strictly accountable." This time, however, John Wilson recommended that the fraternity's expulsion for so long a time be reconsidered. The Student Affairs Committee did reconsider and suspended the chapter until July 1, 1993, allowing it to reapply in August 1992 for renovations that could be completed by the beginning of the 1993–94 academic year.[26] Also, Phi Delta Theta was placed on social probation after damage to the chapter house interior during Homecoming weekend, and the Kappa Alpha national organization put W&L's chapter on social probation for violating the alcohol policy during rush.[27]

The Fraternity Renaissance Program was formally dedicated during Homecoming Weekend in October 1991. Gathered in Red Square between two of the renovated houses, Phi Delta Theta and Sigma Nu, a large crowd heard John Wilson extol the virtues of a revitalized fraternity life and its compatibility with W&L values, and Colonel Murphy observed that things "are coming back around" to the way Greek life should be. The *Alumni Magazine* portrayed the vivid contrast from the past—"living rooms with rotting floorboards and fire-sale modular furniture"—to the present—"Oriental rugs, finely upholstered sofas, and even a decorative houseplant or two." The exteriors had been transformed from appearing like "sections of bombed out Dresden" to "architectural showpieces."[28] By this time, the total cost of the renovations had risen to $13 million, but evidence of success was on the ground. The previous summer, the *Roanoke Times and World News* favorably portrayed similar contrasts in an assessment of the program but focused on the return of housemothers. (While a "nonstudent resident manager" could be other than a housemother, that was clearly the idea.)[29] Buddy Atkins had, in fact, told the *Alumni Magazine,* "It's a false notion that the fraternity decline was a gradual process. With the removal of the house mothers and other controls and constraints things fell apart rapidly. We had untrained, inexperienced kids with no guidance running houses. It was very much like *Lord of the Flies.*" Surprisingly, mature, responsible, and savvy women could still be found to take on the task of housemothers, especially on party weekends, and they were very much a part of W&L's reforms.

In August 1993, John Wilson reported to the trustees that the final three houses (Sigma Chi, Sigma Phi Epsilon, and Delta Tau Delta) would soon be ready for occupancy; "so we have made our schedule and can declare the physical side of fraternity renaissance to be completed." He heaped credit on Frank Parsons for shepherding "this difficult, expensive, and complicated project" to completion. While fraternities and fraternity life would "preoccupy all of us" in the years ahead, "we are on a solid footing once again."[30]

The renovation portion of the Fraternity Renaissance was by any measure a success. The houses were truly revivified, within a framework of ownership and upkeep that helped insure that they stayed that way. But the most important aspects of fraternity reform would always be a work in progress. Issues persisted toward and into the next century—especially problems with hazing and rush. The decision of the faculty in 1995 to push fraternity rush into the winter semester (an idea talked about for decades) brought forth a storm of student objections, but it nevertheless went into effect in January 1997 with the help of some IFC leaders, especially Anthony Mazzarelli. The faculty changed the schedule but did leave to the students the job of developing the rules and regulations. New students would, finally, not be inundated with intense social life during their first months on campus but would have time to settle in, complete their first semester classes, and develop friendships among people not connected to a particular fraternity. As Wilson was fond of pointing out, Robert E. Lee also favored such an adjustment period. After 1995, the new president, John Elrod, launched a major effort to eliminate hazing at W&L.[31]

MANY ISSUES BLAMED on fraternities were pervasive among college students generally and were part of the social and cultural landscape of late twentieth-century America. Washington and Lee's efforts to contend with alcohol, drugs, and problems of sexual harassment and abuse led to a more elaborate disciplinary regimen, as well as to differences of opinion among the trustees, faculty members, and students.

Alcohol was endemic to collegiate social life, and W&L alumni might fondly recall beer-soaked fraternity-house basements on party weekends. Alcohol consumption was difficult to monitor, though student surveys suggested that it had grown through the 1980s and 1990s. The most troubling trend was "binge drinking"—intentionally consuming as many drinks as possible in a short time with the explicit intention of getting drunk and even passing out.[32] A popular game called a "crawl" entailed drinking at place after place until the participants couldn't walk. Drinking before going out for an evening was termed "front-end loading." Drinking was not confined to the weekends, and increasing numbers of women were imbibing more heavily. (W&L women had their own drinking club, "Elixirs.") According to a Harvard Public Health survey, 72 percent of W&L students who had drunk within the previous thirty days said they had "binged" (compared with a national response of 44 percent). Roughly three-quarters also reported a negative personal outcome from drinking—whether it had to do with schoolwork, interactions with others, or unplanned sexual activity. Seventy-seven percent of the W&L class of 2000 said they drank alcohol in high school. Fraternity events were often associated with excessive drinking. Bid Night during the first Winter Rush in 1998 sent five women and five men to the infirmary for alcohol-related problems, three students to the Emergency Room for alcohol poisoning, and two to Intensive Care at Stonewall Jackson Hospital. All but one fraternity violated rules forbidding alcohol in the houses on that evening. Steps were quickly taken to prevent a recurrence on Tear Night, but the offending fraternities were fined only $500 each, a penalty considered far too low by many faculty members. President John Elrod declared alcohol abuse to be "the most serious issue facing the University" and launched a number of initiatives and educational programs to combat it. The board of trustees established in 1997 the Alcohol Steering Committee—composed of students, parents, alumni, faculty, trustees, and outside experts—which attempted to change this aspect of student culture, and the *Alumni Magazine* featured a frank article on the serious alcohol issues at W&L.[33]

Drinking was a long-standing tradition. When the IFC petitioned the trustees in 1951 to permit the return of bars in chapter houses as a means of encouraging responsible drinking, they observed that alcohol consumption "has prevailed in the past, is prevalent at the present, and will continue into the future." Even James Leyburn was not opposed to moderate alcohol consumption in a proper setting by students of legal age. A total ban, Leyburn believed, simply would not work; students should be encouraged to regard drinking in the context of normal, adult social life. President Gaines refused to endorse Leyburn's suggestion that students visit faculty houses for academic discussions over sherry: How could he justify this to the trustees? But he knew that prohibitions on students—just like national Prohibition—only heightened the appeal, even glamour, of alcohol and drove consumption further off campus.

The United States lowered the drinking age to eighteen during the Vietnam conflict, but Virginia raised it again to twenty-one in 1985 after passage of the National Minimum Drinking Age Act, intended to deter drunk driving. For colleges, this posed a major challenge for student discipline, since some undergraduate students could now legally drink and most could not. While W&L alumni, including trustees, sought to curtail student abuse of alcohol rather than eliminate its consumption entirely, they were far less indulgent when it came to the matter of illegal drugs, especially narcotics like cocaine. Alcohol was a legal substance licensed and even sold by the state to those of proper age, but controlled substances and hallucinogens were strictly illegal, with serious penalties for possession, use, and especially selling to others (trafficking). W&L also strictly prohibited them. When students were arrested and convicted of felony drug offenses prior to graduation, the trustees were reluctant to approve the award of their diplomas, at least until their "debt to society" had been paid in full. Student drug use at W&L was, as far as we can know, not unusually high, but it represented different things to different generations. Students tended to see possession of drugs as "stuff people do," but trustees and local prosecutors considered it a serious crime.

Local and state law-enforcement authorities targeted drug offenses, including those on college campuses, and some W&L students were arrested and convicted for possession and use of hard drugs and for selling drugs to others. Except for marijuana possession, all drug offenses were felonies under Virginia law. In May 1984, Wilson called a special faculty meeting to consider additional evidence in the case of one student convicted and sentenced to twelve years in prison, most of which was suspended. The faculty had initially voted to postpone the decision concerning award of the student's degree until pending legal matters had been resolved, and then award the degree. But some faculty protested that the severity of the offense called for a reconsideration of the decision.[34] The board agreed to defer action on the degree until the student's probation was completed or vacated. He served time in jail, and when his probationary period was ended by the circuit court, the trustees approved the award of the degree. This confusion and ambivalence, and the trustees' general preference for harsher penalties for drug offenses, mandated a fresh look at student disciplinary policies.

Generally, the trustees and the faculty agreed on the seriousness of alcohol and illegal drugs and recognized the importance of student self-governance. In light of ongoing problems, they also agreed on the necessity for greater university oversight. The faculty adopted a new drug policy in May 1985. Based on recommendations of the Drug Policy Review Committee, appointed by President Wilson and chaired by Professor Leonard Jarrard, the new policy was adopted with the understanding that it would be reviewed again within a three-year "trial period" by an ad hoc committee appointed by the president.

Under the new policy, the faculty resumed direct authority over student disciplinary matters that had previously been delegated to the University Council. Other than setting the policy itself, the faculty required a report from the dean of students on any completed disciplinary actions on major offenses and emphasized that the disciplinary framework was intended to "promote our educational objectives" and the values of "a special community" at W&L, rather than to enforce external legal and judicial actions. The Drug Policy Review Committee had explicitly recommended that "statutes do not form an appropriate basis for our disciplinary system." Therefore, only two conditions were required for faculty approval of the award of a degree: that the student satisfy all academic requirements and face no further W&L disciplinary actions.

As an indication that disciplinary matters were becoming more complex, the policy also specified which offenses were to be considered "major" and "minor" and how they would be addressed, primarily by the Student Control Committee. Major violations included threats of death or bodily injury, drug possession with intent to distribute, the sale of marijuana for profit, theft and fraud, sexual assault (including "unwanted sexual touching"), vandalism, and the "use of racial, ethnic, religious, or sexual slurs directly to an individual or identifiable group." Minor offenses included less egregious actions "disruptive of the life of the University" and also the "accommodation" sale or distribution of marijuana or providing alcohol to someone not legally eligible to purchase it. Penalties for major offenses included the possibility of expulsion or suspension, now within the purview of the Student Control Committee. A repeated minor offense could be punished by suspension for up to one year. But the faculty emphasized that penalties were not intended as punitive but to encourage a "reformation of conduct." Major offenses were referred to a Certification Committee (the chairs of the Student Control Committee and the Student Affairs Committee and a faculty member of the Student Affairs Committee) to determine how they would be adjudicated. Also, the Student Control Committee followed different procedures depending on the category of the offense—more formal in the case of major offenses, with provisions against self-incrimination and for W&L student advisors to assist the accused (even questioning witnesses), and a two-thirds vote required for conviction. Students could appeal committee decisions to the Student Affairs Committee, which reviewed all penalties, and its decision was final. Though devised to assure fairness, these procedures did not involve legal precedents and other trappings of the judicial system.[35] As the Drug Policy Review Committee reminded the trustees, "The most prevalent and recurrent drug problem on this campus, the most destructive of our academic enterprise, is alcohol abuse."[36]

The new drug and alcohol policies marked a significant transition at Washington and Lee. Previously, only honor violations were considered major offenses that could result in expulsion, and decisions were made exclusively by the Student Executive Committee. Now, a comparatively elaborate set of procedures dealt with an array of student misconduct and determined whether offenses were major or minor. Unlike most universities, the implementation of these policies at W&L still relied heavily on student governance, though the faculty was becoming more involved.

In an April 1986 meeting of the Board Executive Committee with the Drug Policy Review Committee, the trustees again expressed their deep concern about student drug use, including individual possession, which was not included as a disciplinary offense under the jurisdiction of the Student Control Committee. As Wilson stated in a diplomatically worded memo to Jarrard and his committee, the "trustees acknowledge that there may remain a difference in view or emphasis on the question of drug possession" but urged consideration of a more robust approach to this behavior, to more explicitly convey the university's values while not undermining its education mission or counseling function. The trustees appreciated the faculty's shared concern about the seriousness of selling drugs and proposed no changes in the current procedures or policies during the agreed-upon three-year probationary period. The delegation of disciplinary authority to the faculty, the dean of students, and the Student Conduct Committee also continued, but the board asked the Faculty Executive Committee to closely monitor the two years remaining.[37]

Continuing problems with drugs—including arrests and convictions—kept the issue on the front burner. A student, convicted of cocaine possession in September 1985, was sentenced in February to five years in prison with all but six months suspended. He served his sentence in the local jail and was allowed to continue his coursework at W&L even while incarcerated. The Student Conduct Committee reviewed his case, found him guilty of "student misconduct," and placed him on social probation. The board, however, determined that a degree should be awarded only after his probation was completed or terminated. Trustee Tom Touchton commented that alumni, parents, and certainly the trustees were "inclined to take a tougher stance on drug matters than that indicated by the present policy" and that the faculty "should be aware of the opinions and strong feelings of these other constituencies since they are supportive of the University and of the faculty in so many ways."[38] The faculty continued to insist that W&L's disciplinary and academic policies *not* be tied to "prosecutorial or judicial action" or any pending legal matters. Meanwhile, the number of student drug cases continued to grow. A Rockbridge County Grand Jury in September 1987 indicted two current and two former W&L students, along with several others in connection with a "multistate drug network" distributing MDA, a "hallucinogenic designer drug," and other substances.[39] Four W&L applicants for degrees faced pending drug-related charges in May 1988.[40]

The three-year "trial period" for the drug and alcohol policy and its disciplinary procedures ended with only modest changes. In January 1988, Wilson appointed a ten-person ad hoc review committee, chaired by Professor Samuel Kozak, with Dean John serving ex officio. The principal issues included the Student Control Committee's power to unilaterally suspend or expel students and the differentiation of major and minor offenses. Wilson also asked the committee to consider whether the possession of drugs should continue to be treated similarly, despite the differences in penalties in criminal court, and whether (echoing sentiments of the trustees) the current university policy "appears to condone drug possession and use." Finally, he wrote, "I alert you to the continuing interest of the Board of Trustees in all of these matters and the Board's decision to see the highest degree of unity achieved between the Faculty and the Board in the conduct of the University's Drug Policy."[41]

The review committee report, submitted to Wilson on April 26, recommended two major changes: strengthening the guidelines and the role of deans in working with students accused of alcohol or drug offenses, and establishing a new disciplinary committee to address certain cases of misconduct. The dean of students and the dean of the law school would be responsible for carrying out "a graduated system of counseling and referral" for students identified or accused of alcohol and drug offenses. The four steps ranged from a meeting with the student to mandated participation in a treatment program. The dean could expel or suspend a student for failure to comply with any step in the process.

The most significant change was the creation of the Confidential Review Committee, composed of three students and four faculty members appointed by the president, with responsibility for evaluating and responding to "incidents of sexual assault or of ethnic, racial, religious, or sexual harassment, including slurs or unwanted sexual touching." The Student Control Committee, according to the Kozak review committee, was "uncomfortable" dealing with matters of such an "extremely personal and sensitive nature," and students were reluctant to bring matters before the SCC because of concerns about confidentiality and competence to decide such matters.[42] The entire faculty considered these recommendations at a special meeting on May 25.

John Wilson shared his thoughts on these issues with the board throughout his presidency. In 1990, he hoped for a conversation in the next academic year "that will put excessive alcohol use in a fresh perspective. This can't take a puritanical coloration and we certainly don't want to recreate the era of prohibition even if we could." Perhaps, as Tom Wolfe suggested in a board meeting, the "current preoccupation with health and exercise" would cut down on the worst abuses.[43] In 1994, Wilson lamented the new "tradition" of parents placing bottles of champagne under the chairs of their offspring at commencement, and he pledged to put a stop to this "indecorous" practice. This was another case, he suggested, "of giving an inch and losing a yard." He thought the problems with alcohol might actually be growing: "In fact we have created a society in which the abuse of alcohol is now said to begin in the fifth and sixth grades. High school drinking is very widespread and thus the patterns are all in place for real abuse under the comparative freedom of collegiate life."[44]

The changes in student culture, and what earlier generations would doubtless have regarded as reckless behavior, coincided with a loosening of many rules and regulations so that young adults could learn to take responsibility for their own lives. But universities were still expected by parents and the general public to ensure student safety and welfare. In this and so many other areas, the last decades of the twentieth century required university administrations to walk a fine line between conflicting expectations. Given its rural location, active student social life, and ready access to automobiles, W&L was probably fortunate that deaths and injuries from automobile accidents were as rare as they were. But some accidents were severe, and students were killed. Alcohol was often implicated, directly or indirectly. Two incidents were especially troubling, drew much attention on campus, and illustrated the challenges to university policies concerning alcohol and student safety.

On the morning of March 16, 1989, a nineteen-year-old freshman was struck and killed by a hit-and-run driver while walking along a road in Lexington. The police explored an anonymous tip implicating three black males, two of whom were already in jail. The tragedy was gravely compounded with the discovery that the hit-and-run driver was, in fact, a W&L senior student who had been drinking, left the scene of the accident, and called in the anonymous tip to implicate others and conceal his involvement. He was arrested in November. At his trial in August, he received only a six-month sentence and probation. The W&L community was left with much to ponder concerning honorable student behavior and accountability, and the dangers of alcohol.[45]

In preparation for coeducation, W&L adopted additional measures to enhance campus security—including improved lighting, an additional security officer, and dormitory regulations. The university decided early on that women students would not be treated differently from males, especially when it came to curfews, visitation, conduct policies, and individual autonomy. Female residents could decide whether males would be allowed on their residence-hall floor. These measures were similar to those prevailing generally in higher education at the time, as colleges and universities sought a proper balance between safety and student independence. During Homecoming Weekend, on October 13, 1991, an intoxicated freshman female student, carried to her dorm room by friends and put to bed, claimed that an eighteen-year-old male who was not authorized to be on the floor had sexually assaulted her during the night. (Security officers locked the doors to the floor after 11 p.m.) The alleged attacker, found and arrested at the scene, was a VMI cadet who had been in the dormitory previously and was also accused of stealing money from the room of the dormitory counselor. He was indicted on five charges in early 1992. At his trial in March, he was acquitted of sexual assault but later convicted of larceny and released with no further jail time.[46] This event traumatized the victim and raised numerous questions about the criminal justice system, student behavior, and the university's responsibilities for student safety. While the dorm floor was locked at night, some residents left their keys outside the door so they could get in after hours. While students obviously needed to pay more attention to their own safety, the university also realized that institutional security precautions and procedures must be upgraded. The freedom W&L students enjoyed and expected on a presumably secure and open campus was now subject to new restrictions—including controlled electronic access to residence halls.[47]

ONE MATTER NOT directly addressed in discussions about student behavior and discipline had for many years hovered over the relationship between honorable behavior and other student misconduct. A new faculty member, Joan O'Mara, raised questions about alcohol abuse and the Honor System, which she perceived to be "construed by a large percentage of the students as narrowly as possible, as little more than a legalistic prohibition against cheating on exams and plagiarism on written assignments, with little or no relevance to any wider dimensions of the whole life of the person." To some degree, John Wilson concurred: "I have always feared that the largest danger to our Honor System is hypocrisy . . . that is the danger of a widening of the gap between the rhetoric of our system and our behavior in various social settings."[48] The university had discovered that widening the scope of the Honor System to cover many forms of student misconduct was problematic and that serious charges such as rape and sexual assault—while certainly dishonorable—were beyond the purview and experience of the Student Executive Committee. Rather, these allegations would be referred to a new Student-Faculty Hearing Board that could also levy a penalty of expulsion. While clarifying matters in some respects, this arrangement tended to blur the broadly defined concept of personal "honor."

The Honor System was sacrosanct in general and continually questioned, defined, and reconsidered in practice. Robert E. Lee's definition of a "gentleman" obviously extended to the "whole life of the person" and derived its power from its simplicity and even imprecision. It survived into the twentieth-first century because of its compelling abstract appeal—its mystique—but also its adaptation to new times, generations, and circumstances. One important element of the Honor System was that each new student generation would revisit the underlying concepts to ensure their continuing relevance. In practice, it was not applied to all behavior and activity in all times and places, though these limits were not precisely drawn. At the same time, its essential features were retained: implementation entirely by students, a single sanction of expulsion (honor is not divisible), and avoiding a specific code of offenses or conduct, a list of "dos and don'ts." While the lack of specificity ennobled the concept of "honor," it also led to confusion about what was, and was not, honorable, as well as to increasing emphasis on *process*, mitigating against arbitrary and unfair judgments by structuring how things would be done.

The periodic revisions of the "White Book," which first appeared in 1968–69, reflected the details and the continuous reexamination of how the Honor System functioned. It laid out how many members of the Student Executive Committee were required to bring charges of an honor violation, the rights of the accused and his or her advocates to question accusers and witnesses, the operations of a public trial in the case of an appeal (who would preside, how a student jury would be selected, how many votes were required to convict), and what designation would appear on the transcript of those who withdrew or were expelled for honor violations. Maintaining an acceptable balance was no mean feat, especially since offenses were not codified. "Fairness" mandated procedural safeguards and "rights" for the accused—to face and question accusers, construct a defense, consult with an "advocate," and appeal an unfavorable decision to the full student body in open session. In general, and especially after the late 1960s, the process became more formal and the procedures more elaborate.[49]

Most changes were procedure related, but a few were consequential. In May 1984, the Student Executive Committee refused to reintroduce the "tolerance clause"—making the failure to report a violation an honor violation itself—which had been a central component of the system until it was eliminated in the early 1970s. The measure continued to run counter to student attitudes at the time; some students referred to it as a "squealer clause." (Students were now required to either confront a fellow student suspected of an honor offense or report it to a member of the Student Executive Committee.) At the same time, because three of the four students who requested open hearings that year had their convictions overturned, a proposal was made to reduce the number of student jury votes necessary to overturn a committee verdict. This seemed to violate any notion of procedural fairness, stimulated a vigorous dissenting letter from the Student Bar Association of the law school, and was not adopted.[50]

The Honor System encountered increasing difficulties in the 1980s and 1990s, due largely to changing societal expectations and rising litigiousness. While Honor System hearings were formal and elaborate—with the familiar terminology of "trials," "accused," and "convictions"—they were not held in a court of law. Ultimately, the system's success depended on informed support from the entire student community, including a willingness to set aside friendships or sympathies in favor of a noble concept.

The number of honor cases remained fairly steady, usually with no more than three or four convictions per year, but the pattern varied. In 1979–80, the numbers were relatively high: thirty-three honor investigations resulted in fifteen hearings, three voluntary withdrawals, twelve acquittals, and three convictions in honor trials, two of them public. In 1993–94, another unusually active year, twenty investigations led to closed hearings, one voluntary withdrawal, and seven convictions. At such times, questions always arose about how well the student body actually understood the Honor System.

New student orientation, conducted on campus each fall, continued to offer detailed presentations on the Honor System, often in dramatic outdoor settings like the Liberty Hall ruins. Faculty members were supposed to be schooled in the workings of the system and were expected to report suspected honor violations to the Student Executive Committee rather than attempt to resolve the matter themselves. They were also expected to fully explain to their classes the nature of class assignments and the rules of proper scholarly attribution.

The Honor System had been a point of disagreement between students in the undergraduate college and the law school since at least 1970. An editorial in the W&L Law News in 1977 found "little that is honorable about Washington and Lee's 'honor' system." The trials were "procedural horror shows" weighted against the accused, with the executive committee serving as "prosecutor, judge, and jury" reminiscent of "Star Chamber proceedings."[51] The following month, a survey revealed that many law students apparently favored major changes, such as graduated penalties or separate systems for undergraduates and the law school.[52] By far the greatest concern was about procedures and what many law students perceived to be inadequate respect for due process. A subcommittee of the Board of Governors of the Student Bar Association proposed reforms in 1978 that included a codification of honor offenses and guarantees of due process.[53] On the other hand, a Law News article in 1979 predicted that the W&L honor system would likely meet due-process requirements under the fourteenth amendment and cited a number of legal precedents.[54]

As reported in a May 1984 Roanoke newspaper story, "All school year, law students have been complaining that the underclassmen are running the school's cherished honor system in a careless fashion." A recent graduate claimed that the undergraduates "do not understand the constitutional safeguards that we build into our criminal justice system—the innocence of the accused until proven guilty." He also complained that rules of evidence were violated and that the proceedings went beyond the official charges. The thirteen-member executive committee contained only two members from the law school, and the proposal for adding a third member failed due to an insufficient number of votes cast. A proposal to set up a separate honor system in the law school was only narrowly defeated.[55]

It was perhaps inevitable that law students—only a few of whom had received undergraduate degrees from W&L—would judge the honor system by the rules and expectations of the criminal justice system and the courts. Indeed, some alumni had warned that the proliferation of written procedures would lead precisely in this direction. Society in general was more inclined to support due-process rights and be uncomfortable when ill-defined transgressions were punishable by a single penalty, especially in a closed hearing—which were traditional features of a system based on abstract concepts of honor, integrity, and mutual trust.

In the end, justice depended on the judgment, maturity, and commitment of the students. The conviction of a student in the spring of 1992 for what appeared to be a minor transgression (pledging completion of a routine homework assignment that was not completed) highlighted the main issues. The student's family and friends questioned how such a relatively trivial offense could result in expulsion from the university, and their protest led to discussions of the operations of the Honor System, how it differed from honor systems at at other institutions, and whether it provided sufficient protections for the accused party. In particular, how could college students without legal training, the maturity conferred by life experience, and any oversight by university faculty or officials play the definitive role in a matter of such importance to a fellow student?

Wilson and other administrators explained that student responsibility for the Honor System was a long-standing tradition and decisions were not subject to appeal to the faculty or administration. But Wilson was concerned by the questions critics had raised. He sought more information on the history and function of the Honor System and received in July a sheaf of historical materials and an essay prepared by Professor John M. Gunn. Wilson responded that Gunn's reflections "had arrived at a time when I had asked the question of origin and encountered a fairly misty landscape," and he was especially pleased to find evidence of a pledged examination as early as 1858. He asked if Gunn's paper could be distributed to the Student Executive Committee and perhaps members of the faculty. "I think the obligation to be specific in making assignments is a very important one and I found your examples to be very instructive."[56]

The trustees also had questions. In the October 1992 board meeting, student body president Joshua W. McFarland reported that the Student Executive Committee had focused on better means of educating faculty and students on the Honor Code, including, among other things, dividing first-year law students into smaller groups to view and discuss the committee's explanatory video. The orientation of new faculty also now included a meeting with a member of the Student Executive Committee, and two members had accompanied the School of Commerce faculty on a retreat. The committee was also considering revisions to the White Book.[57]

A nine-member White Book Review Committee completed its analysis by May 1994, and Robert K. Tompkins, the new Student Executive Committee president, reported a number of changes in the procedures to better protect the rights of the accused. He also noted efforts to educate the community on the Honor System and to offer better training for advocates of the accused. The committee had, however, made no change "in the current understanding respecting the application of the Honor System to students beyond the boundaries of the Washington and Lee campus and Rockbridge County." At the October board meeting, the new student body president, Kevin S. Webb, reported that White Book revisions were being implemented, including a new guidebook and orientation for investigations, training sessions on honor violations and misconduct matters brought before the Student Conduct Committee and the Student-Faculty Hearing Board, and an Honor System reorientation program for juniors and seniors. Webb had met with Dean Barry Sullivan of the law school to discuss the strength of the Honor System there and was exploring ways to bring the undergraduate and law school campuses together. The Student Executive Committee also sponsored a new video, a campus visit by a national expert on honor systems, and refinements to the procedures. With the board's encouragement, a formal review of the White Book was now scheduled to occur every two years. Hardin Marion told his fellow trustees that he fully supported student responsibility for the Honor System but warned that the board should continue to consider its proper oversight of the Student Executive Committee's procedures.[58]

Could the W&L Honor System survive in its traditional form or would it go the way of other honor systems throughout the country? Indeed, even the nation's service academies—with recent experiences of cheating scandals—had modified their honor codes with graduated penalties and the accoutrement of legal proceedings. But at Washington and Lee the typical graduate still looked upon the Honor System as the single most important, indeed defining, feature of the university. Perhaps Wilson said it best: "I feared a little bit in my first years here that people kept pulling the Honor System up by the roots to look at it, and this is not a healthy way to keep a plant growing." But he concluded that the Honor System remained strong, with a positive impact on individual conduct: "I believe this impact is measured not by the investigations or by the hearings or still less by the convictions, but by the quiet, united observance of the personal integrity doctrine that we don't even see because it's happening every night in study rooms or in the library or wherever the temptation to take a shortcut might be found and is resisted."[59]

THE LATEST SOUTHERN ASSOCIATION of Colleges and Schools reaccreditation self-study—organized around ten major areas, with work assigned to various committees and groups—was re-designated the Long-Range Plan and its developers the Long-Range Planning Committee. The Board Executive Committee reviewed the plan at a special two-day meeting in August 1989, and the document reached the trustees for approval and a lengthy discussion in October.[60]

Concerned about institutional size, the trustees were averse to approving an undergraduate enrollment over 1,600 or abandoning the current target ratio (roughly 6:4) of men to women. A minimum of 1,000 men was important, to support the fraternity system among other things. The Board Executive Committee endorsed student body diversity but without specific numbers or targets. Tom Touchton advocated retaining the "traditional profile" of the W&L student. The committee developed its own priority system for new academic programs and rated some in the arts (an orchestra and visiting artists) in the lowest category, along with neuroscience, which seemed to some more appropriate in a medical school. Frances Lewis spoke in favor of the arts programs, though not necessarily for a greater number of arts majors, and Tom Wolfe defended neuroscience as the "wave of the future" and deserving of the highest priority. Several trustees observed that the faculty members were dissatisfied with the 12–12–6 week academic calendar because of inadequate time in the long semesters. Touchton suggested reverting to a 15–15 arrangement, but Rector Ballengee advised against it. Elrod, the chief academic officer, noted that the president and deans were also unhappy with the current calendar, though some strongly supported the spring term, and the matter would be taken up when the Long-Range Plan was complete. The board decided, with one negative vote, that the undergraduate student body should not exceed 1,600 and should contain at least 1,000 males by the end of the 1990s.[61]

At the same October 1989 meeting, the outlines of the next major fundraising campaign, to be titled "On the Shoulders of Giants," began to take shape. Wilson sought board approval for a $128 million overall target and recommended a ten-year operating budget based upon a successful capital campaign—a budget in which all new capital projects would be funded by gifts and the endowment would grow by $88 million. The board also heard from consultants about next steps and the upcoming feasibility study.[62] The board eventually decided on an overall goal of $127 million, almost twice the amount raised in the previous campaign.

The first, or "quiet," stage of the campaign focusing on potential large donors began in July 1990. By October 1989, $26 million was on the books; by the May 1991 board meeting, $44.5 million had been given or pledged. The number reached $55.5 million by the time of the public announcement in February 1992. The announcement, held at Mount Vernon—home of the university's first major donor—on his birthday, February 12, was attended by more than a hundred guests. It was followed by a reception at the Mayflower Hotel for six hundred people, a campus kickoff at the Lenfest Center on March 6, and a series of campaign "rollouts" in cities and alumni chapters across the country. Trustees Gerry Lenfest and Touchton, national campaign chair and vice chair, were backed by an impressive plan, professional staff, and an array of fellow trustees, alumni chapters, and volunteers.[63] Lenfest, '53, from Pottstown, Pennsylvania, and his wife Marguerite made the lead $3 million gift in 1988 for the performing arts center that would bear his name. This was, to that point, the second largest gift of a living alumnus to W&L (after that of Sydney Lewis). Lenfest also joined with former trustee Houston Harte, '50, to create a $5 million challenge pledge to match, dollar for dollar, contributions to the capital campaign.

The new fund-raising effort certainly rested on the shoulders of the previous Development Program. Each trustee was expected to participate in the effort through personal gifts and by persuading others; nearly fifty of the eighty-six alumni chapters were primed to serve as local and regional hubs, and a detailed communications plan included a video, publications, and full use of the *Alumni Magazine*. Lex O. McMillan III, '72, the executive director of development, and Farris Hotchkiss, a veteran from the trenches of the previous campaign, were key university leaders. The board's Development Committee contributed ideas and actively pushed and monitored the campaign as it evolved.[64]

The two recent capital campaigns were complementary. The first one, ending in 1981, focused heavily on the capital needs of a growing institution and truly transformed the W&L built environment. The new effort addressed remaining capital needs—a performing arts center, a student center, and science building—but the primary focus was on endowment. W&L's reliance on tuition revenue to meet the operating budget was edging beyond the usual 60 percent toward 70 percent, and financial aid funds were dependent on gifts and grants. The campaign goals included $77 million for endowment: $31 million for scholarships, $19 million to endow faculty positions, $14 million for academic programs, and $4 million for the computer center.

The campaign raised more than $100 million by late February 1994, and the target of $127 million was reached a year later. The campaign formally ended on June 30, with an official total of $147 million, and occasioned a formal celebration in October, when major donors were invited to a special event on campus coinciding with the inauguration of John Elrod as W&L's new president.

Hovering just beyond the campaign's time horizon, but very much part of the message, was the upcoming celebration in 1999 of Washington and Lee's 250th anniversary. In 1994, the Board Development Committee recommended publication of a "vignette book" to highlight portions of the university's history in time for the celebration. (This would ultimately become the elegant volume *Come Cheer*, edited by Mame Warren.) Even as donors were recognized and the development effort celebrated, university staff shifted their attention toward the anniversary, virtually incorporating it as a further phase of the capital campaign. In 1996, George Washington's beneficence to Liberty Hall Academy two hundred years earlier was marked by special events and activities. A Washington Society subcommittee—composed of Peter Agelasto, Dan Balfour, and Parke Rouse—arranged for a publication by Rouse, a traveling exhibit of the Peale portrait of Washington and other memorabilia, special presentations on campus, and communications to the news media.

Clearly, the university now relied on continuous philanthropy to secure its future. What had first become evident in the 1971–1981 Development Campaign was now firmly reinforced by "On the Shoulders of Giants": independent higher-education institutions must conduct systematic, intensive, and continuous fund-raising if they hoped to be successful.

ENHANCEMENTS TO campus facilities and infrastructure were less dramatic than those following the Development Program campaign, but they were still significant. A new 71,000-square-foot residence hall for juniors and seniors, costing over $8 million and named in honor of Frank Gaines, opened in August 1988 on the corner of Washington and Nelson streets, opposite the Warner Center. With single rooms, configured in suites, kitchens, meeting space, and an exercise room, it marked another major step toward bringing more students to live on campus.

A long-awaited major addition was built diagonally across from Gaines Hall, next to the old Lexington railroad station. Gaines had mentioned the need for a new university theater or auditorium in the 1930s, and it had appeared in long-range plans at least since 1964, especially as the old Troubadour Theater on Henry Street became less adequate. Preliminary plans for the same area were drawn in the 1970s, but even the ambitious Development Program could not generate the required funding. Finally, in 1987, the university embarked on construction of a $9 million center for the performing arts that dwarfed the earlier proposals. The Lenfest Center for the Performing Arts opened for use in January 1991. The facility provided exceptional new space for drama, music, and dance, and a gallery for showing visual arts. A theater seating 425 people faced a stage, large enough for a ninety-two-piece orchestra, with a shock-absorbing floor suitable for dance. A smaller experimental theater was even more flexible.

The largest new project addressed long-standing academic needs in the sciences. W&L had struggled to maintain a first-rate science program, which enormous advances in biology, chemistry, physics, and geology made increasingly difficult, as did the development of the new field of computer science and breakthroughs in the study of neuroscience and cognition in psychology. Preparations for careers in medicine, dentistry, science, and engineering were central to career aspirations of a rising number of W&L students. In 1962, the

New Science Building—later named Parmly Hall—was a substantial improvement for the time but was inadequate just twenty years later. Entirely new fields—like molecular biology—were developed during those two decades. Furthermore, the thirty full-time science faculty were scattered over four different buildings, and space was scarce for even the most basic faculty and student research, not to mention the space and equipment expected by new faculty members. In May 1992, the trustees moved new science facilities to the top of the priority list, even ahead of a new student center. The eventual plan provided for renovating Parmly and Howe Halls and connecting them with a new, embracing structure that would increase the total gross square footage by two-thirds, at a cost of $22 million. The new science complex—to that time the largest capital project in the university's history—would provide enhanced space not only for each faculty member but also for the undergraduate research that had been a hallmark of W&L's curriculum.[65]

In December 1989, retired US Supreme Court justice Lewis Powell announced the gift of his personal and professional papers to Washington and Lee, setting in motion plans to receive and house them properly. Once again, Sydney and Frances Lewis stepped forward, with a $1 million gift toward a $2 million addition to Lewis Hall that included sufficient space for the papers and also for faculty offices, seminar rooms, a reading room, and offices for Justice Powell, an archivist, and a secretary. The new archives were dedicated over three days in April 1992 with a special conference, a banquet, and a keynote speech by US Supreme Court chief justice William Rehnquist.[66]

COEDUCATION LED TO an immediate and dramatic improvement in W&L's admissions picture. More students—male and female—applied and the academic qualifications of the pool rose, as did the enrollment "yield," or the percentage of admitted students who matriculated. But in many respects, the demographic and geographic profile of entering undergraduate classes remained much the same. In 1990–91, almost half of first-year students hailed from the South (the largest number from Virginia, Maryland, and Texas) and almost a quarter from the Northeast. The majority had attended public high schools. The great majority of those declaring a religious preference were Protestant, and almost a third were Episcopalian or Presbyterian. About 2 percent were Jewish. But the entering class in 1990 included twenty-eight foreign students from twenty-one different countries. The proportion of students from outside the South was growing, reflecting a more national pattern of recruitment and enrollment. A quarter of the entering class expressed no religious preference at all (actually an eight-year low). The retention and graduation rates were markedly better: 88 percent of the original class of 1991 completed their degrees in four years or less, the highest graduation rate in forty years. And the total enrollment was larger and now included women and a smattering of African Americans (3.8 percent of undergraduates in 1990-91).[67]

The university's tuition was increasing, to keep up with inflation and because of greater student demand and rising needs for new faculty and other academic improvements. Undergraduate tuition in 1989-90 was over 42 percent higher than in 1985-86 and over 13 percent higher than a year before. (For the first time, law-school tuition was set slightly higher than undergraduate tuition). This pattern also increased the amount needed for financial aid.

Some aspects of student life came to an end. Perhaps most notably, ROTC was no longer needed to prepare as many leaders in an all-volunteer military, and the small unit at W&L was deactivated in 1991. Student life remained energetic across a wide range of organizations and activities. In 1992-93, twenty-four undergraduate student organizations (including eleven devoted to the performing arts and eight to religion) offered extracurricular opportunities, in addition to sixteen fraternities, four sororities, twenty-two varsity sports, and fifteen sports clubs. More than 70 percent of the undergraduate student body participated in intramural sports and more than 90 percent in the Mock Convention every four years.[68] Satisfaction with campus social life still depended largely on whether one belonged to a fraternity (82 percent of men) or sorority (65 percent of women), and the campus community continued to be somewhat fragmented, without a common campus meeting place. While many sophomore men lived in fraternity houses, the second-year women had to find their own housing, joining junior and senior students scattered in rental accommodations throughout the city and county. Even after all sophomores were required to live in university housing, upper-class students still resided in a variety of apartments in town and rental houses that, over time, acquired their own names (Amityville, Aqua Velva, Bordello, Hooverville, and Rose Hill along them), each with distinctive social reputations. By the summer of 1997, almost half of W&L students lived in dormitories, 18 percent in fraternities, and about a third off campus.[69] Students still gathered on the banks of the Maury River in good weather and for parties at Zollman's Pavilion and in the newly renovated fraternity houses.

Outlets for campus news and student opinion increased, especially as technology enabled easy access to publishing. Frustrations over perceived inadequacies in the *Ring-tum Phi* (including an infamous April Fool issue and what many considered generally insipid reporting) led to the rise of new publications, most notably the *Washington and Lee Spectator* and the *Trident*. Independent of the university and self-supporting, the *Spectator* first appeared in a two-thousand-copy run on Reunion Weekend in May 1989, and it produced five issues in 1989–90 and seven issues the following year. Published by the Campus Reporting Committee, with encouragement and support from the Intercollegiate Studies Institute (whose president, T. Kenneth Cribb Jr., '70, had been a policy adviser to President Ronald Reagan) and the Madison Center for Educational Affairs, the *Spectator* took a conservative stance, especially opposing anything smacking of "political correctness." It pointed out the failings of the *Ring-tum Phi* and kept a skeptical eye on the university administration. Denounced by some as a "right-wing rag," the *Spectator* contributed investigative pieces on W&L affairs and boasted a number of student leaders on its senior staff. Soon a sister—but altogether different—publication joined the list. Also published by the Campus Reporting Committee, the *Trident* first appeared in April 1993 and received funding from the university through the Student Publications Board. The Student Executive Committee allocated almost twice the amount of money to the *Trident* in 1993–94 as it did for the *Ring-tum Phi*.[70]

Other publications supported by the Student Publications Board included the *Calyx* yearbook, the *Ariel* literary magazine, the *Journal of Science* and the *Journal of Politics*. The *Traveller*, a liberal alternative to the *Spectator*, and a Christian magazine, *Common Ground*, were among the independent papers. Over the next decade, even more new publications appeared, including *Una Vox*, *She Says*, the *Seedling*, and the *Political Review*. Whatever their focus or political bent, these publications enlivened campus conversations and also bore the marks of student journalism, including overheated rhetoric produced through usually late-night, caffeinated labors at the keyboard to meet deadlines, with varying success and often with typos.

Student performance groups benefitted especially from the new venues in the Lenfest Center but also appeared in many places throughout the year on and off campus. The Troubadours finally had an excellent space for intimate dramatic plays, as well as musical stage productions, and so did the orchestral performers, vocal and instrumental. Other musical groups—from the mixed chorus and smaller ensembles to the popular a cappella groups like the Sazeracs, Southern Comfort, and Jubilee—seemed more popular than ever.[71]

The Mock Convention remained a vigorous quadrennial event engaging most of the student body, though with adjustments in light of changes in the American presidential campaign system. Given the rising importance of political primaries, the convention was moved earlier in the calendar—from the traditional late spring schedule to late March in 1988 and early March in 1992 and 1996. Drawing up and adopting party platforms continued as part of the process, and a few student delegations attempted—with mixed success—to predict the outcomes of some state primaries based on their research. The news media continued to focus on the W&L event because of its successful record and its primary commitment to accuracy. It was always quite a party, with plenty of photo opportunities and the appearance of notable political personalities. The presidential races in 1984, 1988, and 1992—with Republicans in the White House—offered true tests of the W&L model: a predominantly conservative student body was transformed, however briefly, into committed and enthusiastic Democrats. Most importantly, the successful W&L track record was preserved and extended.

The 1984 convention, held in the Warner Center, followed the usual parade down Main Street with fifty-five floats—almost all pulled by tractors driven by local farmers—and featuring donkeys rather than elephants. Some students took the occasion to protest coeducation; a float with a Native American theme proclaimed "Chief Says No Squaws," and the Virgin Islands entry declared "Virgins Against Coeducation." Another float carried women wearing bunny outfits and fishnet stockings. US senator William Proxmire of Wisconsin delivered the keynote address; other speakers included Sen. Ernest "Fritz" Hollings of South Carolina, Virginia governor Charles Robb, Sen. Jennings Randolph of West Virginia, and the youthful, up-and-coming senator Joseph Biden of Delaware. Discerning the conservative leanings of the crowd and spotting several Nixon stickers in the audience, Biden cheerfully addressed "my fellow Democrats, all five of you" and declared "it's good to be here in the nineteenth century."[72] In the same vein, Charles F. Phillips Jr., Lexington's mayor and a W&L economics professor, welcomed "fellow Republicans and weekend Democrats."[73] The delegates nominated US senator Walter Mondale of Minnesota on the first ballot, with Sen. Gary Hart running second and the Rev. Jesse Jackson third. Sen. Lloyd Bentsen won the voting for vice president, just ahead of US representative Geraldine Ferraro.

Four years later, the convention nominated Governor Michael Dukakis of Massachusetts on the second ballot. US senator Al Gore Jr. of Tennessee was tapped for vice president, but—as evidence of the usual relaxed attention in Mock Conventions to the second position on the ticket—W&L professor Jefferson Davis Futch III eked out the platform speaker, Gov. Bill Clinton of Arkansas, for second place. Atlanta mayor Andrew Young gave the keynote address, and other speakers included Robb, Virginia governor Gerald Baliles, and Lt. Gov. (and soon to be governor) Douglas Wilder. Despite his third place finish behind Professor Futch, it was Clinton who most impressed the delegates with a rousing platform address and later by joining them that evening for partying, dancing, and playing the saxophone at Zollman's Pavilion.

Clinton did not return in person for the March 1992 Mock Convention, but he was nominated on the first ballot, beating out Sen. Paul Tsongas of Rhode Island by only four votes. Michael Dukakis, the parade marshal, arrived late because of bad weather but delivered remarks along with former speaker of the US House of Representatives, Thomas P. "Tip" O'Neil. This time the spellbinding orator was New York governor Mario Cuomo, tempting some in the audience to put him up for the nomination for president. Once again, W&L had chosen correctly, and Clinton's victory in November returned the Mock Convention to the Republicans.

In 1996 students ventured predictions of the outcomes of some state primaries and also found themselves confronted with what seemed a truly open race with no single Republican Party leader or front-runner—a situation that continued up until the real party convention itself. Relying on considerable research, the delegates rose to the challenge and nominated US senator Bob Dole of Kansas for president and Gen. Colin Powell as vice president. Rep. Newt Gingrich of Georgia delivered the keynote, and other speakers included former US vice president Dan Quayle, US senator and W&L alumnus John Warner of Virginia, and secretary of education and conservative pundit William Bennett.

AS FRANK GAINES and others had hoped, eliminating subsidized athletics led to an increase in overall student participation in intercollegiate as well as intramural sports. Athletics continued to be an important element of the individual student experience. Competing together provided lifelong bonds for some students, heightened by the university's small size, and brought together students from different fraternities, majors, and backgrounds.

Given the national hothouse of big-time collegiate athletics, and alumni (and some coaches') dreams of notable success on the court, field, or gridiron, there were occasional complaints about W&L's membership in the Old

Dominion Athletic Conference (ODAC) and in the NCAA's Division III. But students enrolled at W&L partly because they could run cross-country or play tennis while getting an education, and they competed, made memories, and sometimes won conference and even national titles and set individual records. The university expanded and improved its athletic facilities and rose to the challenge of providing athletic opportunities for undergraduate women at a time when mandated gender equity in college sports made this imperative. John Wilson was especially involved in the policies and administration of the university's athletic programs, and he did more than any other single individual during his tenure as president to reaffirm and reinforce the spirit and reality of W&L's commitment to a balanced program of amateur intercollegiate sports.

The full story of athletics at Washington and Lee in the 1980s and 1990s exceeds what can be provided here, but some broad outlines are revealing. William D. McHenry, '54, the athletic director and chairman of the department of physical education since 1971 (after a decade at Lebanon Valley College) presided over all sports and was head football coach for five seasons. With the possible exception of lacrosse, the athletic teams themselves enjoyed limited followings but offered opportunities to train under competent coaches and compete against other college teams. The football team won conference championships in 1981and 1985 under Coach Gary Fallon but had mostly mediocre seasons through the late 1980s and early '90s. Coach Fallon concluded seventeen seasons at the helm in 1994 and died unexpectedly in May 1995 at the age of fifty-six. Frank Miriello replaced him. The men's soccer team, coached by Rolf Piranian, claimed conference championships in 1986, 1989, and 2000. The swimmers were consistent winners under Page Remillard, finishing with a perfect season in 1992–93. The golf team posted a number of winning seasons under "Buck" Leslie, and Gary Franke's wrestlers had a string of winning seasons in the late 1980s, as did the tennis team, which finished second in the Division III tournament in 1986 and won W&L's first national championship in any sport in 1988. The baseball team had a mixed record under Jim Murdock and Jeff Stickey, and posted only two winning seasons between 1982 and 1995. The entire W&L intercollegiate program consistently ranked high in the ODAC.

Lacrosse was the premier W&L intercollegiate team because of its success against national competition in Division I. Its record of seven NCAA Tournament appearances (six consecutively) under Jack Emmer between 1973 and 1980 was unprecedented. Competing at this level with no athletic scholarships was difficult, and Emmer left in 1983 to become head coach at the US Military Academy at West Point. The teams under the new coach, Dennis Daly, completed the transition to Division III in 1987 and made it to the NCAA Tournament but had a dismal 2–11 showing in 1988. Jim Stagnitta joined the athletic staff in 1990 and led the Generals back into lacrosse prominence with twelve consecutive winning seasons and six NCAA Tournament appearances—but in Division III with a mostly new list of opponents.

Coeducation meant new commitments and opportunities in athletics, a challenge addressed in institutional assessments and planning. Were W&L's athletic facilities adequate? Would the legal requirement for gender equity in higher education (Title IX of the Higher Education Act) mean the elimination of some men's sports? And how many new women's sports would there be? The first classes of undergraduate women were determined to make their mark on all aspects of the university, including athletics. Their rates of participation in intercollegiate competition and intramural sports were impressive, especially considering that some women students were relative neophytes. The particular sports were selected partly according to the interests of the women themselves and partly on the university's ability to mount a successful program, the costs, the competencies of existing staff, and the availability of suitable competition.[74]

The first four sports for women, introduced in 1985–86 and shepherded by the new associate athletic director, Cinda Rankin, were tennis, swimming, cross-country, and golf. After a 1–8 season in 1986, the tennis team went 18–1 two years later under Bill Washburn and won the conference championship in 1989 and in all but two of the succeeding years until 2007 under Rankin. Dick Miller coached the women in their first three years of cross-country competition, and Jim Phemister took over from 1988 until 1997, with a particularly impressive performance in 1992. The women's swim team was launched in 1985–86 with only three members, but as in tennis they advanced from an 0–9 season in the first year to a consistent series of winning seasons and conference championships under Remillard until 1990–91 and then subsequently under Coach Kiki Jacobs. Soccer was initiated as a varsity-developmental sport in 1986—when almost a quarter of the entire female enrollment turned out for the team—and began competing within the conference in 1988. Coached by Jan Hathorn, the teams followed a familiar trajectory, beginning haltingly and then posting a consistent winning record in most years, beginning in 1990. Volleyball was introduced in 1988, coached first by Susan Dittman until 1991 and then by Terri Dadio, who took the team to conference championships in 1995, '97, '98, and '99. In 1989, both track (coached by John Tucker) and lacrosse joined the contingent of women's sports. Lacrosse enjoyed a series of successful seasons and conference championships in 1992, '93, and '98 under Hathorn. Basketball was added in 1993–94 and posted a winning record in its first season, coached by Terri Dadio Campbell. While teams were mostly competitive, the next winning season would be in 1999–2000.

Over even a single decade, the memorable athletic events and personalities are legion, and each student involved has his or her own fond recollections. The days were long over when a small number of tenured athletic-department personnel coached a variety of sports. Coaches were now hired on renewable term contracts, though some remained at W&L for many years. The old-timers were able to enjoy the fruits of tenured appointments. Dick Miller celebrated his two-hundredth career cross-country victory midway through his thirty-third season in 1984 and guided his team to the conference championship—and to conference coach of the year honors for the second time in three years. By that time, he had also coached wrestling for nineteen years and been head coach of the tennis and track teams (in more than five hundred total contests), as well as serving as associate athletic director. And he would coach the first women's cross-country team.[75] "Stormin' Norman" Lord was a fitness fanatic before anyone knew about fitness fanatics. He joined the physical education faculty in 1946 and, except for a two-year leave to serve in the Korean War, spent all that time in Lexington and never missed a single day of class because of illness. With a booming voice, a ready whistle around his neck, and a theatrical predilection, he put students through a series of vigorous exercises, after categorizing them by their state of fitness—from "Varsity" to "Better see a doctor" to "I need Coach Lord's help"—marked by different-colored shoestrings. He coached a number of sports over the years, but his mantra was fitness for life.[76]

In addition to fulfilling their principal role as teachers, coaches also did their best to help their athletes and teams win. One memorable example was the so-called Armadillo formation in lacrosse, a 1982 ball-control invention of Coach Jack Emmer to raise his team's chances against the powerful, undefeated, and number-one-ranked North Carolina Tar Heels on Wilson Field. After a 22–8 loss to Virginia, W&L needed something. After gaining possession of the ball, a group of five W&L players would form a tight huddle around it and, basically, stop play until they could spot an opportunity to score against the befuddled opponents. The sight of Tar Heel players and referees clustered around and under the tight tangle of Generals was an unprecedented sight. W&L used the formation through most of the second half, and the score was tied in the fourth quarter. But the Tar Heels won the game 11–8. The Armadillo was short-lived; within two days, the lacrosse rules committee banned it.[77]

Another stroke of coaching ingenuity did not work out so well. At Sewanee in October 1987, the W&L football team was soundly trounced 24–7 in the first half. The team's lack of aggressiveness so upset Coach Gary Fallon that he decided, as motivation, to conduct a full-contact scrimmage during halftime. Two players were injured, one of them sustaining a broken leg and spending several days in the local hospital. The team's play did improve in the second half, but W&L still lost. The situation was compounded by the failure of the coaches to immediately notify the parents of the injured players or to visit the player in the hospital before the team departed. John Wilson was livid: "We portrayed ourselves," he wrote the coach and athletic director, "as callous or indifferent to our amateur athletes and their families."[78] Needless to say, this particular motivational exercise was never repeated.

The roster of individual athletes included All-Americans and national champions. Kevin Weaver, a gifted tailback from Martinsburg, West Virginia, broke W&L's single-season rushing record in 1985, gaining 1,161 yards. He also set a single-season scoring record in the process, and was named the leading rusher in the nation in Division III. The African American student was a chemistry and premed major, and laboratories and other academic demands required him to miss ten of the team's eighteen practice hours per week—a positive commentary on Weaver and W&L's genuine commitment to the student athlete.[79] Among the first women standouts was Elizabeth Miles of Louisville, daughter of a W&L alumnus who would soon be the university's rector. An outstanding swimmer, she, along with the other two members of the women's swimming team, practiced with the men and were vastly outnumbered in almost every meet. Despite going 0–9 in their first year, they still managed to place third in the ODAC championships. Miles, a national leader in long-distance freestyle events, went to the NCAA Division III championships along with five W&L men who also qualified.[80]

The Alumni Association established the Washington and Lee Athletic Hall of Fame in May 1987, and the first class of five inductees was chosen the following May and honored at a banquet in September. The names were familiar—indeed legendary—to anyone who followed W&L athletics, and they covered several generations: Cy Young, '17, winner of sixteen varsity letters in four sports and a former Alumni Association secretary; Walt Michaels, '51, a star of the 1950 football team that went to the Gator Bowl and later a long-time collegiate and professional football coach; Edmund M. Cameron, '24, captain of the football and basketball teams, who became a coach and athletic director at Duke University; Robert W. Spessard, '39, an outstanding basketball player; and Karl E. (Skip) Rohnke, '60, with twelve varsity letters in track and field, swimming, and soccer. The second class, inducted in 1989, included Gil Bocetti, '52, quarterback of the 1950 football team; Richard A. (Cap'n Dick) Smith, '13, baseball coach and athletic director from 1921 to 1954; Norman P. Iler, '37, a star in basketball and baseball; Dominik A. Flora, '58, a multisport athlete nationally recognized in basketball; and Ernest J. (Skip) Litchfuss, '74, an outstanding athlete in basketball and lacrosse. The Hall of Fame continues to the present day, a pantheon of student athletes and others who made significant contributions to W&L's sports tradition.

The traditional notion of the student athlete, a term embedded in modern NCAA rules and regulations, is nowadays increasingly ignored at the highest levels of intercollegiate competition. But the tug, even at W&L, has always been between sport as an element of personal development in an academic environment and as a form of entertainment and public expression of school spirit. The university has always sought a "proper" balance, especially since the events of 1954. W&L's conference affiliation, NCAA divisional status, and the suitability of the university's competition were issues involving this balance—and all were factors in decisions concerning lacrosse.

The national attention paid to the W&L teams' success against top-ranked, larger Division I opponents was difficult to abandon, and the university stuck with it as long as possible. Competing against Virginia, Navy, North Carolina, and Johns Hopkins for the national Division I title was heady stuff for coaches, players, and alumni. But lacrosse had now drifted into the major college universe, dominated by big money and all its compromises and trappings—a universe that W&L was firmly determined to avoid. W&L's biggest challenge was competing in Division I while adhering to the financial-aid policies of Division III (no athletic scholarships). In 1985, the board approved Bill McHenry's recommendation that W&L lacrosse remain in Division I but shift the schedule away from schools that awarded "the full complement" of scholarships to those that shared W&L's general philosophy on sports or, at least, maintained similar academic standards. The 1986 schedule added Dartmouth, Cornell, and Yale; eliminated some traditional rivals like North Carolina and Maryland; and re-

tained others like Virginia and Duke.[81] But the win-loss record of 5–9 under
Dennis Daly was not not far off Jack Emmer's 1983 mark of 5–7. Victories over
Dartmouth and Virginia Tech, and a close game against Virginia were overshadowed by overwhelming losses to Cornell, Loyola, and Maryland-Baltimore
County. The university's Athletic Committee recommended unanimously that
a shift to Division III be made "immediately," and the board approved a request
to the NCAA in June 1986 to do just that, in time for the 1987 season. McHenry
and Coach Daly concurred with Wilson's observation that more subsidization
in Division I lacrosse "is not a direction Washington and Lee is prepared to
follow." Of course, some were disappointed, and a few even preferred giving
athletic scholarships to "dropping down a level."[82] But for the most part the
players looked forward to having a chance to win—which indeed they did,
going 11–4 and to the NCAA Division III tournament in 1987 and returning to
consistent winning seasons under Jim Stagnitta in 1990.

The majority of alumni and fans admired the university's academic reputation and accepted the lessons and decisions of the 1950s. But it was difficult
to live anywhere in late twentieth-century America (especially in the South)
and be impervious to the hype, drama, and media-whipped emphasis on big-
time intercollegiate sports—the championships and bowl games, the celebrity
players, the total commitment of loyal boosters, and the multimillion-dollar
coaches. "It would be great," one 1936 graduate wrote to the *Alumni Magazine*
in 1988, "to look at the sports section of the Sunday paper and see that Washington and Lee had won a game, and with some degree of regularity. It has been
many years since that situation has existed. Needless to say, we 'ole timers' are
proud of the University's high scholastic standards; with the fine athletic traditions held by W&L, however, the present athletic situation is a bit embarrassing."[83] W&L coaches understandably put a high value on athletic performance
and winning, and saw recruitment of skilled athletes as an important part of
their jobs. These pressures perpetuated a certain tension between athletics and
academics, even at an institution like W&L.

If there was ever anyone who had strong credibility in addressing these
issues, it was John D. Wilson. A star defensive back for the 1952 national-
champion Michigan State football team (and Academic All-American), former
provost at Division I Virginia Tech, recipient of the Duffy Daugherty Award
in 1987 from his alma mater, and nominee for the Theodore Roosevelt Award,
the highest distinction conferred by the NCAA, his big-time sports credentials
were impeccable. The barbs aimed at James Leyburn in the 1950s could not be

directed against Wilson, who was just as committed to W&L's student athletes and even more vigorously outspoken on the corruption of big-time college sports. In the *Richmond Times-Dispatch*, he lamented the "huge sums of money being made and spent by top Division I powers," which constituted "a brand new incentive to cheat." He believed that public disclosure of the details— how much money was in athletics and where it went, the graduation rates of athletes—would help solve the problem: "Institutional embarrassment is the only motivation left." He opposed athletic dormitories, freshmen eligibility, and "redshirting" (holding players back to retain their athletic eligibility). He advocated closing programs down for at least two years if they "grievously" violated standards. But he knew any changes would be difficult. The big-time programs had "huge budgets to support, staffs to maintain, large stadiums and coliseums to fill, alumni and fan expectations to fulfill." Indeed, big-time programs had become virtually autonomous enterprises separate from the universities themselves.[84] He knew that was a path W&L would never follow, but it was a scourge on all of higher education.

Even at W&L and in Division III, athletic recruiting was a persistent issue between admissions staff and coaches eager to attract and commit to gifted athletes as early as possible. (The W&L Admissions Office was concerned that formal or informal commitments were made to some athletes before they were deemed academically admissible.) In the spring 1985, Wilson employed this issue to begin a much broader consideration of "the current status of our program and our hopes regarding its future." A "frank exchange" in May was framed by his preliminary list of fourteen questions that included W&L's recruiting practices, athletic affiliations, length of seasons and out-of-season activities, schedules and who should be responsible, the role of financial aid, and the gaps between philosophy and practice among Division III schools. He also wanted to know how much pressure coaches perceived "to compile winning records, year in and year out" and what should be done "to insure that athletic coaches are spared the temptations or fears which patently operate in many Division I schools."[85] He shared his memorandum with the trustees, noting that the athletic staff had apparently been discussing most of these questions "ever since I arrived." While no one had all the answers to the "very peculiar condition" of college sports in the country, "at least we have a chance to remain sane in our program if we can find enough good peers who share our view."[86] In handwritten notes prepared prior to the meeting, Wilson listed even more concerns, focusing on limiting the demands (practice times, out-of-season conditioning, etc.) on student athletes, particularly those who wished to participate in two sports; staff and space problems; recruiting practices; admissions "slots" for athletes (which he further labeled "a bottomless pit"); and whether W&L should maintain thirteen men's sports.[87] Bill McHenry wrote Wilson on May 29 that the coaching staff was eager to improve their relationship with the admissions staff but would appreciate a system of guidelines or preliminary assessments that would facilitate recruiting, perhaps along the lines of those used by Ivy League institutions.[88]

Wilson remained dissatisfied with aspects of W&L's program and turned his attention to the challenges of introducing women's sports. He kept in touch with the athletic-department leadership, as well as with some individual coaches. In 1989, he decided to replace Bill McHenry as athletic director. McHenry took a leave-of-absence in 1989–90, and the next year he returned as head of the Physical Education Department. In the meantime, Dick Miller served as interim athletic director. Wilson wanted the national search to proceed as quickly as possible, looking for "strong leadership in the years ahead to guide us still further along the pathways laid down so well since 1954."[89]

In a memo to the search committee, he revealed his concerns and future expectations (doubtless drawn in part from his personal experience as a student athlete). He noted that the criteria for faculty promotion and tenure could not be applied to the coaching staff, now ineligible for tenure and appointed on three-year moving contracts. But the criteria that often prevailed in athletics were not appropriate either: "coaches live in a world in which success is superficially judged by wins or losses." Such a measure had, in fact, been applied in performance evaluations at W&L, and the new athletic director should rely on "a much fuller examination of the coach as teacher and colleague," especially regarding "congruence of thought and practice with the rules and spirit of amateur athletics in a serious academic institution." The AD should expect coaches to organize the total effort in a given sport, reinforce positive values, ensure "exemplary team behavior on and off the field," develop good intercollegiate relationships and schedules, and "instill esprit or high team morale, especially in adversity." These attributes "form a coherent cluster of desirable characteristics and represent what I will be looking for. Indeed, they represent what I assume we have all been looking for many past years."[90]

The newly organized Athletic Department Liaison Committee of the Alumni Association Board of Directors "emphatically" endorsed a number of goals. These included a "broader and stronger intramural program"; a football schedule that would "more effectively enhance the reputation of the University" and include schools located in areas with substantial numbers of W&L alumni; a rekindling of school spirit currently lacking among undergraduates; a focus on at least one sport to be nationally competitive; and the inclusion of more "nationally prominent schools" on the basketball schedule. They also suggested forming an alumni committee, under the guidance of the Admissions Office and the Athletic Department, to assist in identifying and recruiting skilled athletes.[91] Many of these ideas were not new, and some were shared by the W&L administration, but Wilson cautioned that the committee's recommendations "have not had the benefit of internal reflection." He was particularly dubious about the proposed athletic admissions committee.[92]

In his eagerness to fill the position, Wilson personally entangled himself in the search. The former W&L lacrosse coach, Jack Emmer, was interested in the job and visited the campus in May, even before the search committee had been appointed, and Wilson told Emmer he would be a good candidate. The athletic staff, asked to meet with the finalists and provide comments to the search committee, was less enthused, and the committee's final report to Wilson did not include Emmer's name. Wilson admitted that he "had made some mistakes" in the process and that the timing of Emmer's early visit had been poor.[93] But the search, he also confided, had been successful, resulting in an appointment that fulfilled Wilson's hopes and met all his standards.

Forty-one-year-old Michael F. Walsh, coming from nine years as baseball coach and assistant athletic director at Dartmouth, became the fifth athletic director at W&L on December 1, 1989. He was thoroughly familiar with Division III programs, need-based financial aid, and strong liberal arts institutions. He had the additional perspective of experiencing coeducation at Dartmouth and dealing with the issues of gender equity. He supported contacting potential recruits only if they fit the academic profile of the university, and he described revenue generation through athletics as "deplorable." None of this, however, detracted from his pursuit of athletic excellence and winning.[94] One of Walsh's first tasks was the selection of a new lacrosse coach; Jim Stagnitta, the former head assistant at the University of Pennsylvania, also began his duties on December 1. Walsh and Bill Hartog visited Dartmouth to learn more about the "Ivy League index" for determining academic eligibility of athletes. This system consisted of adding the total of the math and verbal SAT scores, the high-school rank, and other indicators to reach a single number that would be compared to a desirable average of students scores in order to determine if a particular student athlete was admissible. W&L developed a variation of such an index and has employed it successfully, thereby reducing the tension between admissions and the athletic department. Hartog also observed that many more good athletes were admitted through the regular admissions process.[95] Wilson celebrated the new athletic-director appointment, especially because Walsh had "no prior allegiances or friendships or animosities to complicate his work. I hope and pray that he will succeed and bring a new and fresh sense of excellence and style to all our sports programs, from intramural to intercollegiate teams."[96]

One of the early questions posed to Walsh was frequently asked on or off campus: Was the ODAC the best athletic conference for W&L and should the university consider other options? Most complaints revolved around the type and visibility of the other conference members. Walsh's noted that W&L was "a victim of its own geography"; he agreed that there was too much academic disparity among the ODAC schools. W&L was also haunted by its history—still celebrated by many alumni—of competing against major universities, and its aspirations to claim schools like Dartmouth and Amherst as its athletic and academic peers.

The ODAC, founded as the Virginia College Conference in 1975, began with eight members in 1976. The other charter members were Bridgewater College, Eastern Mennonite University, Emory & Henry College, Hampden-Sydney College, Lynchburg College, Randolph-Macon College, and Roanoke College. Several other institutions joined shortly thereafter: Hollins and Sweet Briar for women's sports in 1982, Catholic University in football in 1982 (until 1984), Maryville College in Tennessee in 1980 (until 1988), Mary Baldwin College in 1984 (until 1992), Virginia Wesleyan College in 1989, and Guilford College in North Carolina in 1991. Only about half of these members played football.

Soon after he arrived, Wilson sought to engage with more high-profile opponents and "like-minded" universities in the East and Northeast. Even he was concerned about "the degree to which athletic affiliations shape the public perception of a collegiate institution." He was "absolutely certain that our ODAC affiliation does not aid us, and may in fact detract from the esteem we might otherwise have a claim upon." In response to his queries, the Athletic Committee responded that it would be extremely difficult to regularly schedule "teams from institutions with comparable academic reputations and a Division III NCAA status," and equally difficult to schedule teams within the ODAC—especially in the "minor sports"—if W&L dropped out of the conference. In addition, the costs of scheduling far-away teams would be considerable, also requiring additional time away from classes. Bill McHenry conducted a survey of thirty-seven other schools concerning their interest in scheduling W&L in football. Of the twenty-seven that responded, eight expressed no interest because of distance and cost, and twelve declined because of conference commitments and traditional rivalries. Eight schools expressed an interest if their budgets were increased, an extra game added to their schedules, or if some opening was created by a schedule change. In addition, new athletic conferences of schools in Pennsylvania and Maryland further limited opportunities to schedule nonconference opponents.[97]

Wilson understood but was reluctant to abandon the issue. As for the increased cost of travel, "I would rather play 22 good schools than 26 (or whatever) mediocre ones. That is another way to think about expenditures."[98] W&L's determination—shared by Wilson—not to compete against schools that awarded athletic scholarships (except, of course, for lacrosse, which W&L played at the Division I level in 1985) also limited opportunities. Thus, schools like Davidson and VMI were off-limits. Despite many changes in the intercollegiate athletic landscape over the years, the same basic considerations have led W&L to remain, and compete successfully, in the ODAC.

W&L athletics, even with continuing discussions and some complaints, has followed the athletic philosophy set down after 1954 with considerable consistency. Wilson's message of welcome to fans gathered at Wilson Field—printed in the program of W&L's home football games—summed it up: "The players of today's game are, in every respect, students. That should not need saying but, alas, it is important, in this day of subsidized extravagance, to keep it in mind. They bring athletic skills and energy and teamwork to these grounds on Saturday afternoon. But during the other days of the week, they are mainly concerned with deepening their understanding of themselves, their culture and their natural world."[99]

CHAPTER THIRTEEN

THE UNIVERSITY
AT 250

AS THE 1990S ADVANCED, some distinctive personalities who had helped guide, and even define, Washington and Lee passed into history. Fred Cole died in May 1986 at the age of seventy-four. James Farrar Sr., who influenced so many young people to attend W&L, and who shepherded the first African Americans into the student body, died in 1993, aged sixty-seven. Even non-Chemistry majors knew Professor Keith Shillington, who served on the faculty for thirty-eight years and had somehow acquired the honor of kissing the Homecoming Queen every year on Wilson Field. He was seventy when he died in 1992. William Webb Pusey III, another university stalwart, died at eighty-four in November 1994. In his forty-two years at W&L, he taught German and Russian, founded the East Asian Studies Program, and served as department chair, dean of the College, and acting president. Epitomizing the ideal W&L professor, Pusey was devoted to teaching based on solid scholarship, strongly supported the library, and was a friend to the university's leaders and untold numbers of colleagues and students. When he retired in 1981, the student body established an award in his name to be given annually for outstanding service to the university. Robert Stewart, who died at the age of seventy-seven in 1995, was hired by James Leyburn as W&L's first professor of music. Reportedly, his job interview consisted of playing piano sonatas with the dean of the university.

James Leyburn succumbed to complications from pneumonia in Hagerstown, Maryland, on April 28, 1993, at the age of ninety-one. He retired from W&L in 1972 to his family's Spring Hill Farm in Martinsburg, West Virginia, and served for fifteen years as organist and Sunday school teacher at the Falling

Waters Presbyterian Church, where his father had served as pastor. He later moved to a nearby retirement community, where he walked four miles a day, worked on his memoirs, kept his usual tally of the books he had read or reread that year, and even published a book in 1989, *The Way We Lived: Durham, 1900–1920*. He kept in touch with many former students and colleagues, and in his later years occasionally returned to campus. After one of his last visits, in 1986, he expressed delight about coeducation and relief that the transition had gone so well. He supported John Wilson's efforts to bring more students to live on campus and to reform the fraternities, which he called "the greatest problem on campus just now."[1] A former student, Lex McMillan, visited Leyburn in July 1992 and found him as inquiring as ever, asking about university matters and life in Lexington, and recalling his first meeting with Frank Gaines and his fond relationship with Frank Gilliam.[2]

Leyburn's death and interment in the Falling Waters Presbyterian Church burial ground brought forth an outpouring of sentiment from former students and colleagues who had been moved by his passion for learning and his quiet integrity. John Wilson termed him a "monumental figure," and a memorial tribute adopted by the faculty quoted from his final address at the time of his retirement, when he invoked the "duty to right injustice, to build true communities of isolated individuals, to open paths of opportunity to those less privileged so that they, too, might live richly."[3] Former W&L journalism professor Paxton Davis wrote in the Roanoke newspaper "that no one played a greater part in Washington and Lee's development except Robert E. Lee, and both, it is worth noting, made academic broadening their central concern, not football, fund-raising or the construction of new buildings."[4] Only a few of his specific policies were realized, though his ideas and example are inscribed in what the university is today. Perhaps the most notable of Leyburn's legacies was his insistence on the things that were truly most important, which inspired others to do likewise. The comments about him were in some ways as much about the higher aspirations for the university community generally. The tributes were also, of course, to a great teacher who saw dignity and promise in every individual and lamented the misfortune of the unchallenged mind. Fittingly, the trustees put his name on the library, which was dedicated in May 1994 at an event attended by hundreds of people, including eighteen members of his extended family.[5] Leyburn's final lecture of the academic year, "The Death of Socrates," was legendary. But he was probably most remembered for his annual address to freshmen on the Greek ideal of arete, or "excellence in all that is admirable." (It was always well received at W&L since Leyburn also emphasized the contrast with Sparta, with a glance toward VMI.) The words were memorable, of course, but maybe even more important was this quiet, dignified man's passion for truth and obligation, for "the JOY of mental activity and excellence."[6]

JOHN WILSON'S RETIREMENT from W&L in 1995 signaled, if not the end of the era, the completion of a challenging, successful, and enormously consequential presidency. It had not been easy. Coeducation was, by any measure, a great success. The Fraternity Renaissance may not have changed student culture, but it definitely ensured the university's control over the houses themselves and provided greater leverage to deal with student misconduct and inspire better behavior. Efforts toward greater social and economic diversity in the student body enjoyed limited success but were conscientious and persistent. The struggles with alcohol abuse, sexual harassment and assault, and ensuring a campus culture of civility and respect resulted in new policies and procedures, though not complete solutions, and they continued at W&L as they did throughout American higher education well into the next century. Wilson eloquently reaffirmed W&L's commitment to student athletes, in opposition to the corruption of big-time college sports. He also took justifiable pride in new academic programs like computer science, neuroscience, and Russian studies, and directed greater attention to the arts. The realization of a true campus performance center occurred in large part because of Wilson's close relationship with Gerry Lenfest, and the new science complex was essential to the university's future success. Finally, the "Shoulders of Giants" campaign met its ambitious goal and further embedded a genuine and continuing "culture of philanthropy" in the university community. As Wilson looked to the future, the most pressing university needs had been addressed. It was a good time to step down.

Another of John Wilson's legacies—perhaps even more important than policies, programs, or bricks and mortar—was a quality of mind, a way of approaching and analyzing issues that was thorough, thoughtful, open, and collegial, as well as courageous and authoritative when circumstances required it. He shared his reflections with others and was as likely to call upon Shakespeare as on higher-education statistics to explain his thinking and justify his proposals. He understood W&L and its traditions and which things were most worth preserving. A humanist to the core, he possessed healthy self-confidence and a sense of humor. All in all, he was one of W&L's best presidents, who could—along with Frank Gaines, Fred Cole, and Bob Huntley—lay claim to preserving the university by helping to transform it.

John and Anne Wilson moved back to Blacksburg, where they had many friends from their years at Virginia Tech. They returned not long thereafter to live in Lexington, where they were pleased when a large new art and music building, to be constructed alongside the performing arts facility and supported by a new $15 million gift from Lenfest, was named in their honor in 2001. John Wilson died on March 2, 2013. He was eighty-one years old. At a memorial service in Lee Chapel the following day, President Ken Ruscio termed Wilson's presidency "a genuine milestone in the history of the institution" which "laid the groundwork for so many of the important things that we have accomplished and will continue to accomplish in years to come."

A NEARLY YEARLONG presidential search was launched as soon as Wilson notified the board of his wish to step down. The search committee, chaired by former dean of the college William Watt, and the trustees' selection committee, chaired by Rector A. Stevens Miles Jr., sifted through 137 candidates, arriving at eleven semifinalists and then four finalists. Among the four interviewed in Charlotte, North Carolina, in January 1995 was John Elrod, the current dean of the college and vice president for academic affairs. Elrod, a Kierkegaard scholar and former chair of the philosophy department at Iowa State, had arrived in 1984 to begin a fruitful decade as leader of the faculty and second ranking administrator at W&L. He and his wife, Mimi, hailed originally from Georgia and quickly adjusted to life in Lexington. He had been involved in all the challenges and changes in these years and was well regarded by colleagues, alumni, students, and particularly the faculty. But it was not at all certain that he, as a member of the current administration, would be selected as president. That had occurred only once—with Huntley's appointment—in over a century.

The decision was announced to some six hundred people gathered in Lee Chapel on February 24. Huntley had written Wilson the day before, complimenting him on a job well done and wondering "about who is next." In his response, Wilson described the scene. "John Elrod's appointment was the best kept secret in Lexington. . . . The trustees were seated in two rows across the 'stage' in Lee Chapel and the place was full of students and faculty. The spontaneous standing ovation that greeted the announcement by Steve Miles validated the whole process" that had kept totally confidential the identities of the other three finalists. "Anyway," Wilson observed, "it was a good process and it produced an exceptional result."[7]

W&L's chief academic officer thus entered the president's office as a familiar academic leader with great local support. He and Mimi were well known in the university and the community. Their regular informal dinners with students were appreciated and would continue in Lee House. He was almost always the first one in the office, famous for sending e-mail messages at 5:30 in the morning, and regularly exercised at lunchtime. Mimi would continue her work in the Office of Special Programs. All in all, it seemed like a virtually seamless transition that would keep the university moving forward in the directions Wilson had established.[8]

Elrod was especially committed to broadening and deepening the international dimensions of the W&L curriculum, seeing to the best and most complete use of the new science facilities, working for better accommodations for art and music and the university's sororities, and—perhaps most of all—completing the construction of the long sought and long delayed student center project, all of which was detailed in a five-year plan and strategic planning process that had begun at the end of Wilson's term. The Chemistry and Geology Departments moved into the new science center in 1996, followed by Biology and Physics into the renovated Howe Hall and Computer Science and Physics into Parmly Hall in 1997. The new indoor athletic pavilion—the Duchossois Tennis Center—was dedicated in 1997, and work began to thoroughly renovate the museum in Lee Chapel. The most important new academic addition, also in 1997, was the Shepard Program for the Interdisciplinary Study of Poverty and Human Capability, which would become a mainstay of the curriculum and provide service opportunities for students. By 2000, the new sorority houses were up and the multilevel parking garage adjacent to the Warner Center was completed. The admissions picture continued to be highly positive. But problems and issues also have their own momentum. Alcohol abuse, sexual harassment and assault, and fraternity transgressions persisted as elements of student culture. President Elrod was especially intent on curtailing the abuse of alcohol, which he declared the most serious problem facing W&L, and also on eliminating hazing in the fraternities, often fueled by alcohol.

The university observed its 250th anniversary in 1999. John Elrod presided over a yearlong schedule of special events, concerts, meetings, and presentations that celebrated how far W&L had come since the founding in 1749. Activities included an Alumni College focused on the oral history of W&L in July 1998, special "250th vacation cruises" from Stockholm to Barcelona in August, the usual special occasions of Founders Day in January (featuring former Harvard president Derek Bok), and the law school commencement in May (featuring US Supreme Court chief justice William Rehnquist). A Hampton Court Gala was held in London, along with a conference by the Center for Academic Integrity (featuring US senator John Warner, '49), and a Bicenquinquagenary Ball. A special exhibit of the photographs included in the lavish, heavily illustrated, large-format, 331-page book, *Come Cheer for Washington and Lee: The University at 250 Years,* edited by Mame Warren, was opened in August 1998.[9] Reunion Weekend was a significant culminating event, especially the dinner on May 1, 1999, when over ten thousand people (3,000 in Lexington) gathered to watch "Live from the Lenfest Center," a seventy-minute presentation broadcast over satellite to 7,000 people in fifty-five locations throughout the country. The broadcast, co-hosted by Roger Mudd, '50, and Cecily Tynan Badger, '91, of WPVI-TV in Philadelphia, featured remarks by Elrod, James Ballengee, and current Rector J. Frank Surface; performances by the University Chorus, Chamber Singers, and Jazz Ensemble; and awards presented to Sidney M. B. Coulling, Francis P. Gaines (posthumously), and present and former presidents of the Student Executive Committee.[10] Not surprisingly, a new major fund-raising effort arose in the wake of these celebrations: the Rising Generation Campaign, launched in October 2001 with a $225 million goal.

When Elrod was interviewed for the *Alumni Magazine* in 2000, at the five-year mark of his presidency, he expressed satisfaction with the strategic planning process, new academic programs, and progress thus far to address "the challenge to students to manage alcohol responsibly." Elrod was no fan of prohibition but hoped to "change the culture" that accepted the irresponsible use of alcohol. Similarly, he continued the effort to persuade the fraternities "to live up to the ideals they espouse." The university "Commons" project was now proceeding, with VMDO architects from Charlottesville (the same firm employed for the Fraternity Renaissance) retained for the design and funding provided from the sale of tax-free bonds and donor gifts. But much remained to be done, and the presidential agenda was lengthy.

The interview also addressed the deeply troubling fact that Elrod had been battling cancer for eighteen months and was then undergoing chemotherapy at the M. D. Anderson Cancer Center in Houston. He embraced this latest challenge with his usual determination and optimism. The treatments seemed to be working, and he and Mimi were "determined to keep our lives as normal as possible." He said he gained strength from the responsibilities of his office, "staying focused and thinking as little as I can about my illness is my salvation."[11] But the cancer spread, and his energy declined. Less than a year after the interview appeared, on July 27, 2001, President John Elrod died. He had requested that he not be eulogized in Lee Chapel, but the outpouring of grief and sympathy for Mimi and the family swept the campus, the Lexington community, and the extended W&L family. Given his abiding interest in students and their success, the trustees named the new student center the Elrod Commons.

Professor Larry Boetsch, named Elrod's successor as dean and vice president for academic affairs (after the brief interim appointment of Lad Sessions), assumed the role of acting president until a proper search could be conducted. A university mourning the passing of its president now worked diligently to get back on track.

SEVEN DECADES AFTER Francis Pendleton Gaines walked toward his inauguration in Lee Chapel, Washington and Lee had become a different place. Despite renovations and expansion, the chapel, the Colonnade, Doremus Gymnasium, the Graham-Lees residence hall, and many faculty houses on campus still remained and would be entirely familiar to even the oldest graduates. Small classes, student access to faculty members, and the Honor System remained hallmarks of the university's character and identity. Many traditions persisted, but not without changes and adaptations to a new national and international milieu. The most important traditions remained at the core, but in seventy years the university had been transformed.

Some changes could be traced in the usual measurements of institutional size, scope, composition, and capacity. Total fall 2000 enrollment reached 2,069, including 363 law students. Women now accounted for over 45 percent of undergraduates and 41 percent of law school enrollment. African Americans constituted almost 4 percent of the total student body, but W&L's enrollment remained overwhelmingly non-Hispanic white. Many fewer students than in 1930, however, declared affiliation with a religious denomination: Presbyterians and Episcopalians were still the major denominations, accounting for over a third of those who expressed a preference, and over 28 percent were

Roman Catholic. Almost a third declared no religious preference at all. W&L had always been geographically diverse, with strong representations from Virginia, the Middle Atlantic region, and the South, but also drawing students from throughout the country, especially the Northeast. In 2000, W&L students hailed from forty-seven states and thirty-one foreign countries, with the greatest numbers from Virginia, Maryland, Texas, Pennsylvania, New York, and North Carolina. Thirty-eight students were from California and twenty-eight from Illinois. The Greek tradition persisted as a dominant element of campus social life; 78 percent of men and 68 percent of women belonged to fraternities and sororities. The Assimilation Committee was long gone, along with anything resembling a student-imposed dress code, and new technologies shaped life and work throughout the campus. The university had also experienced many decades of nonsubsidized intercollegiate athletics, a situation Francis Gaines would have especially appreciated.

The university's faculty was much larger, more diverse, and by most measures even better qualified. Of the 212 total faculty in 2000, about half were at the rank of professor, and almost a quarter were women. The curriculum was greatly expanded in size, scope, and variety but still focused on the liberal arts at the undergraduate level and on academic breadth and successful practice in the law school. The spring term remained a distinctive and innovative feature of student learning. W&L continued to depend on its former students for essential support, counting on the loyalty and generosity of 21,000 living alumni. Giving to the Annual Fund, which had followed a steady path upward since the fund was established, now topped $4 million a year. The endowment stood at almost $740 million, and W&L was ranked twelfth among the top twenty-five national liberal arts colleges in the annual *US News and World Report* survey in total endowment and eighth in endowment per student.[12]

These measures imparted obvious truths about W&L and its progress, but they only gave a general idea of the university. A key question was whether, given all these changes, it retained its long-standing purposes and spirit. The hope was that Washington and Lee had become stronger and better, transformed in many respects but not in its central character. The hope seemed to be realized. Traditions had to be adapted to new circumstances in order to survive, and changes were essential if W&L was to enter the pantheon of top national liberal arts colleges. Between 1930 and 2000, W&L had also benefited from the leadership and dedication of four different individuals who faced different challenges but could be regarded among the university's best presidents. Gaines, Cole, Huntley, and Wilson each made significant contributions, addressing the most pressing challenges during their time and bringing distinction to Washington Hall. If W&L, laden with tradition and reluctant to change, was resilient in the face of adversity—as Sidney Coulling said—it was the presidents who had led the way, who did what had to be done, who pressed forward and inspired others to do likewise. Collectively, these four presidents provided W&L with leadership in challenging times that few other universities could rival.

One thing seemed certain at the dawn of a new millennium: the university rested on a solid foundation and was well positioned for the years ahead, even as some doubted that liberal arts institutions could weather new economic, technological, and cultural trends. The challenges, adjustments, controversies, and resilience experienced over seventy years had at least verified the truth of the university motto. Washington and Lee was best served when it was "not unmindful of the future."

APPENDIX

Board of Trustees Membership, 1930–2000

George Walker St. Clair* (R)	1901–1939
Harrington Waddell*	1915–1940
Rev. William McClanahan White*	1915–1934
William Alexander MacCorkle*	1918–1930
John William Davis*	1921–1949
Judge Charles J. McDermott	1922–1941
James Randolph Caskie* (R)	1924–1967
George Bolling Lee*	1924–1948
Walter Lapsley Carson*	1926–1959
Newton D. Baker*	1928–1937
William McChesney Martin	1928–1949
Judge Louis Spencer Epes*	1929–1935
Gov. George Campbell Peery* (R)	1929–1952
Francis Pendleton Gaines (P)	1930–1959
Robert Henry Tucker (AP)	1930–1930
Herbert Fitzpatrick* (R)	1931–1957
Fowler McCormick	1933–1944
Dr. James Morrison Hutcheson* (R)	1935–1965
Harry St. George Carmichael*	1938–1949
Oscar Caperton Huffman*	1938–1941
Dr. John Newton Thomas* (R)	1938–1973
Homer Adams Holt*	1940–1969
Clarence R. Avery*	1941–1953

NOTES

ABBREVIATIONS

PP   Presidential Papers
BOT   Board of Trustees
AA   VP for Academic Affairs and Dean of the College

Unless otherwise noted, all referenced archival documents, papers, and other material are located in Washington and Lee University Special Collections, James G. Leyburn Library.

PROLOGUE

1. All quotations and information on W&L's early history are from the definitive source on the university to 1930, Ollinger Crenshaw's *General Lee's College: The Rise and Growth of Washington and Lee University* (1969; reprint, Baton Rouge: Louisiana State University Press, 2017).

2. Junkin died in 1868, and in 1925 he was reinterred in the Lexington cemetery near the grave of his son-in-law, Confederate general Thomas J. "Stonewall" Jackson.

CHAPTER ONE

1. *Alumni Magazine,* Nov. 1930, pp. 18–19.

2. "Address to ODK Assembly," Dec. 17, 1963, Gaines Papers, box 11, folder 82.

3. *Southern Newspaper Publisher's Association Bulletin,* Jan. 19, 1952, pp. 20–21.

4. Virginius Dabney, unpublished essay, Gaines Papers, box 10, folder 66.

5. William S. Powell, ed., *Dictionary of North Carolina Biography,* vol. 2 (Chapel Hill: University of North Carolina Press, 1986).

6. George Washington Pascal, *History of Wake Forest College,* vol. 3 (Wake Forest, NC: Wake Forest College, 1943), p. 388.

7. John W. Davis to George W. St. Clair, Oct. 25, 1929. Quoted in William H. Harbaugh, *Lawyer's Lawyer: The Life of John W. Davis* (New York: Oxford University Press, 1973), p. 396.

8. Robert Henry Tucker to Gaines, Feb. 24, 1930; Gaines to Tucker, Feb. 28, 1930, PP, Gaines, box 17, folder 284A.

9. Tucker to Gaines, June 10, 1930; Gaines to Tucker, undated, PP, Gaines, box 17, folder 284A.

10. Arthur M. Cohen and Carrie B. Kisker, *The Shaping of American Higher Education: Emergence and Growth of the Contemporary System,* 2nd ed. (San Francisco: Jossey-Bass, 2010), p. 123.

11. US Department of Education, National Center for Education Statistics, 1992.

12. Cohen and Kisker, *Shaping of American Higher Education,* pp. 181–82.

13. Smith to John W. Davis, quoted in Harbaugh, *Lawyer's Lawyer,* pp. 395–96.

14. George E. Denny to Judge Louis S. Eppes, Personal and Confidential, Sept. 5, 1930, Treasurer, Subject Files, box 1.

15. Details of John W. Davis's life and career are drawn from Harbaugh, *Lawyer's Lawyer.*

16. *President's Report,* May 1933, p. 2. *President's Reports*—usually printed and widely distributed, often as issues of the university *Bulletin,* during the Gaines presidency—are archived in PP, Gaines. These annual, semiformal documents were discontinued in the Coles administration.

17. *Preliminary President's Report for the Trustees,* May 28, 1940, including Gaines, "Washington and Lee University, 1930–1940: A Review of a Decade," p. 1, PP, Gaines.

18. These figures are taken from the reports of the university treasurer contained in the annual *President's Reports* from 1930 to 1939.

19. Gaines, "Washington and Lee University, 1930–1940," p. 1.

20. Gaines, *Digest of President's Report,* 1933, p. 1.

21. BOT minutes, Jan. 19, 1932.

22. *President's Report,* May 1934, p. 2.

23. BOT minutes, Oct. 29, 1932; June 4, 1934; June 6, 1935; Oct. 12, 1935.

24. "Special Information on Salaries," Report to the Southern Association of Colleges and Secondary Schools, PP, Gaines, box 16, folder 264.

25. Gaines, *Digest of President's Report,* 1932, p. 1.

26. BOT minutes, Jan. 19, 1939.

27. Gaines, *Digest of President's Report,* 1932, p. 2.

28. Gaines, "The New South Thinks of the Old," address to the annual dinner of the Southern Society of New York City, Dec. 10, 1930, pp. 1–4, Gaines Papers, box 9, folder 109.

29. Gaines, "After College, What?," address to the Association of Virginia Colleges, Richmond, Feb. 10–11, 1933, Gaines Papers, box 9, folder 71.

30. Gaines, "Continuity and Change on the Campus," address to the Association of Virginia Colleges, Richmond, Feb. 9–10, 1940, Gaines Papers, box 10, folder 76.

31. *Preliminary President's Report,* May 25, 1939, p. 4.

32. Louis Menand, *The Marketplace of Ideas: Reform and Resistance in the American University* (New York: W. W. Norton, 2010), pp. 32–43.

33. *Washington and Lee Catalogue, 1930–1931,* p. 54.

34. *President's Report,* May 1934, p. 2.

35. BOT minutes, June 11, 1936.

36. Gaines to John W. Davis, Aug. 28, 1936, PP, Gaines, box 8, folder 130.

37. *Washington and Lee University Bulletin,* May 1930.

38. Frank J. Gilliam, "Report of the Dean of Students," *President's Report,* 1939, p. 23; Gaines, "Washington and Lee University, 1930–1940," p. 2.

39. Gaines, "Opening Address to Students," Sept. 15, 1933, rough typescript notes, Gaines Papers, box 9, folder 71.

40. Gaines, "Washington and Lee University, 1930–1940," p. 3.

41. Cohen and Kisker, *Shaping of American Higher Education,* p. 133.

42. *President's Report,* May 1936, pp. 2, 8, 15.

43. *President's Report,* Dec. 15, 1939, pp. 24–25.

44. *Preliminary President's Report,* May 25, 1939, p. 2.

45. In addition to Washington and Lee, the original Southern Conference included Alabama, Auburn, Clemson, Georgia, Georgia Tech, Kentucky, Maryland, Mississippi State, North Carolina, North Carolina State, Tennessee, Virginia, and Virginia Tech. They were joined a year later by Florida, Louisiana State, Mississippi, South Carolina, Tulane, and Vanderbilt, as well as Sewanee in 1923, VMI in 1924, and Duke in 1929. Athletic conferences changed frequently even then, and in 1933 thirteen schools left to form the Southeastern Conference. Seven more left in 1953 to form the Atlantic Coast Conference.

46. *President's Report,* May 1935, p. 2.

47. Gaines to Herbert Fitzpatrick, Jan. 17, 1935, PP, Gaines, box 17, folder 282.

48. Clarence Sager to Gaines, Nov. 12, 1937, and Dec. 21, 1937; Gaines to Sager, Nov. 18, 1937, PP, Gaines, box 24, folder 391.

49. "Report of Special Committee on Athletics," Apr. 25, 1939, appended to *Preliminary President's Report,* May 25, 1939; *Preliminary President's Report,* May 25, 1939, p. 3; Gaines, "Washington and Lee University, 1930-1940," p. 4.

50. "Report of the School of Law," in *President's Report,* May 15, 1931, pp. 42–48.

51. Ibid.

52. "Report of the School of Law," in *President's Report,* May 1935, p. 4.

53. "Report of the School of Law," in *President's Report,* May 1936, pp. 18–19.

54. *President's Report,* May 1933, p. 2; and *President's Report,* May 1934, p. 3.

55. *President's Report,* Oct. 1940, pp. 5–6.

56. Gaines, "Washington and Lee University, 1930–1940," p. 2.

57. Gaines to Dr. George Bolling Lee, Judge Charles J. McDermott, and Mr. Oscar C. Huffman, Nov. 29, 1938, PP, Gaines, box 10, folder 196.

58. Gaines, memo to BOT, Dec. 15, 1939, PP, Gaines, Memos to the Board. These memoranda, including some correspondence with individual trustees, are contained in separate folders according to date. They are referenced henceforth as Memos to the Board.

59. James N. Veech to John W. Davis, Mar. 26, 1935, and Newton D. Baker to James N. Veech, Mar. 29, 1935, copies in AA, Dean of the College, Faculty Matters, Student Activities (General), 1935–79, box 4, folder 78.

60. Gaines, memo to BOT, Apr. 2, 1935, copy in AA, Dean of the College, Faculty Matters, Student Activities (General), 1935–79, box 4, folder 78.

61. Homer A. Holt to Gaines, Aug. 17 and Sept. 16, 1943; C. R. Avery to Gaines, Aug. 21, 1943; and Joseph T. Lykes to Gaines, Aug. 30, 1943, PP, Gaines, Memos to the Board.

62. Gaines to John W. Davis, Aug. 28, 1936, PP, Gaines, box 8, folder 130.

63. Gaines, memo to BOT, Dec. 15, 1939, p. 2, PP, Gaines, Memos to the Board.

64. Gaines's "confidential" letter of Apr. 4, 1936; Nicholas Murray Butler's telegram to Gaines on Apr. 9; Gaines's response to Butler of Apr. 14, PP, box 17, folder 285.

CHAPTER TWO

1. *President's Report,* Oct. 15, 1940, pp. 6–7.

2. Gaines, memo to BOT, May 29, 1941, p. 3, PP, Gaines, Memos to the Board.

3. *President's Report,* Oct. 15, 1941, pp. 3–4.

4. *Ring-tum Phi,* Dec. 19, 1941.

5. *War Stories* contains a wealth of information and recollections of W&L men serving in World War II. This was a special edition of the *Calyx* yearbook, covering the classes from 1925 to 1950, published about 1995 by the Alumni Office.

6. AA, Dean of the College, Faculty Matters, Administration WW II, 1941–50, box 1, folder 6.

7. Gaines to Thurman D. Kitchin, Apr. 22, 1943, PP, Gaines, Subject Files, Law School, 1944–50.

8. William McChesney Martin to Gaines, Apr. 17, 1944, PP, Gaines, Subject Files, Law School, 1944–50.

9. Gaines to John L. Newcomb, May 1, 1944, PP, Gaines, Subject Files, Law School, 1944–50.

10. *President's Report,* Oct. 8, 1943, pp. 6–7.

11. Gaines to Robert W. Hodges, Apr. 16, 1942, PP, Gaines, folder 148.

12. Gaines, "Washington and Lee and the War: A Plea to Alumni," *Washington and Lee University Bulletin* 41 (Feb. 16, 1942).

13. Gaines to Joseph T. Lykes, Dec. 17, 1942, PP, Wilson, Correspondence, Lykes Endowment, box 20.

14. Gaines, "Confidential Memorandum to the Board: Factors Governing Student Enrollment," Mar. 16, 1942, PP, Gaines, Memos to the Board.

15. *President's Report,* Oct. 8, 1943, p. 7.

16. Recollections of Dr. Robert F. Stephens, '47, in *War Stories.*

17. Recollections of Don Murray, '43, in *War Stories.*

18. Gaines to BOT, May 11, 1942, PP, Gaines, Memos to the Board.

19. Gaines's and Tucker's remarks, and much of the foregoing, in *President's Report,* Oct. 15, 1942.

20. Rupert N. Latture, "Report of the Dean of Students," *President's Report,* Oct. 8, 1943, pp. 18–19.

21. Gaines, memo to the BOT, Dec. 1, 1942, PP, Gaines, Memos to the Board.

22. Gaines, memo to the BOT, June 17, 1943, PP, Gaines, Memos to the Board.

23. Norman Lord, interview by Mame Warren, Apr. 16, 1996. All cited interviews by Mame Warren are located in the Mame Warren Collection, W&L Special Collections.

24. *War Stories,* pp. 95–96.

25. Edwin Gaines, interview by Mame Warren, Jan. 13, 1999.

26. James R. Caskie to Gaines, Feb. 11, 1943, PP, Gaines, box 33, folder 486.

27. Clifton A. Woodrum to Gaines, Feb. 16, 1943; Gaines to Woodrum, Feb. 18, 1943, PP, Gaines, box 33, folder 486.

28. R. P. Hobson to Gaines, Oct. 15, 1945; Gaines to Hobson, Oct. 24, 1945, PP, Gaines, box 32, folder 483.

29. *President's Report,* Oct. 8, 1943, p. 9.

30. Gaines, memo to the BOT, Feb. 11, 1947, PP, Gaines, Memos to the Board.

31. "Education in Review," *New York Times,* Sept. 5, 1948.

32. All of these considerations are contained in Gaines, memo to the BOT, May 17, 1946, PP, Gaines, Memos to the Board.

33. Gaines, "Special Memorandum to the Board of Trustees," marked confidential, Oct. 4, 1948, PP, Gaines, Memos to the Board.

34. Gaines, memo to the BOT, May 17, 1946, p. 3, PP, Gaines, Memos to the Board.

35. John W. Davis to Gaines, May 27, 1946, PP, Gaines, Memos to the Board.

36. William McChesney Martin to Gaines, May 27, 1946, PP, Gaines, Memos to the Board.

37. James Ballengee, interview by Mame Warren, Mar. 28, 1996. The author can personally testify to the longevity of these "temporary" postwar prefabricated units, since he and his new bride made their first home together in Hillside Terrace more than twenty years later, in 1964–65. The monthly rent then was $38, including all utilities except telephone. They were torn down in 1975.

38. Clayton E. Williams to Gaines, May 5, 1947; Joseph A. McClain Jr. to Williams, Mar. 13, 1947, PP, Gaines, Subject Files, Law School, 1944–50.

39. John C. Hervey to Clayton W. Williams, Sept. 14, 1948, PP, Gaines, Subject Files, Law School, 1944–50.

40. Gaines to John W. Davis, Oct. 12, 1948; Gaines to John C. Hervey, Oct. 26, 1948, PP, Gaines, Subject Files, Law School, 1944–50.

41. Dean G. D. Hancock, *President's Report,* 1945, pp. 12–13.

42. Gaines, memo to the BOT, June 7, 1949, PP, Gaines, Memos to the Board. For details of the bicentennial and alumni fund-raising efforts, see the *President's Reports* for 1947, 1948, and 1949.

43. Gaines, memo to the BOT, Feb. 22, 1949, PP, Gaines, Memos to the Board.

44. Gaines, memo to the BOT, July 21, 1950, PP, Gaines, Memos to the Board.

45. *President's Report,* 1947.

46. "L. J. Desha Report," *President's Report,* 1947, pp. 9–10.

47. Ballengee, interview.

48. *President's Report,* 1948, p. 4.

49. Gaines to George Biggers, John D. Ewing, and James B. Stahlman, Apr. 2, 1946; Walter C. Johnson to Gaines, Apr. 5, 1946; Henry P. Johnston to Gaines, Feb. 26, 1946, and June 5, 1946, PP, Gaines, box 496, folder 170.

50. For biographical details, see Richard Greening Hewlett, *Jessie Ball duPont* (Gainesville: University of Florida Press, 1992), and "Biography" in the Jessie Ball duPont Papers, W&L Special Collections.

51. Jessie Ball duPont to Frank and DuVergne, Dec. 15, 1937, Jessie Ball duPont Papers, Correspondence, 1937, box 61, folder 11; Jessie Ball duPont to the Gaineses, Feb. 15, 1938, box 68.

52. Hewlett, *Jessie Ball duPont*, p. 136.

53. Gaines to Jessie Ball duPont, undated; duPont to Gaines, Mar. 25, 1937, Jessie Ball duPont Papers, Correspondence, 1937, box 61, folder 11.

54. Gaines to Jessie Ball duPont, undated [1950], Jessie Ball duPont Papers, Correspondence, box 129, folder 9.

55. Jessie Ball duPont to Gaines, Nov. 5, 1952, Jessie Ball duPont Papers, Correspondence, box 138, folder 6.

56. Edwin Gaines, interview by Mame Warren, Jan. 13, 1999.

57. Gaines, memo to the BOT, July 21, 1950, PP, Gaines, Memos to the Board.

58. Gaines to Philip F. Howerton, Dec. 18, 1944, PP, Gaines, box 14, folder 237.

59. Paul K. Conkin, *Gone with the Ivy: A Biography of Vanderbilt University* (Knoxville: University of Tennessee Press, 1985), pp. 440–43.

60. Marvin M. Cullom to Gaines, May 15, 1946; Gaines to Cullom, May 22, 1946, PP, Gaines, box 16, folder 299.

61. Gaines to J. E. Smitherman, Feb. 20, 1947, PP, Gaines, box 497, folder 186.

62. Douglas S. Freeman to Gaines, Apr. 6, 1945; Gaines to Louis Spillman of the *Waynesboro News-Virginian*, Apr. 10, 1945, PP, Gaines, box 28, folder 423.

CHAPTER THREE

1. Gaines to the BOT, Aug. 29, 1950, and record of responses, PP, Gaines, Courses, ROTC, box 1, folder 1.

2. Gaines, "Personal and Confidential" to Harry F. Byrd, Nov. 20, 1950; Byrd to Gaines, Nov. 24 and Dec. 6, 1950; Gaines to BOT, Jan. 9, 1950, PP, Correspondence, ROTC, folders 1 and 2.

3. Gaines to Gen. Hoyt S. Vandenberg, Feb. 13, 1951; US Air Force to Gaines, Apr. 20, 1951, PP, Gaines, Subject Files, series 2, ROTC—Proposal and Application, 1951.

4. Gaines to Maj. Gen. Hugh M. Milton II, Nov. 27, 1953, PP, Gaines, Correspondence, ROTC, folder 3, box 1.

5. Gaines to "Messrs. Chenery, Lykes, and McDonald," Dec. 1, 1952, PP, Gaines, Memos to the Board, 1952–54.

6. W. Brown Patterson, "The Educational Vision of the Founders and the Development of the Curriculum at the University of the South," in Gerald L. Smith and Samuel R. Williamson, eds., *Sewanee Perspectives on the History of the University of the South* (Sewanee: University of the South, 2008), pp 144–45.

7. US Department of Education, National Center for Education Statistics, 1992.

8. Frank J. Gilliam, "Report of the Dean of Students," *President's Report*, 1951, p. 23.

9. Gilliam, "Report of the Dean of Students," *President's Report*, 1952, p. 24. Additional student data are drawn from subsequent *President's Reports*.

10. For excellent biographical profiles, see A. Prescott Rowe, "A Life of Service to His University," *Alumni Magazine*, Aug. 1963, pp. 2–7; and "Our Good, Gray Dean: Frank J. Gilliam, 1895–1976," *Alumni Magazine*, Apr. 1976, pp. 1–7.

11. "End of an Era with Cy Young," *Alumni Magazine*, Summer 1958, pp. 2–3.

12. Donald E. Smith, "Report of the Director of University Development," *President's Report, 1953–54*, pp. 26–30. Also see subsequent reports in *President's Reports* for 1955–56, 1956–57, and 1957–58.

13. BOT minutes, Jan. 26, 1957, Jan. 18, 1958.

14. Mary Coulling, interview by Mame Warren, Aug. 16, 2010. Both Mary Coulling and her husband, Sid, attribute this change in direction to the incoming presidential administration, but Fred Cole's appointment did not occur until June 1959.

15. Mary Coulling, interview.

16. These and other details are contained in Lex McMillan, "Notes from a Visit with Dr. Leyburn," July 29, 1992, James G. Leyburn Papers, Death Notices and Tributes. These notes were the basis for an article in the *Alumni Magazine*, Fall 1992, p. 30.

17. William W. Pusey III to Fred C. Cole, memo concerning faculty seniority, Aug. 23, 1962, AA, Faculty Files, Leyburn, 47–72.

18. Virginius Dabney, unpublished essay, 1953, PP, Gaines, folder 66.

19. Sidney M. B. Coulling III, "Presentation to the Board of Trustees on the University Mission Statement," Oct. 1993, PP, Wilson, box 14, Coulling, Sidney (Mission Statement).

20. McMillian, "Notes from a Visit with Dr. Leyburn."

21. "Report of the Dean of the University," *President's Report*, 1948, pp. 10–14.

22. James G. Leyburn, "Remarks to the Faculty Discussion Group, November 20, 1947," Leyburn Papers, box 1, folder 3.

23. Ollinger Crenshaw to Robert McLean Jeter Jr., July 20, 1947, and Sept. 28, 1954, Ollinger Crenshaw Papers, box 320, Letters.

24. Leyburn, various memoranda to the faculty, Leyburn Papers, box 32, folder 136.

25. James G. Leyburn, "A Plan for An Ideal College," Mary Baldwin College, *Alumnae News Letter*, Apr. 1948, pp. 3–7.

26. L. W. Adams, "Report of the Dean of the School of Commerce and Administration," *President's Report, 1957–58*, p. 20.

27. Mrs. John B. Trevor to Gaines, Dec. 6, 1946; Gaines to Wilbur L. Tilden, Nov. 20, 1946; Gaines to Herbert Fitzpatrick, Nov. 5, 1946, PP, Gaines, box 17, folder 279.

28. Gaines to G. D. Hancock and R. H. Tucker, Nov. 6, 1946, PP, Gaines, box 17, folder 279.

29. Obituary of O. W. Riegel by Wolfgang Saxon, *New York Times*, Aug. 28, 1997.

30. These and subsequent quotations taken from O. W. Riegel, "Hacking It," chap. 8, "The Waiting Years I," c. 1935–41 (draft).

31. William W. Pusey III discusses these and other fictional works connected to Washington and Lee in a pamphlet, *Washington and Lee University in Fiction* (W&L University Library, 1988). Also see M. Gary Coleman, "W&L in Fiction: The University's Three Novels Stir More Than a Few Good Memories," *Alumni Magazine*, Mar. 1980.

32. Marshall Fishwick, "Shenandoah Receives Bryher Award," *Alumni Magazine*, Dec. 1952, p. 13.

33. John D. Macguire, "Report on Religious Activities," *President's Report*, Oct. 1953, p. 36.

34. "World-Famous Historian Joins Faculty," *Alumni Magazine*, Winter 1958, pp. 2–4. Toynbee's celebrity drew large crowds to his lectures, but some complained that he was a rather boring speaker.

35. *Ring-tum Phi,* May 16, 1958.

36. The 1944 convention was canceled because of the war and a depleted student population. An unsigned document prepared in preparation for the convention of 1948 further noted about 1944: "Students probably thought Roosevelt would be president forever so what's the use anyway." *Record of W&L Mock Political Convention,* Mock Convention, 1940–56, box 1A.

37. Townsend Oast to Mr. and Mrs. J. T. Engleby, Apr. 16, 1952, Mock Convention, 1940–56, box 1A.

38. Gaines to Rev. Maurice S. Sheehy, May 7, 1956, PP, Gaines, Mock Convention, 1940–56, box 1A.

39. Hardin Marion, interview by Mame Warren, July 19, 1996.

40. The leading study of white collegiate fraternities, from which these observations are drawn, is Nicholas L. Styrett, *The Company He Keeps: A History of White College Fraternities* (Chapel Hill: University of North Carolina Press, 2009).

41. Ibid., pp. 126–27.

42. Ibid., pp. 240–41.

43. Ibid., p. 148.

44. Gilliam and Leyburn to Gaines, Apr. 2, 1949, AA, Dean of the College, Faculty Matters, Dean Leyburn, Miscellaneous 1949–54, box 1, folder 28. Also see "Tentative Basis for the Development of Non-Fraternity Club Facilities at Washington and Lee," AA, Dean of the College, Faculty Matters, Fraternities, 1949, box 2, folder 50.

45. Leyburn to Lewis Adams, Sept. 23, 1950, AA, Dean of the College, Faculty Matters, Student Activities (General), 1935–79, box 4, folder 18.

46. *Ring-Tum Phi,* Dec. 5, 1952.

47. The W&L Interfraternity Council to BOT, undated, appended to a letter from James G. Leyburn to L. W. Adams, Mar. 21, 1951, AA, Faculty Files, Leyburn, '47–'72.

48. Leyburn to Lewis Adams, Sept. 23, 1950, AA, Dean of the College, Faculty Matters, Student Activities (General), 1935–1979, box 4, folder 18.

49. Leyburn to Members of the Executive Committee, July 15, 1955, AA, Faculty Files, Leyburn, '47–'72.

50. "Stricter Rules Are Set Up," *Alumni Magazine,* Fall 1958, pp. 13, 20; "University Appoints Proctor," *Alumni Magazine,* Winter 1959, p. 18.

51. Brooks G. Brown III, letter to the student body, Aug. 1964.

52. Anonymous, "A Sociological Study of the Washington & Lee Student Body," 1952, Leyburn Papers, box 2, folder 136.

53. James G. Leyburn, "Report of the Dean of the University," *President's Report,* 1952, pp. 8–9.

54. James G. Leyburn, "Report of the Dean of the University," *President's Report,* 1953, pp. 7–8.

55. Gaines, "ODK Address," Dec. 17, 1963, Gaines Papers, box 11, folder 82.

CHAPTER FOUR

1. "This Was the Year," *Alumni Magazine,* Nov. 1950, pp. 15–17.

2. "Many Alumni at 'Gator Bowl," *Alumni Magazine,* Mar. 1951, pp. 5–7.

3. See John Sayle Watterson, *College Football: History, Spectacle, Controversy* (Baltimore: Johns Hopkins University Press, 2000) and Edward L. Ayers, *The Promise of the New South: Life After Reconstruction* (New York: Oxford University Press, 1992). A perceptive examination of football in one southern liberal arts college is Woody Register, "Remembering Ninety-Nine Iron: A Historical Perspective on the Legendary Football Team that Won Five Games in Six Days," in Gerald L. Smith and Samuel R. Williamson Jr., eds., *Sewanee Perspectives on the History of the University of the South* (Sewanee: University of the South, 2008), pp. 345–404.

4. Mike Stachura, "The Legacy of the Beechenbrooks," *Alumni Magazine,* Spring 1989, pp. 19–20, 37–40.

5. Jim Wamsley, *Roanoke Times,* June 8, 1969, reprinted in *Alumni Magazine,* Aug. 1969, p. 4.

6. Charles J. McDermott to Gaines, Nov. 6, 1933, PP, Gaines, box 498, folder 195.

7. Minutes of the Faculty Executive Committee, 1930–64, AA, box 807.

8. *Ring-Tum Phi,* Nov. 2, 1937.

9. Lynchburg Alumni Association to Gaines et al., Jan. 13, 1939, PP, Gaines, box 24, folder 392.

10. See Andy Thomason, "One Man Had a Plan to Keep Money Out of College Sports. Here's What Happened," *Chronicle of Higher Education,* Aug. 12, 2014. Graham's protégée, William Friday, became president of the University of North Carolina and one of the strongest advocates of integrity in intercollegiate sports.

11. Gaines to R. A. Smith, Mar. 12, 1934, PP, Gaines, box 16, folder 261.

12. Gaines to R.A. Smith, W. E. Tilson, H. K. Young, Nov. 4, 1935, PP, Gaines, box 16, folder 261.

13. Gaines to Clarence L. Sager, Nov. 18, 1937, PP, Gaines, box 24, folder 391. Also see the draft of the plan to establish the "Washington and Lee Alumni Scholarship Fund."

14. Clarence L. Sager to N. K. Young, Nov. 11, 1937, PP, Gaines, box 24, folder 391.

15. Clarence L. Sager to Gaines, Nov. 12, 1937, PP, Gaines, box 24, folder 391. This was the letter that occasioned Gaines's reply on November 18.

16. Gaines to J. Morrison Hutcheson, Dec. 16, 1937, PP, Gaines, box 24, folder 391.

17. Gaines to Clarence L. Sager, Jan. 6, 1938, PP, Gaines, box 24, folder 391.

18. Gaines to Herbert Fitzpatrick, Jan. 17, 1935, PP, Gaines, box 17, folder 282.

19. R. A. Smith to Gaines, May 21, 1942, PP, Gaines, box 16, folder 261.

20. Edward E. Brown to R. A. Smith, June 11, 1945; James R. Caskie to Edward E. Brown, June 25, 1945, PP, Gaines, box 24, folder 385.

21. Randolph G. Whittle to Gaines, Nov. 10, 1945, box 24, folder 385.

22. BOT minutes, Jan. 18, 1946, referring to the minutes of Oct. 12, 1945.

23. Athletic Committee Resolution, Oct. 9, 1945, PP, Gaines, box 24, folder 385.

24. Gaines to the Alumni of Washington and Lee, 1945, PP, Gaines, box 24, folder 385.

25. Register, "Remembering Ninety-Nine Iron," pp. 388–89.

26. Alexander Guerry to Gaines, Dec. 3, 1945; J. R. Cunningham to Gaines, Dec. 10, 1945, PP, Gaines Papers, box 24, folder 387.

27. Gaines to Alexander Guerry and President Charles E. Diehl, Jan. 3, 1946, PP, Gaines Papers, box 24, folder 387.

28. Alexander Guerry to Gaines, Jan. 5, 1946, PP, Gaines Papers, box 24, folder 387.

29. See Paul R. Lawrence, *Unsportsmanlike Conduct: The National Collegiate Athletic Association and the Business of College Football* (New York: Praeger, 1987).

30. Draft of NCAA questionnaire, completed in Gaines's own hand, dated Nov. 12, 1948, PP, Gaines, box 24, folder 390.

31. John E. Pomfret to Gaines and the Presidents of six other Virginia universities, Apr. 25, 1949, PP, Gaines, box 24, folder 390.

32. Clayton E. Williams to Gaines, June 14, 1949, PP, Gaines, box 24, folder 388.

33. Gaines to Clarence P. Houston, June 20, 1949, PP, Gaines, box 24, folder 390.

34. Clarence P. Houston to Gaines, Oct. 14, 1949, PP, Gaines, box 24, folder 390.

35. Gaines, memo to the BOT, "Special Report on the Athletic Situation," June 7, 1949, PP, Gaines, Memos to the Board.

36. Clayton E. Williams to Gaines and the BOT, May 24, 1950, PP, Gaines, Athletic Correspondence, box 1, folder 3.

37. Clayton E. Williams to the BOT and Acting President James G. Leyburn, June 6, 1951, PP, Gaines, Athletic Correspondence, box 1, folder 2.

38. "Personal and confidential" memorandum from Gaines to the Athletic Committee of the BOT, Dec. 9, 1950, PP, Gaines, Athletic Correspondence, box 1, folder 2.

39. "W&L Football: Another Way," by Fred Hinton, *Roanoke Times*, Apr. 25, 1972. This article was part three in a series on various approaches to college football.

40. Gaines to Gordon Gray (president of the University of North Carolina), Jan. 22, 1952, PP, Gaines, Athletics Correspondence, box 1, folder 3.

41. Lewis F. Powell Jr. to Gaines, Oct. 16, 1951; Gaines to Powell, Oct. 17, 1951, PP, Gaines, Athletics Correspondence, box 1,folder 2.

42. Letter from seven Richmond alumni to Gaines, June 5, 1952, PP, Gaines, Athletics Correspondence, box 1, folder 3.

43. Gaines to BOT Athletic Committee, Nov. 8, 1951, PP, Gaines, Athletics Correspondence, box 1, folder 2.

44. Gaines to BOT Athletic Committee, Dec. 4, 1951, PP, Gaines, Athletics Correspondence, box 1, folder 2.

45. Leyburn to Richard A. Smith, Dec. 15, 1951, AA, Dean of the College, Faculty Matters, 1950–80, box 1, folder 2, Absence Regulations.

46. Gaines to Paul H. Wofford Jr., Nov. 27, 1951, PP, Gaines, Athletics Correspondence, box 1, folder 2.

47. Beverly A. Davis to Gaines, Nov. 29, 1951, PP, Gaines, Athletics Correspondence, box 1, folder 2.

48. Gaines to H. C. Byrd, Jan. 28, 1952, PP, Gaines, Athletics Correspondence, box 1, folder 3.

49. Gaines to W. D. Bain Jr., Apr. 3, 1952, PP, Gaines, Athletics Correspondence, box 1, folder 3.

50. Clayton E. Williams to Gaines and the BOT, Apr. 18, 1952, PP, Gaines, Athletics Correspondence, box 1, folder 3.

51. Gaines to the BOT Athletic Committee, May 12, 1952, PP, Gaines, Athletics Correspondence, box 1, folder 4.

52. Charles R. McDowell, professor of law and the chairman of the committee to Boylston Green, president of the University of the South, and seventeen other presidents, Oct. 2, 1952, PP, Gaines, Athletics Correspondence, box 1, folder 3.

53. Gaines to John R. Cunningham, George M. Modlin, John L. Plyler, Dec. 8, 1952, PP, Gaines, Subject Files, Series 2, Southern Conference.

54. Frank Gilliam to Gaines "re Athletics," Dec. 10, 1952, PP, Gaines, Athletics Correspondence, box 1, folder 3.

55. H. Gray Funkhouser to Gaines, Jan. 10, 1953 (Gaines's response, June 18, 1953); N. C. Evans to Gaines, Nov. 3, 1953 (Gaines's response, Nov. 9, 1953); Robert P. Hobson, Nov. 10, 1953 (Gaines's response, Nov. 30, 1953), PP, Gaines, Athletics Correspondence, box 1, folder 5.

56. "Report on the Football Situation at Washington and Lee for the Athletic Committee," appended to Gaines to Dr. J. Morrison Hutcheson of Richmond, Oct. 5, 1953, PP, Gaines, Athletics Correspondence, box 1, folder 5.

57. "An Analysis of Present Program," showing financial results from 1951–52, 1952–53, and projected for 1953–54, PP, Gaines, Athletics Correspondence, box 1, folder 3.

58. James R. Caskie, "The Athletic Decisions: Background and Meaning," *Alumni Magazine,* Dec. 1954, p. 14.

59. *Ring-tum Phi,* June 2, 1954. An excellent summary of these events was initially presented to the Fortnightly Club in Lexington by Frank A. Parsons, who graduated in 1954 and was appointed W&L's director of publicity in September: "Turning Back the Clock: Thirty Years Ago a Major Controversy Raged on W&L's Campus," *Alumni Magazine,* Sept. 1984, pp. 13–17. Parsons later served as assistant to three W&L presidents and as editor of the *Alumni Magazine.*

60. *Alumni Magazine,* June 1954, pp. 2–3.

61. Gaines to Robert P. Hobson, June 5, 1954, PP, Gaines, Subject Files, Honor Code Violations, 1954, series 2.

62. *President's Report, 1953–54,* pp. 1–2, PP, Gaines, Subject Files, series 2, President's Reports.

63. A statement by Rector James R. Caskie clarified many details in "The Athletic Decisions: Background and Meaning," *Alumni Magazine,* Dec. 1954, pp. 13–15.

64. Carl Wise to Gaines, July 10, 1954; Carl Wise to Gaines, July 14, 1954, PP, Gaines, box 19, folder 329. On July 16, after several conferences with Wise, Gaines responded on July 16 that he would "simply file that letter until after the next meeting of the Board of Trustees."

65. Caskie, "The Athletic Decisions: Background and Meaning," p. 14.

66. Letter in *Richmond Times-Dispatch,* July 30, 1954.

67. The text of this letter—undated, untitled, and unaddressed—is available in PP, Gaines, Athletics Correspondence, box 1, folder 7.

68. A statement Gaines sent to every alumnus and member of the student body on Aug. 18, 1954, accompanied this memorandum; PP, Gaines, Athletics Correspondence, box 1, folder 6.

69. Caskie, "The Athletic Decisions: Background and Meaning," p. 13.

70. C. William Pacy to Gaines, Aug. 9, 1954, PP, Gaines, Athletics Correspondence, box 1, folder 6.

71. Gaines to C. William Pacy, Aug. 18, 1954, PP, Gaines, Athletics Correspondence, box 1, folder 6.

72. Paul J. B. Murphy Jr., '49, to W. L. Webster, president of the W&L Alumni Association (undated but probably in 1954), PP, Gaines, Athletics Correspondence, box 1, folder 8.

73. F. O. Funkhouser and Goodloe Jackson, *Richmond Times-Dispatch,* July 30, 1954.

74. "Rouse Asks W&L Alumni to Aid Football's Return," *Richmond Times-Dispatch,* Aug. 18, 1954.

75. Leyburn to Cy Twombly, July 30, 1954; Cy Twombly to Leyburn, Aug. 6, 1954, Leyburn Papers, Athletic Affairs Correspondence, box 2, folder 17.

76. "Leyburn Voices Amazement at Reports on W&L Dispute," *Roanoke Times,* Sept. 16, 1954.

77. Ollinger Crenshaw to Robert McLean Jeter Jr., Sept. 28, 1954, Crenshaw Papers, Letters, box 320.

78. Letter to Gaines, the trustees, other administrators, and the *Ring Tum-Phi,* Oct. 13, 1954, Leyburn Papers, Athletic Affairs Correspondence, box 2, folder 18.

79. David W. Foerster to Leyburn, Oct. 13, 1954; Leyburn to Foerster, Oct. 21, 1954, Leyburn Papers, Athletic Affairs Correspondence, box 2, folder 18..

80. Jack B. Porterfield to James R. Caskie, Dec. 16, 1954, PP, Gaines, Athletics Correspondence, box 1, folder 8.

81. Edgar F. Shannon Jr., "Commends Action of W&L's Trustees," *Richmond Times-Dispatch,* Aug. 4, 1954.

82. "Statement from the Alumni Board of Trustees," *Alumni Magazine,* Mar. 1955, pp. 15–16.

83. Parsons, "Turning Back the Clock," p. 16.

84. Walter A. Groves to Gaines, Oct. 26, 1954; John R. Cunningham to Gaines, Oct. 6, 1954; Gaines to John R. Cunningham and John L. Plyler, Oct. 11, 1954; Edward McCrady, Nov. 8, 1954, PP, Gaines, Athletic Correspondence, box 1, folder 8.

85. E. P. Twombly, *President's Report,* 1955–56, pp. 42–44.

86. "Report of the University Committee on Intercollegiate Athletics 1954–55," to Gaines and the BOT, May 30, 1955, PP, Gaines, Athletics Correspondence, box 1, folder 10.

87. W. M. Hinton to Gaines, May 31, 1958; Gaines to Frontis W. Johnston, June 10, 1958, PP, Gaines, Subject Files, series 2, Southern Conference.

88. University "Sports News" release, Mar. 28, 1956, PP, Gaines, Athletics Correspondence, box 1, folder 11.

89. Robert I. Peeples and Don Luria to Gaines, Dec. 15, 1956, PP, Gaines, Athletics Correspondence, box 2, folder 12.

90. William M. Hinton to Gaines, Apr. 30, 1957; Frank J. Gilliam to Gaines, May 4, 1957, PP, Gaines, Athletics Correspondence, box 2, folder 12.

91. J. Morrison Hutcheson to George E. Burke, Jan. 22, 1958, PP, Gaines, Athletics Correspondence, box 2, folder 13.

92. Lewis F. Powell Jr. to Gaines, Jan. 31, 1958, PP, Gaines, Athletics Correspondence, box 2, folder 13.

93. Gaines to Lewis F. Powell Jr., Feb. 5, 1958, PP, Gaines, Athletics Correspondence, box 2, folder 13.

94. Lewis F. Powell to Gaines, Feb. 17, 1958, PP, Gaines, Athletics Correspondence, box 2, folder 13.

95. Gaines to BOT, Jan. 30, 1958, PP, Gaines, Athletics Correspondence, box 2, folder 13; BOT minutes, Jan. 18, 1958.

96. Caskie and Gaines, "The University's Athletic Policy," *Alumni Magazine,* Feb. 1958.

97. Sidney Coulling, interview by Mame Warren, Aug. 16 and Sept. 2, 2010.

98. Walter Bingham, "A Sport for Gentlemen," *Sports Illustrated,* Nov. 6, 1961.

99. Washington and Lee, *Bulletin, The Third Century: A Report for the 212th and 213th Years, 1960–1961–1962,* Feb. 1963, p. 52.

100. "W&L Budget Low But It's Not Cheap," *Roanoke Times,* Apr. 25, 1972.

101. "Era of Hero Is Long Gone," *Roanoke Times,* Apr. 25, 1972.

102. Mike Stachura, "The Legacy of the Beechenbrooks," *Alumni Magazine,* Spring 1989, pp. 39–40.

CHAPTER FIVE

1. "Au Revoir, Dr. Gaines," *Alumni Magazine,* Summer 1959, pp. 4–5, 24. Also, see a selection of newspaper editorial comments, pp. 22–23.

2. John W. Davis to John S. Munce, Dec. 8, 1928, PP, Cole, box 1, folder 3.

3. Minutes of the Trustees' Committee on Presidential Succession, Oct. 30, 1958, and Nov. 21, 1958; James R. Caskie to Huston St. Clair, Dec. 5, 1958, PP, Cole, box 1, folder 3.

4. "The Future of Washington and Lee," PP, Cole, box 1, folder 3.

5. Minutes of the Presidential Succession Committee, Jan. 17, 1959, PP, Cole, box 1, folder 3.

6. Ollinger Crenshaw to Robert McLean Jeter Jr., Aug. 8, 1958, and Feb. 19, 1959, Crenshaw Papers, Letters, box 320.

7. John Minor Wisdom to Joseph Lykes Jr., Jan. 13, 1959 (on Lykes Brothers Steamship Company stationery); William B. Wisdom to James R. Caskie, Jan. 23, 1959; Ollinger Crenshaw to Joseph L. Lanier, Nov. 12, 1958, PP, Cole, box 1, folder 5.

8. Minutes of the Presidential Succession Committee, June 3, 1959, and June 4, 1959, PP, Cole, box 1, folder 3.

9. Clarence L. Mohr and Joseph E. Gordon, *Tulane: The Emergence of a Modern University, 1945–1980* (Baton Rouge: Louisiana University Press, 2001), pp. 87–91, 140–47, 164–80.

10. Hamilton Crockford, "W&L President Studies Hard," *Richmond Times-Dispatch,* May 8, 1960.

11. Both Pusey's and Cole's addresses were published by the university, PP, Cole, box 2, folder 20.

12. Fred C. Cole, "Comments on the Functions of a University," *Journal of Medical Education* 36, no. 8 (Aug. 1961): 883–87.

13. Fred C. Cole, Founder's Day Remarks, Jan. 19, 1962, PP, Cole, box 4, folder 33.

14. Fred C. Cole, Remarks to Alumni, Oct., 1959, PP, Cole, box 4, folder 36.

15. US Department of Education, National Center for Education Statistics, 1992.

16. Fred C. Cole, memo to the BOT, June 1, 1960, PP, Cole, Memoranda to the Board, 1959–1960–1961.

17. Frank Parsons, interview by Mame Warren, Sept. 4, 1990.

18. BOT minutes, Jan. 21, 1967.

19. William W. Pusey III, "Report for 1962–63 of the Dean of the College," AA, Dean of the College, Faculty Matters, Deans Reports, box 2, folder 29.

20. Fred C. Cole, "Memorandum to the Faculty," appended to a cover memo to the BOT, Mar. 25, 1960, PP, Cole, Memoranda to the Board, 1959–1960–1961.

21. Fred C. Cole, Report to the BOT, 1961, PP, Cole, Subject Files, Series 2, President's Reports.

22. BOT minutes, Jan. 21, 1961.

23. Useful data on enrollment and other areas can be found in "Background Information," assembled for a special meeting of the board of trustees in Washington, DC, Apr. 4–5, 1970; a copy is in Commerce School, Miscellaneous, folder 3, Board of Trustees, 1970–81.

24. Pusey to Cole, June 25, 1964, PP, Cole, Subject Files, series 2, President's Reports.

25. These and other quotations and data are from the Washington and Lee *Bulletin, The Third Century: A Report for the 212th and 213th Years, 1960–1961–1962*, Feb. 1963, pp. 12–13.

26. Fred C. Cole to the BOT, Feb. 12, 1964, and Aug. 28, 1964, PP, Cole, Memoranda to the Board.

27. "New Financial Aid Program Is Established," *Alumni Magazine*, July 1960, p. 12; "Washington and Lee's Financial Aid To Undergraduates Shows Big Gain," *Alumni Magazine*, Dec. 1962, p. 26. Also, see James D. Farrar, "Needs for Increased Student Financial Aid, 1960–1961," and "Student Financial Aid," Dec. 1, 1959, PP, Cole, Subject Files, series 2, Scholarship and Student Financial Aid.

28. "Notes on Plans and Projections," prepared for a special meeting of the board of trustees on Apr. 4–5, 1970, in Washington, DC, pp. 9–10, a copy is in Commerce School, Miscellaneous, folder 3, Board of Trustees, 1970–81.

29. "Washington and Lee University Self-Study Report for the Southern Association of Colleges and Schools, 1964–1966," (hereinafter referred to as "SACS Self-Study, 1964-1966"), p. 263.

30. See James W. Whitehead to Cole, May 30, 1963, PP, Cole, Subject Files, series 2, Scholarship and Student Financial Aid.

31. BOT minutes, Jan. 20, 1962.

32. See minutes of Special Committee of the Board of Trustees, Sept. 18, 1965 and the Special Committee's "Report to the Board of Trustees," PP, Cole, Miscellaneous Material, 1965. Also, see an undated memorandum clarifying W&L's position on external grants in addition to information contained in a Carnegie Foundation study of federal programs in higher education, both used by the Special Committee in its deliberations, and BOT minutes, Oct. 9, 1965. Only Trustee Joseph E. Birnie voted against the resolution.

33. BOT minutes, Jan. 15, 1966.

34. "Notes on Plans and Projections," p. 11.

35. Fred C. Cole to the BOT, May 29, 1961, PP, Cole, Memoranda to the Board, 1959–1960–1961.

36. BOT minutes, July 25, 1964.

37. "A Lee College?" *Alumni Magazine*, Feb. 1965, pp. 4–8.

38. Louis Menand, *The Marketplace of Ideas: Reform and Resistance in the American University* (New York: W. W. Norton, 2010), pp. 25–52.

39. Ollinger Crenshaw to Robert McLean Jeter Jr., Dec. 22, 1961, Crenshaw Papers, Letters, box 320.

40. Washington and Lee Faculty minutes, Mar. 15, 1962, and Apr. 16, 1962.

41. "Statement to be Read by the Chairman of the Curriculum Committee to the Faculty, March 1, 1962, on the Proposed Revised B.A. Curriculum," AA, Dean of the College, Curriculum Studies, 1960–64, box 1, folder 4. The reference to James was Pusey's marginal comment on the draft of this statement.

42. Frank Parsons, interview by Mame Warren, Feb. 29, 1996. "A State of Institutional Philosophy for Washington and Lee University," in "SACS Self-Study, 1964–1966," pp. 97–100.

43. "SACS Self-Study, 1964–1966," pp. 458–59.

44. Detailed minutes of the "Joint Session of Board of Trustees and Self Study Committee for Study of Self Study Report, Aug. 14–16, 1966, The Homestead, Hot Springs," PP, Huntley, Subject Files, Board of Trustees, 1.

45. "Report of the Visiting Committee to Washington and Lee University," AA, Dean of the College, Curriculum Studies, 1964–69, box 2, folder 19.

46. Undated memo to Members of the Faculty from the Curriculum Committee, AA, Dean of the College, Curriculum Committee, 1967–71, Distribution Proposals. Also see minutes of the Curriculum Committee in the same file.

47. Washington and Lee Faculty minutes, May 1, 1969.

48. Henry S. Roberts and Edgar W. Spencer, "Why is the New Curriculum Desirable?" *Alumni Magazine,* Winter 1970, pp. 21–24.

49. Geology professor Edgar W. Spencer to Gregory T. Armstrong of Sweet Briar College, Apr. 21, 1970, AA, Dean of the College, Curriculum Committee, 1967–71, Correspondence Concerning Curriculum Revision. Spencer also enclosed a summary of the benefits of the calendar.

50. Questionnaire and responses appended to an undated (probably Nov. 1969) memorandum from David B. Dickens, chairman of the Foreign Study Committee, and widely distributed to faculty members, AA, Dean of the College, Curriculum Committee, 1967–71, box 2, Foreign Study Curriculum Review.

51. Washington and Lee, *Bulletin, The Third Century: A Report for the 212th and 213th Years, 1960–1961–1962,* Feb. 1963, p. 38.

52. Charles V. Laughlin, "A Day's Work," *Washington and Lee Law Review* 16 (1959).

53. This and much subsequent information on the law school is taken from the "SACS Self-Study, 1964–1966," pp. 194–208.

54. Stuart B. Campbell, of the Virginia Board of Law Examiners, to Charles P. Light Jr., Sept. 6, 1966, PP, Subject Files, Law School, 1951–72.

55. Michael H. Cordozo to Charles P. Light Jr., Apr. 16, 1964, with attachment, "Report to the Dean and Faculty of Washington and Lee University School of Law by Samuel A. Beatty and Michael H. Cordozo," PP, Cole, Subject Files, Law School 1964.

56. Homer A. Holt to Charles P. Light Jr., May 11, 1964, PP, Cole, Subject Files, Law School 1964.

57. "Selected Statistics for Representative Private, Liberal Arts Colleges, 1966/67," PP, Cole, Subject Files, Library, 1966–68, section 2.

58. Henry E. Coleman Jr. to Fred C. Cole, Dec. 15, 1964, PP, Cole, Subject Files, Library, 1960–68, Section 1.

59. "More than a collection of books . . . a happy place to learn and relax," interview by Maurice D. Leach Jr., *Alumni Magazine,* Sept. 1974, pp. 1–7

60. "Improved Science Accommodations Strengthen University's Program," *Alumni Magazine,* Dec. 1962, p. 2.

61. "Notes on Plans and Projections," pp. 1–8.

62. James Whitehead, interview by Mame Warren, Nov. 9, 2009.

63. Frank Parsons, interview by Mame Warren, Sept. 4, 2009.

64. Board Executive Committee special meeting minutes, Mar. 28, 1966; BOT minutes, executive session, May 14, 1966.

65. "SACS Self-Study, 1964–1966," pp. 395–404.

66. BOT minutes, May 18 and Oct. 19, 1968, Jan. 18, May 16 and 17, 1969.

67. "SACS Self-Study, 1964–1966," pp. 404–10.

68. University news release, May 22, 1967, PP, Cole, box 3, folder 29. A unanimous faculty resolution praising Cole was transmitted by Robert E. R. Huntley to the board of trustees. Faculty resolution, June 12, 1967, PP, Cole, Memos to the Board of Trustees, 1965–1966–1967. Also see letter to Cole from the president and six former presidents of the W&L chapter of the American Association of University Professors, June 1, 1967, PP, Cole, box 11, folder 138.

69. William W. Pusey III to Cole, Nov. 17, 1967, and Feb. 1, 1968, PP, Cole, box 11, folder 144.

70. Robert E. R. Huntley, "The Way We Were," *Rockbridge Historical Society Proceedings* 10 (1980–89).

71. Parsons, interview.

72. Sidney Coulling, interview.

73. Parsons, interview.

CHAPTER SIX

1. R. A. Smith to R. M. Murphy, Oct. 2, 1923, PP, Gaines, box 24, folder 394.

2. *Ring Tum-Phi*, Oct. 10, 1923.

3. Henry Louis Smith to William A. MacCorkle, Oct. 11, 1923; Smith to Carroll N. Gibney, Oct. 12, 1923, PP, Gaines Papers, box 24, folder 394.

4. Gaines to R. A. Smith, Dec. 15, 1937, PP, Gaines, box 16, folder 261.

5. Gaines to BOT, Nov. 9, 1949, PP, Gaines, box 14, folder 388.

6. Herbert Fitzpatrick to Gaines, Nov. 14, 1949; James R. Caskie to Gaines, Nov. 10, 1949; Huston St. Clair to Gaines, Nov. 15, 1949; J. Morrison Hutcheson to Gaines, Nov. 10, 1949; John Newton Thomas to Gaines, Nov. 15, 1949; and John W. Davis to Gaines, Nov. 14, 1949, PP, Gaines, box 14, folder 388. While St. Clair voted in favor of the 1964 board statement to open admissions to students regardless of color, both Caskie and Hutcheson voted against it. A baseball game was scheduled in Lexington on April 12, 1951, between W&L and the University of Michigan (which had a black player) with apparently at least preliminary university approval, but it was rained out.

7. Clarence R. Avery to Gaines, Nov. 26, 1949, and Edward E. Brown to Avery, Nov. 17, 1949, PP, Gaines, box 14, folder 388.

8. Gaines to Ralph C. Hutchison, Jan. 27, 1950, PP, Gaines, box 14, folder 388.

9. The definitive account is Raymond Arsenault, *Freedom Riders: 1961 and the Struggle for Racial Justice* (New York: Oxford University Press, 2007).

10. For the full story, see Diane McWhorter, *Carry Me Home: Birmingham, Alabama: The Climactic Battle of the Civil Rights Revolution* (New York: Simon and Schuster, 2001).

11. Melissa Kean, *Desegregating Private Higher Education in the South: Duke, Emory, Rice, Tulane, and Vanderbilt* (Baton Rouge: Louisiana State University Press), p. 6.

12. Ibid., p. 90.

13. A. G. Lively to Gaines, Nov. 6, 1950; Gaines to Lively, Nov. 8, 1950, PP, Gaines, Subject Files, Law School, 1944–50.

14. Special Committee on Racial Discrimination, American Association of Law Schools (AALS), "Interim Report for 1954" and "Final Report for 1954."

15. David F. Cavers to Gaines, Feb. 4, 1955, PP, Gaines, Subject Files, Law School, 1944–50.

16. Gaines to James Caskie and Homer Holt, Dec. 5, 1955, PP, Gaines, Subject Files, series 2, Racial Question, 1954–56.

17. Gaines, "Statement on Non Discrimination in Law School," undated document in PP, Gaines, Memos to the Board, 1955–56.

18. Gaines to James Caskie and Homer Holt, Feb. 28, 1956; Caskie to Gaines, Mar. 1, 1956; Holt to Gaines, Mar. 1, 1956, PP, Subject Files, series 2, Racial Question, 1954–56.

19. Kean, *Desegregating Private Higher Education in the South*, p. 68.

20. Biographical details are taken from Joel William Friedman, *Champion of Civil Rights: Judge John Minor Wisdom* (Baton Rouge: Louisiana State University Press, 2009.) See, also, Jack Bass, *Unlikely Heroes: The Dramatic Story of the Southern Judges of the Fifth Circuit Who Translated the Supreme Court's Brown Decision Into a Revolution for Equality* (New York: Simon and Schuster, 1981), and Deborah Marquardt, "Judge John Minor Wisdom's Mighty Pen," *Alumni Magazine*, Fall 1998, pp. 19–22.

21. Friedman, *Champion of Civil Rights*, and Bass, *Unlikely Heroes*, pp. xi–xii.

22. John C. Jeffries Jr., *Justice Lewis F. Powell, Jr.* (New York: Charles Scribner's Sons, 1994), p. 24.

23. Ibid, pp. 170, 180.

24. Powell, "Civil Disobedience: Prelude to Revolution?" *U.S. News and World Report*, Oct. 30, 1967, pp. 66–69; "A Lawyer Looks at Civil Disobedience," *Washington and Lee Law Review* 23, 1968: 205–31.

25. Jeffries, *Justice Lewis F. Powell Jr.*, pp. 297–98.

26. Arsenault, *Freedom Riders*, p. 542, chap. 7, and epilogue. I am indebted to Roy T. Matthews for sharing Maguire's recollection of his conversation with Coffin. Before returning to Connecticut, Coffin and Maguire were interviewed for a story that appeared in *Life* magazine. Arsenault points out that Maguire and the other Freedom Riders from Alabama, white and black, could not safely return to the state for some years thereafter.

27. BOT minutes, Oct. 13–14, 1961. A confidential summary and report, "Matters Pertaining to Proposed Appearances at Washington and Lee University by the Rev. Martin Luther King and General University Policy on Visiting Lecturers," with a limited number of copies, was prepared for the board on October 20, 1966, for consideration at its meeting at the Homestead. Also containing copies of news reports and other related documents, it was placed in the University Archives by Dr. Allen W. Moger, chairman of the Committee on Lectures. Unless otherwise noted, this is the documentary source for information on this matter. PP, W&L Presidents, 1935–70, Restricted.

28. BOT minutes, Jan. 20, 1962.

29. "Reader Questions Motives for Inviting Ellison Here," *Ring-tum Phi*, Nov. 7, 1963.

30. *Ring-Tum Phi*, Oct. 6, 1966.

31. A. W. Moger to Mrs. William L. Howell, Oct. 20, 1966. Included in "Confidential Summary."

32. A. W. Moger, handwritten cover sheet, "Confidential Summary."

33. Kean, *Desegregating Private Higher Education in the South*, p. 235.

34. John Chavis, a free black man, had attended Washington College in 1802, but this was little known in the mid-twentieth century and had no bearing on the university's admissions policies or student body.

35. Kean, *Desegregating Private Higher Education in the South,* p. 177.

36. Frank Parsons, interview by Mame Warren, Sept. 4, 2009.

37. Three student research efforts on the integration issue at W&L are helpful: Juarez New-some, "The Desegregation Process at Washington and Lee University," a paper written for Professor Holt Merchant, Mar. 23, 1992; John Thompson "Jay" White, "Battling Southern Heritage: A History of Blacks at Washington and Lee," honors thesis, 1996; and Gordon LA, "The Racial Integration of W&L and VMI: A Comparative Study," 2005 Summer Undergraduate Research Institute, VMI. Copies of all three can be found in Special Collections, W&L Misc., Washington and Lee University: Black Students.

38. Roger Paine, "Approach to Desegregation Topic of Mixed Discussion," *Ring-tum Phi,* Feb. 11, 1964.

39. "We Shall Overcome," *Ring-tum Phi,* Feb. 11, 1964.

40. Kenneth P. Lane Jr., "An Unjust Attack," *Ring-tum Phi,* Feb. 14, 1964.

41. Telegram from Lyndon B. Johnson to Fred Cole, July 2, 1964; telegram from Cole to John-son, July 2, 1964; James R. Caskie to Cole, July 3, 1964; *Richmond Times-Dispatch,* Aug. 19, 1964, PP, Cole, National Citizens Committee for Community Relations, DC, 1964, box 9, folder 129; Jessie Ball duPont Papers, box 202, folder 14. Cole prepared a statement for the *Lynchburg Advance* that he had accepted the appointment as a civic duty in response to "a direct request from the President of the United States."

42. A good summary of the decision and its implications is the draft of an article, intended for but never published in the *Alumni Magazine,* written by Frank A. Parsons: "The Matter of Admissions . . . ." A typescript draft of the article is available in PP, Huntley, Subject Files, series 2.

43. BOT minutes, July 24, 1964.

44. Huntley, interview by Gordon LA, June 29, 2005, in LA, "The Racial Integration of W&L and VMI," pp. 28–29. Also see White, "Battling Southern Heritage," p 39.

45. BOT minutes, Oct. 24, 1964.

46. Frank A. Parsons, "The Matter of Admissions . . . ," draft manuscript, in PP, Huntley, Subject Files, series 2. The draft carried a subhead noting the request from the Alumni Board that "a Complete Account of the Matter and Its Significance" be printed in the *Alumni Magazine.*

47. Lewis F. Powell to Frank A. Parsons, Dec. 12, 1964, PP, Subject Files, Admissions Policies (including integration), 1964–79.

48. "A Question of Admissions . . . ," *Alumni Magazine,* Fall 1964, p. 3. This citation and oth-ers from the *Alumni Magazine* are confusing because an identical publication—the *University Magazine*—was published in the Winter 1965—as part of the *Washington and Lee Bulletin* 64 (Feb. 1965). The *University Magazine* was the front section of the *Alumni Magazine* (everything but alumni news, etc.), offered in a separate form for other audiences, such as parents, students, and the general public. To simplify matters, I cite only the *Alumni Magazine.*

49. One trustee had notified (future trustee) Jack W. Warner of Tuscaloosa, Alabama, immedi-ately after the board action and asked him to share his thoughts with Cole and the other trustees. In Warner's opinion, from a purely "business point of view," as a private institution W&L could afford to be truly independent and defer any action for the moment, gaining additional support in some quarters and guarding against a future swing of the pendulum "the other way." Jack W. Warner to Fred Cole, July 16, 1964, Jessie Ball duPont Papers, box 202, folder 14.

50. "In Lee's Spirit," *Washington Post,* Nov. 3, 1964.

51. All quotations from this discussion are taken from detailed minutes of "Joint Session of Board of Trustees and Self-Study Committee for Study of Self-Study Report, Aug. 14–16, 1966, the Homestead, Hot Springs," PP, Huntley Papers, Subject Files, Board of Trustees. (Neither John Minor Wisdom nor Lewis Powell attended this meeting.)

52. Dennis Haston and James Farrar Sr., interviews with Juarez Newsome, Jan. 1992, in "The Desegregation Process of Washington and Lee University," pp. 9–11.

53. Cole notified the board about this request in August 1966 and noted that that assistance would be offered, but at no cost to the university.

54. The news story announcing the admission of Haston and Smith appeared in many newspapers. See "2 Negro Students Accepted by W&L," *Richmond Times-Dispatch,* Aug. 22, 1966.

55. Huntley, interview by Gordon LA, June 29, 2005, in LA, "The Racial Integration of W&L and VMI," p. 32. Also see interview by Theodore C. DeLaney of Kenneth Satlin, a close friend and classmate of Leslie Smith, "Leslie Smith and Kenneth Satlin," W&L Miscellaneous, Washington and Lee University: Black Students.

56. Walter Blake, interview by Mame Warren, May 2, 1977.

CHAPTER SEVEN

1. James T. Patterson, *The Eve of Destruction: How 1965 Transformed America* (New York: Basic Books, 2012).

2. Tony Judt, "Meritocrats," *New York Review of Books* 57, no. 13 (Aug. 19, 2010): 4.

3. BOT minutes, Jan. 23, 1965.

4. Frank Parsons, "Conventional Dress—Will It Continue?" *Alumni Magazine,* Dec. 1965, pp. 2–3, 9, 19.

5. Cole's address was reprinted in its entirety, with photographs of current campus fashions, in *Alumni Magazine,* Dec. 1965, pp. 4–8. Trustee Lewis Powell requested that Cole's remarks be reprinted and widely distributed, even to other colleges, foundations, and private schools under the imprimatur of the trustees. BOT minutes, Oct. 9, 1965.

6. Parsons, "Conventional Dress—Will It Continue?"

7. "Alumni Return, Look, Listen, Inquire, Spar, and Speak Up," *Alumni Magazine,* Dec. 1967, pp. 2–5.

8. "A Matter of Coats and Ties: A Lengthy Debate Reconstructed," *Alumni Magazine,* Dec. 1967, pp. 8–12.

9. Tom Wolfe, interview by Mame Warren, Apr. 19, 1996.

10. "Cocktail Party Kicks Off Homecoming-Openings," *Ring-tum Phi,* Oct. 13, 1961.

11. "SACS Self-Study, 1964–1967," p. 302.

12. "Report by the Dean of Students to the Board of Trustees' Meeting, July 26, 27, 1965," PP, Huntley, Subject Files, Board of Trustees, 1.

13. James D. Farrar to Frank Gilliam, Sept. 22, 1961, AA, Dean of the College, Faculty Matters, Fraternity Rushing and Schedule, 1961–65, box 3, folder 52. (Numbers for 1962 were added in pencil to the chart.)

14. Herman B. Wells to Cole, Nov. 3, 1966; Cole to Wells, Nov. 16, 1966; Edward C. Atwood Jr. to Cole, Nov. 15, 1966, PP, President's Office, Subject Files, Fraternities, 1966–70.

15. Huntley to William T. Bringham, May 31, 1968, PP, President's Office, Subject Files, Fraternities, 1966–70.

16. Edward C. Atwood Jr. to Huntley, Apr. 20, 1968, PP, President's Office, Subject Files, Fraternities, 1966–70.

17. "SACS Self-Study, 1964–1966," pp. 305–6.

18. Ibid., p. 292.

19. This description is taken from the Student Executive Committee statement in 1968–69.

20. John M. Gunn, "An Essay on the W & L Honor System," Sept. 1992, was sent in response to President John D. Wilson's enquiry about the history and evolution of the Honor System. See, also, Wilson to Gunn, Sept. 21, 1992, PP, Wilson, box 13, Honor System, 1960–94.

21. Atwood to Cole, May 23, 1966, PP, Wilson, box 13, Honor System, 1960–94.

22. Atwood to Cole, Mar. 22, 1966, PP, Wilson, box 13, Honor System, 1960–94.

23. Frank Gilliam to Cole, undated, PP, Wilson, box 13, Honor System, 1960–94.

24. See Gunn, "An Essay on the W & L Honor System." Gunn wrote, "It is my judgment that a person who is unwilling to cooperate with the Honor System, even if she/he has major reservations about it, should not accept a position on the faculty of Washington and Lee" (p. 5).

25. "SACS Self-Study, 1964–1967," pp. 284–86.

26. Gunn, "An Essay on the W & L Honor System," p. 2.

27. Neil Kessler's article was reprinted as "The Honor System: *Semper Idem?*" in the *Alumni Magazine,* Jan. 1969, pp. 12–13.

28. William W. Pusey III to Fred C. Cole, Feb. 1, 1968, PP, Cole, box 11, folder 144.

29. Steven R. Saunders to Richard Nash, Mar. 3, 1968, Mock Convention Files, 1968.

30. Cole to BOT, Oct. 22, 1965, PP, Cole, Memoranda to the Board, 1965–1966–1967.

CHAPTER EIGHT

1. Robert E. R. Huntley, "The Way We Were," *Rockbridge Historical Society Proceedings* 10 (1980–89): 595–96.

2. Frank Parsons, interview by Mame Warren, Feb. 29, 1996.

3. "A Day of Rain and Affirmation," and "The President Wears Loafers," *W&L Magazine,* Winter 1968, pp. 1 and 14–16.

4. William C. Friday, "Address," PP, Huntley, Inauguration, box 2.

5. Huntley, "Inaugural Remarks," PP, Huntley, Inauguration, box 2.

6. The rate of college enrollment increased significantly after 1984, despite predictions to the contrary based on the number of eighteen-year-olds in the population, but the outlook at the beginning of the 1970s suggested losses of enrollment approaching 15 percent through the mid-1990s.

7. These opening enrollment figures are from the chart called "Enrollment Trends" in the *Report of the Registrar, 1984–1985.* The total opening enrollment figures differ somewhat from previously announced numbers because of adjustments for transfers, exchange students, and so on.

8. The persistence numbers, going back to the class of 1955, are contained in *Report of the Registrar, 1980–1981.*

9. The "Self-Study Report of Washington and Lee University, 1978" (hereinafter referred to as "SACS Self-Study, 1978"), pp. 139–40. The verbal SAT scores of the entering class had declined from 596 in 1967 to 540 in 1977, and in math from 628 to 590 (p. 87).

10. William M. Hartog, "Admissions: Strong Today, But . . . ," *Alumni Magazine,* Oct. 1980, pp. 3–8, 18–21.

11. "SACS Self-Study, 1978," pp. 287–88.

12. Ibid., pp. 125–26.

13. "W&L is a Major Center for East Asian Studies," *Alumni Magazine,* Apr. 1977, pp. 10–12.

14. "Report on the Fine Arts," "Fine Arts Update," PP, Huntley, Subject Files, series 2, Trustees, box 1, Misc. Board Papers, 1974–83.

15. W. Patrick Hinely, "University Theatre: New Directions in Playmaking," *Alumni Magazine,* July 1976, pp. 10–15.

16. BOT minutes, May 25, 1974.

17. "SACS Self-Study, 1978," pp. 147–48.

18. James Lewis Howe, "'Wahrheit ind Dichtung': Washington and Lee Has Narrow Escape from Becoming Co-educational," *Alumni Magazine,* Dec. 1939, pp. 5, 18. The word *co-education* was sometimes hyphenated in letters, documents, and publications, but *coeducation* is the dominant usage. I have eliminated the hyphen hereafter unless it appears in publications.

19. Lou Hodges to Huntley, Feb. 28, 1969, with signed petition of Feb. 5, 1969 attached, PP, Wilson, box 10A, Coeducation at W&L.

20. "A Decade of Progress," *Alumni Magazine,* Feb. 1970.

21. Huntley to C. Walton Rex, Mar. 24, 1970, PP, Wilson, box 10A, Coeducation at W&L.

22. Huntley to Hodges and members of the committee, Apr. 8, 1969, PP, Wilson, box 10A, Coeducation at W&L.

23. BOT minutes, May 16, 1969.

24. "Cooperation May Be Key to Coed Problem," *Dallas Morning News,* July 19, 1968.

25. BOT minutes, Oct. 4, 1969, Jan. 17, 1970; "University Report, 1974–75," *Alumni Magazine,* Oct. 1975, p. 1.

26. Nancy Weiss Malkiel, *"Keep the Damned Women Out": The Struggle for Coeducation* (Princeton: Princeton University Press, 2016); Louis Hodges, "Question: Should W&L Go Coed?" *Alumni Magazine,* Winter 1970, pp. 14–16.

27. James. D. Farrar to Huntley, Mar. 23, 1970, PP, Huntley, Subject Files, series 2, Trustees, box 1.

28. "The Report of the Committee on Coeducation at Washington and Lee University," submitted to the BOT for their special meeting, Apr. 4–5, 1970, PP, Wilson, Coeducation.

29. "The Girls—They Came, They Conquered; And It's Quite Possible They'll Be Here For Good," *Alumni Magazine,* Apr. 1970.

30. "Outlook and Review," *Ring-tum Phi,* Mar. 1, 1972.

31. BOT minutes, May 26, 1973, and Oct. 30, 1973.

32. BOT minutes, Jan. 12, 1974.

33. BOT minutes, May 24, 1974.

34. Minutes of the Trustee Coeducation Study Committee, Dec. 7, 1974, Trustees, Study Committee on Coeducation; Trustee Study Committee on Coeducation Report, vol. 1, Summary Volume, Aug. 1975, PP, Wilson, Coeducation, box 10A.

35. Robert W. McAhren to Select Committee of Trustees on Coeducation, Apr. 16, 1975; McAhren to the faculty, Apr. 21, 1975; and copies of the six additional responses, Trustee Study Committee on Coeducation, folder 1.

36. A summary of faculty responses from Robert W. McAhren to Select Committee of Trustees on Coeducation, Apr. 16, 1975, Trustees, Study Committee on Coeducation, folder (con'd 1). A similar summary (with respondents not identified) was circulated to the faculty on April 21, 1975.

37. Jefferson Davis Futch to McAhren, Apr. 30, 1975; Hodges to McAhren, Apr. 24, 1975; James M. Phemister and Lawrence K. Hellman to McAhren, Apr. 30, 1975, Trustee Study Committee on Coeducation, folder (con'd, 2).

38. Ibid.

39. Summary and Overview, Trustee Study Committee on Coeducation, Trustee Study Committee on Coeducation, pp. 5–6.

40. "SACS Self-Study, 1978," p. 91; BOT minutes, Jan. 31, 1976.

41. "W&L Will Remain a Men's College," *Alumni Magazine,* Jan. 1976, p. 9.

42. James Edward Scanlon, *Randolph-Macon College: Traditions and New Directions, 1967–2005* (Ashland: Randolph-Macon College, 2013), pp. 139–47.

43. Mary D. Beaty, *A History of Davidson College* (Davidson: Briarpatch, 1988), pp. 389–90.

44. "Law Women: Bringing a Diversity of Perspective," *Alumni Magazine,* May 1976, pp. 8–10.

45. Much of this discussion based on Mame Warren's interview with Robert Huntley, Apr. 23, 2009, pp. 18–20.

46. "University Report, 1974–75," *Alumni Magazine,* Oct. 1975, pp. 1–15.

47. The accreditors had made many demands before. Among other things, they consistently recommended that the law faculty be compensated on a separate—and higher—scale than other professors, which W&L resisted. They also brought early pressure to bear on the university to admit African Americans before W&L and many other southern law schools were prepared to do that.

48. Robert Stevens, *Law School: Legal Education in America from the 1850s to the 1980s* (Chapel Hill: University of North Carolina Press, 1983), pp. 199, 205–9.

49. Ibid., p. 235.

50. Huntley, interview.

51. Ibid.

52. Roy Steinheimer, interview by Mame Warren, May 27, 2010.

53. Millard H. Ruud (Association of American Law Schools) to Huntley and Steinheimer, June 23, 1980; James P. White (American Bar Association) to Huntley and Steinheimer, Aug. 18, 1981, PP, Wilson, Law School General File, folder 4.

54. Steinheimer, interview.

55. BOT minutes, May 29, 1971.

56. Steinheimer, interview.

57. Sally Wiant, interview by Mame Warren, Apr. 9, 1996.

58. "SACS Self-Study, 1978," pp. 289–90, 294.

59. "School of Law, Dean's Report, 1979–80," *Washington and Lee Fact Book, 1979–80.*

60. "Capital Fund Campaign Gets Under Way," *Alumni Magazine,* Fall 1958, pp. 14–15; "Capital Fund Drive Passes Two Million Mark," *Alumni Magazine,* July 1960, p. 13.

61. BOT minutes, May 14, 1966.

62. Deborah Marquardt, "This is Your Life Frank Parsons," *Alumni Magazine,* Summer 1999, pp. 21–27; Neil Pentifallo, "Frank Parsons: W&L's Man Behind the Scenes, *Ring-tum Phi,* Sept. 21, 1978.

63. See Deborah Marquardt, "GentleMan Caller," *Alumni Magazine,* Summer 2001, pp. 14–19.

64. BOT minutes, Oct. 14, 1967.

65. BOT minutes, May 18, 1968; "Physical Planning at Washington and Lee University Status Report, July, 1968," PP, Huntley, Subject Files, series 2, Trustees, box 1.

66. An entire special issue of the *Alumni Magazine* (Apr. 1971) was devoted to the new campaign and its goals.

67. Huntley to Frances and Sydney Lewis, Dec. 11, 1971, PP, Huntley, Correspondence, Misc. 1969–71.

68. Excerpts from the "Meeting of the Washington and Lee Achievement Council," Oct. 29, 1971, PP, Huntley, Subject Files, series 2, Trustees, box 1; Huntley, "The Way We Were," p. 602.

69. Development Committee minutes, Jan. 11, 1974, PP, Huntley, Subject Files, series 2, Board of Trustees, box 2.

70. Huntley, interview.

71. BOT minutes, Jan. 30, 1976; Development Committee minutes, Oct. 21, 1976, PP, Huntley, Subject Files, series 2, Board of Trustees, box 2.

72. "Fredericksburg Philanthropist Bequeaths $11 Million to Washington and Lee," *Alumni Magazine,* Jan. 1976, pp. 1–2, 6–7, 9; and Rupert N. Latture, "A Memorandum" noting President Gaines's relationship and influence with many large donors, Jan. 19, 1976, submitted to the BOT meeting on Jan. 30–31, 1976.

73. William Washburn to Richard D. Haynes, July 12, 1974, PP, Wilson, box 3, Alumni Board, folder 2.

74. "Report to the Committee on the University Alumni Program," May 9, 1975, PP, Wilson, box 3, Alumni Board, folder 2.

75. Minutes of the Development Committee Meeting, Mar. 16, 1979, PP, Huntley, Subject Files, series 2, Board of Trustees, box 2.

76. "Development Program Success: A Promise Is Kept As 10-Year Fund-Raising Effort Exceeds Its Goal by $5 Million," *Alumni Magazine,* Jan. 1982, pp. 1–3.

77. Farris Hotchkiss to BOT, Aug. 12, 1982, PP, Huntley, Memoranda to the Board of Trustees, 1979–82.

78. Minutes of the Development Committee Meeting, May 21, 1982.

79. Minutes of the Combined Meeting of Development and Planning Committees, Oct. 15, 1982.

80. "The Dedication of Lewis Hall" and "The Saga of 'Jockey John' and the Judge," *Alumni Magazine,* May 1977, pp. 1–2, 13–15. The 1824 dedication of Washington Hall is covered in Crenshaw's *General Lee's College.*

81. "Contracts Are Awarded for the New Library," *Alumni Magazine,* Sept. 1976, pp. 4–5; Robert E. R. Huntley, "Reflections on the Decision to Build the New Library," p. 6.

82. "The Squirrel Memo," *Wall Street Journal,* Oct. 24, 1974.

83. *Ring-tum Phi*, Sept. 14, 1978, and Jan. 11, 1979.

84. Institutional Planning Committee minutes, Mar. 16, 1979, Oct. 31, 1980, and May 21, 1982.

85. Mary Tyler Cheek to Huntley, June 3, 1977.

86. Leslie Cheek Jr. and Mary Tyler Freeman Cheek to Huntley, June 20, 1977.

87. Huntley to Mr. and Mrs. Leslie Cheek Jr., June 20, 1977.

88. Huntley to BOT, Aug. 17, 1977.

89. BOT minutes, Oct. 21, 1977.

90. I am indebted for all information and details to James M. Whitehead, *A Fragile Union: The Story of Louise Herreshoff* (self-published in two editions, 2003 and 2006), with an introduction by Tom Wolfe.

91. In addition to Whitehead's account and other catalogues of the collection, see Thomas V. Litzenburg Jr., *Chinese Export Porcelain in the Reeves Center Collection at Washington and Lee University* (London: Third Millennium, 2003). The Herreshoff paintings were featured in a special exhibition in the Corcoran Gallery of Art in Washington, DC, and frequently go on tour. Pieces from the porcelain collection have been loaned to many museums and exhibitions, including 200 items in a nationwide Smithsonian tour celebrating the national bicentennial. An archeological dig conducted by W&L faculty and students at the site of the Liberty Hall ruins, essentially undisturbed since the building burned, uncovered shards of Chinese export porcelain, similar to those in the Reeves Collection, used by students some two-hundred years earlier.

92. See "SACS Self-Study, 1978."

CHAPTER NINE

1. Joshua B. Freeman, *American Empire: The Rise of a Global Power, the Democratic Revolution at Home, 1945–2000* (New York: Viking, 2012), p. 260.

2. *Ring-tum Phi*, Sept. 30, Oct. 17, Nov. 7, and Nov. 14, 1969.

3. Freeman, *American Empire*, p. 278.

4. *Lexington News-Gazette*, May 6, 1970; *Ring-tum Phi*, May 6, 1970. The *Alumni Magazine* carried a lengthy summary of these events, written by Frank Parsons, "Between a Rock And a Hard Place—Eight Days in May," June 1970, pp. 1–15. I have drawn much of my account (and many quotes) from this thoughtful and detailed summary, as well as from newspaper reports and university documents. The term "eight days in May" was used by students, probably inspired by the title of a 1964 movie, "Seven Days in May."

5. "EC Endorses Petition to Withdraw Troops," *Ring-tum Phi*, May 6, 1970.

6. Robert E. R. Huntley, interview by Mame Warren, May 14, 1996.

7. *Ring-tum Phi*, May 13, 1970.

8. Frank Parsons to Lewis F. Powell Jr., Apr. 26, 1982, PP, Huntley, Letters on Resignation.

9. Huntley, interview.

10. "Student Leaders Condemn 'Irresponsible' Activities," *Ring-tum Phi*, May 13, 1970.

11. Huntley, "A Message to Parents of Washington and Lee Students," May 13, 1970, PP, Correspondence with Parents, 1958–70; Glenn Azuma and Peyton Gravely to Parents, May 14, 1970, PP, Huntley, Demonstrations 1970, box 1, folder 3.

12. James M. Whitehead, *A Fragile Union: The Story of Louise Herreshoff* (self-published in two editions, 2003 and 2006).

13. *Richmond Times-Dispatch,* May 28, 1970.

14. "Professors Disagree With W&L Letter," *Richmond Times-Dispatch,* June 6, 1970.

15. Severn Duvall to Hugh F. White Jr., June 25, 1970, PP, Huntley, May Demo 1970, box 1, folder 2.

16. The theft of the ceremonial University Mace from the President's Office later in the month, and the suggestion that it had been burned, especially aggravated the faculty. Indeed, the mace was missing from the commencement ceremony, but it was later anonymously returned without damage.

17. Robert S. Keefe, "The Free University Forum: It Had 'Some Good Learning' On Highly Personal Subjects," *Alumni Magazine,* June 1970.

18. "Radical Change at W&L," *Roanoke Times,* June 9, 1970.

19. See Virginius Dabney, *Mr. Jefferson's University: A History* (Charlottesville: University Press of Virginia, 1981), pp. 507–29. Dabney attributed much of the protest at UVA to the urgings of "Marxist extremists."

20. James Edward Scanlon, *Randolph-Macon College: Traditions and New Directions, 1967–2005* (Ashland: Randolph-Macon College, 2013), p. 79.

21. Paul K. Conkin, *Gone With the Ivy: A Biography of Vanderbilt University* (Knoxville: University of Tennessee Press, 1985), p. 628.

22. W. E. James to William C. Washburn, Aug. 9, 1970, PP, Huntley, May Demo 1970, box 1, folder 2. The "form" paragraphs that Huntley incorporated into his responses are found in PP, Huntley, May Demo 1970, box 1, folder 7.

23. The board statement was included as part of the Parsons *Alumni Magazine* article, p. 11.

24. Student Executive Committee, "Recommended Faculty Guidelines for the Honor System," Nov. 1970.

25. Neil Kessler, "The Honor System: *Semper Idem?*" *Alumni Magazine,* Jan. 1969, pp. 12–13.

26. BOT minutes, May 29, 1971. Also see "Honor System Reaffirmed," *Alumni Magazine,* July 1971, p. 1.

27. "EC President Swede Henberg Hits In Loco Parentis At Parents' Weekend Meeting," *Alumni Magazine,* Feb. 1970.

28. Lewis G. John, "Question: What Is Today's Student Like?" *Alumni Magazine,* Winter 1970, pp. 25–27.

29. Sidney M. B. Coulling, "So W&L Isn't What It Used to Be; But With What Are You Comparing It?" *Alumni Magazine,* Jan. 1973, pp. 13–15.

30. "Five Student Body Presidents Discuss Life at W&L Today," *W&L,* Sept. 1974, pp. 12–15.

31. See the "Working Paper" and related documents in AA, Dean of the College, Faculty Matters, Social Function Committee, 1961, box 4, folder 93.

32. Documents relating to these matters are found in AA, Dean of the College, Faculty Matters, University Council, 1970–78, box 5, folder 3.

33. The University Council's new policies and standards were also presented to the board. See PP, Huntley, Board of Trustees Meeting, Jan. 31–Feb. 1, 1975.

34. Minutes of the Faculty Executive Committee, Mar. 25, 1974, AA, Dean of the College, Faculty Executive Committee, 1960–83, box 820.

35. Drinking at W&L," *Alumni Magazine,* May 1981, pp. 14–15.

36. "President Huntley's Speech, Special Student Assembly," Dec. 4, 1968, PP, Wilson, box 36, Drugs. Also see "W&L Focuses on 'Pot' Problem," *Richmond Times-Dispatch*, Dec. 8, 1968.

37. This account is based on the comprehensive report from Dean of Students Lewis John, provided to Huntley on July 12, 1973, which Huntley shared with the trustees on July 24 and which can be found in PP, Huntley, Memos to the Board, 1973–74. This was reprinted as a special report, "Drug Cases Pose Complex Problems for the University Community," *Alumni Magazine*, Sept. 1973, pp. 10–13.

38. Report by Edward C. Atwood Jr. to the BOT meeting on July 26–27, 1965, PP, Huntley, Subject Files, Board of Trustees, box 1.

39. "Fall Campus Changes Will Be No Less Significant Than They Were A Hundred Years Ago Under Lee," *Alumni Magazine*, Aug. 1970, p. 2.

40. The *Alumni Magazine*, Mar. 1971, was devoted to a discussion of the fraternity situation at W&L.

41. "Fraternities Fall on Hard Times," *Roanoke Times*, May 17, 1970.

42. Ibid.

43. A draft letter, dated Apr. 13, 1970, PP, Huntley, Subject Files, Fraternities 1966–70.

44. Robert S. Keefe, "After an Era of Tumult, Fraternities Are Different—Yet Not So Different," *Alumni Magazine*, Mar. 1976, pp. 5–9.

45. University Council, "Policy Statement on Fraternities, Feb. 25, 1976," presented to the BOT meeting in May 1976.

46. Dan Murphy, Coordinator of Fraternity Affairs, to the presidents of each fraternity, Mar. 31, 1978, with new provisions of the Student Affairs Committee, adopted on Feb. 2, appended, PP, Subject Files, Fraternities 1978–79.

47. The original motion before the faculty, the University Council Action of May 3, 1979, and substitute motion adopted by the faculty can be found in PP, Subject File, Fraternities, 1979. See, also, AA, Dean of the College, Faculty Executive Committee, 1960–83, box 820.

48. "Fraternity Improvements," *Alumni Magazine*, Sept. 1980, pp. 1–2.

49. James D. Farrar to Huntley, Oct. 2, 1969, PP, Admissions Policies (including integration), 1964–79.

50. Robert Huntley, interview by Mame Warren, Apr. 23, 2009.

51. William Hill, interview by Mame Warren, May 4, 1996.

52. Eugene Perry, interview by Mame Warren, Apr. 16, 1996.

53. "Campus Activism? Yes . . . But with a Vital Difference," *Washington and Lee Alumnus*, Aug. 1969, p. 5.

54. SABU Pamphlet, 1970, in Special Collections, also included in Jay White's honors thesis, "Battling Southern Heritage: A History of Blacks at Washington and Lee."

55. White, ""Battling Southern Heritage," p. 61.

56. Huntley, interview by Mame Warren, May 14, 1996.

57. Gordon LA, "The Racial Integration of W&L and VMI: A Comparative Study, 2005 Summer Undergraduate Research Institute," pp. 38–40, Special Collections, W&L Miscellaneous, Washington and Lee University: Black Students.

58. Juarez Newsome, "The Desegregation Process of Washington and Lee University," paper for History 363, Mar. 23, 1992, Special Collections, W&L Miscellaneous, Washington and Lee

University: Black Students. Newsome conducted telephone interviews with a number of the black students involved.

59. "Black Culture Week," *Alumni Magazine,* Apr. 1973, pp. 20–21.

60. See Huntley to BOT, Jan. 21, 1977, PP, Huntley, Memos to the Board of Trustees, 1974–78; "Black Students Protest Honor Code Trial at W&L," *Roanoke Times,* Jan. 20, 1977; "University, Blacks Hold Ongoing Talks," *Lexington News-Gazette,* Jan. 26, 1977.

61. "Minority Cultural Center dedicated in Oct.," *Alumni Magazine,* Nov. 1982, pp. 19–20.

62. Walter Blake, interview by Mame Warren, May 2, 1997.

63. Robert S. Keefe, "The Little Quarterly That Helps Shape American Literature," *Alumni Magazine,* Dec. 1972, pp. 6–7.

64. Huntley to BOT, Aug. 14, 1968, PP, Huntley, Memos to the Board of Trustees, 1968–69.

65. W&L Office of Sports Information, news release for Jan. 5, 1970.

66. Jack Emmer to Huntley, Sept. 7, 1978, PP, Huntley, Subject Files, series 2, 541.

67. William M. Hartog to Bill McHenry, Mar. 31, 1982, PP, Wilson, Athletics, 1980–88, box 32, folder 3.

68. Samuel R. Spencer Jr. to Huntley, May 29, 1978; Huntley to Spencer, June 26, 1978, PP, Huntley, Subject Files, series 2, box 541.

69. Bill McHenry to Huntley, with memorandum from Jack Emmer attached, May 21, 1982, PP, Wilson, Athletics, 1980–88, box 32, folder 3.

70. Bill Achnier, "Campus Close Up: Washington and Lee University," *Coach and Athlete,* Nov. 1976, pp. 10–12.

CHAPTER TEN

1. Fred Cole to Huntley, Dec. 29, 1982; Huntley to Cole, Jan. 3, 1983, PP, Cole, box 11, folder 144.

2. BOT minutes, Feb. 13, 1982.

3. Ballengee to the BOT and Trustees Emeritus, Apr. 8, 1982; and Sidney Coulling to Members of the Presidential Search Advisory Committee, Mar. 18, 1982, PP, Wilson, box 1, Presidential Search Committee 1982.

4. "Wilson Elected President," *Alumni Magazine,* Sept. 1982, pp. 1–7.

5. Robert Mottley, "Without Fear or Favor," *Alumni Magazine,* Fall 1994, pp. 14–15.

6. Jeffrey Hanna, "'I Do Solemnly Swear . . . ' The Inauguration of President John Delane Wilson Brightens a Rainy Day," *Alumni Magazine,* July 1983, pp. 1–5.

7. "The Inauguration of John DeLane Wilson," with complete remarks from Bartlett and Wilson, University Archives.

8. Wilson to BOT, Jan. 25, 1983, Memos to the Board. All of Wilson's memoranda to the Trustees are filed in folders by date and contained in Box 1, PP, Wilson.

9. Sally Wiant, interview by Mame Warren, Apr. 9, 1996. Wilson's memorandum was probably a copy of or similar to his first monthly communication with the trustees.

10. John R. Thelin, *A History of American Higher Education* (Baltimore: Johns Hopkins University Press, 2004), p. 318. See, generally, chap. 8, "Coming of Age in America: Higher Education as a Troubled Giant, 1970 to 2000," pp. 317–62.

11. Wilson to Members of the Monday Luncheon Group, July 21, 1983, PP, Wilson, Memos to the Board.

12. Wilson to the BOT, Aug. 16, 1983, PP, Wilson, Memos to the Board.

13. E. Stewart Epley, "Treasurer's Report," *Alumni Magazine,* Jan. 1985, pp. 12–16.

14. "Institutional Long-Range Plan (I), 1990–2000," pp. 1–2, PP, Wilson, box 565, Board of Trustees Material, 1994–95.

15. Huntley to James H. Clark, Nov. 8, 1973, PP, Huntley, Memos to the Board of Trustees, 1973–74.

16. College and University Personnel Association (CUPA), *1983–84 National Faculty Salary Survey by Disciplines and Rank in Private College and Universities,* PP, Wilson, box 14.

17. *Fact Books.*

18. Wilson to BOT, Nov. 25, 1986, PP, Wilson, Memos to the Board.

19. "Institutional Long-Range Plan (I), 1990–2000," pp. 3–8.

20. Wilson to BOT, Mar. 1, 1989, PP, Wilson, Memos to the Board.

21. "Institutional Long-Range Plan (II), 1990–2000," p. 81.

22. Wilson to Members of the Faculty, Aug. 25, 1987, with attachment, "Faculty Evaluation Procedures," PP, Wilson, box 30, Faculty and Staff, folder 1.

23. Sidney M. B. Coulling, "Moving a Graveyard: W&L Faculty Approves Curriculum Revision," *Alumni Magazine,* May 1983, pp. 1–2.

24. Charles Cox, "Still a Fortress of the Liberal Arts, W&L Bucks National Trend, Wins," *Richmond Times-Dispatch,* June 24, 1984.

25. Anne Coulling, "West Meets East: From Humble Beginnings, East Asian Studies Are Flourishing," *Alumni Magazine,* May–June, 1986, pp. 2–7.

26. "Celebration of the Arts," *Alumni Magazine,* Summer 1991, pp. 5–7.

27. "The Woods Creek Gap: How Wide is the Separation Between the Law School and the Undergraduate School?" *Alumni Magazine,* May 1981, pp. 1–7.

28. "Rick Kirgis Is Appointed New Law Dean," *Alumni Magazine,* Mar. 1983, pp. 1–2.

29. Wilson to BOT, Feb. 9, 1988, PP, Wilson, Memos to the Board.

30. Brian D. Shaw, "Putting the School of Law on the Map," *Alumni Magazine,* Fall 1988, pp. 8–12. See also a lengthy transcribed telephone interview Bezanson gave in May 1988, forwarded with Bezanson to Wilson, July 19, 1988, PP, Wilson, box 20, Law School Correspondence, 1988.

31. Bezanson to Wilson, Mar. 21, 1989, PP, Wilson, box 20, Law School Correspondence, 1989.

32. "ABA/AALS Site Evaluation Self-Study Report," 1993, copy in PP, Wilson, box 29.

33. Bezanson to Wilson, Oct. 14, 1991, PP, Wilson, box 20, Law School Correspondence, 1991.

34. Wilson to Bezanson, May 30, 1989; Bezanson to Wilson, May 1, 1989, PP, Wilson, box 20, Law School Correspondence, 1989.

35. Bezanson to Wilson, May 23, 1990, PP, Wilson, box 20, Law School Correspondence, 1990.

36. Bezanson to Wilson, Mar. 19, 1992, PP, Wilson, box 20, Law School Correspondence, 1992. Bezanson noted W&L's determination "to be unique as a national law school, with small size, intimate, rigorous, and writing-intensive education, and a very fine faculty of genuinely devoted teachers who, at the same time, are thoughtful, productive, and nationally-recognized scholars." This was hardly a limited ambition!

37. "Institutional Long-Range Plan (I), 1990–2000," pp. 97–101.

38. Jeffrey G. Hanna, "The Newest Science: Computers Find a Place in the Liberal Arts," *Alumni Magazine,* July–Aug. 1985, pp. 11–13.

39. "W&L adds new department in computer science," *Alumni Magazine,* Mar. 1984, p. 24.

40. "Institutional Long-Range Plan (I), 1990–2000," pp. 28–29.

41. Jeffrey G. Hanna, "Yes, They Really Are *Students:* "Non-traditional Undergrads add Diversity to Classroom," *Alumni Magazine,* Jan.–Feb. 1985, pp. 1–4.

42. The ABD program was one of the university's efforts to increase diversity in the classroom and recruit minorities to the regular faculty.

43. "W&L Actively Recruits Minority Law Students," *Law News,* Nov. 13, 1986.

44. Karl M. Funkhouser, *Alumni Magazine,* Aug. 1988, p. 47.

45. Center for Assessment and Policy Development, "Opening Closing Doors, Closing Opening Doors: Efforts to Increase African American Student Access and Success in Six Southern Liberal Arts Colleges," Mar. 1993, PP, Wilson, box 13, Atlanta Meeting . . . CAPD Report.

46. Wilson to Sherry Magill (acting executive director of the duPont Fund), Apr. 20, 1993, PP, Wilson, box 13, Atlanta Meeting . . . CAPD Report.

47. See John W. Kuykendall (president of Davidson College) to Sherry Magill, Apr. 30, 1993, PP, Wilson, box 13, Atlanta Meeting . . . CAPD Report.

48. Sidney Coulling, remarks to the Board, PP, Wilson, box 14, Coulling, Sidney (Mission Statement).

49. Wilson to Sidney Coulling, Oct. 25, 1993, PP, Wilson, box 14, Coulling, Sidney (Mission Statement). Coulling added that he had responded to an inquiry from Rector A. Stevens Miles Jr. concerning the university's history and religion, noting that the 1988 Mission Statement made no mention of religion at all.

50. "Alumni, Prospective Students Attend Minority Weekend," *Alumni Magazine,* July 1990, p. 27.

51. These "success stories" were highlighted in "Without Rancor: The Story of Desegregation at Washington and Lee and What's Happened Since," by William Cocke and Deborah Marquardt, *Alumni Magazine,* Summer 1998, pp. 17–23.

52. Rosalyn D. Thompson to Wilson, June 30, 1986, PP, Wilson, Student Correspondence, 1984–88.

53. Wilson to Rosalyn D. Thompson, June 30, 1986, PP, Wilson, Student Correspondence, 1984–88.

54. Wilson to John Elrod, Farris Hotchkiss, Rick Kirgis, and Larry Peppers, Aug. 19, 1986, PP, Wilson, Faculty and Staff Memos, box 30, folder 1.

55. Robert G. Holland, "Universities of Much Diversity But Scant Brain Function," *Richmond Times-Dispatch,* Apr. 14, 1991.

56. William R. Cogar, "Why Scrutiny of W&L Will Benefit the University," *Richmond Times-Dispatch,* Sept. 22, 1991.

57. Wilson to the BOT, Sept. 27, 1991, PP, Wilson, Memos to the Board.

58. Randy Bezanson to Wilson, Sept. 17, 1991, PP, Wilson, box 20, Law School Correspondence, 1991.

59. Bezanson to Wilson, May 16, 1991, PP, Wilson, box 20, Law School Correspondence, 1991.

60. Bezanson to Wilson, Oct. 14, 1991, PP, Wilson, box 20, Law School Correspondence, 1991.

61. Bezanson to John Elrod and David Howison, with copy to Wilson, May 16, 1991, PP, Wilson, box 20, Law School Correspondence, 1991.

62. Wilson to the BOT, Aug. 15, 1991, PP, Wilson, Memos to the Board.

63. Bezanson to Betsy Levin of AALS, with copy to Wilson, Oct. 8, 1991; Wilson to Bezanson, Oct. 10, 1991, PP, Wilson, box 20, Law School Correspondence, 1991.

64. Wilson to the BOT, Sept. 27, 1991, PP, Wilson, Memos to the Board.

65. "Defending Diversity," *Law News,* Sept. 5, 1991.

66. Wilson to BOT, May 30, 1990, PP, Wilson, Memos to the Board.

CHAPTER ELEVEN

1. Two trustees—T. Hal Clarke and J. Alvin Philpott—were unable to attend, but both participated by telephone. Tom Wolfe, a new trustee elected in January, was not yet sworn in.

2. James M. Gabler to Wilson, Nov. 2, 1982; Wilson to Gabler, Dec. 30, 1982, PP, Wilson, Coeducation Issue, box 11. The voluminous materials on every aspect of W&L's consideration and implementation of coeducation—including correspondence, studies from other universities, and admissions data—are primarily contained in PP, Wilson, boxes 7, 10A, 10B, 11, and 12. Materials relating to coeducation are also found elsewhere, in trustee, presidential, and faculty files.

3. Farris Hotchkiss to Wilson, "Coeducation Considerations," Jan. 26, 1983, PP, Wilson, Coeducation, box 11. Hotchkiss also provided a copy of his memorandum on coeducation of Apr. 17, 1975.

4. James Whitehead to Wilson, Jan. 17, 1983, PP, Wilson, Coeducation Misc., box 12, folder 1.

5. E. C. Atwood to Wilson, Jan. 27, 1983, PP, Wilson, Coeducation Misc., box 12, folder 1.

6. William J. Watt to Wilson, "Gabler Letter Concerning Coeducation" (undated), PP, Wilson, Coeducation Misc., box 12, folder 1. As did some others, Watt referred specifically to Alexander W. Astin's book, *Four Critical Years: Effects of College on Beliefs, Attitudes, and Knowledge* (1977), in which Astin suggested that students performed better in single-sex environments.

7. W. C. Washburn to Wilson, Jan. 28, 1983, PP, Wilson, Coeducation Misc., box 12, folder 1.

8. Robert W. McAhren to Wilson, Mar. 11, 1983, PP, Wilson, Coeducation, box 10K.

9. Pamela H. Simpson to Wilson, Apr. 15, 1983, PP, Wilson, Coeducation, box 11.

10. "Coeducation on the Table," *Alumni Magazine,* Nov. 1983, pp. 1–2.

11. *Newport News Daily Press,* Oct. 2, 1983.

12. *Richmond Times-Dispatch,* Oct. 3, 1983.

13. Wilson to BOT, Oct. 11, 1983, PP, Wilson, Memos to the Board.

14. "Alumni Leadership Conference, *Alumni Magazine,* Nov. 1983, pp. 34–35.

15. "Coeducation on The Table," *Alumni Magazine,* Nov. 1983, pp. 1–4. Presidential leadership, as Nancy Weiss Malkiel concludes, was crucial everywhere: "Presidents needed to convince their boards to embrace coeducation. They had to harness faculty support; they needed to deal with alumni who had very strong views about coeducation; they needed to mobilize the internal planning and execution to make coeducation happen; and they needed to find the necessary resources." With skillful leadership, "the easier it was to imagine, and then move the institution to embrace, a different future." Malkiel, *"Keep the Damned Women Out": The Struggle for Coeducation* (Princeton: Princeton University Press, 2016), pp. xvii–xviii.

16. "Coeducation on The Table," *Alumni Magazine,* Nov. 1983, p. 4.

17. BOT minutes, Oct. 22, 1983.

18. Wilson to Members of the BOT, "Undergraduate Coeducation at Washington and Lee," Oct. 19, 1983, pp. 1–21, PP, Wilson, Memos to the Board.

19. Quoted in Wilson to Members of the BOT, Nov. 16, 1983, PP, Wilson, Memos to the Board.

20. Personal communication by Dick Sessoms to the author.

21. "Front Lawn" Supplement, "Dead End? The Question of Coeducation," *Ring-tum Phi,* Nov. 3, 1983.

22. Wilson to Members of the BOT, Nov. 16, 1983, PP, Wilson, Memos to the Board.

23. Jeffrey M. Stone to Wilson, Nov. 14, 1983, PP, Wilson, Coeducation, box 10A.

24. Kenneth P. Ruscio to Wilson, Oct. 20, 1983, PP, Wilson, Coeducation, box 10A.

25. James M. Ballengee to Wilson, Personal and Confidential, Nov. 3, 1983, PP, Wilson, Coeducation, box 10A.

26. Farris Hotchkiss to Wilson and University Relations Group, Dec. 19, 1983, PP, Wilson, Coeducation, box 10A.

27. Frank Parsons to Alice F. Emerson, president of Wheaton College, Apr. 15, 1987, PP, Wilson, box 14, WE–Wlt Misc. Wheaton, in Norton, Massachusetts, was considering coeducation and sought to benefit from W&L's experience.

28. Jeffrey G. Hanna, "The Admissions Race Is On: As the Numbers Go Down, the Competition Heats Up," *Alumni Magazine,* Jan. 1984, pp. 5–15.

29. Peter A. Agelasto III, "A Message from Your Alumni Board President"; Jack W. Warner, "Jack Warner's Letter on Coeducation," *Alumni Magazine,* Jan. 1984, pp. 1, 2–3.

30. Wilson to Farris Hotchkiss, Jan. 5, 1984, PP, Wilson, Coeducation, box 10A.

31. See Lewis John to Wilson, Jan. 24, 1984; Richard B. Sessoms to Wilson, Jan. 23, 1984; Lewis John to Wilson, Jan. 27, 1984, PP, Wilson, Coeducation, box 10A.

32. J. D. Farrar to Wilson, Jan. 27, 1984, PP, Wilson, Coeducation, box 10A.

33. Toni M. Massaro to Wilson, Jan. 13, 1984, PP, Wilson, Coeducation, box 11.

34. BOT minutes, Feb. 3 and 4, 1984.

35. Wilson to BOT, Feb. 13, 1984, PP, Wilson, Memos to the Board, 1982–87.

36. Mary Bishop, "College Try: W&L Head Bucks Tradition on Coeds," *Roanoke News,* Feb. 5, 1984.

37. William M. Hartog, "Demographics 1982–1992, Highlights," PP, Wilson, Coeducation, box 10A.

38. See William Hartog to BOT, "Admissions Operation 1978 to 1983," Feb. 1, 1984; "Highlights: Admissions Yields 1965–83"; "Secondary School Counselor Survey: A Report for the Board of Trustees," Feb. 3, 1984, PP, Wilson, Coeducation, box 12.

39. Wilson's handwritten list, "Coeducation," in PP, Wilson, Coeducation, box 11.

40. Wilson to Members of the Executive Committee, Mar. 14, 1984, PP, Wilson, Coeducation, box 11. Wilson also sent copies of this memorandum to all other members of the board, for information and comment.

41. Mike Allen, "Students, Faculty Disagree," *Ring-tum Phi,* Apr. 24, 1984.

42. Jack W. Warner to "Selected Alumni and Friends of Washington and Lee University," Apr. 20, 1984, PP, Wilson, Coeducation, Box 11. After the coeducation decision was made, Jack Warner accepted the new reality and continued his strong loyalty and financial support to Washington and Lee.

43. E. Waller Dudley to James M. Ballengee, Apr. 25, 1984, PP, Wilson, Coeducation, box 11.

44. Christian A. Compton to Wilson, May 7, 1984, PP, Wilson, Coeducation, box 11.

45. Wilson to Marshall Fishwick, May 7, 1984, PP, Wilson, box 32, Fishwick.

46. Farris Hotchkiss to Wilson, May 14, 1984, PP, Wilson, Coeducation, Richmond Visit with Lewis Huntley, box 11.

47. Wilson to J. B. Sowell Jr., May 1, 1984, PP, Wilson, Coeducation, Richmond Visit with Lewis Huntley, box 11.

48. Wilson, "Thoughts on Coeducation and W&L," an undated list Wilson wrote out in long hand and then had typed, probably in May 1984, PP, Wilson, Coeducation, box 11.

49. BOT minutes, May 24, 25, and 26, 1984.

50. Copies of the letter and the responses were provided by Mark B. Davis Jr. to the author and will be placed in W&L Special Collections.

51. "Washington & Lee Studies Opening Its Doors to Women," *Washington Post,* July 2, 1984.

52. "Coeducation Polarizes W&L," *Norfolk Virginian Pilot,* July 1, 1984.

53. BOT minutes, July 14, 1984.

54. "Another Historic Moment: After 235 Years, W&L Charts a New Course," *Alumni Magazine,* July 1984, pp. 3–7.

55. "Statement of the Board of Trustees, Washington and Lee University," July 14, 1984, PP, Wilson, Memos to the Board.

56. Transcript, "News Conference on Coeducation, The Commerce School Building, July 14, 1984," PP, Wilson, Coeducation, box 10A.

57. Bill Hartog, interview by the author, June 17, 2015.

58. Stephen M. Finley, letter to the editor, *Alumni Magazine,* July 1984, p. 48.

59. "Now It's 'Children' of Alumni," *Alumni Magazine,* July 1984, p. 8.

60. Wilson to the Faculty, July 18, 1984, and Wilson to University Staff, July 19, 1984, PP, Wilson, Faculty and Staff, box 30, folder 2.

61. See Wilson to Robert L. Spivey, president of Randolph-Macon Women's College, and identical letters to other presidents, July 16, 1984, PP, Wilson, Coeducation, box 10A.

62. Robert G. Holland, "W&L's Act of Evolution," *Richmond Times-Dispatch,* July 17, 1984.

63. Wilson to Members of the Faculty and Administration, "Subject: The Coeducation Steering Committee," Sept. 10, 1984.

64. BOT minutes, Oct. 27, 1984.

65. Wilson to BOT, Sept. 14, 1984, PP, Wilson, Memos to the Board; *Roanoke Times and World-News,* Sept. 11, 1984.

66. "Plans for Coeducation Proceeding," *Alumni Magazine,* Mar.–Apr. 1985, pp. 47–48.

67. Richard Sessoms, personal communication to the author.

68. William E. Brock to Wilson, Oct. 22, 1984, PP, Wilson, box 15, Brock Family.

69. Wilson to Marshall Fishwick, Nov. 19, 1984, PP, Wilson, box 32, Fishwick.

70. Wilson to Marshall Fishwick, Apr. 1, 1985, PP, Wilson, box 32, Fishwick.

71. "Preliminary Research Report to Washington and Lee University," Southeastern Institute of Research, Inc., May 9, 1984, PP, Wilson, Coeducation, box 10A.

72. Letters from Rufus Kinney and Richard F. Cummins, *Alumni Magazine,* Mar. 1984, p. 55.

73. Letter from Raymond D. Smith Jr., *Alumni Magazine,* May 1984, p. 51.

74. Letter from Pryse Roy Elam, *Alumni Magazine*, July 1984, pp. 51–52.

75. Mary Bishop, "Welcome to W&L," *Roanoke Times and World-News*, "Extra" section, Sept. 1, 1985.

76. "Final Admissions Figures Indicate Most Successful Year Ever," *Alumni Magazine*, July–Aug. 1985, p. 22.

77. "A Grand Entrance: The Class of 1989 Ushers in a New Era," *Alumni Magazine*, Sept.–Oct. 1985, pp. 2–4.

78. "W&L Women Get Diplomas," *Roanoke Times and World News*, June 2, 1989.

79. "W&L Graduates First Coed Class; 'Great Time' United 96 Women," *Richmond Times-Dispatch*, June 2, 1989.

80. Eric Randall, "Women Fare Well at W&L," *Roanoke Times and World News*, May 28, 1989.

81. Peter Baker, "When Tradition Bows to Modern Realities," *Washington Post*, Apr. 14, 1990.

82. See "Coeducation Review Committee Final Report," Sept. 1994, and subcommittee reports in PP, Wilson, box 32, Coeducation, folders 1 and 2. Also PP, Elrod, box 6, folder 1, Coeducation Transition Committee.

83. Wilson to Alice F. Emerson of Wheaton College, Apr. 7, 1987, PP, Wilson, box 14, WE-Wlt Misc.

84. "Subcommittee Report on Student Political Life," PP, Wilson, Coeducation Reports, box 32, Student Life.

85. "Institutional Long-Range Plan (I), 1990–2000," June 20, 1989, PP, Wilson, box 565, Board of Trustee Material, 1994–95.

86. Anne Schroer-Lamont, interview by author, July 28, 2015.

87. "Sexual Abuse Survey Results Released," *W&L Law News*, Oct. 4, 1990.

88. Schroer-Lamont, interview.

89. *Ring-tum Phi*, Oct. 22, 1992, and Nov. 12, 1993.

90. "Report on Faculty and Administration," Coeducation Review Committee, PP, Wilson, box 32, folder 1, Coeducation, pp. 1–12.

91. Women Faculty/Administrators Discussion Group to the Committee to Enhance Faculty Quality, May 31, 1989, PP, Wilson, box 606, Women's Issues.

92. Larry Peppers to Professors Margand and Wiant, June 2, 1989, PP, Wilson, box 606, Women's Issues.

93. Anne C. Schroer-Lamont to Wilson, June 1, 1995, PP, Wilson, box 30, Retirement Letters.

94. John Elrod to BOT, "Coeducation Review Committee Final Report," Oct. 2, 1995, PP, Wilson, box 16, Coeducation Review Committee Final Report.

95. Elrod to Faculty and Staff, May 28, 1996, PP, Wilson, box 16, folder 2, Faculty Memos.

96. Wilson to Pamela H. Simpson, Oct. 14, 1994, PP, Wilson, box 36, folder 1, Fine Arts,.

97. Wilson to Anne C. Schroer-Lamont, June 12, 1995, PP, Wilson, box 30, Retirement Letters.

CHAPTER TWELVE

1. Wilson to BOT, Oct. 11, 1984, PP, Wilson, Memos to the Board.

2. Wilson to Members of the Advisory Committee (including Mr. Herrick), Apr. 1, 1985, PP, Wilson, box 30, Faculty and Staff Memos, folder 1.

3. Wilson to Members of the Advisory Committee and Members of the Central Administrative Staff, Oct. 18, 1985, PP, Wilson, box 30, Faculty and Staff Memos, folder 1.

4. Wilson reflected in detail on the enrollment and gender-balance issues in a letter to Omer L. Hirst, Aug. 26, 1985.

5. Wilson to Members of the Central Staff, "Skylark Meeting: Sept. 4–5," Aug. 1, 1986, PP, Wilson, box 30, Faculty and Staff Memos, folder 1.

6. Wilson to BOT, Feb. 21, 1988, PP, Wilson, Memos to the Board.

7. Wilson to Members of the Central Staff, "Skylark Meeting: Sept. 4–5," Aug. 1, 1986, PP, Wilson, box 30, Faculty and Staff Memos, folder 1.

8. Wilson to Marshall Fishwick, Apr. 25, 1983, PP, Wilson, box 32, Fishwick.

9. BOT minutes, May 21, 1983.

10. Wilson to Members of the Board of Trustees, Sept. 21, 1983, PP, Wilson, Memos to the Board.

11. Wilson to Marshall Fishwick, Nov. 7, 1983, PP, Wilson, box 32, Fishwick.

12. Wilson to the BOT, Sept. 24, 1985, PP, Wilson, Memos to the Board.

13. Wilson to Marshall Fishwick, Jan. 28, 1985, PP, Wilson, box 32, Fishwick.

14. Tom Touchton, interview by Mame Warren, Jan. 27, 1997.

15. Brian Shaw, "A Greek Revival? Alumni Fraternity Council's Symposium Cites Problems, Promise," *Alumni Magazine,* Nov.–Dec. 1986, pp. 3–6.

16. Touchton, interview.

17. "A New Beginning For Fijis," *Alumni Magazine,* Nov.–Dec. 1986, pp. 6–7.

18. Wilson to Members of the Faculty, Jan. 20, 1988, with appended copy of Paul J. B. Murphy Jr. to Fraternity Chapter Presidents and House Corporation Presidents, PP, Wilson, box 30, Faculty and Staff Memos, folder 1. While momentum was developing for further action, fraternity problems continued. In a letter to one fraternity-house president, Wilson called attention to the behavior that freshman might learn in the fraternity houses: "Too many of them are coming back to the dorms only to break windows and trash the hallways. We have taught that this is somehow neat or macho behavior. And, of course, it is utterly puerile and boring." Wilson to Jay Mackley, Nov. 18, 1987, PP, Wilson, Student Correspondence, 1984–88.

19. BOT minutes, Jan. 29–30, 1988.

20. Wilson to BOT, July 6, 1988, and Leroy Cole Atkins II to W&L Fraternity Presidents, June 30, 1988, PP, Wilson, Memos to the Board.

21. BOT minutes, Oct. 21 and 22, 1988. W&L already owned three fraternity houses and the land on which many others were located.

22. Wilson to Friends of Washington and Lee, Jan. 18, 1989, PP, Wilson, Memos to the Board.

23. Wilson to BOT, June 5, 1989, PP, Wilson, Memos to the Board.

24. Wilson to BOT, Jan. 26, 1990, PP, Wilson, Memos to the Board.

25. "Fraternity Renovations Begin," *Alumni Magazine,* July 1990, pp. 5–7.

26. *Ring-tum Phi,* Jan. 18, 1992, and Feb. 27, 1993.

27. *Alumni Magazine,* Winter 1992, p. 25.

28. Mike Stachura, "Fraternity Renaissance: A Change From Within," *Alumni Magazine,* Winter 1991, pp. 10–15.

29. "'Mothers' Aim to Make W&L Frats More Like Home," *Roanoke Times and World News,* June 2, 1991.

30. Wilson to BOT, Aug. 26, 1993, PP, Wilson, Memos to the Board.

31. Matt Jennings, "Renaissance Mazz," *Alumni Magazine,* Spring 1997, pp. 25–27.

32. Binge drinking was sometimes defined as five drinks in a row for men and four for women, and usually resulted in extreme inebriation.

33. Deborah Marquardt, "Everybody Drinks in College," *Alumni Magazine,* Spring 1998, pp. 26–29.

34. Wilson to Members of the Faculty, May 17, 1984, PP, Wilson, box 30, Faculty and Staff, folder 2.

35. Anne Coulling, "New Drug Policy: Faculty Votes Changes to University's Disciplinary System," *Alumni Magazine,* July–Aug. 1985, p. 21.

36. BOT minutes, May 25, 1985.

37. Wilson to Leonard E. Jarrard, Apr. 24, 1986, reprinted in BOT minutes, May 24, 1986.

38. See BOT minutes, May 22 and 23, Oct. 23 and 24, 1987.

39. *Lexington News Gazette,* Sept. 9, 1987.

40. Lewis G. John to Trustees Academic Affairs Committee, May 19, 1988.

41. Wilson to Professor Samuel Kozak et al., Jan. 4, 1988, PP, Wilson, box 30, Faculty and Staff Memos, folder 1.

42. Ad Hoc Committee of Review to Wilson, Apr. 26, 1988, PP, Wilson, box 30, Faculty and Staff Memos, folder 1.

43. Wilson to BOT, June 5, 1990, PP, Memos to the Board of Trustees.

44. Wilson to BOT, June 16, 1994, PP, Memos to the Board of Trustees.

45. *Lexington News Gazette,* Mar. 22, 1989; *Ring-tum Phi,* Mar. 23, Sept. 7, Nov. 2, and Dec. 4, 1989, Jan. 11, Aug. 30, and Sept. 27, 1990.

46. *Lexington News Gazette,* Oct. 16, 1991; *Ring-tum Phi,* Jan. 9, Feb. 6, Mar. 12, and Apr. 23, 1992.

47. The victim's family filed a lawsuit against the university, which was eventually settled on Apr. 10, 1995.

48. Joan O'Mara to Wilson, Oct. 1, 1990; Wilson to O'Mara, Oct. 15, 1990, PP, Wilson, box 30, Fine Arts, folder 2.

49. This pattern is well documented in a review of actual honor cases and decisions by Kevin K. Batteh, '95 and '98L, and president of the Student Executive Committee in 1997–98. See Batteh's paper, "Washington and Lee's Honor System: A Case Study of the Evolution of an Alternate Legal System," Spring 1998, Special Collections.

50. *Ring-tum Phi,* May 3, 10, and 17, 1984.

51. "An Honorable System?" *W&L Law News,* Nov. 10, 1977.

52. "Honor Poll Shows Student Disfavor," *W&L Law News,* Dec. 8, 1977.

53. "SBA Submits Honor Reform," *W&L Law News,* Feb. 23, 1978.

54. "Legal analysis considers Honor Code litigation," *W&L Law News,* Sept. 27, 1979. The article also predicted that lawsuits against the Honor System would increase. See also "EC Discusses Honor Code," *Ring-tum Phi,* May 29, 1980.

55. Mary Bishop, "W&L Justice: Law Student-Undergrad Conflict Spills into Honor System," *Roanoke Times and World News,* May 20, 1984. Also see *W&L Law News,* Apr. 6 and 20, and Oct. 18, 1984.

56. Betty Kondayan (Acting Special Collections Librarian) to Patricia Dunn (the President's Office), July 21, 1992; John M. Gunn, "An Essay on the W&L Honor System," Sept. 1992; Wilson to Gunn, Sept. 21, 1992, PP, Wilson, box 13, Honor System, 1960–94.

57. BOT minutes, Oct. 30–31, 1992.

58. BOT minutes, May 27–28, Oct. 28–29, 1994, and May 26, 1995.

59. "Five Years Later: A Conversation with President John D. Wilson," *Alumni Magazine*, Apr. 1988, p. 7.

60. BOT minutes, Oct. 19, 20, 21, 1989.

61. In January 1994, Wilson framed many of the same issues as part of a proposed five-year plan and recommended an average target undergraduate enrollment of 1,600 and law school enrollment of 360—eliminating enrollment targets by sex in the interest of both quality and fairness. Wilson to BOT, "Five-year Planning Proposal," Jan. 24, 1994, PP, Wilson, Memos to the Board.

62. BOT minutes, Oct. 19, 20, 21, 1989.

63. Dick Abderson, "On the Shoulders of Giants," *Alumni Magazine*, Spring 1992, pp. 4–9.

64. See Development Committee minutes, 1990–95.

65. Dick Anderson, "Physical Science: Building the Case for a New Facility," *Alumni Magazine*, Fall 1993, pp. 27–31.

66. "Powell to Give W&L His Collection of Papers," *Alumni Magazine*, Apr. 1990, pp. 2–4; "A Fitting Tribute," *Alumni Magazine*, Summer 1992.

67. *Fact Books*, University Archives, Special Collections.

68. "W&L Undergraduate Factoids—Aug. 26, 1993," included with Wilson to Members of the BOT, Aug. 26, 1993, PP, Wilson, Memos to the Board.

69. Evan Atkins, "It Takes a Village," *Alumni Magazine*, Summer 1997, pp. 15–19.

70. Dick Anderson, "The New Student Journalism," *Alumni Magazine*, Winter 1994, pp. 26–32.

71. "Singing for Their Suppers," *Alumni Magazine*, Spring 1993, p. 35.

72. *Lexington News-Gazette*, May 16, 1984.

73. *Roanoke Times and World News*, May 12, 1984.

74. Wilson to Cinda Rankin, Dec. 18, 1986, PP, Wilson, Athletics, 1980–88, folder 2.

75. "Dick Miller Captures No. 200," *Alumni Magazine*, Nov. 1984, p. 16.

76. "Lord, Keep Us Fit," *Alumni Magazine*, Feb. 1987, pp. 11–13.

77. William Cooke, "The Day of the Armadillo," *Alumni Magazine*, Summer 1992, pp. 18–20.

78. Wilson to Gary Fallon and Bill McHenry, Nov. 4, 1987, PP, Wilson, Athletics, 1980–88, folder 1.

79. "A Record Season," *Alumni Magazine*, Feb. 1986, pp. 15–17.

80. "Women Swimmers Get Off to Fast Start," *Alumni Magazine*, Apr. 1986, pp. 28–29.

81. "Lacrosse Remains Division I," *Alumni Magazine*, Aug. 1985, p. 30.

82. "I to III," *Alumni Magazine*, Aug. 1986, pp. 10–11.

83. George W. Harrison, letter to editor, *Alumni Magazine*, Aug. 1988, p. 47.

84. Bill Millsaps, "The State of College $port$," originally in the *Richmond Times-Dispatch* and reprinted in the *Alumni Magazine*, May–June 1985, pp. 10–11.

85. Wilson to Members of the Department of Athletics, Apr. 23, 1985, PP, Wilson, Misc. Files, box 14, Athletic Meeting, May 31, 1985.

86. Wilson to Members of the BOT, May 27, 1985, PP, Wilson, Memos to the Board.

87. Wilson, handwritten outline for "Athletics Meeting," PP, Wilson, Misc. Files, box 14, Athletic Meeting, May 31, 1985.

88. William D. McHenry to Wilson, May 29, 1985, PP, Wilson, Misc. Files, box 14, Athletic Meeting, May 31, 1985.

89. Wilson to Members of the Athletic Faculty and Staff, June 22, 1989, PP, Wilson, box 29, Athletic Dept. Search Letters.

90. Wilson to Members of the Athletic Director Search Committee, July 17, 1989, PP, Wilson, box 29, Athletic Dept. Search Letters.

91. J. Richard O'Connell to William J. Watt, Aug. 4, 1989, PP, Wilson, box 29, Athletic Dept. Search Letters.

92. Wilson to William Watt, Aug. 7, 1989, PP, Wilson, box 29, Athletic Dept. Search Letters.

93. Wilson to William P. Englehart Jr., Oct. 12, 1989, and to Joseph P. Keelty, Oct. 24, 1989, PP, Wilson, box 29, Athletic Dept. Search Letters.

94. "Committed to Excellence," *Alumni Magazine,* Dec. 1989, pp. 11–16.

95. Bill Hartog, interview by author, June 17, 2015.

96. Wilson to William P. Englehart Jr., Oct. 12, 1989, and to Joseph P. Keelty, Oct. 24, 1989, PP, Wilson, box 29, Athletic Dept. Search Letters.

97. Samuel J. Kozak (Chair of the Athletic Committee) to Wilson, Jan. 15, 1985, PP, Wilson, box 29, Athletic Situation—ODAC.

98. Wilson to Samuel J. Kozak, Feb. 4, 1985, PP, Wilson, box 25, Athletic Situation—ODAC.

99. W&L home football game program in PP, Wilson, Athletics, 1980–88, folder 1.

CHAPTER THIRTEEN

1. James G. Leyburn to Rupert N. Latture, Sept. 4, 1986, Leyburn Papers, box 1, folder 1.

2. The full notes (in the Leyburn Papers) were edited and appeared as "Notes from a Visit with Dr. Leyburn," *Alumni Magazine,* Fall 1992, p. 30.

3. "A Memorial Tribute to James Graham Leyburn, 1902–1993," by O. Kendall White Jr., William A. Watt, John M. McDaniel, and Lex O. McMillan III, Leyburn Papers, J. G. Leyburn, Death Notices, Tributes.

4. Paxton Davis column in *Roanoke Times and World News,* copy in Leyburn Papers, 1947–72, Faculty Files.

5. "Leyburn + Socrates = God," *Alumni Magazine,* Summer 1994, pp. 7–8.

6. James G. Leyburn, "To the Freshmen," Sept. 12, 1972, PP, Wilson, box 13, Honor System. Leyburn retired in 1972.

7. Huntley to Wilson, Feb. 23, 1995; Wilson to Huntley, Mar. 17, 1995, PP, Wilson, Correspondence—H, box 15.

8. Brian Shaw, "Family Man," *Alumni Magazine,* Spring 1995, pp. 10–14.

9. Mame Warren, ed., *Come Cheer for Washington and Lee: The University at 250 Years* (Lexington: Washington and Lee University, 1998).

10. *Alumni Magazine,* Summer 1998, Summer 1999.

11. Deborah Marquardt, "A Conversation with President John Elrod," *Alumni Magazine,* Fall 2000, pp. 16–19.

12. These data are taken from the *Fact Book, 2000–2001.*

SOURCES AND
ACKNOWLEDGMENTS

This book relies extensively on primary source materials in the Washington and Lee University Archives and Special Collections in the James G. Leyburn Library, to which I was given unfettered access. Divided into record groups according to administrative area (President, Treasurer, Deans, Registrar, etc.) and activity (Mock Convention, Athletics, etc.), the archives include the usual range of official documents and reports, such as the *Fact Books,* president's reports, trustee meeting books, faculty minutes, and Southern Association of Colleges and Schools self-study reports and supporting documents. They also contain a rich store of official memoranda and personal correspondence. (John Wilson's presidential papers are especially extensive, personal, and revealing of the man and his thinking.) These are supplemented by collections of individual papers, newspaper clippings, audio recordings (invaluable to appreciate the florid oratory of President Francis Gaines), videos, catalogs, and all manner of university and student publications (including the *Ring-tum Phi, Calyx,* and *Alumni Magazine*). All the images in this book are from Special Collections or the W&L Office of Communication and Public Affairs. The university has begun the process of digitizing portions of these materials to make them accessible online. The President's Office provided me with more recent minutes of the board of trustees and its committees, not yet officially placed in the archives but available there in many of the trustee books for specific meetings.

The interviews with university officials, faculty members, and former students, conducted by Mame Warren and housed in Special Collections, are useful for their individual impressions of key events and decisions but are especially important for insights into aspects of university life—including recollections from veterans returning after World War II, participants in the student demonstrations in 1970, and early African American students. Without these interviews, the necessary research for this book would have been more lengthy and difficult, and one hopes the collection will be expanded.

The papers of important individuals held in Special Collections have been extremely helpful. The Francis P. Gaines Papers contain family letters, speeches, appointment books, and even his poetry. The James G. Leyburn Papers include personal correspondence, speeches (though regrettably not his most famous encomium to the Greek ideal), grade books, the lists he kept of all the books he had read or reread, and even specific instructions for his funeral service. The Jessie Ball duPont Papers contain a wealth of correspondence to and from this major benefactor of higher education and other cultural and charitable endeavors, as well as material related to her service on the board of trustees and a stream of personal correspondence with Frank and Sadie Gaines. Unfortunately, the university has few collections of personal papers from notable members of the faculty, apart from their university-related correspondence. Two collections are therefore all the more valuable. The O. W. Riegel Papers include many items, in particular the rough draft of his unpublished reminiscence, "Hacking It." Riegel delighted in his clandestine irreverence toward authority and orthodoxy, but he was also a shrewd observer and one of W&L's most significant faculty members. Ollinger Crenshaw's Papers include materials relating to his work on *General Lee's College,* but his personal views on matters concerning the university, and life in general, are found in correspondence with a former student, Robert McLean Jeter Jr. Thanks to Jeter's son's gift of Crenshaw's letters to W&L, we now have access to the thoughts of another long-time senior faculty member on university policy and life over several decades.

Published work about national events and higher education since 1930 is enormous in variety and extent. The books and articles I have specifically relied upon are detailed in the notes. Works of particular importance for this volume include, of course, Ollinger Crenshaw, *General Lee's College* (New York: Random House, 1969) and *Come Cheer for Washington and Lee: The University at 250 Years,* with excellent essays and wonderful photographs edited by Mame Warren (Washington and Lee University, 1998). Also see Nicholas L. Styrett, *The Company He Keeps: A History of White College Fraternities* (Chapel Hill: University of North Carolina Press, 2009); Melissa Kean, *Desegregating Private*

Higher Education in the South: Duke, Emory, Rice, Tulane, and Vanderbilt (Baton Rouge: Louisiana State University Press, 2008); Robert Stevens, *Law School: Legal Education in America from the 1850s to the 1980s* (Chapel Hill: University of North Carolina Press, 1983); and John R. Thelin, *A History of American Higher Education* (Baltimore: Johns Hopkins University Press, 2004). Nancy Weiss Malkiel's important book, *"Keep the Damned Women Out": The Struggle for Coeducation* (Princeton: Princeton University Press, 2016), which focuses on Harvard, Princeton, Yale and other prominent American universities, as well as Oxford and Cambridge in England, provides an essential context for understanding considerations and challenges similar to those encountered at W&L, but it appeared too late to inform this book. Excellent biographies cover the lives of four people very important to W&L: William H. Harbaugh, *Lawyer's Lawyer: The Life of John W. Davis* (New York: Oxford University Press, 1973); John C. Jeffries Jr., *Justice Lewis F. Powell, Jr.* (New York: Scribner's Sons, 1994); Joel William Friedman, *Champion of Civil Rights: Judge John Minor Wisdom* (Baton Rouge: Louisiana State University Press, 2009); and Richard Greening Hewlett, *Jessie Ball duPont* (Gainesville: University of Florida Press, 1992).

For general and specific information on other colleges and universities, especially for comparisons to W&L, see Gerald L. Smith and Samuel R. Williamson Jr., eds., *Sewanee: Perspectives on the History of the University of the South* (Sewanee: University of the South, 2008); Paul K. Conkin, *Gone with the Ivy: A Biography of Vanderbilt University* (Knoxville: University of Tennessee Press, 1985); Clarence L. Mohr and Joseph E. Gordon, *Tulane: The Emergence of a Modern University, 1945–1980* (Baton Rouge: Louisiana State University Press, 2001); Virginius Dabney, *Mr. Jefferson's University: A History* (Charlottesville: University of Virginia Press, 1981); James Edward Scanlon, *Randolph-Macon College: Traditions and New Directions, 1967–2005* (Ashland, VA: Randolph-Macon College, 2013); and Mary D. Beaty, *A History of Davidson College* (Davidson, NC: Briarpatch Press, 1988).

A committee of selected alumni was charged in 2009 with developing criteria for a new university history, selecting an author to undertake it, and overseeing it as it evolved. I am indebted to its members—Dan T. Balfour, Roy T. Matthews Jr., John M. McCardell Jr., Courtney A. Penn, Alston Parker Watt, and its coordinator, James D Farrar Jr.—for the opportunity to do this work. The Class of 1966 fiftieth-reunion gift to "Collect and Preserve the University's History" provided support not only for the publication of this book but for the essential and continuing work in W&L Special Collections to enhance and manage the university's archival resources. Though this book was written at the invitation of the university, it is my book, and I am responsible for all the information, interpretations, and errors it contains. At the same time, I am extremely grateful to the university for its support and to the many people who have made the writing of this book possible.

I owe much to the staff of the James G. Leyburn Library and especially those in Special Collections, who have been like an extended family during my more than six years of work on this project; they have been essential to the undertaking. My thanks to Thomas E. Camden, Vaughn Stanley, Lisa McCown, Seth McCormick-Goodhart, Edna Milliner, Byron Faidley, and Alston Cobourn for their assistance, guidance, and encouragement, with extra appreciation to Seth and Lisa—and Patrick Hinely, the university photographer—for help with the images, culled from the enormous number in the university's collections. Mame Warren, whose scores of interviews were extremely helpful, also advised me concerning the university's historical collections, based on her work as editor of *Come Cheer for Washington and Lee: The University at 250 Years.* My friend and fellow historian, Bruce M. Stave, author of *Red Brick in the Land of Steady Habits: Creating the University of Connecticut, 1881–2006* (Lebanon, NH: University Press of New England, 2006), helped me assess and shape this task in the beginning. My thanks also to those in the President's Office, especially Katherine Brinkley, who efficiently printed, assembled, and distributed many drafts of the manuscript; she deserves her own publishing imprint. I am also grateful for research assistance to Henry Nicholas "Lex" Luther, '14, a work-study student.

A diverse group of individuals—including current and former faculty members and administrators, almost all of them alumni—read all or part of various drafts of the manuscript and offered corrections and suggestions large and small. They helped me avoid errors and ensured my humility: professional historians Roy T. Matthews, I. Taylor Sanders, Theodore C. DeLaney, and J. Holt Merchant, as well as Daniel Balfour, Farris P. Hotchkiss, Richard B. Sessoms, Lew John, Waller T. "Beau" Dudley, and Uncas McThenia. I am also indebted to Paul R. "Rand" Dotson, Lee Campbell Sioles, and Neal Novak at the Louisiana State University Press, and my diligent copyeditor, Julia Ridley Smith, for her patience and dedication to clarity, consistency, and brevity. They can all, hopefully, recognize and appreciate the improvements they inspired in the book. I also thank Mark Davis for sharing with me a copy of his book, *Solicitor General Bullitt* (Louisville, KY: Crescent Hill Books, 2011), and information about

Gaines and John W. Davis, their work together on the board of the Carnegie Endowment for International Peace, and their influential circle of friends. My personal interviews with William Hartog and Anne C. Schroer-Lamont on aspects of admissions, coeducation, and student life were also very helpful.

I was fortunate to meet on several occasions during my work on this book with two major figures in W&L's history who were in retirement in Lexington: Bob Huntley and Frank Parsons. Huntley remained the confident, frank, gracious raconteur, and Parsons the more reflective jack-of-all-trades with a touch of wit. Huntley died on December 10, 2015, and Parsons on January 28, 2016, followed within a month by Sid Coulling and Lou Hodges. I regret that I was not able to meet with John Wilson, who died on March 3, 2013. Their passing truly marked an end to an era in the W&L history they had done so much to define. I am pleased that they can, to some degree at least, live on together in this book.

Ken Ruscio was nearing the end of his entirely successful, decade-long presidency as my work on this book was concluding. His ability to communicate what is important about W&L, and why tradition and transformation go hand-in-hand, is at least the equal of any of his predecessors. He provided enthusiastic support for this project, and I regret that I must leave his story to a future historian.

The person with whom I worked most closely from the beginning is James Farrar Jr., the secretary of the university and senior assistant to the president. Literally brought up on the W&L campus, Jim reflects the spirit of the place, just as his parents did. He gets things done. Work on this project was a pleasure, in large part because of Jim's consistent help and support; in times of trouble I would want him to share my foxhole. We have developed a friendship and discovered much about W&L together.

Especially in later life, one can better appreciate the cumulative influence of mentors and friends, not just on matters of career but also on life and ways of thinking. This book is dedicated in part to my mentors: Ollinger Crenshaw at W&L, my graduate advisors George B. Tindall and George E. Mowry at the University of North Carolina at Chapel Hill, and my postdoctoral advisor David Herbert Donald at the Johns Hopkins University. I deeply appreciate my association with close friends and superb historians, with whom I have imbibed much history over the years, along with many other things. Somehow, pondering the historical craft and the nature of truth in the context of marriages, children, travels, and new jobs over decades expands the mind while keeping everything moored to reality. My closest friend, and sometime coauthor, David R. Goldfield and I have been at this since 1970, and I am happy to say that we persist and even kid ourselves that we are getting better. I also value my close friendship with Peter Kolchin since our days at the Institute of Southern History at Johns Hopkins in 1971. Two of our comrades—Howard N. Rabinowitz and Raymond A. Mohl—now deceased, are greatly missed and remembered for their intelligence, decency, and passion for history and belief in its importance.

My wife Mardi and I lived the first year of our married life—and my senior year—in what Bob Huntley termed the post–World War II "paper huts" of Hillside Terrace. A recent graduate of Wellesley College, she commuted to teach fifth grade at Stuart's Draft Elementary School, attended university events, and occasionally served tea in Lee House. She knows W&L. Apart from being my loving partner of more than fifty years and raising two superb children, she is a discerning and persistent critic, research assistant, and the first reader of whatever I write. After more than fifty years, she remains essential and still inspires.

INDEX

Note: Italicized page numbers refer to photographs.